AFRICAN AMERICAN POWER AND POLITICS

The Political Context Variable

Socialization - pg 113
political context variable - pg 9

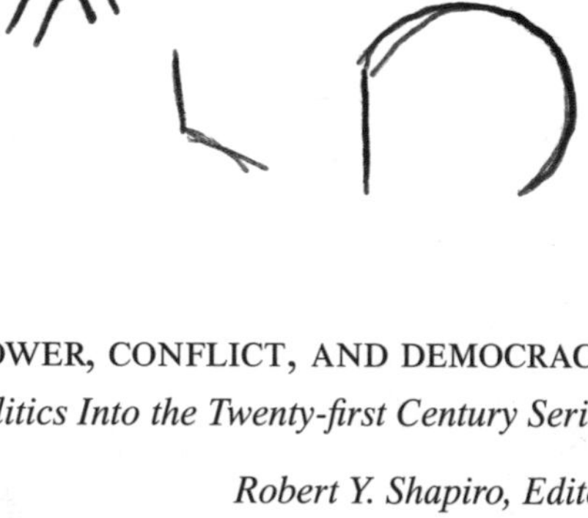

POWER, CONFLICT, AND DEMOCRACY

American Politics Into the Twenty-first Century Series

Robert Y. Shapiro, Editor

POWER, CONFLICT, AND DEMOCRACY:
AMERICAN POLITICS INTO THE TWENTY-FIRST CENTURY

ROBERT Y. SHAPIRO, EDITOR

This series focuses on how the will of the people and the public interest are promoted, encouraged, or thwarted. It aims to question not only the direction American politics will take as it enters the twenty-first century but also the direction American politics has already taken.

The series addresses the role of interest groups and social and political movements; openness in American politics; important developments in institutions such as the executive, legislative, and judicial branches at all levels of government as well as the bureaucracies thus created; the changing behavior of politicians and political parties; the role of public opinion; and the functioning of mass media. Because problems drive politics, the series also examines important policy issues in both domestic and foreign affairs.

The series welcomes all theoretical perspectives, methodologies, and types of evidence that answer important questions about trends in American politics.

POWER, CONFLICT, AND DEMOCRACY: AMERICAN POLITICS INTO THE TWENTY-FIRST CENTURY

John G. Geer, *From Tea Leaves to Opinion Polls: A Theory of Democratic Leadership*

Kim Fridkin Kahn, *The Political Consequences of Being a Woman: How Stereotypes Influence the Conduct and Consequences of Political Campaigns*

Kelly D. Patterson, *Political Parties and the Maintenance of Liberal Democracy*

Dona Cooper Hamilton and Charles V. Hamilton, *The Dual Agenda: Race and Social Welfare Policies of Civil Rights Organizations*

African American Power and Politics
The Political Context Variable

HANES WALTON, JR.

COLUMBIA UNIVERSITY PRESS NEW YORK

Columbia University Press
Publishers Since 1893
New York Chichester, West Sussex

Library of Congress Cataloging-in-Publication Data

Walton, Hanes, 1941–
African American power and politics : the political context variable / Hanes Walton, Jr.
p. cm.—(Power, conflict, and democracy)
Includes bibliographical references and index.
ISBN 0-231-10418-9 (cloth).—ISBN 0-231-10419-7 (paper)
1. Afro-Americans—Politics and government—Case studies. 2. Afro-Americans—Civil rights—Case studies. 3. United States—Politics and government—1981–1989—Case studies. 4. United States—Politics and government—1989——Case studies. 5. United States—Race relations—Case studies. 6. Conservatism—United States—History—20th century—Cast studies. 7. Republican Party (U.S. : 1854–)—History—20th century. 8. Democratic Party (U.S.)—History—20th century. I. Title. II. Series.
E185.615.W315 1997
323.1'196073—dc20 96-35063
CIP

Casebound editions of Columbia University Press books are printed on permanent and durable acid-free paper.

Printed in the United States of America

c 10 9 8 7 6 5 4 3 2 1
p 10 9 8 7 6 5 4 3 2 1

To
Professor Tobe Johnson,

a Morehouse man, Columbia-trained Phi Beta Kappa scholar, and author, who returned to his alma mater to teach brilliantly, research with distinction, and render great service to his students, the department, and the discipline of political science,

for

serving as an exceptional example of what can be accomplished at a small, prestigious African American college and in the larger world of scholarship

CONTENTS

FIGURES

TABLES

FOREWORD

William H. Boone

Hanes Walton's book is timely for it comes at a point when all of the forces once sympathetic to the black agenda have moved to fortify the new context. Federal agencies have reinterpreted rules in order to undermine previously race-conscious policies. We have recently been treated to the United States Department of Education's attack on educational scholarships targeting specific racial groups. The federal courts are more likely to respond to individual rather than group concerns and less likely to accept class action suits to redress harm. Earlier arguments in support of integration have been turned on blacks as weapons to dismantle and make obsolete the nation's traditionally black institutions of higher education, particularly the state-funded schools.

If there was a golden age for African American politics, it was probably the period following World War II through the mid-1970s. During this period the modern contextual framework of black politics began to form, eventually coalescing into its most productive period, the 1960s, with the passage of civil rights legislation and the expansion of the black middle class. While racial discrimination did not disappear from the societal context, excessive, overt racism became an American embarrassment. Presumably, whites did penance by allowing blacks to help shape the context in which the new political game would be played. In large measure, however, that context was racially defined.

By the mid-1970s, America found itself in the midst of an economic decline. An unpopular war had concluded in a defeat for the United States. The backdrop for the beginning of the Reagan-Bush era was one in which America was depicted as having lost its leading status in the world. A white backlash began to occur. To some whites, it appeared that one group (blacks), with the assistance of the federal government, was being given a disproportionate advantage over other groups (whites). In their view, the context in which the national political game was being played, and the rules by which it was being played, had shifted to their disadvantage. The rules therefore had to change.

The groundwork for such changes began to take shape with the election of Richard Nixon; however, the 1980 election of Ronald Reagan provided the ultimate answer to the uneasiness being experienced by white America. The Reagan and Bush administrations unshackled the constraints that had been placed upon overt racist practices as a result of the civil rights and affirmative action eras. It especially unshackled those constraints in the federal structure. Many whites interpreted the actions of these Republican presidencies as a signal. Some described the neoconservative political context as a step toward reclaiming the nation from those who had brought it into a state of disrespect and mediocrity.

The context in which America practiced politics changed considerably during the course of these administrations. At the highest levels of government, policies were enacted and rhetoric was cast about which had as their purpose the creation of wedges between racial and ethnic groups. To help legitimize the altered context, neoconservative black intellectuals were given a home inside the Reagan-Bush Republican party as well as in conservative think tanks across the country. This cadre of black intellectuals was able to create an aura of acceptance by blacks of the new context. They were able to appropriate the rhetoric of the civil rights movement to justify Reagan-Bush governmental policies which deemphasized the need for federal intervention in resolving the problems affecting blacks and dismantled governmental initiatives to implement such programs. Thus, an intellectual framework was established which had the effect of decimating 30 years of black consensus politics.

The Reagan-Bush years effectively disrupted the black political context and, in so doing, rendered problematic the traditional tactics of black politics. Race-consciousness as a tactic was turned on its head. President Bush's nomination and the subsequent confirmation of Clarence Thomas as an associate justice to the United States Supreme Court is but one illustration of the way in which the Republican conservative leadership was able to pit the old ways against the new. A considerable number of black organizations which had called for a black to replace retiring black Justice Thurgood Marshall, found themselves dumbfounded when that call was answered with the nomination of Thomas, a black whose views and actions ran decidedly counter to the established racial precepts. The old-line black groups and leaders had placed themselves in a "race box," and they could not climb out of it. Bush's maneuver left these African American organizations, politicians, and intellectuals directionless and fumbling for a rationale in their opposition to Thomas. Clearly, the Bush administration had changed the context and parameters of the discussion.

The Thomas affair is graphic proof of the lack of a progressive response by African Americans to the changed political context of the Reagan-Bush era. In this light, the 1992 presidential victory of the Democrats may not be reason to celebrate, nor should blacks assume that Bill Clinton's victory marks a return to the pre-Reagan-Bush context. After all, the conservative wing of the Democrat party won the election, not its moderate-liberal wing. For twelve years this wing argued that, in order to win the presidency, the Democrats needed to mirror the Republican party. Since Clinton's victory, it has remained true to that cause. For this reason, the context in which black politics is waged must change once more. In this book, in a clear and insightful manner, Hanes Walton explains the nature of that effort.

PREFACE

• • • • • • •

The aim of this innovative work on the role, function, and influence of the political context variable in African American politics is to be both comprehensive and systematic in its coverage and analysis of that variable. Moreover, this volume moves beyond the definition, delineation, discussion, and description of this variable at the micro and macro dimensions and explores how the political context as a political variable impacting political behavior can be altered and transformed from one that is fairly racially tolerant, inclusive, and pluralistic, to one that is abrasively and aggressively intolerant, exclusive, and hierarchical. Thus, the concern is with "who" and "how" and "when" the political context can be transformed and not just with the variable itself and its manifestations at the individual and collective levels.

This work focuses upon the Reagan-Bush (1980–1992) and Clinton (1992–1996) presidencies as the forces seeking to transform the political context and the political tactics and strategies through which the first two presidents sought to alter the political milieu in order to diminish and render ineffective African American politics. Analysis of the Clinton presidency provides a chance not only to make partisan comparisons but also a chance to see how a Democratic president relates to the legacy of his party's past role in structuring the political context as well as responding to the transformed changes and challenges left by a Republican era.

The roots for this work were laid with the help of Professor J. Clay Smith, Jr. and his lovely wife, Patricia Grace Smith. Professor Smith, a life-long traditional Republican and Patti, a life-long Democrat and currently chief of staff to the associate administrator of Commercial Space Transportation in the Federal Aviation Administration, have been of immense value in helping me develop, structure, and sharpen the political context variable as an analytical tool for evaluating and appraising the Reagan-Bush and Clinton presidencies and their impact upon the African American community and its politics. The Smiths and I discussed this in numerous conversations. In addition, Professor Smith and I held many discussions either in his office at the Howard University Law School, in his classroom there, or in my former offices and classrooms at Savannah State College. His insights, and his incomparable collection of clippings, letters, and other documents about African American Republicans and African American politics have been invaluable. The Smiths, two well read and well-tuned political observers and activists, vividly demonstrate that all learning does not take place in the classroom, and that political science professors can still learn new ideas and insights outside of the regular academic process, structured as it is by books and articles. Patti Smith's evaluations of the recent activities of African American Republicans were especially insightful. I owe them both a real debt of gratitude for sharing their intellectual reflections and for their careful, practical analysis of this era.

The Smiths are both careful scholars born of the struggles of the 1960s.

> [Patricia Grace Smith] had been among the dozen black students assigned to integrate Tuskegee High School twenty-eight years earlier [and one who] testified . . . as a fourteen-year-old in Judge Johnson's courtroom after all the white children had pulled out to avoid integration, before Tuskegee High School mysteriously burned to the ground.[1]

Patti has written: "Justice worked that day when Judge Johnson listened intently to what we all had to say . . . and ultimately when the Judge handed down his decision that the state of Alabama has an obligation to educate us as it did others."[2] Her current scholarly work still looks at the question of justice for the African American community.[3]

Professor J. Clay, author of the recent *Emancipation: The Making of the Black Lawyer 1844–1944,* deals with questions of justice in his scholarly writing in both the legal sphere and the political process arena. Several of these works will be discussed in this Preface and in the volume.

Prior to my interactions with the Smiths, I was greatly influenced by my college and graduate school professors who insisted that the political context was an integral part of African American politics. In graduate school, Professor Samuel DuBois Cook emphatically included the political context among the variables discussed in his courses on American politics and political philosophy. His wisdom on the subject was pioneering and unexcelled. Another professor of mine, Harold

Gosnell, demonstrated the power of the political content, particularly in his classic work on the African American political experience, *Negro Politician.*[4]

Others, like Emmett Dorsey, Nathaniel Tillman, Jr., Robert Martin, and Morris Lovett, never forgot to mention or write about the powerful role of the contextual variable in the African American political experience. Additional graduate school professors like the late Bernard Fall, Brian Weinstein, and Joseph Cooper brought this variable to my attention in international relations, African politics, foreign affairs, and public policy. To all these teachers, I express my wholehearted thanks.

At the start of my undergraduate training in political science at Morehouse College, Professor Robert Brisbane made it quite clear that the political context was a viable and critical variable in the African American political experience. Professor Brisbane was teaching us just as the sit-ins, marches, and demonstrations of the 1960s started. He has written about these realities in the context in an earlier era.[5]

Also at Morehouse, Professor Tobe Johnson provided a different perspective on the political context variable by revealing its role and function in public bureaucracies and public administration. He taught us that the political context was not just a variable in the political process, decision making institutions, and public policy, but it was also a variable in public agencies. As a teacher he sought to "foster the values of reasonableness and rationality," "stay abreast of the professional developments" in the discipline, "be useful to the profession by serving on national boards and committees" and exemplify the "higher principles of a Morehouse graduate." He succeeded in both his teaching effort and superb scholarship as well.[6]

However, once the political context variable became the lens through which I would analyze the contemporary political scene, I was burdened with the practical matter of doing the case studies to confirm the reality of the political context variable in the African American community. For assistance in this area, I must thank the host of people who helped me prepare the essays that appear in this volume. Again, I am thankful to the Smiths for the many leads, documents, clippings, and contacts they so generously supplied me, an overburdened professor working at a small historically black college with few resources. I thank each of my students who worked on these essays, particularly for their efforts in surveying the people of Pinpoint, Georgia, the birthplace of Clarence Thomas, the second African American Supreme Court Justice. They braved many practical difficulties to complete this survey. LaShawn Warren was in charge of in this effort, and I cannot say enough good about her. Another student, Victor Cooper, was quite helpful when we visited Pinpoint, Georgia.

I also called upon the help of several of my former students. Professor Oliver Jones, Jr., the head of the political science department at Florida A & M University joined this effort. Professor Ronald Clark, an educator in Maryland, assisted, as did Professor Marion Orr, of Duke University's political science department.

I would also like to mention the efforts and assistance of my colleagues: Cheryl M. Miller, who provided numerous news clippings; Joseph P. McConnick, II, who sent me several documents and materials; Leslie Burl McLemore, who sent me materials; Kenneth Jordan, who coded, entered, and analyzed the data from the Pinpoint, Georgia survey; Tasha Owens, who obtained electoral data that had been refused me by the Metropolitan Planning Commission of Savannah, Georgia.

In the midst of this project, I switched schools, moving from Savannah State College to the University of Michigan. Most of the research as well as the writing of the two essays written with my undergraduates had taken place while I was at Savannah State College. The manuscript was drafted at the University of Michigan. Of my colleagues here, Professor Steven Rosenstone helped with data collection; he also read and critiqued two of the case studies.

Beyond the University of Michigan, I want to thank Professor Robert C. Smith and Wilbur Rich for a host of fine insights and marvelous leads. Thanks to my four contributors, Katherine Tate of Ohio State University, Michael Dawson of the University of Chicago, and Paula D. McClain and Steven Tauber of the University of Virginia. Their vision expanded the scope and coverage of this volume.

In the final stages of preparing the manuscript, a crisis arose regarding microfilm borrowed from the University of Georgia. Thanks to the efforts of Joia Ellis-Dinkins, Margaret Mitchell-Ilugbo, and Dr. Guy Craft, I was able to make use of the microfilm copy of the Claxton weekly newspaper, the *Claxton Enterprise,* from 1979–1994.

Margaret Mitchell-Ilugbo did her usual fine job in deciphering my handwriting, and Ms. Greta Blake deserves praise for her irreplaceable skills in preparing the tables and figures. Dr. Guy C. Craft was endlessly helpful at Savannah State College Library. Finally, I would like to thank D. K. Anderson. She knows the reason why.

My sincere thanks and appreciation to my wonderful college classmate, fraternity brother, and insightful human being, Dr. Thomas J. Washington, III, for his late night calls and good humored conversations.

Lastly to my family, particularly the boys, Brandon and Brent, for my late hours and long absences from their little league games, my thanks for their patience and good cheer. To my brother Thomas N. Walton and his wife Geanelvin, I offer my sincere appreciation for their continued support and good cheer.

Hanes Walton, Jr.
University of Michigan
July, 1996

INTRODUCTION
The 104th Congress–The Perspective of the Chairman of the Congressional Black Caucus

• • • • • • •

Congressman Donald L. Payne

Author's Note: The reader should be aware that this reflective assessment of the 104th Congress was written on March 10, 1995, three months into the session. For the first time in forty years, Republicans had captured the House of Representatives; they elected a fervent conservative, Newt Gingrich, as Speaker. Gingrich declared that he would continue the Reagan revolution and proposed a series of sweeping contextual changes, many outlined in the Contract with America, that would affect both the House and the country.

The 104th Congress included the largest number of African Americans (38 Democrats and 2 Republicans). Yet, for the first time in forty years, they were in the political minority and the chairman of the Congressional Black Caucus had to map out a battle plan for the session.

Thus the reader encounters here the chairman's outlook and perspective at the beginning of the legislative session. This Introduction illuminates how African American leaders and spokespersons react to the potential impact of new and impending contextual changes.

Congressman Payne's introduction is an excellent historical illustration of the political context variable in African American politics. Moreover, it offers unique insights and perspectives into the 105th Congress because the Republicans are still in control.

The 1994 mid-term elections ushered in a new era in Congress and, regretfully, a new attitude based on the belief of those brought to power that they had a mandate from "angry white men" voters.

I want to reflect on the Congressional Black Caucus's (CBC) work in the 104th Congress. It was a real privilege for me to be elected to the chairmanship of the Caucus, and I have found it to be an exciting challenge. As you probably know, one of the first acts of the new Republican majority was to pass a bill shutting down the Caucus and other vocal Congressional groups. I likened it to the aftermath of a coup, where the first thing you do is to silence the opposition. But we have survived, in a reconfigured form, and we are more determined than ever to be the moral voice and conscious of Congress even though our offices were closed and our funding was restricted by the Speaker.

The CBC and the Contract with America

The Caucus believes that the "Contract with America" is an all-out attack on basic rights which will have an absolutely devastating effect on all of our nation, but particularly on African Americans. Efforts to promote inclusion are being falsely portrayed as strict numerical mandates. Sweeping changes in the structure of our laws and the content of our constitution are being enacted with minimal debate, and in some instances, without even full hearings. The 4th Amendment was weakened two weeks ago by saying that several warrants are really not totally necessary anymore.

The so-called balanced budget amendment could deny school lunches to over 7 million children. Over 2 million young children and pregnant women would lose nutritional assistance through the WIC Program. This is a program that is so successful that the CEOs of a number of major corporations, including Prudential, Bell South, and AT&T, traveled to Washington in 1991 to testify in favor of funding for WIC before the House Budget Committee.

We have gotten a preview of how the Republicans intend to balance the budget through the rescissions they have proposed for this year's budget. They propose to eliminate entire programs which for some people are a matter of basic survival, such as the Low Income Home Energy Assistance program. This program gives temporary help to elderly and low-income families who are unable to pay their utility bills. In my home state of New Jersey, the elderly or disabled make up 45% of the participants. Summer jobs for youth are also being totally eliminated. Thousands of low-income youth who could be productive, instead being idle this summer, stand to lose. Punishing people because they are poor will make life for low-income families more stressful, but it will do very little to address our fiscal problems.

What the new Republican Congress is doing is taking the same formula that failed in the 1980s and trying to sell it again. We were promised in the 1980s that if we cut domestic spending, increased defense spending, and enacted large tax cuts, the budget would magically be balanced in four years.

But consider this—in the 200 years from the time George Washington served as our first President to the day that Jimmy Carter left office, the accumulated national debt was $908 billion. After only twelve years of Reagan-Bush economic policies, the national debt quadrupled to nearly $4 trillion!

As we race through the Contract with America, fundamental rights that have served our nation well over the years are being shredded. This past week, Congress voted to discard our present system of justice and replace it with the so-called "English rule" whereby the loser in a lawsuit is required to pay the expenses of the other party.

It was pointed out by my colleague Congressman John Conyers, a distinguished member of the Black Caucus, that just recently, the normally conservative British magazine, *The Economist,* called for the abandonment of the "English rule" because only the very wealthy can afford the costs and risks of most litigation under this rigid system.

All of us recognize that frivolous lawsuits are a problem, but to administer such a drastic and unbalanced solution makes no sense.

Another case of over-reaction is the rush to enact term limits for members of Congress. There are members who have stayed for many years, but they are the exception rather than the rule. In fact, over half of the current members of the House were elected in 1990 and thereafter. In the 104th Congress, there are 87 new members in the House, a dramatic turnover achieved without the imposition of term limits. Somehow, voters are being persuaded that we should abandon our current system of free elections and enact a mandate limiting the number of times voters can send their representative to Congress.

Term limits represent a real threat to minorities, who are just now catching up and being represented in greater numbers in the political process. Voters already have the power to go to the polls and vote out of office any official whom they no longer want to represent them. Why should Congress now decide that they know better than the voters what is best for them?

The CBC and the Third World

In African/Caribbean Affairs, the CBC has been very active. We take exception to an article in the March 6, 1995 issue of the *Baltimore Sun* that portrayed Africa as a troubled continent left on its own.

Although the article portrays Somalia and Rwanda as setbacks, I would like to inform you of CBC efforts to assist in each of these situations. You may recall at the end of the Bush administration that CBC members, Mervyn Dymally, John Lewis, Barbara-Rose Collins, Butler Derrick and myself traveled to Somalia. We informed the American people first hand of the suffering there. We feel that we helped to convince President Bush to intervene militarily in Somalia. I return three more times and later spearheaded a fund raising effort in New Jersey that netted over 3 million dollars of pharmaceutical supplies. While some will argue that the peacekeeping mission went wrong, others recognize that thousands of lives were saved from starvation.

Regarding Rwanda, former Chair of the CBC, Kweisi Mfume, and I sent three letters to President Clinton. We urged more positive American leadership at the United Nations (UN) Security Council to stop the genocide in Rwanda. The United States has been accused by such renowned groups as OXFAM/UK and Human Rights Watch as stalling in the UN. Finally, and in desperation, our letter of June 16 informed the President that members of the CBC would not participate in the forthcoming White House conference on Africa if the administration did not focus its energies on stopping the genocide. This got the President's attention, and was followed by a high level meeting at the White House between Caucus members and Secretary of State Christopher, National Security Advisor Tony Lake, UN Ambassador Madeleine Albright and USAID administrator Brian Atwood. I feel our action contributed to our quick humanitarian response to the refugee situation in Goma, Zaire, and Tanzania.

I need not go into detail on the CBC's positive role in returning President Aristide back to Haiti under the leadership of Charlie Rangel and Major Owens. I believe the press had given us due credit along with Randall Robinson.

More recently, we have played a major role in again saving the Subcommittee on Africa Development Fund by persuading Ben Gilman and Henry Hyde, and with a meeting with the new Speaker, Newt Gingrich. As CBC Chairman I sent a letter to Senator Mitch McConnell, Chairman of the Senate Appropriations Subcommittee on Foreign Operations. McConnell had proposed a $110 million recision cut in the currently approved 1995 budget of 800 million dollars. With the help of both Republican and Democratic friends we were able to forestall this entire cut both in the Senate and House. The hard fought $800 million African Development Fund is still safe. But, we must still be aware that the same effort will be needed in next year's budget process.

The CBC and Institutional Politics

The Caucus has played an active role in a number of key issues this year. We insisted that Dr. Foster's nomination for Surgeon General proceed, despite criticism from right-wing idealogues. We conferred with him and then encouraged the White House to step up its efforts. We also met with Vice President Gore and Dr. Foster. On another matter, after the new Chairman of the House Rules Committee took down a portrait of the late Claude Pepper, a great champion of civil rights and the elderly, and replaced it with a painting of a renowned segregationist, former Congressman Howard Smith of Virginia, we staged a successful sit-in, demanding the portrait be removed.

We have been outspoken on the issue of affirmative action, which Republicans have chosen to use as a "wedge issue" because it is divisive and misunderstood by most Americans. The affirmative action directives in the law, for the most part, simply encourage the consideration of the qualifications of minorities and women when hiring decisions are being made.

The CBC and A Modest Re-Empowerment Proposal

We are engaged in a very serious and critical debate in Congress about the direction of this nation. When African Americans mobilize for action, they can effect the debate as well as the direction of the nation. For instance, in the post-Civil War era, 70% of blacks were registered to vote; but in our most recent Presidential election, in 1992, almost 70% of young blacks did NOT exercise their right to vote. Let's work on turning those numbers around again.

PROLOGUE
The Conceptualization of a Variable

• • • • • • •

Kenneth A. Jordan and Modibo M. Kadalie

The plethora of studies addressing the political context variable during the past four decades have all examined the contextual effects of race from a unidimensional perspective: almost invariably, scholars investigating this phenomenon have looked at the voting behavior of whites as a function of African American residential density and have relied exclusively on aggregated rather than disaggregated data to support their findings. Commencing with V. O. Key Jr.'s seminal work of 1949, *Southern Politics,* most studies have focused on the negative reaction white voters have exhibited in areas of relatively higher levels of African American population density as measured at the county or state level. The literature dealing explicitly with the racial dimension suggests that one should expect a negative relationship regarding the impact of African American densities on the voting behavior of whites regardless of whether the unit of analysis or level of aggregation is a neighborhood, precinct, county, state, or region. The level of geographical aggregation notwithstanding, the dependent variable throughout most analyses is the vote choice made by white voters while the independent variable has remained African American residential density.

A critical question that remains unanswered regarding the political salience of race is how has the contextual influence of race on the voting behavior of African Americans been affected by white population density and white political behavior?

Limitations of Past Research

Theoretically, contextual analysis stresses that individual behavior is affected by the social and political milieu and not just by individual attributes or characteristics.[1] This approach poses several theoretical and methodological weaknesses and shortcomings. Studies that provide strong evidence for the conclusion that African American density acts as a negative contextual influence on white voter behavior violate the methodological rules of commission as well as omission. The essence of contextual models generally, and the African American concentration hypothesis in particular, relates environmental characteristics to individual behavior and thus commits an ecological fallacy. The inability of those studies clearly to validate or reject the African American concentration hypothesis stems from ambiguities inherent in their reliance solely on aggregate data. In other words, when the African American population is viewed in this sense, it negates the presence as well as the views of unregistered voters as well as the politically inactive by lumping all African Americans together as if they are a monolithic group. The inherent danger in this approach is to attribute to the individual characteristics that are a function of their environment rather than the individual. It therefore becomes imperative to exercise extreme caution when using aggregate data to infer individual-level relationships.

The contextual effect hypothesis also omits or ignores the possible contextual effect of white demographic concentration on the political behavior of African Americans.

White scholars examining this concept have largely ignored how whites have systematically engaged in political activities that have had a negative impact on African American life in general and African American political behavior in particular. When one considers the consequences of such racist practices as poll taxes, southern voter registration methods, the grandfather clause, and legislative districting, it becomes inconceivable how white scholars examining the political context of race could ignore or disregard the behavior and the responses of African Americans to these issues. Current vote dilution techniques, re-registration procedures, and racial gerrymandering are a few current examples.

When studies find that whites living in geographical areas with high proportions of African Americans are more likely to support candidates and issues that are antithetical to African American political interests, they ignore the behavior of whites in areas where the concentration of African Americans is low and wrongly argue that in counties with fewer African Americans whites do not vote or act against African Americans. Frank Parker's *Black Votes Count: Political Empowerment in Mississsippi After 1965,* Lawrence Hanks's *The Struggle for Black Political Empowerment in Three Georgia Counties,* and James Button's *Blacks and Social Change: The Impact of the Civil Rights Movement in Southern Communities* are recent studies that reveal that size and location are not always the key variables in inhumane policies.

The dynamics of the racial threat thesis, which argues wrongly that rural areas with small African American populations would be relatively less concerned with the perpetuation of the racial status quo, ignores antagonism toward the electoral empowerment of African Americans and resentment of the threat to white political hegemony. Support for this point is provided in the study of the 1990 Senate race between David Duke and Senator Bennett Johnston in Louisiana which found that the African American concentration among registered voters in a parish was found to be positively linked to the rate of white voter registration.[2] Given the electoral empowerment of African Americans, racist whites pursued, as a strategy designed to take advantage of the dynamic of racial threat, a policy of mobilizing an overwhelming majority of white voters to enhance their probability of success. This would depend on a large percentage of the white electorate residing in high percent African American contexts. However, throughout much of this century, the number of southern whites living in such contexts has been declining.[3] While the difficulty with such a racist strategy is evidenced by the ultimate failure of the Duke campaign in 1990 and his subsequent failure in the gubernatorial race in 1991, Duke did win a seat in the state legislature. Thus the racial threat hypothesis still retains some explanatory power.

It is also very important to point out that Key's research postulated that this phenomenon was essentially an attitude or behavior that was unique to the black belt or predominantly rural areas in the deep south where African Americans constituted a substantial proportion of the population. More specifically, the locus of Key's assertions was the rural county with a large African American population. "It is not the Negro in general," Key observed, "that provides the base for white Democratic unity in national affairs; it is fundamentally the rural Negro in areas of high concentrations of colored population."[4] It is clear that studies of the political context variable in relation to the political demography of the South has largely ignored the role of racial hostility as an explanatory variable and accentuated the potential effects of the level of African American concentration. Studies hypothesizing the linkage between African American concentration and racial hostility, specifically the willingness to vote for a racist candidate, remains operative in the South, no doubt, but such studies have failed to point out that such racial antagonisms is not unique to the black belt but is equally salient in other regions. Although the conclusion that African American density measured at the precinct level behaves as a positive contextual influence on white voter behavior was arrived at by Carsey in his analysis of the contextual effects of race on white voter behavior using data on the 1989 New York city mayoral election, it was posited that the main difference between the literature which reports a negative influence of African American densities on white voter behavior and those studies that find a positive contextual effect on voter behavior is the level of aggregation at which the contextual effect on voter behavior is measured.[5] Carsey further asserts that studies finding a positive effect measure the contextual variable at something akin to the neighborhood level which makes it easy to visualize an environment in which direct social interaction takes place on a daily basis, thus leading to Carsey's conclusion that it is the interaction that is responsible for producing the positive relationship. If this premise is valid, why did Dinkins suffer such a lopsided defeat in his re-election bid in 1993 in view of the fact that the political topography of the city remained the same. This helps to point out the danger in using the racial concentration hypothesis, regardless of the level of aggregation, as an independent variable when attempting to predict white voter behavior.

There are those white pundits who argue that whites will vote for African Americans if they hold mainstream values. By mainstream, they mean right wing ultra conservatives such as African American Republican congressmen Gerald Franks and J. C. Watts, whose political views are no different than whites who take positions that are inimical to African American progress and advancement. They also claim that you do not have to redraw congressional districts in order to integrate Congress. History simply does not bear this out: there have been only two African Americans elected to Congress from the state of Georgia in the last one hundred years.

While Key elaborated that "it is the whites of the black belt who have the deepest and most immediate concern about the maintenance of white supremacy,"[6] Carsey's study on the contextual effects of race on white voter behavior in the New York mayoral election of 1989 found that, although strong evidence exists for the conclusion that African American density measured at the precinct level behaves as a positive contextual influence on white voter behavior, one should not lose sight of the fact that an overwhelming majority of whites in New York city did not vote for Dinkins.

The political context variable has been inadequately conceptualized to mirror only how whites "threatened" by higher African American concentrations have expressed their fears through the ballot. The terms threat and fear are used as a ruse for racist whites bent on projecting perceptions of racial concentrations among African Americans as negative and thus transferring the burden emanating from those perceived threats and fears to the African American population.

Finally, almost all previous studies have employed the percent of the population that is African American as an indicator of racial concentration rather than the percentage of all registered voters classified as African American. When measured this way, the racial concentration hypothesis appears illogical in view of the fact that only a small percentage of the African American population are registered voters. Racial concentration within the pool of registered voters is a more direct measure of threat to white political dominance than is a simple measure of overall population racial balance.[7] It appears reasonable that a more compelling argument for the behavior of whites within the political landscape is more an appeal of ideological extremists such as David Duke and George Wallace to simple racism rather than either demography or geography.

Conceptual Ambiguity

A reconceptualization of the political context variable is necessary because there may be no true contextual effect at all. A critical question is not only whether a contextual effect exists, but if so, why? Contextual analysis has been faulted for ignoring the intervening variables that more fully explain how the context affects individual behavior.[8] We must be able to identify the attitudinal linkage that accounts for any contextual effects observed. It may be that whites from counties with higher proportions of African Americans display more conservative attitudes toward candidates and issues that are germane to the African American community simply because they differ in relevant individual-level characteristics such as racism and hostility toward African Americans. Unless we can rule this out, we cannot conclude that a contextual effect is present. Moreover, an identification of precise socio-economic characteristics and environmental settings that one should expect to produce a positive or negative race-based contextual effect on voter behavior is still, at this stage in the methodological process, problematical. Nonetheless, the literature strongly supports a measurable link between social interaction and the contextual effects of race on voter selection and choice in the electoral process.

The critical question remains, if context influences behavior through processes of interpersonal influence, then why have white scholars failed to show in their research how white attitudes, behaviors, and demographic concentrations have affected African American voter behavior or how African Americans have responded to the racial character of the local context?

The prevailing assumption in this volume is that whites fear African Americans and that the effects of racial threat on the political behavior of whites manifests itself in political activities and voting patterns that are inimical to African American life in general. The role of racial hostility, specifically, the willingness of whites to vote for a racist candidate, and the general disaffection of whites toward policies that promote African American advancement are deemphasized as plausible explanations of the racial concentration hypothesis. The relationship between racial concentration and perceptions of African American threat appears spurious at best but nonetheless continues to be used as a mechanism to mobilize large segments of the white population in registering to vote in support of militant segregationists. Racial issues remain significant in the relationship between African Americans and whites.[9] The shape of legislative districts, the existence of a runoff primary, racial desegregation, and affirmative action programs remain highly controversial. Although race has been a dominant political cleavage in the United States for most of its history, racially specific issues appear to produce a more contextual effect than demography or geography on voter behavior and choice. For example, the impetus for the candidacy of the segregationist George Wallace for the presidency of the United States in 1968 was spurred by the passage of landmark civil rights legislation in 1964 and 1965.

Without a doubt, one of the most significant pieces of legislation to be passed in this century for empowering African Americans was the Voting Rights Act of 1965. The effect of this act was to mobilize African Americans in many counties with large African American populations which previously had resisted African American voting and had provided strong support for militant segregationists.[10] Racist whites reacted to this landmark court decision not because of the racial composition of their area of residence but because of the perceived threat to white political hegemony.

In a study on attitudes of Democratic activists toward the 1984 Jesse Jackson candidacy, the author concluded that white Democratic activists from counties with greater concentrations of African Americans were more negative toward the Jackson candidacy because they were more politically conservative and perceived negative consequences from Jackson's candidacy.[11] Such consequences include the perception that such electoral victories for African American candidates would diminish white political control. This analysis left unanswered the important question of what percent of the white activists became activists as a result of the Jackson candidacy? It is illogical and racist to conclude that African American population density caused white voters to become actively involved politically. A more reasonable explanation for their negativism toward Jackson is first because he is an African American and secondly because of his liberal views on civil rights and other race related issues.

Detrimental Effects of One Dimensional Conceptualization

While political topography is multidimensional, the political context variable ignores the reaction or the responses of African Americans to contexts in the white community. For example, it fails to analyze how African American voters respond to white population density and distribution. Aside from providing only a unidimensional analysis, it disregards the empirical and theoretical contributions to be gained from exploring the dimensions of African American voting behavior.

The analytical techniques employed to analyze the political context variable assume that the structural determinants of white political behavior are racial/demographic rather than economic or political. This sets a dangerous precedent for young scholars in search of methodological paradigms that are holistic in scope. The political context variable fails to take into account other confounding and intervening variables that mitigate against the African American residential concentration hypothesis. Moreover, one must also be cognizant of the fact that Key's analyses of the political context variable only used correlation analysis as the statistical basis of his argument. His research was therefore limited to the extent that only the statistical association between variables rather than predictability could be inferred. Although statistically, the relationship between white voter behavior and African American population density could show a very strong or significant relationship, other confounding or intervening variables could account for such a relationship thus rendering any statistic produced an artifact at best due to the spuriousness of the relationship. Most contemporary studies examining this phenomenon have relied on the use of multiple regression analysis to predict the probability of white electoral and political behavior as a function of African American residential density.[12] The results have been inconsistent and inconclusive. It should be pointed out that only the variables included in the regression models can have an explanatory impact while other significant variables capable of producing a positive or negative contextual effect may be omitted. For example, the contextual effects of such relevant variables as racial hostility, history, ethnicity, social interaction, and aspects of one's social experience may not get entered in the equation.

Scholars have examined only a portion of Key's assertion made nearly fifty years ago that the "racial tenor of Southern Politics varied with the concentration of blacks in the local context." Although traditional southern views on race and an overriding commitment to African American subordination, as argued by Key, were politically rooted in the old plantation areas of the deep south, the black belt, Key maintained that what sustained the Jim Crow system was not the racial attitudes of nonaffluent and uneducated whites but the political power and leadership of propertied elites committed to a form of social control that centered on the racial subordination of African Americans.[13] When Key wrote, the politics of the South was essentially the politics of race.

The racial concentration hypothesis lacks credibility in a system whereby white attitudes and behaviors toward African Americans are shaped by the resolve to maintain socio-economic and political control regardless of the levels of residential density. To view African American population density as a causal variable is to diminish the impact of simple racism. Further research is needed to determine more clearly the multidimensional nature of the political context variable.

AFRICAN AMERICAN POWER AND POLITICS

The Political Context Variable

I

OVERVIEW

• • • • • • •

Hanes Walton, Jr.

Context, as a deterministic variable in political behavior and politics, is *invisible.* For most political theorists it is a given and usually taken for granted. Most scholars who research and write primarily at the microanalytical level omit it due to the fact that their work focuses on individual psychological attributes. For those who work at the macroanalytical level, with its focus on institutions such as the state and its apparatuses, omission of the political context variable occurs most frequently because it is not institution-bound, nor does it help to make a case for institutions vis-a-vis individuals as the locus of analysis.

Some political scientists do research and write solely from a focus on the context variable. For the most part, however, their work has been directed either at the individual or the institutional level, and not much cross-fertilization has taken place. At best, political context has been just one more interesting variable in the ever-expanding pool of variables available for analysis. Rarely if ever has any use been made of the context variable as a tool with which to analyze and assess the African American political experience, and the infrequent forays that have been made are limited and narrow. None have isolated the influence of context nor have any analyzed its impact on the African American political experience. Basically, this experience has been probed using a multiplicity of other variables, including demographic, sociological, psychological, cultural, economic, organizational, and, most recently, feminist variables.

It is possible, especially in a behaviorally centered discipline like politics, to discount the significance of presumably irrelevant variables and consign them to the realm of the nonessential. While that would be a grave epistemological and paradigmatic error, the nominal status of the context variable in the discipline in general and in African American politics in particular clearly demonstrates that such errors can exist and perpetuate themselves. The contributors to this volume contend that failure to address and explore the variable of political context leaves one's grasp of African American politics deficient.

In order to systematically and comprehensively conceptualize political context as either an independent or a dependent variable, one must have both a plan of analysis and a scheme for ordering the structure of analysis of the variable so that an assessment and evaluating of the data can be made. Without these only an uneven, incomplete portrait of the context variable in African American politics will emerge. The overriding purpose of this book is to provide readers with a holistic picture.

Given such a task, knowledge of the means by which this plan and scheme are developed becomes paramount. For Mack Jones, who writes about the need in the study of African American politics to pay strict attention to epistemological matters, conceptualization clearly helps to determine the structural ordering.

> The process of social science inquiry [involves] the construction of frames-of-reference to guide problem formulation, prescribe the level of analysis, determine the criteria of evidence, stipulate the appropriate methods and techniques to be used, and [determine] which regularities constitute "problems." All of these operations are purposive and normative.[1]

On this point, Lenneal Henderson, in his seminal work on African American political experience, notes the following:

> Certainly, who says what about black politics should become part of any consideration about *the study* of black politics . . . because part of the debate about *the study* of black politics is whether . . . a significant difference [exists] in the motivations, assumptions, hypotheses, biases, and conclusions which finally become part of the research of this subject.[2]

Thus, for Henderson as well, not only is conceptualization important in how the study of African American politics will be structured, but the structural ordering that emerges from this conceptualizing provides insights into the "motivations, assumptions, hypothesis, biases, and conclusions" that undergird the plan of analysis taken.

Again, Mack Jones writes: "A political science grounded in the black definition of reality would of necessity raise different questions from those that emanate from the prevailing paradigm."[3] In other words, researchers investigating the political experience of a particular subcultural community must begin with a definition of the concept born of the community being studied. And that is where this book begins. Simply put, the structure of this research and the plan of analysis are rooted in the nature, scope, and significance of the political context variable in the African American political community.

This book is divided into nine parts. Each part begins with an overview relating the particular topic area to the political context variable and to the overall analysis. Each part has at least one detailed paper. Given the enormous role and importance of the American political process in the African American community, the longest section is Participation, the dominant focus of this work.

It is hoped that this structure will provide readers with a view of the political context variable as it affects and is affected by every aspect and feature of the American political system.

At the onset, the single chapter in part one, Definition, provides an understanding of the meaning of the political context variable as it has been described in the academic political science literature. It then moves on to discuss the meaning and definition of the variable within the African American community specifically; the differences and similarities in these definitions, past and present, is explored. This paper concludes with a discussion of how the context variable can be operationalized and then measured in every dimension of the political science discipline and in the American political system as a whole.

Once the variable has been defined and described, the next step is to outline the techniques and procedures used for gathering data about the variable and for empirically assessing and evaluating that data. This is the focus of part two: Methodology. Two distinct approaches to the study of race and politics have emerged from the literature over the years.[4] One focuses on African American political activity as a means of empowerment. The other, the "race relations" approach, deals with system maintenance over empowerment. Both approaches have cultivated their own distinctive methodologies. But readers must be ever mindful that methodological concerns are not necessarily neutral, and that methodology is not always constructed to generate valid knowledge. It can be used, given a researcher's "motivations, assumptions, hypothesis, biases, and conclusions," to provide misleading, even fraudulent, results. Therefore, the first paper in this section explains how, depending on the approach taken, different results, and consequently different interpretations of and conclusions about the role and significance of the context variable on African American politics, have been generated. The first paper raises and addresses some questions about the methodology of political science research in a racialized society, while the second describes the methodology employed in the research undertaken for this book.

The focus then shifts to the American political system itself. If, as John Hope

Franklin and Genna Rae McNeil write, the Constitution of the United States is indeed "a living document" and the Supreme Court, in its role as interpreter of the Constitution, has had to be "concern[ed] with the problems of race in order to provide racial justice and civil rights," there is no better place to begin analyzing the changing African American political context than with an investigation of the nature of constitutionalism in the United States.[5] The single chapter in part three, Constitutionalism, describes the institutions, individuals, and interest groups that attempt to shape constitutional interpretations during efforts to transform the African American political context. Significant attention is devoted in this analysis to the Reagan-Bush years.

The next step is to focus on the cardinal component of any democracy: the individual citizen. Modern behavioral research suggests that one of the ways to assess and validate the significance of individuals as movers and shapers of the American political system is to look at the political culture, socialization, and opinions of American voters. This necessarily involves a detailed examination of the attributes, self-categorization, and psychological predispositions of these voters. The parts on Culture and Socialization and the first paper on Participation seek to do just that, relative to a focus on the African American voting populace.

The first of these takes a major politically transformative event of the Reagan-Bush era, the Los Angeles riots of 1992,[6] and probes the political, philosophical, and ethical motives guiding the behavior of some of the African American individuals involved. Rarely have Black urban uprisings been studied much beyond their economic, racial, and psychological implications. This paper marks a departure from the extant research.

Socialization investigates the effects of political forces on a subcultural community—specifically, the protest resignations of two African American elected officials in the rural south during the Reagan-Bush years. Again, the tendency in the academic political science literature is to concentrate on permanent socialization agents such as schools, family, media, and peer groups on individual and group political behavior.[7] By stressing the importance of a short-term factor, this section offers some pioneering insights.

The first paper in Participation, on political opinion, describes how the political attitudes of African American voters have fluctuated during periods of political context transformation. Public opinion of a nearly monotholitic group, like African Americans on certain political issues, as it socio-political-legal context is being transformed in negative ways, is not stable and permanent, even in its opposition to the transformers.

If one is to gain information on and insights into the transformation of a group's political context, one must analyze the process or processes designed for both maintenance and change of the political system as a whole. In the United States and other democracies, this is the process of voting, with its concomitant political campaigns, colorful political personalities, party partisanship, third parties, political party conversion, and interest-group politics. Nearly all previous analyses of African American partisan politics have revolved around blacks and the Democratic party,[8] partly because most African Americans are Democrats and partly because the party itself has held the presidency for all but twenty-eight years since the New Deal. To offer readers a novel standpoint from which to view the transformation of the African American political context, the papers in this section highlight the politics and political efforts of African American Republicans during the Reagan and Bush presidencies. The other principle guiding this section is that, to unearth important aspects of the context variable in African American politics, one should not look simply at African American political participation at the presidential, congressional, senatorial, gubernatorial and mayoral levels, but in political parties, interest groups, campaigns, and conventions.

One paper provides a rare look at African American involvement in interest-group politics in the White House and the Justice Department during the Bush presidency. Another chapter analyzes how the transformed political context of the era influenced the political campaigns of African American candidates at the grassroots level. This is followed by an examination of African American voting patterns, and, with it, a case study of an instance when the usually heavily Democratic voting pattern of African Americans was broken. In this case, Black voters backed a Republican mayoral candidate even while Republican party politics at the national level were producing negative consequences for the African American community. This paper asks: Under what conditions and circumstances will African Americans in a transformed political context vote for the transformers of that context? The next paper analyzes Black support for the Republican party in the tiny rural backwater community in which Supreme Court Associate Justice Clarence Thomas was raised to determine whether the nomination of an African American to the Supreme Court influences political party conversion at the community level.

Another paper explores political campaigns in which explicit instead of implicit appeals that exploit race and racial cleavages are used for partisan gain.[9] The data presented offer insights into how such appeals affect African American voting behavior in a transformed political context.

The following two papers examine the context variable at the congressional level. Where one of these focuses on the Republican party's financial support of African American GOP congressional candidates during the Reagan and Bush years, the other addresses a major electoral breakthrough: the election of the first African American woman, Carol Mosely-Braun, to the United States Senate.

The tenth paper in this section offers a comprehensive analysis of African American political participation in and responses to Ross Perot's bold, dramatic, and very significant third-party run at the presidency. The concluding paper of this section looks at the success and failures of the presidential campaign of an

African American political leader, attempted at the height of the Reagan-Bush period of political transformation. That candidate, L. Douglas Wilder, ran as a Democratic contender in the 1992 elections.

Having looked at participation, we next ask: What role do decision-makers play in shaping the aspirations, concerns, and interest of African American voters and candidates? This section, Decisions, offers two papers. The first, in its discussion of the fledgling Clinton administration's early confrontations with the transformed political context left behind by Reagan and Bush, focuses on Clinton's political appointments. Unable to pass major social legislation and economic initiatives for the benefit of the African American community which was so badly burned by the Republican contextual revolution, Clinton, like so many presidents before him, adopted the strategy of appointing prominent African Americans to government positions in order to pacify this community of voters and respond to its needs.[10] The second paper examines the events that have transpired since the Republican party, even more intent on transforming the political context for African Americans and other minorities, took over the 104th Congress.

Discussion of the influence of political decision-makers leads to an analysis of public policy production. The two papers on Policy concern the effects of a transformed political context on both domestic, particularly urban, as well as foreign policy. The first of these papers continues the focus on urban unrest as it concentrates specifically on fiscal urban policies of the Reagan, Bush, and Clinton presidencies. It offers a unique perspective due to the comparison it draws between Republican and Democratic presidents in a transformed political context. In the second of these papers the question becomes: Given that the Republicans successfully transformed domestic policy during the Reagan and Bush years, what successes did they have in transforming foreign policy, and how did African Americans respond to these Republican efforts? The role and function of African American foreign policy elites and organizations are thoroughly evaluated and analyzed in this regard.

In the closing section, Prospects, the depth and breadth of the African American political landscape are pulled together in a brief summary and conclusion which also offers a glimpse into the future.

Collectively, these papers provide the reader with an array of testable propositions about the American political context and the African American political context variable. Perhaps more importantly, they offer directions for future investigations of this under-explored variable.

This empirically based work is launched by well-informed perspectives from the realms of theory and practice in the form of the introductory commentary offered by leading political science scholars William H. Boone, Kenneth Jordan, Modibo Kadalie, and by Congressman Donald L. Payne, chairman of the Congressional Black Caucus. Their opening statements lend much to the scope and direction of this work, and aptly set the tone for the analysis that follows.

PART I

DEFINITION

Political context, as a variable in the African American political community, is a concept awaiting definition. In the mid-eighties it was shown that most of the key concepts born of the behavioral revolution in political science had to be reformulated, re-conceptualized, and redefined to adequately explore and explain African American political behavior.[1] Political context is no different.

The working definition developed for this study has been rooted in and derived from the African American political experience. The political context variable is defined in this volume as a thesis which postulates that political behavior at either the individual or the group level is not independent of the political environment (a particular time period and a particular place) in which it occurs.

Once a definition has been developed in light of the African American political experience a full-fledged conceptualization can be made. But in mapping out the conceptualization of the defined variable, it is essential to pay strict attention to the unique features of the variable. The race attribute has a special relationship to its cultural base. The conceptualization of the African American political context variable for this study demonstrates the unique features and make theoretical allowances for them.

Following the definition and conceptualization is the overview of ways in which the variable was transformed in recent Republican and Democratic administrations. Finally, this paper closes with an emphasis on the scope of this volume: how the political context variable shapes African American political behavior in all the aspects of the American political process, including decision-making and policy. It also presents examples of contextual transformation by the three presidents—Reagan, Bush, and Clinton—under study.

2

THE POLITICAL CONTEXT VARIABLE

The Transformation Politics of the Reagan, Bush, and Clinton Presidencies

• • • • • • •

Hanes Walton, Jr.

Political context as a variable offers the thesis that political behavior, at either the individual or group level, is not independent of the political environment (i.e. a particular time period and a particular place) in which it occurs.[1] Although this is the working definition for this book, there are many variations on the definition. In his first book on political participation, Lester Milbrath tells us that "Environmental impact on behavior is indirect, meaning that it is always mediated by personality."[2] However, by the second edition of the book Milbrath and Gael write:

> environmental factors shape human behavior independent of the personal traits of an individual. . . . There are a variety of contextual or environmental variables that could affect political participation [and among them are] the cultural milieu, the social-structural character of the community, and the political setting.[3]

While they specify some of these contextual variables, they could add such important ones as national leadership (presidential and congressional), ideological preferences, and public opinion on race and policy proposals.

Another definition says that the political context variable "is any effect on individual behavior that arises due to social interaction within an environment."[4] This definition equates "social interaction" with the political context: "contextual effects as construct here are due to social interaction within particular environments and social contexts are created as a result of these interactions."[5] But the crucial reality here in both definitions, the persistent one or the recently revised one, is that the political context is itself static and the characteristics are dynamic. This is a fundamental intellectual failure given the political experiences of racial, ethnic, and political minorities (and to a great extent majorities) in American's long and ever changing political history.

Although several scholars have made the point that the political context can change, definitions tend to characterize the variable as static and unmoving. "The impact of these environmental factors on participation can be changed or influenced by the design of the Constitution and political system of a nation."[6]

John Books and Charles Prysby conclude their study:

> We believe that more emphasis should be placed on how the context changes over time. The possibility that changes in the contextual variable rather than this absolute value have the greatest impact deserves explicit consideration.[7]

Then they observe:

> There are very few examples of research hypothesizing that the extent of certain behavior is related to the degree of change in some contextual variable, but there are social reasons to believes that changes in contextual characteristics are as important as their absolute values.[8]

Still, while these authors note this reality and assert its importance, particularly for future studies of the political context, they themselves keep their static definitions. This is a costly mistake. A static definition of the political context limits its applicability as well as the researcher's epistemological outlook.

Therefore we refine our working definition to include both the static and dynamic features of the political context variable. The political context variable, which influences and shape political behavior at either the individual or group level, is both dynamic and static as are the elements in the context and the relationship between change and the context is reciprocal.

The other, possibly greater, conceptual flaw in the definition of the political context in the scholarly literature is in its understanding and grasp of race as a political contextual variable.

About race as a factor in the political context Books and Prysby tell us: "Studies of political behavior in the United States also have considered another important aspect of the social composition of the context: The racial make up of the community."[9]

Another analyst writes: "Race has been a dominant political cleavage in the United States for most of its history. Currently, no other cleavage within the electorate divides voters more sharply than does race."[10] After having said this, the author declares: "However, the importance of race goes beyond describing how individuals of a particular racial group behave. A substantial body of research demonstrates that race also produces a contextual effect."[11] While it is true that this substantial literature exists, it is unidirectional, focusing only on white responses.

Thomas Carsey in a succinct summary of this literature finds "we have two strong and well-respected research traditions in political science that lead potentially to conflicting expectations regarding the impact of black densities on voting behavior of whites at the neighborhood level."[12] The first of these is described by V. O. Key: "white voters living in increasingly black counties and/or states became increasingly likely to vote in a manner considered hostile to black interest."[13] The second tradition, which is more general and pays less attention to the racial factor in the context, declares that non-group (non-black) members will vote in a manner considered positive and friendly to black interests.

A pioneering article explains these two traditions:

> While a strong literature reports a negative effect of black densities on white voter behavior at the county and state levels, when measured at the precinct and borough levels, we find a positive effect.
>
> The contextual effect of race may not be so different from the contextual effects of factors like partisanship, ethnicity, or social class.[14]

Despite this finding, Gerald C. Wright, Jr. "examine[d] southern voting patterns for Wallace in the 1968 presidential election and found that whites were more likely to vote for Wallace when they lived in counties with large black populations."[15] In the same year, William Keech in his analysis of Tuskegee, Alabama and Durham, North Carolina found "similar effects"[16] and "Matthews and Prothro's study of southern politics in the early 1960s found similar contextual effects for several race-related attitudes."[17] During Jesse Jackson's 1988 campaign to capture the Democratic party's presidential nomination,

> the political attitudes of southern political activists were significantly affected by the racial composition of the county: white Democratic party activists from counties with a high proposition of black voters were more likely to hold conservative views on a variety of race-related issues.[18]

A recent analysis continues this look at how African Americans in the context influences white voting behavior by looking at white voter registration rates in Louisiana: "Higher black concentrations are associated with a decline in the percentage of white registered voters who are Democrats and an increase in the percentage who are Republicans."[19]

Collectively, every single piece of the literature looks at the contextual effect of race on white political behavior. None of the literature looks the other way. And the empirical findings and therefore generalizations which emanate from this literature leave the distinct impression that what is important and of the highest priority is that the mere presence of African Americans in the context significantly influences and impacts white political behavior—nothing else matters. Moreover, given this one-way conceptualization of race composition in the political context and the preponderance of the literature on this point, there arises a clear cut sense of what Mark Jones calls the "anticipation and control needs . . . of the dominant majority."[20] For in this one-sided literature is not only a set of "shared beliefs about the subject matter [and a] consensus on the range of appropriate questions to be asked," there is finally "shared normative assumptions on basic . . . issues."[21] These "shared normative assumptions" about the political context become a dominant orthodoxy that ultimately creates and sustains a public discourse which takes as the norm the wishes, preferences, and bias of the white political majority as the right and proper way to think about this political variable. This normative public discourse displaces and submerges the viewpoint that whites in the context, as either a majority or minority, impact and influence African American political behavior. While one academic recognized the unidirectional approach in this vast literature, he wrote: "thus, while social contexts are important to blacks as well as to whites, an analysis of the role of social contexts in shaping the political behavior of blacks awaits some other investigation."[22]

Recently, two groups of African American political scientists have attempted to determine if the social (political) context played an influential role in shaping African American political behavior. One group discovered that the mere presence of African American mayors in the political context heightened the racial consciousness of the members of the African American electorate and increased their political mobilization.[23]

The second group found in lower income neighborhoods in Detroit, Michigan that the greater the incidence of poverty in the African American neighborhood, the lesser the degree of political participation and mobilization.[24] The finding from the Detroit study was in direct opposition to the insights of the finding of a white political scientist who used Buffalo, New York as his neighborhood context. From this study, he asserted:

> In many instances blacks also live in lower status neighborhoods, but the relationship between their political behavior and their neighborhoods is largely spurious—other factors are quite obviously responsible for these differences.[25]

Hence, poverty in the context does not shape African American political behavior. Exactly how he arrived at this conclusion is unclear since he deleted all the African American respondents from his study.[26]

Although these two rather recent studies reveal for the first time how the political context shapes African American political behavior, the next step has yet to be taken towards explaining how whites in that political context shapes African American political behavior.

Besides the definitional and conceptual problems, there is the methodological one. In his *Southern Politics,* V. O. Key, Jr. empirically correlated African American population densities with aspects of white political behavior at macrolevel (counties). This empirical methodological aspect not only pervades the book but became the overriding theme and theoretical device for explaining southern politics. Although surely not Key's fault, most subsequent academics have accepted his measurement methodology as the only way to empirically assess the political contest variable at the macrolevel. This has lead to the erroneous proposition in the discipline that racial population densities are the only variable of the political context. Nothing could be further from the truth.

Another measurable aspect of the political context variable is the organizational one, which in the South is the one-party system. In fact, it is the bedrock of southern politics. It is of such importance that Key devotes three of five parts of *Southern Politics* in an explicit manner to it and the other two parts in an implicit manner: like the population density aspect, this other aspect pervades the book and part one of the book begins with this focus. On this aspect of the political context variable, Key let it be known that southern black belt whites, a small and very discipline elite, used a single organization, the Democratic party (today it is the Republican party), to change the regional and then national political context. He empirically measured this aspect of the variable at the macrolevel also. But over time, this fundamental aspect of the variable got lost or dropped. The reason is simple.

Of the two aspects of the political context variable at the macrolevel, the organizational aspect was measured by relying "heavily on cartographic evidence and on scattergrams of aggregate data to explore the nature of party factions in the South."[27] Such an innovative use of maps and the spatial placements of county votes made the subsequent use of this aspect of the political context variable more difficult in linear measurement technique like regression analysis which, unless otherwise noted, is a cross-sectional measurement device. Key's cartographic and scattergram measuring devices used an interrupted time series—before and after. Key's measurement devices used two or more points in time, making them dynamic and thereby showing change from one point to another. Regression analysis on the other hand is usually static and population densities as expressed in percentages representing a single time point, like an election year or a single decade.[28] Hence, the organizational aspect of the political context variable, because of the complexity in measuring it, got misplaced by subsequent scholars who explored the racial threat hypothesis instead. It was no longer used in the analytical and explanatory equations of this variable at the macrolevel. Thus, the political context variable became methodologically devoid of one of its central defining aspects at the macrolevel. This diminished the usefulness of this variable to explain the political process and illuminate other categories of variables, like the sociological, economic, and psychological ones. The loss crippled the ability of scholars to find a satisfactory definition and measuring technique of the political context variable at the microlevel.[29]

Therefore, reflected in our refined definition and conceptualization of the political context variable is the rudimentary acknowledgement that the variable can influence and shape political behavior of both African Americans and whites. Next, the political context variable contains an organizational aspect, political parties, which effect both African Americans and whites. In this volume our concern is with the ways in which the white majority or minority can transform the political context of the African American community and its political behavior.

Transforming the Political Context Variable

Having set forth the definition and the conceptualization of the variable, the next logical step is to ask how whites can change and alter the context for African Americans. To begin to structure the answer to "how," one can go directly to one of the intellectual fathers of the context variable, V. O. Key, Jr. In his classic on southern politics, he established beyond a shadow of a doubt that the mere presence of African Americans in the context shapes white political behavior and he followed his findings to their logical conclusion that the political behavior of a white minority shapes African American political behavior in the post-Reconstruction era. Historically, the white political minority changed the context by altering the rules, disenfranchising African Americans,[30] and instituting the public policy of informal and formal (legal) segregation for all of southern society.[31] And finally they altered political party membership and the bases of party competition in the region. The Democratic party became the party of white supremacy; the Republican party found little support in the white electorate. Hence, the Democratic party became hegemonic throughout the region.[32] Whites induced contextual changes at the legal, cultural, social and finally the organizational level, effectively removing African Americans from the political process, the Fifteenth Amendment to the Constitution notwithstanding. Overall, Key's formulation of the political context variable in *Southern Politics* showed both sides of the political coin. Yet his disciplines and proponents severely restricted and circumscribed his formulation.

But after his classic in 1949, Key added to his formulation of the political context variable and it is to these additional insights that we now must turn for an answer to our research question of how can the political context be changed, not only by a southern white minority, but by whites in general. Key writes:

> Politicians may, in effect, invest group attributes with political significance. Appeals to group interest, prejudices, and pride are part of the stock-in-trade of the politician who often labors mightily to make the voter conscious of his social characteristics in order that they may determine his political preference.[33]

What Key reveals is that politicians and political leaders as well as political parties can take an attribute, like race, which is prevalent in the context, give it a top priority in the political campaign, and thereby accentuate it positively or negatively. A negative emphasis, either by explicit or implicit racial appeals, cleaves the political context and the groups become polarized as public opinion changes as a result of these campaigns; these opinions manifest themselves in changes of public policy as well as the preferences for certain policies. Once this happens, African Americans find themselves in not only a modified legal and political environment, they find their rights diminished and consistently under attack, federal assistance and legal protection reduced, and economic benefits and compensatory support policies discontinued. The political context has been transformed.

The civil rights era of the 1960s had a substantial positive impact on the political context of the African American community. But the Reagan and Bush presidencies attacked and eliminated many of the reforms created in that period, negatively transtorming the political context of the African American community. A Democratic administration followed these Republican presidents. This administration had the option of rolling back the transformation, going along with the transformation, or doing a little of both; since this was a centrist rather than a liberal democratic administration, it was not clear which option or options would be implemented. These different administrations provide a unique opportunity to explore and evaluate the political context variable.

The Politics of Contextual Transformation: The Reagan, Bush, and Clinton Presidencies

Contextual transformation and retransformation didn't simply began with the Reagan, Bush, and Clinton presidencies. There is a long and uneven history of national leaders, parties, and governmental institutions changing the political context for African Americans in negative and positive fashions.

In the colonial period nine (69%) of the original thirteen colonies never denied the vote to free men of color. But when the revolutionary war transformed these thirteen original colonies to states governed by the Articles of Confederation, only four (31%) states permitted free men of color to vote.[34] In states like Pennsylvania and North Carolina African Americans initially had the right to vote but the state legislatures revoked that right in New Jersey in 1807, Connecticut in 1818, North Carolina in 1834, and Pennsylvania in 1838.[35] Although New York never denied the right, it placed a $250 property qualification on free men of color to vote in 1821.[36] (Table 2.1)

In the formative years of the new nation, these patterns continued:

TABLE 2.1

The Voting Rights of Free Blacks in the Thirteen Original Colonies: The Colonial and Revolutionary Eras

Colony	Vote denied from the outset	Vote eventually denied	Vote never denied	Colonial status
The Colonial Era				
Massachusetts			x	Royal
New Hampshire			x	Royal
Rhode Island			x	Self-governing
Connecticut			x	Self-governing
New York			x	Royal
Pennsylvania			x	Proprietory
New Jersey			x	Royal
Delaware			x	Proprietory
Maryland			x	Proprietory
Virginia		x		Royal
North Carolina		x		Royal
South Carolina		x		Royal
Georgia		x		Royal
Total		4	9	
The Revolutionary Era				
Massachusetts			x	
New Hampshire			x	
Rhode Island			x	
Connecticut		x		
New York			x	
Pennsylvania		x		
New Jersey		x		
Delaware	x			
Maryland		x		
Virginia	x			
North Carolina		x		
South Carolina	x			
Georgia	x			
Total	4	5	4	

Status of the colonies from Rebeca Brooks Gruver, *An American History* (1981). Suffrage information from *The Development of Sentiment on Negro Suffrage to 1860* (1912). *Neglected History: Essays in Negro History by a College President* (1969).

> With the exception of Maine, none of the states that entered the Union after 1800 permitted blacks to vote in general elections. . . . By 1860, only Massachusetts, Maine, New Hampshire, Vermont, and Rhode Island allowed blacks to vote on the same terms as whites.[37]

Of the state government's ability to transform the political context for African Americans in the formative years of the new nation, a legal scholar tells us:

> Because the national government exercised limited functions during the nineteenth century, state and local governments were far more significant in determining the rights that blacks enjoyed. Moreover, in defining these rights, states operated virtually without restraint by the national government.[38]

Yet it was not only the state governments in this period that transformed the political context for "Free Men and Women of Color." The Supreme Court did so in the *Dred Scott* decision,[39] and Congress did after the Civil War with the thirteenth, fourteenth, and fifteenth amendments.

But the fact that white governments at different levels in the federal system can transform the context variable in either positive or negative ways is only half the story. Political parties, interest groups, political candidates, elected and appointed officials can also transform the political context for African Americans. Lets look for a moment at the Democratic party one hundred years ago, led by President Grover Cleveland. Listen as Richard Valelly and Jeffrey Tulis mark the moment:

> A century ago, Democrats regained control of both the White House and Congress for the first time in thirty-six years, since the Buchanan administration of 1857–1861. The Cleveland administration promptly moved to roll back the several statutes enacted during Reconstruction to implement the Fifteenth Amendment. They did this in the 53rd and 54th Congresses, 1893–94.
>
> The Repealer made it considerably easier for Southern conservatives to engineer a massive transformation of the Southern electoral system. New rules—literacy tests, grandfather clauses, good understanding tests, poll taxes, and the like—drove black Southerners out of electoral politics.[40]

Collectively these examples reveal that Key's astute observation and empirical finding that attributes in the context can be activated to transform the political context is understated in terms of race. Concerning race there are longstanding cultural beliefs. These can be articulated to mobilize individuals in a negative manner, and these beliefs can in addition sustain the transformation of the political context of African Americans in a negative way by political institutions. It must be added to Key's insight that some contextual attributes, like race, are much stronger culturally based than others. For these, transformation can come from a greater number of political entities and sources than for other, weaker culturally based attributes.

The inherent features in the American political culture that give birth to these sustaining values and beliefs about race were there at the creation and founding of the nation.

By affirming the slavery of African Americans, the founding and constitutive document, the Constitution, combined democracy and tyranny simultaneously. Foreign political observers such as James Bryce, Alexis de Tocqueville, and Gunnar Myrdal have all noted this dual reality. Yet the prevailing consensus, fostered in part by Louis Hartz's influential work, *The Liberal Tradition in America,* is that America is literally all about equality. In her recent address to the American Political Science Association, its first female president, Judith Skhlar, reminded the profession of this dual tradition which has never disappeared. She writes:

> American political theory . . . has been charged with an obsessive and unconscious commitment to a liberal faith that prevents it from asking profound and critical questions.[41]
>
> Until the Civil War Amendments America was neither a liberal nor a democratic country, whatever its citizens might have believed. . . . This country had embarked upon two experiments simultaneously: one in democracy and the other in tyranny.[42]

John Hope Franklin tells us:

> Those who wrote the Constitution brought with them to Philadelphia not only a century and a half of experience with slavery but also a similar period of discrimination against blacks who were *not* slaves. If the framers of the Constitution gave no attention to blacks who were free, it was not because they believed that there should be no distinction among the peoples. Rather, it was because of the framers' preoccupation with slavery at a time when continued discrimination against free blacks was assumed.[43]
>
> One looks in vain at the entire miserable period from the writing of the Constitution to the outbreak of the Civil War to find any indication that the Founding Fathers, the fledgling government of the United States, or the great leaders of the nation in the first half of the nineteenth century pursued a policy looking toward any semblance of citizenship or equality for free black Americans.[44]

Franklin concludes that one of the enduring legacies that the Founding Fathers bequeathed to future generations of Americans was a moral ambiguity about race.[45]

Cultural values and beliefs about race predates the formation of the new nation, and these beliefs informed the Founding Fathers, permeated the organizing documents—the Declaration of Independence and the Constitution—and structured the new nation. Although the Revolutionary War led to the abolition of slavery in the northern states and "transformed slavery from a national to a sectional institution,"[46] it was treated as a national institution in 1775 and at the 1787 Constitutional Convention in Philadelphia.

Despite the fact that the South lost the Civil War and despite President Lincoln's Gettysburg Address, southern regionalism continued the moral ambiguities and thereby the cultural values and beliefs present at the founding. Folklore, plays, movies, novels, social customs, and religion perpetuated the myth of the "lost cause." This myth held that southerners had fought in a noble cause and that the participants in that "lost cause" were heroes and heroines. For the nation, the South became the repository of cultural beliefs and values about race. Although Gary Wills has argued that President Lincoln's words at Gettysburg remade America, it is obvious that President Lincoln's effort to reshape the Constitution didn't offset or diminish the southern regionalism that said otherwise.

> The Gettysburg Address has become an authoritative expression of the American spirit—as authoritative as the Declaration itself, and perhaps even more influential, since it determines how we read the Declaration. For most people now, the Declaration means what Lincoln told us it means, as a way of correcting the Constitution itself without overthrowing it. It is this connection of the spirit, this intellectual revolution [and] by accepting the Gettysburg Address, its concept of a single people dedicated to a proposition, we have been changed.[47]

In this competition for the public mind Wills posits that southern regionalism has lost: "The proponents of states rights may have arguments," he opines, "but they have lost their force, in courts as well as in the popular mind."[48] Wills concludes by asserting: "Lincoln changed the way people thought about the Constitution."[49]

Not only didn't the South lose this battle for the public mind, southern leaders like George Wallace moved north in his 1968 and 1972 campaigns and found considerable electoral support for the values and beliefs about race so embedded in their regional culture. Southern ideas had northern adherents.

Noting the earlier efforts of Republican candidate Barry Goldwater,[50] drawing significant lessons from George Wallace's northern forays and President

Nixon's victorious use of his southern strategy in 1968, in 1980 Republican strategist Kevin Phillips developed not only a new political arithmetic for Republican presidential hopefuls, but a southern Republican strategy that had national implications based on mobilizing voters around race in the political context.[51] These efforts mobilized not only individuals in the South but also individuals geographically far removed. As a result, others inside the Republican party drew valuable lessons about the cultural base of the race attribute.

As governor of California from 1966 to 1974, Ronald Reagan made repeated trips to the South, speaking "to Chambers of Commerce, groups of businessmen gathered in Brownville, Lake Charles, Kosciusko, Johnson City, Cullman, Macon, Perry, and Falls Church and places in between."[52] As Greenshaw writes:

> Ronald Reagan had already made one unpublicized tour through the Southland, touching places in Alabama, Mississippi, and Louisiana. He told small gatherings about the qualities of this man Goldwater, and he showed off his own great qualities as far as they were concerned. Then he went back to California where he sat down with a group of Republican businessmen and started planning his debut as a [presidential] candidate.[53]

From this pre-positioning strategy, Reagan and the Republican party developed their crucial political technique, the re-introduction of racial cleavages for partisan political advantage. Reagan launched this effort by starting his presidential campaign in Philadelphia, Mississippi, were the three civil rights workers James Chancy, Michael Schwerner, and Andrew Goodman were brutally murdered during the Freedom Summer of 1964. At the Nashoba County (Mississippi) Fair in 1980, Reagan spoke in explicit terms about states rights and other issues dear to the old south. With these frequent trips to the South, Reagan was immersing himself in the cultural beliefs and values that this region had sustained and promoted about race. He was also learning how to gain political support and backing from this region by discovering first-hand which code words for race would work. Explicit racial appeals were giving way to implicit ones due to the African American civil rights movement and the success of the Voting Rights Act of 1965. In an era before the rise of focus groups and the changing of political rethoric, Reagan's first-hand experiences were invaluable. The only thing that he needed was to determine if these appeals would work outside of the South.

> Ronald Reagan, the former governor of California and opponent of the 1964 Civil Rights Act, held the state's rights philosophy of the right wing of his party and promised to reduce the federal commitment to civil rights enforcement and the Great Society economic programs that have benefited blacks substantially.[54]

Political commentator William Schneider says: "Reagan's victory confirmed the Republican party's shift to the right. It gave party control to the conservatives who first emerged as a protest faction against the party establishment in 1964."[55] And the sole purpose of this hard turn to the right was simple: "The Republican new right has tended to attract many former conservative Democrats, particularly in the South and West. . . . Strom Thurmond, Jesse Helms, John Connally, S. I. Hayakawa, and Ronald Reagan were all once Democrats who, as conservatives, found themselves out of place in their party."[56]

Electoral scholar Walter Dean Burnham shows us that in the 1980 election, "Reagan and his allies [won] through an integrated conservative revitalization program."[57] He writes:

> The Reagan legacy is likely to be particularly long lasting . . . through the federal *courts.* . . . Reagan's judicial appointments were different: They came from the ideological right, not just from the ranks of Republican-affiliated lawyers. By the end of his eight years, Ronald Reagan had appointed more than half of all federal judges.[58]

Burnham argues that the goals and objectives of

> the Reagan Revolution are . . . essentially, to achieve the dismantling of the domestic functions of the American national state (i.e. the federal government); and moreover in such a way as to make it as difficult as possible for any subsequent political generation to put this Humpty-Dumpty back together again.[59]

But what did this mean for African Americans and their political context? One political scientist makes this observation about the direction of the "Reagan Revolution" for African Americans and their political context:

> Although Ronald Reagan took the fewest legislative actions of any president, his executive actions were unparalleled . . . The Reagan administration returned civil rights to the forefront of the domestic policy agency . . . However, Ronald Reagan's policy was one of contraction rather than expansion and thus reversed the direction that civil rights policy had taken during the past generation.[60]

Steven Lawson writes that the second Reagan administration "proved no more promising to Afro-American political advancement than did the first"; indeed, he contends, "the Republican administration went further in antagonizing blacks than even its opponents had expected."[61] Clearly, the Reagan presidency changed the political context around the variable of race, at the electoral level and the governing level.

When the presidential mantle passed from Reagan to his vice president, George Bush in 1988, the political and social context remained under siege. In the presidential campaign, Bush continued to "stroke" the white, male (and particularly southern) electorate with his use of the infamous "Willie Horton ads." Of this, one scholar writes:

> To portray a black male who "killed" one white male, stabbed a second, and raped a white woman as a typical criminal is inaccurate. Rather, my point is that raising the fear of whites that they are likely to be murdered or raped by blacks is unjustified. It is racist to identify William Horton's action as somehow typical, as George Bush did when he said that the Horton case had "come to symbolize, and represent . . . the misguided outlook of my opponent." Moreover, disproportionate portrayal of blacks as criminals play on racial fears.[62]

Crime became one of the implicit code words in the campaign. And when this code word was employed with the word liberal, the dreaded code word for "racially sensitive," Bush defeated the Democratic presidential candidate, Michael Dukakis. The electoral techniques developed during the two Reagan presidential elections paid off handsomely for the next Republican hopeful. And in all three of these presidential elections, the southern based cultural values and belief about race had proven not only successful but transferable from the South to the rest of the nation. Implicit racial appeals would play everywhere and with nearly every political group in society.

Therefore Bush, like Reagan, began governing with these concerns in mind. The Bush administration, though much less strident about racial issues than the Reagan administration, continued the policy of non-enforcement of civil rights laws and regulations. While Bush advanced a mixed appointment policy of designating hard liners and soft liners in terms of African American conservatives, his appointment of Clarence Thomas to replace Thurgood Marshall on the Supreme Court was clearly demonstrative of the context-changing strategy that had been initiated during the Reagan years. Thomas was a hard-line conservative operative within the Reagan administrations, serving at HEW and two terms on the EEOC. He had also attended the Fairmont conference. This conference, which took place one month after Reagan's election, was orchestrated by his friend and future cabinet member, Edwin Meese. It brought together a new group of African American leaders to embrace and espouse conservative philosophy and programs as the solution to problems in the African American ghetto, underclass, and middle class. The conference also made clear that this ideology would be a prerequisite for political appointments in the new administration. Shortly thereafter, Thomas denounced his own sister, and by implication other

African Americans, for receiving welfare assistance, a pronouncement that was to resurface along with Anita Hill's charges of sexual harassment to fan the flames of his controversial nomination hearings.[63]

Additionally, the Bush presidency carried forward the practice of vetoing restorative civil rights legislation. Reagan had vetoed such legislation in 1987; Bush followed suit in 1990.[64] Only mild or watered down civil rights legislation would prevail during the latter's term.

While the presidency was undermining and undercutting the civil rights victories of the sixties, it was not alone. The Supreme Court joined in altering the context in which the interests of the African American community were viewed. Reagan had installed a conservative majority on the Court which set out to disavow affirmative action as a remedy for discrimination, eliminate federal contract set-asides at the local and state level,[65] and diminish the depth and breadth of the 1964 Civil Rights act (which was later repaired in part by the 1987 and 1991 Civil Rights Restoration acts).[66] In addition, the Court changed the burden of proof in discrimination cases from effect to intent, and treated both African American voting rights and reapportionment disputes as affirmative action cases rather than as matters of constitutional rights.[67]

Only the Democratic-controlled Congress sought to minimize the thrust of Republican presidential leadership. Although Congress confirmed the majority of the conservative African American Reagan-Bush appointees, it tried, through the use of its oversight and budgetary powers, to thwart some of these appointments.[68] And Congress passed the two Civil Rights Restoration bills. In the case of the 1987 bill, it overrode Reagan's veto to enact the legislation. While it failed to override Bush's veto of similar restorative legislation in 1989, Congress was able to effect a compromise bill in 1990.[69] Similarly, Congress reduced the budget of the Civil Rights Commission when its chairman, Reagan hard-liner Clarence Pendleton, an African American, attacked comparable pay for women and called African American civil rights leaders "the new racists."[70]

However, Congress approved the Reagan tax cut and his reductions in spending for social programs. It also approved Reagan's appointment of Pendleton and later Walter Allen to the Civil Rights Commission, Samuel Pierce (a relative softliner) to HUD, and a host of conservative African Americans to federal judgeships.[71] Moreover, Congress did little to move President Bush to establish a national urban policy, not even in the wake of the Los Angeles riots.

Thus, while Congress's efforts were mixed, they were, on the whole, less negative in changing the political context of the African American community than were Reagan and Bush and the Supreme Court. Let us look at some of the specific ways in which these presidents went about altering the context.

President Reagan began almost immediately by demanding, creating, and promoting a new African American leadership. Ideology, particularly Republican conservatism, became the criterion by which this leadership was appraised. African American political hopefuls could not only not avoid expressing the conservative ideology of the Republican party line, but they had to carry it out while in office. Secondly, the Reagan presidency, with its immoderate use of the federal budget veto and modification of regulatory procedures and rules to achieve political ends, effectively lessened, or refused to enforce, existing civil rights laws and rules.[72] The Reagan administration launched a full-scale attack on the Civil Rights Commission, reconstituting it with ideologues more to its liking. It appointed African American conservatives to token positions within the federal bureaucracy, charging them with the task of promoting programs of restraints, denials, and cutbacks in affirmative action, equal employment opportunity, and other race-sensitive policies. Reagan himself sought to derail efforts to honor Martin Luther King, Jr. with a national holiday, but eventually conceded and approved legislation enacting King's commemoration. In his second term, Reagan continued to alter the political context within both the African American and white communities. Under his watch, the public mood toward racial inequality changed from one of concern to one of outright rejection. "Blame the victim, not the government," was the prevailing notion of the day.

Indeed, if ambitious African Americans of the era aspired to quick advancement of their political careers, they needed only adhere, as the Fairmont conference and the subsequent Fairmont papers revealed, to a special kind of political correctness: a general political conservatism that eschewed civil rights policies and programs, and that attacked the various civil rights leaders who were lobbying the new president for the maintenance and support of the political context of the civil rights era. The new African American conservative Republicans had to be outspoken in this regard, and had to, at every occasion possible, deny that the government was the solution. Like their mentor, President Reagan, they had to see government as the problem.

Moreover, the aspirants' espousal of the Reagan brand of political correctness took precedence over all other qualifications and achievements. Experience, talent, mentorship, or length of party affiliation were not as important as this political correctness. Traditional African American Republicans who failed to join the new bandwagon were swept aside or quickly removed from office and eliminated from the list of potential appointments. At the Equal Employment Opportunity Commission, the nomination to the chairmanship of one such dissident member, J. Clay Smith, Jr., who had been critical of the Reagan program, was pushed aside to make way for the appointment of an African American conservative, William M. Bell. William Raspberry, a columnist at the *Washington Post,* described the situation:

> Smith is a hard-working black Republican who was appointed to the EEOC in 1977. He has been acting chairman since March. In the normal course of things, he would have seemed a natural for a White House appointment to a full term as chairman. Instead, he has been languishing

> on the job for most of the year, doing what he can to hold the commission together . . . maybe the problem is that Smith disagrees with the administration's stand against affirmative action, or that he has fought (successfully) the OMB proposal to slash the EEOC budget.
>
> Ironically, Bell is on record as sharing the administration's opposition to special employment consideration for minorities because they are minorities. But in nominating him, the administration is practicing preference of the most egregious sort. If Bell were white, it is inconceivable that he would have been nominated for any important management post.[73]

These African American Republicans were placed in strategic governmental positions, particularly at the Civil Rights Commission, the EEOC, and the Office of Civil Rights in HEW. Then like-thinking African American Republican operatives were installed in benefits agencies such as the food stamp and welfare programs to blunt any criticism of racism on the part of the Reagan administration. The next step was the courts, regulatory agencies, and service bureaucracies. The emphasis was on sub-cabinet positions, hidden but powerful and potentially effective in undermining and undercutting the political framework built during the 1960s and 1970s.

> Reagan administration apparently see no conflict between promoting black conservatism and policies that reverse civil-rights rulings of the past . . . while most black Americans are resigned to a grim new era of race relations, conservatives (Republicans) feel they are in the best position to reshape black politics since the 1930s.[74]

"The Southern Way" on race questions was transformed into "the American Way." New code words were fashioned for whites to blame and devalue African Americans, and attempts were made to demonstrate that old line African American leaders did not speak for the masses.[75]

To ensure that this contextual transformation would survive, white and African American conservatives were selected to the federal and Supreme Court benches. This effort gave the contextual change a constitutional and legal support system base.

The Reagan administration captured and took control of the regulatory rule-making apparatus. By executive order, Reagan placed full responsibility for promulgation and implementation of civil rights laws under the authority of the Office of Management and Budget (OMB). As a last ditch measure, the president vetoed new civil rights bills.

The fiscal cutbacks, reductions in force, and eliminations of antipoverty and social welfare programs during the Reagan and Bush years virtually ensured that the goal of the African American community for economic stability and progress would crumble and fade. The economic crisis in the nation's predominantly

FIGURE 2.1

Reagan-Bush Era Techniques and Procedures for Contextual Change and Potential Net Results

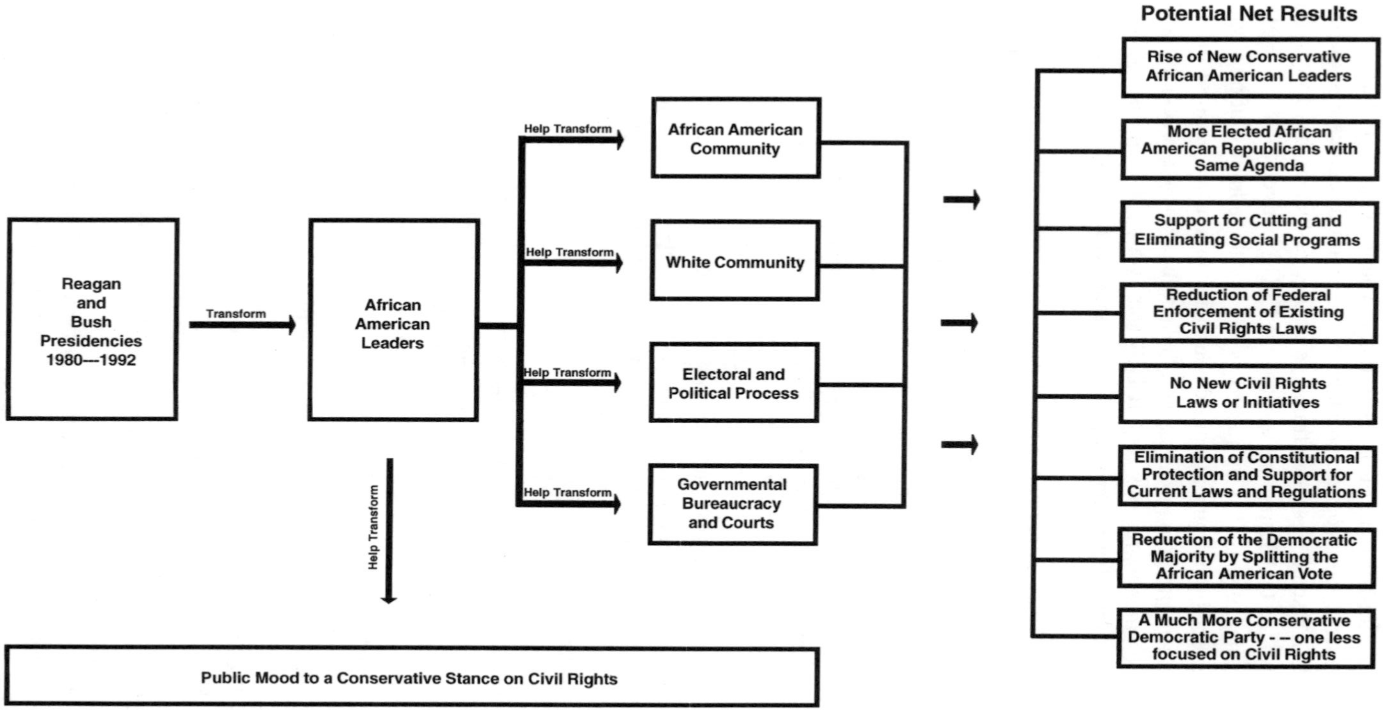

African American inner cities was exacerbated, and a new plague of drugs swept through these blighted urban areas. African American crime rates soared, as did unemployment.[76] However, the Reagan-Bush administrations sought to address the problems of drugs, crime, and unemployment by building more jails and prisons.

Bush's campaign manager, Lee Atwater, who assumed the post of party chairman after the 1988 elections, calculated during the campaign that about 15% of the African American vote would be needed to provide the Republicans with a victory. This support would have doubled the percentage of African Americans affiliated with the party. The Republicans went after the African American middle and upper classes. Atwater himself went after African American college graduates and alumni, starting with Howard University. This proved to be a disaster and ended in one of the strategy's first failures.[77]

Along with the political recruitment of African Americans came the political promotion and electioneering of African American conservative Republican candidates. Men like Alan Keyes in Maryland and Maurice Dawkins in Virginia ran for the Senate in 1988. Others mounted conservative congressional campaigns. An unexpected victory came when African American Republican Gary Franks wrested a congressional seat in Connecticut from the liberal white incumbent by running as an extremely conservative candidate with regard to social and economic issues.[78] This was the only white congressional district in the entire country to elect one of these conservative African American Republicans to office. Four years later, a white district in Oklahoma elected a former football star, J. C. Watts, to Congress. The majority of these candidates went down in electoral defeat in both African American and white congressional districts. Thus, little contextual change was effected via this route.

The election of African American conservative Republicans to Congress was only a very small part of the overall effort to send more Republican conservatives to Congress. While this larger effort was much more successful, contextual change in this regard was further mediated and dampened by Democratic control of both houses of Congress.

In summary, the techniques and procedures for contextual change included transforming (1) the Republican party, (2) African American leadership within that party, (3) public attitudes and mood, (4) the federal bureaucracy and courts, and (5) the electoral process. Every base was covered in this comprehensive effort to halt and, where possible, roll back the civil rights advances made by African Americans. One traditional African American Republican, who saw all of this coming and denounced it, told party strategists that this approach would lead to a failure to build an equitable two-party system and effectively recruit African Americans. His pleas and perceptive forecast went unheeded.[79]

Figure 2.1 summarizes the techniques and procedures that the Reagan and Bush presidencies employed to effectuate contextual change. Operating through the Republican party and their own presidencies, these leaders shaped the political process, the federal bureaucracy, and judiciary.

The figure sets forth some eight potential results. This volume asks whether or not African American power and political behavior permitted these potential net results to be attained.

In 1992, the Reagan-Bush era came to an unexpected end. "*Southern Republicanism at the presidential level has at least one major flaw; it can be significantly reduced by a native son presidential candidate.* Both Carter and Clinton candidacies provide evidence that this flaw exists."[80] Bill Clinton of Arkansas heightened the impact and influence of the native son variable by choosing as his vice presidential running mate, Al Gore, from Tennessee. In the 1988 election, Tennessee gave the Republican party a nine percent advance over the Democrats. With a native son on the ticket, Tennessee in 1992 "shifted back to the Democratic column, giving the party a 5 point plurality. . . . Again, a native son reversed party fortunes in his own state."[81] In 1992, the Democratic party broke, if only temporarily, the Republican grip on the solid south and fractured their alliance at the presidential level. But, in order to sway the South back into the Democratic fold, the party's leadership had to embrace the cultural values and beliefs about the region just as strongly as the Republicans had.

After the party nominee Michael Dukakis was defeated at the polls in 1988, the conservative wing of the party reconstitutioned itself into a group known as the Democratic Leadership Council (DLC), which worked to move the party to the right of center. Bill Clinton of Arkansas was among the DLC's founding members.

The first expression of his fidelity to the southern culture came during the primary and the general election campaigns. Throughout both campaigns, Clinton and his allies deliberately distanced himself, in a rude and callous fashion, from Jesse Jackson, who had come to be viewed as the leader and spokesperson of the liberal wing after failing in his bid for the Democratic nomination in 1988. Clinton went before Jackson's own Rainbow Convention and "openly criticized [Sister Souljah] for reportedly saying in wake of the Los Angeles riots, that blacks should stop killing each other and start killing whites."[82] This political retoric and political symbolism told southern Democrats and northerners what they waned to hear. This earned Clinton credentials as a centrist candidate.

The most tell-tale sign of the impact of the racial conservatism of the Reagan-Bush era lies in the fact that Democratic candidates and nominees made no major speeches or concessions to the African American community during the entire 1992 presidential campaign. As president, Clinton has not provided any symbolic or substantive rewards to the African American community. The first example of this can be seen in Clinton's selection of African American attorney and civil rights leader Vernon Jordan as co-chair of his transition team. Although vocal during the Carter administration, Jordan was neither visible nor vocal,

FIGURE 2.2

Political Groups and Organizations in President Clinton's Governing Coalition, 1992–1996

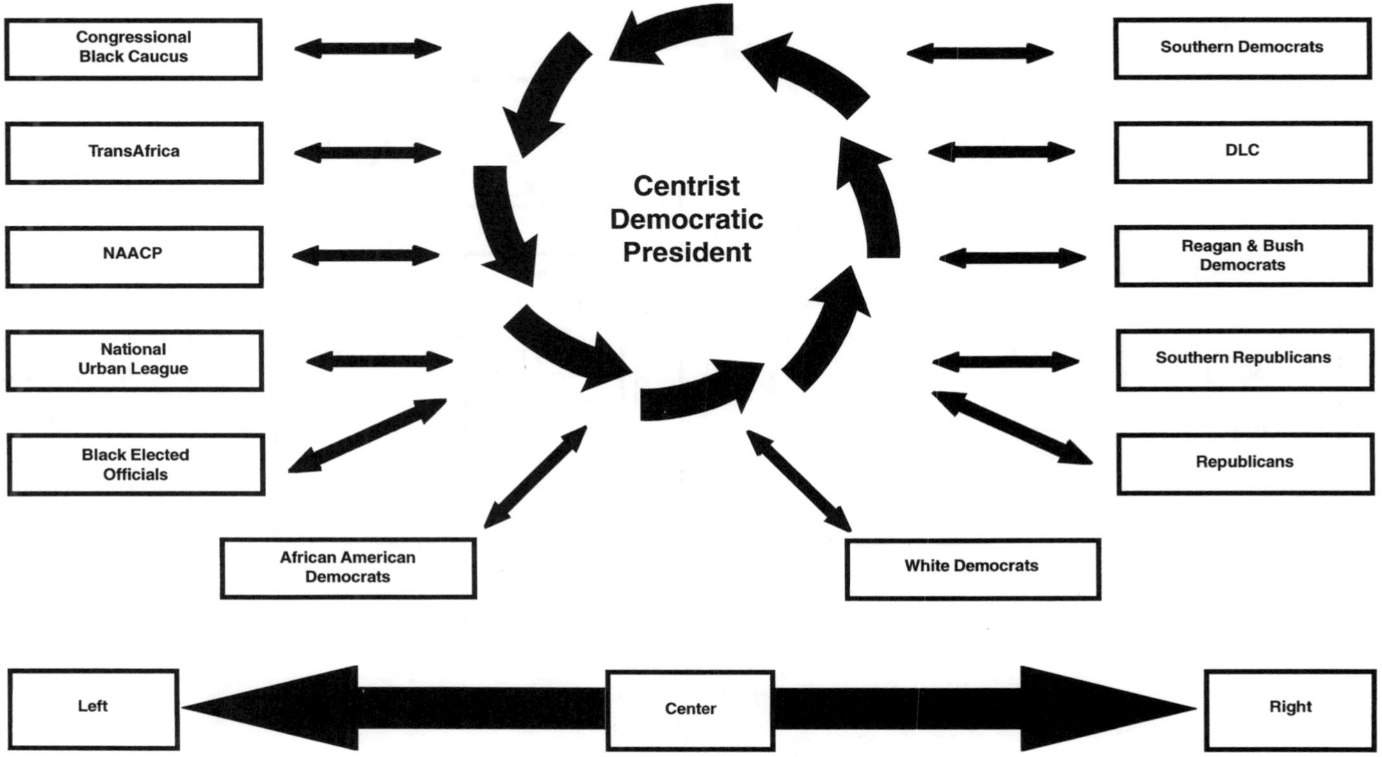

FIGURE 2.3

African American Political Strategies to Obtain Federal Intervention at the State Level to Eliminate Slavery and Racial Discrimination, 1800–1865

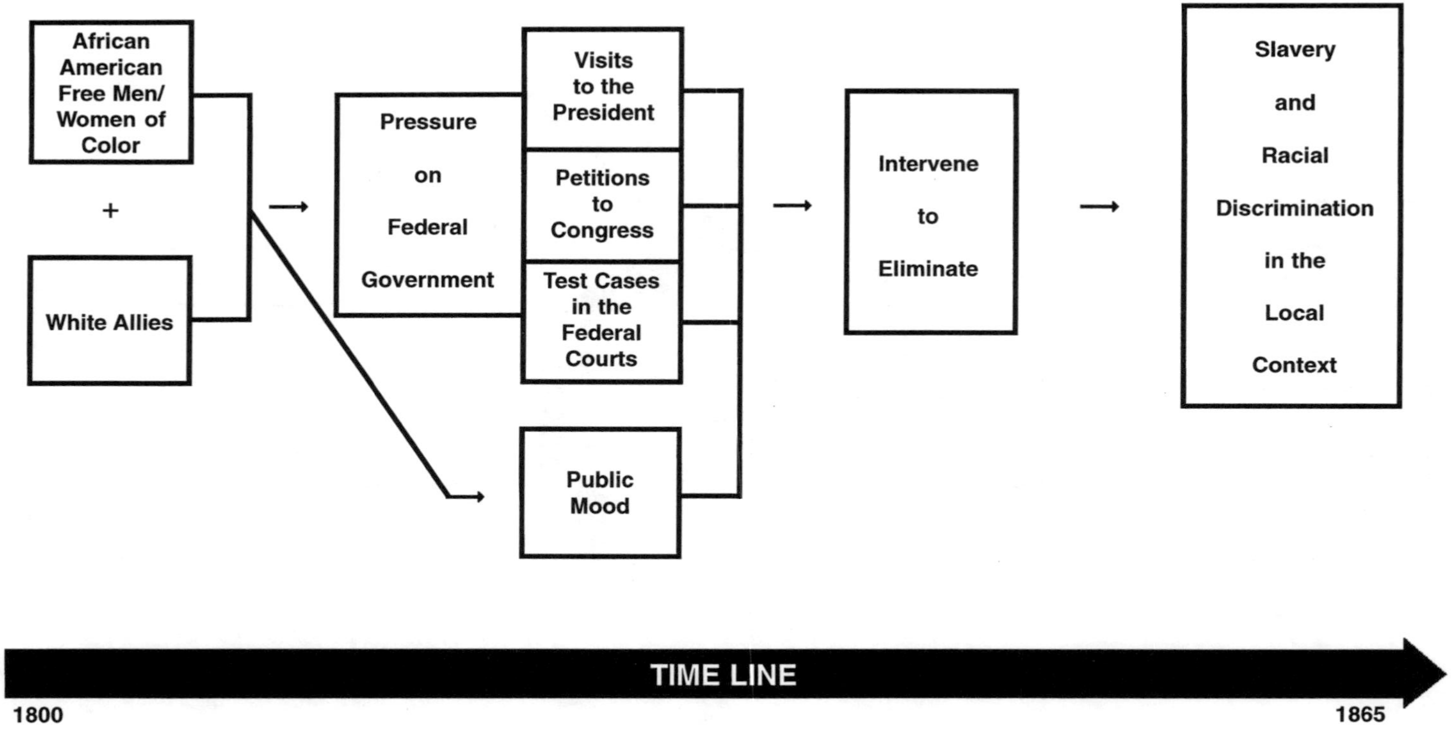

even from the sidelines, during the Reagan-Bush era. Such a choice, even at the symbolic level, raises questions about contextual transformation. The significance of Clinton's four African American cabinet appointees in the Departments of Commerce, Veteran Affairs, Energy, and Agriculture is diminished because these posts are not ones that can most effectively reverse the contextual setbacks created by the outgoing administrations.

Figure 2.2 reveals the political cross pressures that a centrist Democratic president must contend with. The President must oscillate between the forces on his right—the Reagan and Bush Democrats, the Southern Democrats, mainstream Democrats, his own DLC, and the political criticism of the Republican party—while on the left, he must face the Congressional Black Caucus, TransAfrica, and other African American interest groups and a very few white congressional liberals and supporters. Overall, Clinton has stayed right of center. And when the Democratic party lost control of both houses of Congress in the 1994 mid-term elections, President Clinton was vigorously and vocally attacked by the DLC and his concessions to the right included firing the outspoken African American Surgeon General Jocylen Elders, a reassessment of affirmative action policies, drastic cuts in social welfare programs.

His political behavior concerning race raises some fundamental questions about what a centrist Democratic president can do in the wake of a Republican contextual revolution. How can he counter and confront such a revolution? Or is he interested in countering such a revolution or merely interested in maintaining some of his electoral coalition partners? Exactly how much can a centrist candidate achieve in the wake of strong right wing ideologies?

African American Political Behavior and Contextual Change

In periods of massive contextual change, where the political context is changed to negatively impact African Americans, what is their resultant political behavior?

Figure 2.3 summarizes such action historically. African Americans who were free undertook (1) visits to see Presidents and ask for their assistance in stopping or reversing the contextual change; (2) they sent petitions to Congress; (3) they tried test cases in state and federal courts; and (4) they sought to alter the public mood toward abolition and non-racial discrimination.

This figure tells us that the political context variable is not only influencial, but that it shapes African American political response and action. Eventually, African American efforts in conjunction with others ended slavery. But then came segregation.

In the fifties and sixties, African Americans once again launched a counter contextual revolution which ended the segregation context and ushered in the current era of desegregation.

The African American political experience has existed in the political contexts of slavery, segregation, and desegregation, but the Reagan-Bush era was a period of "intense racial conservatism implemented by Republican presidents" unlike no other period in American history. The Clinton administration provides us with a rare opportunity to further assess and evaluate this variable in a post-transformed contextual period.

PART 2

METHODOLOGY

Achen and Shively define contextual analysis as research that "describes the effect of characteristics of individuals' environments on their behavior."[1] The authors go on to specify that these contextual effects are "group properties [that] actually influence behavior in some social domain," principally via "communication among individuals in a group."[2] The exploration of the impact of context or environment on African American political behavior is the focus of this book. We assert that political context is one of the systemic variables influential in the shaping of African American political behavior: scholars must henceforth conceptualize it as such, gathering data that can reveal and explicate the contextual variable, and, in their data analyses, testing and probing for its diverse manifestations. Lastly, the relationship between contextual and individual-level variables must be noted and interpreted.

The analysis of context as a variable in African American political behavior demands an appropriate and sound methodology. Such analysis turns on the researcher employing a methodology that determines and pinpoints the contextual effects of white political behavior upon African American political behavior. Before there can be theory testing there must be theory building. That is, theoretical models must first be available that identify crucial variables and their relationships before empirical estimations can be conducted to test and measure these relationships. These theoretical models set forth testable propositions emanating from previous investigations.

Examination of the few contextual analyses of African American political behavior that have been conducted reveals that these studies are, for the most part, both unidirectional and unidimensional. None offer an empirical estimation of the effects of white political behavior upon that of African Americans. There is no theory building, nor is there any theory testing. In this book, our task will be to develop a series of testable propositions from a comprehensive set of case studies so that careful testing of these propositions can be undertaken in the future. In this way we hope to bring readers one step closer to fully understanding the variables shaping African American political behavior.

Before describing our case study methodology we must reflect upon another epistemological approach for anlayzing the effects of race in the political context: the race relations approach. In the race relations approach, white political behavior is the organizing and dominant priority, not African American empowerment efforts.[3] Of this approach, Donald Matthews, the only academic in the field who has explicitly addressed this issue, asserts: "Negro goals and political objectives should not be studied in isolation but in terms of their relationships to white opinion and political demands."[4] Thus, for Matthews and a host of white scholars who subscribe to this view, African American politics cannot be studied alone as a separate entity unto itself. For these academics, the focus must be upon the relationship between the races and how African American empowerment efforts might affect white political behavior.

Only one percent of the articles published in the two leading journals in the discipline, *American Political Science Review* (from 1906 to 1990) and *Political Science Quarterly* (from 1886 to 1990), a total of 27 articles each, have been devoted to analysis of the race attribute in American politics.[5] Not only have the major journals in the field paid scant attention to this subject, but the overwhelming majority of these articles have taken the race relations approach.[6] Among the few articles that have had African American political empowerment as the primary focus can be found some clues about the ways in which the contextual variable has influenced African American political behavior.[7] Although none of these articles are works of contextual analysis nor designed to measure contextual effect, they nonetheless provide significant insights on the impact of political context on the African American community.[8] The present work extends and expands their focus using a methodology appropriate to this epistemological outlook.

Scholars operating in the midst of a contextual counterrevolution who wish to maintain this illusion while advocating partisan theories learn to become quite adroit at manipulating a crucial and critical feature of modern scholarship: methodology. Methodology, simply put, is comprised of the techniques and procedures used to gather, analyze, and interpret data. The keystone assumption is that the more scientific one's research is, the more reliable and truthful it is. Purportedly, what researchers determine via rigorous application of methodological techniques is achieved by the techniques and not by the designs and dictates of human motives and prejudices. Nothing could be farther from the truth.

The methods used by political scientists to gather, analyze, and interpret data on African American politics have been scrutinized and evaluated in at least three works. My earlier work, *Invisible Politics: Black Political Behavior,* demonstrates the limitations and failures of the application of behavioral methodology to the study in a comprehensive, systematic fashion. In it, I conclude by suggesting that many of the techniques and procedures as well as the concepts, theories, and frameworks of this methodology must be reformulated to be of effective use in delineating the African American political experience.[9] Another work, "Paradigms and Paradoxes: Political Science and African American Politics," by Michael Dawson and Earnest Wilson, looks at a variety of contemporary social science paradigms (Marxism, social choice, Weberian analysis, modernization, pluralism, and nationalism) in terms of their usefulness to this analysis.

> Some paradigms are more likely than others to treat racial politics as an important and serious subject. In all cases, however, we did want to show how the subject matter was handled by the paradigms, even if racial politics was not necessarily central to a paradigm's theoretical concerns.[10]

Prior to these two works, Donald Tryman, in a pioneering work on racial politics, argued that "developmental and modernization theories of comparative politics can be redefined and then productively applied to [African American] politics."[11] Tryman strongly advocates the potential of this approach, and he provides one of the best summaries of the strengths and weaknesses of modernization theory to be found anywhere in political science literature.[12]

Beyond these two critiques of methodology and one overview analysis, there have been some smaller efforts. Several analysts have reviewed the edited volumes on African American politics and have noted numerous shortcomings.[13] Some claim that these works do not adequately connect with African American political theory and thought. Others note that they offer no suggestive methodological approaches or techniques, nor did their editors explain the methods they chose to use.

However, the work of Mack Jones is a unique effort in the methodological realm. His writing does not center on specific methodological techniques or procedures but rather on the nature of the African American political experience and the necessity to construct a paradigm from that experience rather than adopt dominant methodology. Jones looks at epistemological conceptualization rather than methodology, noting that:

> scholars so committed would not begin their critiques of mainstream political science simply by looking for procedural errors, biases, misplaced emphases, ulterior motives, or similar academic transgressions. . . . In-

> stead, they would begin by challenging the existing corpuses of political science literature in its entirety.[14]

This book contends that there is a national political context and at least four subnational contexts: state, county, local, and a combination of these three, known as regional context. It also contends that during their respective terms of office, Presidents Reagan and Bush, and to a lesser extent Clinton, tried to transform and restructure the national political context. Yet a federal system, unlike a unitary one with centralized authority, does not provide the opportunities for a coordinated, uniform, systematic transformation of the political context. Even when local context does become similar to national context, the change itself can be due to very different reasons. Thus efforts at transformation are uneven and fragmentary, and the response of African Americans to these efforts will be likewise.

Few African Americans foresaw the coming of the transformation of the political context that occurred during the Reagan-Bush administrations. One who clearly did was J. Clay Smith, Jr. in his prophetic article: "A Black Lawyer's Response to the Fairmont Papers."[15] Although Professor Smith sounded the alarm, even the most alert opponents of the conservative Republican counterrevolution did not develop a reaction strategy immediately.

How well or poorly could the African American political community, its political elites, and leadership work, with or without allies, to prevent two presidents, allied with African American conservatives, from transforming the political context so as to disadvantage that community and its recent political achievements? How can any community whose political landscape is targeted for contextual transformation gear up to challenge that incursion? In all fairness to African American leaders, the Reagan-Bush approach was a new and formidable. Notwithstanding, the answers to these questions remain an important part of the definitional component.

The United States is structured by federalism, which is an embedded tradition that manifests as legal realities. It is driven by politics and societal leaders, and it interacts with other minor political contexts—in this case, the African American political context—to either advantage or disadvantage it. Although the constitutional parameters of the United States are supposedly fixed and permanent, the nation's political context keeps transforming and redefining these parameters at the most fundamental and basic level: the level of rights, liberties, and freedoms.

This feature of contextual transformation by the majority is the unique and distinctive aspect of the political context variable in the African American political experience. Surrogate measures must be developed for these constitutional fundamentals and embedded traditions at the attitudinal and behavioral levels and for the organizational machinery and its leadership which launches and mobilizes these redefinitions and contextual changes. Such measures must be considered if an empirical rendering and reading of the political context variable is to be made.

How to conceptualize a methodological approach to investigating the effect of the political context variable in the African American community during the Reagan-Bush (and now Clinton) eras? Better yet, what methodology would do justice to the exploration of the specific components of that context as well as to the interaction between the contextual transformers and their targets? What approach permits one to best assess and evaluate political realities when the political context has been transformed?

The paradigms explored by Dawson and Wilson are singularly inappropriate for this task. The major traditional methodologies—legal, institutional, and philosophical—are also deficient in terms of their ability to address and explore the political context variable. For these reasons, the case study method had to be deployed. This method, which is widely used in political science although it did not originate in that discipline, allows the exploration and gauging of the different levels of political context, the different areas of context being transformed, and the successes and failures of those attempting the transformation. At the same time, it allows one to appraise the response of the target community and its political operatives. Moreover, this methodology, while only a focus procedure in that it looks at but a single political entity at a time, is quite flexible in the measurement techniques that can be employed to delineate the focus area under study. Hence, a variety of quantitative and qualitative techniques can be employed in analyzing the political context using case study methodology.

The case study approach is also flexible in terms of qualifying what an analyst can use as data sources. The focus, however, must stay upon the case under examination. Therefore, different essays in this volume use different data bases in their exploration of the context variable in African American politics. This makes for a detailed assessment of this variable as well as a rich and diverse one as well.

The case study methodology has a long history in the African American political experience and has produced some enormously rich insights and ideas. However, during the Reagan-Bush era of political contextual transformation, methodology was employed to serve the transformers. According to Mack Jones,

> Studies undertaken in this context yield only information that may be useful in determining how the black presence may be managed to minimize stress in the system, and not information about how the system might be transformed to serve black interest.[16]

Professor Jones is perceptive indeed. Methodologies are not neutral, and they are clearly not neutral when race has been elevated to a context transforming variable. He continues:

> Starting from the assumption that the system is near perfect, with optimum institutional arrangements, political scientists are predisposed to view most problems as transient, resulting from routine societal maturation and ame-

> nable to solutions through existing arrangements. The system, by definition, is sound. Persistent and recurring problems that defy such solution are not perceived to be systemic. Instead they are viewed as accidents of history, as the result of deficiencies of those in whom the problems are manifested, or as some combination of the two. Since the paradigm defines them as nonsystemic, such problems are also to be resolved without systemic change.[17]
>
> Driven by the dictates of the dominant paradigm, such studies necessarily view black life through the eyes of its adversaries. These adversarial studies are taken as authentic and universally useful descriptions of black political life, when in fact they are only caricatures by those for whom the black presence is a problem. The caricatures are built around the presumed pathologies of black life. Such scholarship is bereft of prescriptive insights.[18]

In a period of contextual transformation one is apt to find scholarly studies that claim race is not a factor, or is of only minimal consequence, in the transformation. The two papers here address these methodological problems. Chapter 3 addresses the issue of whether race is a factor in contextual counterrevolutions from a historical perspective. For example, two recent books looking at Republican leaders of different eras disclaim that race was a factor by first conceptualizing the matter out of existence.

> Goldwater was neither a racial bigot nor, in principle, a segregationist. . . . Although [he] was thus neither racist nor segregationist, his racial conservatism had a powerful appeal to anti-civil rights forces that had been deserted by the national Democratic party.[19]

Another example can be found in David Lisio's comments about President Hoover:

> Ignorant about racism and its workings, Hoover thus unwittingly became its captive. He was not a bigot with a lily-white southern strategy, as the standard interpretation argues. Indeed, Southern lily-whites were the first to recognize this fact. Instead a combination of ignorance about racism and his utopian idealism worked against both himself and black Americans.[20]

Both apologists disclaim that their man is a bigot. Each offers a ready-made excuse as to why race is not the controlling variable in contextual change, and both offer methodological techniques to substantiate their point. At least, so they think.

Chapter 4 addresses the problem of race as a minimal factor. In these studies, usually undertaken by race relations specialists in political science, an empirical estimation of the race factor is made in conjunction with numerous other variables. In every case, the race variable had only minimal impact. In these instances, the variable is analyzed away.

Thus, in periods of contextual counterrevolution, methodologies can either conceptualize or analyze race away.

Therefore, to overcome the methodological problems and weaknesses so prevalent in earlier studies of contextual revolutions and counterrevolutions in American politics, this study opts not only to conceptualize the race factor as bidirectional in the political context but to employ a case study methodology at the foundational level of political inquiry, that is, the theory-building level. In so doing, potentially testable propositions suitable for the second level, that of theory testing/empirical estimation, will be developed.

3

AFRICAN AMERICAN POLITICS
A Case Study Methodological Approach

• • • • • • •

Hanes Walton, Jr.

Political context and its transformation during the Reagan, Bush, and Clinton eras, can be much more thoroughly investigated using case study methodology than with a broad overview or survey approach, if theory building is the ultimate purpose of the study. Case studies are the building blocks for any discipline and particularly for an area that is unexplored and unassessed. In a barren and undiscovered intellectual terrain, basic mapping, formal parameters, and useful guideways and promising paths must be fashioned. Case studies permits the establishment of intellectual frontiers.

A case study is an analytical research study which is focused on a single reality. Robert Yin provides a more technical definition.

> A case study is an empirical enquiry that (1) investigates a contemporary phenomenon within its real-life context; when (2) the boundaries between phenomenon and context are not clearly evident; and in which (3) multiple sources of evidence are used.[1]

This is precisely the manner in which the case study methodology in used in analyzing the political context in the African American experience. Moreover the case study approach has as one of its strengths, "its ability to deal with a full variety of evidence—documents, artifacts, (systematic) interviews, (participant) observation," aggregate data, quantitative analysis, and political history.[2]

Finally, "the case study is preferred in examining contemporary events" and the Reagan, Bush, and Clinton administrations are such, and case studies "are generalizable to theoretical propositions and not to populations or universes," which is the very essence of this study.[3] Theory building about the political context variable in the African American experience drives this book. Hence, connections between variables is critical for any understanding of the research problem. But before we began with a comprehensive and systematic analysis of contemporary events in the American political process and system, it is essential that we assess and evaluate pioneering case studies that have emerged in previous periods of contextual transformation. It is to these extant early case studies that we now turn.

Data and Methodology

The key question to be explored here is: Did scholars and academicians use the case study methodology to analyze the last major partisan contextual revolution, which occurred during the Kennedy-Johnson era (1960–1968)? How much will these case studies, when aggregated, tell us about the political and contextual changes of that period? How much can we infer from the Kennedy-Johnson era to the current one, and what can we learn from both in terms of understanding how African American politics responds to contextual change?[4] It seems that contextual counterrevolutions are inevitable, given African Americans' apparent need to have their constitutional and legal rights established by partisan political majorities—first the Republicans, and recently the Democrats. This is one of the fundamental realities that separate African American politics from white American politics: the latter group, having had its essential constitutional rights established at the point of creation of the political system, has been free to spend its political efforts and resources trying to advance and advantage itself and its interests within the system. African Americans, on the other hand, must spend most of their political time and energies trying to create political majorities amenable to extending African Americans' rights. The case study methodology is of paramount utility to more clearly identify and explicate contextual upheavals in the political arena.[5]

To explore the first question, we must conduct a content analysis of the case studies of the Kennedy-Johnson era and reconstruct the African American political experience of that era. Key questions are: when did case studies of that political experience take place, who sponsored and supported such studies, and how did such studies evolve over time? This will enable us to put case studies of the Reagan-Bush era into proper perspective as well as reveal how earlier events led to and undergirded the Kennedy-Johnson years. The following bibliographic overview illuminates the rise and evolution of case studies on African American politics, a necessary step before we can aggregate the case studies of the Kennedy-Johnson era and paint a portrait of that period and time. Our methodology will be a content analysis of those studies and the aggregation of those single-case findings.

Case Study Methodology in African American Politics: A Bibliographic Overview

As shown in figure 3.1, the American Negro Academy (ANA), an "organization of authors, scholars, [and] artists . . . for the promotion of letters, science, and art," founded March 5, 1897, in Washington, D.C., was the premier organization to utilize, in a major way, the case studies approach to examine African American politics. Its first priority was to promote "the publication of scholarly work" by and about African Americans.[6] From its establishment until its demise in 1924, the Academy produced four major book-length monographs (although it announced five) and 22 occasional papers.[7] With regard to these papers, the historian of the organization makes this observation:

> Between 1897 and 1924, the ANA published twenty-two occasional papers on subjects related to the culture, history, religion, civil and social rights, and the social institutions of black Americans. While the quality of the papers varied, all of them help to illuminate the many ways in which, during the first quarter of the twentieth century, an important segment of the small community of educated American blacks attempted to intellectually defend their people, justify their own existence, and challenge ideas, habits, attitudes, and legal proscriptions that seemed to be locking their race permanently into an inferior caste.[8]

However, of these 22 case studies, five, or 23 percent, are relevant to African American politics. They include Occasional Paper Number 6, "The Disfranchisement of the Negro" (1899); Number 11, "The Negro and the Elective Franchise" (comprised of six chapters) (1905); Number 16, "The Ballotless Victims of One-Party Government" (1906); Number 21, "The Shame of America, or the Negro's Case Against the Republic" (1924); and Number 22, "The Challenge of the Disfranchised: A Plea for the Enforcement of the 15th Amendment" (1924). Not only are these case studies rich in careful reflection and analyses of the political context which African Americans faced at those moments in history, but they cogently describe how a revolution of the political context in post-Civil War America was being led by the South via the process of disenfranchisement of African American voting rights and the deprivation of their rights to participate in the American political process. Perhaps most im-

FIGURE 3.1

The Evolution of the Case Study Method in African American Politics and Its Sponsors and Supporters

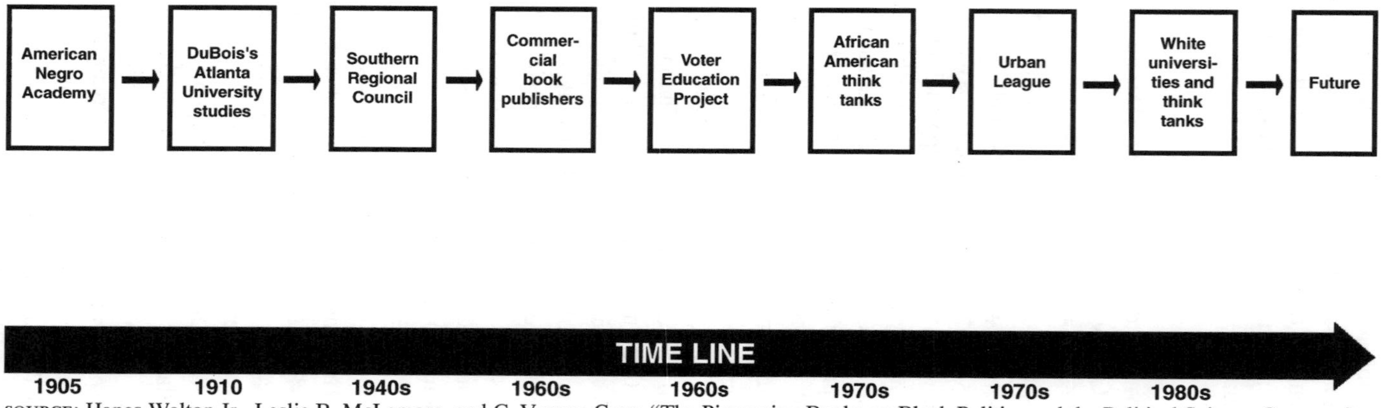

SOURCE: Hanes Walton Jr., Leslie B. McLemore, and C. Vernon Gray, "The Pioneering Books on Black Politics and the Political Science Community, 1903–1965," *National Political Science Review* 2 (1990): 196–218.

portantly, these papers show that the transformation of the political context does not have to be instituted by the president, Congress, the courts, or even the federal bureaucracy, but can be undertaken by a coalition of state governments and their people. Simply put, a region of the country, the South, fostered the transformation of the political context.[9]

Atlanta University's W. E. B. DuBois was the next to launch a series of case studies on the African American community, which he conducted and directed himself.[10] Surprisingly, while most of DuBois's Atlanta University studies explored economic, social, legal, and moral issues, they did not investigate in any detail the African American political experience. DuBois was one of the founding members of the American Negro Academy, but did not pen any of their studies on African American politics. Given DuBois's commitment to racial uplift, for which the studies were supposed to provide a scientific underpinning, his lack of attention to political issues has suggested to some that no significant political activity by African Americans was going on during the period of these early studies. However, this lack of concern by DuBois is more the result of a conscious effort on his part to avoid clouding his case studies with politics than it is an indicator of political inactivity.

Following the ANA and Atlanta University studies, a white organization, the Southern Regional Council (SRC), produced a number of significant case studies on African American suffrage in the late 1940s and early 1950s. It also produced a work, *The Federal Executive and Civil Rights,* in 1960. Of the SRC's earlier case studies, two by Margaret Price, *The Negro Voter in the South* and *The Negro and the Ballot in the South,* and one by Luther Jackson, "Race and Suffrage in the South Since 1940," are most frequently sought after.[11] These works provide some empirical rendering of the African American electorate before the Voting Rights Act of 1965.

Just as the turbulent decade of the 1960s began and the African American political context began to change anew, commercial book publishers such as McGraw-Hill and Holt, Rinehart, and Winston, began to publish single case studies on African American politics.[12] Their output, while small, produced nearly a dozen well-known case analyses of the changes taking place in African American communities in several southern states.

The Voter Education Project followed suit with its newsletters on African American politics in the South.[13] This African American voter mobilization organization would later be joined by African American think tanks such as the Joint Center for Political Studies (JCPS), the Urban League, and eventually white universities and think tanks. Overall, numerous organizations and groups have sponsored and supported case studies of the African American political experience, but their track records have been generally uneven and sketchy. Perhaps the most prolific and enduring of these organizations has been the Joint Center for Political Studies, founded in 1970. The JCPS has also been the most consistent and persistent in the area of sponsoring and developing monographic case studies on African American politics. Although it has done little work that isolates and analyzes the political context variable, the JCPS has been most active in focusing on African American political participation and office holding,[14] annually publishing the *National Roster of Black Elected Officials.* Along with several such books and directories, it has also issued a long list of case study monographs. One of these monographs focuses on Jesse Jackson's 1984 presidential campaign.[15] The JCPS was not very active during the Reagan-Bush era, publishing only a few studies from 1980 to 1992, and most of these studies provide little systematic or comprehensive analysis of the African American political context. One of these case studies stresses the need for African American self-help efforts along with governmental initiatives.[16]

The major limitation of the JCPS case studies is that they rarely focus on and thereby fail to isolate the contextual variables. Moreover, because the Center was not founded until 1970, it "missed" the Kennedy-Johnson contextual revolution. To conduct a contextual analysis of the Kennedy-Johnson era and thereby test the first research question, attention must be given to the case studies produced during these years by commercial publishing houses.

Case Studies of African American Politics Produced During the Kennedy-Johnson Contextual Revolution

Prior to their publication by commercial publishing houses, these seven case studies had been commissioned and guided by the Case Advisory Committee of the Eagleton Institute of Political Studies in Practical Politics at Rutgers University.[17] They were prepared "under the general editorship of Paul Tillet of the Eagleton Institute of Politics staff with the assistance of the Case Advisory Committee."[18] The Eagleton Institute strove to "introduce the case method, already applied successfully to business and public administration curricula, into the teaching of American politics." The cases it chose to analyze were "lucid, dispassionate recounts of actual political activity, . . . built on materials not found between hard covers, materials hitherto locked in the oral tradition of politics."[19] Above all, they were selected to fulfill teaching needs and to motivate student interest. The Case Advisory Committee was comprised of five political science professors, four political science department chairs, a dean and a director. Among the departmental chairs were administrators from Princeton, Georgetown, and Berkeley. Small colleges, like Chatham College, Douglass College, and Florida Atlantic University were also represented. Nonetheless, while the committee reflected a fair geographical academic cross-section, no African Americans or other minorities served.

Although the Institute itself published numerous case studies, six of its case studies were published by McGraw-Hill. A seventh study, not undertaken by the

Institute, was published by Holt, Rinehart, and Winston.[20] Two of these seven case studies were conducted by African American political scientists. At the time that they wrote their studies, both these authors were working at predominantly African American universities: G. James Fleming taught at Morgan State University in Baltimore, while Charles V. Hamilton was on the faculty at Tuskegee University in Alabama. Their respective studies look at the efforts of two African American communities, one urban and one rural, to empower themselves politically. In terms of geography, two of the seven commercially published studies have a northern focus (New York and Baltimore), while the rest explore events in the South (the cities of Atlanta, Memphis, Durham, and Tuskegee; and the state of Louisiana).

Table 3.1 indicates that the seven case studies fall into three major categories. Four of the studies come under the electoral category. These case studies dealt with African American electoral politics: two with city elections (Fleming and Wright), one with a congressional election (Haygood), and one with voter registration at the city level (Hamilton).

The next category, "protest politics," includes two studies by Walker and Sindler which explore the use of protest politics and tactics in changing the political context of segregation in the South. The studies examine mass desegregation mobilization strategies in two major southern cities. Describing his study, Sindler writes that it "treats the interaction of youth groups, other elements of the protest movement, and the white community leadership in Durham, North Carolina."[21] Walker's book-length study follows essentially the same paradigm.

The last category includes only one study, by Pinney and Friedman. Their study focuses on the legislative activity of white political leaders in Louisiana to maintain segregation in the public schools. Additionally, it examines the relation-

TABLE 3.1

Categories of Case Studies of the Kennedy-Johnson Contextual Revolution, 1960–1968

Categories	Authors		Percentage of whole
Electoral	Fleming, Haygood Wright, Hamilton	(4)	57%
Protest	Walker, Smaller	(2)	29%
Legislative	Pinney and Freidman	(1)	14%
Total		(7)	100%

For an analysis of the Eagleton list of practical case studies, see Hanes Walton Jr., Leslie B. McLemore, and C. Vernon Gray, "The Pioneering Books on Black Politics and the Political Science Community, 1903–1965," *The National Political Science Review* 2 (1990): 196–218.

ship of African American voters to such well-organized and well-orchestrated legislative activity, and offers some insights into the NAACP's legal efforts against segregation.

These seven case studies cover the period from 1960 to 1965, spanning the initial and middle years of the Kennedy-Johnson era. In that sense, they are not completely comprehensive, nor are they systematic; yet, they are quite diverse, rich, and attentive to the major areas in the African American community undergoing contextual change—and quite representative as well. Therefore, we can answer our first research question in a positive manner. There is a strong correlation between what appeared in the seven case studies and what was happening in the Kennedy-Johnson contextual revolution. This era first saw school desegregation, then desegregation of public facilities in the South, and finally change in the electoral area. Each of the case studies covers at least one of these three major categories. Hence, for the first question we find significant support.

The Nature of Contextual Change Described in Case Studies from the Kennedy-Johnson Era

What do these case studies tell us about the political contextual changes that occurred during the Kennedy-Johnson era? To answer that question, let us first look at this era in terms of its constitutional and legal context.

The Supreme Court's 1954 decision in *Brown v. Board of Education* set into motion the forces that would eventually bring about school desegregation in the South. This ruling meant that states could no longer maintain public schools segregated on the basis of race. The Court's later decisions to uphold African American protest efforts to desegregate the city buses in Baton Rouge, Louisiana, and then Montgomery, Alabama, sent additional signals to both African American and white communities that protest politics might be employed to change the political context from one that nurtured racial segregation to one that fostered racial equality, particularly where African Americans did not have the electoral power to do so.[22] However, it was the federal government's intervention in Little Rock, Arkansas, to uphold the Court's decision, and the passage of the civil rights acts of 1957 and 1960 (which were, in effect, voting rights acts) that clearly demonstrated to the South that a contextual revolution was about to start and that the federal government might intervene to ensure such contextual changes.[23] By signalling that change in the area of civil rights would be coming from the federal government and, most importantly, from the Oval Office itself, the Kennedy and Johnson administrations altered the public mood with regard to race relations.[24] Moreover, African Americans themselves, through the work of civil rights leaders such as Martin Luther King, Jr., organizations such as the

Student Nonviolent Coordinating Committee (SNCC), and activities such as sit-ins and Freedom Rides, were constantly signalling that they would be the forerunners of this contextual change.[25]

The sociopolitical environment during the Kennedy-Johnson era was clearly either in the midst or on the verge of contextual change when the seven case studies under discussion were undertaken. Each of these studies explored in their own unique way the nature of that change as it was taking place.

In the leadership category, Pinney and Friedman's study shows how one southern state, through its legislative process, sought to impede and stop the forces of change bent on eliminating segregation in the public schools. They further describe how African Americans, without positions of power in the electoral process, eventually succeeded in changing the segregation context through the legal process by using the legal system to outmaneuver the entire state legislative effort.[26] In the protest politics category, the two studies by Sindler and Walker show how, in Durham and Atlanta, a new group of civil rights protestors, African American college students, were spurred to enter the political process in their respective cities through the only means available: protest. This type of politics re-energized the extant African American leadership and eventually led to the desegregation of public facilities in the downtown areas of these two cities.[27] Thus the political context in Durham and Atlanta was changed. Local and outside elements, operating in a political atmosphere in which change was believed possible, engineered a contextual revolution at these sites.

With one exception, the case studies in the electoral category, like those in the protest group, demonstrate the roles that African American individuals and groups employed to change the political context that barred them from the electoral area and the fruits of such participation. The Hamilton study looks at the protracted struggle undertaken by African Americans in Tuskegee through their organization, the Tuskegee Civic Association, to register sufficient voters to join the local political process and gain power in city government. In Tuskegee, the majority was African American, but all local political power was in the hands of whites who were extremely resistant to efforts to alter the sociopolitical status quo.[28] Fleming's electoral case study looks at the efforts of African Americans in Baltimore to elect African Americans to the city council. While all the events Fleming describes took place before the passage of the 1965 Voting Rights Act, his study clearly reveals that African Americans knew and understood the importance of changing the political context in order to gain electoral power. In Baltimore, the African American population realized that getting out the vote and wresting political representation at City Hall were essential for changing the political context and their plight.[29] William Wright examines a similar African American electoral drive in Memphis in 1959.[30] As he maintains:

> This case study of the 1959 public works commissioner contest attempts to explain the Negro strategy within the context of earlier Negro political experience and the local political environment, the way in which it was executed, and the white reaction to it.[31]

Wright analyzes all aspects of the local context, describing and defining the final outcome of the election. Although the African American candidate lost the election, Wright shows that African Americans took the leadership role in this pioneering attempt to alter the political milieu.

The last study in this category examines African American involvement in a political machine in the North, New York City's Tammany Hall, and looks at efforts to re-elect an African American representative, Adam Clayton Powell, to Congress. A review of this case study described it thus:

> Another volume to appear in this time frame on the congressman was a skewed journalistic account of Tammany Hall's attempt in 1958 to "deny the Democratic nomination to the Harlem Congressman." In 1956, Powell urges his voters to support Republican Dwight Eisenhower for president, although Powell himself stayed on the Democratic ticket. Then on 8 May 1958, the congressman was indicted for income-tax evasion. On 15 May, a week later, Tammany announced that they would not back the congressman. The effort failed, and Powell beat the machine candidate by a margin of three-to-one. This journalistic account, while quite descriptive, tries to portray Powell as a true political scoundrel.[32]

This study recounts how African Americans sought to stop the local contextual changes (i.e., the removal of an African American elected leader with one hand-picked by white leaders, and the inventive use of political tactics by the African American community leadership), and an illustration of how whites tried unsuccessfully to engineer these changes with the help of an African American leader and his supporters.

When we aggregate these seven case studies, what do they tell us about contextual changes in the Kennedy-Johnson era? First, they demonstrate that the federal government, through its branches (the Congress, the Supreme Court, and the presidency) can effectuate contextual change in the political environment. Second, they show that African Americans can and do help to initiate contextual changes as well as defend themselves against such changes. Third, they show that whites will resist contextual change if they fear it will modify their way of life, even if that way of life is found to be unconstitutional. Fourth, these studies reveal that African Americans employed a variety of strategies—electoral, protest, and legal—to change illegal and unconstitutional contexts. Fifth, we see from these case studies that African Americans are sometimes successful in their efforts, as in Atlanta and Durham, and sometimes fail, as in Baltimore and

Louisiana. Hence, contextual change can be both negative and positive for African Americans, and both types of change can occur simultaneously.

Once again, the case studies approach has yielded strong and positive support for the second research question. Relevant studies produced during the Kennedy-Johnson era, while they do not provide a comprehensive portrait, do provide critical insights and evidence about the nature of political contextual change prior to the Reagan-Bush era.

Conclusions

As these case studies reveal, presidents, along with other branches of government, can and do initiate and implement contextual changes in the sociopolitical arena. Moreover, the individuals and groups (i.e., races) caught up in any contextual revolution do not only respond to it, but they can initiate a revolution or counterrevolution of their own.

In both the Kennedy-Johnson and the Reagan-Bush eras, race was a central variable in the contextual revolutions these presidents sought to inspire. The former, however, sought to promote change to improve the life of African Americans, while the latter tried to arrest and reverse such contextual expansion. In the present era, the Clinton administration has inherited the remnants of these two contextual revolutions. President Clinton has the option of returning the support of his party and the government to a contextual revolution committed to expanding African American civil rights and advancement, or he can opt to let the contextual changes of the Reagan-Bush era remain intact. Regardless of his approach, another contextual revolution is surely in the offing. However, after four years of the Clinton administration, if one takes into account his lack of a call for policy initiatives and his failure to support any new regulatory procedures to protect the African American community, it seems that the latter option has basically prevailed.

4

AFRICAN AMERICAN RACE RELATIONS POLITICS
The Failure of Empirical Methodology

• • • • • • •

Hanes Walton, Jr.

Change in the American political context, especially when it is the result of deliberate efforts, as it was during the Reagan-Bush era, involves changes in the political process, not only at the attitudinal, cultural, constitutional, participational, decisional, bureaucratic, and policy levels but also at the methodological level. Political science scholarship also changes during such a transformation, because intellectual and academic support must be provided for the new political rhetoric, visions, and promises. The best way to create new political alternatives and objectives is to change political science scholarship at one of its most fundamental levels—the level of methodology. The techniques and procedures for data analysis must be revised so that they will present the factual data of the changed political context in the bold new light of that very context.

Political posturing demands academic legitimacy[1] so that those who make claims to the political context can claim to be neutral. Political scholarship and the backing of academic political scientists often become the foundations for politicians' arguments and symbolic assurances of the rightness of their policies. As the focus of this scholarship changes, the data analysis techniques employed by scholars to prove their interpretations of political data change as well.

For instance, when slavery as an institution was transformed during the antebellum period in the South in the political context from a necessary evil to a positive good, academic and intellectual support was brought to bear to justify this new political order. Political science scholars, like other players in the political and social order, were promoted into this service. Remarking on the bold switch in scholarship that occurred during that period, Samuel D. Cook has noted:

> The defense of slavery began with an apologetic view of it as a "necessary evil" and ended up with the assertion that it was a "positive good," even for the dehumanized and brutalized slaves robbed of political and constitutional rights and moral autonomy. The ambiguous conscience of the country required either that slavery be completely abolished or that the institution of slavery be "moralized" and slaves completely dehumanized. The latter was the tragic course taken, but the democratic, humanistic, and idealistic impulses of the land, after much anguish and struggle, reversed the course. Slavery collapsed, but racial injustice continued in different forms and on new levels of being.[2]

Moving ahead to the Reagan-Bush era, one sees again an instance in which political science scholarship and academic procedures were enlisted to support efforts to change the political context. In the case of the Reagan-Bush administrations, these efforts focused on discrediting the traditional civil rights leadership of the preceding eras and reintroducing racial divisiveness for partisan political gain.

Regarding this first objective, the incoming Reagan administration let it be known before it officially took office that it wanted a "new" and "different" African American leadership. At the Fairmont conference, for example, the newly elected President Reagan, his personal counsel, Edwin Meese, III, and other neoconservative Republican operatives and strategists called for "a new African American leadership."[3] The initiator of the conference, H. Monroe Browe, also noted that the meeting "appears to have been instrumental in stirring a national debate on issues concerning blacks and minorities—on who speaks for blacks, and where future progress may be found."[4] Meese spoke to the same point, referring to a conferee's mention of "a new corps of trans-ethnic political leaders" as "a really valuable concept" and "the diversification of black leadership" as "the start of political and philosophical maturity."[5]

Shortly after the Fairmont conference, a pseudo-academic and scholarly essay by Linda Lichter appeared with a title that came directly from the remarks of H. Monroe Browe: "Who Speaks for Black America?" This essay argued that the "old" African American leadership—those undiversified, immature, and homogenized leaders—were badly out of step with the African American masses, and no longer spoke for African Americans.[6] Those African Americans sponsored by the Reagan administration and the conservatives were the new leadership, this article contended. Indeed, it called for all that Meese had called for at the conference—a "change in thinking . . . in self-participation . . . in leadership, and . . . in varieties of political orientation."

Of Lichter's scholarship and methodological techniques, another group of scholars working in the same area of survey research had this to say:

> Lichter . . . reporting on a 1985 survey of a random sample of six hundred blacks, presented a portrait of black attitudes that is considerably different from that in most other surveys. It reveals less awareness of structural obstacles, greater approval of individualism, and an altogether more conservative electorate than either we or others have found. Estimates can vary, of course, depending on sampling procedures.[7]

Lichter's polemical study based on flawed scholarship (a random sample of six hundred African Americans would have a sampling error too great to substantiate its findings) was published in one of the leading conservative journals, *Public Opinion.*[8]

In the legal area, one author tried to show that African Americans' demands for civil rights were "disabling America."[9] As he saw it, the civil rights, equal opportunity, and affirmative action regulations and laws "imposed" on the American public placed greater cost and limitations than benefits on society, and ultimately reduced excellence and the quality of individual achievement.[10]

Legal arguments of this type were followed in the social policy and public policy literature. Nathan Glazer agreed that there were limits to social policy.[11] In a similar vein, Charles Murray argued that race-based public policy caused its recipients to lose ground.[12] Not all of the scholarship supportive of the changed political context of the Reagan-Bush era came from conservative Republican scholars or academicians who claimed neutral or "balanced" stances. Some come from Democrats and liberals. For example, civil rights lawyer Frank Parker maintained that works such as those described above were biased scholarship.[13]

In the area of constitutional studies, another academic, Abigail Thernstrom, argued in 1987 that governmental protection of the voting rights of African Americans was a form of affirmative action and therefore reverse discrimination; hence, it should be reversed.[14] This was one of the demands of the Reagan-Bush era, and Thernstrom's position supported the Republicans' policy desires. Thernstrom had earlier advanced the Republican-supported argument that the individual-level model of constitutional relief was better than the group-based model, even though African Americans had suffered in the American political system as a group.[15]

In the realm of party politics, several members of the academic community argued forcefully and, for some, persuasively, that the failure of the Democratic party to win the White House during this period of Republican ascendancy was due to the Democrats' support of African American concerns and issues that angered whites, forcing them to realign and attach themselves to the Republican party. The blame for this was put at the feet of the African American electorate and their civil rights leaders, particularly at the feet of Jesse Jackson, who mounted two Democratic presidential campaign bids in 1984 and 1988. Sentiments such as these represented the intellectual wisdom of the day during the Reagan-Bush era, and tomes espousing these arguments appeared regularly.[16]

Scholarly political science interest in the matter of race did not start with the advent of the Reagan-Bush era. The study of race and race relations was formally institutionalized in the University of Chicago's Department of Sociology in the 1920s.[17] The perspective and concerns formalized in these courses have since found their way into other academic disciplines, notably political science.

Race and politics has long been a concern of political science.[18] There have emerged in political science scholarship two major traditions around the intellectual study of race and politics. The oldest and most dominant tradition is the race relations approach. Cheryl Miller and Joseph P. McCormick II, in their study of the literature on this subject in the leading journals, define works of race relations politics as those that:

> emphasize an implementation strategy to obtain peaceful and consensual relations between the two races, even if the result is the domination of one and the subordination of the other. The race relations politics category includes those works which value and highlight stability over conflict, gradual and moderate change over radical, strident, or disruptive change. It is work confined to limited political adjustment in the context of existing institutions.[19]

The other tradition is African American politics, a scholarly tradition that spans a much shorter timeframe. Works in this category, as defined by Miller and McCormick, address African American political empowerment. "The prominent question here," they write, "is whether or not a specific course of action increases the power of the African American community."[20] This category of political science scholarship is thus not as concerned with whether a course of action will hurt or harm the white community as is race relations scholarship, whose primary concern with regard to any initiative or policy is how it will affect the white community, not how it will benefit the African American community.

With respect to methodology, both of these traditions have employed the behavioral as well as older traditional political science methodologies. Methodologies notwithstanding, the ideological notion of progress, as in "we are making and will continue to make progress in race relations in this country," prevails in the first approach. However, race relations studies always minimize the influence and impact of race in the political and social and economic equation, and the

FIGURE 4.1

The Continuum of Two Research Traditions

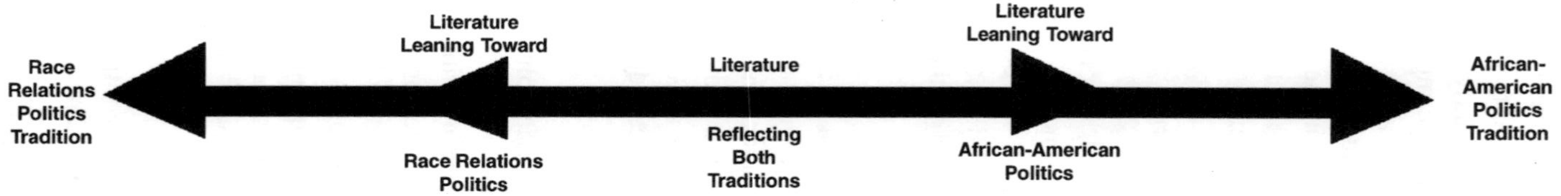

Adapted from Hanes Walton Jr., Cheryl M. Miller, and Joseph P. McCormick II, "Race and Political Science: The Dual Traditions of Race Relations Politics and African American Politics," in John Dryzek, James Farr, and Stephen Leonard, eds., *Political Science and Its History: Research Programs and Political Traditions* (New York: Cambridge University Press, 1995), 145–174.

idea that race is not a causal or determinant variable is an essential tenet of these studies. Academics in this tradition are always seeking and exploring some factor (or factors) other than race to be the dominant and causal factor in determining the outcome of the American political process.[21] In their view, individual merit is, in the final analysis, the basis for all advancement, privileges, and achievements. Despite race relations scholars' protestations to the contrary, race has been important and a delimiting feature of American democracy in the view of advocates of the scholarly tradition. Scholars who employ both behavioral and traditional methodologies confirm this thesis. It is to this use of political science methodology during the Reagan-Bush era that we now turn.

Data and Methodology

Did the academics of the race relations school of political science scholarship, in their work on race and politics during the Reagan-Bush era, use empirical methodologies to minimize and diminish the impact of race as an explanatory variable? Moreover, did their scholarship support and undergird the desires of the Reagan and Bush administrations to transform the political context? Findings to this effect would provide insights into not only the role of academic scholarship in supporting contextual transformation but also into how this academic scholarship deploys and implements methodologies that help substantiate the "correct" political doctrine. While it is widely known that scholarship is often modified (yielding what is called, in the academic community, revisionist studies), little is known about the role of methodology in producing such works.[22] With regard to the role of methodology in the study of race and politics specifically, even less is known because this aspect has not been a major concern until recently.[23] Therefore, the study of the transformation of the political context of the African American community must include an analysis of how various methodologies, particularly empirical ones, were used to downplay race as a key variable. Figure 4.1 illuminates the major analytical steps and procedures to be employed in this paper to assess the use and role of methodologies in race relations studies during the Reagan-Bush era.

The creation of a timeline/timeframe delineating the major African American political events that took place before and during the Reagan-Bush era is a useful first step in assessing the role of methodology in the race relations studies that emerged during that period.

There are a number of forces which influenced and shaped the nature of the discipline over time. Figure 4.2 is a chronological chart of concurrent historical forces in: (1) the African-American political community; (2) racial ideologies; (3) the dominant socio-political system; and (4) disciplinary trends. The figure provides a baseline and a fairly dynamic picture of internal and external (disciplinary) events and concerns occurring in the four major areas.

FIGURE 4.2

African American Political Events, Racial Ideologies, the Sociopolitical System, and Disciplinary Trends, 1619–1990s

TIME YEARS	AFRICAN-AMERICAN POLITICAL EVENTS
1863	Emancipation Proclamation
1861---1865	Civil War
1865	Thirteenth Amendment
1868	Fourteenth Amendment
1870	Fifteenth Amendment
1875	Civil Rights Acts
1877	Presidential compromise and end of black Reconstruction
1883	Supreme Court nullifies the Civil Rights Acts
1890---1902	Era of disenfranchisement
1895	B. T. Washington's Atlanta compromise address
1896	Plessy v Ferguson
1901	Last African American, George White, leaves Congress
1903	The Soul of Black Folks published
1905	Niagara Movement organized
1906---1925	Race riots and lynchings
1909	NAACP organized
1910	National Urban League formed
1915	Grandfather clause outlined (Guinn v U.S.)
1927---1932	Initial white primary cases
1928	Oscar Depriest elected to Congress (Republican)
1934	Arthur L. Mitchell elected to Congress (Democrat)
1941	President Roosevelt issues executive Order 8802 creating FEPC
1942	William Dawson elected to Congress
1944	Adam Clayton Powell, Jr. elected to Congress
1944---1948	White primaries outlawed (Smith v Allwright and Rice v Elmore)
1947	President Truman creates Committee on Civil Rights
1955	Martin Luther King, Jr. and the Montgomery bus boycott
1957---1964	Three new Civil Rights Acts
1965	Initial Voting Rights Acts
1967	Election of first black big city mayors
1972	Shirley Chisholm run for President
1974	California and Colorado elect black Lt. Governors
1984 and 1988	Jesse Jackson's run for the Presidency
1989	Virginia elects first black Governor, L. Douglass Wilder

TIME YEARS	RACIAL IDEOLOGIES AFRICAN-AMERICAN/WHITE
1619---1865	Black Nationalism/White Supremacy ↓
1870---1920	Black Nationalism and Integration/ Social Darwinism ↓
1920---1960	Race Relation Thought(ism) ↓
1970s Present	Race Pluralism and Integration/ Race Relation and Integration

TIME YEARS	DOMINANT SOCIO-POLITICAL SYSTEM
1619---1865	Introduction of Slavery
1866---1896	Rise and Institutionalization of Segregation ↓
1909---1954	Challenges to the Racial Status Quo ↓
1954---Present	Efforts Toward Full and Complete Desegregation

TIME YEARS	DISCIPLINARY DEVELOPMENT & BLACKS IN THE PROFESSION	METHODOLOGICAL ORIENTATIONS
1870---1880	Prehistoric and Origins ↓	Deduction Approach ↓
1880---1903	Formative Years ↓	Historical-Comparative ↓
1886	Political Science Quarterly starts ↓	
1903	Formation of American Political Science Association ↓	
1906	American Political Science Review starts ↓	
1954	Ralph Bunche: President of APSA ↓	Behavioralism ↓
1970s	Committee on Status of Blacks ↓	
1980s	Summer Institute for African American Students	Post-Behavioralism

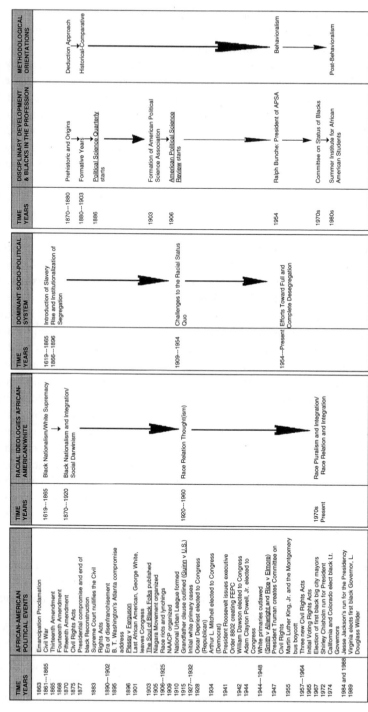

The historical events adapted from Alton Hornsby Jr., *Chronology of African History* (Detroit: Gale Research, 1991); political science data taken from Albert Somit and Joseph Tanenhaus, *The Development of American Political Science: From Burgess to Behavioralism* (Boston: Allyn and Bacon, 1967).

The vertical dimensions of figure 4.2 show milestones occurring from 1619 (the introduction of slavery to the American colonies) through 1990. Movement across the chart permits a comparison of similarities and concurrent happenings affecting the larger political system, the African-American community, and the political science discipline.

Figure 4.3 is derived from figure 4.2 and depicts four major forces (interacting with each other) and their linkage to the two traditions of the study of race.

Table 4.1 reveals two significant facts about the presidential speeches and the articles used for figure 4.3. Only three of the seventy-nine presidential addresses this research encompasses even mention the word "Negro" (or "black" or "African American"). Table 4.1 reveals the total number of articles, book reviews, and special features that each of the two journals have devoted to the African-American political experience. Single articles deal wholly with African-Americans, while combination articles focus on African-Americans as well as other racial or ethnic groups. Given the diverse and diffuse nature of the

FIGURE 4.3
A Conceptual Schematic of the Key Variables Affecting the Discipline Through Time, 1619–1990s

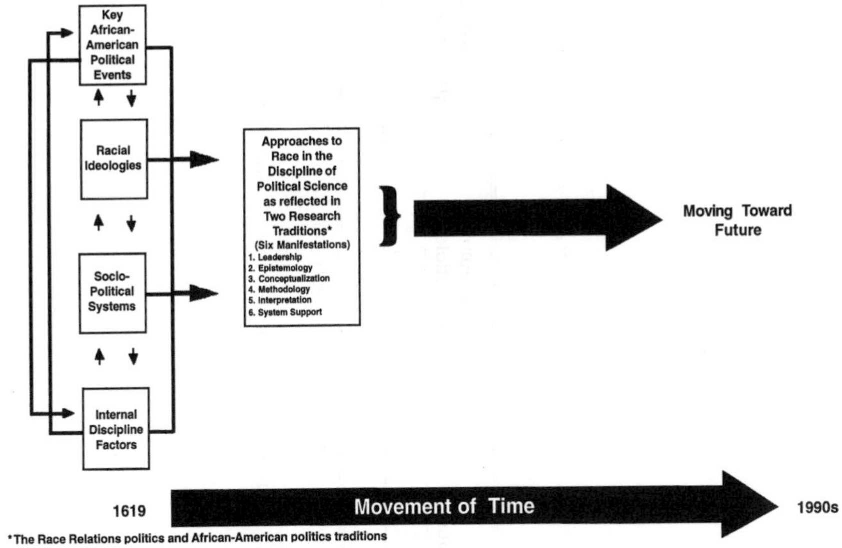

Adapted from Hanes Walton Jr., Cheryl M. Miller, and Joseph P. McCormick II, "Race and Political Science: The Dual Traditions of Race Relations Politics and African American Politics," in John Dryzek, James Farr, and Stephen Leonard, eds., *Political Science and Its History: Research Programs and Political Traditions* (New York: Cambridge University Press, 1995), 145–174.

TABLE 4.1

The Quantity of Data on Race and Politics in Two Political Science Journals, 1886–1990

Journal	Total Number of Articles	Articles		Book Reviews		P.A.	P.E.
		Single	Combination	Single	Combination		
Quarterly	2,474	27 (1%)	33 (1%)	131	93	3	39
Review	3,683	27 (1%)	31 (1%)	144	102	0	2

P.A. = Presidential Addresses; P.E. = Political Events Section

SOURCES: *The Political Science Quarterly* (1886–1990) and *The American Political Science Review* (1906–1990).

combination articles and book reviews, the analysis which follows is limited primarily to single articles.

Both the *Political Science Quarterly* (*Quarterly*) over 105 years, and the *American Political Science Review* (*Review*) in 85 years, have published an identical number (N = 27) of race-related articles. The other striking feature of table 4.1 is the small number of articles devoted to the African-American political experience over time. Both journals committed only about two percent of their coverage (total of single and combination articles) to the issue of race and politics.

We categorize the presidential speeches and journal articles into the two research traditions, acknowledging the existence of gradations, nuances, and overlap of normative values and political perspectives that in some cases the two categories subsume. When the combined fifty-four articles are categorized by research tradition, the dominant focus reflected in the journals becomes clearer. Table 4.2 shows that most of the twenty-seven single articles of each journal fall into what we have defined as the race relations politics tradition. Little more than a third of the articles were concerned with ways to enhance and improve the political power of African-Americans.

Given the small number of articles over nearly a century, we explored the temporal dimension by decades. When did these fifty-four articles appear? Table 4.3 displays the total number of articles per decade and their placement in the two traditions. It reveals that articles addressing race and politics from a race relations politics perspective began rather early and have maintained a dominance in the political science literature. This category of articles has occurred in a cyclical pattern. Articles in the African-American politics tradition were few

TABLE 4.2
The Number and Percentage of Articles in Each of the Dual Research Traditions, 1886–1990

Categories	Number	Percentage
The Political Science Quarterly		
Race Relations Politics	16	59.3
African American Politics	11	40.7
Total	27	100.0
American Political Science Review		
Race Relations Politics	17	63.0
African American Politics	10	37.0
Total	27	100.0

SOURCES: *The Political Science Review Quarterly* (1886–1990) and *The American Political Science Review* (1906–1990).

and far-between before the 1940s. What one finds particularly in the 1960s and 1970s is a dual perspective, with race relations politics articles appearing along with African-American politics articles. Articles in these two traditions began to appear in more nearly equal numbers with the growth in the number of African-American political scientists. When the Reagan-Bush and Clinton eras took place, there was a strong tradition among political scientists to use a methodological approach, dubbed here as a "race relations" approach, to deny or diminish the fact that race is a factor in contextual revolutions.

These studies provide the data base for the present analysis. Four focus areas emerge: (1) electoral events, (2) political party events, (3) legal and constitutional decisions, and (4) public policy events. We shall evaluate the methodologies used in these studies, specifically looking at how these studies treat race as a variable in the explanatory equation and intellectual interpretation of the findings. Proceeding in this manner will yield an analysis and exploration of the research hypothesis that will be both systematic and comprehensive.

In sum, the data base with which this assessment and analysis of the methodologies used in political science race relations studies will be conducted includes

TABLE 4.3

The Number of Articles in Each of the Dual Traditions by Decade, 1886–1990

Decades	Tradition Number Per Quarterly		Tradition Nunber Per Review	
	Race Relations Politics	African-American Politics	Race Relations Politics	African-American Politics
1880s	0	0	--	--
1890s	3	1	--	--
1900s	2	0	3	0
1910s	1	1	0	0
1920s	0	0	0	0
1930s	1	1	1	1
1940s	0	1	0	3
1950s	1	0	1	0
1960s	4	1	3	0
1970s	3	3	7	3
1980s	0	3	2	2
1990s	1	0	0	1
TOTAL	16	11	17	10

SOURCES: *The Political Science Review Quarterly* (1886–1990) and *The American Political Science Review* (1906–1990).

the sundry academic studies that were produced during the Reagan-Bush era. This data base will be organized into four basic areas in order to discern the patterns, trends, and unique features of the varied methodological procedures.

Electoral Events and Empirical Methodology

Two years into the first Reagan administration, a massive campaign to put African American mayor Thomas Bradley into the governor's mansion in California was undertaken.[24] To some, Bradley's personality, his nonaggressive behavior and mollifying demeanor, fit the mold of an African American candidate who could amass and maintain white support. He had earlier proven that he could garner such support by prevailing in the highly competitive contest for the mayor's seat in Los Angeles, where African Americans make up only one-third of the voters. However, when the votes for the 1982 California gubernatorial race were tallied, Bradley lost by a very small margin.[25] Yet the pre-election polls and surveys had projected a Bradley victory.

Why did he lose? Was it due to racism or the failure of African Americans to turn out for Bradley? Analyst after analyst during the period under question failed to cite "racism" as the major explanatory variable. Empirical methodology could not even pinpoint the role that racism played in this campaign. Thus, the research attributed Bradley's defeat to the conclusion that he lost because he took African American voters for granted and simply did not reach out to campaign for their votes as vigorously as he should have. Simply put, Bradley lost because of African Americans, not racism. Once again, empirical methodology failed to discern the chief cause. As one observer wrote: "A number of factors have been proposed to explain the Bradley loss. These range from negative opinions of Bradley's wife to the large turnout of voters against the proposal to ban handguns." Although it is true that in a close election, any one or a combination of factors can be "fatal,"[26] in the case of this election, every explanation was offered except race, despite the fact that, as Henry notes, "In California [in 1982], Democrats retained control of the legislature, strengthened their grip on the Congressional delegation, and elected every statewide partisan officer below the rank of governor."[27] Thus, in an election otherwise marked by a Democratic sweep, the African American Democrat lost.

Another significant example can be found in the analysis of the results of a mayoral contest in New York City. This time the situation was reversed. An African American Democrat, David Dinkins, won, but his winning was not attributed to racial variables. In one case, Arian, Goldberg, Mollenkopf, and Rogowsky, in their study of the election using an empirical methodology known as regression analysis, have shown that race, race riots, and several racial incidents such as the Bensonhurst, Howard Beach, and Central Park jogger episodes had nothing to do with Dinkins's election. At the outset, these authors claim that their book:

> seeks to shed light on what motivated the voters of New York City to elect their first black mayor in the fall of 1989 and why they did so by the closest of margins with vast numbers of defections from traditional Democratic voting patterns. At first glance, "race" would appear to be the obvious explanation but we believe that single word says both too much and too little. Race is not a sufficient explanation because important groups in New York City did not vote along strictly racial lines.[28]

They also write: "First race was certainly a major factor in these elections, but not principally in the way that people usually think."[29] Apparently, they wish to have it both ways. They continue: "so yes, race did matter, in fact a great deal. But it mattered least in its most blatant form of racism, pure and simple."[30]

This is not, however, the entire truth, for Arian et al. later drop the "race" variables from their statistical analysis, concluding, for example, that "while the Bensonhurst incident certainly had an impact on the momentum of the campaign and the mood of the city, it is harder to measure its precise impact on the electorate."[31] In other sections of their book, where they use multivariate techniques to ascertain the dominate independent variables, race is once again left out: "We assessed the relative weights of factors bearing a shift using linear regression analysis. However, we excluded the dominant elements of racial mistrust and party identification from the equations in order to reveal the effect of other variables."[32] By so doing, race is clearly not going to show up in the list of dominant variables. Nonetheless, these authors draw the following conclusion:

> In sum, defections from traditional Democratic voting pattern in 1989 had strong roots in race-based mistrust. However, fear about crime and a weariness with corruption also worked heavily against Dinkins as a black Democrat.[33]

Yet this does not show up in their statistical model. Then, in the final chapter, where they are assessing the role of divisive issues on the outcome of the election, racial issues are not built into the regression equations as an independent variable.[34]

No wonder empirical methodology failed in this case. A major variable was simply not explored in the model. The reality in this and other instances is that, during the Reagan-Bush era, race as a factor in African Americans' political defeats and political victories could not be confirmed by empirical methodology as having even played a role. Four years later, when Dinkins lost his re-election bid, similar studies appeared.

Political Party Events and Empirical Methodology

In 1984, Jesse Jackson entered the Democratic primaries seeking the party's nomination for president. Although Jackson ran an exceptional if not unusual campaign, marred only by the "Hymie-town" flap over a derogatory remark about Jews, he failed to gain the party's nomination,[35] which went to former Vice President Walter Mondale.

Why did Jackson lose? One academic account avowed that the Rainbow Coalition leader was an "African American racist."[36] Others claimed that Jackson's flawed character was the problem[37]; that his blackness "got in the way"[38]; and that his politics (and that of African American leaders generally), because it lacked a class analysis and approach, severely constrained and undermined his effort.[39] For all of these academics, Jackson lost because of Jackson. He was, in their final analysis, his own worst problem.

But while many were attempting to explain Jackson's electoral defeat in terms of his personal attributes, others were busy trying to prove that the overall election defeat (in the primary and general elections) had occurred because the demands Jackson and other African Americans had made on the Democratic party had alienated it from one of its traditional coalitional groups: the white south.[40] First appeared an academic book chapter that espoused this unsupported position.[41] Later, this contention would be put forth in a major book entitled *Race and the Decline of Class in American Politics.* As Huckfelt and Kohfeld, the authors of that book, write:

> Political commentators were curiously reluctant to focus on the racial divide. They stressed the high level of support for Jackson among whites, evidently based on an implicit assumption that he would fail to receive *any* white support. Yet, when attempts were made to explain why he did not receive a higher level of white support, the explanation generally avoided race. Commentators seriously argued that whites were reluctant to support Jackson primarily because of his lack of experience in foreign affairs! These convoluted efforts to avoid race in the explanation of Jackson's difficulties among whites produced some curious racial overtones. If whites judged Jackson to be lacking in foreign policy expertise, why did blacks support him? Were blacks unable to make judgments regarding foreign policy? If blacks supported Jackson *because* he was black, it is difficult to argue that race was unrelated to the reason that whites generally *failed* to support him.[41]

Therefore, these authors argue, "the decline of class as an organizing principle in contemporary American electoral politics is directly related to the concurrent ascent of race," even though they had earlier stated:

> It has become abundantly clear that the politics of race serves both to disguise and to disrupt the politics of class. Racial politics serves as a disguise for class politics because, above all, the unifying impetus behind the politics of race is the disadvantaged status of blacks in society. Thus, the politics of race is fundamentally anchored in the politics of class.[42]

In Huckfelt and Kohfeld's view, Jackson, in his 1984 and particularly his 1988 campaign, kept this subterfuge going with his emphasis on race rather than class issues. His candidacies illustrated "the strains of race and class that define the political dilemma of the Democratic party."[43] Moreover, his efforts failed to attract and maintain the electoral support of lower-class Democratic voters. Hence, they write:

> The new Republican party, sired by Barry Goldwater and sustained by Ronald Reagan, is an intentional or unintentional response to the politics of race, a curious blend of populist rebellion and conservative social backlash that frequently falls short of adequately representing the business, upper, and middle-class interest that formed the core of Eisenhower's party.[44]

Huckfelt and Kohfeld could not decide whether the Republicans had "intentionally" or "unintentionally" used race or racial tensions to recruit low-income voters to the GOP. However, they do note that this scrambling for the low-income vote disrupted the Republican party, straining to appeal simultaneously to upper- and lower-class interests.

Thus the variable of race not only caused the Democratic party to lose, it also created a major, long-term dilemma for the Republican party. Yet, nowhere in Huckfelt and Kohlfield's statistical analyses, their model, or their data-gathering efforts do they once reveal how African Americans and Jackson accomplished this feat. While they mention that Jackson got only upper-middle-class support but not lower-class support, not once do they provide any evidence or proof of this claim. They merely assume it to be true and then proceed to show the consequences.[45] Additionally, their analysis is ahistorical in that they never show how southern demagogues traditionally have used "race baiting" to mobilize the Democratic party and how Republicans have reverted to the same tactic in modern times to forge winning coalitions, at least at the presidential level. Notwithstanding, these authors conclude that "race is not a legitimate basis for partisan conflict in democratic politics and an electoral system structured in term of race is destructive of democratic values."[46] Empirical methodology thus had failed again.

Following Huckfelt and Kohlfield's book came other academic and popular analyses that claimed the Democratic party lost ground during the Reagan-Bush era as a consequence of African Americans. However, the empirical findings of these studies would not include racism as a major factor and variable in the intellectual equation.[47]

Legal/Constitutional Events and Empirical Methodology

Numerous controversies emerged in the legal and constitutional area during the Reagan-Bush era. The background to one of these was the Supreme Court's decision in *South Carolina v. Katzenbach* (1966) to support and sustain the 1965 Voting Rights Act. This marked the first decision declaring the constitutionality of the act, and sanctioned most of the act's section 4 and all of section 5, which addressed the English-language provision and pre-clearance of any new law or regulation pertaining to voting rights, respectively.[48] According to Grofman and Davidson, the controversy surrounding the Court's decision involved "a combination of historical, normative and legal-technical issues."[49] Davidson continues:

> Perhaps the key dispute is over whether the act and related case law have evolved into a mechanism for enforcing "affirmative action" quotas. In particular, to what extent has the proviso included in the 1982 Amendments denying a right to proportional representation been violated in cases such as *Thornburg v. Grigles* (1986)? . . . In addition to debate about normative and policy questions, there has been considerable dispute over the legal standards that ought to govern voting rights cases, especially with respect to the operationalization of the three prongs of the *Grigles* test for vote dilution under section 2 of the Act.[50]

The lead work in opposition to the Voting Rights Act and its continued implementation was conducted by political scientist Abigail Thernstrom, who attempted in 1979 to establish the act's "odd evolution" and unconstitutional base in an article published in *The Public Interest,* a conservative policy-oriented magazine. Commenting on Thernstrom's article, Kousser notes the following:

> Although [Thernstrom] approved of the original act, she argued (albeit without presenting evidence) that after *Allen v. State Board of Elections* in 1969 it had become a tool in the hands of Justice Department attorneys with a "vested interest" in mandating districts as section 5 remedies for at-

> large dilution and annexation of white suburbs, remedies that in her view amounted to "proportional racial representation."[51]

The act, Thernstrom warned, was "creating a host of new problems," and in spite of the opportunity for it to expire in 1982, it seemed:

> well on its way to becoming . . . a permanent part of our political landscape. It was not the canards of aging reactionary southerners that the Republican opponents of the amendment embraced during the debates of 1981–82 but Thernstrom's argument and those of academicians such as law professors Donald Horowitz and Williams Van Alstyne, political scientists Timothy O'Rourke and John Bunzel, and philosophers Barry Gross and Michael Levin.[52]

In her subsequent book, entitled *Whose Votes Count: Affirmative Action and Minority Voting Rights,* Thernstrom continues her argument that voting rights is a form of affirmative action. Indeed, in her view, voting rights protection clauses for African Americans and other minorities are, plain and simple, a form of reverse discrimination.[53] Yet she neither employs empirical data to support that contention and ascription, nor does she establish the disappearance of racism in empirical terms—two elements that are critical to support such an argument.[54]

Nonetheless, Thernstrom's argument was expanded by others and introduced into the Reagan-Bush era debate over the federal civil rights regulatory apparatus. The position taken by conservative Republican strategists and scholars was that these regulatory agencies had advanced the state at great cost to "nonparticipants," that is, those who were not the victims of racism.[55] Again, not even the slightest use of empirical methodology was engaged to determine either the enduring presence or the disappearance of racism to substantiate these arguments. Those who opposed the constitutionality of the Voting Rights Act during the Reagan-Bush and Clinton years failed to employ empirical methodology to show the disappearance or the declining significance of racism in the American political process. On the other hand, many of the expert witnesses in the voting rights cases that both pre- and post-dated the 1965 Voting Rights Act used empirical methodology—regression analyses and, at times, double regression techniques—to show the continual existence of racism in voting patterns and to convince the courts of the persistence of this cultural reality.[56] For example, the empirical work done by Frank Parker in 1990 clearly established the continuance of racism in the electoral process in Mississippi.[57]

Yet the conservative argument contended that there was little need for the civil rights regulatory, enforcement, and administrative apparatus because the kinds of racism that made this apparatus necessary no longer existed, and that, in effect, the bureaucrats involved in this apparatus had little or nothing to do.[58] Lacking supportive evidence, their real intent was to create a new constitutional majority that embraced the distortion of the historical record and the dismissal of factual data.

Public Policy Events and Empirical Methodology

During the Reagan-Bush era, a number of academics and scholars writing in the area of public policy attempted to refashion the political context by attacking the social, economic, and regulatory policies enacted during the Kennedy-Johnson era. Their attacks involved some unusual arguments, and, like their colleagues in the legal and constitutional arenas, most failed to use empirical methodology to prove their theses that these policies constituted some form of reverse discrimination or were detrimental to the very people they purported to assist.

One of the first works of this kind to appear was Thomas Sowell's *Civil Rights: Rhetoric or Reality,* published in 1984, that decried the existence of civil rights policies.[59] Not only did this work not involve even the minutest effort at empirical methodology, it quickly disappeared from the academic landscape. Essentially it was itself a rhetorical effort, but it set the stage. Later that same year, another controversial policy book, Murray's *Losing Ground,* appeared. Murray's book, instead of focusing its attack on civil rights policy alone, blasted every major public policy initiative designed to assist African Americans.[60] Although Murray used empirical techniques, he did so in a fraudulent way. His book is an example of the kind of nonempirical nonresearch popular during the Reagan-Bush era, in which arguments against anti-racism public policy initiatives were put forth without establishing the collapse of racism.

Then there is Hugh David Graham's historical look at the creation and the evolution of civil rights policy.[61] Essentially drawing upon materials from the presidential archives from Kennedy to Nixon, Graham's argument is that the well-meaning and well-intended policies of the Democratic administrations preceding Reagan and Bush had gone awry in the judicial and implementation process. In their final form, he posits, these policies had become uncontrollable, worrisome things that exceeded the intentions of their original framers—indeed, of the constitution itself. Instead of being helpful, Graham contends, the civil rights policies created during the Kennedy-Johnson era had become harmful and counterproductive, and, for all intents and purposes, constituted various forms of reverse discrimination against white Americans.[62] He even suggests that without some of these policies racism would have died a natural death. Yet neither in his analysis of presidential and congressional documents nor his focus on court cases and the federal bureaucracy does Graham take any quantitative or qualitative notice of the effect or continuance of racism. Somehow, to Graham and other scholars of the Reagan-Bush and Clinton eras, the critical and crucial variable of race was no longer a feature of contemporary America.[63]

Conclusions

During the Reagan-Bush and Clinton eras, several academic works denied the presence or influence of racism in the electoral, partisan politics, legal/constitutional, or public policy areas. Empirical methodologies were either omitted, ignored, or disavowed as a means of testing for the influence and impact of race as an independent variable. Indeed, the apparent genius of the race relations studies arm of political science scholarship during the Reagan-Bush and Clinton eras is that, even in a period during which the behavioral revolution had revolutionized the discipline to employ more quantitative measures and techniques to test variables in a multivariate way,[64] these studies either dismissed or minimized empirical techniques that could have tested for and quantified the existence or absence of the variable of race. Yet these pundits proclaimed, without empirical substantiation, that America had come of age—that racism was no longer a determinant of the life chances of African Americans. The promulgation of this myth worked exceedingly well for the political context transformation Reagan and Bush had set into motion. It allowed these administrations, while claiming to be pursuing race-neutral policies, to introduce racial cleavages into the political process for partisan gain and further disadvantage African Americans. Moreover, the academic and intellectual communities provided support for the Reagan-Bush contextual transformation, even though the basis of that transformation was factually flawed.

The Reagan and Bush administrations' intent in transforming the African American political context was to build larger political majorities that could undermine and undercut the constitutional victories of African Americans which had been gained via the support and efforts of earlier political majorities despite the moral legitimacy of these claims and victories.

PART 3

CONSTITUTIONALISM

Ultimately, efforts to transform the African American political context involve the transformation of the constitutional foundations of the American political system. There are at least two ways to do this. One method calls for a transformation of the Constitution itself via amendments. Throughout American history, scores of legislative proposals have attempted to do this, but the success of such efforts have been slight. The second method, changing the way and manner in which the Constitution is interpreted, has met with greater success and has therefore become the option of choice for most politicians.

There are several dimensions to this latter approach. One strategy involves stacking the Supreme Court and the other federal courts with jurists whose politics reflect those of the ruling political party until they form a clear-cut majority. This strategy was pursued during the Reagan-Bush era and it had great success.[1] As Barbara Luck Graham states, President Reagan "attempted to influence constitutional interpretation by aggressively pursuing its social and civil rights agenda through the appointments of conservative federal judges."[2] This task was furthered, Graham notes, by Reagan's efforts to politicize the solicitor general's office "by trying to persuade the Supreme Court to overturn important precedents in the civil rights area through advocating a jurisprudence of original intent."[3]

The Reagan-appointed attorney general, Edwin Meese, III, declared early in President Reagan's first term on November 15, 1985, how federal judges should go about implementing "original intent." As attorney general Meese saw it:

> The approach this administration advocates is rooted in the text of the Constitution as 'illuminated by those who drafted, proposed and ratified it . . . in the main a jurisprudence that seeks to be faithful to our Constitution—a jurisprudence of original intention, as I have called it—is not difficult to describe. Where the language of the Constitution is specific, it must be obeyed. Where there is a demonstrable consensus among the framers and ratifiers as to a principle stated or implied by the Constitution, it should be followed. Where there is ambiguity as to the precise meaning or reach of a constitutional provision, it should be interpreted and applied in a manner so as to at least not contradict the text of the Constitution itself.[4]

The Bush presidency continued the approach. Attorney General Meese offered as further justification for this concept this insight:

> At issue is a way of government. A jurisprudence based on first principles is neither conservative nor liberal, neither right nor left. It is a jurisprudence that cares about committing and limiting to each organ of government the proper ambit of its responsibilities. It is a jurisprudence faithful to our Constitution.[5]

Despite the insistence of this conservative Republican, some federal judges objected and one wrote: "On most issues, to look for a collective intention held by either drafters or ratifiers is to hunt for a chimera."[6] Federal Judge Irving Kaufman, of the Second Circuit Court of Appeal, states:

> As a Federal judge, I have found it often difficult to ascertain the "intent of the farmers," and even more problematic to try to dispose of a constitution question by giving great weight to the intent argument.[7]

Meese and the Republican President did not respond to this criticism.

But what of criticism from the African American community? Professor Matthew Holden, Jr. points out that the original Constitution has a problem when it comes to the matter of race on both its "principle" and "usage" levels. He writes:

> The American Constitution "of usage" [and] the real Constitution, has reflected a racial hierarchy. The dominant group, defining itself mystically as the "white race," has sought to achieve, maintain, and reinforce an

hegemony or hierarchy over other persons and groups defined as not white.[8]

From this perspective, Constitutions in the most general sense stipulate which members of the political community are entitled to all available measures of deference and material benefit, which members can claim only partial benefits . . . which subjects are to be ruled, and which are mere resources to be used.[9]

Understood in this manner, in the original intent of the founders at either the level of principle or at the level of usage, racial bias was a problem. And to accept "original intent" as conceptualized by Attorney General Meese and insisted on by the Republican president was, in the eyes of some critics, to accept a racial hierarchy. But this criticism also went unanswered. The contextual transformation of the Constitution continued unchanged during the Reagan-Bush and Clinton eras.[9] Clinton, for instance, responded to Republican presidential hopefuls Gov. Pete Wilson and Senator Phil Gramm by reviewing and then dropping the federal government's affirmative action policies. After these candidates lost their party's nomination, President Clinton did not reverse his action.

Another means of establishing a new constitutional doctrine involves changing the political and legal discourse and then asserting that said discourse is what the Founding Fathers originally desired. The first step in this process is the launching of incessant attacks on Supreme Court decisions. During the Reagan-Bush era, these attacks were aimed at the recently established rights and liberties extended to African Americans via Supreme Court decisions and legislative actions of the civil rights era. These Republican administrations sought and found ways, legal and extralegal, to undercut the civil rights, equal opportunity, and affirmative action laws and legal decisions of the 1950s, 1960s, and 1970s. Both Reagan and Bush, in raising suspicions about the validity and morality of these rulings and laws, suggested that the majority of the American people were opposed to them. Later majority public opinion, established through polls and surveys, offered support for these suspicions. Despite the legitimacy of these protective legal and legislative mandates, politicians and bureaucrats hesitated in their support of them. With chaos and confusion about African American civil rights and liberties abounding in both the public mind and the government, a new constitutional doctrine of inequality emerged under a new guise.

Constitutional inequality is defined here as all attempts to have the federal courts declare any remedies that seek government intervention, including affirmative action, busing, quotas, and set-asides, as unconstitutional. During the Reagan, Bush, and Clinton eras, Republicans sought to advance the idea that any remedy to ameliorate racial discrimination with government help does not advance equality as much as creating new inequalities by disadvantaging white Americans. The contextual revolution sought to have embedded in law the idea that all government-backed reform of racial discrimination was a form of constitutional inequality.

Almost immediately after coming into office in 1980, the Reagan administration began its attack on affirmative action and other government-sponsored remedies. Affirmative action was dubbed reverse discrimination and therefore unconstitutional, and equality was claimed to be less important than liberty. When the latter idea failed to immediately catch hold, the concept of equality was then bifurcated into two categories: (1) equality of opportunity and (2) equality of results. Equality of results became the focus, at least in the academic and scholarly literature.

These efforts had their roots in earlier attempts to recast constitutional intent. Beginning in the postcolonial period, the proslavery forces won certain victories in shaping the Constitution such that it protected their peculiar institution.[10] This legal protection stayed in the document until dislodged by the abolitionists and their allies.[11] Since the Civil War,

> the struggle between the constitutional problack forces and the constitutional antiblack forces has been recurring and sporadic, but the struggle has covered the entire spectrum of rights and privileges in this country, running from a definition of citizenship sights to voting principles and running for public office.[12]

While, to date, the "antiblack" forces have suffered the greatest reverses, the Supreme Court has given this loose confederation several significant victories, including some of recent note like the *Bakke* decision and the ruling in *Richmond v. Croson.*[13] This type of bias in the legal system led one observer, Marcus Pohlmann, to note that "blacks end up dependent both on white-created legislation and the administration of those laws."[14] Pohlmann's comments suggest that the racial makeup of the court assures that the antiblack forces are more likely to win even if ideology is not a factor, as it was during the Reagan-Bush era.

As Graham noted, "clearly, ideological and policy position considerations emerge as the most significant factors in determining who sits on the Supreme Court under the Reagan administration."[15] Ideology was also the determining factor for the Bush administration's African American Supreme Court nominee, Clarence Thomas, who was confirmed, in part, precisely because he was a conservative.[16]

The legal and political discourse continues, and many neoconservative scholars and academics continue to advance questionable theories of constitutional inequalities while other academics struggle to apply affirmative action to voting rights.[17] Still others deploy themselves as "expert witnesses," offering new theories of "limited representation," another form of constitutional inequality.[18] Hence, the struggle to reinterpret the Constitution is well under way. Several of the Thomas-aided Court majorities that diminish voting and prisoner rights have gone unchallenged by the Clinton administration.

Among the forces seeking to advance constitutional inequality are African American conservatives. This is their role, as designed at the Fairmont Conference, and several moved swiftly to advance and play that role, including J. A. Y. Parker, president of the Lincoln Institute, an African American conservative think tank. On June 10, 1985, shortly after Reagan's second term began, Parker sent out a mass mailing

> [a] mailgram concerning the possible resignation of Associate Justice Thurgood Marshall [and] solicited money so that the Lincoln Institute can do research to identify "black conservatives" for the United States Supreme Court should Thurgood Marshall, who is black, retire.[19]

Parker added:

> As the head of the Lincoln Institute, I strongly feel that Justice Marshall's replacement must be a conservative Black American. Repeat, a conservative Black American.
>
> But you can be certain that the powerful liberal establishment will wage an intensive public campaign in support of a replacement of Thurgood Marshall who is just as liberal.
>
> Even some liberal Republicans within the Reagan administration may promote a liberal Black American as a replacement for Justice Thurgood Marshall with the purpose of appeasing Black radicals like Jesse Jackson.
>
> You and I must not let this happen.
>
> We must have a Black American who takes a strict constitutional view. View similar to that of High Court Jurists William Rehnquist, Sandra Day O'Connor and Chief Justice Warren Burger.
>
> I believe that President Reagan will listen to the findings of Black conservatives. He will listen to the Lincoln Institute . . . Please send your check to me today.[20]

As this mailgram shows, African American conservative operatives were willing in several ways to assist the Reagan-Bush constitutional and political transformations. Another African American Republican took Parker and his mailgram to task. J. Clay Smith, Jr. wrote:

> Are these [Rehnquist, O'Connor, and Burger] the only legal role models that you can refer to? If you are trying to educate the public to your persuasion, then why can't you provide the name of a single black judge or lawyer as a model against which to measure Supreme Court worthiness?[21]

5

AFRICAN AMERICAN POLITICS AND THE CONSTITUTION

Neoconservative, Neoliberal, and African American Conservative Theories of Constitutional Inequality

• • • • • • •

Hanes Walton, Jr.

Political context, when it is transformed as it was during the Reagan-Bush era, involves efforts to reshape and reorient constitutional doctrine, interpretation, and application. At times, these efforts might include modification of the Constitution itself via new amendments or, as during the Reagan-Bush years, the threat of potential or proposed amendments. However, the period from 1980 to 1996 saw less of an effort to modify the Constitution and more of an effort to reshape and reorient constitutional doctrine.

Emerging out of the civil rights movement efforts of the 1960s and early 1970s were several congressional, presidential, and bureaucratic techniques designed to implement civil rights laws and shore up their constitutional foundations. By the 1970s, the United States had extended certain constitutional rights and liberties to African Americans via the Civil Rights Law of 1964, the Voting Rights Act of 1965, the Open Housing Act of 1968, and the Equal Employment Opportunity Act of 1972. With these laws, African Americans were supposed to gain and exercise the same constitutional privileges of liberty and equality that all other Americans had long enjoyed. To make real these legal rights, the federal government developed a series of rules, regulations, and guidelines designed to ensure equality and justice for African Americans.[1]

It was these implementation devices that the anti-egalitarians of the Reagan-

Bush era were after. They sought to prove that there was no constitutional basis for these techniques and procedures, while simultaneously striving to alter the Constitution so that there would be no support or foundation for them. In their rush to judgement and their intellectual, academic, and political myopia, they deliberately overlooked the continuing and new forms of institutional racism that were evolving to confront the recent victories of the civil rights movement.[2] But this myopia and several of the theories of constitutional inequality had appeared prior to the advent of the Reagan-Bush era. Attacks upon African American civil rights achievements were well under way and operative during the preceding Democratic administrations, but these assaults had been scattered, their arguments sketchy, and their theories furtive and fragmentary. What the Reagan-Bush administrations did was to embrace these polemical fringe theories and bring them, no matter what their shortcomings and weaknesses, into the mainstream. Under Reagan and Bush, these new theories of constitutional inequality received legitimacy. The stage was being set for change in the political context.

Data and Methodology

This paper asks whether or not the nature and scope of the constitutional theories propounded by such political groupings as the neoconservatives,[3] neoliberals, and African American conservatives supported and furthered inequality in America. Did the arguments advanced by these three groups and their allies seek to deny the usefulness and validity of the techniques and procedures designed to implement the civil rights victories of the 1960s and 1970s? The answers are to be found in the writings (books, articles, essays and commentary) of the key leaders in the three political groups. For the sake of brevity, however, it will be necessary to select a single representative from each grouping.[4]

The Neoconservative Theory of Constitutional Inequality: Nathan Glazer

Perhaps the first academician to launch a theory of constitutional inequality in recent times was Nathan Glazer, and he did so some five years before the Reagan administration.[5] Glazer's chief argument was that affirmative action, a tool of the Kennedy presidency, was a form of reverse discrimination. He arrived at this position by asserting that "the consensus of the middle 1960s has been broken, that it was and remains the right policy for the United States—right for the groups that had suffered and in some measure still suffer, from prejudice and discrimination and right for the nation as a whole."[6]

What was this dead consensus? According to Glazer, the "thrust for equality [had] shifted from the legal position of the group to the achievement of concrete advancement in economic and political strength"; hence this supposed consensus "was merely for political equality, not economic equality or group parity."[7] Nowhere, however, does Glazer define or even show the existence of a consensus—neither in public opinion, the courts, Congress, the civil rights community, or the presidency—he merely asserts the existence of one. Then, on the basis of this fake consensus, he builds a curious and strained argument about constitutional inequality. He writes:

> In 1964, we declared that no account should be taken of race, color, national origin, or religion in the shaping of voting, jobs, and education (1968, we added housing). Yet no sooner had we made this national assertion than we entered into an unexampled recording of the color, race, and national origin of every individual in every significant sphere of his life. Having placed into law the dissenting opinion of *Plessy v. Ferguson* that our Constitution is color-blind, we entered into a period of color-and group-consciousness with a vengeance.[8]

This argument, like the one about a consensus, is both a pretense and a fabrication. The idea of a color-blind Constitution did not begin in 1896 with the dissenting opinion in *Plessy v. Ferguson.* But Glazer makes it appear that it did, and that it came from an dissenting opinion that was, at the time, questionable.

Having made this argument, Glazer moves to another point. Using the EEOC (Equal Employment Opportunity Commission) procedure of generating statistics to show patterns in job discrimination, Glazer posits yet another unsubstantiated position:

> The downgrading of acts of discrimination in the legal and administrative efforts to achieve equality for blacks and other minority groups in favor of statistical pattern-seeking has some important consequences. It is one thing to be asked to fight discrimination against the competent, hard-working, and law-abiding; it is quite another to be asked to fight discrimination against the less competent or incompetent and criminally inclined. The statistical emphasis leads to the latter. Undoubtedly even those of lesser competence and criminal inclination must be incorporated into society, but one wonders whether this burden should be placed on laws against discrimination on account of race, color, religion, or national origin.
>
> The emphasis on statistics, rather than personal discrimination, raises another problem. The argument from statistics without cases is made . . . only because it is an easier argument to make, and will lead to more sweeping remedies.[9]

Glazer thus makes a preposterous leap in logic and academic reasoning to assert—using extreme analogies, examples, and, in this case, extreme assertions as proof—that affirmative action will lead to the advancement of the "less competent or incompetent and criminally inclined" over the "competent, hard-working and law-abiding."

Moreover Glazer asserts that the affirmative action approach is in violation of the Constitution. He argues that "this new course threatens the abandonment of our concern for individual claims to consideration on the basis of justice and equity, now to be replaced with a concern for rights for publicly determined and delimited racial and ethnic groups."[10] "This course," in his view, "is not demanded by legislation. Indeed, it is specifically forbidden by national legislation—or by any reasonable interpretation of the Constitution."[11]

But what is "reasonable interpretation of the Constitution"? Glazer does not explain this in his writings, thus one must assume that he is referring to his own personal interpretation.

Glazer, as one of the first contemporary neoconservatives to argue for constitutional inequality, contended that the individual basis of Constitutional rights had been violated by a new technique for group remedies. For him, affirmative action was reverse discrimination and therefore constitutionally invalid.

Glazer was not content merely to fabricate his ideas about reverse discrimination; he insisted on promoting them and on urging other scholars to do the same. During the Reagan-Bush era, he advanced the notion that voting rights for African Americans was a form of affirmative action and encouraged another academic (Thernstrom) to write a scholarly advocacy text on this position. Thernstrom states:

> When I was still almost wholly preoccupied with domestic concerns, Nathan Glazer took me out to lunch and encouraged me to get to work. My preliminary conclusions about minority voting rights were published in *The Public Interest,* the journal he co-edits.[12]

Not only did Glazer shepherd Thernstrom's book, he endorsed it in several places and contended that it was not a work of scholarly advocating, which it obviously was. In his own book, Glazer had focused on the areas of employment, busing, and housing in his efforts to verify the presence of reverse discrimination; but his work was perceived as polemical by most in the academic community. Thernstrom's illogical patchwork of anti-affirmative action and antiegalitarian ideas, while it received severe criticism in some quarters, was met with praise and awards in others. In this manner, Glazer continued to popularize his ideas.

Glazer resurfaced during the Reagan era as a consultant to the Civil Rights Commission. In this capacity, he continued to raise the issues he talked about in his earlier books and other writings.[13]

The Neoliberal Theory of Constitutional Inequality: Hugh D. Graham

In his 1990 work entitled *The Civil Rights Era,* Hugh D. Graham writes: "Classic liberalism's injunction to stop doing evil could not seem to repair the collective damage quickly enough to bring equal opportunity to these historically victimized citizens in their lifetime."[14] He continues: "Liberalism's historic command not to discriminate could not achieve its goal of a color-blind society because the racism of the past had become institutionalized."[15] As a representative analysis of neoliberal thought, Graham's assertions show that the neoliberals rest their case on two bases that are distinctively different from those of the neoconservatives. First, while the neoconservatives essentially rest their case on the supposed distinctions that the Founding Fathers made between liberty and equality, the neoliberals fall back on classical liberal theory. In the neoliberal view, government should play a non-interventionist role in society. They criticize civil rights proponents, techniques, and procedures if they call for an activist government role in the promotion of social policy. Secondly, the neoliberals tend to deplore racism and racists, denouncing in strong language the legacy of racism in society. The neoconservatives, on the other hand, usually claim that it no longer exists, that it has been finally and safely put to rest.

As Graham writes: "by 1970, the civil rights coalition was displacing the original formula of equal treatment for individuals with a formula of proportionally equal results for groups."[16] In Graham's view, the "emerging compensatory theory and [its] proportional model of equitable relief was . . . forged in the crucible of black protest" and "the newly evolving doctrine of protected classes was immature."[17] Thus, for the unfortunate victims of racism, neoliberals—while they understand that African Americans suffered discrimination as a group and claim they want to help—prefer the individual model of relief instead of a group-based model of regulatory relief.

Graham, like his mentor Glazer, sees a specific moment when the civil rights movement changed:

> The fundamental shift of goals and means that distinguished Phase I from Phase II, then, was the shift from "soft" to "hard" or from positive-sum to zero-sum affirmative action. The shift was from a goal of equal treatment with positive assistance, such as special recruitment and training efforts, to a goal of equal results or a proportional distribution of benefits among groups. This shift created the tension, captured by the polls, between Phase II's preferential treatment and the American consensus for equal opportunity and against equal results through minority preferences.[18]

He notes that in the so-called first phase, the individual or "retail" model of relief prevailed. Civil rights regulatory organizations "would respond to the initiatives of others on a case-by-case, 'retail' basis, rather than take the initiative to attack broad 'wholesale' patterns of discrimination in large firms, unions, and entire industries." By phase II, however, things changed:

> The EEOC's complaint-response model symbolized to the EEO community the trivialization of the nation's most pressing domestic and moral concern. To them it rang of the voluntarism of a largely neutered agency. They were stunned by the impracticality as well as the moral inappropriateness of the studied, case-by-case, retail approach to an outrageously obvious and massive continuation of wholesale job discrimination against minorities.[19]

For Graham and other neoliberals, this supposed change created a model of group-based relief that somehow violated the Constitution. In their view, the individual-based and focused Constitution could not and should not grant group-based relief. Although it has, in the past and since, granted group-based relief (to farmers, child laborers, poor, elderly, disabled, veterans), the neoliberals claim that the Constitution cannot, without being itself destroyed, grant group-based racial relief. By making this questionable argument, the neoliberal advocates of this theory advanced yet another notion of constitutional inequality.

Like Glazer, Graham would later extend his thesis to voting rights, where he argues that "unlike the issues generated by affirmative action in employment or higher education, . . . voting rights policy has seemed immune from widespread public distemper."[20] As he sees it, however, Section 4 of the Voting Rights Act "is as radical and effective an innovation as Title 2, which represented an unprecedented intrusion by federal authority on local prerogatives, an intrusion quickly sustained by the Supreme Court under Chief Justice Earl Warren."[21] For Graham, affirmative action policy in voting rights laws took the form of "giving preference to selected minorities in electoral districting or arrangement."[22] Thus, the neoliberals, following the path blazed by the neoconservatives, became advocates of constitutional inequalities.

During the Reagan-Bush years, the Department of Justice shifted the focus of proof in civil rights violation cases from showing the effects of racism to showing its intent, a much harder case to prove. With this new procedure in tow, Graham writes, the Reagan administration effectively restructured the involvement of lawyers working with the federally funded Legal Services Corporation (LSC) in costly voting rights discrimination lawsuits. Long before the end of his administration, President Reagan ordered the Legal Services Corporation "to discontinue challenges to discrimination in voting on the grounds that this work is 'political.' " The Bush administration continued this attack on the LSC, Graham notes, "including a ban on legal support to communities challenging election studies." Overall, "The Reagan-Bush administrators have been uniformly hostile to reforms designed to increase voter participation." Clearly, they were emboldened by these magical theories of constitutional inequalities.[23] Graham took the position that the state promoted these reforms beyond their legislative parameters, ultimately violating constitutional standards.

The African American Conservative Theory of Racial Neutrality: Thomas D. Sowell

With the advent of the Reagan administration and as a result of the Fairmont conference, the idea of race-neutral public policy rose to prominence. Such policies were proffered as the ideal vehicles to advance and assist African Americans. The Reagan-Bush era of the 1980s and early 1990s was to be different from the preceding decades that produced such policies, which, in the eyes of African American conservatives such as Thomas Sowell, were self-defeating.

Sowell, in his book, *Civil Rights: Rhetoric or Reality,* begins his critique of race-based public policies (i.e., civil rights laws) by noting that:

> one of the must central—and most controversial—premises of the civil rights vision is that statistical disparities in incomes, occupations, education, etc., represent moral inequalities, and are caused by "society."[24]
>
> Another central premise of the civil rights vision is that belief in innate inferiority explains policies and practices of differential treatment, whether expressed in overt hostility or in institutional policies or individual decisions that result in statistical disparities.[25]

He identifies one more problem:

> A third premise of the civil rights vision is that political activity is the way to improving the lot of those on the short end of differences in income, representation, in desirable occupations, or institutions, or otherwise disadvantaged.[26]

In Sowell's view, public policies that help and assist African Americans in terms of voting and political participation are not guaranteed constitutional rights, but simply another form of race-based public policy. He and other African American conservatives would contend these have no constitutional standing. This is indeed a clever approach: to deny that African American voting rights have any legal foundation. It is both a narrow analytical perspective and one that is ahistorical and anecdotal, with no empirical basis or validity. At best, it is simply Sowellian, designed like the theories of Glazer and Graham to substantiate a personal vision. Collectively, these three end up at the same conclusion—that government-backed reforms to do away with racial discrimination is constitutionally wrong and creates inequalities—although their starting points, examples, routes, and logic are all different.

Sowell strives to show that race-based public policies, specifically those designed to assist African Americans, lack "general validity" and cannot possibly help those that they are designed to help.[27] As he claims:

> we have questioned the validity and appropriateness of shaping a general civil rights vision as the law of the land for all groups from the highly unusual experience of blacks. Now the question can be confronted as to how well that vision serves the group in whose name it was first invoked.[28]

For Sowell, social policies specifically designed for African Americans represent a double-edged sword. These policies harm African Americans in two ways, either "directly as blacks or indirectly as members of the general society," Sowell writes. On one hand:

> Resentment in the white community, and sometimes other minority communities, is likewise heightened when particular laws, programs or policies are publicly labeled as benefits for blacks. . . . even the most trivial, explicitly racial [policies] will provoke resentments that can easily lead to fervent crusades.[29]

On the other hand, Sowell contends: "[affirmative action] benefits primarily those blacks already more advantaged, making more disadvantaged blacks worse off."[30]

What, then, is productive social and public policy in the African American conservative view? Sowell is quite clear:

> Benefits that blacks receive as members of the general society produce neither the same political gain for black leaders nor build up the same resentments in the white population. No doubt the G.I. Bill after World War II had an almost revolutionary effect on the ability of blacks to attend college, but it produced neither racial strife nor political breast beating by black leaders.[31]

Elsewhere, he writes:

> Earmarked benefits for blacks provide some of these hate groups' strongest appeal to whites, however little these earmarked policies actually help blacks, either absolutely or compared to more general social benefits. They have the same potential for racial polarization.[32]

In sum, African American conservatives argue, race-neutral public policies or "more general social policies" would help African Americans more in both the short and the long run than would race-conscious public policies. But the implication is that race-based public policies are unconstitutional, while race-neutral ones are not.

Thus, Sowell's views represent still another theory of constitutional inequality. His book is a clear-cut argument against civil rights public policies as being both illegal and unconstitutional as well as counterproductive, for in it he writes that "the civil rights revolution of the past generation has had wide ramifications, . . . and . . . [it] has also altered the very concept of constitutional law and the role of courts."[33] In all of his writings, Sowell equates affirmative action with quotas, declaring that quotas are unconstitutional because the Constitution is based on individual rights.

Conclusions

The views of these three theoriticians provide support for our research question that new ideas of constitutional inequality surfaced during the Reagan-Bush era and were mainstreamed by these two presidencies. Indeed, Reagan and Bush used these theories to transform the political context and disadvantage African Americans. Upon close examination, each theory has been shown to attack and criticize civil rights and affirmative action policies, even to the extent of considering the Voting Rights Act of 1965 unconstitutional.

PART 4

CULTURE

A contextual revolution is not only aimed at legal principles and precepts, it also targets individuals in terms of their beliefs, values, and attitudes. Transforming the political context means changing the political culture and its attendant subcultures.

> Since culture and all that the concept implies . . . are abstracted from the behavior of man, they are surely subject to change by man. If culture is man-made or other than "neutral," the individual is free to change it.[1]

Having indicated that cultures and their value and belief systems can be changed, Eulau turns his attention to belief systems and cultural orientations.

> Often these beliefs have only symbolic functions with few consequences for actual political action. But under certain conditions . . . beliefs have an important effect on the political order. In the American South, the belief that Negroes are impulsive, childlike, over-emotional, short on intelligence and initiative, docile, easily frightened, or incredibly superstitious has been the most pervasive single factor in political behavior. That this belief in "white supremacy" is neither rational nor subject to disproof does not

> negate its effectiveness in giving meanings to political orientations as well as actions.[2]

This cultural orientation was elevated to national politics in the 1980s and early 1990s, when long-held, dormant beliefs about race were mobilized for political gain by conservative Republicans. For whites, the Reagan-Bush era, with its adroit use of racial symbols, code words, and African American conservative operatives, was a period during which a resurgent view of race was put into force in American society.

In *Plessy v. Ferguson,* constitutional inequalities had been interpreted as constitutional,[3] injustice was presented as justice, which was restricted to persons with a particular skin color, and subordinated to racism. Moreover, the racial majority, in its actions and relationships to the racial minority, was right and its cause just. Justice, therefore, had a new foundation. This is what happens when the political context is transformed so as to disadvantage a specific group: cultural values and beliefs are changed, and dominant as well as latent positions are permitted to resurface. The cultural values of the impacted group (in this case, African Americans) are reactivated to assist in their sociopolitical defense.

This changing of cultural values in the African American subculture was what the Reagan-Bush Republicans did not want to happen. They activated African American conservatives to tell the African American community that the new values were acceptable and that injustice was now justice. At the Fairmont conference, the founding convention for new African American leadership, one participant, Oscar Wright, explained this value shift thus:

> you do not need new special laws to protect black people. Racial discrimination is not a matter of law. The Thirteenth through Fifteenth Amendments to the Constitution made the legal barriers null and void. You do not need social legislation for American citizens.[4]

In the Republicans' view, voices like Wright's were supposed to offset and still the emergence of critical cultural voices from within the African American community. And African Americans were supposed to accept these voices and the changing concept of justice in the land.

Similarly, there were voices in the white community that provided support for the abbreviation and destruction of justice and moral values in the U.S. According to Aaron Wildavsky:

> It is this belief—not in equality underdefined nor in just one kind of equality, but in the *mutual reinforcement of opportunity and results*—that I think made the United States truly exceptional. Another way to describe U.S. exceptionalism is the way that liberty . . . is held to be compatible

> with equality.... So adherents of U.S. individualism understand that Liberty can conflict with equality and vice versa.[5]

This political scientist's preference is for an equality of opportunity that, when "meticulously followed, would lead to an approximation of equality of results."[6] This discussion suggests that it is somehow natural for those who insist on liberty (i.e., justice in a restricted fashion, as argued by neoconservatives, neoliberals, African American conservatives, and Reagan-Bush Republicans) to clash with those who demand equality; that this is somehow the natural order of things, the rational way, the essence of American exceptionalism. Wildavsky emphasizes equality of opportunity (justice restricted) over equality of result because the former express "national character" and reflect"national cultures and value system."[7] "Opinions," continues Wildavsky, "are themselves a part of the culture, controlling the direction and force of change,"[8] and they are likewise essential to the political culture. "Put most simply," he concludes, "the political culture serves to identify and to make safe and/or desirable for the individual a wide range of 'socially acceptable' political viewpoints."[9]

Hence transformation of the political context means transforming both the majority political culture and the minority political subculture. But inside the political subculture that the majority desires to change exist defensive mechanisms that have evolved over many years. These mechanisms may not be able to halt the transformation in the majority culture, but they can hinder this transformation in their own community, and, by resistive behavior, send a signal to the majority community. A single mouthpiece or a few are simply not strong enough to overcome these protective mechanisms.

Despite the large number of studies on political culture in general, few have recognized and detailed the African American subculture, and these few have all come from African American scholars. Such works fall into two categories: synthesis or empirical studies. (The pioneering work on political culture, *The Civic Culture,* was a five-nation survey of natoinal political attitudes. *Race, Class, and Culture* by Robert Smith and Richard Seltzer, and the article by Allen, Dawson and Brown are empirical studies of political culture in the African American community.) In the first type, pioneered by Charles Hamilton and Matthew Holden, a major dominant characteristic of African American culture is shown to be its strong moral/religious component.[10] A later synthesis study by Charles Henry demonstrates, in a qualitative way, that African American politics is unique and different from the overarching American politics because African American political culture, with "its rootedness in a black church tradition that blends sacred and secular vision, provides and endows African American people's political activities with a 'moral vision' that is not found in mainstream American politics."[11] It is this moral/religious tradition that affixes justice on a permanent rather than a relative basis in this subculture.

Moreover, it was precisely this moral/religious element in African American political culture that would resist the Reagan-Bush era's vision and conceptualization of justice. Three major works of this era, *Running for Freedom: Civil Rights and Black Politics in America Since 1941, Civil Rights and the Reagan Administration,* and *African Americans at the Crossroads: The Restructuring of Black Leadership and the 1992 Elections,* all make the case that the oppositional and electoral politics of this era were grounded in the values and beliefs of the African American political culture. Justice in the African American tradition, according to the synthesists, meant fairness and equity not "might (read: the racial majority) means right."

The conclusions in the synthesis studies are based on both qualitative and empirical/quantitative data. For example, three African American scholars (Richard Allen, Michael Dawson, and Ronald Brown), via a national survey of African Americans, identified this moral/religious component in the African American belief system and noted its ability to shape African American political behavior.[12] They offer convincing empirical support for their findings. Two other scholars, using a supplemental sample of African Americans that was part of an annual national survey sample, also noted the influence of this component, concluding that subcultural variation cannot be totally explained by race or class but by specific characteristics inherent in a community's culture.[13] They too offer empirical data to support their position.

There is another dominant feature and reality. As noted by William Cross, Jr., in one of the most important books of the Reagan-Bush era, "Blacks are fundamentally bicultural in perspective, while whites are primarily monocultural."[14] W. E. B. DuBois called this African American dualism "double-consciousness" and the novelist Richard Wright dubbed it "double vision." In recent years, psychologists have refined and used this concept to assess African American culture.[15] They also find African Americans to be biculturally competent. Cross adds:

> At the conclusion of [my] study, I pointed out that if one used the information generated by the social-network and content analysis to predict racial-preference patterns in Black and white children, it would be reasonable to assume that the two groups of children would "play back" reality in a manner similar to the way in which reality had been presented to them. A categorical same-race preference would be predicted for whites as a group, and "split," or dual, pattern for Blacks as a group. Such patterns would show the ontogeny of a white-oriented monoracial reference group orientation in whites, and a biracial reference group orientation or bicultural competence in Blacks.[16]

Biculturalism is inherently more complex and difficult to transform than monoculturalism, especially when it is combined with a strong moral/religious characteristic, as is the case of the African American subculture. Therefore, not only could the simplistic strategy of using African American "mouthpieces" to espouse the conservative doctrine not transform the concept of justice in the African American community, but those whites who subordinated justice to race would be roundly resisted and called into question as well. This is what happened in the 1992 Los Angeles riot.

Typically, race riots, that is, all such riots involving significant numbers of African Americans, past or present, have been explained in terms of the characteristics of the persons who participated in them, in hopes of isolating the causes of such insurrection. As Cross notes,

> The initial "riot studies," which focused on Watts, produced results that argued that relative deprivation, rising expectations, and reactions to economic stress accounted for the origins of riots. . . . The deprivation, frustration, reaction to stress theories suggested that a certain threshold for stress was triggered by environmental conditions, and that Black people exploded under the burden of oppression.[17]

Perhaps most importantly, these "riot studies," in the way that they were conducted, created personality profiles of the rioters that established and "helped to popularize a profile of black militants along the lines of . . . the 'riffraff' theory of Black militancy"[18] and as the cause of riots themselves. Cross, again:

> The essential elements of this characterization involve the perception that Black militancy and radicalism follow from experiences of frustrations and social alienation and are more prevalent among psychopathic personalities, the chronically unemployed, and the underclass. For example, [Ann] Wortham depicts the militant [rioter] as "unjust and unnatural," "parasitical," "disillusioned and alienated," "a terrorist," "the Prince of anti-mind, anti-morality and anti-life," a person with "little ego strength," a person who "has a fondness for risks and no qualms about doing bodily harm to individuals," and finally, a "hoodlum and criminal . . . whose violent behavior is an act of violation."[19]

Besides Wortham, other African Americans such as Martin Kilson and Thomas Sowell support this theory. (In fact, in recent political science work, Kilson has used it to advance a new conception of African American political leadership,[20] effectively depriving African American leadership of its cultural roots and placing it in a self-hatred mode.) Yet, despite these ascriptions, there is more to African American riot behavior than criminality. As long as the profile methodology is used, however, little else will be found. When one approaches civil unrest and urban rioting from the standpoint of African American culture, with its moral/religious and bicultural elements, clear-cut ethical and moral dimensions of this phenomenon emerge. Another voice besides criminal action or mere frustration can be heard in the midst of these acts—the voice of justice and morality.

This section seeks to explore the 1992 Los Angeles riots via data obtained from public opinion polls rather than profile studies of the people involved in the rioting. Its focus is on the nature, scope, and cultural meaning of riot activism—on the "other voice" described above. Like earlier studies, this examination found a relationship between a people's opinions and their political culture, and will attempt to explore it.

6

AFRICAN AMERICAN POLITICAL CULTURE

The Moral Voice and Perspective in the Recent Urban Riots

• • • • • • •

Hanes Walton, Jr.

Late in the afternoon on April 29, 1992, a Simi Valley jury containing no African American members acquitted (on all but one count) the four white police officers accused of excessive force in the beating of African American motorist Rodney King. Before dusk that evening, the largely African American and Latino community of South Central Los Angeles erupted with anger, rage, and violence. The end result of these two profoundly searing and inseparable events was the single most destructive "race riot" of this century.[1]

The Reagan-Bush method of transforming political context involved the use of race as political currency and capital. When people of color are discounted, when their political, economic, and social goals are marginalized, oppression ensues. Once a race is devalued, injustice and moral relativism increase due to the ascribed differences in races. The value of one race over another becomes inflated in this type of political context and members of the more highly valued race can thus bargain more successfully for goods, services, and benefits than can those whose race is undervalued. In such a market, justice works in the interest of the dominant race. However, resistance and rebellion, in some form or fashion, are bound to emerge from within the ranks of the devalued racial group. It is inevitable; it is simply inherent in the nature of intergroup relations.[2] Yet, the resistance of subordinate groups to injustice or oppression, especially when it is manifest in unconventional or protest behavior, is usually viewed and treated by dominant groups as simple displeasure, as minor grievances with life changes and conditions. Thereby, dominant groups can reduce the moral force of the subordinates' arguments, making these grievances and arguments appear more the expression of something like anger and passion unleashed by exceptional forces and realities. This was clearly seen during the Reagan-Bush era, wherein conclusions about the nature of the resistance that was spawned by people of color were so mediated by the media that the moral dimension and voice was all but lost.

Resistance has, among other things, a cultural base. The values that undergird it emerge out of the matrix of the cultural formulation inherent in the overall community. Over time, communities create their own cultures, and it is culture that permits a community to become empowered as an actor or player in the political arena. It is culture that provides the ideas, beliefs, and attitudes with which a community evaluates and apprises the surrounding world and determines how its members should act and react to the positions and postures taken by others. Culture contains some moral and/or ethical standard about humankind, about life, and about reality. The reduction of the moral dimension of riot behavior to individual- and personal-level factors as well as group-level ones removes a community-made culture with a moral vision from the overall assessment and evaluation of the situation. This type of reductionistic approach in political science analysis has taken two distinct forms.

First, because the urban uprisings of the 1960s coincided with the behavioral revolution in the discipline, African American riot behavior was analyzed from the standpoint of the individual and framed within psychological theories of individual interaction and reaction.[3] Ideas about relative deprivation, diffusion and contagion, and group resentment were quickly pressed into service. Three decades later, such individualistic explanations abound.

Secondly, African American reaction and resistance to injustice and subjugation has been treated by political science analysts as less an individual reality and more a group response and form of political protest.[4] There is a longstanding tradition of various forms of political protest in America. Drawing essentially from the realities of the civil rights movement, protest has been acknowledged as an acceptable form of political expression for African Americans when all other channels were closed. Two presidential commissions—the McCone Commission, which was organized in the wake of the 1965 Watts riots, and the Kerner Commission, [5] Their reports argued that there was a justified base to the reactions and forms of resistance evidenced during those insurgencies; even these blue-ribbon commissions acknowledged that behind the riots were a valid set of causes and determinants.

Perhaps the riots-as-political-protest concept was carried to its ultimate conclusion by James Button, who sought to determine in empirical terms the nature of governmental response to these acts of resistance. If government failed to respond to conventional politics such as voting, party participation, and interest group activity, Button queried in his research, would it respond to African American riot behavior? He checked and found that it did. Yet he noted that even so-called "liberal" policies established in response to African American demands included repressive measures. "The shift in federal policy to the 'Liberal' approach," he writes, "meant combining both guns and butter for the ghetto."[6] As he further noted,

> while the antipoverty agency responded quickly and immediately with funding increases for several riot cities . . . [eventually] federal financing of riot control training and equipment for local policies were initiated, and intelligence-gathering networks were established or enlarged.[7]

In the final analysis, Button concludes, riot protest, while it is political and in fact evolves from grievances and disenchantment with the political system, is ultimately less productive than other forms of political protest, if not counterproductive.

Both these two approaches fail, even in the vaguest way, to illuminate and bring to bear the moral dimensions of rioting as a form of political protest. Both fail to articulate the moral voice of this form of protest in the policy sphere. In short, both categorical political science approaches precluded the possibility that behind African Americans' dissatisfactions, grievances, and disenchantment were a set of cultural beliefs and values that might have preconditioned riot-behavior responses. To date, however, academic and scholarly studies have limited these responses to shortcomings of the system. How these shortcomings impact thoughts about the delivery of services dismisses the aggrieved race and its cultural beliefs about justice.

Communities often develop, and the African American community in particular has developed, a sense of justice that can be played out in unconventional ways. The marches and demonstrations led by the Reverend Martin Luther King, Jr., can be seen as one way by which the African American community played out its sense of justice and morality. Riot behavior is clearly another means by which it displays the same. Morality and culture, while not discontinuous, can be expressed by discontinous events such as riots.

Data and Methodology

The research question to be explored in this essay is whether the concerns and issues expressed by African Americans during and after the riot can be linked to a moral and ethical dimension in African American political culture. Academicians and scholars prior to this attempt have cut their focuses short, limiting their data bases to the opinion-survey responses of aggrieved individuals. The main reason for this is inherent in the race relations perspective so dominant in social science, particularly political science, literature. In this perspective, the role of research and researchers is to minimize race as a explanation for social phenomena.[8] Another explanation can be found in the failure of modern survey research on African Americans and racial attitudes to structure and develop for their analyses the cultural matrix and components of African American public opinion.

Essentially, researchers have been content to use standardized opinion surveys, with some modifications, to tap into the minds and moods of African Americans.[9] However, reliance on such instruments has yielded only a partial illumination of the key components of African American public opinion.[10] Even a modified survey such as the National Black Election Survey, when analyzed, gives rise to delineation of but a limited view of the African American belief system.[11] The primary research technique for analysis of opinion data involves regression analysis of independent variables to determine the strongest and most influential factors. As always with this method, only a few factors emerge. Other studies utilizing this technique have focused on single variables such as inequality and are more disconcerting than useful, as these surveys extract these concepts from the contexts which give them meaning.[12]

Finally, there is the matter of the pursuit of differences. All academics, save the creators of the National Black Election Survey, in doing political survey research and polling, have utilized both an African American and a white set of subsamples. Similarly, their data analyses and interpretations are driven by a comparison of whites and African Americans. For example, as one set of academics attests in offering their findings, "we are interested in making explicit comparisons between the ways racial inequality is viewed by black and white Americans, but the NBES surveyed only blacks." Later, they write, "Only by devoting careful attention to the views of blacks as well as whites can we reach accurate conclusions about Americans' racial attitudes."[13]

Such studies unequivocally contend that African American attitudes only provide meaningful knowledge and insights if they are expressed with, and in relationship to, the attitudes of whites. These comparisons dominate the literature. Using such an approach delimits the sundry other possibilities in African American public opinion. Things other than the differences in African American and white opinion and attitudes do not get studied and reported.

This paper seeks to fashion a new path for research into the links between

African American riot behavior, public opinion, political protest, and community culture. The empirical data base for this investigation is drawn from a public opinion survey of individuals living in the African American community in Los Angeles both before and after the riots. As its authors report:

> Since 1986, the Survey Research Center at UCLA's Institute for Social Science Research (ISSR) has conducted an annual survey. From 1986 to 1991, the survey covered a three county area, including Los Angeles, Ventura, and Orange counties. Beginning in 1992, the area sampled was restricted to Los Angeles county and hence the project is now titled the Los Angeles County Social Survey [LACSS].[14]

Essentially, the 1992 LACSS was "a countywide random-digit dial telephone survey of adults living in households," conducted by the ISSR. The interviews, which took place both before and after the Los Angeles riots, were structured in the following manner:

> The pre-verdict/rebellion interviewing took place from February 3, 1992 until April 29, 1992, at approximately 3:30 p.m., yielding a total of 963 interviews. The post-verdict/rebellion interviewing extended from that time until July 29, 1992, yielding a total of 906 interviews. Thus, 51.5% of the interviews were obtained prior to the verdict/rebellion and 48.5% in its aftermath.[15]

Although this data source is unique it is limited to the inhabitants of Los Angeles county. Therefore, the second data base is the June 22–30, 1992, post-verdict/riot Home Box Office/Joint Center for Political Studies (HBO/JCPS) poll, a national telephone survey of African Americans' perspectives on a wide range of public policy issues.[16] The sample size of that survey was 750.[17]

Thus this paper engages in secondary analysis of the LACSS and HBO/JCPS data. However, I am concerned less with the standard secondary analysis approach and more with using this methodological procedure to produce an empirical rendering of the hurt, anger, and despair that emanated from the verdict and that the riot/political protest reflected. This investigation will use empirically based opinion clusters and issue categories to probe the Los Angeles African American community's cultural realities to determine if a linkage can be found between the recent violent uprisings and that community's long-standing moral values and beliefs. Did the impetus to riot/rebellion rest on some moral or ethical dimension inherent to the African American community's political, social, and cultural matrix?

Figure 6.1 explains how this analysis will proceed. Step one involves verdict, a matter of justice and law, which led to the riots. Step two, the secondary analysis of the public opinions expressed by participants in and observers of the

FIGURE 6.1

Three Steps in Searching for a New Perspective on African American Violence

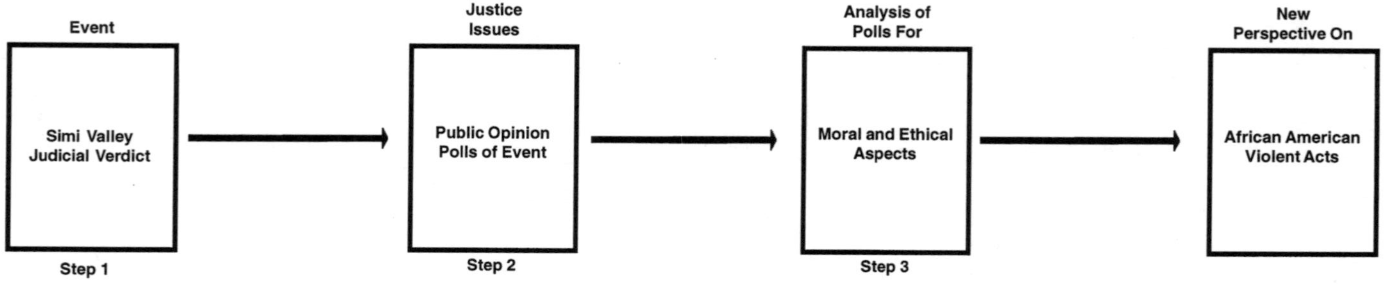

riot, leads to a tabular representation of the two surveys' reduction of the justice issue to matters of individual and group concern and to a review of public textual materials that examine the African American community's cultural, moral, and ethical components.[18]

Justice and Injustice in Public Opinion Polls of African Americans: Local and National Surveys of the 1992 Los Angeles Riots

A judicial verdict set off the riots in Los Angeles in April 1992. Therefore, the question of justice is central and critical to any assessment of the evolution of the rebellion/resistance. Public opinion polls and surveys should have asked their respondents basic questions about matters of justice and injustice in America, but the post-verdict surveys—the LACSS and HBO/JCPS polls—asked questions that were only marginally related to this area. For example, the HBO/JCPS survey report noted the following:

> nine percent of those surveyed expressed the opinion that the rioters in LA were justified because of the Rodney King verdict. . . . Half those surveyed, however, expressed somewhat ambivalent feelings, indicating that they did not approve of the rioters' behavior, but that they understood their frustration and anger.[19]

The HBO/JCPS questions were not so much concerned with the justice/injustice issue as they were with the rioters' individual realities. The LACSS did not do much better, although it did ask a series of questions that attempted to tap into the respondents' attitudes and opinions—not about justice or injustice, but about the frustration and anger that were exemplified by the riots. This individual-level approach foreclosed a look at the moral dimensions of the African American community's reactions.

Indeed, neither survey, either the national or the county one, dealt with the event which preceded the riots in a focused manner. At best, the questions asked were indirectly and tangentially related to the issue of whether justice had been served in the trial of the four white policemen. The issue of justice or injustice in America is not one that pollsters and survey analysis traditionally have been concerned with.[20] Moreover, when such survey questions have been developed for African Americans, the focus has not been on "justice" but on "equality," and essentially on "inequality," a less meaningful matter. Thus, one could not expect the surveys generated in response to the Simi Valley verdict to be equipped to address the basic and fundamental issue that launched the riots in Los Angeles—the issue of justice and injustice in the city since the Watts riots of the 1960s.

To determine the frustration and anger of the Los Angeles situation, one has to tease them out of the six categories of questions generated by the LACSS. These categories are: (1) life in Los Angeles; (2) crime and punishment; (3) the verdict and the riot; (4) poverty and racial inequality; (5) ethnic group, alienation, and equality in America; and (6) dimensions of prejudice, stereotyping, and social distance. Of these six categories, only categories three, four, and five included questions that were even remotely related to the injustice of the verdict.

The LACSS survey report noted that responses to questions in category two, which focused on issues of crime and punishment, "[confirmed] many of the speculations commentators made following the Simi Valley police brutality verdict that blacks would grow more pessimistic about the treatment they could expect from a white-dominated social institution."[21] Responses to questions in the third category (about the verdict and the riot) revealed that fully 95% of African Americans surveyed disagreed with the verdict. Indeed, over two-thirds of the African American respondents interpreted the disturbances "as a protest against unfair conditions."[22] On the whole, the survey report concluded, African Americans appeared to be "strongly inclined to see the verdict as part of an ongoing and systematic pattern of injustice that blacks face when dealing with the criminal justice system."[23] Moreover, a "strong and uniform rise in black alienation from American social institutions is the single cleanest and most consistent change observed for any of the items we have examined."[24]

These findings serve as a springboard to insights into the opinions and attitudes that indirectly touch upon the justice/injustice issue. Table 6.1 encompasses three related questions. The first question asked African American respondents to appraise the acquittal verdict: overwhelmingly, they found justice absent from that decision. The second question asked their opinions about the entire justice-dispensing system: most believed it to be flawed with regard to moral issues. Finally, question three asked for African American respondents' appraisals of the behavior of the rioters: the riot was mainly seen as a way of raising objections against both the unfairness of the verdict and against the justice system itself.

The findings presented in table 6.2 show African Americans to have perceived the injustice and unfairness of the verdict and the American justice system as rooted in societal realities. American society overall, as reflected in the respondents' opinions, was seen as basically unjust and dishonest in its dealings with people of color; as a result, its institutions were deemed inherently unfair.

Table 6.3 is another composite representation of African American public opinion emanating from the riot area. In their responses to three questions, African American respondents generally viewed none of society's institutions as being designed to resolve and implement justice. In short, the respondents believed that federal, state, and local courts are simply in "no position to serve the common good," and that they serve only the special interests of whites.[25]

Taken collectively, these three tables tell us that African Americans can

TABLE 6.1

African American Public Opinion on Justice in the Verdict and the Riot: A Composite View

Question	The Verdict as a Justice Issue	Strongly Agree	Agree	Neither Agree Nor Disagree	Disagree	Strongly Disagree	Totals	N
C-11	Now I have some questions to ask you about the Rodney King case. First, how did you feel about the jury verdict acquitting the four police officers accused of beating Rodney King? Do you personally strongly agree, agree, neither agree nor disagree, disagree or strongly disagree with the jury verdict?	.5	1.4	1.8	20.6	75.7	100.0	437
C-12	Second, how about the statement that blacks usually don't get fair treatment in the courts and criminal justice system? Do you strongly agree, agree, neither agree nor disagree, disagree or strongly disagree with that statement?	44.2	35.5	6.1	11.1	3.1	100.0	425
		Mainly Protest	**Looting and Street Crime**		**Half and Half Protest and Looting**			
C-14	Fourth, some people say these disturbances are mainly a protest by Blacks against unfair conditions. Others say they are mainly a way of engaging in looting and street crimes. Which of these statements seem more correct to you? (IF VOLUNTEERED, 50/50 mixture)	67.5		22.8		9.7	100.0	412

Adapted from Laurence Bobo, et al., "Public Opinion Before and After a Spring of Discontent: A Preliminary Report of the 1992 Los Angeles County Social Survey," (Los Angeles: UCLA Center for the Study of Urban Poverty—Occasional Working Paper Series, September, 1992), Tables C-11, C-12, and C-14.

TABLE 6.2

African American Public Opinion About Problems with American Society: A Composite View

Now I will read several statements. Please tell me whether you strongly agree, agree, neither agree nor disagree, disagree or strongly disagree with the following statement.

Problem With Society	Response	Pre	Post	% Difference
American society owes people of my ethnic group a better chance in life than we currently have?	**Strongly agree**	21.0	34.2	+13.2
	Agree	33.7	41.2	+7.5
	Neither Agree nor Disagree	13.6	7.9	-5.7
	Disagree	25.5	14.0	-11.5
	Strongly Disagree	6.2	2.6	-3.6
	Total	100.0	99.9	
	N	(243)	(228)	
American society just hasn't dealt fairly with people from my background?	**Strong agree**	17.1	27.8	+10.7
	Agree	46.5	48.0	+1.5
	Neither Agree nor Disagree	9.8	7.0	-2.8
	Disagree	22.9	14.1	-8.8
	Strongly Disagree	3.7	3.1	-.6
	Total	100	100	
	N	(245)	(227)	

Adapted from Laurence Bobo, et al., "Public Opinion Before and After a Spring of Discontent: A Preliminary Report of the 1992 Los Angeles County Social Survey," (Los Angeles: UCLA Center for the Study of Urban Poverty—Occasional Working Paper Series, September, 1992), Tables C-23 and C-26. Percent differences were calculated by the present author.

TABLE 6.3

African American Public Opinion About Problems with American Political Institutions: A Composite View

Problem with Political Institutions	Response	Pre	Post	% Difference
How much confidence do you personally have in the Federal Government in Washington, D.C. at the present time: Would you say a lot of confidence, some confidence, or not much confidence:	**A Lot**	4.9	5.2	+0.3
	Some	25.8	3.9	-1.9
	Not Much	69.3	70.3	+1.0
	Total	100.0	99.4	
	N	244	230	
How much confidence do you personally have in the state government in Sacramento at the present time: Would you say a lot of confidence, some confidence, or not much confidence?	**A Lot**	3.6	3.9	+0.3
	Some	37.2	34.6	-2.6
	Not Much	59.1	61.5	+2.4
	Total	99.9	100.0	
	N	241	231	
How much confidence do you personally have in the local government in your city or county at the present time?	**A Lot**	6.5	5.6	-0.9
	Some	46.1	38.5	-7.6
	Not Much	47.3	55.8	+8.5
	Total	99.9	99.9	
	N	245	231	

Adapted from Laurence Bobo, et al., "Public Opinion Before and After a Spring of Discontent: A Preliminary Report of the 1992 Los Angeles County Social Survey," (Los Angeles: UCLA Center for the Study of Urban Poverty—Occasional Working Paper Series, September, 1992), Tables C-4, C-5, and C-6. Percent differences were calculated by the present author.

appraise the failures and shortcomings of their government, even in surveys and polls that are not directly designed to tap their opinions on certain key issues. They further show that these respondents' evaluations stem from some of the values and ideas embedded in the African American political culture. In sum, these tables provide empirical evidence that the African American community not only has a different point of view of society and its institutions, but its point of reference is also beyond that of the majority political culture.

The Relationship of African American Public Opinion to the African American Political Culture: The Linkage of Protest Behavior to a Moral Dimension

Psychologist William Cross, in analyzing the African American psyche and personality, has developed and advanced the notion of African Americans as "bicultural."[26] His theoretical postulate updates W. E. B. DuBois's notion of the African American's "double-consciousness"—the result of existing in both the American and the African American cultural matrices. Cross's refinement of DuBois's concept permits one to see that African Americans and other oppressed people—because of this capacity for cultural absorption, creation, and innovation—can create their own communities with their own cultural standards within the larger, dominant community. Inside this community subculture, Cross contends, exists a moral imagination that includes the community's views about morality.

"Morality," according to Thomas McCoullough, "refers to commonly accepted rules of conduct, patterns of behavior approved by a social group. It consists of beliefs about what is good and right held by a community with a shared history."[27] Not only has the African American community over time developed a community culture with its own set of moral principles and precepts, its spokespersons have articulated and iterated these principles and precepts through the jeremiads of the African American political sermon. As Charles Henry writes:

> The Afro-American jeremiad evolved out of the Anglo American jeremiad as an explanation for the collective suffering of black people. . . . As such the black jeremiad both explain black sufferings and provides a culturally acceptable protest against the black condition.[28]

He continues:

> More recently, Martin Luther King, Jr. and Jesse Jackson have linked America's moral mission to its treatment of people of color. The success of these men as leaders is firmly rooted in the black church tradition—in

> both black and white denominations—which links the moral lessons of the Bible to current political events.[29]

As David Howard-Pitney put it: "The black jeremiad always strives to speak to and within a changing American consensus and yet it is usually at the forward edge of that consensus, prodding it toward even more thorough and inclusive social change."[30] Thus, the African American cultural community is shown as having a moral dimension that can generate, activate, and sustain social outrage, political protest, and nonviolence as well as violence, resistance, and rebellion. Indeed, the resistance raised by African American spokespersons such as King, Malcolm X, and recently Jesse Jackson has included both violent and nonviolent approaches as means of advocating and advancing this moral dimension.

Yet, when considerable numbers of African American public-opinion survey respondents discuss riot behaviors as "a wake-up call" for America, pollsters often fail to account for the moral view of justice historically held by the African American cultural community. This moral dimension, one that an oppressed people developed to sustain their day-to-day existence under conditions of slavery and second-class citizenship, sees justice as being comprised of compassion, equity, and equality. Moreover, this moral viewpoint recognizes the differences in the spirit and personality of diverse groups of people while simultaneously embracing the similarities that exist between all human beings.At the same time, this concept abounds with paradoxical contradictions. This moral dimension of the African American community is, at best, a composite of many forces; indeed, it is much more complex than recent scholarship would have it appear. While most non-African American political scientists have, remarkably, defined the African American concept of justice as an individual phenomenon,[31] African Americans themselves generally define it as a community phenomenon.

Thus, the poll respondents had a vision of justice and what it should mean, and their vision expressed itself in the context of a racialized society. In this sense, then, rioters create a public dialogue and set the basis for the discussion in that public dialogue. Others, however, are free to enlarge, dismiss, or restate the issues in the dialogue. The specific vehicle by which the public dialogue may be launched may be either violent or nonviolent, internal or external. The Simi Valley verdict (an external event) activated the violence and public dialogue in Los Angeles.

Notwithstanding, mainstream public opinion specialists and politicians often seek to deflect or avoid this dialogue in order to define and control the situation. As a result, much is lost and forgotten. When public attention and discussion is turned away from the moral and ethical dimension, notes Glenn Tinder: "It expresses a willingness to pass over legitimate grievances." This, he continues, "is not only beyond the capacity of most of us, it can be asked whether it is reasonable and prudent. Does it not mean that people can get away with anything?"[32] When a community has a continuing set of legitimate grievances, it sets and creates community-specific cultural standards for evaluating and assessing community members' status in the larger society as well as their responses when these grievances have been exacerbated. These standards become the cornerstone of the community's collective political mind. They also motivate the behavior of community members. Moreover, such cultural principles and precepts can also shape political behavior differently within communities.[33] Thus we see a linkage and a relationship between African American public opinion and African American political culture, regardless of whether the former is expressed in nonviolent public dialogue or violent rebellion or rioting. Attempts to obsfucate such a relationship are, in a sense, attempts to dominate and subordinate, to retain the political hegemony or craft "the official story." As James Scott writes:

> The dominant never control the stage absolutely, but their wishes normally prevail. In the short run, it is in the interest of the subordinate to produce a more or less credible performance, speaking the lines and making the gestures he knows are expected of him. The result is that the public transcript is—barring a crisis—systematically skewed in the direction . . . represented by the dominant.[34]

In the case of Los Angeles in 1992, the African American public dialogue was anything but one of quiet obedience. Rather, it was "an inchoate scream of rage . . . a finely drawn and highly visual image of an apocalypse, a day of revenge and triumph, a world turned upside down using the cultural raw materials" of the African American community.[35] Yet the resultant public transcript, as reshaped by the Bush administration and local officials, presented this African American political protest event as devoid of an essential cultural characteristic—namely, the moral/ethical dimension.

Conclusions

Empirical data offer support for the hypothesis that a relationship exists between African American public opinion/action and culture. Although the data would not allow us to fix the specific parameters of that linkage and relationship, it does provide support for a suggestive confirmation.

When race becomes political capital and currency, as it did during the Reagan and Bush administrations, it also becomes a topic in the public dialogue. With the advent of the riots in Los Angeles, when the Simi Valley verdict redefined the concept of justice/injustice and discounted legitimate grievances confronted by the African American community, the issue of race was returned to the forefront of that dialogue. Acting out of their own community's cultural rendering of morality, African Americans were compelled to remind the powers-that-be, in forceful terms, that the view and version of justice adopted and promoted during the Reagan-Bush era—a justice based on race and a kind of moral relativism—would be contested. Thus we see that when a transformed political context leads to a negative redefinition of the societal concept of justice, subcultural perspectives will find ways to enter this skewed discourse, even if they fail to alter it.

PART 5

SOCIALIZATION

The political context of a society or community is suffused with both agents of and the consequences of efforts at political socialization. In an open and democratic society, this process of political teaching and learning is an unending process. Researchers examining this area have concentrated almost exclusively on the permanent agents of socialization, such as school, family, peer groups, and media. They have tended to overemphasize the long-term and long-range effects of political socialization while virtually ignoring nonpermanent agents and their short-term effects. However, these are precisely the aspects of socialization that must be addressed when examining a transformed political context.

During their twelve years in office, presidents Reagan and Bush sought to drastically transform the African American political context. African American politicians, for their part, had to react, and quickly, to these transformational efforts by resocializing their community, particularly African American voters. Long-term political objectives had to be dropped for short-term ones. The African American community had to be mobilized by nonpermanent socializing agents to express their moral outrage and opposition to this negative Republican manipulation.

This section asks the following questions: What are the nonpermanent agents of African American political socialization and how do they operate in the short term? How are these short-term socializing forces activated? What values, beliefs, and attitudes available to long-term socializing agents can be used to direct and structure short-term agents and effects?

Very little is known about the relationship between long- and short-term socializing forces in the African American community. Early in the 1980s, however, a work that spoke directly to this issue of relationships and linkages suggested that the Black church exerted strong long-term influences as a political socializing agent, and that, for African Americans, religion was a core factor in their political value system. This work also suggested that nonpermanent socializing agents like the civil rights movement could draw upon these religious core values to mobilize African Americans to address short-term situations.[1] Recent research has offered empirical evidence to support this postulate. According to Laura Reese and Ronald Brown, "Two different messages appear to be present at places of worship—one promoting civic awareness, the other political activity,"[2] Although this is attenuated by gender,[3] both African American men and women derive from their religiosity core values that lead them to see the power differentials between white and blacks. The core values inherent in the long-term socialization force of religion can be adapted by nonpermanent agents within short time frames.

African American political leaders do not have a wide variety of techniques and processes available to them when conditions call for heightened racial consciousness, rapid political mobilization, and significant resocialization within their communities. However, they have employed many less well known and unconventional tactics with varying degrees of success. As Samuel DuBois Cook remarks:

> the political life of blacks has not been exhausted in alienation from and victimization by the American political system . . . [African Americans] . . . searched the forest and backyard and back streets of organizational life for the key. They labored mightily in the largely barren fields of petitions, memorials, resolutions, proclamations, propaganda, moral suasion, conciliation, anguished cry, and feeble organizations.[4]

It is to one of these unorthodox political socializing techniques that we now turn. First we remind readers that the study of political socialization encompasses the study of political context. John Books and Charles Prysby are emphatic on this point:

> Another important cousin of contextual analysis is the study of political socialization. Those studying the socialization of individuals into political roles deal with many of the same factors and mechanisms as students of social (political) context do.[5]

Moreover, they assert that socialization studies, such as the one to be undertaken in this section, "share with contextual analysis a concern for some of the varied ways in which aggregates and social units affect individuals."[6]

Bearing this in mind, this section examines one of the many short-term political socialization strategies employed by African American political leadership: the "protest resignation." The question to be pursed: What in the political context leads to a protest resignation by African American leaders, and how do such resignations socialize the Black community?

permanent socializing agents

family, school, church, ~~[illegible]~~ media

~~non permanent~~

social protests

protest resignation

CRA 1964

VRA 1965 Poll taxes, literacy tests

NAACP

Brown v Board

EEOC

Reconstruction Amendments

13, 14, 15

pg. Political socialization differs by race.

- Blacks don't have oppor. to est. perm. socializing agents

- early focus on majority, of socialization assumed it was same as minority

7

AFRICAN AMERICAN POLITICAL SOCIALIZATION
The Protest Resignations of Councilpersons Jerome Woody and Renee Baker

• • • • • • •

Hanes Walton, Jr., Oliver Jones, Jr., Pearl K. Ford

If political socialization is the process of transmitting political values and beliefs from one generation to another, then political resocialization and counter-socialization are the processes whereby these values and beliefs are reoriented and refashioned. The are also the routes by which subcultural groups like the African American community alters, adapts, or avoids the political mores of the dominant majority culture, which has long sought to force them to accept a status that is not only politically but also socially and economically inferior and subordinate.[1]

Analysis of the national political context should reflect multiple streams of political socializing efforts rather than a single strand. However, research on political socialization has focused for the most part upon the socialization processes and efforts of the majority. Moreover, these studies have generally tended to infer that what holds true for the majority applies equally to subcultural groups. Given the nation's history of slavery and segregation and the lingering presence of institutional racism, differences between members of minority and majority groups are inevitable at even the most basic level of values and beliefs about individual worth and meaning. Indeed, African American "political socialization occurs differently and leads to different results."[2] The failure of the empirical research to uncover this crucial fact—that, when it comes to politics, African Americans are socialized differently—leads to a related problem: nonpermanent forces have frequently exerted strong socialization effects upon the African American community, yet nowhere in the academic political science literature have these agents been identified or even considered.

African American have had few opportunities to establish or control permanent socialization institutions such as major media or educational organizations. Thus, out of sheer necessity, African American political leaders have relied upon or resorted to nonpermanent agents and institutions to socialize and resocialize their communities politically.

> During the sixties, black leaders like Martin Luther King, Jr., taught blacks through mass demonstrations and movements, using single galvanizing events instead of long-term formal processes to overcome centuries of powerlessness so that blacks would become social and political forces acting for their own betterment.[3]

Drawing upon data derived almost completely from studies involving members of the dominant cultural majority, researchers have long contended that the agents of political socialization found to be permanent, stable, and enduring among the majority had a similar role and effect within minority communities. This perspective also led to the supposition that, across racial and ethnic groups, nonpermanent political socialization agents had no meaningful effect. Thus, few studies have been done on alternative socializing agents such as the church, language, political personalities, major societal crises, or events.

Empirical researchers Aldon Morris, Shirley Hatchett, and Ronald Brown have noted that early research on political socialization, which focused on the dominant cultural majority, tended to be more concerned with "stability and constancy" in the political system than with justice and injustices.[4] In their pioneering study on the political socialization aspects of the civil rights movement, they found that "the research on blacks has been insensitive to the continuities of the black political process," and that "persistence-perspectives of black socialization are unable to explain sudden mass changes in political consciousness and mobilization."[5] In addition, their study revealed:

> By focusing on system-maintenance variables such as political efficiency, trust, political interest, and attachment to traditional political authorities, political scientists have, for the most part, failed to consider . . . the disorderly side of politics to which locked-out groups are usually constrained.[6]

The modern civil rights era, which began in Montgomery, Alabama, in 1955, was both a political and social protest. As Morris, Hatchett, and Brown maintain, "political protest is a form of power behavior initiated by groups excluded from the established political order," and "social protest has always been, and continues to be, an enduring component of the black experience."[7] Thus, in their view, "the Montgomery bus boycott was a ground breaking political development," that "provided a method and a blueprint of resistance beyond the boundaries of traditional political behavior."[8] Via such counter-socializing tactics as "boycotts, sit-ins, marches, demonstrations, filling up the jails through arrests [and] mass meetings," the African American community was resocialized into a new political consciousness. Indeed, a new political reality was achieved that clearly displaced that created by the ensconced socializing agents of the dominant white society. Morris, Hatchett, and Brown conclude, "The [civil rights] movement itself was a tool of political socialization. Its mass tactics required people to learn and execute new forms of political behavior."[9] It also "played an important role in resocializing other groups—white students, women, immigrant farmworkers, Hispanic Americans [and] Native Americans to the politics of protest."[10]

Despite the trailblazing insights and findings of this pioneering article, Morris et al. fail explicitly to mention and discuss a significant socializing agent within the African American community: African American political leaders. It is clear that, not only during the civil rights era but during other periods in African American history, appointed and elected African American political leaders have, through their presence, behavior, and actions, politically socialized the African American community.[11] However, to more fully understand their role, we explore one of the many unheralded political counter-socialization strategies employed by these leaders: the use of the protest resignation.

African American leaders have long used protest resignations to send a specific message to their communities and to white communities as well. Long before African Americans would use this tactic successfully at the electoral level, a few African American appointed political leaders used it. For example, during World War II, the esteemed African American lawyer, William Hastie, was appointed a civilian aide to the secretary of war to investigate complaints from African American servicemen about the Army's policy of racial discrimination. What Hastie found so appalled him that he resigned his appointment in protest and then actively criticized the Army once back in civilian life.[12]

A protest resignation is the act of removing oneself from a position on a board, commission, or other body in direct response to an act, custom, or law passed by that body which violates the interests, norms, or ethical standards of one's political constituency or one's personal standards. Not only does protest resignation challenge undesirable conditions, but it is designed to dramatize and bring attention to concealed political realities. By confronting the issue publicly, African American political leaders who utilize this tactic alert the African American community in an effort to reform or nullify such realities.

Claxton, Georgia, known for its fruit cakes and its annual Rattlesnake Roundup, presents an appropriate site for an empirical study of the political socialization effects of this tactic during an era of political context transformation. Located in rural Evans county, Claxton is the county seat and the largest city in this lower-middle Georgia area. During the Reagan-Bush and Clinton years, two African American council persons in Claxton used protest resignations to politically socialize both the African American and white communities.[13]

The Political Context in Evans County, Georgia, and its County Seat: The City of Claxton

The Data and Methodology

The data base for this investigation was drawn from: (1) city and county demographic data; (2) city election data; (3) transcripts of interviews with the two African American councilpersons and the mayor of Claxton, (4) content analysis of articles published in the city's newspaper, the *Claxton Enterprise* for the period 1979–1995,[14] and the newspaper of the closest metropolitan area, the Savannah *Morning News and Evening Press* during the periods of the protest resignation (for correlative data); (5) the text of the lawsuit filed by the American Civil Liberties Union (ACLU) against the city of Claxton, along with the judge's order in the case; and (6) the city's charter. These data sources should provide all of the information needed to conduct a detailed empirical analysis of both the political context in Claxton and the effectiveness of protest resignation as a political socialization strategy in that context. They should also provide some testable propositions about the ways in which such nonpermanent socialization agents effect the substance and direction of African American politics.

The Site

Evans county was formed from several adjoining and surrounding counties on August 11, 1914 and named for a Confederate general. Figure 7.1 reveals that from the 1920 until the 1990 census, the mean African American population in the county stood at 36 percent. That percentage peaked at 38 percent in 1960 and has been slowly declining ever since. In 1990, the population of Claxton was 34 percent African American. Figure 7.1 shows that the African American population in Claxton has gradually grown from one-fifth of the population to one third.

These demographic data tell us little about the impact of racism, racial discrimination, and racial subordination in the political context of Evans county. However, census data for 1990 are suggestive of the conditions faced by the area's African American population. They reveal that the African American per

FIGURE 7.1

Percentages of African Americans and Whites in Evans County and Claxton, Georgia, 1920–1990

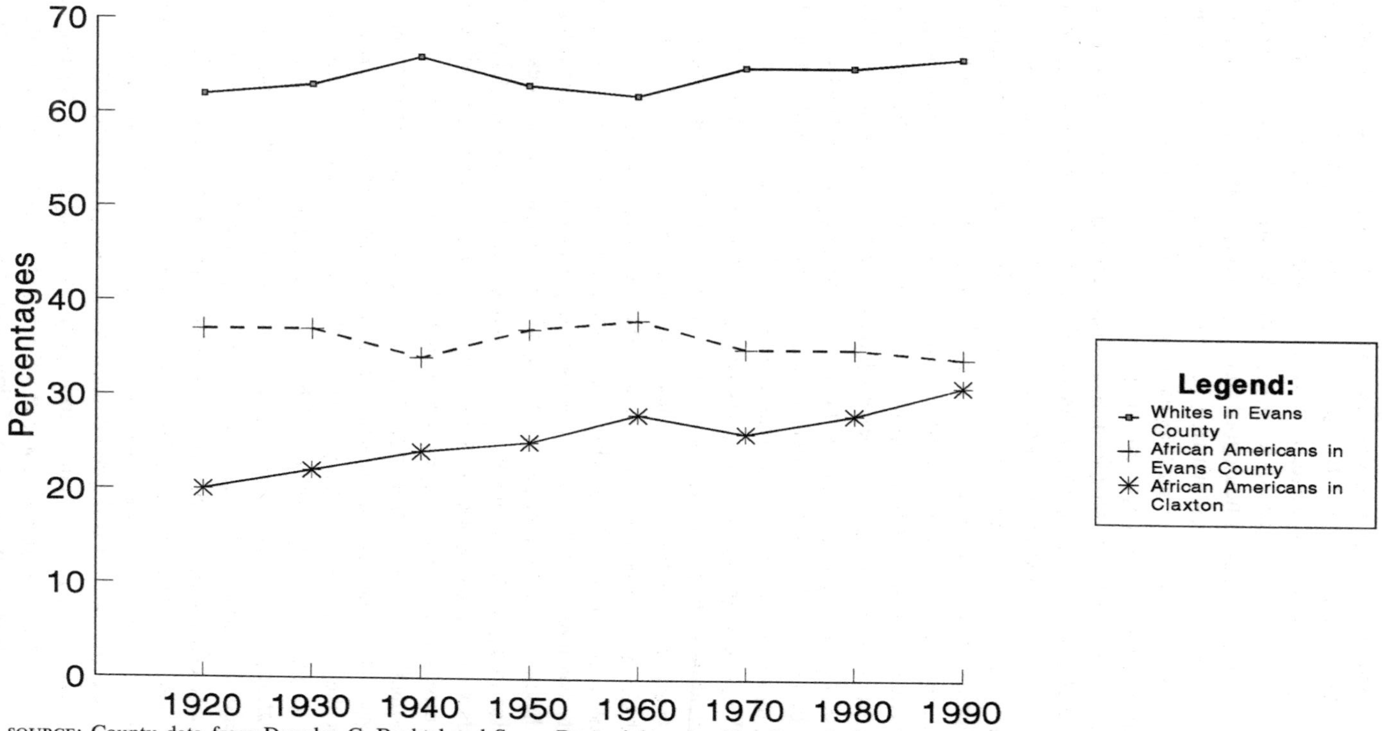

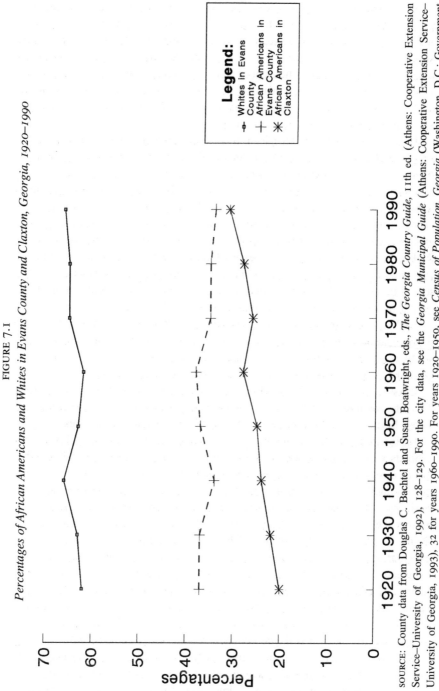

SOURCE: County data from Douglas C. Bachtel and Susan Boatwright, eds., *The Georgia Country Guide,* 11th ed. (Athens: Cooperative Extension Service–University of Georgia, 1992), 128–129. For the city data, see the *Georgia Municipal Guide* (Athens: Cooperative Extension Service–University of Georgia, 1993), 32 for years 1960–1990. For years 1920–1950, see *Census of Population, Georgia* (Washington, D.C.: Government Printing Office, 1920–1950).

capita income in the county at that time was about $5,700 a year compared to $12,000 for white residents. A full 42 percent of the African American population was at or below the poverty level as opposed to 16 percent of whites. Married households comprised 53 percent of the county's African American households, female headed household were 44 percent, and male-headed households 6 percent. For whites, married households comprised 87 percent of the total, with the remainder consisting of female-headed households (11 percent) and male-headed households (2 percent).

In 1990, the African American and white unemployment rates were 12 percent and 4 percent, respectively. As for education, 87 percent of the county's African American residents had a high school education or less compared to 74 percent of whites. Ten percent of the white population had a college education or higher compared to only 4 percent of the African American population.

Thus, on every indicator in 1990, the white population of Evans county was much better off than the African American one. And until 1985, the 1965 Voting Rights Act not withstanding, whites held all of the political power in both the city and the county municipal governments, including every position on the school board, the city council, and the county commission. It took a 1983 legal suit by the county's African American citizens to change that.[15]

As V. O. Key, Jr., has shown in his influential *Southern Politics,* the South's preoccupation with race, racial discrimination, and racial subordination relegated white corruption, political mismanagement, and policy failures to the background along with a host of other social, economic, and legal ills.[16]

Claxton has faced unbelievable municipal problems throughout its history. The city has long been plagued by a series of political mishaps and misadventures. Fiscal crises have bedeviled the city's leadership for decades. In mid-1979, for example, just as the Reagan era was about to commence, Claxton city officials were forced to borrow $150,000 not only to "cover outstanding debt" but to meet current "operating expenses as well."[17] Later, at a September 1980 city council meeting, it was revealed that the city owed $24,000 to local businesses. That meeting ended with "no remedy to paying the present debt . . . as was the initial intent of the [meeting]."[18] Two years later, Claxton was still trying to dig its way out of debt,[19] but with little progress. An audit of city expenditures in 1983 revealed that the city's general revenue fund had been overspent by $30,961.60, and its revenue sharing fund by $5,283.30. According to the city clerk, this was due to the fact that many local businesses had gotten behind on their utility bills, yet their utilities could not be turned off "because the city [owed] them more them they [owed] the city." Mayor Perry Lee DeLoach commented that the city council "could offer him no relief."[20]

A series of federal and state grants during the Reagan-Bush era helped the city back to some degree of financial solvency. But after the Reagan and Bush presidencies had given way to the Clinton era, financial problems continued to haunt Claxton.[21] In 1993, the city clerk revealed that the city faced a $112,000 budget deficit from the previous fiscal year. She noted that "the money needed for the deficit would be loaned to the city's general fund from the gas budget."[22]

Claxton also has a history of voting irregularities. During the 1979 mayoral and council elections, the Georgia Bureau of investigation (GBI) was called in to investigate allegations of "mishandling" of absentee ballots.[23] Following the GBI's probe, the district attorney asked for a thorough investigation of the case.[24] By the last year of the Bush era, 1992, there was still talk of voting irregularities in local elections.[25]

Other persistent problems give cause for concern about the political context in Claxton. The city habitually submits poorly prepared and improperly filled out applications for state and federal funds, which have been repeatedly rejected.[26] The ineptness includes a botched 1981 attempt by the city to annex a predominantly African American section of Evans county in order to attract federal funds.[27] In addition, there have long been clashes and feuds between the mayor and city council members and among council members.[28] Questions have long been raised about the mayor's and councilmembers' repeated absenteeism.[29] To add to this list, in 1989 the mayor, despite the ethical and legal objections of some councilmembers, voted to break a deadlock and give city contracts and favors to other councilmembers.[30]

In 1984, when the Ku Klux Klan petitioned to hold a march in Claxton, the mayor consented. He did state, however, that he would allow the Klan only one rally, and if any Klan members re-entered town after the rally, they would be arrested. By contrast, a similar "one time only" privilege was not extended to a group of African American demonstrators in 1992 who were attempting to rally the community to have a local street named for Dr. Martin Luther King, Jr.[31]

All of these conflicts—despite the presence from 1968 to present of a long-term incumbent mayor, Perry DeLoach, who, by his own account, was the "fairest" and "most equal representation-oriented mayor in the United States"—give ample reason to doubt the calibre of leadership in Claxton. In an extended interview with the authors, Mayor DeLoach claimed that no other white mayor enjoyed better relations with his black constituents than he.[32] Ironically, he cited the city's recent successes in obtaining community development block grants (CDBG) as evidence of his lack of racism; yet these successes can be attributed more to the local economic stagnation and deficit conditions than to delusions of racial harmony.[33]

Despite this plethora of problems—financial, electoral, administrative, legal, and ethical—the Claxton city council and its mayor were unrelenting in their efforts to challenge and block the rights and liberties granted African Americans under the Civil Rights Act of 1964, the Voting Rights Act of 1965, and the Housing Act of 1968. They sought to deny and delay these rights at the fundamental level in every way possible. Indeed, the racism practiced by Claxton's ruling politicians was so pervasive that in 1994 it attracted the attention of the national media.[34]

In 1980 the city council attempted to block the construction of a federally funded public housing project targeted for a poor, primarily African American, neighborhood even though this action put the city at risk of having to pay high attorney's fees as well as of losing other federal funds.[35] The case went to court, and even after the judges ruled in the federal housing authority's favor, the council refused to give up. It tried to rezone the land; when that failed, it voted to cancel the project's building permit.[36] The city wound up in court again, incurring some $5,000 in legal costs to no avail: the housing authority won again.[37]

Also in 1980, members of the city council caused an uproar when they made disparaging remarks about the "minority participation on a board empowered to administer a block grant for which it had applied." African American civic leaders in Claxton were offended by the council's remarks and found them "slanderous."[38] Once again, the the bigotry of Claxton's white political leaders cost the city the grant from the state.

In 1983 the council entered into a costly court battle over reapportionment. At the time, Claxton's elected officials were elected districtwide, an electoral procedure prevented African Americans from winning office at either the county, city, or school board level.[39] Immediately after the suit was filed by African Americans and the ACLU, the Mayor created a biracial committee to develop a plan which would be acceptable to whites. The committee's plan was rejected by the African Americans and the ACLU and the City filed its response to the court."[40] Once again, the council's resistance to African American empowerment proved costly. Its legal fees for contesting the redistricting plan came to $6,600.[41]

In 1986, the first year after African Americans were elected to the city council in Claxton, a request was made to make Dr. Martin Luther King, Jr.'s birthday a paid holiday for city employees (in the same year that the state and federal holiday went into effect). The city council, however, was unyielding. The vote was 5 to 2 in opposition. Only the two newly elected African American councilpersons, Jerome Woody and Louise Glover Williams, voted for the measure. The white councilmen raised the city's lack of finances as justification for their position. They later compromised nominally, agreeing to "let those who wanted to take a day off with vacation pay or a day without pay to do so."[42]

The newspaper editorialized against the efforts of Councilman Woody, citing what they dubbed Woody's "poor judgement" in the matter:

> Claxton City Councilman Jerome Woody told his fellow council members Monday night that he wanted the city's approval of a paid holiday recognizing Dr. Martin Luther King's birthday so that our city could avoid

> adverse publicity and change Claxton's image as a town of racial disharmony. If those were the councilman's intentions, he failed miserably.
>
> We simply feel that Mr. Wood's refusal to seek compromise on the question ruined any good intentions that he had.[43]

In 1992, the city council refused a request to have a street renamed after Dr. King. Louise Williams presented the council with a petition with 90 signatures—nearly all of the residents of Church Street, the street whose name the bill proposed to change.[44] According to newspaper accounts, Mayor DeLoach "deemed the request out of the question." Councilwoman Williams then pressed the mayor and council for "an official decision" on the petition, but failed to get their endorsement[45] Councilman Woody, in an interview, revealed that the mayor admitted to him that Church Street could not be renamed because the largest white church in the city was located on it, and the congregation would not allow the church to have a black man's name in its address. The mayor was himself a member of this church and its mailing address is on another street.

Councilman Woody revealed how Mayor DeLoach later shrewdly made himself appear to be a friend and benefactor of the African American community. After the petition had been defeated, the mayor received a letter from the president of the Claxton chapter of the NAACP asking that a narrow strip of a side street be named in honor of Dr. King. The mayor responded positively, claiming that this action was an indication of his appreciation of the African American community and his responsiveness to it.[46]

The newly elected African American councilpersons were appointed by the mayor to symbolic and insignificant positions on the historical society, biracial, Christmas decorations, and chamber of commerce committees. As a later African American councilwoman noted, these were "lightweight" appointments that failed to provide African American officials with any significant insights into city problems and business. For nearly a decade, African councilmembers' requests for better committee assignments were ignored by the mayor and the senior white councilmembers.[47]

In 1995, faced with the dramatic protest resignation of Councilwoman Renee Baker, Mayor DeLoach named Woody and Williams as the chairs of the city's fire and police department committees. However, these advances were short-lived. Soon afterward, a white police officer made a questionable arrest in the African American community. After Councilwoman Williams mounted an extensive investigation, including summoning the chief of police to a council meeting to defend the officer's actions, the mayor reorganized the city council, giving the committee chairpersons' powers over to the city clerk. Opposition and objections to this move by African American councilmembers were strong. Councilwoman Williams noted that the city clerk "already holds a multitude of jobs at City Hall, including city clerk, bookkeeper, drug program director,

planning and zoning administrator, supervisor of elections, and personnel director."[48] She was also a member of the local school board and the wife of the police chief, whose office she would thus be charged to oversee. The wisdom of this act is dubious at best.

When councilpersons Baker and Williams asked that the city pay their membership fees and housing expenses for the Georgia Association of Black Elected Officials' annual conference (totaling $225 each), Mayor DeLoach opposed the request, citing a council measure prohibiting "city-paid membership in various organizations" except civic or community groups that had been approved just hours before Baker and Williams made their requests.[49] Prior to this, the city had routinely paid for many of the professional expenses of council members. The mayor also denied both councilwomens' request for regular monthly "financial reports" so that "each elected official" would know "the day-to-day financial affairs of the city." He also refused to provide them with a meeting agenda two days prior to each meeting, as they had earlier requested. As he indicated, "We're not going to start conducting the city's business on the streets before it's brought to full council."[50]

To this day, Mayor DeLoach or his representatives hand-deliver meeting agendas to council members just two hours before meetings are scheduled to begin. Members who ask for more time to consider a surprise matter listed on the agenda are refused. Not only does this mayoral action show a complete disregard for the city charter,[51] it is a blatant usurpatation of power for the express purpose of keeping the council's African American members in the dark—even if that means the whole council must arrive at meetings unaware and unprepared to fully conduct the city's business. Mayor DeLoach's tactic is used in other rural Georgia townships to promote the ineffectiveness of newly elected African American officials.[52]

Finally, there was the problem of rude and high-handed behavior displayed by the mayor and the five white councilmen for their African American peers on the council. When African American councilmembers took exception, they were accused of inflaming race relations and setting back racial "progress."[53]

But the mayor's and councilmen's actions against African American empowerment were not merely isolated behavior. As the Reagan-Bush era wore on, the local newspaper began to shift from a rather neutral and inactive position to a more negative and aggressive one. A number of pejorative political cartoons began to appear in its pages, cartoons that depicted African Americans like Atlanta Mayor Andrew Young and the Rev. Jesse Jackson in a negative light.[54] The newspaper hired an editorial columnist who declared in his opening slavo: "Well, it's official, my hero, Pat Buchanan, is running for president."[55] This columnist presented a continuing series of articles that attacked African American leaders, derided federal government support and protection of African American rights (indeed, the federal government itself); linked African Americans to crime; disparaged the Supreme Court's rulings in favor of integration, affirmative action, and reapportionment; and attacked "liberals" and their presumed leader, then-presidential candidate Bill Clinton.[56] The Reagan-Bush contextual revolution served only to bolster a posture that had long hampered and delayed African American empowerment in Claxton and elsewhere and gave white city officials, especially those in the rural South, just the backing they needed to mount bold demonstrations of anti-black sentiment.

Such was the political context in Claxton, Georgia during the Reagan-Bush years. It was a city beset with an impressive array of municipal problems, but these problems were not its primary concern. Hindering African American empowerment, even if it meant exacerbating the city's longstanding financial weakness, was.

Socialization to African American Empowerment

Reagan and Bush were transforming the political context for African Americans by diminishing and derailing the advances resulting from the civil rights movement just as the African Americans in Claxton were beginning to reap the fruits of that movement.

How do African Americans with few resources socialize themselves to politically mobilize their communities? Prior to the 1984 elections, the African American political leadership of Claxton took a variety of steps to raise their constituents' political consciousness and behavior. They used cultural activities such as Black History Month as a platform to bring in speakers, usually African American elected officials from neighboring communities,[57] but also such notable figures as Jaqueline Jackson, the wife of Reverend Jesse Jackson.[58] They also held a voter seminar to educate African American voters about the 1984 electoral contest.[59]

With political consciousness-raising efforts under way, Claxton's African American community began to organize for power. Organizations such as the Georgia State Coalition of Black Women, the Local Gladiators Club,[60] Concerned Citizens for Better Government for Evans County, and the NAACP, launched a variety of political efforts in the city and county. The Coalition and the Gladiators began a voter registration drive. The Concerned Citizens group filed a reapportionment suit, and the NAACP filed a discrimination suit against the county school board.[61] Then the community took the final step, nominating Louise Williams, a native of the city and a graduate of the county high school, for an at-large city council seat in November, 1983. She came in third, in last place. However, a victorious reapportionment suit (from at-large to district elections) soon changed all that, particularly when the courts approved a redistricting plan in 1984.[62]

This plan divided the city into two voting districts, one predominantly black and one predominantly white. Two new seats were added to the council to

TABLE 7.1

African American City Council Candidates in Claxton, Georgia, 1983–1995

Candidate	Districts	Vote	Results
	1983		
Louise G. Williams	At Large	159	Lost
	1984		
J.C. Banks	1	73	
Mary Harper	1	75	Won*
Louise G. Williams	1	54	
Jerome Woody	1	76	Won
	1985		
Renee Baker	1	75	Won
Mary Harper	1	25	Lost
Louise G. Williams	1	32	Lost
	1986		
William Stewart	1	39	Lost
Louise G. Williams	1	68	Won
Jerome Woody	1	54	Lost
Sinclair Miller	2	51	Lost
	1987		
Renee Baker	1	***	Unopposed (won)
	1988		
Louise G. Williams	1	***	Unopposed (won)
	1989		
Renee Baker	1	***	Unopposed (won)
	1990		
Louise G. Williams	1	***	Unopposed (won)
	1991		
Renee Baker	1	***	Unopposed (won)
	1992**		
Booker T. Hagan	1	20	Lost
Vernella Welch	1	27	Lost
Jerome Woody	1	43	Won
	1995		
Vernella Welch	1	54	Lost
Jerome Woody	1	74	Won

Election results taken from various issues of *The Claxton Enterprise* from 1983–1995 and from data provided by the City Clerk.

**Harper, the second-largest vote getter, was elected to the Council for one year.*

***The 1992 election was a special election to fill the vacancy created by the resignation of Councilwoman Renee Baker.*

****No election is held when there is no opposition.*

accommodate the representatives elected from the new black district; the original five seat remained in the hands of voters from the white electoral district. In December 1984, the city held new elections.[63] Because only two individuals from the newly created African American district could take seats on the council and four individuals ran, the city's election rule was that the highest vote-getter would win a full two-year term and the second highest vote-getter would win a one-year term. Table 7.1 lists the African American candidates who have run for Claxton city council since 1983.

Mary Harper, a member of the Georgia Coalition of Black Women, won a one-year term in the 1984 election, while Jerome Woody won a two-year term. In 1985, Harper lost to Renee Baker in a three-way contest.[64] The following year, Jerome Woody was defeated by Louise Williams, who had been the very first African American to run in the city, in the 1983 elections.[65] Baker and Williams served on the city council unopposed until Baker resigned in 1992 and a special election put Jerome Woody back on the city council. Since that time, Woody and Williams have represented District One. No African American has been able to win in District Two.

At his first council meeting in January 1985, newly elected Councilman Jerome Woody threatened to resign from the council due to what he claimed were "irregularities in committee assignments."[66] The newly elected African American council persons, Woody and Harper, were "placed on newly created ad hoc committees and not on any of the council's standing or regular committees. . . . Woody was assigned to start and head a committee for housing in the private sector and to represent the city of Claxton in the Small Business Administration 503 Committee."[67] When Councilman Woody objected to these placements, Mayor DeLoach responded: "I am the mayor and I make appointments . . . I have no apology of the appointments." Councilwoman Mary Harper responded to Councilman Woody by saying: "I resent your putting words in my mouth. I have worked with the mayor for years, you don't have to speak for me."[68] Woody did not carry out his threat. Nonetheless, the stage had been set.

In the years following Woody's initial protest, Claxton's African American councilpersons repeatedly voiced displeasure at their committee assignments. Councilwoman Baker was especially pointed in her frequent public challenges to the mayor in this regard.[69] Baker, who worked at the local bank and held a B.S. degree from Georgia Southern University, often noted that the white councilman who headed the finance committee had less than a high school education. She maintained that she felt a tremendous sense of political impotence with her own assignments. Despite Baker's obvious qualifications and experience, Mayor DeLoach was unyielding.

Finally in February 1992, after six years of being refused better committee assignments, Councilwoman Baker resigned her seat in protest.[70] The only vote against accepting her resignation was cast by the only other African American member of the council. When the council offered to call a special session for

Baker to discuss her grievances, she declined, claiming that they knew full well her grievances.

In the best tradition of paternalistic southern white politicians,[71] Mayor DeLoach claimed in an interview with the authors that he "was shocked beyond imagination" at Baker's actions. Still, he steadfastly held on to the view that his appointment powers were absolute.

However, the mayor's resistive action revealed that he was not really knowledgeable of the mandates of the city's charter. Section A, Article II of that Charter sets out the mayor's appointive powers:

> The Mayor shall have the right and authority to name all of the city appointments to all boards and commissions; however, the appointments are subject to the approval of the council. The Mayor shall further have the right and authority to name all committee chairpersons from the membership of the council and designate to them the administrative assistance necessary to run their departments.[72]

Thus by law, the Claxton mayor's appointive powers are not as absolute as Mayor DeLoach has been implementing them or as he represented them to us. Those powers must be shared with the council.

This illustrates an enduring problem in the South: the law is and has been interpreted to mean what powerful individuals want it to mean, particularly when race is involved. Such was the case in Claxton.

Clearly, Councilman Woody's initial threatened resignation socialized the actions of the other African American councilmembers. Councilwoman Baker stated that she hoped her resignation would raised the African American Claxton community's awareness of their elected officials' lack of real power. She also hoped that it might help those who seek elective positions in Claxton to gain a better understanding of the political arena there.[73] Thus, she saw her protest resignation as a means of transmitting values to another generation of African Americans, and of educating the public by passing on a set of beliefs about the realities of power and the possibility of sharing that power.

All of the remaining African councilmembers confided in interviews with the authors that they too had contemplated resigning from heir elected positions in light of the mayor's and the white councilmembers' racist tactics. Councilwoman Williams, however, indicated that Baker's resignation would have a "devastating" impact on the African American community. Nonetheless she noted that, "It's just getting worse . . . As a black leader, I cannot represent my people."[74] For these reasons, she, along with the other African American elected officials, came to view protest resignation as a means of serving notice to white political figures of their failure to cooperate and compromise with their African American fellow citizens and lawmakers. They also saw it as a way of informing their constituents in District One that African Americans in Claxton were being denied their full, fair, and meaningful representation in local government affairs.

While these data do not permit us to compare how protest resignations affect and influence African Americans at the individual and collective levels, they do suggest that the African American political figures involved were aware of the socializing influence of their actions. Just as important as Baker's action was to Claxton's African American community, it also sent a message to the local white community and its elected leadership that tactics of disempowerment will not be suffered endlessly or accepted silently without political resistance. Later in the year when the matter of committee appointments resurfaced, Mayor DeLoach stated: "I'm going to make those appointments based on the job the person can do and who can get it done the best."[75] There is no example of this ever being done as far as the African American councilpersons are concerned. When they were given power, it was administratively taken away.

Conclusion: Empirical Propositions from a Case Study

This case study has revealed that, in some southern localities, it took nearly two full decades for African Americans to exercise the rights and liberties they had won during the 1960s. Some southern politicians were not compliance-minded about either federal laws or Supreme Court decisions, and neither were political leaders at the national or executive levels.

The data emerging from the Claxton study flies in the face of the scholarly consensus about vehement opposition to African American political empowerment waged by whites in the black belt south. According to Key, it was the size of the African American population that intensified white southern racism and racial opposition to African American progress. The case of Claxton shows that the size of the African American population never really mattered as a factor in local white politicians' resistance to African Americans attaining their full civil and political rights—African Americans were outnumbered by whites more than two to one. Moreover, the Claxton picture of African American rural political empowerment efforts has been repeated elsewhere. A recent analysis of a similar rural Georgia county reveals great similarities and suggests a degree of similarity across the state's black belt and non-black belt counties.[76] Although African American rural empowerment efforts are numerous in the South,[77] it is necessary to return to our Claxton case study for more insights. As Claxton's African American voters sought to exercise their rights, the city's white politicians sought to undermine these efforts.

One of the major testable propositions emerging from this case study is that protest resignations—either threatened or actual—will affect the elected leadership if the original conditions which cause it to be employed are not corrected. A second testable proposition evolving from this case study is that protest resignation has an impacts not only at the elite level but at the mass level as well. Values and belief about public virtue and public trust and public facts are conveyed by this tactic. Thus in subsequent studies on the political context variable in African American political socialization, researchers can probe for the values and beliefs that are conveyed by these protest resignations. It should also be possible in subsequent analyses of protest resignations as a socializing device to see what influence this tactic has on the race-consciousness of the African American community, how racial ideology is impacted, and how racial belief systems are sustained, appropriated or reorganized.

The political empowerment efforts of Claxton's African American elected officials, and subsequently their tactics, were neither a response nor a reaction to Reagan's and Bush's efforts to change the political context of a targeted group: they were simply the initial signals of a delayed movement just getting under way. The contextual revolution of the Reagan-Bush era provided the atmosphere, the examples, and the procedures being used at the national level to disempower African Americans. In such instances, groups that are trying to empower themselves often turn to innovative and creative devices and tactics to socialize the struggle for empowerment. One of these tactics may be protest resignation, and it might just be influential enough to transmit values to both elite and the community, to say nothing of wider audiences beyond the local political context. Indeed, protest resignations have a long and rich history in African American political life,[78] and the case of Claxton is just a continuation of that tradition.

PART 6

PARTICIPATION

Contextual transformation is attempted at not only the academic, intellectual, constitutional, and cultural levels but also within the political process. Transformation of the individuals and organizations involved in the political process, of electoral arrangements and procedures, and of the outcomes of the process ultimately means the transformation of the process itself, at its various levels (federal, state, county, local, and regional). This transformation will be uneven and, at times, uncoordinated and scattered, but not necessarily unsystematic.

One of the chief tools used to enhance African American political participation was the Voting Rights Act. As Steven Lawson notes, "The major political battle between Reagan and his civil rights opponents occurred over the renewal of the Voting Rights Act." He continues: "with the Act due for renewal in 1982, with Reagan in the White House, and with Republicans in control of the Senate, the bill's supporters took the precaution of starting their efforts a full year in advance." The Reagan administration "took a position on renewal that conformed with its opposition to race-conscious affirmative action remedies."[1] President Reagan sought to persuade the Senate to modify the renewal bill by adding an amendment that would require an "intent" rather than an "effect" test to substantiate evidence of discrimination. His efforts failed, however, and the Act was renewed for twenty-five years.[2]

In his second term, Reagan went after voting rights activists themselves. As Lawson relates:

> In the aftermath of Reagan's reelection, the Justice Department indicted eight long-time civil rights activists in Alabama on criminal charges that were viewed as an attempt to roll back black political power. The government contended that the accused had engaged in vote fraud by improperly soliciting and casting absentee ballots in the heart of the State's black belt area.[3]

The suit was brought by an African American. Conservative whites in the locality, notes Lawson, "took advantage of these generational and ideology splits within the black community." These whites "were looking ahead to the upcoming 1986 election, which featured Senator Jeremiah Denton, a Republican who had opposed renewal of the Voting Rights Act in 1982." He further adds that Denton "thought his chances would be stronger if black leaders came under attack and the black electorate felt discouraged from going to the polls."[4] Yet this tactic also failed: Denton lost; nationwide, the African American electorate helped the Democrats to regain control of the Senate in 1986.

Despite the setbacks Reagan experienced, his Republican successor followed his lead. During Bush's 1992 reelection bid, the Justice Department indicted voting rights activists in Democratic opponent Bill Clinton's home state on similar charges of absentee vote fraud.[5] Clearly, participation was a target for transformation by the Reagan-Bush Republicans. However, these efforts did not exhaust their repertoire of exclusion tactics; numerous other techniques were employed in this regard.[6]

One of these tactics emerged in the arena of African American group politics. Much of this collective activity had a civil rights focus and targeted the federal government.[7] All of the major decision-making branches of government were being lobbied by civil rights organizations. To counter these efforts, first the Reagan, then the Bush, presidency politicized the civil rights bureaucracy by appointing critics of traditional civil rights policies to head up those agencies and offices that addressed these concerns.[8] This tactic of "appointment sabotage" forced the civil rights organizations into confrontation and dispute with the very agencies to which they had formerly turned for redress and assistance. Because the energies of civil rights groups and their leaders were consumed in fighting for their own survival and fighting against these "captive" bureaucracies in the federal government, they could not attack other African American problems and crises.

Regarding Reagan-Bush era efforts to attract African Americans to the Republican party, Martin Kilson has argued: "In short, we need a new cadre of what I call trans-ethnic black political leaders, both liberal and conservative, but especially the latter."[9] The Republican party began recruiting African Americans during these administrations with the stipulation that new members be decidedly conservative. African American Republican Gloria Toote said:

> The failure of the Republican party in the past has not been its lack of commitment. It has been its inadequacy in communicating with the poor. It is that simple. We are very, very poor at public relations. . . . The obligation now is greater than ever, for this administration is going to bring about a dramatic change. Program upon program will be exorcised. There is no question of that. The failure of so many programs is evident.[10]

In other words, Reagan-Bush era African American Republican conservatives who sought affiliation with and advancement in the party had to maintain, and maintain loudly, that government was the problem.

For example, the Reagan administration appointed an African American, Samuel J. Cornelius, to head the Department of Agriculture's Food and Nutrition Division, which oversees the Food Stamp program. Prior to this appointment, Cornelius had been charged with abolishing the Community Services Administration, which funded hundreds of programs for low-income people across the country. Upon taking the job, Cornelius asserted that he was going to "clean house." "There are a lot of people getting food stamps who don't qualify," he stated, "And I intend to get rid of them and make it possible for those who deserve the stamps to get them."[11] Yet Cornelius soon had a change of heart. He began arguing for an increase rather than a reduction in food stamp programs serving low-income urban areas and was summarily removed from his post and has since passed into political oblivion.[12]

Other African American political appointees and party affiliates whose political allegiance did not waver and who found it not too difficult to disadvantage African Americans remained in their places.[13] African American politicians, even some of questionable background, were recruited to the Republican party as long as their views followed the party's line.[14]

Although the transformation process was bent on truncating and redirecting African American political participation, it had unintended consequences. It revived a fading political figure in the American political process: the southern demagogue. This is a politician whose stock-in-trade, in the words of V. O. Key, is "to subordinate to the race question all great social and economic issues that tend to divide people into opposing parties."[15] Southern demagogues generate their political capital from and derive political successes by exploiting the race issue. Their prominence had faded with the civil rights revolution, but the Reagan-Bush era, with its emphasis on re-introducing racial cleavages for partisan gain, saw the return of such notable southern demagogues as David Duke.

Another unintended consequence was the counter-mobilization of African American political forces. In their pioneering recent work on political participation, Steven J. Rosenstone and John Mark Hansen argue that because Reagan's proposals threatened the "interests of so many people, politicians, groups, that activists took to the field."[16] In the case of African Americans, the major player in this field was the Reverend Jesse Jackson.[17] As Rosenstone and Hansen further remark, "Mobilization of citizen participation around specific issues is common in local politics."[18] Reagan and Bush thus became the issue, and African Americans entered the political process in numerous ways to make their political voices heard and increase their participation in the political process. They ran for the Senate and for the presidency and approached third-party politics with renewed enthusiasm and sophistication. African American political participation became increasingly innovative and aggressive. The contextual revolution that the Reagan-Bush Republicans had envisioned did not evolve into the one-way process they had hoped for.

With the coming of the Democratic Clinton administration and its centrist politics and policies, the onslaught in the area of political participation set into motion by the Reagan-Bush presidencies continued nearly unabated. On June 19, 1995, the Supreme Court in the *Miller v. Johnson* case (94–631) declared that the Georgia majority African American 11th Congressional District was a "racial gerrymander and thus violated the equal protection clause as interpreted in *Shaw v. Reno.*[19] President Clinton made a major effort to shape African American political opinion on crime. He spoke to groups of African American ministers and clergy, urging them to make an assault on crime. Here a political leader was instructing moral leaders and telling them how to advocate ethical and religious values so as to shape subcultural behavior. But this public relations policy and posture was not extended to the white religious community. Nor was it reflected in the Clinton-sponsored Crime Bill.

Then there was the matter of his "juggling acts" with his African American political nominees and appointees to cabinet and subcabinet positions to satisfy his Republican critics as well as his own Democratic critics in the Democratic Leadership Council (DLC). The end results was a new "litmus test" for African American democratic political appointees, i.e. silent individuals on race, moral, and civil rights issues—which in many ways approximates that launched by Reagan and the Fairmont conference.

In response to President Clinton's wavering and equivocating, African American voters stayed at home in the 1994 congressional elections and the Democrats lost control of both houses of Congress. In his analysis of the Democrats' major loss, this centrist president never publicly mentioned his administration's inadequate responses to the Reagan-Bush contextual revolution and its legacy. In fact, soon after the election he fired his outspoken African American Surgeon General, Jocylen Elders. His administration continued to move to the right to assuage his DLC supporters and the resurgent Republican Congress forced him further right and away from checking the Reagan-Bush legacy.

Immediately upon capturing both houses of Congress, Republicans began a full scale attack on affirmative action policies.

Two Republican presidential hopefuls, Governor Pete Wilson and Senator Phil Gramm, made opposition to affirmative action the centerpiece of their campaigns while all of the contenders, including the African American Alan Keyes, fully embraced the Republican stance on the issue. The aggressiveness of the Republicans on this issue set into motion two major reactions.

First, it caused the Clinton administration to began a high-level review of affirmative action and a promise to change the policy remedy as quickly as possible. On July 19, 1995, President Clinton came out for a modified form of affirmative action and urged governmental agencies to implement the new policy. The second, and perhaps, unintended consequence, was that a traditional African American Republican, Arthur Flecther, who had served in various capacities under several Republican presidents beginning with Nixon, announced his candidacy for the Republican nomination in 1996. He simply called himself the Affirmative Action candidate. It was a new day, and an innovative effort on the part of African Americans. Yet Flecther never entered the primaries. African American political commentator Alan Keyes did run in most primaries but was shut out of televised debates in South Carolina and Atlanta, Georgia. As conservative as most of the other contenders, Keyes charged that racism still existed in the party after being arrested in Atlanta for trying to enter the TV studio. (He was later released and charges were dropped.)

8

AFRICAN AMERICAN POLITICAL OPINION
Volatility in the Reagan-Bush Era

Michael C. Dawson

> It is clear to most reductionist intellect that black people think differently from one another, it is also clear that the time for undiscriminating racial unity has passed.[1]

Political context, when it is transformed, affects the political opinion of African Americans. African American political opinion has been more volatile in the past few years than it has been for several decades. Just in the period between 1991 and 1992, we have seen George Bush achieve both a modern record level of presidential approval for a Republican president and a modern record low level of approval for all presidents—lower than Nixon's approval during Watergate or Reagan's during the recession of 1982–83. During the same brief time span, African Americans' normally solid identification with the Democratic party swung by 30 points, dipping below 50 percent for the first time in the modern era in early 1991 but climbing back to over 70 percent by mid-1992. Since 1988 a steadily increasing number of African Americans have classified themselves as political independents. Twenty percent or more have consistently identified themselves as independents since 1990; this figure reached a high of nearly 40 percent in early 1991. The only "mainstream" indicator of party politics among African Americans that has not varied much during the past few years has been their affiliation with the Republican party, which traditionally has hovered below 10 percent. Thus, African Americans' growing dissatisfaction with the Democratic party has not resulted in growing strength for the Republicans but rather with both long- and short-term increases in the percentage of African Americans who see themselves as independents. These trends are described in Figure 8.1.

Party politics is not the only area in which African American political opinion has exhibited volatility. As Toni Morrison argues in her introductory essay to a collection of African American scholarly reflections on the Anita Hill-Clarence Thomas controversy, intense debate occurred within the black community as a result of this conflagration.[2] Several essayists in that collection noted that class, gender, and ideological cleavages within the black community were fully activated by the Thomas hearings.[3] Then, only half a year later, that community and the nation were again rocked by the widespread rage unleashed in the wake of the travesty of justice that occurred in Simi Valley.

Evidence from the pioneering work of Larry Bobo and his colleagues shows that large shifts in black opinion occurred after the acquittal of the four police officers and the subsequent rioting—particularly among upper-income African Americans. Their polls reveal an increasing certainty on the part of well-to-do blacks that America is a racially unjust society and a rising sense of alienation. Indeed, significant numbers of upper-income blacks noted that they were more

FIGURE 8.1

Black Party Identification and Presidential Approval, 1991–mid-1992

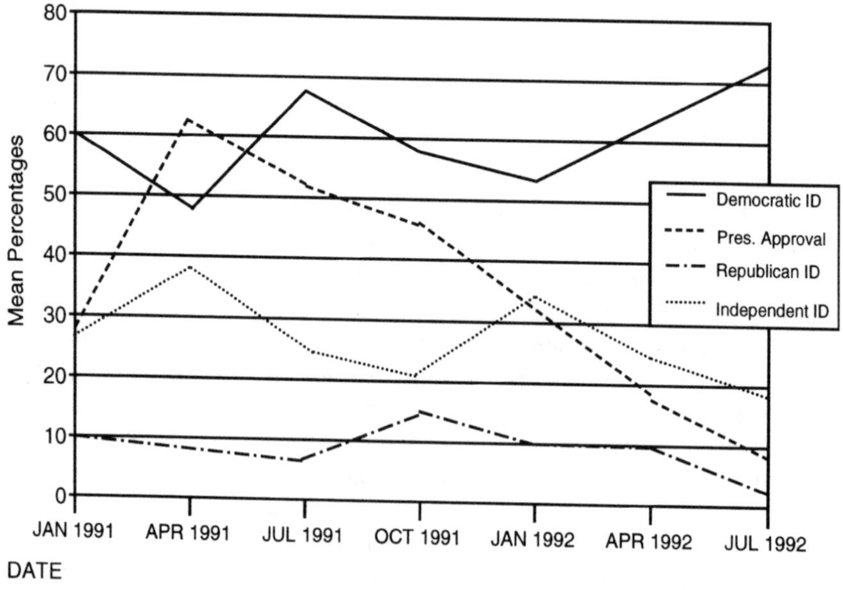

convinced than ever that the remaining racial inequalities in American society were due to racial discrimination. At the same time, other surveys conducted in Los Angeles both before and after the riots show that not only do large gaps exist in income and other measures of societal status between blacks and whites, but similarly large gaps exist between blacks and Asian-Americans and blacks and Latinos. The following findings illustrate the racial gulf in political opinions about the riots: over 67 percent of African Americans, but only 43 percent of Asians, 39 percent of Latinos, and 37 percent of whites viewed the Los Angeles rebellion as an act of "mainly protest." On the other hand, 56 percent of whites, 52 percent of Latinos, 51 percent of Asians, but only 23 percent of blacks saw the rebellion as best characterized as looting and/or crime.[4]

What is the cause of these increasing racial divisions within American political opinion and the parallel increase in the volatility of African American political opinion in particular? The most popular response to that question is that, as most social science theories would predict for any group, steadily increasing economic divisions within the black community are finally becoming reflected in that community's political activities.[5] Other political science scholars have argued that the peculiarities of the Bush administration may have caused the swings in black political opinion related to the party system.

Others contend that the advent of the Reagan administration represented a profound watershed in American politics. Reagan led the Republican party to a series of victories that reversed decades of both economic and racial policies. The great majority of African Americans believed Reagan's civil rights and affirmative action policy reversals represented a severe blow to African Americans, and many considered the Reagan presidency to be extraordinary hostile to African American group interests.[6] This perception of the Reagan administration was reflected in the very low approval ratings Reagan received from African Americans.[7]

President Bush continued Reagan's campaign tactics and policy initiatives while making more sophisticated use of symbolic politics. Bush showed that he was more willing to meet with black leaders, including Jesse Jackson. Yet he finally signed a much weakened version of the Civil Rights Restoration Act in 1991 only after extracting severe concessions from advocates of a strong bill. It was also Bush—the public opinion "beneficiary" of "popular" military interventions in Panama and Iraq—who nominated the profoundly conservative Clarence Thomas to replace Thurgood Marshall on the Supreme Court.

Certainly, the Reagan-Bush administrations pushed the political climate in this country far to the right of the political spectrum, and African Americans were not immune to the political trends that occurred in the larger political arena. I will directly test the hypothesis that this directly affected African Americans' identification with the American political party system. Specifically, I will test the proposition that African Americans' identification with the Democratic party declined during the Reagan-Bush era. Increasing polarization in the black community and the advent of the Reagan-Bush era tell only part of the story. Much of the volatility seen in African American political opinion is due not only to the changes that occurred within the black community during this time but also to a factor viewed by African Americans as a structural failure in the American political system.

This structural change, which has accelerated greatly in the past four years, has led both major political parties to publicly distance themselves from African Americans. The resulting political isolation has intensified divisions within the black community. For example, former Marxists such as Earl Ofari Hutchinson, who wrote a seminal essay on the "myth of black capitalism," now advocate black capitalism and alliance with the Republican party (as does national talk show host Tony Brown) as the correct response to the Los Angeles rebellion.[8] Thoughtful African American scholars such as Ronald Walters, chair of Howard University's political science department, have suggested that African Americans seriously consider supporting the 1992 candidacy of political independent Ross Perot—who once advocated establishing a perimeter around the barrios and ghettos of Dallas and house-to-house searches for contraband. Of course, many African American commentators who urged blacks to consider Perot did so not because of his political stances but to try and force the two major parties to address the political needs of African Americans. Others (quietly) urged the black community to enthusiastically support the Democratic contender, Bill Clinton, despite any strong focus on Clinton's part on urban issues or economic policies aimed at the poor.

Political isolation thus led to dismay and despair as the strategic choices confronting African Americans during the 1992 elections began to be viewed as extremely limited. It is primarily this systemic context—that of a growing political, economic, and social crisis African Americans face—that structures African American opinion and is responsible for the volatility in African American political opinion.

I further argue that politically relevant class and status divisions have existed within the black community for quite a while and that conflict between African American women and men over issues of gender and politics has also been endemic. These political conflicts have been, to a significant degree, invisible outside the black community both due to a lack of interest on the part of those outside that community and to the active efforts of many African American leaders and institutions to maintain a facade of racial unity.[9]

What is presented in this paper should be taken as preliminary speculations derived from an empirical base of very recent studies by myself and colleagues across the nation. Much more detailed work is needed before more systematic inferences can be drawn.

Data and Methodology

The racial group interests model has served as the main framework for my previous research on African American politics.[10] This framework for analyzing African American political choices is based on the following assumptions. First, until the mid-1960s, race was clearly the decisive factor in determining the opportunities and life chances available to virtually all African Americans despite their individual or family social and economic status. Consequently, it was much more efficient for African Americans to determine what was good for the group and use group status, both relative and absolute, as a proxy for individual utility. It was also efficient to use group status as a proxy not only because of the relative ease with which a candidate, piece of legislation, or public policy could be analyzed vis-a-vis their effect on African Americans, but because the information sources available in the black community (such as media outlets, kinship networks, community and civil rights organizations, and especially the preeminent institution in the black community, the church) would all reinforce the political salience of racial interests and provide information about racial group status and politics.

Second, the psychological theories of attribution and self-categorization suggest that individual-level psychological processes reinforce the salience of racial politics for African Americans. Information that either minimized intragroup differences or exaggerated intergroup differences could thus be more easily accepted than information that contradicted current images of the importance of race in politics. Errors in information processing and biases in decision making would thus tend to favor racial explanations of the social world. The salience of one's racial identity (or any other group identity) is seen as a function of the cognitive accessibility of information pertinent to that identity and of the fit of that identity with social reality. This latter feature suggests two ways in which racial identity can become less salient for African Americans. If, particularly for the new black middle class, race becomes less alien in their own lives, then racial politics should become less important. This is essentially the process described by social scientists such as Dahl.[11] On the other hand, information about the political, economic, and social worlds of African America could become less accessible to African Americans. This could be due to individual blacks, particularly middle-class ones, moving out of the black community.[12] But information can also become less accessible as a result of breakdowns in the social networks in the black community, as has happened in some of the most economically devastated inner-city neighborhoods.[13] This is particularly important in the context of understanding the effects of neighborhood poverty on black politics.

Generally, we should expect the importance of the combination of the cognitive phenomenon of accessibility and fit to slow the process of political diversity among African Americans. Exit from the black community is much harder for

African Americans than was similar mobility for European-ethnic groups in the early twentieth century or for Asians or Latinos today.[14] Moreover, the perception of a racially hostile political and social climate helps to counteract economic information and reinforce the salience of racial group politics for African Americans.

It is upon these assumptions that a framework was developed for analyzing African American political choices. However, if poor African Americans become more isolated in America's poorest communities, one would expect to see the residents of those communities exhibit significant political divergence from blacks who reside elsewhere.[15] Yet there are several ways by which bias can be introduced into the utility calculus. To the extent that either perceptions of individual utility or group interests are noisy (large), one would expect more reliance on heuristics.[16] To the extent that formal and informal institutions are strong in a given black community, and individual African Americans have strong ties to these networks, one would expect perceptions of racial group interests to play more of a role in calculations about political decision making. The role of institutions in reinforcing the importance of racial group interests would thus lead to greater cognitive availability of psychological constructs supporting a racial group utility calculus. This is due to the availability heuristic which suggests that construction and retrieval of more prominent and available memories and other cognitive structures bias the decision-making process in the direction of utilization of racial group conflict.[17] Therefore, if African American institutions emphasize racially oriented analyses of political candidates, policies, and social programs, perceptions of the utility of group calculus are more likely to be heightened vis-a-vis individual calculus. In this instance, the type of racial belief system explicated by Allen would also bias decision making in favor of racial group calculus.[18]

In general, Dawson found perceptions of racial group interests to be a major force in shaping African American politics.[19] Examination of data from the National Black Election Study of 1984–88 (NBES) leads me to suggest that two aspects of group interests were particularly important. First was the respondents' perceptions that their fates were linked to that of the race as a whole. Second was their belief that whites were economically better off than blacks. Indeed, an integral aspect of the development of perceptions of African American group interests has been the relative and absolute economic status of African Americans. Since slavery the political fate of African Americans has been tied to the economic status of the race. These two factors presuppose each other, and together they powerfully predict much of the micro-level political behavior and political opinion of African Americans. Except in two domains (black nationalism and African American support for policies of economic redistribution), socioeconomic status has not been found to play a major role in this shaping at the micro-level.

The measures available to the research community have not been adequate to fully test theories of micro-level African American politics. For example, previous surveys have lacked adequate measures of the validity of African American information sources and the perception of importance of different types of organizations in the African American community. Perceptions of African American group interests along a variety of issue domains have not been included in the overwhelming majority of surveys. However, even with the crude measures that we now have, this framework has been proven to explain powerfully a variety of African American micro-level political behaviors ranging from support for black nationalism, identification with the two political parties, voting behavior, and support for various public policies.

One reason this framework has been relatively useful for helping explain African American political behavior is because, even through the 1980s, large numbers of African Americans continued to believe that what happens to the race as a whole personally affected their lives. A construction of linked fate was therefore needed to measure the degree to which African Americans believe that their own self-interests are linked to the interests of their race. Additionally, measures of relative group status, particularly economic status, are essential for understanding African American perceptions of racial interests.

The National Black Election Study of 1984–88 allows one to show both the basic underpinning of African American group interests and the role these interests played in shaping African American political behavior and beliefs during the period of the study. The NBES was a national telephone survey comprised of 1,150 interviews sampled from the adult African American population. It remains the most comprehensive political survey of the African American population ever attempted. (A full description of the survey and of the other surveys upon which it drew may be found in several sources including Dawson, and Gurin and her colleagues' study of Jesse Jackson's presidential campaign.[20])

In the NBES, the concept of linked fate was measured in both 1984 and 1988. The study also measured African Americans' perceptions of their relative economic status compared to that of whites. In 1984, for example, 73 percent of all African Americans in the NBES sample responded affirmatively to the question, "Do you think what happens generally to the black people in this country will have something to do with what happens in your life?" The comparable figure for 1988 was 76 percent. The NBES also measured the degree to which African Americans perceived economic disparities between blacks and whites. Not surprisingly, 65 percent of African Americans during both years of sampling believed that blacks are in a worse economic position than whites.

My own work has shown the presence of a strong linkage between these two measures. Further, I have shown earlier that whether an African American believes his or her own fate is linked to that of their race as a whole is not predicted by either socioeconomic status or gender. Rather, it is predicted by the degree to which an African American individual is integrated into black community organizations and tied to black information networks in addition to that individual's assessment of the relative economic status of African Americans.[21]

Recent Trends in African American Political Opinion

Through 1988, African American political opinion was viewed as relatively stable, particularly in areas such as partisanship, presidential approval, and voting behaviors that reflected African Americans' self-placement in the American political universe. As several observers of the politics of race have noted, the 1964 election marked a watershed event in the long history of race and American politics.[22] By 1964, the two parties had clearly become identified with opposing sets of racial policies. We can still see these differences reflected in contemporary African American presidential approval, party identification, and issue positions.

During the 1988 election, however, African Americans' perceptions of their racial interests yielded large majorities for the Democratic party. Figure 8.2 displays black and white trends in presidential approval while figure 8.3 displays the percentage of blacks and whites who identified with the Democratic party.

FIGURE 8.2
Black and White Presidential Approval, 1961–1992, by Calendar Quarter

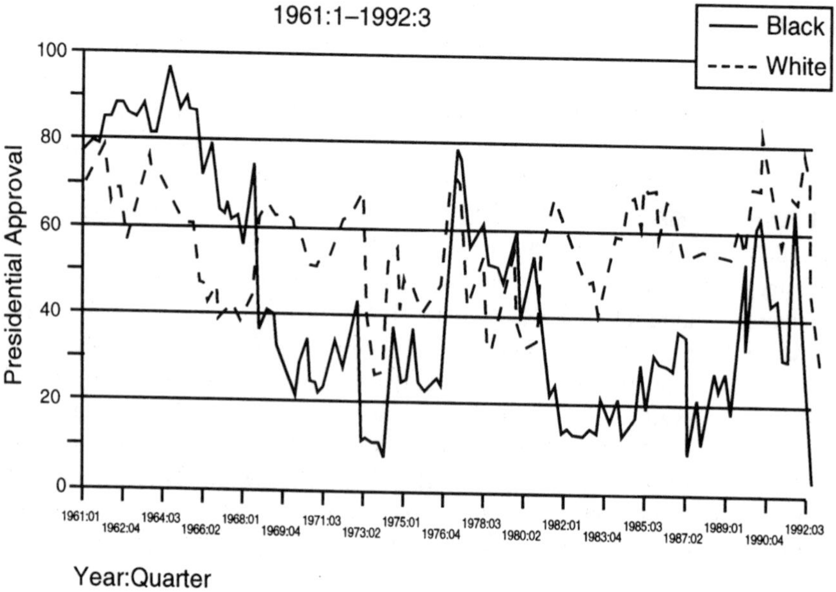

These figures help to illustrate two major aspects of black political behavior and opinion: (1) the Democratic party and Democratic presidents could count on substantial support from the black community until the early 1990s, and (2) African American political opinion was often the opposite of white political opinion. That an extremely large gap exists between black and white political opinion is a fact of American political life.

Several examples will be presented to outline the contours of African American political opinion and the racial divide in American political opinion. The following presidential approval and party identification data covering the period 1961–1990, in addition to the data used in figures 8.2 and 8.3, come from a data set acquired by Roper, who used standard Gallup Poll questions but disaggregated the responses by respondent race.[23] Racial differences in presidential approval can be seen in the following averaged statistics for each of the following presidents.

We see the same pattern of large racial differences in party identification: (1) Black Democratic party identification during each of the following presidents' administration:

(a) Carter	84%
(b) Reagan	73%
(c) Bush	67%

FIGURE 8.3

Black and White Democratic Supporters, 1961–1992, by Calendar Quarter

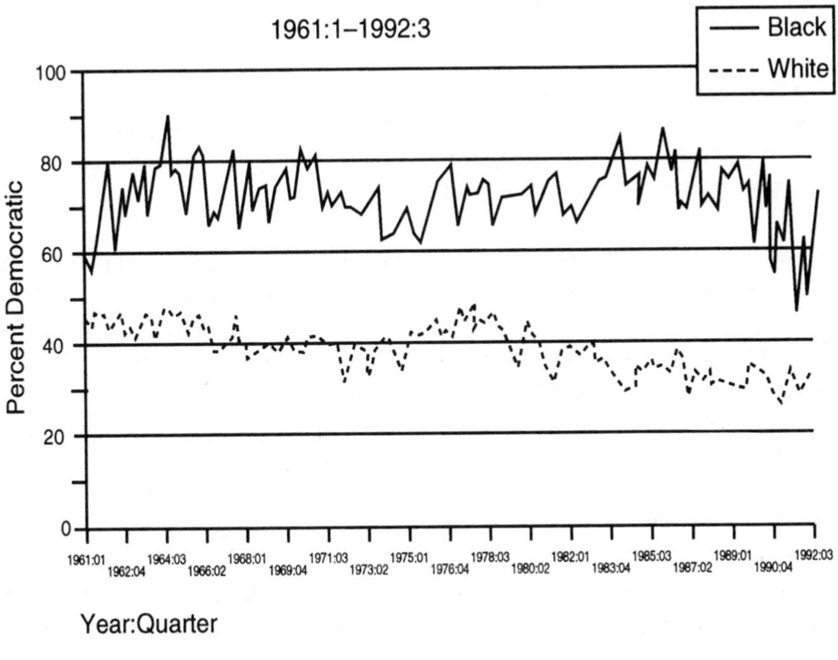

(2) Combined black and white Democratic party identification:
  (a) Carter 42%
  (b) Reagan 41%
  (c) Bush 32%

(3) Black Republican party identification during each of the following presidents' administration:
  (a) Carter 7%
  (b) Reagan 6.5%
  (c) Bush 10%

(4) Combined black and white Republican party identification:
  (a) Carter 17%
  (b) Reagan 28%
  (c) Bush 25%

Similar patterns emerge from the 1988 NBES data when we look at racial differences in issue positions, not only on racial policy but on a variety of other issues. In 1988, African American respondents tended to support programs that would require economic redistribution.[24] Fifty-seven percent of African Americans supported a policy of government-guaranteed jobs and good standard of living, compared to 11 percent of whites, a 36 percent racial gap on this issue. Sixty-five percent of blacks supported increased spending on services to the unemployed, while 24 percent of white respondents did not—a 41 percent gap.

African Americans' opinions of the need for a strong social safety net in 1988 matched that of Martin Luther King, Jr. a generation ago. Dr. King believed that the government and society should play a major role in eliminating poverty and promoting economic justice. As he stated in 1968:

> There is nothing but a lack of social vision to prevent us from paying an adequate wage to every American citizen. . . . There is nothing except shortsightedness to prevent us from guaranteeing an annual minimum—a *livable* income for every American family.[25]

Not surprisingly, even larger gaps can be found in the realm of racial policies. A large percentage of African Americans, 70 percent, supported increased spending on programs to help blacks. By contrast, only 14 percent of whites expressed this opinion, resulting in a racial gap on this policy of 56 percent. Ninety percent of African Americans supported the proposition that the government should see to it that blacks get fair treatment in jobs while 46 percent of whites supported this position, resulting in a 44 percentage-point racial gap for this question. African Americans supported the preferential hiring and promotion of African Americans (65 percent), while Whites did not (11 percent)—a 54 percentage point difference.

The tendency on the part of many African Americans to support strong governmental efforts to bring about racial equality was also an integral part of

King's program by 1967. King strongly believed in strong employment goals based on the percentage of minorities in a given city.[26] Under his leadership, the Southern Christian Leadership Conference developed Operation Breadbasket to try to increase minority hiring.

The racial divide in political opinion is often reproduced in racially polarized voting behavior in national, state, and local elections. King argued that these divisions began before the riots, during the period following the Selma march in early 1965. He described the basis for the emerging racial split as follows:

> When Negroes looked for the second phase, the realization of equality, they found that many of their white allies had quietly disappeared. Negroes felt cheated . . . while many whites felt that the Negroes had gained so much it was virtually impudent and greedy to ask for more so soon. The paths of Negro-white unity that had been converging crossed at Selma, and like a giant X, began to diverge. Up to Selma there had been unity to eliminate barbaric conduct. Beyond it the unity had to be based on the fulfillment of equality, and in the absence of agreement the paths began to inexorably to move apart.[27]

From 1964 to 1988, the racial divide in mainstream American politics was solid. The Democratic party was clearly identified with African Americans and the Republican party with white racial interests—a fact that helped produce Republican dominance in presidential approval and led African Americans to support liberal to radical racial and economic policies. Economic as well as racial issues were highly salient for African Americans. As shown in table 8.1, issues such as those surrounding gender politics, along with other social issues that were less salient along the racial dimension, manifested much more variation within the African American community and exhibited much smaller gaps with white political opinion. This pattern, which remained stable for over three decades, has since begun to unravel.

Why is African American Political Opinion so Volatile?

Many explanations have been offered: one such explanation cites the increasing economic polarization within the black community. For example, opinion divisions among African Americans of different economic strata have been shown in the degree to which support is voiced for economic redistribution and for the political and social separation from whites. As figure 8.4 illustrates, more than one-third of African Americans whose family incomes fell below the poverty line in 1988 supported the formation of an independent black political party. Conversely, only 1 of 10 African Americans whose incomes did not fall below the poverty line were willing to support the formation of such a party. Multivari-

TABLE 8.1

Differences Between Black and White Public Opinion, 1988

Issues	Whites	Blacks
Supports increased spending on government services	33	63
Supports decreased defense spending	31	47
Supports government health insurance	39	49
Believes that government should see to providing jobs and a good standard of living	21	57
Believes men and women should have equal role	68	68
Supports increased spending on:		
- social security	53	82
- food stamps	16	49
- fighting A.I.D.S.	71	83
- protecting the environment	64	58
- financial aid to college students	39	72
- assistance to the unemployed	24	
- childcare	53	78
- public schools	61	83
- care for the elderly	73	90
- the homeless	61	90
- the war on drugs	74	82
Supports decreased federal spending on:		
- aid to Nicaraguan contras	50	51
- star wars	40	53
- space and scientific research	31	25
Approves of U.S./Soviet nuclear treaty	90	71
Opposes use of U.S. military to protect oil shipments	32	50
Supports greater cooperation with Russia	43	42
Opposes limits on foreign imports	34	22
Political Identification		
Considers self a liberal	27	41
Considers self a Democrat	40	83
Likes something about the Democratic party	51	63
Dislikes something about the Democratic party	48	20
Likes something about the Republican party	52	22
Dislikes something about the Republican party	47	50
Candidate and Public Figure Evaluations		
Likes something about Bush enough to vote for him	59	190
Dislikes something about Bush enough to vote against him	52	47
Likes something about Dukakis enough to vote for him	44	61
Dislikes something about Dukakis enough to vote against him	63	22
Disapproves of Reagan's handling of his job as president	34	75
Thinks Jackson would make the best Democratic candidate	13	59
Feels extremely cold towards Bush		

ate analysis confirms that African American support for a black political party drastically falls as income and education increase.[28] However, the greater the perception by blacks of a link between one's own fate and that of the race, the stronger the support for black political autonomy and a black political party.

Moreover, economic status has been shown to be an important determinant of black political opinion in two instances. In the first instance, although most African Americans, regardless of status, support policies of economic redistribution, when such a policy directly impacts the interests of high-status African Americans, the redistributive effect is relatively small. More dramatic divisions along economic lines can be found when African Americans disagree about which tactic or strategy best advances the interests of the race. Thus, whether African Americans should abandon the two parties and start a party of their own, or whether African Americans should politically and socially distance themselves from whites, are questions that the black poor are much more likely to answer in the affirmative.

As the work of Cohen and Dawson highlights, there is also a spatial component to the political relevance of economic division within the black community. These researchers have shown that the politics of African Americans who live in neighborhoods with poverty levels of 30 percent or greater differs significantly from that of African Americans who live in less devastated neighborhoods, even after controlling for individual economic status.[29] Thus, they conclude, as economic inequality increases among African Americans, so the divisions deepen within the black community about which way forward and with whom.

FIGURE 8.4

Support for the Formation of an Independent Black Political Party, by Level of Poverty

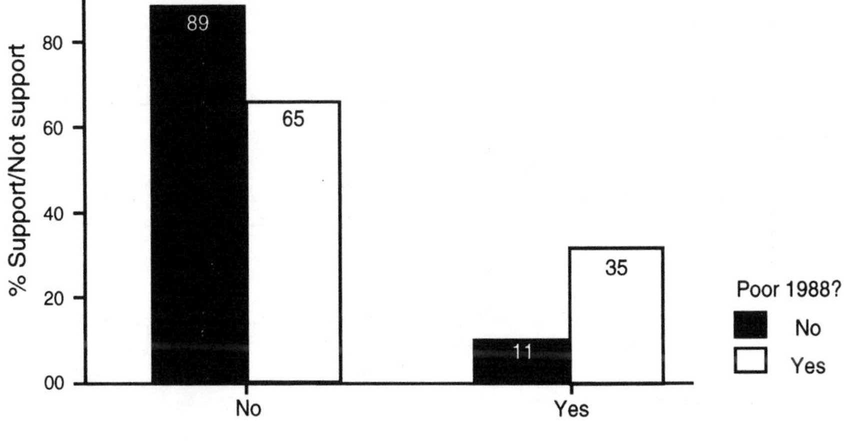

The volatility of African American political opinion is caused to a significant degree by severe deterioration in the political and economic systems within which African Americans find themselves as well as growing economic divisions within the black community. Through most of the 1980s, most African Americans identified unemployment as the major problem facing the black community. As figure 8.5 displays, black unemployment continues at disastrous rates. Moss and Till present a generally despairing view for the prospects of significant improvement in black male joblessness.[30] Given the economic restructuring described by Johnson and his colleagues, the likelihood of continued attacks on the employment stability of urban black workers could well intensify in the future.[31] As always, employer discrimination such as that reported by Kirschenman and Neckerman continues to contribute significantly to the deterioration of the economic fortunes of a sizable segment of the black community.[32] Neither party appears willing to champion either a major progressive restructuring of the economy, which would necessitate significant federal intervention, or significant strengthening of programs advancing racial equality.

Then there are the several politically relevant status divisions that exist within African America. These divisions are generally masked in most political analyses because many analysts prefer to concentrate on partisanship—that is, the strong identification of the racial interests of African Americans with the

FIGURE 8.5
Black and White Unemployment Rates, 1954–1991, by Calendar Quarter

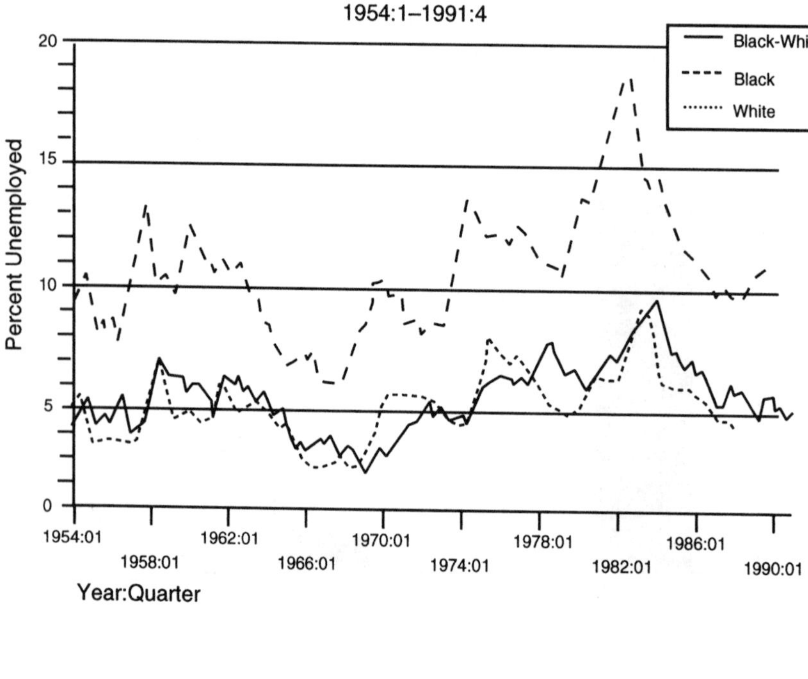

Democratic party. This traditional affinity has produced a false perception of homogeneity in African American political opinion. Consequently, when African Americans have become disaffected with the Democrats, it has been perceived that these disillusioned blacks, lacking anywhere else (i.e., any other viable party alternative) to turn, have chosen to withdraw from the political system entirely. Yet, during the Bush administration, the Republican party was able to win over significant numbers of African Americans as some sectors of that population became more conservative—no more than 6% supported Reagan and nearly 10% supported Bush. However, while the Bush presidency received a record high level of public approval (over 60 percent in early 1991), Bush received the modern low for black presidential approval (7.5 percent in July 1992). Statistical models of black presidential approval clearly show that Bush's high approval ratings were caused by very brief jumps in support for his presidency during the Panama and Iraq campaigns. In both cases, black approval rapidly declined to the traditional low levels of black support for modern Republican presidents. As analysis of black party identification has shown the Republicans have made very few gains among African Americans in contemporary times.[33]

However, there has been a growing African American dissatisfaction with the Democratic party since the mid-1980s. Analysis of the 1984 and 1988 NBES survey results reveal that fewer African Americans believed in 1988 that the Democrats worked very hard on black issues. Since 1988, *Newsweek* has reported a large increase in the percentage of African Americans who argue that there would be no difference between a Democratic and Republican administration when asked, "Would a Democratic administration do more to help blacks get ahead, or would it not be much different from the current Republican administration?" This dissatisfaction with the Democratic party has been reflected in the large jump in the number of African Americans who in the Bush years identified themselves as independents. This number rose from 9 percent during the Carter administration to 11% during the Reagan presidencies, and to 22% during the Bush administration. Current poll results show the tendency continuing in the Clinton years.

Can we determine if the shift in black partisanship is a response to the politics of the Reagan-Bush era? Table 8.2 presents results from a multivariate analysis of the influences on African Americans' identification with the Democratic party between January 1961 and December 1991.[34] These results show that for every quarter that Reagan and Bush were in office—everything else being held constant—black Democratic party identification declined by three percentage points. In the absence of countervailing influences such as the rise in the gap between black and white unemployment and the steadily increasing unpopularity of President Reagan during his tenure and the fluctuating popularity of President Bush, black Democratic identification could be expected to decline rapidly.[35] Yet blacks still represent a greater share of the Democratic party than

TABLE 8.2
The Determinants of Black Democratic Identification, 1961–1991

Independent Variable	Dependent Variable Percentage Black Democratica Identification Coefficient (SE)
Reagan-Bush era	-2.88 (1.73)
Difference Black/White Unemployment Rates	-1.29 (.34)
Change in Consumer Price Index	1.70 (.93)
Democratic Honeymoon	10.15 (4.34)
Republican Honeymoon	0.51 (3.31)
Watergate	-1.99 (2.60)
International Rally Events	.93 (.92)
American Killed in Action (X1000)	-.04 (.06)
Presidential Approval	.11 (.03)
Past Value of Democratic Identification	.14 (.09)
Constant	59.80 (6.66)

n=123
Adjusted R^2 .19

Data set assembled by author. Economic data are from the Cicibase Econometric Database. Presidential approval and party identification data are from the Gallup Organization. Notes: The estimates are OLS estimates derived using the Regression Analysis for time series program.

the Republican party, even though blacks represented on average less than 3% of those who identified themselves as Democrats during the 1980s.

However, the volatility of African American political opinion is not due to Republican successes, but rather to a shift in the party system since the mid-1980s. The Democratic response to the national Republican electoral successes—based as those successes were on race-baiting, the use of racial code words, and racial conservatism—has been to distance the Democratic party from African Americans and platforms such as urban policy and economic redistribution that have become identified with African Americans. Today's situation is similar to that of the early twentieth century and the late 1950s where both parties were seen as trying to distance themselves from black Americans and their issues. During each of these periods and to various degrees, African Americans had few allies and fewer options within the American political system. Both parties were apparently hostile toward African Americans, and African American politics was marked by increased volatility.

Discontent and Dismay

Upon review of the political and economic climate that has been developing since the 1970s, it should come as no surprise that 47 percent of the respondents in the 1984 NBES did not believe that much real change had occurred during the preceding twenty years in terms of eliminating discrimination.

Another 40 percent of the 1984 respondents believed that African Americans will never achieve full social and economic equality in this country. This is the context in which contemporary black politics exists, and it is one of escalating racial conflict and ongoing debate.

The Los Angeles riots are an example of what happens to African American political opinion when violent racial conflict occurs. Bobo and his colleagues recorded strong shifts in African American political opinion after the acquittal of the four Los Angeles police officers.[36] Apparently, the jury's decision and the ensuing rebellion served to reinforce many African Americans' view of the political and economic system as one devoid of racial justice. The Anita Hill-Clarence Thomas confrontation, which preceded it also served to intensify political debate within the black community. Yet, while the Los Angeles disturbances sparked debates on the survival of African Americans given the current trajectory of the American political economy, the Hill-Thomas debate raised the question not only of who is worthy of being put on the "black" agenda, but of who can consider themselves "black."

The Nixon-Ford strategy of splitting off a segment of the black community was followed by the Reagan-Bush strategy of demonizing African Americans. Yet some African American academics, among them Martin Kilson, who in 1981 were urging possible alliances with the Republicans and praising "new black leaders" such as Thomas and the late Clarence Pendleton were attacking the Reagan administration by 1983. The basis for their reversal seems clear: unless one was totally in agreement with the Reagan program, one was a "bad Negro." Bad Negroes were the cause of many of the nation's domestic ills ranging from poverty, to crime in the streets, to being a member of those greedy, special-interest civil rights groups which were intent on looting the national treasury. At the national level, this strategy was electorally very successful.

As the Democrats responded to the aggressively racial strategy of the Republicans, it became clear to key actors of both parties that either attacking or removing African Americans and their interests from the national political agenda was a successful strategy. This shift, which has become increasingly evident over the past few years, has helped to highlight the divisions and debates within the black community. As competing groups struggled to have their interests included as part of the black agenda, Los Angeles exploded.

The debate over the Los Angeles riots is similar to that which ensued from the violent activity exhibited by the black poor during the 1963 Birmingham protests. In an historical analysis of the political activity of the black poor in Birmingham, Robin Kelley argues that the different social realities of the black poor and segments of the black working class in Birmingham led them to adopt different tactics, violent tactics, than the civil rights leadership who considered them "riff-raff." In particular, many of their grievances as a class were with the police, and that was the focus for many of the violent confrontations.[37]

One of the key features of the preceding two decades' emphasis on electoral politics was that gender and class divisions were submerged due both to the racial gulf in politics, as seen in political opinion and electoral data, and appeals of black elites to unite behind "our" candidate. There was also the implicit social contract within the black community which held that emphasis on electoral activity at both the national and local levels would benefit the entire community. However, at neither level has this contract been fulfilled. Reducing African American unemployment by a mere 2.4 percent over four years—the difference in black unemployment during the Clinton presidency—does not make much difference if the starting unemployment rate is the 12 to 20 percent African Americans have experienced during most of the 1980s and 1990s. Moreover, African American mayors in city after city, from Los Angeles to Newark, have also been cutting services and jobs. As electoral options become less attractive and more risky, increased debate and uncertainty will lead to greater volatility. As African Americans consider political arenas other than electoral, whether it be the Supreme Court or the streets, gender and class divisions will be harder to suppress and keep in the closet. The cries of "what is best for the race" are much noisier and diverse. The continued deterioration of the American political economy has important consequences for black women as well as black men, a fact some social scientists seem to overlook. Only by understanding how the restructuring of the American political and economic systems work their way through the interactions of race, class, and gender can African Americans hope to forge a political agenda that has some chance of addressing the crises of the black community.

What Next?

I have argued elsewhere that the future of African American politics will be structured by the economic and racial climates of the next several decades.[38]

Unfortunately, I believe that the most pessimistic scenario—the one I call the "politics of isolation"—is the one most likely to evolve. The consequences of a continued deterioration in both the economic and racial climate would be the increasing political and perhaps spatial isolation of African Americans. The inner cities and near suburbs would become hopelessly impoverished communities, politically powerless and physically isolated from the rest of American society. Residential segregation would continue to prevent all but a few African Americans from escaping the black ghetto. The African American middle class would be increasingly vulnerable as politicians in the mold of Jesse Helms and David Duke capitalize more and more on white frustration and racism in their efforts to reverse the hard-earned gains garnered as a result of the civil rights and Black Power movements. Radical politics would flourish not only among less affluent African Americans but could spread to their middle-class peers.

However, intense debate over agendas, strategy, and tactics are also highly likely in the face of this bleak and volatile scenario. The relative lack of power of the black community will cause some to argue (incorrectly, in my view) that the African American agenda should be narrowed to only "core" issues. African Americans' participation in third party and other independent political movements is also likely to increase, perhaps leading to the creation of an independent black political party.

The flames over Los Angeles severely distressed the black community both internally and in terms of its relationship with white America. Numerous middle-class African Americans gave personal testimonials following the Simi Valley verdict, stating that despite their accomplishments the verdict reinforced their feelings that African Americans had no chance of justice in this nation. There were significant gaps between the emphasis African American and white leaders put on the events in Los Angeles. White national politicians of both political parties were soon bent, once again, on ignoring urban and racial issues.

Significant internal divisions are evident over what tactics to pursue to rectify the problems of the black community. As the gulf in economic, social, and political dimensions between African Americans and whites increases, the potential for widening divisions within the black community and for that community's isolation from the rest of the nation increases as well. In such an environment, another legacy of the Reagan-Bush regime, one would expect not only continued volatility in African American political opinion but also heightened potential for its fragmentation.

9

AFRICAN AMERICAN PRESSURE GROUP POLITICS

The Reformulation of a Reply Brief to the Supreme Court by J. Clay Smith, Jr., Robert Goodwin, and Elias Blake

• • • • • • •

Hanes Walton, Jr.

African American political and social history is filled with incidents in which apparently innocuous devices and efforts have wreaked havoc in the black community. African Americans have developed systems of detection that are centered either in groups, organizations, or institutions, or, should the aggregate sentinels fail, in a single individual[1]. Figure 9.1 shows the structure of this two-tier system. The first tier includes the traditional civil rights organizations: the NAACP, the Legal Defense Fund, and the Urban League. It also includes the educational watchdog organizations: the United Negro College Fund (UNCF) and the National Association for Equal Opportunity in Higher Education (NAFEO). Finally, this first tier includes political and legal groups such as the Congressional Black Caucus (CBC) and the National Bar Association (NBA). At the second tier stand attentive individuals within the African American community. These strategically located individuals (as opposed to placed, for no one gives them their role, they merely assume it) remain vigilant to currents that might harm or disadvantage the African American community and its institutions. Their main role is to sound the alarm and mobilize the first-tier groups.

Once some new overt or clandestine attack is detected a call to action and collective mobilization is set off in the African American community. But the outcome always hangs in the balance. As a racial minority, African Americans

FIGURE 9.1

Key Organizations in the Two Tiers Defending African American Public Higher Education

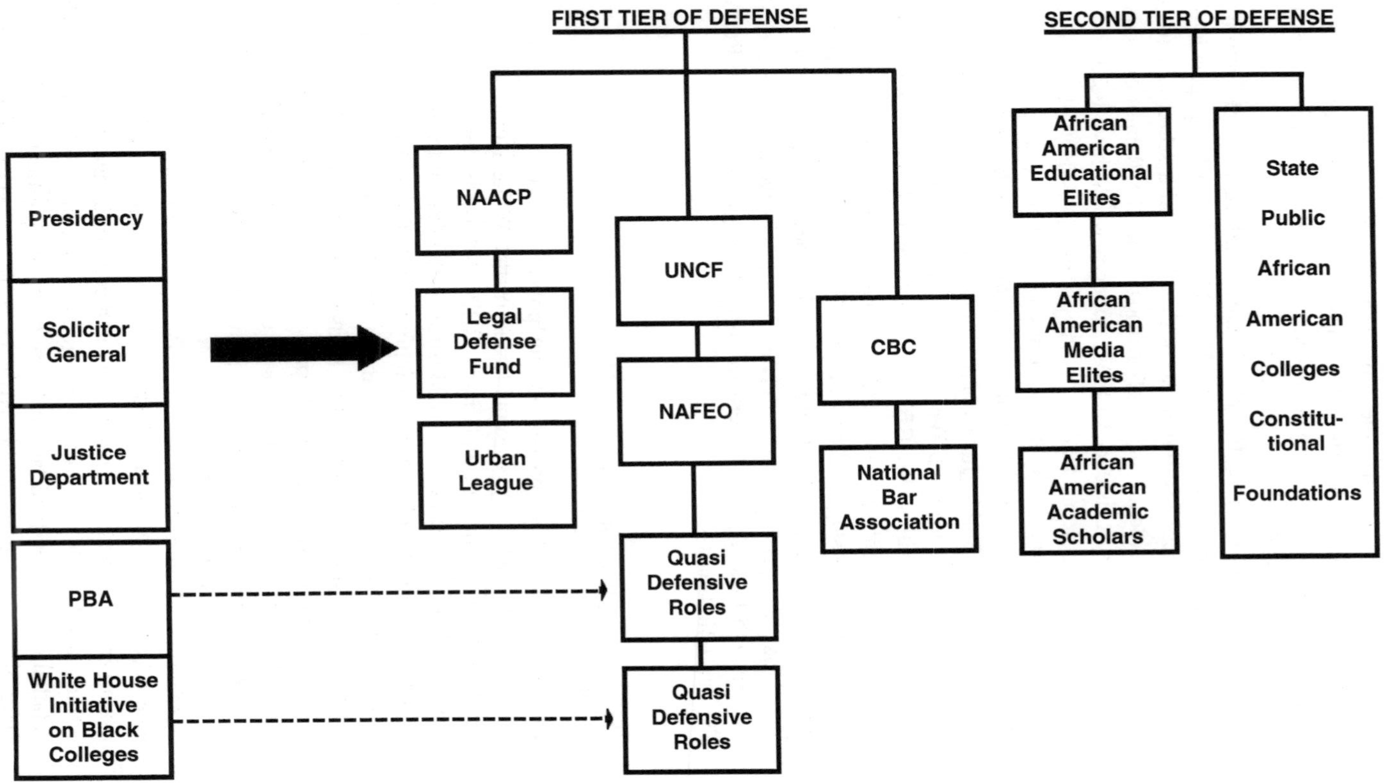

can never be certain that the adversary can be overwhelmed. Retreats are necessary, and the community regroups to fortify itself against renewed onslaughts. Even when African Americans achieve a victory, it is often a pyrrhic one. Justice does not always prevail.[2]

Although the struggle for maintenance and support of historically black public colleges and universities (HBPCUs) both predates and postdates the Bush administration, these institutions were the object of a secret assault engineered by the Bush presidency in October 1992. Had the Republican conservatives prevailed, the very existence of these colleges would have been in jeopardy. A lone sentinel, Dr. Elias Blake, Jr., the former president of Clark College in Atlanta and a legal researcher who has worked for years on issues related to African American colleges, sounded the alarm. Blake and a few troops, like attorney J. Clay Smith, Jr., Robert Goodwin, Executive Director of the U.S. Department of Education's White House Initiative on Historically Black Colleges and Universities (WHIHBCU), and former Howard University president James Cheek fought a pitched battle to stave off the attack. Their battle plan was comprised of two stages, almost all of which took place behind political closed doors: (1) to expose and bring to public view the attempt to destroy the HBPCUs, and (2) to reformulate the device that would have constitutionally undermined these African American institutions—in this case, a Reply Brief to the Supreme Court.

Data and Methodology

Did African American pressure-group politics affect the outcome of a secret maneuver by conservative Republicans in the White House during the Bush presidency to impair and undermine HBPCUs? To explore this question in an empirical way, it is necessary to construct a reliable and valid data base. In this instance, the Justice Department's reply brief to the Supreme Court—in its two versions, one before and one after the intervention of African American pressure groups—is both the "instrument of transformation" of the political context and the key data source for this chapter. Additional data are derived from the Supreme Court decision in the case of *United States v. Fordice* (formerly *Ayers v. Mabus*). These three documents provide the crucial evidence bases and the outcome materials for this study.

Other pertinent documentary sources supplement these data bases. Goodwin, who was running President Bush's Points of Light Foundation in June 1992, when I interviewed him, shared with me a copy of a memo he had written while serving at WHIHBCU (hereafter referred to as the Goodwin Memo). This memo detailed day-by-day (and later hour-by-hour) the political negotiations that took place behind the scenes of the HBPCU crisis. Ms. Hazel Mingo, who replaced Goodwin as director of WHIHBCU, provided me with the following documents:

President Bush's Executive Order 12877, which established WHIHBCU on April 28, 1989; available minutes of WHIHBCU board meetings; the 1990 annual federal performance report on executive agency actions to assist HBCUs; a list of federal agency representatives on the board; a list of members of the group called the "President's Board of Advisors (PBA) on Historically Black Colleges and Universities," a quasi-governmental agency established by Executive Order Number 12677 and chaired by Cheek; and a number of correlative items about the initiative's activities.[3] In addition to these documents and materials, she searched her news clippings and press releases files to no avail.[4] Ms. Mingo also promised me a copy of the PBA's initial report to President Bush, writing in response to my request: "with reference to the Advisory Board's report to the President, the deadline for submission has been extended until August 1, 1992. We will forward a copy of the document as soon as it is available for release."[5] The report was never released to the public, but the available documents provide a clear paper trail of the people and governmental units involved.

Smith's fully documented and scholarly chronicle of events (hereafter referred to as the Smith Document) provides lengthy and profound coverage of the African American pressure group's efforts. It was Smith, who served as legal counsel to the National Association for Equal Opportunity in Higher Education (NAFEO), an umbrella organization of African American public colleges, who brought the nature of the behind-the-scenes struggle to save HBPCUs to my attention. He had long been critical of the Bush administration's manueverings against HBPCUs and was the legal "point man" for the African American pressure group involved in the October crisis. In addition to this document, Smith provided me with a copy of NAFEO's amicus curiae (friend-of-the-court) brief and other useful documents pertaining to the *Ayers* (later *Fordice*) case as well as clippings from newspapers and relevant journalistic publications.

Additionally, a professor of public policy, Cheryl Miller of the University of Maryland-Baltimore County, long an observer of the struggle of African American colleges, sent me clippings on the commentary that surfaced in key educational and judicial journals about the *Ayers* case and the Supreme Court's ruling. Leslie McLemore, a professor of political science at Jackson State University, a resident and political activist in the state where the case originated (Mississippi), also supplied me with useful documents and materials on the legal machinations and ramifications of the case.

For insights into the interaction of so-called African American pressure groups and the White House players in the struggle to "reform" the reply brief, I conducted interviews with Smith, Goodwin, and Blake.[6]

These documents and interviews provide the basis for the content analysis methodology used in this search to determine the influence of an African American pressure group on White House decision makers around the issue of the fate of the nation's HBPCUs in an era of contextual transformation. The insights derived may be useful in developing at least a preliminary theory about African American pressure group politics in a specific era.

African American Pressure Group Politics: An Overview of the Literature

African American political scientist Ralph Bunche was the pioneer scholar in the investigation and analysis of African American pressure group politics.[7] His work focused on (1) the identification of African American interest groups, (2) the strengths and weaknesses of these groups' lobbying tactics and techniques, and (3) their policy successes and failures. For all practical purposes Bunche set the direction for research in this area; his approach was no different from that of other mainstream scholars such as Arthur F. Bently and Peter Odegard.[8]

Following Bunche's work, there appeared a rash of works that were singularly focused on the NAACP.[9] The 1960s and 1970s witnessed an expansion from a focus on the premier civil rights organization to investigations of other groups such as SNCC, CORE, the National Welfare Rights Organization, and the Urban League, along with more studies on the NAACP. However, even though the scope broadened, most of the new single-organization studies were undertaken by race relations specialists and academicians. Consequently, these studies were concerned primarily with organizational imperatives and offer minute details about organizational in-fighting and leadership problems, concluding that the groups' failures to achieve their objectives could be attributed to internal dissension and conflict.[10]

African American political scientists began themselves producing works on African American interest group politics following the Bunche approach. For example, in his work, "Negro Interest Group Strategies," Harry Bailey divides African American pressure groups into two categories: middle-class political groups and nonviolent direct-action groups. Into the first category he places the NAACP; groups like SCLC, CORE, and SNCC fit into the second category, which he concludes have been most successful.[11]

Following these scholarly forays evaluating the tactics and procedures of African American pressure groups, interest shifted to the nature of the protests raised by organizations involved in the fading civil rights movement. This focus was more the concern of African American historians than anyone else.[12] It gradually gave way to a review of the role of African American pressure groups in the voting rights struggle of the late 1970s and early 1980s.[13] A host of more specialized pressure groups, such as organizations of African American elected officials (i.e., the Congressional Black Caucus, the National Conference of Black Mayors, and the Georgia Association of Black Elected Officials), captured some attention and fostered some analysis,[14] but they were overshadowed by the scholar's concern with the voting rights issue.[15]

Another point of departure was taken by scholars such as James Jennings in their work on African American pressure group activity at the grass roots level in America's urban centers. They explored the efforts of crusading African American community activists and a newly emergent set of protest organizations on behalf of those poor and marginalized African Americans caught in the nation's slums and hobbled by the rising drug and crime culture. The future course and struggles of these organizations and individuals, with their new strategies of self-reliance—an outgrowth of the retrenchment of government during the Reagan-Bush era—are only partially understood and realized. Thus there is much research yet to be done.[16] The final chapter on these new urban grass roots pressure groups is yet to be written.

Overall, the literature on African American interest and pressure groups is fragmentary and unsystematic. It is predominantly focused upon civil rights pressure groups—their strategies, strengths, and weaknesses, singularly and collectively. Moreover, it is basically devoid of the insights and intellectual substance that would help readers to frame a vision of nontraditional (or nonclassical) pressure group activity, particularly in an era of contextual transformation. The current literature provides little in the way of theoretical propositions about African American pressure group politics in such eras primarily because the variables of leadership, tactics, and procedures have superseded that of context.

Local Context as a Force in Shaping National Context

Contextual transformation does not simply start at the national level. On the contrary, regional (particularly southern) and local contexts generate pressures and ideas that bubble up to the national level. Many times, these local ideas have been percolating, indeed simmering, for years; and they become the trigger for national political actions and contextual transformation efforts. Paul Light is a student of how presidents set their agendas. In his view:

> The sources of ideas are often the sources of political pressure. As presidents set the domestic agenda, they face considerable lobbying from outside interests. . . . Ideas do not enter the White House under neutral conditions. The vast majority of ideas enter the domestic policy process with some pressure attached. . . . Interest groups, executive agencies, even White House staff may add to the clamor for a specific idea. Although interest groups, the parties, and the media are only a limited source of new ideas, they are formidable sources of pressure.[17]

This is particularly true for interest groups when they are part of the president's winning electoral coalition.

> Interest groups are approached in a somewhat different light. Whereas the President attempts to maintain contact with party leaders, there is a conscious effort to avoid interaction with most interest groups. Unless the interest group is a key member of the President's electoral coalition, there is only limited contact.[18]

Light further notes that even when these interest groups are a part of a president's winning electoral coalition, they "operate most effectively at the subterranean levels . . . influencing the White House staff and the President."[19] In this way, they become a driving force in determining the president's agenda as well as a force in getting the president to alter the political context in their favor. Beginning in the Reagan years and continuing through the Bush presidency, the South was such an interest group and part of the winning electoral coalition. Therefore, when the Reagan-Bush presidencies responded via transformation of the political context, they were, for all intents and purposes, responding to their constituencies.

The most persistent area seeking contextual maintenance was the state of Mississippi,[20] which sought during the Reagan-Bush years to continue "its policy of de jure segregation in its public university system . . . despite the Supreme Court decisions in *Brown v. Board of Education* I and II."[21] Private African American petitioners initiated a lawsuit, *Ayers v. Mabus,* in 1975 with the United States Department of Justice joining the case on behalf of the plaintiff, charging that "state officials had failed to satisfy their obligation under . . . the Equal Protection Clause of the Fourteenth Amendment and Title VI of the Civil Rights Act of 1964 to dismantle the dual system" of higher education in Mississippi. At the District Court level, the African American petitioners argued that "in various ways the State continued to reinforce historic, race-based distinctions among the universities." The respondents argued that the state had "fulfilled its duty to disestablish its state-imposed segregation system by implementing and maintaining good faith, nondiscriminating, race-neutral policies and practices in student admission, faculty hiring, and operations."[22] After twelve years of attempts "to reach a consensual resolution through voluntary dismantlement" all of which failed because the state plans favored or were biased toward the white universities, the suit went to trial in 1987. By the time the trial was over, some 71 witnesses and 56,700 pages of exhibits had been presented. Based upon this evidence, the District Court found "that current actions on the part of the defendant (state) demonstrate conclusively that the defendants are fulfilling their affirmative duty to disestablish the former de jure segregated system of higher education."[23]

The case subsequently went to the federal Court of Appeals. The local context was slowly and gradually moving to the national level.

As the federal district court's decision continues, "The Court of Appeals reheard the case en banc and affirmed the decision of the District Court with a simple exception. . . . It did not disturb the District Court's findings of fact or conclusions of law."[24] In the Court of Appeals's view, "the record makes clear that Mississippi has adopted and implemented race neutral policies for operating its colleges and universities and that all students have real freedom of choice to attend the college or university they wish."[25] In the view of J. Clay Smith, however, race-neutral methodology had prevailed to maintain a system of constitutional inequalities.[26]

African Americans had lost at two levels in the judicial system. On November 13, 1991, the case was argued by Attorney Alvin O. Chambliss before the Supreme Court.

The Supreme Court handed down its decision on June 26, 1992. In an 8-1 decision, the Court indicated that "the primary issue in this case is whether the State has met its affirmative duty to dismantle its prior dual university system." After stating the main legal issues involved, the findings stressed that "we do not agree with the Court of Appeals or the District Court, however, that the adoption and implementation of race-neutral policies alone suffice to demonstrate that the State has completely abandoned its prior dual system."[27] For the Supreme Court, the equal protection clause of the Constitution was "offended by sophisticated as well as simple-minded models of discrimination." Hence, "the existence of a race-neutral admissions policy does not mean that such a policy alone cures the constitutional violation of a dual system." In fact, "even after a state dismantles its segregative admissions policy," the decision stated, "there may still be state action that is traceable to the State's prior de jure segregation and that continues to foster segregation."[28] The Court's position was clear:

"Our decision establishes that a State does not discharge its constitutional obligations until it eradicates policies and practices traceable to its prior de jure dual system that continue to foster segregation."[29]

In the Supreme Court's reading of the facts in *Ayers v. Mabus,* several surviving aspects of Mississippi's prior dual system were constitutionally suspect. Even though such policies may be race-neutral on their face, the Court decreed, "they substantially continue constitutional inequalities," and still had a "discriminatory taint."[30] As the Court subsequently ordered, "because the District Court and the Court of Appeals failed to consider the State duties in their proper light, the cases must be remanded."[31] The state of Mississippi was held to be "in violation of the Constitution and Title VI"; and the Court ordered remedial proceedings conducted.[32]

The local context had reached the national level. Yet, in this instance, the Supreme Court refused to let the local context become nationalized, even though the Court had been remade, during the Reagan-Bush years, through the appointment of a conservative majority to that body.

African American Pressure Politics and the Bush White House

Reagan's vice president, George Bush, defeated the Democratic challenger Michael Dukakis in the 1988 presidential election,[33] and promised to continue to transform the political context of racial divisiveness that his predecessor had launched.[34] The South, as a part of Bush's winning election coalition, fully expected that issues would be resolved in their favor or that its interests would be supported. By the time *Ayers* arrived for resolution at the Supreme Court in 1991, since African Americans had not been a central part of the Republican electoral coalition, the only decision the Bush administration had to make was how best to support the interest of its electoral constituency, which included Mississippi and the South. White House operatives seized upon the most immediate and appropriate means, the filing of a writ of certiorari (a request to be heard by the Supreme Court) in the *Ayers* case. The language and legal nuances in this brief set off the alarm and the ensuing mobilization of African American pressure groups.

Although the deadline for filing for certiorari was February 25, 1991, the Justice Department filed its brief requesting the Supreme Court to hear the *Ayers* case on January 28. Prior to filing its brief, the Justice Department held meetings with attorneys Alvin O. Chambliss, Jr. and Robert Pressman, co-counsel for Mr. and Mrs. Ayers and the other plaintiffs. At these meetings, the attorneys attempted to persuade the Department to align its brief with the legal themes of the petitioners. Other meetings took place between Solicitor General Starr, Smith (as NAFEO's counsel), Blake, Julius L. Chambers, and Janell M. Byrd of the NAACP Legal Defense Fund; attorney William Coleman, and others. As Smith notes: "This brief took a more narrow view as relates to the liability of Mississippi's discriminatory conduct than the arguments urged by petitioners and NAFEO, but it supported [the] plaintiff's petition for certiorari." Consequently, a counter-petition for certiorari was filed by NAFEO, the National Bar Association, and the Congressional Black Caucus. After receiving the sundry petitions for certiorari, the Supreme Court agreed to hear the *Ayers* case on April 15, 1991.[35]

The struggle over the Justice Department's brief began in earnest when Elias Blake, after reading that document, sounded the alarm by calling NAFEO and PBA members Goodwin and Smith.[36] Already, on November 20, 1990, Smith notes the following:

> concerned that the Justice Department, which had been in and out of the *Ayers* case over the years, would make no effort to support the anticipated petition by plaintiffs for review to the United States Supreme Court of the decisions in *Ayers III,* [I] sent a letter to Kenneth W. Starr, the Solicitor General, asking him to give the Ayers decision *a very hard look.*[37]

In his letter, Smith stressed that the race-neutral methodology used by *Ayers,* if allowed to stand, would "eventually close all of the historically Black public colleges."[38] Realizing that his letter would have little impact on the Solicitor General, Smith sent copies of the letter to NAFEO members (HBCU college presidents) and key civil rights lawyers and groups who were unaware of the ramifications of *Ayers,* especially its potential effects on HBPCUs. He informed Dr. Samuel L. Myers, the president of NAFEO,[39] of his concerns, as well as leaders of other civil rights groups, including the NAACP, the Legal Defense Fund, a few black Republicans, the National Bar Association, and the Congressional Black Caucus. Figure 9.2 reveals the people and groups that were mobilized into action by Smith to reform the Justice Department's brief.

As the Justice Department was developing its brief, Smith, in consultation with Blake, was assembling a team of young, bright African American lawyers including Erroll D. Brown, Cynthia R. Mabry, and Lisa C. Wilson to prepare the petition for the African American pressure groups. By May 1991, Smith's team had been extended to include attorney William A. Blakey; Professor Stephen Halpern of the State University of New York-Buffalo; and Professor Alfred D. Mathewson of the University of New Mexico Law School. Their goal was to file NAFEO's brief on the merits of African American public colleges a month before it was due.[40]

The Justice Department's position on the nation's historically black public colleges had also become the center of attention and concern for the members of the PBA. On June 26, 1991, just a few days before the Department filed its brief, Dr. James Cheek, the group's chairman, sent a letter to President Bush informing him of a resolution adopted by the PBA "for your immediate and urgent attention." The resolution read, in part:

> We convey to you our grave and urgent concern that the legal position of the federal government in the *Ayers v. Mabus* case, presently being finalized by the Solicitor General's office . . . does not reflect constructively and productively on the HBCUs, nor on all other HBCUs, similarly situated in the United States.[41]

The White House did not immediately respond to Cheek, an influential African American Republican and supporter of President Bush, prior to the filing of the Department of Justice's brief. On June 27, 1991, Thurgood Marshall announced that he was retiring from the Supreme Court. Justice Marshall's announcement rocked the African American community. It also meant that possibly no black person would be on the Supreme Court when *Ayers* was decided. Given the antiblack sentiment demonstrated by the Reagan and Bush administrations in a number of areas[42] and a number of troubling decisions handed down by the Supreme Court in the area of civil rights,[43] the plight of the HBPCUs heightened the concerns of African Americans, concerns that did not abate when President Bush announced the nomination of Judge Clarence Thomas as Justice Marshall's successor to the Court on July 1, 1991.[44]

The Department of Justice's brief was filed a week or so after the Thomas

FIGURE 9.2

Key Pressure Groups and Agencies, and the Lines of Communication, in Reformulating the Reply Brief to the Supreme Court

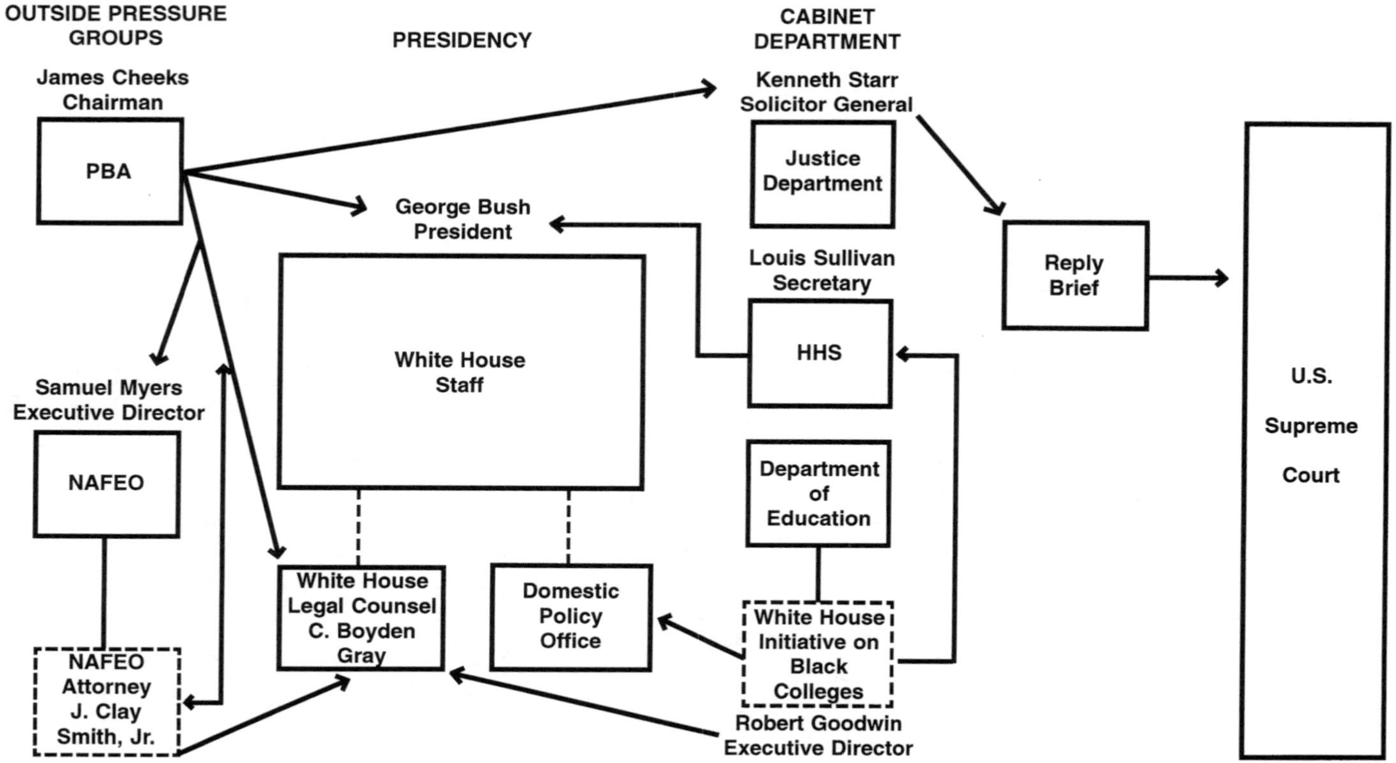

nomination. Soon after, word spread throughout the civil rights community that the brief, though supportive of the black plaintiffs, contained some hidden bombshells that would, if adopted by the Supreme Court, undercut HBPCUs. It was suspected that the Justice Department's brief was substantially watered down from the brief recommended to the Solicitor General by John R. Dunne, the assistant attorney general for civil rights in the Department.

Perhaps the clamor surrounding the Justice Department's brief accelerated a belated response to Cheek's letter. On August 2, 1992, Nelson Lund, Bush's associate counsel, informed Dr. Cheek of the President's strong support of black colleges, stating that "the role of such institutions in a sound educational system is not, however, at issue in the *[Ayers]* case." Regarding the funding of HBPCUs, a matter that was not specifically raised in Cheek's letter, Lund stated that "eliminating duplicative programs, which the Government argues is required by the law, may well as a practical matter, resulting in increased funding for formerly all-black institutions."[45]

Given Smith's interpretation of portions of the brief, the representations of Lund were not received with confidence. In fact, the PBA, spurred to action by Elias Blake, wondered how a brief that could have such potentially adverse consequences on HBPCUs had been filed without any consultation with the PBA. This matter received much discussion during a meeting of the PBA held in early September 1991.

At that meeting, Dr. Arthur E. Thomas, vice-chairman of the PBA and president of Central State University, issued a statement saying, "the record will show that Historically Black Colleges and Universities have earned the right to continue to exist."[46] Indeed, the tone of Thomas's statement was one of heightened concern about the future security of HBCUs. Referring directly to the Department of Justice, Thomas wrote:

> In addition to the position being taken by the states as it related to Historically Black Colleges and Universities, there are "mixed" signals coming from the Federal government. The President demonstrates support for the HBCUs through his support of the [United Negro College Fund], the establishment of this Board, his Executive Order No. 12677, and other initiatives. However, at the same time, the U.S. Justice Department is sounding a retreat from assistance to public HBCUs. No greater example of that can be found than in the recent Solicitor General's Brief on behalf of the U.S. in the Mississippi Higher Education case.[47]

The next day, September 10, 1992, the PBA met with President Bush. Robert Goodwin of WHIHBCU described their concerns:

> In our September Board meeting, which was held in concert with the Annual Fall Congress which is held by the White House Initiative Office

> there was a meeting scheduled with the President that was intended to basically establish some level of dialogue with him about the general progress that was being made or not being made, as the case may be, in regards to federal funding going to the HBCU community. That was the stated purpose of the meeting. But it was determined in preliminary conversations with members of the Board that we ought to take this opportunity to again express our concerns to the President about the way that this case was going.[48]

Goodwin described the meeting:

> On Monday, September 10, the President met with his Board of Advisors. Immediately prior, he met with a subset of the nation's education writers, at which time he was asked about the *Ayers* case. He said, "we support historically black colleges. . . . I don't want anything passed or added that would detract from what I think is a very specific and important role for these historically Black colleges. And our administration will not be taking new steps to make things more difficult there."[49]

Later that afternoon, an ad hoc group of PBA members, Goodwin, and Smith met with Lund and C. Boyden Gray, the White House legal counsel.

> Mr. Gray indicated: (1) that he, too, was unfamiliar with the case, (2) that there was sufficient time to affect the government's position, (3) that he would research the case, (4) that he sought the input of the NAFEO Council, (5) that his instructions from "his boss" were to try to "fix" the problem, and (6) that he would advise the ad hoc group of his finding. Therefore, the President's legal counsel deferred the discussion to the President's associate counsel, Nelson Lund.[50]

During this meeting, Cheek informed Gray that he had just met with President Bush and John Sununu, the President's chief of staff. Cheek told Gray that the President had reaffirmed his commitment to black colleges and had expressly stated that he had not directed any change in domestic policy, nor recommended any change in legal policy to alter those views.[51] Why, Cheek asked, had the Justice Department veered from Bush's existing policy of enhancing these institutions? Gray deferred this question to Lund, stating that he was not familiar with the details of the case. This, however, was questionable, as the college presidents would later comment, because it seemed highly unlikely that Gray would be unfamiliar with a brief that could have such an adverse effect on black colleges and that would be decided in 1992, an election year. Lund referred to his earlier letter to Cheek and stated that the brief would have no adverse effect on HBPCUs or HBCUs.

As NAFEO legal counsel, Smith explained the group's legal position on the *Ayers* case during this meeting. He indicated that one of the most important and historical, as well as most vexing, issues surrounding the survival of the HBPCUs was the question of disparate state funding based on race. He noted that some of the language in the Justice Department's brief on *Ayers* was radically different from any brief that had been filed by the Department in previous desegregation cases involving the equal protection clause. In effect, based on the language in the brief, racially discriminatory funding in Mississippi's system of higher education was sanctioned by the Constitution. He referred to the following excerpt from the brief:

> we discern [no] independent obligation flowing from the Constitution to correct disparities between what was provided historically black schools—in term of funding, programs facilities, and so forth—and what was provided historically white schools. . . . There can be no question that the historically black colleges share the distinctive trait of a shameful history of inadequate state funding. What is not clear is why the Constitution demands that, at this late date, the State turn its energies to redressing an historical imbalance in spending on those institutions, rather than on ensuring that each of its young people be free to choose among all that the State has to offer, limited only by ability and not by race. . . . As a practical matter, moreover, it will be an enormous, and endlessly litigious, undertaking to ensure that there are no longer any spending disparities.[52]

This language, Smith explained to Gray, sent a clear signal to the Supreme Court that funding of HBPCUs on the basis of race was not covered by the Fourteenth Amendment. In his view, such an interpretation could have far-reaching ramifications for the faculties, students, and potential students of these schools. It was feared that the states would allow black public colleges to "wither and die on the vine." Smith further informed Gray and Lund that the language in the brief invited the Court to limit the exercise of judicial review in matters of disparate public higher education funding based on race because of the perceived demands that would be placed on the courts.[53] He reminded Gray that civil rights cases should be treated no differently than other complex civil matters such as antitrust litigation.

The last issue raised by Smith at this meeting was NAFEO's objection to footnote 39 of the Justice Department's brief. This note, buried near the end of the brief, explained the difference between duplication in facilities and disparity in facilities and funding in language that Smith claimed was confusing and not based on any principals of law. The language suggested that blacks, like whites, would choose to attend historically white schools if Mississippi's dual-system of higher education was ended, and added that "disparities . . . are not segregation in effect." Smith urged that the footnote be deleted.[54]

Gray stated that he was not prepared to respond to the technical issues raised by Smith and he suggested that the group's concerns be put in writing. On September 13, 1991, Cheek sent a detailed legal analysis to Gray via Smith.[55] Thirteen days later, Myers sent a second opposing legal analysis to the White House.[56]

According to Goodwin, at the September 10 meeting with the PBA, the President indicated "that he was unaware of the potentially disastrous consequences of the case and wanted to devote staff time necessary to understand the issue and intervene, if possible."[57] On September 26, Michael Williams, the African American Assistant Secretary of Education,[58] informed Goodwin that, despite the Cheek and Myers statements, the government's reply brief, a copy of which he had just received, was virtually unchanged from the original.[59] Goodwin immediately notified Cheek and both initiated plans to convene a second meeting of the relevant parties.

As of early October 1991, there had been no movement by the Bush administration to address the concerns of NAFEO or the PBA, and no action had been taken by the White House to follow up on the September meetings. The inaction on the part of the White House, possibly due to the administration's miscalculation of the depth of the concerns raised by the nation's black college presidents, prompted Cheek to enlist the support of Louis W. Sullivan, the Secretary of the Department of Health and Human Services and the only African American in the President's Cabinet. On October 2, 1991, Cheek sent a letter to Secretary Sullivan:

> On September 9, 1991, several of the presidents of HBCUs and I met with the President at the White House to express our concerns about critical portions of the Department of Justice's brief before the United States Supreme Court in *United States v. Mabus*. . . . We were shocked to learn that when the United States Supreme Court decided to hear the appeal . . . the Department of Justice radically changed a twenty-year position abandoning the enhancement remedy. The brief went even further to voluntarily assert that nothing in the constitution required a state to correct past acts of racial discrimination by an enhancement policy remedy. In short, the Department of Justice now argues that black colleges, their faculties and students, long denied equal funding by a discriminating state, are now without a remedy to correct past discrimination. The brief even suggests in so many words that even if HBCUs were equally funded, that Whites would not attend them.[60]

Cheek concluded that if the Court accepted the reasoning of the brief, public black colleges were doomed, and private black colleges would soon meet a similar fate.[61]

The continued inaction of the White House showed that the office of the

President's legal counsel had not taken the Cheek and Myers communications seriously. On October 5, Cheek informed Gray that he had learned that Gray had communicated to Sullivan and other officials in the Bush administration that Smith and the PBA had " 'dropped the ball' [regarding our] promise to provide you with specific language that we wanted placed in the Department of Justice Reply Brief." Additionally, he related, "we are being told that you are reporting to Secretary Sullivan and others that, to date, you have received nothing from me."[62] Cheek continued:

> Many of my colleagues and I are deeply troubled that you appear to treat this matter with recklessness indifference and in a manner that ill serves the President. . . . We hope you will exhaust every option available to you and your colleagues to spare us all the pain and grief that are certain to flow from the misrepresentation of the policies of the President. . . . One option is to have the Department of Justice . . . in its reply brief, inform the Supreme Court that it is withdrawing pp. 31 and 33 of its brief already before the Court. Another option, and one which we prefer, is for the Justice Department to withdraw from the case.[63]

A few days after Cheek's letter reached Gray, Anita Faye Hill, a professor at the Oklahoma University School of Law and former member of Clarence Thomas's staff at the Equal Employment Opportunity Commission, disclosed that Thomas had sexually harassed her while she was employed at EEOC. From October 7 to 11, every newspaper in the nation was reporting on the most sensational news story ever to break about a nominee to the Supreme Court.[64]

On October 7, Goodwin and Cheek told Smith that a meeting with the Solicitor General would occur that day at 1 p.m. at the Department of Justice. At the meeting, representatives of NAFEO, the PBA, Secretary Sullivan's office, and Milton Bins, the chairman of the Council of One Hundred, a black Republican group, would at last be able to express their concerns about the language in the Department's reply brief directly to the Solicitor General, Kenneth Starr.

Judge Starr was accompanied to the meeting by three of his aides. He sat at the head of a long table flanked by Cheek on his left and Smith on his right. Cheek and Smith took different approaches during the meeting. Cheek was firm in his assertions that Starr's brief had to be either revised or withdrawn because it threatened the survival of HBPCUs and was apparently inconsistent with the President's domestic policy. Cheek's position, that these colleges had to be enhanced and supported and that they had a constitutional right to exist, seemed to irk Starr,[65] who defended his brief and challenged the group to show him just how his brief would hurt the colleges.

Smith's role was to provide details on the legal position of the group. He reminded Starr that he had set forth his concerns about the Fifth Circuit's opinion on *Ayers* in a letter to him on November 20, 1990. Smith then reviewed the language of the brief with Starr in the same manner that he had reviewed it with Gray in the September 10 meeting. His argument was supported by the NAFEO presidents present, who provided Starr with additional information about the realities their institutions faced. One of the presidents told Starr that claims that the Constitution did not prohibit disparities in funding of white and black colleges were already being "tossed in our faces."[66]

The meeting lasted an hour, but little headway was made. After it ended, the African American attendees retired to the Marriott Hotel to assess the meeting and determine whether or not the group should issue a press release criticizing the Bush administration's reversal of its enhancement policy for HBPCUs. The group could not agree on the press release but they agreed that the legal position in the original brief had to be withdrawn in the reply brief which was due to be filed in the Supreme Court by October 9.

As the countdown for the filing of the reply brief drew near, telephone calls were made and the Smith's legal analysis of the situation was circulated to key, and to certain sympathetic black political operatives within the Bush administration. Students on some of the HBPCU campuses were poised to begin protests to save their schools. Clarence Thomas, in the meantime, was about to face the nation regarding Anita Hill's sexual harassment allegations.

Some HBPCU presidents who had pledged their support for Thomas and who had lobbied on his behalf even after Hill's claim, began to assess the damage to their reputations if President Bush did not intervene to declare his position on the *Ayers* brief. Franklyn Jenifer, the president of Howard University, had "assured the White House" that he would support the Thomas nomination. While Jenifer claimed that he had "[spoken] favorably about Thomas on his own volition" even after being criticized by Democratic members of Congress, he "later refused to go along with . . . a group of black college presidents to issue a formal endorsement of Thomas."[67] No doubt reluctance to support Clarence Thomas increased when the press reported that yet another black woman had charged Thomas with sexual harassment as well.[68]

On the afternoon of October 8, Cheek called Smith to ask him to contact Gray once again. As Smith recalled:

> I called Mr. Gray, who was not available, around midday. I was anxious about the conversation because I knew that this discussion was critical to the fight that had been waged regarding the brief. Mr. Gray returned my call and we began to talk about the brief and I took him line-by-line through the objectionable portions of the brief, ever reminding him of the unexplainable shift in the administration's enhancement policy, a shift that I believe had caught the President, but not all of his advisors, by surprise. The conversation was cordial, but in one instance it became pointed during my instruction to Mr. Gray on the law as I understood it. He said, "You know, we are not dumb," and I shot back, "And neither are we!" I

> informed Mr. Gray that the State of Mississippi had specifically relied on the objectionable language in their brief before the Supreme Court, so that this was sufficient proof that the language in the brief of the Department of Justice could be interpreted against the HBCUs. Mr. Gray, voicing concern, informed me that another meeting was to be held at the Department of Justice the next day and that a representative from the Office of Management and Budget and a person from his staff would be present to present some alternatives. In the meantime, I informed Mr. Gray that pages 32–34, and 41 note 39 of the Department of Justice's brief should be withdrawn or disavowed in the Reply Brief.[69]

In fact, the state of Mississippi had referred to the language in the Justice Department's brief in its own brief in support of its case.[70] The two parties' positions remained firm, and the conservative operatives in the White House simply would not budge.[71] However, on October 9th, the day the reply brief was to be filed, a third and final meeting was held between the ad hoc African American pressure group and the Republican bureaucrats. Cheek; several members of NAFEO including Calvin Burnett, president of Coppin State College, and James E. Lyons, Sr., president of Bowie State College; two representatives from Secretary Sullivan's office; a representative from the Office of Management and Budget; Nelson Lund; Milton Bins; Franklyn Jenifer; and others met again with Solicitor General Starr and three members of his staff. Again, Starr indicated that the objectionable language in the original brief would not be withdrawn or disavowed in the reply brief. After he left the meeting, Lund remained to answer questions, yet few questions were asked. Starr had answered the only question that mattered.

Finally the representative from the Office of Management and Budget, the agency with responsibility over grants and other funding issues, made a presentation to the group. He told the group of other funding avenues available to black colleges at the federal level. At that point, the group's patience ended. "We are not real estate!" exploded Smith,

> We are here on principle, the principle that disparate funding of HBCUs as against historically white colleges in Mississippi and other states based on race violates the Constitution. Receiving money solely at the federal level as an alternative to protection under the Equal Protection Clause was not what this meeting was to be about.

It was clear to Smith and the others that if the language in the July brief was not altered, something historically greater than dollars would be lost, and that something was equal protection for HBPCUs under the Constitution. After the meeting, Cheek, Goodwin, and Smith again retreated to the restaurant lounge of the Marriott, and Cheek resolved to draft and send a telex to President Bush criticizing him for his administration's flip-flop on this issue. Minutes after the telex was sent, Smith received a call in the lounge. As he recalls: "I [couldn't] remember the name of the person who called me. Quite frankly, I was not expecting a call at all. The person, I believe, was from either the White House or from the Solicitor General's office." The caller read to Smith a portion of the text that was to be filed as the Justice Department's position in its reply brief:

> More broadly, it is incumbent on the State of Mississippi to eradicate discrimination from its system of higher education. Over the years, that discrimination manifested itself in a deprivation of equitable and fair funding to historically black institutions, which sought faithfully, and under difficult circumstances, to serve the interests of black students in Mississippi. Those students were deprived of the unfettered choice demanded by the Equal Protection Clause. Indeed, those historic disparities operated to deprive prospective students of all races of the full range of choices that would have been theirs to enjoy but for the State's discriminatory practices. The time has now come to eliminate those disparities and thereby unfetter the choice of persons who can hereafter choose freely among the State's institutions of higher learning.[72]

The caller further indicated that the footnote that was to appear after the above statement would read as follows: "Suggestions to the contrary in our brief, U.S. Br. 32–34, 41 n. 39, no longer reflect the position of the United States." As Smith recalls: "I asked the caller to reread the footnote. Then I told him that I had one small addition to add. He told me that no changes could be made as this language had to be cleared and approved by the President."[73] Smith told the caller that he was satisfied with the language, and then asked him to reread it to Cheek, who concurred.[74] The concerns of the African American pressure groups had finally been addressed.

A week later, the day after Clarence Thomas had been confirmed by the Senate in a vote of 52–48,[75] the *Chronicle of Higher Education* quoted Oswald P. Bronson, president of Bethune-Cookman College and chairman of NAFEO's board, as stating that had the Justice Department's position "gone before the Supreme Court without clarification, it could very well have spelled the epitaph for the historically black college community."[76] On October 11, Goodwin, who had played an important role supporting both the President and the black college presidents, stated:

> We can all [breathe] a collective sigh of relief that the vigorous efforts by the President's Board of Advisors (PBA) on HBCUs, this office, and the leadership and membership of NAFEO and UNCF have resulted in the Justice Department (DJ) modifying its reply brief. . . . In our judgement, a severely damaging precedent . . . has been averted. . . . There are many

> heroes to be credited, i.e., PBA Chairman Dr. Jim Cheek [who] remained focused, steadfast and resolute throughout this arduous process. . . . J. Clay Smith was brilliant in his legal prowess through these crucial deliberations. It must also be properly noted that the HBCU community owes a great debt of gratitude to Secretary Lou Sullivan, who played a pivotal role in the sensitive negotiations with the White House.[77]

During the presidential campaign of 1992, President Bush's decision ordering the Solicitor General to reform the Justice Department's brief to reflect his civil rights policies toward black colleges was characterized by Republican conservatives as an "unusual order."[78]

Some Testable Propositions from the Case Study

Amicus curiae, or "friend of the Court" briefs are among the many weapons in the arsenal of techniques and strategies used by African American political pressure groups to influence and affect the political context. Such briefs, according to Harvey Mahood, submitted in legal cases of critical importance to the interests of the African American community, "represent a more indirect route to judicial influence." In Mahood's view, "Amicus briefs are interest group inputs to court personnel of additional data and arguments relevant to an impending judicial decision. . . . Though less costly and less time consuming than litigation, the submission of a brief has its limitations [and] strength."[79] Mahood further notes that "the high-water mark in Amicus briefs submitted to the Supreme Court occurred in the *Bakke* case (1978)."[80]

In Timothy J. O'Neill's pioneering study of these briefs, we learn of the strength of such legal activity in pressure group politics:

> The Bakke case attracted one of the largest set of Amicus Curiae in the history of the Supreme Court. One hundred seventeen organizations alone or collaboratively submitted fifty-one "friends-of-the-court" briefs, ensuring a broader expressions of arguments, evidence, social interest, and concerns than the advisory process of two-party conflict normally allows.[81]

The federal government (that is, the Department of Justice) also files amicus briefs in various cases before the federal courts. Or the Department of Justice can file a reply brief through the Solicitor General and in consultation with White House legal counsel, after the plaintiff and the state have filed their briefs. In these reply briefs, the Justice Department can either support the position taken in the amicus brief or it can disavow or modify its original stand.

In the mid-1970s, prior to the Reagan-Bush era, the Justice Department had filed an amicus brief in support of the contentions and positions of the African American petitioners in the Mississippi *Ayers* case. That support had changed by the time the case finally came before the Supreme Court. By that time, members of the new Bush administration, particularly key staffers in the Solicitor General's office and the office of the White House legal counsel, altered the language of the earlier brief and thereby modified the government's and the President's previously announced position in support of HBPCUs.

As Executive Director of WHIHBCU, Robert Goodwin had to relate all of his concerns about the issues surrounding the *Ayers* case through the Office of Domestic Policy. Despite Goodwin's best efforts, he was stymied at all turns. Similarly, the efforts of PBA chairman James Cheek to gain access to President Bush proved as unsuccessful as Cheek's efforts to persuade the Solicitor General or legal counsel to reform the government's brief. The only available route to the President was through Bush's lone African American cabinet official, Louis Sullivan. As Goodwin plainly states:

> Once we found all avenues of access deliberately blocked, we then started to basically start a fire that eventually reached the President and eventually caused the President, we think personally, to intercede causing the Solicitor General to reverse his earlier positions.[82]

"Presidential access for interest groups," argues one student of the process, "shall be viewed as a product not only of interest group demands but of presidential initiatives."[83] He continues by noting that such groups "can alert presidents to potential 'fire storms' of opposition or the impending actions that might be detrimental to administration goals."[84] Such observations reveal very little about the situation described in this chapter, however. In this case, presidential access for two African American pressure groups—one private (NAFEO) and one public (the WHIHBCU/PBA)—was achieved by taking an alternative route, a back road through the Cabinet to the President. The President had to intervene personally to stop members of his own staff from taking a position to which he had previously and publicly stated he was opposed.

Lobbying the President was also a more complex and costly project than most members of the African American pressure groups had imagined. Early in 1992, as NAFEO and the members of the PBA waited for the decision of the Supreme Court, it was learned that Goodwin, who as executive director of WHIHBCU had provided staff and resources to the PBA, had been fired from his position because of the role he had played in getting the Justice Department to reform its brief in the *Ayers* case. Goodwin's dismissal led PBA chairman Cheek to conclude that African American colleges were operating "in a hostile environment,"[85] a view widely shared by other HBCU presidents.[86]

On June 26, 1992, the Supreme Court issued its decision in *United States v. Fordice,* the final name of the *Ayers* case, which had been renamed with the

1991 election of Kirk Fordice to the governorship of Mississippi.[87] Legal Defense Fund attorney Alvin O. Chambliss, Jr. argued and won the case, with eight justices deciding in favor of his clients and one opposing. The ruling was significant because, for the first time, the Court extended the application of *Brown v. Board of Education* to higher education. Moreover, it rejected race-neutral policies as sufficient means of disproving present-day discrimination. Further, the Court inferred that policies "such as discriminatory funding of HBCUs on the basis of race, that affect free choice of all citizens to attend public colleges, denies Equal Protection under the Constitution."[88]

Although the Court's decision was not as specific on the HBPCU question as NAFEO would have liked it to be, Smith concluded that the decision could have been much worse.[89] According to Smith,

> NAFEO entered this case to establish the educational soundness and justification for the class of citizens, faculty and alumni of [HBPCUs]. That was the purpose of my November 20, 1990 letter to Kenneth W. Starr, the Solicitor General, and that was the point of both of the briefs that we filed in *United States v. Fordice.* Our objective was more difficult than that of the petitioner's because we supported their arguments, ones that we believed in, and attempted to show that the neutral principle methodology used by the State to establish nondiscrimination in a number of areas shielded them per se from judicial review of their past policies . . . of discriminatory funding of Black colleges. . . . I think that our brief sensitized the Court, even the one justice in dissent, [to the fact] that Black colleges, opened to all citizens who chose to attend them, may not be underfunded by the State in a discriminatory manner because they are predominately Black.[90]

In this case, access to the President was blocked even for the entities (the WHIHBCU and PBA) that the President had created specifically for that purpose. Even after gaining access to the President and winning a difficult court contest, the injured group continues to suffer. Several southern states (i.e., Louisiana and Alabama) have since presented renewed challenges to issues similar to those that figured in the *Fordice* case. Moreover, these states are also claiming that they cannot implement the decision passed down by the Court in *Fordice,* nor can they implement it fairly.[91] Their efforts are merely maneuvers to maintain the dominance of the local—that is, southern—context in political affairs. Since 1992, the Louisiana and Alabama cases have begun moving through the federal courts, and Mississippi is claiming it has no money to implement the Supreme Court decision. Time will tell if this was a pyrrhic victory.

In the final analysis, the research hypothesis—that African American pressure-group politics can be and were mobilized to resist the secret maneuvers of conservative forces to alter the political context—was supported and sustained.

10

AN AFRICAN AMERICAN GRASS ROOTS POLITICAL CAMPAIGN

Campaign Manager Richard Smiley and Candidate Barbara J. Mobley

• • • • • • •

Hanes Walton, Jr.

Political context is inherent in political campaigns and competition. In this examination of the changed American political context during the Reagan-Bush era, three crucial questions emerge about the nature of political campaigns. First, did the Republicans' efforts to redesign and restructure the political context affect state and local political campaigns involving the African American community? Second, did these campaigns change to meet the changing political context or did they change to address the issues and realities peculiar to their own local political context? Our third question is: how were issues of gender and race played out in the politics of the African American community during the Reagan-Bush years? To determine the answers we focus on a specific campaign, an electoral battle that involved two African American women candidates who competed in both the Democratic primary and run-off elections for a seat in the state legislature.

African American political campaigns are the least examined topics in African American politics. They have been studied in relationship to other political realities, but not as political entities deserving of their own special analysis and attention. Many analyses of African American presidential,[1] congressional,[2] gubernatorial,[3] and mayoral[4] contests, have described the characteristics and components of these campaigns, but usually only in passing and as part of a larger analytical scheme.

The exception to this pattern is former civil rights activist and Georgia Senator Julian Bond's pioneering monograph, *Black Candidates: Southern Campaign Experiences,* which was penned just as African Americans began entering the political process en masse in the aftermath of the civil rights movement.[5] Bond's work captured some of the initial campaign efforts of African Americans and served, in the words of Vernon Jordan, then director of the Voter Education Project (VEP), as a "guide [to be used] by other black candidates in the South."[6] Bond examined dozens of campaigns conducted under a broad range of circumstances.[7] He interviewed candidates and analyzed political contests that pitted African Americans against other African Americans or against whites in both rural and urban sections of the South for offices ranging from local magistrate to Congress. Bond's monograph offers insights into African American grass roots political campaigns and about the political context of the mid- and late 1960s and permits us to explore the local and national political contexts that preceded the Reagan-Bush era and thereby make some comparative reflections.

Data and Methodology

Four of six criteria of African American grass roots campaigns were derived from Bond's work: first, the campaign must be southern, local, and small-scale. Second, the candidate had to have little or no prior political experience. He or she could not be well-financed nor have a well-organized or professionally managed campaign organization. Essentially, such a campaign had to have an "amateur spirit" about it. Third, it had to take place in a predominantly African American district; although whites could be present in the district, they could not be the majority of registered voters. Fourth, the major media forces in the district could not have played a significant role in the campaign; that is, the contest was not of major interest or concern to the media. The fifth and sixth criteria were not derived from Bond's study. That the representative campaign had to have engaged an experienced grass roots campaign manager was included based on recent African American political experience. The role of campaign managers has changed in the two-and-a-half decades since the publication of the Bond monograph. The last criterion—that the candidate had to be a woman—was employed to control for the impact and saliency of the gender issue during the Reagan-Bush era.

The newspapers of several southern urban areas were monitored to identify a campaign that most closely matched these six criteria for a grass roots political campaign. A campaign in Decatur (DeKalb county), Georgia, in a newly reapportioned state legislative district, provided such a match. It met the geographical criteria; was waged in a predominantly African American district; pitted two poorly financed African American women candidates against each other; and the candidate's campaign manager, Richard Smiley, had broad experience in grass roots campaigns. One aspect of the campaign deviated from our criteria: nearby Atlanta's largest newspaper, *The Journal-Constitution,* did have some interest in the race because the incumbent was under indictment, alleged to have taken bribes.

In addition to meeting the criteria, this race afforded us the opportunity to look at the involvement of another well-known grass roots organizer, the Reverend Hosea Williams, who served as his candidate-daughter's campaign manager. Indeed, DeKalb county was the elder Williams's "home turf." He himself had been elected state representative in the county's District 54 (a position he held from 1974 to 1984). (Since 1990, he has served as county commissioner of District 3.) Ironically, Williams had also helped to train his daughter's opponent's campaign manager, Richard Smiley, during the civil rights movement days.

Extensive interviews were held with the key principals—campaign manager Smiley and his candidate, Attorney Barbara J. Mobley—and statistical analysis of election returns were undertaken. In addition, a content analysis was made of the newspaper articles about the race and the candidates that appeared in the Atlanta and Decatur papers.

The Political Evolution of a Grass Roots Campaign Manager: The Case of Richard Smiley

Richard Smiley began his career as a civil rights activist in the rural south at age sixteen. As he recalls:

> Well, I'm from Selma, Alabama, and right after the 1965 Voter Bill was passed, I was working with the SCLC, King's organization, and we started doing voter registration all over south Alabama. . . . And then after voter registration, we did the first "get out to vote" for black candidates that ran in Alabama. We did a seventeen-day tour where black candidates were running in Alabama.
>
> I left Selma [and] I came to Atlanta in 1965 where Hosea Williams had a [voting rights effort] called the SCOPE Project (Summer Community Organization for Political Education) where mostly white students came from the north and were introduced to the black culture in 1965.[8]

It was through his summer work with Williams that Smiley learned the rudiments of African American grass roots campaigns. His political education was interrupted by the Mississippi "March Against Fear" in 1966.[9] Due to the intensity of the march and the pressures put upon him as an organizer, Smiley eventually stopped his civil rights activism. Soon after the march, he received a fellowship to attend a private high school in California. After high school, he attended college in Utah, later returning to California, where he lived and worked for eighteen years.

Smiley continued to pursue his interest in politics. He assisted in Pat Hillard's successful 1975 campaign for the school board in south San Francisco in a 41-percent black district. In 1973, as part of the requirements for his degree from the University of Utah, he returned to the South to work as a summer intern for Atlanta's Congressman Andrew Young, whom he knew from his early civil rights days. He returned the next year to work for Young's congressional campaign. During that campaign he was reunited with Williams, who was coordinating the "get-out-the-vote" efforts for Young.

In Atlanta, Smiley looked for a job in the city and county governments, only to be told that in order to land such a position, one had to get involved with the local political campaigns or become a part of the local political circles. Smiley signed on with Young's second race for mayor. This was only his second time working with a campaign in an urban setting. Young won in 1983, but Smiley did not get a job in the new Atlanta administration as he had hoped. He did get a job in the Fulton county government.

Up to this point, all of Smiley's political experience in campaign politics was as a supporter and participant in rural and urban campaigns, not as a campaign manager and leader. All of that would change in perhaps one of the most controversial and well-publicized African American congressional campaigns to take place to date: the 1986 congressional race for the Fifth District in Atlanta between Julian Bond and John Lewis, two former SNCC associates.[10] In that race, Smiley would get the chance to move from participant to leader.

In his job with the county, Smiley often talked with C. T. Martin, who worked in the county's voter registration office. In one such conversation, Martin told Smiley that he was going to be John Lewis's campaign manager in the race against Julian Bond and asked for Smiley's help. As Smiley recalls,

> At that point, John did not have that much support, so anyone around could end up with a role. . . . John had about ten to twelve people to carry the . . . campaign. Thus I became the field operations manager. In that campaign, Martin really taught me a lot about campaigning, particularly in terms of grass roots campaigning or peoples' kind of campaigning. And with John Lewis it was a peoples' campaign due to the fact that Julian was well-financed.[11]

Bond had the backing of the black and white Atlanta establishments, including Young and former mayor Maynard Jackson.[12] Yet Lewis won the election.

Smiley was soon enlisted to chair the campaign of John Lewis, Sr. (no relation to the victor) for the third city council district in Atlanta. In 1988, Smiley headed Jesse Jackson's presidential campaign in Georgia, an effort that took him around the state. In 1989, he became deputy campaign manager for

Shelia Brown's bid for the Atlanta city council at-large seat. Ms. Brown had never run for a political office before, and had as her opponent a white candidate named Charles Huddelston, who, Smiley recalls, "had a campaign budget of more than $100,000 and most of the 'big time black leaders' behind him."[13] Brown won.

In 1990, Smiley became a coordinator for a white candidate, Jim Pannell, for lieutenant governor of Georgia. It was a major statewide race and Pannell was only known in the southern part of the state. The obstacles facing his candidate proved too difficult to overcome; after losing that election, Smiley took 1991 off.

Political Setting and Context in the State Legislative District

A 1992 state legislative race gave Smiley the chance to display the leadership skills he had acquired in a wide variety of campaigns in rural, urban, and statewide races. The prize in this grass roots campaign was a seat in the Georgia state legislature representing District 69 (Decatur and surrounding areas), formerly House District 50. Prior to reapportionment, this district had been represented by a ten-year incumbent, Frank Redding, who was first elected to serve the district in 1982 and had won re-election four times. In 1992, however, a new reapportionment law went into effect and new areas were added. The newly enlarged district added both African American and white neighborhoods. Thus in 1992 Redding was faced with the challenge of running for re-election in a significantly modified and reapportioned district.

A portion of the newly created district had been represented by Juanita Williams, the wife of civil rights activist Hosea Williams. However, when the new district was redrawn, Mrs. Williams was completely cut out of the district and could not run again. Rev. Williams, whose grass roots political organizing was legendary, was angered and decided that his daughter, Elizabeth, who lived in the new district, should run for the seat formerly held by his wife. She qualified for the race on the last day.

The political context of this race changed just four months before the July 15 Democratic primary. In February, Redding was indicted for vote selling and extortion in the case of a bill, proposed in 1987 and defeated in 1988, that would have made it illegal to serve alcohol at strip clubs, virtually putting those bars out of business.[14] Allegedly, an undercover Georgia Bureau of Investigation agent, posing as a lobbyist seeking to derail the bill, gave Redding a $1,000 cash payment in the hallway of the State Capitol. A second payment, captured on videotape, was made at a downtown hotel after the 1988 legislative session. The case against Redding had been reopened just days before the statute of limitations ran out and was presented to a grand jury. This placed Redding and his

TABLE 10.1

The Racial Composition of Georgia State House District 69 by Number of Registered Voters and Percentage of the Total

Precincts	African American Voters	%	White Voters	%
Tilson	281	98	7	2
Wadsworth	1,503	86	249	14
Rainbow Park	165	82	36	18
Candler	1,088	87	160	13
Toney	967	92	84	8
Casa Linda	840	93	61	7
Knollwood	784	76	253	24
Hooper Alexander	658	65	362	35
Winnona	562	33	1,160	67
Midway	370	43	494	57
Midway Park	217	34	423	66
East Lake	878	87	130	13
Forrest Hill	155	15	893	85
Total	8,468		4,312	
Mean	651	(69)	332	(31)

SOURCE: DeKalb County Elections Office, 1992.

campaign for the reapportioned district seat under both a cloud of suspicion and the media spotlight. Two weeks after his indictment, Redding voluntarily stepped down from his House seat, but he did not resign.[15] Even under indictment, however, he qualified to run as a candidate in the primary. In July, right before the Democratic primary in District 69, the judge declared a mistrial after the jury failed to agree on a verdict.[16]

Another candidate was local attorney Barbara J. Mobley. Mobley, who ran a private legal practice in Decatur, had long been involved in several community organizations and groups, and two groups devoted to dealing with women's issues, particularly the battered spouse problem. In addition, she had been very active in her church and its sundry outreach efforts. She also had Richard Smiley as her campaign manager in this grass roots campaign.

Table 10.1 depicts the racial composition of the district and the home precincts of the three candidates in the Democratic primary.

Smiley's Political Strategies and Techniques

David Canon claims that"experienced politicians respond to the structure of political opportunities and generally attempt to follow the path that will ensure their smooth advancement," while:

> Amateurs, at least in the aggregate, are less strategic in their decisions to run for office. Often they do not have as much at stake (i.e., losing the base office), so they may be drawn into an election by benefits less tangible than electoral success.[17]

The ambition theory does not offer a good explanation about amateurs in politics and particularly about African Americans in politics. Critical for the recruitment of African Americans into politics was the emergence of open political opportunity structures. Before the passage of the 1965 Voting Rights Act, at least in the South, there were few such structures. Hence, political ambition, at least in the African American political context, had to be subordinated. Bond's monograph from an earlier period notes the importance of community need and demand; political ambition is not indicated as a significant driving force. As many an African American political challenger has discovered, "amateurs may have fewer opportunities to run if experienced challengers exploit the uncertainty created by new district lines and voters who are not familiar with the incumbents."[18]

How did the political novice Barbara Mobley decide to enter the race against a ten-year incumbent, especially when her friends, neighbors, and personal acquaintances were urging her to the contrary? Mobley recalls:

> Richard [Smiley] had prepared me to hear from people, whom I thought were friends, that it was impossible for me to win against . . . the incumbent. They told me not to take it personally. They were just sharing their honest opinions with me. . . . Some of my friends were really concerned, quite frankly about my safety and about my law practice. . . . Those issues were brought up and the question was asked, whether it was really important enough for me to risk things I had built my reputation in the community on, because the campaign against such an incumbent might damage me.[19]

How, then, was Mobley recruited to run?

> The reason I got involved was because in 1990 when I went to the polls to vote for a state representative in my district, the two choices to me were not choices, real choices, for the people in the district. So I, along with other people, complained about the fact that we had not had good represen-

tation by the previous state representative, Frank Redding. His challenger at the time was a black Republican, George Robinson. Mr. Robinson's campaign was strictly negative and did not attract a lot of support for him, although some people were tired of Frank. So, I complained about it, talked to some friends about it. I really had not at that time thought about getting involved, but wanted to support somebody. And the suggestions kept coming, why don't you run? Eventually I did.[20]

In Mobley's case, the political opportunity, a community need and demand, and individual interest were all present.

As a political novice, how did Mobley recruit such a seasoned campaign manager? Again, Mobley is candid:

> Richard had been involved in political campaigns on several levels. He was one of the first people to suggest I should run and I told him no, I don't think so, I could perhaps support somebody. Then from time to time when I would see him he would always ask, ready to get the campaign started, or say something in reference to my running. So last year I attended a conference that State Representative Frank Redding attended. His demeanor and response to some concerns, primarily women's issues, proved to be the decisive acts on his part that made me know that I really should get in the race. So I talked with Richard about it. In January I called him. I was looking for him, and I found him, and I called him and told him I wanted to talk to him about the race, and that is how it happened. I didn't know anybody else personally.[21]

There were other factors that led Mobley to choose Smiley as her campaign manager.

> I am a member of the Atlanta Women's Political Caucus and there were some other women candidates with whom Richard had worked, such as Sheila Brown, who is a member of the Atlanta city council. He also co-managed Juanita Hicks, the woman who is the clerk of the Superior Court in Fulton county. I knew that he was involved in field operations for Jesse Jackson's campaign in the state of Georgia. I heard things from people who were more involved politically than I, about people who could be trusted to run your campaign, especially if you didn't have a lot of money. So his name came up a couple of times. Finally, I talked to a couple of other people about it and then called him.[22]

Similarly, Smiley was recruited to the campaign for reasons other than sheer ambition. He describes his involvement in the campaign:

> In '92, this friend of mine called me up and asked me, "Do you remember you asked me to run in 1988 for state representative?" I told my friend, the Representative-elect from DeKalb county, that I really had no interest in working on any campaigns. I was sort of frustrated with the campaigns that I had worked on. I just did not see any progress, I didn't see any personal progress. I didn't see any progress in terms of the black community. But, I told her, I said, well I committed myself to you in 1988, and I always try to keep my commitments. So, we set a meeting . . . I asked her if she was serious about winning and why she thought she could win.[23]

After several meetings aimed at getting to know his candidate, Smiley agreed to become her campaign manager if she would go to Selma to the twenty-fifth anniversary of the march that led to the 1965 Voting Rights Act.[24] As he recalls:

> We started out, I knew that Barbara had worked in some voter registration drives, sororities, did some other social things. But I called Barbara and said, "Barbara, we need to go to Selma, Alabama." I said, "They are having their twenty-fifth anniversary march in Selma." And she said, "Why do I need to go to Selma?" I said, "We can meet some people from your district from there." So we got in the car and went on to Selma, Alabama. We went to Selma, well, Barbara had never been to Selma, I didn't know if she was a little nervous or not. The purpose of Selma was to let Barbara get a feel of the work that black folks went through for the right to vote. I think a lot of black politicians forget about people dying. Sometimes I think that even the so-called people who worked during the civil rights movement forgot about the sacrifices that people made for the right to vote. So I don't know whether Barbara understood the purpose of the trip.[25]

Mobley recalls:

> You see, Richard came from Selma. He thought that it was important to go because he had been intimately involved in the civil rights movement and he knew that people like congressman John Lewis would be there. . . . So, I didn't think it was necessary to go to Selma, but he thought it was important and after we got to Selma I appreciated the trip a bit more. Even all the way down there I kept saying, "Richard, I don't see why it is necessary for us to go to Selma." Sometimes he would make decisions about things that would ultimately be important in my campaign. He said, "It may not make sense initially to go, but towards the end you'll see that it was really a part of the whole strategy."[26]

At this point in his career, campaign manager Smiley did not simply want to put his well-honed skills behind another political amateur and make him or her a winner who would simply go into office and do little for the African American community. Smiley was putting a condition on his recruitment into another political campaign. At least in some races, community interest is as important as the individual candidate's self-interest. And the candidate in this instance had to accept Smiley's conditions because she was a political neophyte who knew she needed an experienced grass roots campaign manager like Richard Smiley.

The political science literature tells us that three aspects of an amateur's background hurt his or her chances of getting into office: "the absence of prior campaign experience, low name recognition, and a general preference among voters for candidates who have prior experience."[27] As Canon notes, although "these obstacles are not insurmountable . . . successful campaigns . . . indicate that large expenditures on consultants, staff, and advertising permit amateurs to overcome initial deficits."[28] With money in short supply, only an effective campaign strategy directed by a seasoned veteran can help the political amateur get the job done in a grass roots campaign.

Smiley implemented a comprehensive grass roots strategy against the well-funded incumbent and another candidate whose campaign was being managed by her civil rights hero father. After having educated his candidate to the political necessity of demonstrating a real commitment to helping the community, Smiley began the process of making her visible.

> We came back from Selma to Decatur, [and] I said Barbara, now the next thing is that nobody knows you! I said, you know, we have a few friends who know that you are a lawyer, but those are not the people who are going to vote for you. I said what we have to do is to do a visibility campaign and we must start out by going door to door.[29]

Mobley remembers as well:

> I was less than a neophyte because I had no name recognition, except among my immediate neighborhood, my church, my sorority, and a couple of other social and civic organizations that I was active in. . . . In Richard's mind the most important thing was to get my name out there. He said we needed to start in my precinct. To him it was very, very important to win my home precinct. So we started going door to door on my street. . . . I was going door-to-door to introduce myself and find out what issues were priority issues in this precinct.[30]

Smiley trekked along with his candidate on these walking tours because he believed that even a well-intentioned person could lose a campaign going door-to-door if it was not done right. Along the way, Smiley trained Mobley in effective door-to-door campaigning.

The second feature of Smiley's strategy was that neither he nor his candidate were to mention the name of the two opponents in the race. Instead,

> We would always say we were running for the seat when someone would ask who we were running against. We would say that Frank Redding use to hold the seat or something of that nature. We would try not to deal with our opponent.[31]

Third, Smiley launched Mobley's campaign nearly four months before the qualifying date. Smiley believed that political amateurs have to use every opportunity to acquire name recognition. Moreover, such a long-term strategy would give his candidate a chance to equalize the forces that the incumbent could bring to bear on the race. Thus, Smiley started the campaign early, working first in his candidate's own precinct, and moving quickly on to other precincts. By the time Mobley qualified for the primary, her campaign had covered half the precincts in the district.

Smiley contends that the political amateur must mix his or her techniques in a grass roots campaign:

> One thing that Barbara and I decided was whether we had volunteers or not, we were going to win the election. Barbara and I were going to do something every day. We would do shopping centers, we would do two or three shopping centers. Then we would do door-to-door on a street. They thought we had hundreds of people working, and sometimes, there was no one out there but Barbara and I. Then we would hit another neighborhood. Then when we had a group of people, we would do a whole bunch of things. But we never did stop. Never. We always stayed on the case day-by-day. To a certain point, people thought that we were the incumbent.[32]

After April 27, when Mobley qualified for the primary, Smiley stepped up the pace of her campaign by posting yard signs, sending mailers, and staffing telephone banks. Most important, he sent his candidate out to the churches to meet the voters.

> I went to most of the churches in the district, especially the African American churches. Sometimes we would call ahead to tell them we were coming, other times, we had this preprinted card that said, "Visiting with you today is Attorney Barbara J. Mobley, candidate for the State House." At all the churches except one, I was introduced and after church was over, I would stand there shaking hands. The other part of that campaign strategy with churches was that Richard and a team of volunteers always

> hit the parking lots with flyers while I was [inside]. So when they came out, in addition to having met me they had some literature on their cars.[33]

Smiley's church strategy was different for the African American and the white communities.

> Once again, I had to rely on my campaign manager's understanding of the campaign process because in my mind, I should be campaigning in the white precincts the same way I campaigned in the black precincts. He explained to me that there was a fundamental difference in approach. One of the differences is that in white churches, there was not the expectation of white voters that the campaign would extend to covering their cars with campaign literature, as opposed to the black community. It was an expectation of these district communities to receive information in its own distinctive way. So, we didn't leaflet any predominantly white churches. I attended one predominantly white church and at that church, I was not introduced, although I did pass out cards. I stayed after church service and individually introduced myself. The reception, however, was cool.[34]

Smiley and his candidate built a biracial coalition. Whites volunteered to campaign for Mobley in white communities and introduce her to their friends and neighbors. Campaign mailings approached the two communities in different ways.

> Also, the fact that I was endorsed by both of the major Atlanta papers, the *Atlanta Journal* and the *Atlanta Constitution,* my campaign manager thought in the black community that it really was not a big deal. He thought that in our community it could have been the kiss of death to say that you carried both of those endorsements. But in the white community, carrying those two endorsements was valuable. I think that helped.[35]

This matter of endorsements brings up another point about Smiley's grass roots strategy. Typically in most African American local election campaigns, candidates strive for endorsements from various community groups, leadership organizations, social clubs, political leagues, alliances, and sundry ad hoc political coalitions and political celebrities. Much time and energy are devoted to trying to win these endorsements.

> We didn't ask for any endorsements. That is one thing that I told Barbara: I do not believe in endorsements. . . . Endorsements used to be a big thing when black folks first started registering to vote. Starting in Atlanta back in the early sixties and the late fifties, you had a group of blacks who put out a ticket and black folk would vote for the candidate on their tickets. I

> think that over the years black folks have become more sophisticated. They don't want you to tell them who to vote for. I think tickets turn people off. I think you have to go out and run your individual campaign. . . . So I think tickets really work against you in the black community. I think endorsements work against you.[36]

Smiley maintains that endorsements can bind and hinder a candidate after the campaign has been won. "We ran on our own merit. Afterwards, so and so couldn't come up and say 'I endorsed you.' They still can't take credit for it. Nor can they make demands because they were part of the winning coalition."[37]

There was one final strategy in this grass roots campaign that Smiley believed was critical to a campaign run in a majority African American district. That strategy was "to remind people of the punch number" (the candidate's number on the ballot). As he notes:

> I think punch numbers are very important in the black community. We had people going around saying I know the punch number is 35, that is all, they didn't even have to think about the name, when they go in the polls, they just punch. So, that number was very important and we got lucky when we got our yard signs, we were lucky enough to get the punch number put on it. Most of our opponents didn't get their punch number put on their signs until the last two or three weeks of the campaign. So we had a long period of time with our punch number out there. Everyone remembered our punch number. They might not or could not remember Barbara's name, but they remembered to punch number 35. So, that was one reason that we hesitated on getting the signs made up because we wanted to get them made up early, but I said that punch numbers were going out in a few days so let's wait. Our brochures had punch numbers out the first day they came out. We had 2,000 brochures made up with our punch number.[38]

It had been Smiley's experience that even if a candidate's efforts to get voters to recognize his or her name are not successful, getting them to remember the candidate's punch number will.

> I just think that in the black community whether you can read or write, you know how to count. I think that a number is very important. You don't have to think that much about a number. So I think psychologically it is a little easier to deal with.[39]

Employing this array of strategic insights, procedures, and techniques, Smiley and Mobley met Redding and Williams in the July 15 Democratic primary. Mobley came in first, Williams second, with Redding a clear-cut loser. However, the closeness of the vote for Mobley and Williams necessitated a run-off between the two women. Table 10.2 reveals the story of the primary and run-off results.

The run-off was set for August 11. Smiley saw the run-off election as a challenge and another opportunity to display his skills:

> That Wednesday after the election, we started a telephone bank from 5 to 9 o'clock. Barbara and I went out and did shopping centers, and we did precincts that we lost. We started to go door-to-door in the precincts, because Barbara and I were kind of upset because we should not have lost that precinct. We worked hard in that precinct. We lost it by 30 something votes. But we should not have lost it. So we went back to that precinct that next day. Every day on, we did shopping centers, door-to-door, telephone banks, that is all we did. Except we did a couple of things different. We started doing human billboards in the mornings. Barbara would go out there, say from 7:00 in the morning until 8:30, and we had thank you for your vote on July the 15th, and need your support on August 11th. Barbara did at least two or three major freeway entrances. We got a lot of response. People would wave back, blow their horns, give a thumbs up and other signs of support. Out of it all, we received one thumbs down. As a human billboard, Barbara would dress real brightly, smile a lot, hold up her campaign sign on a stick in one hand and wave with the other hand.
>
> The other thing we did on both election days, which I don't normally do, we ran telephone banks from 8:00 to 6:30. We had telephone banks going all day. I think what happened was the people that work at night we woke up and reminded them to go to the polls. I think it was really rare that we got 1,735 votes in July and come back and get 1,725, almost the identical votes and precincts. I don't know if we could ever do it again. But we did it this time. I think Barbara and I were compatible in terms of candidate versus campaign manager. I think we both were aggressive.[40]

Mobley beat Williams in the run-off election despite the fact that Redding endorsed Williams's candidacy and allowed Williams to put his picture in her literature. From the aggregate election evidence, Redding's 900 voters from the primary did not switch to Williams in the run-off, as Williams's vote totals in the run-off barely increased. Without a Republican opponent in the November general election, Mobley captured the seat for the 69th House District. Her grass roots campaign, under the leadership of an experienced campaign manager, had prevailed.

As the newly elected State Representative, Mobley had this to say about her campaign manager's plan:

> Richard as a manager did not write the whole campaign plan down on paper. To me, it was piecemeal with him, he had this grand plan and I still have not seen the plan. We just executed it. I do believe that he had a plan,

TABLE 10.2

Results of Democratic Primary and General Elections in Georgia State House District 69, 1992 and 1994

1992 Election						
Precincts Totals	**Barbara Mobley**	**%**	**Elizabeth Williams**	**%**	**Frank Redding**	**%**
Democratic Primary						
3,865	1,735	44.9	1,167	30.2	963	24.9
General Election						
2,812	1,725	61.3	1,087	38.7	0	0
1994 Election						
Precincts Total	**Barbara Mobley**	**%**			**Melvin Butler**	**%**
Democratic Primary						
2,120	1,758	83.0			362	17.0

SOURCE: DeKalb County Elections Office, 1992–1994.

but [because] of concerns . . . about the security of the campaign office [and] spies in the campaign . . . he didn't write it down. Nevertheless, it was obviously there.[41]

Conclusions

We have found support for our research hypothesis that local elections do not necessarily respond to national influences. The redesigned and reshaped political context that had been established by the Reagan-Bush presidencies had little or no influence on the 1992 elections in Georgia's House District 69. Although Hosea Williams and the Reverend Ralph David Abernathy had endorsed Reagan during the 1980 elections, no evidence of the Reagan-Bush political agenda was apparent in this local race. Even Reverend Williams's advertisement for his daughter, calling upon African Americans to "Vote for Family Values"—a recurrent Republican theme—seems less a product of the Reagan-Bush emphasis than a reflection of the campaign realities in District 69. This election, and perhaps numerous others like it in other predominantly African American districts across the country, turned on the issues, personalities, and political contours that generated them rather than on national mainstream issues, thus lending support to Tip O'Neill's dictum that "all politics is local."

Aggregate election data reveal that the gender issue was not important in this particular electoral contest, having apparently been "canceled out" by the appearance of two women in the race. The gender of the candidates was not the sole factor operating in this case; nor was the incumbent's indictment a significant issue in the Mobley-Williams contest.

In 1994, with a Democrat in the White House, Smiley and Mobley once again conducted a grass roots campaign. Neither Clinton nor the Republican Contract with America became issues in Mobley's re-election. The issues remained local ones. Table 10.2 reveals the similarities of the two races.

From our case study of the campaign leadership style of Richard Smiley, we were able to delineate the key aspects and components of grass roots campaigning in the African American community. Comparing this 1992 election campaign with some of the earlier political campaigns waged by African Americans in a changing political contextual environment, we can see perhaps one of the most important similarities: namely, that Smiley and Mobley's campaign focused less on southern government and more on the candidate. In Bond's day, southern government officials at the state, county, or local levels, fought and resisted the emergence of African American officeholders. In the Reagan-Bush era, these forces resided in the high echelons of national government. However, national government officials did not intrude into this particular campaign.

11

THE AFRICAN AMERICAN REPUBLICAN VOTE IN A SOUTHERN MAYORAL ELECTION

• • • • • • •

Hanes Walton, Jr., LaShawn Warren, Damon E. Elmore, Amy Y. Graham, Simone Green, Victor Cooper, Kimberlynn Hendricks, Sesley Jones, Renita D. Lipscomb, Stephanie Williams, and Renia Williams

Beyond the national political context, there are the regional, state, county, and local ones. These different political contexts may overlap, remain separate and distinct or collide and compete with each other. The linkages and relationships between these different contexts must be understood in order to grasp the rich diversity of African American politics.

As the Reagan and Bush administrations were attempting to redesign and reshape, from the national level, a new political context for African Americans, blacks in Savannah, Georgia (Chatham county)[1] dropped their traditional Democratic partisanship and became Republican voters, at least in the mayoral context. Wielding the balance of power in the 1991 mayoral elections, these African American voters helped this traditionally Democratic southern city to elect its first Republican mayor in 21 years. This Republican victory came without warning. No one expected it, least of all the Democratic mayor, the Republican mayoral candidate, and the Reagan-Bush political operatives. However, the answer to the question of why African Americans in Savannah voted Republican when that party, at least on the national level, was doing and had done as much as it could to harm and hinder the African American drive for liberty and equality rests in the local political context, not the national one.

As Figure 11.1 reveals, for five of the six mayoral elections in Savannah

FIGURE 11.1
Winning Pluralities in Savannah Mayoral Elections, 1966–1991

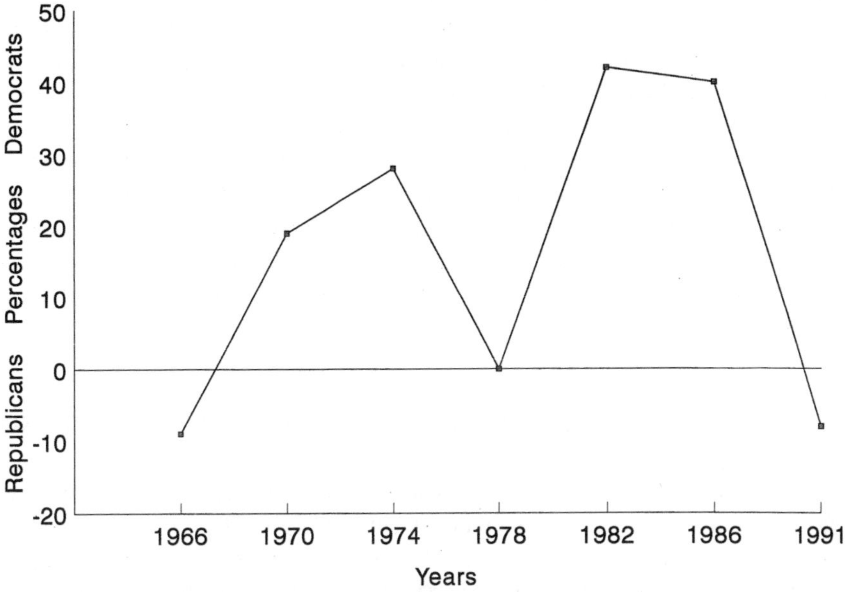

Calculated from the Consolidated Returns, Savannah, Georgia Municipal Elections, Board of Elections, Chatham County, Georgia.

since the passage of the 1965 Voting Rights Act, the Democrats won the mayoralty. In 1978 the Republicans did not even field a candidate at all. All this came to an end in 1991.

Data and Methodology

The data for this case study of the 1991 mayoral race in Savannah were derived from three sources: (1) election returns obtained from the Chatham county Board of Elections, (2) content analysis of the local African American and white (mainstream) newspapers during the campaign, and (3) interviews with local political elites (i.e., the incumbent mayor, several mayoral candidates, and other political participants). Analysis of the election returns enabled the empirical rendering of trends in African American electoral behavior in Savannah since the passage of the Voting Rights Act in 1965. This data also provided information about the nature, scope, and significance of the shifting partisan alignments that occurred within Savannah's African American community. Since no voter survey or polling data was available, analysis of local newspaper accounts revealed the mind and mood of Savannah's politically active population and political opinion makers. Interviews with some of the key actors in this mayoral drama, in both the African American and the white communities, provide insights into the political interactions of the candidates, the community, and the voters. These three distinct databases have been integrated into a coherent whole to systematically analyze the similarities and differences between local and national political contexts. As a result, a portrait of the linkages between various political contexts within the African American community emerges.

The outcome of this election—a major change in the local political context—heightens the drama of the local reality for researchers. Occurring as it did in the midst of the Republican party's drive to forge a new national context for African Americans, the 1991 Savannah mayoral election provides a rare opportunity to examine first-hand the relationship between diverse political contexts.

African American Democratic Partisanship in a Southern City

As table 11.1 shows, the Democrats, with the aid of the African American vote, gained control over the mayorship in Savannah in 1966. The Democrats won the next four elections by increasingly larger percentages each time. In 1991, however, the Republicans, who had rarely received more than a third of the city's vote in recent years, abruptly ended the Democratic streak, capturing more than a third of the African American vote in the process. Clearly, the political context had changed between 1966 and 1991.

African Americans had been voting in Savannah since shortly after the Civil War, despite the state's poll tax, which was demanded of every registered voter regardless of color. Reading and interpretation tests, character tests, and whites-only primaries failed to thwart Savannah's African Americans in registering and voting.[2] The 1965 Voting Rights Act, at least in the local political context, served to enlarge the size of the African American electorate in Savannah and increased its political influence.

The increased voting numbers did not result in immediate influence for Savannah's African American community after 1965. The first fruits of the act were not harvested until the 1968 elections. In that race, one African American, Bobby L. Hill, was elected to the state legislature; and another, the Reverend L. Scott Stell, was elected to the Chatham county commission. However the power of the vote was not to empower African Americans in this southern setting.[3] These victories became possible only after both of these political bodies had been reapportioned to create African American majority districts. While reapportionment helped the fledgling African American political movement, it likewise constrained it by focusing the energies and mobilization efforts of the county's African Americans on a single seat or office. Overall, it had a channeling effort.

In addition, the city had not followed the county or the state legislature in

TABLE 11.1

Total Number and Percentage of the Democratic and Republican Vote in Savannah Mayoral Elections, 1966–1991

Years	Total Voting	Republican Vote	%	Democratic Vote	%	Winners
1966	30,513	16,630	(55)	13,883	(46)	Republicans
1970	26,016	11,665	(45)	14,351	(55)	Democrats
1974	25,364	9,177	(36)	16,187	(64)	Democrats
1978	No Election*	No Election		No Election		Democrats
1982	22,947	6,751	(29)	16,196	(71)	Democrats
1986	20,815	6,140	(30)	14,675	(70)	Democrats
1991	31,700	17,199	(54)	14,501	(46)	Republicans
Mean	26,256	11,260	(42)	14,966	(58)	

The returns for each year were taken from The Consolidated Returns, Savannah, Georgia Municipal General Elections, issued by the Board of Elections of Chatham County.

**In 1978, the mayor and his surrogates worked both the white and African American communities to discourage challengers. Thus no election was held. This is a rare occurrence in a major urban area, except in Southern politics.*

reapportioning its voting districts by the time the next round of mayoral elections occurred in 1970. During this campaign, the mayor and the city council all ran at large.[4] Indeed, slating was the chief political tactic used in the city's mayoral races. The Republican and Democratic mayoral candidates each picked a slate of six council persons to run together, and each candidate would work not so much for himself or herself but for the entire slate. In the primaries, different partisan slates generally competed against each other. In the general election, the two party's slates vied for control of the city.

In the 1970 mayoral elections, the incumbent mayor, a Republican, put together an all-white slate of councilmen. Just prior to the election, the Democrat hopeful, John P. Rousakis, quietly met with the head of the local NAACP to cut a deal.[5] Rousakis sought the African American vote and offered the NAACP the opportunity to choose one African American for the Democratic slate. The deal was accepted.[6] Boles Ford, a local businessman popular in both the African American and white communities in Savannah, was put forth as the candidate for alderman. In the election, Ford beat his Republican opponent 13,497 to 10,774, and he came very close to equaling the total number of votes received by Rousakis (14,351)—a difference of only 854 votes. The smallest possible African American vote in this contest was 8,007 votes.

In the next mayoral election, in 1974, candidates again ran at large on political slates. Rousakis added another African American to his slate, businessman Roy L. Jackson. The Republican slate offered no African Americans. The Democratic slate won, with Ford getting 15,194 votes to 8,130 for his Republican opponent, and Jackson getting 14,618 to his opponent's 8,527. Rousakis received 16,185 votes. Again, the difference between the mayor's and the African American candidates' votes was small.

The real fireworks in this campaign occurred in the Democratic primaries when another local African American businessman, Enoch Mathis, attempted to develop his own Democratic slate to challenge that of the incumbent mayor.[7] The local NAACP leadership, grateful for a second council seat and doubtful that the African American electorate could successfully rally behind one of its own, opposed this effort. So did the two African American councilmen. The Mathis slate eventually pulled out of the Democratic primary and entered the general election as an independent slate; however, the same forces that thwarted it in the primaries kept the slate off the general election ballot on a technicality.[8]

This incident says much about the nature and significant of political slating. First, it exposes slating as a blocking device that builds political coalitions and networks prior to the primaries and virtually assures the failure of insurgent slates. It also shows how slating permits political elites and party insiders to hand pick African American candidates. At best, the African American electorate serves merely to rubber stamp the party's pre-slated choices, thus limiting its power and political presence and dampening the potential of an emergent African American electorate to a select few.

The city finally reapportioned its voting districts prior to the mayoral election of 1978. Under the new apportionment, the city council was enlarged from six to eight seats, six of which were elected by district and two of which were at-large seats. Of the six districts, three districts were predominantly white and three were predominantly African American. The two at-large seats were projected as winnable by either race. Yet numerous court decisions have created districts since it is virtually impossible for an African American to win at large. No black currently holds an at-large seat. The city's reapportionment plan was not submitted to the Justice Department for clearance prior to its enactment, as required under Section Five of the 1965 Voting Rights Act. As an observer of the local political scene in Savannah, I earlier noted the following:

> When the city of Savannah decide to annex part of the county and reduce black political strength in the city from more than fifty percent to below forty percent, the city fathers held a local referendum, but did not let citizens in the area to be annexed vote on their own fate. The newly-ratified city government had eight aldermen, two of them black; the old board had consisted of six aldermen, two being black. Blacks went from holding one-third of the aldermanic board to holding one-fourth. The formation of this new city government was submitted to the Justice Department as an accomplished fact, not for advance approval, which was in clear violation of civil rights rules and regulations. . . . Even though several national newspapers covered this violation, nothing was done. Columnist Jack Anderson suggested that the reason was that the Attorney General, Griffin Bell was from Georgia, and his son had been hired at a huge salary by the city to be an attorney for the school board.[9]

The African American community was split over the reapportionment plan. Eventually, the opposition chartered a bus and took a group of people to Washington, D.C., to meet with Assistant Attorney General Drew S. Days. As Assistant Attorney General, Days could have stopped the Savannah plan from going into effect; yet, this group persuaded Days that they could live with this plan that circumscribed African American voting power because they wanted to embarrass and hold up to ridicule that segment of the African American leadership that had supported the incumbent mayor's proposal. They hoped that the ramifications of adopting such a plan would cause the African American community to abandon it old-line leaders, but it did not; nor did this young, brash group of new leaders have enough resources or media clout to successfully usurp the old-timers' power. By the next election, however, they would make a major grasp for municipal power by running an African American for mayor.

In 1978, incumbent mayor Rousakis and his slate, in both the primary and general elections, ran unopposed. Every time a potential candidate even remotely talked about surfacing, they were either disuaded or offered a reward not to run.

Since Rousakis won his third term unopposed, there is no way to assess the trend in the African American vote in this election.

By 1982, several members of the mayor's slate, particularly two African American members, faced opposition in the Democratic primary. In the general election, Rousakis won, with an African American vote of 9,172. Five white council members (including the two at-large seats) and only three African American council members were elected. Power in this municipal government thus remained firmly in white hands.

The Influence of the Jesse Jackson 1984 Presidential Campaign

A pioneering study of David Dinkins's 1989 election as mayor of New York city, devotes an entire chapter to Jesse Jackson's 1988 presidential campaign to show how this earlier national campaign set the stage for Dinkins's victory in the local context. Jackson's campaign efforts in New York City (and elsewhere) focused on increasing the registration and mobilization of African Americans and other voters of color. Further, it united previously divided forces, not only different classes within the African American community and different ethnic groups in the city, but various political elites in the city.

> The 1988 presidential primary and general elections in New York city had a number of fundamental implications for the approaching 1989 mayoral elections. First, they showed that a popular and effective black candidate could assemble the magic number of votes in a Democratic primary, namely a plurality over 40 percent. Such a margin would avert a two-person run-off campaign that a black might not win and, for the first time in the city's history, send a black Democratic nominee into the general election. Jesse Jackson's victory in New York city set off a flurry of think-pieces and political strategy discussions among the would-be supporters of David Dinkins for mayor.[10]

In Savannah, four years earlier, there was such a groundswell of support for Jackson presidential campaign that, during his initial visit to Savannah, 14,000 African Americans turned out to hear him speak at the Savannah Civic Center, even though the center only holds 10,000. The 4,000 who could not get in to see or hear Jackson waited in the parking lot during the entire program. Jackson used this opportunity to urge Savannah's African Americans to register and vote. Local African American leaders, the majority of whom were essentially dependent upon the incumbent mayor for their power base, had failed to keep African Americans registered in proportion to their numbers. The local NAACP's earlier voter registration thrust had diminished over the years to a mere symbolic and perfunctory one, adding at most only a few hundred African

Americans to the voting rolls in the years preceding the Jackson campaign. Only a few weeks after Jackson's visit, hundreds were put on the rolls.[11] Consequently, Jackson won the city, county, and congressional district in the Savannah area. This victory in Georgia, his first of the campaign, enabled him to qualify for Federal Election Commission funds and thereby keep his presidential candidacy alive.[12]

Jackson's 1984 campaign affected the local political context in Savannah in three ways. First, it substantially increased African American voter registration. Second, it increased African American political mobilization. No local candidate had ever energized blacks in Savannah to participate in politics to such an extent. Finally, it raised African American political consciousness in terms of leadership. By example and through his rhetoric, Jackson emboldened some of Savannah's local African American leaders to run in the future for the top political offices in the city, county, and district.

One of the factors that launched the first Jackson campaign was the contextual revolution that Reagan was attempting to put in motion. Jackson in turn attempted to derail this revolution at the national level, and his efforts eventually filtered down to the local context. One more transition set was needed, however, the seeds for which were also planted during Jackson's initial presidential race.

The Black Mayoral Challenge in 1986

Long before Mayor Rousakis even announced his intention to run again, he received the endorsement of key African American leaders in Savannah. Working through his political surrogates and operatives, Rousakis had asked all of the city's African Americans of note to join him for a breakfast meeting in December 1985. At the end of that meeting, the mayor's operatives asked for and received from the attendees verbal and written endorsements of him and his efforts. However, at the city's celebration of the first Martin Luther King, Jr. national holiday observance in January 1986, with Mayor Rousakis in attendance, the Reverend Bennie Mitchell, the organizer of the observance (which was funded by the city and the mayor's office), issued a defiant call for an African American mayor for the city. Some in the audience perceived Mitchell's suggestion as bold, daring, timely. Others viewed it as embarrassing, in bad taste, and a negative influence on race relations, and they rushed to apologize to the mayor. Rev. Mitchell stood his ground, however, and the African American community reacted.

After several trial balloons, all of which fizzled, a former two-term city alderman, Roy Jackson, chose to run for mayor. Jackson had lost his seat in 1982 when Savannah's community retired all of its first-generation African American aldermen. Although Jackson had performed admirably as an alderman, Rousakis's African American allies began an incessant and increasingly shrill attack against him and the idea of a black mayor. They highlighted the fact that Jackson had lost his previous seat. They attacked his motives, personality, ability, and sincerity, and floated nasty rumors about his personal life.

The incumbent mayor's campaign slogan was "Teamwork Works," even though none of the African American councilmen chose to be on his team this time out. The three African American council members met privately with Rousakis prior to the beginning of the campaign to determine what concessions the mayor planned to give the African American community in return for their political support. According to Alderman Otis Johnson, his response was "nothing—he would simply run on his record."[13]

Behind the barrage of criticism launched against Savannah's first African American mayoral candidate, Rousakis quietly worked the African American middle-class community in Savannah, sponsoring free disco dances, boat rides, and barbecues in black neighborhoods and attending African American functions. The net effect of Rousakis's heightened presence in Savannah's African American community, combined with the criticism of Jackson, caused that community to become significantly fragmented and deadlocked. To break this deadlock, three African Americans—businessman Bennie Polote, attorney Clarence Martin, and Reverend Mitchell—formulated a strategy to achieved unity. Polote, Martin, and Mitchell had approached several other well-known national African American political celebrities, all of whom refused to help. Only Reverend Jesse Jackson decided to put his prestige and national standing on the line. He arrived two days before the election, and in that brief time he broke the deadlock and shifted the allegiance of the city's African American community to Roy Jackson. The Democratic primary resulted in a surprise tie, and a run-off election had to be held.

Between the primary and the run-off elections, a period of about two weeks, Reverend Jackson rallied the troops in the three African American districts. These districts (1, 2, and 5) had a 52 percent turnout rate in the primary. In the run-off, the turnout rate was 57 percent, a 5-percent increase. In terms of actual votes, Roy Jackson received 1,974 more votes in the run-off than he received in the primary from these three districts. From the other three districts, he received 769 votes in the run-off. Overall, Jackson received 8,588 votes in the primary and 11,769 votes in the run-off.

Reverend Jackson's efforts were not enough. Prior to this election, Savannah's white voters, previously content to let the city's African American voters return the incumbent white mayor to power time and time again, were essentially non-voters in municipal elections. Yet, when they realized that Savannah's black voters were about to abandon the incumbent and put one of their own in office, the city's whites rushed to the polls and overwhelmingly supported the embattled incumbent. Rousakis won the election by 9,229 votes. The 1986 Democratic Party run-off election in Savannah involved the greatest number of voters ever in that city, including primaries and general elections. Some 33,173 voters turned out. Although about 40 percent of the African American vote stayed with the incumbent mayor, the city's old-line coalition had fallen apart, and the stage was set for African American Democrats to switch their vote to the Republican party.

The African American Republican Vote in the 1991 Mayoral Election

Rousakis, who had earlier convinced the state legislature to extend his term by a year, sought yet another term in 1991. His previous victory over a major African American challenger and the fear of another white voter backlash discouraged others in both the African American and white communities from running. He himself felt nearly invincible.[14] Things looked much the same politically in Savannah at the outset of the campaign. However, there was one significant change in the local context.

Rousakis had effectuated three alliances at three different levels in the African American community. First, there was his alliance with the city's old-line civil rights leaders. His second alliance was with Savannah's middle-class African American voters. He had cultivated this alliance through personal contacts such as telephone calls from this office as well as visits to dances, house parties, club socials, and yard parties. This union also included a number of cooperative efforts with fledgling African American businessmen who needed city contracts, loans, and other assistance to stay afloat. The third political alliance was with the African American aldermen and other elected officials, who curried personal and community favors.

Missing was an alliance with the low-income sector of the African American community. Under Rousakis, benefits—so-called "progress" monies—were directed to the city's upper- and middle-class blacks. Savannah's low-income African Americans saw public housing deteriorate, public health services shut down, and public sector jobs and employment decrease. Federal funding to urban areas in general were curtailed during the Reagan-Bush era, and Savannah felt the cutbacks in particular. Drugs became a major new source of income. As Savannah's crime rate soared, so did its murder rate, becoming one of the nation's highest. And all of the murders were occurring within the community's inner city, which was predominated by African Americans.

Initially, the mayor gave the problem of crime in Savannah's impoverished inner-city African American community over to African American leaders, letting them carry out a high profile but low resource, bumper-sticker-type public relations campaign against "black on black crime." Mayor Rousakis only minimally involved his office in addressing these issues.

With his old electoral coalition in tatters—with the three African American aldermen refusing to join the mayor's slate—Rousakis was faced in the 1991 primary election with a strong challenger from the white community, three weaker challengers from the African American community, and a challenge from a white political newcomer. The first African American candidate to announce

TABLE 11.2

The African American Vote in the 1991 Savannah Democratic Mayoral Primary: Votes from Three African American Aldermanic Districts

Candidates	Race of Candidate	Votes from the Districts in 1986 Election*	Votes from the Districts in 1991 Election	Differences	% of Total
John P. Rousakis	White	5,890	2,922	-2,968	43
Brook Stillwell	White	2,556	2,915	+359	39
Willie E. Brown	African American	6,650	2,015	-4,635	78
Bobby L. Hill	African American	NC	1,722	--	82
Howard E. Alls	African American	NC	729	--	74
Ben Hubby	White	NC	358	--	27
Total		15,096	10,661		

The returns for each year were taken from The Consolidated Returns, Savannah, Georgia Municipal General Elections, issued by the Board of Elections of Chatham County.

NC = not a candidate in this election.

was former State Representative Bobby L. Hill. Hill, an attorney who had fallen upon hard times and personal misfortunes, had been, at his peak, a charismatic local leader. Numerous character questions were raised early in Hill's candidacy, however, but he felt he had the support to win. African American alderman Willie Brown, who had run for one of the three at-large seats in 1986, entered the race. Brown had also experienced personal problems that raised some character issues during the campaign. The third African American candidate, Howard Alls, a successful and youthful local attorney, entered the race to give the African American community at least one candidate with a clean record. Among the Democrats, the mayor's major white challenger was Brooks Stillwell, a long-time city alderman and heir apparent to the mayor who decided that he simply could not wait in the wings any longer. Another white challenger, Ben Hubby, was a physician who ran as a reformer seeking to clean up the city's image as a drug- and violence-ridden city.

It is possible to discern the general outline of African American voting behavior in this municipal election by examining voting trends in three of the city's six voting districts: districts 1, 2, and 5. African Americans comprised 97.4 percent of the electorate in District 1, 81.2 percent in District 2, and 75.2 percent in District 5.[15] The total number of votes cast in these three districts was significantly lower, by nearly a third, in 1991 (10,661) than it had been in 1986 (15,096). Moreover, the challengers are shown to have received, collectively, nearly the same number of votes awarded to the incumbent. In this race, one of the African American challengers received only a few hundred votes less than the well-financed incumbent and challengers.

As the "Differences" in table 11.2 show, the African American electorate was obviously much less enthused about both the incumbent and his African American challengers than it had been in the past. Further, the "Percent of Total Vote" reveals that the three African American mayoral candidates received most of their votes from the African American community; whereas the white challengers amassed a substantial level of support from Savannah's African American voters, blacks were not their major source of support.

The vote for the three African American mayoral candidates (4,466) was 42 percent of the total votes in these three districts. When that figure is added to the number of votes cast for the white challengers to the incumbent (7,381), it becomes clear that more than two-thirds (69 percent) of Savannah's African American voters were looking for something—and someone—different.

Because a substantial portion of Savannah's white votes went to the challenger Stillwell, the Democrats were forced into a run-off election, which was held on July 15. Prior to this election, the incumbent, who came in second behind Stillwell in the primary, floated rumors about Stillwell's potential racism, claiming, among other things, that his opponent belonged to a whites-only club. Although Stillwell denied these charges and resigned from the club, he did not attempt to establish an alliance with the city's key African American political leaders or make concessions to the African American community. This gave

TABLE 11.3

The Minimum African American Vote and Percentage in the 1991 Savannah Mayoral Election

Districts	Rousakis	African American Democratic Vote	%	Weiner	African American Republican Vote	%	Total African American Vote	Turnout %
1	3,165	2,946	(69)	1,516	1,297	(31)	4,243	52
2	2,581	1,171	(68)	1,963	553	(32)	1,724	28
3	2,281	620	(68)	3,052	379	(31)	999	38
4	2,277	174	(68)	4,830	79	(31)	253	40
5	2,445	664	(68)	1,562	194	(31)	859	13
6	1,353	368	(68)	3,637	451	(31)	819	56
Total	14,102	5,944	(67)	16,560	2,953	(33)	8,897	

The returns for each district were taken from The Consolidated Returns, Savannah, Georgia, Municipal General Election November 5, 1991 (Board of Elections of Chatham County) for the incumbent Mayor John P. Rousakis and Republican challenger Susan Weiner. The second, fourth, fifth, sixth, and seventh columna were calculated. To arrive at our bases for estimating, we used the Metropolitan Planning Commission in 1990. Using these data, we took the number of whites in Districts One and Two and subtracted it from the total number of votes received in those districts by the Mayor and the challengers. This procedure meant that we accorded white voters a 100% turnout rate, and what vote was left had to be all African American. We totaled the two numbers and then divided that by the total number of nonwhite registered voters to get our turnout rate, as well as the percentage for the Democratic and Republican parties.

We calculated a mean from the turnout rate for District 1 (52) and District 2 (28). It was 40%. Then we took the lowest percentage for each party, 68% for Democrats and 31% for Republicans, to calculate every other category except for District 4 as explained below. For instance, in District 3 we took the Rousakis vote to 2,281 x .40 = 912.4 x .68 = 620. We followed a similar procedure for the Republican candidate.

**For District 4, we had to follow a different procedure because the number of African American registered voters was only 640. Hence, it was 640 x .40 x .31 = 174 and 640 x .40 x .31 = 79.*

Rousakis an opening, and once again he engaged his African American operatives and alliances in an effort to forge a winning coalition. The African American vote carried the day for him in the run-off, a fact that Rousakis, without making any concessions or promises to the African American community, publicly acknowledged. He was now primed for the general election.

Previously, general elections in Savannah had rarely been contested. In 1991, the Republican candidate, Susan Weiner, was a newcomer to town and politically inexperienced. Rousakis was overjoyed. Weiner, he maintained, was "the ideal candidate to defeat in the general election."[16]

The Republican challenger took a proactive stance in the face of the city's crime and murder epidemic. Every time a murder took place in an African American neighborhood, Weiner arrived with the police and emergency medical squads to express sympathy for the family and community members involved. Rousakis called her presence at these events a political stunt. However, Reverend Mitchell and one of the African American county commissioners, Deanie Frazier, who had previously been a strong supporter of the mayor in his 1986 campaign against Roy Jackson, endorsed her. In turn, Rousakis denounced Frazier and Mitchell.

All of the other African American leaders in the city either remained silent or endorsed the incumbent. Given what the Reagan-Bush era had done to African Americans, these leaders could not bring themselves to abandoning their Democratic partisanship, even though a crime wave and murder crisis was destroying their community and the Democrat they had endorsed and supported for many years would not do anything to help. Weiner's announcement of her anti-crime campaign did not dislodge the African American leaders. It did, however, dislodge African American voters.

> After declaring herself "not one of the boys downtown" and mounting a campaign against the old guard, Weiner, a political newcomer, toppled the 24-year incumbent, John P. Rousakis, and became the first female mayor of a major Georgia city.
>
> Weiner, 46, broke other barriers, too: Besides being a native New Yorker, she is a Republican in a city that has traditionally voted for Democrats. She won her new job, in large part, by staging an anti-crime campaign that appealed to voters horrified by Savannah's 59 homicides in 1991, an all-time high for the quiet coastal city of 137,000. Her all-volunteer, rainbow coalition campaign reached disenfranchised voters—chiefly women and blacks . . . eager to quench what Weiner calls the city's thirst for change.[17]

The changed local political context and the Republican candidate's response to it caused a dramatic change in African American voting patterns and behavior in Savannah. Between the run-off and the general election, nearly three thousand African American voters in Savannah switched from the Democratic party to the

Republican party. As table 11.3 reveals, the largest number of African American Republican voters come out of the first district, the area where most of the city's low-income housing was located and where the crime wave was the greatest. This shift caught the African American leadership, and the incumbent, by surprise. Rousakis would have won had these blacks not crossed over. African Americans voting for the Republican were the balance of power in this local election.[18]

Attorney Clarence Martin has long held that the Rousakis mayoralty produced few meaningful returns to Savannah's African American community over the years. Martin, one of the bright young African American political strategists who had worked for years to break Mayor Rousakis's grip on the city's African American electorate, had this to say about the unraveling of the long-standing Democratic electoral coalition:

> It started to collapse in earnest with the African American mayoral campaign of former alderman Roy L. Jackson. And while he made it to and through the primary, but lost the run-off election in the 1986 contest, his efforts provided members of the African American community, both leaders and masses, with a terrific lesson that was both instructive and useful in that African Americans could run citywide and be successful. Thus, those African American voters who had de-aligned from the Rousakis coalition were not ready to rejoin it at the next election. . . . Another force that strained the old Rousakis coalition in the 1991 primary and run-off election was the number of white voters who had grown weary of the incumbent mayor that went to the white aldermen now running for mayor, Brook Stillwell.
>
> Dissatisfied white voters had no place to go, and because of race in their culture and consciousness, they could not bring themselves to support the African American candidates . . . an attractive white candidate moved them out of the coalition with ease.
>
> Although two groups were pulling away from the coalition simultaneously, the African American voter did rejoined the old Rousakis coalition in the run-off because of an uncertainty about Brook Stillwell's commitment to the community. He was still an unknown political commodity. Yet the whites who had pulled away, with Stillwell, did not want to return to the old fold after their candidate went down to defeat in the run-off election.
>
> It all came together in the 1991 general election and the coalition collapsed. The Republican candidate was a woman, and attentive women, white and African American, moved to support this new female candidate. This candidate also gave the disgruntled whites a place to go. And finally, the African American voter who had stayed with the mayor in the run-off deserted him for this new female candidate.

As he concludes: "With these three groups, African Americans, women, and whites, all exiting the coalition at the same time, the mayor was put out of his office and a new day dawned in the city."[19]

Conclusion

An enterprising Republican newcomer reached out to Savannah's African American community and, while its leadership did not respond, one-third of its voters did, and changed things. Low-income African Americans, at the grass-roots level, took the initiative in trying to solve their own problems. They were, in this election, ahead of their own leadership.

The reshaping of the political context at the national level brought African Americans into the Republican party fold, but not for the reasons that party had hoped. While the Republicans were looking to recruit upper-income and middle-class African American conservatives, in Savannah they actually attracted low-income, unemployed, and underemployed African Americans who were tired of being robbed, murdered, and opposed by their own people.

Traditionally, African Americans have supported the party that best serve their needs and deal with issues pertinent to their communities. In the southern city of Savannah, since the Voting Rights Act of 1965, the Democratic party platform was most ideally suited to meet those needs. Consequently, for 21 years, Democrat John P. Rousakis held the mayoralty. Over the years, Rousakis had many opportunities to address directly the issues of crime, unemployment, drugs, and the rapid deterioration of the African American community. Repeatedly, however, he neglected to take any action. As a result, he paved the way for his defeat. African American voters were forced to deviate from their traditional Democratic partisanship to select a candidate who was responsive to the needs of their community. The black vote, combined with the relatively weak vote of the city's Republican bloc, gave Susan Weiner the edge she needed to win over Rousakis's traditional supporters.

However, in her four years in office, Mayor Weiner did not follow through on her anti-crime stance, and although she expanded her base in the white community she refused to expand it in the African American community. In 1995, John Rousakis enlisted his longtime allies in the African American community and entered the Democratic primary. Two African Americans also entered the primary: Frances Bright Johnson, head of the NAACP political advisory council, and alderman Floyd Adams. Only one African American minister, Rev. Matthew S. Brown, endorsed Adams. To the surprise of Rousakis and his near-universal support by the African American leadership, Adams won the African American vote and the primary.

Adams defeated Mayor Weiner by 260 votes in the general election. She refused to concede, claiming irregularities at the polls. After a recount, the chairman of the local Republican party conceded the defeat.

On January 2, 1996, the first African American mayor in the city's 263-year history, Floyd Adams, Jr., was inaugurated at the Savannah Civic Center.

12

AFRICAN AMERICAN REPUBLICAN PARTISANSHIP
Alignment and Dealignment

• • • • • • •

Hanes Walton, Jr.

A party engaged in transforming the political context at any level cannot possibly initiate and fully implement its ambitions without recruiting new party members and supporters. Volumes have been written about partisan identification and partisan realignments, yet African American partisan behavior remains a virtual enigma.[1] In their pioneering work on African American party behavior, Patricia Gurin, Shirley Hatchett, and James S. Jackson make the following claim:

> Black leaders have continuously worried about dependency, first with the Republican Party, and later with the Democratic Party. In repeated elections, they have warned black voters not to allow one party to take their votes for granted. . . . For these reasons, black leaders have always been ambivalent about the major political parties. They did not exhibit unswerving loyalty to the Republican party before the New Deal, nor to the Democratic party afterwards.[2]

The advent of the Reagan-Bush era served to further complicate the picture of African Americans' political party alignment and dealignment behavior.[3]

> Several scholars have noted that beginning with the Nixon presidency, Republican standard-bearers have worked systematically to undermine the achievements of the 1960's civil rights revolution. . . . The first Nixon administration took steps that signalled to the black community that a major shift in federal civil rights policy was taking place.[4]
>
> The retreat from presidential support for civil rights was completed by Ronald Reagan. . . . This administration disagreed with and thus tried to reverse prior civil rights policy. [African Americans] saw the Reagan administration systematically working to reverse the legal gains for which blacks had struggled throughout history and finally won in the 1960s. At least as important in the political thinking of blacks was the Reagan administration cuts in social programs. These cuts disproportionately affected blacks, who are preponderantly in the low-income population. Black opposition to Reagan, already widespread in 1980, grew over the course of his first administration.[5]

The Reagan plan continued under the Bush presidency,[6] as exemplified by the Willie Horton advertisements and Bush's nomination of Clarence Thomas to the Supreme Court.

Given this tendency on the part of the Republican party under Reagan and Bush to introduce issues of race and civil rights for partisan gain, a very simple question can be raised: Did African Americans align or dealign themselves with the Republican party during the Reagan-Bush era? How much of the puzzle of African American political party behavior can be solved by analyzing African American Republican party partisanship during the twelve years of these two administrations?

Unraveling this puzzle is difficult in part because the Reagan-Bush Republican strategy to transform the political context was twofold. Simultaneously with its efforts to disadvantage certain classes of African Americans, the party was also working to attract African American membership.

From the outset, the Reagan administration spread the word that it wanted African American leaders and supporters of a certain political persuasion and predisposition.[7] Additionally, Lee Atwater, chairman of the Republican National Committee, repeatedly let it be known that the party would recruit conservative, middle- and upper-class African Americans.[8] Thus, while African Americans generally were shunned by the Republicans along policy lines, they were invited to join the modern Grand Old Party along class and ideological lines. This select party recruitment has not been the experience of any other group within the American political process, and it marked a radical departure from what had been the African American experience in the Republican party before the Reagan-Bush era.[9]

During the early years of the Reagan-Bush era, the chairman of the Republican National Committee, Lee Atwater, replaced the GOP's traditional recruitment approach with a much narrower one that better suited the party's purpose of contextual transformation. While some traditional African American Republicans acquiesced or supported the Reagan-Bush recruitment thrust, others objected to it. Among this latter group was J. Clay Smith, Jr.:

> If Black people are going to support the Republican party, they need to see that the results of the Reagan administration's economic and social programs benefit them. . . . It is time for Black Republicans who do not share the views of Thomas Sowell and the Fairmont Papers to stand up and be counted and to demonstrate to Black Americans as well as the leadership of the Republican party that we represent the majority view. If we do not . . . the Republican party will never be a viable alternative for the Black community.[10]

For more insights about African American Republican partisanship, let us look at some individual perspectives. Attorney Michael Pratt of Savannah, Georgia tells why he aligned with the Republican party in 1982.

> I started off [in 1974] helping to form a Young Democratic Club at the University of Georgia Law School and finally achieved the presidency of the State's Young Democrats. But over that course of eight years, I finally came to the realization that there was not a whole lot of difference between the parties—Southern Democrats and Southern Republicans. There were some professed philosophical differences . . . but basically you are dealing with people and it is these individual people with those individual ideas that make the impact and make the difference. So I decided, looking at the political situation in the South, that the black vote was being taken for granted by the Democratic party and discounted by the Republican party. I arrived at the conclusion that more African Americans needed to be in both parties in order to make both parties more responsive to the specific needs that addressed African American concerns.[11]

On joining the Young Republican Party, he found "that you had some progressive young people" in the organization and "some regressive as well." Yet, "the attitude toward me was more progressive and more young people were coming into the party with a balanced feeling toward race." These young people wanted to build a strong party in the South and for that they needed black voters. They were trying to reach out to attract blacks into the party and find out what would bring more blacks to vote for Republican candidates in the South.[12]

Pratt ran for probate judge of Chatham county in 1984. He won the primary over a white Republican challenger and garnered between 35 and 45 percent of the white vote. In an interview with the author, he said, "the regressive faction in the party put up this challenger because they didn't want to see the party expand to included African Americans." However, Pratt lost in the general election to the white Democratic candidate.[13] In 1984, a presidential year, African Americans in Savannah voted a straight Democratic ticket, giving Republican candidate Pratt, in his own home districts, no more than 30 to 33 percent of their vote.

Pratt mounted another bid in 1988, running for a state house seat held by an African American female incumbent. Pratt had grown up in this district, which had a black majority. Although the incumbent had been significantly challenged in a previous election, in his own words, Pratt was "soundly trounced in this election." Once again African Americans in the midst of a presidential election voted a straight Democratic ticket. "It was the Republican label that had done me in . . . I was not able to overcome the Republican label" and the "stigma it carried in the African American community."

In 1992, Pratt ran for the newly created 11th congressional district in Georgia. In the Republican primary, he faced an African American minister, Otis Smith, and a white farmer, Woodrow Lovett. He captured enough votes to win a spot in a run-off with Lovett but in that run-off he lost. Lovett lost the general election to Cynthia McKinney. In 1994, she faced another white farmer in the Democratic primary. After she won, he filed a suit that became known as *Miller v. Johnson,* in which the Supreme Court unseated McKinney by declaring the district a case of racial gerrymander.

Pratt was an African American who aligned with the Republican party during the Reagan presidency not because of Republican conservatism, but due to a sense of pragmatism and the needs of the African American community.

Another individual perspective is that of county commissioner Richard Riley of Bryan county, Georgia. He had won his seat as a Democrat in this majority white community where he had been an outstanding high school basketball player. During the Bush presidency, he switched parties and aligned with the Republicans. But before the end of the Bush term, he rejoined the Democratic party and lost the ensuing election. After an interview where it was remarked that some of his ideas sounded like those of Republicans, he went about his political district putting the word out that he might consider joining the Republican party.[15] The word spread and shortly thereafter he got a message from one of former Republican Senator Mack Mattingly's political operatives to attend a luncheon meeting with some of the key Republicans in the state.[16] At the luncheon meeting, the political pitch was made that if commissioner Riley would come out and switch parties, the Republicans would provide great media coverage and the party, which had big plans for him, would set them into motion. As the local Republicans saw it, Riley had cross-over appeal. Here was an African American elected official who had won in a white district in the South.

Two weeks after the luncheon meeting, Riley was told that he was one of six people chosen to greet President Bush, when he visited Brunswick, Georgia that week. The following week, Riley was invited to the White House to participate in a Rose Garden affair, where he met with the chairman of the Republican National Committee, Lee Atwater. In his own words, commissioner Riley "was caught up in the national Republican movement." He was given the red carpet treatment and shortly after his return to Bryan county, he called a news conference which, with Republican help, became a media event. Here, he announced his switch to the Republican party.

His motivations were several. First, "Reagan and Bush had brought patriotism back to middle class white Americans, which whites appreciated very much. In addition, this white middle class was now in the Republican national movement. Hence, electorally the switch made sense." Second, he felt that "African Americans were not negotiating enough for their vote." And in order to do so, African Americans needed to be in both parties. Lastly, he was enjoying himself as a Republican.

Riley's switch came in the midst of a gubernatorial election that the Republican party was making a major effort to win. The party saw 1992 as its best political chance to capture the state house since 1966,[17] the first year since Reconstruction that a Republican won the popular vote (although he lost when the Georgia legislature decided that state law demanded a majority of the vote).[18] In 1992 Republican political ambitions were running high, not only at the state level, but the local one as well. The euphoria had also touched commissioner Riley. He too wanted higher political office. But his ambition ran into opposition from local leaders.

These local leaders, who did not hold office, were connected with former Senator Mack Mattingly, and wanted to enter electoral politics. They felt they had done Riley a favor by connecting him with the top party leadership and that he now owed them a favor. One of the local leaders came to him and demanded that Riley chair his political campaign. When Commissioner Riley voiced his own political ambition, he was threatened. He was told to take the campaign chairmanship or else his re-election bid would be sabotaged because his entire constituency was white. Commissioner Riley was caught up in local hardball Republican politics which demanded that he put his own political plans and ambitions on hold and use his good offices and political visibility to advance the political ambitions of local white Republican operatives. As Riley hesitated, the political heat increased. He was confronted with a demand that he go on local radio and television talk shows to fully endorse and support other white Republicans despite their past history, character, and abilities. He had to do blanket endorsements.

With his political future hanging in the balance, commissioner Riley called a news conference, and switched back to the Democratic party. The local Republicans lost in their electoral efforts, but several did prevail in the 1994 election. Riley paid the price for non-conformity and political infidelity. The national Republican movement to attract African Americans to the Republican party was undone, at least in Bryan County, Georgia by local Republican politicos. Ambition among Republican hopefuls, long out of office, proved their undoing.

In 1992, a group known as the Freedom Republicans filed a lawsuit asking "the Federal Election Commission to hold back every dime of the money it gives to the Republican National Committee until Blacks are more fairly represented in the party."[19] The Freedom Republicans, headquartered in Brooklyn, New York, with some 1,000 members, noted that each party gets "about $11 million of Federal money for its nominating Convention."[20] The Freedom Republicans wanted the Federal Election Committee (FEC) money withheld because the Republican party's rules "make it difficult for members of racial and ethnic minorities to become members of the Republican National Committee and to attend the party's convention as voting delegates."[21] At the time of the suit, there were three African Americans on the Republican National Committee's 165 member voting committee and "all three are from the Virgin Islands."

Federal District Court Judge Charles R. Richey sided with the Freedom Republicans and noted that the delegate selection process of political parties was covered by the Civil Rights Act of 1964, Title VI. This title "forbids discrimination under any program or activity receiving federal finance assistance." However, the FEC had not written any civil rights rules or regulations for political parties.[22] As a result of the suit, it now had to.

Thus at the very moment the Republican party launched its efforts to attract African Americans, current African American party members were suing to make the party more inclusive.

Table 12.1 reveals the percentages of African Americans in every presidential election from 1952 to 1992 who categorized themselves as Republicans. The table gives an indication of the flux in African American alignment and dealignment taking place on the national level. The strongest alignment occurred during the Bush presidential campaign. This alignment trend in the presidential years is repeated at the Congressional level, particularly in 1982, 1986, and 1990. By the time of the Clinton campaign, the alignment trend had shifted to a dealignment one.

However, the data in table 12.1 is party identification and does not reflect party voting by African Americans.[23]

Overall, political party recruitment is based on issues, policy outputs, and benefits.[24] Given the ambivalent nature of the Republicans' Reagan-Bush era recruitment efforts, exactly how did African American political party behavior respond? Did the Reagan-Bush era recruitment efforts of the Republican party lead to the development of a two-party system within the African American community?

In Florida, party registration data have traditionally been disaggregated by race and county. Indeed, Florida has kept such records systematically and comprehensively since 1946,[25] two years after the *Smith v. Allwright* Supreme Court decision abolished the practice of whites-only primaries in the South.

TABLE 12.1

Percentage and Total Number of African American Republicans in Presidential and Congressional Elections, 1952–1994

Presidential Election	% (N)	Congressional Election	% (N)
1952	17 (29)***	1954	22 (22)
1956	20 (29)	1958	22 (35)
1960	20 (34)	1962	15 (16)
1964	8 (13)	1966	11 (15)
1968	** (5)	1970	** (6)
1972	11 (29)	1974	** (7)
1976	6 (17)	1978	8 (18)
1980	8 (15)	1982	** (4)
1984	9 (22)	1986	7 (23)
1988	12 (32)	1990	12 (31)
1992	8 (26)	1994	10 (20)

SOURCE: Center for Political Studies, National Election Studies, 1952–1994.

**The percentage for each election is a composite of the Strong Republican, Weak Republican, and Independent Republican categories.*

****The estimated actual numbers are less than 10, and therefore the % is unreliable.*

******These are the estimated actual numbers.*

Therefore it is possible to discern the number of African American Democrats, Republicans, and other-party voters registered in each county. These data allow me to analyze the alignment and dealignment of Florida's African American voters over time and especially during the Reagan-Bush years.

The state of Louisiana has kept voter registration data by race for more than a century, but only since 1988 has it maintained these statistics by voters' party affiliation. Therefore, data is available from this state for at least part of the period under scrutiny. With this longitudinal, disaggregated data, my analysis will provide perspectives on how African Americans responded to the Republican party's recruitment efforts in two southern states where race was inherent in the political culture. Whereas the Florida data is presented in the official primary reports and again in the general election report during every two-year election cycle, Louisiana reports party registration data on a quarterly basis. However, the Louisiana data is reported herein on a yearly basis.

Because the total universe of data for these two states was available for analysis, this chapter employs descriptive rather than probability statistics, which are more appropriate for a sampling of a total universe of data. Moreover, both graphic and tabular analyses have been utilized to further delineate the trends and general parameters of the party alignment and dealignment of African American voters during the Reagan-Bush era.

African American voters registered as Republicans during the years 1980 to 1992 will be referred to as being aligned with the Republican party. The voters who leave a party will be referred to as having dealigned themselves from that party. Given the aggregate nature of the data, I was able to determine precisely the number of aligned and dealigned African American voters for each time-frame under analysis.

African American Party Politics in Florida: An Historical Overview

"In urbanization for example, may be found a major explanation of Florida's relative unconcern about the Negro. While the state's politics is by no means free of Negro-baiting, the dominant attitude on the race question is comparatively mild." The basic reason for this state of affairs, according to Key, was that "Florida is not only unbossed, it is also unled."[26] H. D. Price, another political scientist, agreed with Key and adds this observation about participation in the mid-1950s:

> Florida's Negro voters, now comprising ten percent of the state electorate, are playing an important part in presidential and gubernatorial elections [within the Democratic party]. They are an accepted factor in local politics in a growing number of counties.[27]

The 1956 gubernatorial primary threatened to cause an upheaval in the traditional state politics. In this campaign, coming two years after the Supreme Court's ruling in *Brown v. Board of Education,* the majority (three of four) of the Democratic party candidates made race an issue by taking a firm stand for maintaining segregation. Only one candidate, Leroy Collins, refused to take a similar stand:

> Negro leadership lined up behind Collins in 1956. [The] importance [of this] can be assessed from the black Democratic registration which had risen to an all-time high of 128,437. A solid black vote for a major gubernatorial candidate was of great importance in placing [Collins] in the run-off or in giving him a majority.[28]

Astute white candidates, Jacobstein notes, "generally solicited the black vote while reassuring whites that they are not pro-Negro. Usually they met privately with black leaders, giving them such assurances as they could."[29] "Using considerable discretion," Collins "continued to solicit the black vote, despite the difficult racial situation into which [the leading segregation candidate] had maneuvered him."[30] When he won, with solid African American support, he could thus assure his white supporters that he had promised African Americans nothing.

Race, when it threatened to surface in Florida politics as a result of the changed political context, was effectively maneuvered out of political existence. The state was able to sidestep a divisive and volatile matter and continue its tradition of limited focus on racial issues throughout the 1960s.[31]

Annie M. Hartsfield and Elston Roady, two political scientists residing in Florida, noted that Florida's African American population made impressive gains in voter registration during the 1960s. By 1970, they report, 56.2 percent of the state's African Americans of voting age (21 years) were registered to vote compared to 39 percent in 1960.[32] African American voter registration was still below that of whites (60 percent in 1960 and 64.2 percent in 1970). Indeed, during the 1960s there were two counties, Gadsen and Jefferson in north Florida, whose populations were majority African American but whose voter registration rolls were comprised of more whites than blacks. African American registered voters in these two rural, sparsely populated, counties comprised only 40 and 35 percent of their voter rolls, respectively. This pattern, which was routine for the South, was one of the factors behind the 1965 Voting Rights Act.[33]

In Florida's urban counties, however, the situation was different.

> Dade (Miami) County with 57,675 Negro registrants and Duval (Jacksonville) County, with 42,183 Negro registrants have the largest number of Black voter participants. . . . The strength of the Negro voter as a group does not appear formidable or forceful in any county, yet the participation of the Negro in the past five years has had a definite effect on the outcome of several Florida elections.[34]

Following the passage of the Civil Rights Act of 1964, white voters in northern Florida reversed their previous unbroken support for the Democratic nominee in the 1964 presidential elections, choosing instead to either support the Republican candidate, Arizonan Barry Goldwater, or refusing to vote entirely.[35] At the same time,

> in other counties greatly increased Negro registration and about solid voter participation for Johnson gave the Democratic presidential nominee the first victory for that party since Truman's plurality victory in 1948. . . . And the pattern of Negro voting observed in the 1964 election was repeated in the 1968 presidential contest [when] between 85 and 95 percent of the Negro voters supported Humphrey in the 1968 election.[36]

Although none of these scholarly observers of African American politics in Florida state it explicitly, they implicitly note that, from 1946 to 1970, African

American voters were strong supporters of the Democratic party and the vast majority registered as Democrats.

African American Republican Partisanship, 1964–1992: A Statistical Overview

Table 12.2 reveals the total number and percentage of African American Republicans in Florida over 14 different state election periods. Table 12.3 shows the

TABLE 12.2

Number and Percentage of African American Republicans in Florida, 1964–1992

Years	Number of African American Republican Partisans	Percent of African American Partisans	Percent of Republican Partisans	Percent of Grand Total
1964	15,054	6	4	1.0
1966	14,420	5	3	1.0
1968	*13,443	4	2	1.0
1970	11,961	4	2	0.4
1972	12,063	3	1	0.4
1974	12,414	4	1	0.3
1976	13,364	3	1	0.3
1978	12,725	3	1	0.3
1980	14,847	3	1	0.3
1982	15,146	3	1	0.3
1984	19,215	3	1	0.3
1986	21,716	4	1	0.4
1988	**24,898	4	1	0.4
1990	27,348	5	1	1.0
1992	32,322	5	1	1.0
Mean	17,396	4	2	.6

SOURCE: Tabulation of official votes by Secretary of State, 1964–1990, General Election Returns.

**In 1964, the Secretary of State did not report the breakdown of registered voters by race in the tabulation of official votes cast in the general election. The racial breakdown is reported in the tabulation of official votes for Florida primary elections. Each year thereafter it is reported in both the primary and general election returns.*

***In 1988, the Secretary of State again breaks the traditional pattern and reports the racial breakdown not in the official tabulation of results but in a list entitled "Voter Registration." In this list, there is for the first time a racial breakdown for all third parties as well.*

TABLE 12.3

Number and Percentage of African American Alignment and Dealignment with the Republican Party in Florida, 1966–1992

Years	Number of African Americans Aligning with Republican Party	Percent of Alignment	Number of African American Republicans Dealigning	Percent of Dealignment
1966			634	4
1968			977	7
1970			1,482	11
1972	102	1		
1974	351	3		
1976	950	7		
1978			639	5
1980	2,122	14		
1982	1,299	8		
1984	3,069	16		
1986	2,501	12		
1988	3,182	13		
1990	2,450	9		
1992	4,974	15		
Mean	2,100	10	933	7

Adapted from the various tabulations of official votes by the Secretary of State. Calculations prepared by author.

number of African Americans who joined or left the Republican party from 1966 to 1990. After the 1964 election campaign, when the Republican party was being led by its anti-civil rights presidential candidate, Barry Goldwater, the number of African American voters in the state who were registered as Republicans started to decline. Goldwater's impact is quite clear. The resulting decline, or dealigning process, continued until Richard Nixon assumed the presidency in 1972, whereupon it began to increase until midway through President Jimmy Carter's term of office. At that point, in 1978, the number of African Americans registering as Republicans slowed and dropped significantly. However, Carter's regionalism failed to dissuade 950 African American Floridians from joining the Republican party during his presidency. Beginning in 1980, African Americans in the state began to register increasingly as Republicans, with their numbers hovering around the four-percent mark of all registered African American voters in the state and at about one percent of all Florida Republicans. Black Floridians attached themselves to the GOP in unprecedented numbers throughout the

TABLE 12.4

Number and Percentage of African American Republicans in Louisiana, 1988–1992

Years*	Number of African American Republican Partisans	Percent of African American Partisans	Percent of Republican Partisans
1988	17,022	3	NA
1989	17,204	3	NA
1990	19,016	3	NA
1991	19,776	3	NA
1992	21,287*		

SOURCE: Secretary of State's Office.

**The 1992 data were collected and reported only for a three-month period, through March 27, 1992.*

Reagan-Bush years, despite the party's selective recruitment policies and these presidents' efforts to turn back the clock on civil rights.

Table 12.4 illustrates the realities of African American political party alignment in Louisiana during the Bush presidency. As in Florida, Louisiana's African American voters increasingly aligned themselves with the Republican party from 1988 to 1992, although their numbers never rose above the three percent level.

In Table 12.5 the Louisiana data is further disaggregated to reveal the actual number of African American Louisianans who aligned with the Republican party during the Bush years.

Although some of these findings parallel those reported in Florida, overall

TABLE 12.5

Number and Percentage of African Americans Aligning with the Republican Party in Louisiana, 1989–1992

Years	Number of African Americans Aligning with Republicans	Percent of Alignment	Number of African Americans Dealigning with Republicans	Percent of the Dealignment
1989	182	1	0	0
1990	1,812	10	0	0
1991	760	4	0	0
1992	*1,511	7	0	0

SOURCE: Louisiana Secretary of State's Office.

**The 1992 data were collected and reported only for a three-month period, through March 27, 1992.*

the numbers in Florida are greater. While Florida experienced some dealignment in the early years of the Bush administration, the GOP in Louisiana saw absolutely no dealignment among its African American partisans.

Conclusions

While registration data from these two states reveal the precise numbers of African American voters who registered as Republicans, these data do not reveal, at least not at the individual level, what factors motivated these individuals to align with the GOP or join the Reagan-Bush crusade. Further analysis of the Florida party registration data by race can provide additional information on the Republican party's overall mobilization within the African American community.

Table 12.6 shows the number of new African American voters entering the party process from 1966 through 1992. With the exception of 1970 and 1990, two non-presidential-election years, these numbers were significant. The first sharp increase in new party registrants came after the 1965 Voting Rights Act. The next two sharp increases came during the presidential election years of 1972 and 1976. Beginning in 1980, Reagan's first year as president, and continuing to 1992, African American Republican party affiliation increased substantially. Clearly the Reagan-Bush contextual counterrevolution had an impact on African American voters, most of whom had previously been Democratic partisans.

Yet table 12.6 shows that Democratic party registration among African Americans in Florida was much greater. In only one election cycle during the Reagan-Bush era (1988) was African American party registration less than 95 percent Democratic. This lopsided identification of African Americans with the Democratic party is reflective not only of traditional voting patterns but also of the counter-effects of the Reagan-Bush Republican policies. These policies increased the number of African American Republican party identifiers, but they likewise increased the number of African American Democratic party identifiers. For (approximately) every three African American Republicans that the Reagan-Bush effort netted, they sent seven or more to the Democrats.

Table 12.7 confirms this same general observation for Louisiana. As more and more new African American voters came on board, the overwhelming majority signed up as Democrats. The seemingly much higher mean of 29 percent Republicans and 71 percent Democrats in Louisiana for the period from 1988 to 1992 is due to the fact that 100 percent of the state's African American voters registering in 1989, at the time of David Duke's campaign, registered as Republicans. The average Republican figures for the other three years was only about 5.7 percent of the total registered voters. Once again, the data suggest that Reagan-Bush era Republican party policies both attracted African American

TABLE 12.6

The Total Number of Voters and Number and Percentage of New African Americans Registering as Democrats or Republicans in Florida, 1966–1992

Years	Total Number of New African American Voters	Number of New African American Republicans	Percent of Total	Number of New African American Democrats	Percent of Total
1966	59,051	0	0	59,051	100
1968	10,036	0	0	10,036	100
1970	0	0	0	0	0
1972	55,936	102	0.2	55,834	99.8
1974	4,390	351	8	4,039	92
1976	54,350	950	18	53,400	82
1978	8,561	0	0	8,561	100
1980	41,565	2,122	5	39,020	95
1982	41,142	1,299	3	39,843	97
1984	90,625	3,069	3	87,556	97
1986	2,501	2,501	100	0	0
1988	18,697	3,182	17	0	0*
1990	19,614	2,450	15	0	0*
1992	19,492	4,974	26	8,492	44**
Mean	32,766	2,100	5	36,583	95

Adapted from various tabulations of official votes by the Secretary of State.

*Decrease in three years.

**Does not total 100 because a considerable number of African Americans registered as third-party voters or as independents.

TABLE 12.7

The Total Number of Voters and Number and Percentage of New African Americans Registering as Democrats or Republicans in Louisiana, 1989–1992

Years	Total Number of New African American Voters	Number of New African American Republicans	Percent of Total	Number of New African American Democrats	Percent of Total
1989	*	182	100	0	0
1990	21,281	1,812	8	19,469	92
1991	14,472	760	5	13,712	95
1992	40,310	1,511	4	38,799	96
Mean	25,354	1,066	29	23,990	71

Adapted from data provided by the Louisiana Secretary of State's Office.

voters to their fold as well as mobilizing many more African Americans to vote Democratic.

At worst, one could conclude that the Reagan-Bush efforts to transform the political context backfired. At best, their efforts met with only partial success. While they did change African American political party behavior, generating more and greater African American identification with the Republican party, they likewise sent more African Americans running to the traditional party of choice, the Democrats. In the case of these two southern states, the transformation of the political context cut both ways.

13

AFRICAN AMERICAN POLITICAL PARTY CONVERSION

The Impact of the Clarence Thomas Nomination on the Party Partisanship of the Residents of his Hometown

• • • • • • •

Hanes Walton, Jr., LaShawn Warren, Damon E. Elmore, Amy Y. Graham, Victor Cooper, Simone Green, Kimberlynn Hendricks, Sesley Jones, Renita D. Lipscomb, Stephanie Williams, and Renia Williams

Voters either change their party affiliation at the onset of a major new political era, or they switch as the era evolves.[1] Partisan moorings can give way or be broken loose by societal events, salient issues, charismatic political personalities and candidates, or bold new party stances. In some cases, the party of transformation, in its programs and policies as well as the posturing and rhetoric of its political spokespeople, may be overtly or covertly opposed to the goals of certain groups. For example, during the Reagan-Bush era, the Republicans sought to portray African Americans' centuries-long drive for liberty and equality as a zero-sum game. The conversion of African Americans from their traditional Democratic party allegiance to identification with the Republican party of the 1980s was a difficult but not impossible task. Some African Americans did align themselves with the Reagan-Bush Republicans, and the reasons for this lie in the unique appeal the GOP made to the African American community during this era.

Throughout the history of American party politics, both major parties have made overt, racist, anti-African American appeals to the white electorate while simultaneously making covert appeals for support to the African American electorate. As a case in point, about a century ago, the Democratic party, led by Grover Cleveland, captured control of the White House and Congress (1893–94) and immediately went about rolling back legislation that had earlier been passed to facilitate implementation of the Fifteenth Amendment, which gave African Americans the right to vote.[2] Similarly, from 1980 to 1992, the Reagan-Bush Republican party was bent on transforming the political context so as to disadvantage African Americans.

Although both parties in both eras engaged in anti-African American policies and rhetoric, noticeable numbers of African Americans converted to the Democrats in the 1890s and the Republicans in the 1980s, despite their platforms and practices.

> In a sense, the challenge facing Democrat Cleveland [in 1884] resembled the challenge confronting Republican Ronald Reagan a century later. Both men led political parties distrusted by the great majority of blacks—parties that argued against a strong federal role in the enforcement of racial equality—and both presidents sought to allay black fears of the new administration and build up a cadre of black supporters.[3]

Lawrence Grossman notes that, upon taking office, President Cleveland recognized black support for his candidacy by appointing African Americans to the diplomatic corps.[4] Cleveland also invited Frederick Douglass and his white wife to dinner at the White House.[5] However, when Cleveland was running for reelection in 1892, he made overtly racist appeals to whites to win their votes while reaching out to African American voters as if there were no contradiction.

> In 1892, with former President Cleveland running once again against President Harrison, the Democrats raised the specter of a Republican revival of the federal election bill. Advised by his campaign manager to exploit the issue, Cleveland recalled "the saturnalia of theft and brutal control which followed another federal regulation of state suffrage." The solidification of ties between northern and southern Democrats in opposition to federal protection of black voters led some blacks who had previously backed the Democrats to switch sides. . . . But this had no impact on northern Democrats.
>
> The Democrats won in a landslide. The new administration repealed the remaining federal election laws; . . . and southern states were now free, with no fear of federal interference, to find ways to disenfranchise their black citizens—even while the Fourteenth and Fifteenth Amendments remained in the Constitution.[6]

The *New York Sun* commented: "The possible loss of the votes of the few colored men . . . counts for nothing against the great duty which the Democracy owes to Democratic principles, and to the happiness and fortunes of millions in the South."[7] In the midst of such racist campaign rhetoric and statements, African Americans almost abandoned the Democratic party. A few, however, continued to support the Democrats. The Democrats won a landslide victory. According to Grossman:

> Indeed, what is surprising is the large numbers of blacks who campaigned for the Democrats in 1892 despite the situation in the South. Democrats exploited black grievances over patronage and argued that the Republican high tariff positions hurt blacks by raising prices on foods they had no choice but to buy.[8]

After the elections, the Cleveland administration repealed the remaining federal elections laws, which meant that the southern states were free once again to find ways to disfranchise their African American citizens despite the Fourteenth and Fifteenth Amendments.[9]

A century later, while simultaneously seeking the electoral support of African American voters, the Reagan-Bush presidencies sought to undercut the civil rights laws of the 1960s and 1970s. Again, some African Americans did convert and join the Republicans despite that party's disregard for and opposition to issues of racial equality and justice.

Historically, both major parties have sought to convert African Americans to their ranks by employing two strategies: (1) political appointment of African Americans to federal positions and (2) appeals to middle and upper-class, conservative African Americans. This chapter targets the first strategy by focusing on the following research question: Does a party's political appointment policy influence the degree of African American conversion to that party, regardless of its stance on racial issues?

Periods of great partisan change are commonly described in the literature as eras of "critical realignment." That is, "the majority of the voting electorate severs its old, long-standing, durable, and basically predictable, partisan alignment and realigns itself with a new political party."[10] To some historians and political scientists, the realignment of African American voters from the Republican to the Democratic party during the New Deal was due to partisan conversion. Others see African Americans' realignment with the New Deal Democrats as the result of that party's efforts to mobilize new African American urban voters.[11]

Recently rediscovered election return data permitted an empirical test of the conversion-mobilization hypothesis in the city of Boston during the New Deal.[12] The Boston data facilitated one of the first explicit studies of critical realignment at the local level. They also reveal how partisan organizations can best craft winning electoral coalitions, either through mobilizing new voters, converting existing voters, or some combination of the two.

Gerald Gamm claims that most scholars "seem convinced that conversion, rather than voter mobilization, was fundamental to the realignment among blacks."[13]

> Among those who have considered the issue, then, there appears to be a consensus that blacks were realigned at least by 1936, and that realignment was a classic example of voter conversion. Indeed, even Kristi Anderson, the foremost proponent of the mobilization argument, finds conversion in her study of Chicago's black population.
>
> There is no evidence from Boston's black precincts to support such conclusions. Turnout among the city's blacks was never remarkably low and it rose steeply after 1932. While black Bostonians were indeed realigned in 1936, or perhaps even 1934, that realignment represented largely a mobilization of new voters, especially of women. It was that mobilization, not a large-scale conversion of former Republicans, that fueled the development of a Democratic majority in the black community in Boston.[14]

Although the Boston political environment does not support, in Gamm's view, the conversion thesis, some conversion apparently did take place. While we cannot test the realignment theories of conversion or mobilization that took place during the New Deal, Gamm's findings compel further exploration of the relationship of race-based political appointment practices to African American party conversion and loyalty. Indeed, the present analysis represents the first time that the assumptions and presuppositions about the conversion effect of party appointment have been tested with regard to African Americans.

During the Reconstruction era, when it ceased sponsoring and supporting major civil rights policies for African Americans, the Republican party initiated the strategy of appointing African Americans to minor domestic and diplomatic posts so as to maintain the loyalty of the African American electorate and political elites.[15] The Democrats were quick to adopt this strategy as well, beginning with the Cleveland administration in 1884.

> President Cleveland recognized blacks in his appointments to the Diplomatic Corps. He adhered to the tradition, instituted by Republican presidents, of appointing blacks as ministers to the "black" nations of Haiti and Liberia, and named another black as consul in Luanda, Angola.[16]

This strategy has been used successfully by both parties over the years as political patronage to either maintain African Americans' loyalty or convert them to their ranks. It was significantly employed during President Carter's administration, and President Reagan's Attorney General Edwin Meese clearly used it to lure African Americans to the Republican party during that administration, as did President Bush. The current Clinton administration has gone even further than its predecessors in this regard, disbursing political appointments as a substitute for public policy that responds to the demands of African Americans. The critical question remains: is the tactic of appointment an effective means of drawing and maintaining the partisan loyalty of the African American electorate?

Data and Methodology

Did President Bush's 1992 nomination of Clarence Thomas to the Supreme Court influence significant numbers of the African American residents of Thomas's hometown of Pinpoint, Georgia, to abandon their traditional alliance to the Democratic party and join the Republican party? That is, as a consequence of this appointment of one of their own, did Pinpoint's African American community realign itself with the Republican party? If so, what can be inferred to the larger setting? If not, why not? Lastly, what would any change in alliance tell us about the nature and scope of African American partisan conversion in an era of contextual transformation of the political environment? In early February 1992, four months after the Senate confirmed Clarence Thomas's nomination to the Supreme Court on October 15, 1991, the authors (a professor and twelve senior political science majors at Savannah State College) began to plan an empirical analysis of these research questions.

Like Savannah, Pinpoint is located in Chatham county, less than five miles from Savannah State's campus. Our curiosity was piqued by a statement that appeared in an article on the front page of the local newspaper. In that article, Leola Anderson Williams, Clarence Thomas's mother, stated that she would vote for President Bush in the next election.[17] After scrutinizing Williams's comments, I decided that a local-context exploration of the conversion thesis was possible.

After a thorough examination of the aggregated election return data for the county, the research team concluded that it would be too difficult to isolate the African American electorate in Pinpoint because the precinct in which the majority of the city's African Americans lived was populated by both African American and white residents. We therefore decided to utilize survey methodology and conduct direct interviews with African American members of the Pinpoint community. Thus, the first step was survey construction. From my past experience of developing surveys for the African American community,[18] I was convinced that a composite instrument consisting of well-known questions on political partisanship and participation and questions developed specifically for the local or state context would be most effective for our purposes. Hence, we utilized 19 questions on (1) demographic matters, (2) political partisanship, (3) voting behavior, (4) major issues, and (5) presidential evaluation, drawn from the National Black Election Survey (NBES),[19] and merged these items with 12 questions specifically addressing the impact of Thomas's nomination on the partisan behavior of Pinpoint's African American residents, for a total of 31 close-ended questions.

The students helped in the selection and placement of the questions as well as the pretesting of the survey instrument among the Savannah State College student body. After refining the survey instrument, the team conducted an on-site evaluation of the Pinpoint community to assess the number of African American households and become familiar with the area. One member of the team, whose family had a number of friends from the area, acted as liaison. Most of the residents were amenable to talking with us.

Next, we mapped out our survey strategy. Instead of doing a sample of the residents, we decided to survey the entire community, or total universe of Pinpoint's African American population of approximately 44 households. Many of the families lived in extended family arrangements, and several indicated that they wanted one survey to suffice for their entire extended family. We therefore modified our strategy to accommodate the desires of the residents, and accordingly, members of these families provided unitary responses to our questions.

Demographically, Pinpoint, as the newspapers depicted it during the Thomas hearings, is a small, impoverished hamlet on the outskirts of Savannah. Overall, it is an isolated, tight-knit, low-income community. Nearly everyone knows everyone else; likewise, everyone knows Clarence Thomas's family. Pinpoint is a one-street community with lots of unpaved streets running off the main thoroughfare. Pinpoint is bounded on the west by a saltwater marsh, on the east by a large trailer park, on the south by a causeway leading to posh Skidaway Island, and on the north by a major white residential development. Formerly, the community's residents crabbed and fished the rivers, creeks, and marsh beds in the area. There was a small canning factory that prepared seafood for shipment throughout the country, but over-fishing brought that enterprise to a standstill in the late 1960s. Pinpoint residents generally work in nearby Savannah.

There is a small community center as well as a small county-maintained playground and a private African American clubhouse located on the marsh. On weekends, the community center brings together many of the residents for a pot-luck fish, oyster, and crab meal. This gathering provides both a recreational and a social outlet for the community's residents. There is also a small Baptist church on the northern fringe of town.

Moving systematically from household to household, we conducted our survey from July 4, 1992, until February 25, 1993. We worked primarily on weekends, near midday and in the early evenings on Saturdays, because that was the only time the whole team could get together and because that was when most of the city's residents could be found at home. Although the survey itself took very little time to conduct, most residents were eager to talk to the students.

Most also offered them food; hence, the majority of these otherwise brief interviews turned into sessions several hours long. Generally, only one or two interviews could be conducted per weekend session.

Thomas's mother, Mrs. Williams, and his sister, Mrs. Emma Mae Martin, were both included in the survey, but they were interviewed last, after all the other residents of Pinpoint had been surveyed. We also conducted extended (about 45-minutes long) taped interviews with these two women. Mrs. Martin still resides in Pinpoint in the house of their grandfather, Myers Anderson. Thomas's mother resides in Savannah.

Altogether, we obtained a total of 30 complete surveys and two in-depth interviews of Thomas's sister and mother;[20] these survey responses and the interviews provide the database for this inquiry. Professor Kenneth Jordan of Savannah State College's Social Science computer lab developed our code book and assisted me in preparing and analyzing this data using SPSS-PC statistical software.

African American Political Party Conversion: The Pinpoint Case

Table 13.1 reflects the demographic and partisan profile of Pinpoint's African American citizens. Most of them, 63.3 percent, are women. The majority have a high school education or less. Pinpoint is primarily populated by elderly people, most of whom are over 50 years of age. The mean annual family income is between $25,000 and $34,000, derived primarily from blue-collar jobs. The majority of the population belong to the sole Baptist church located in the community.

Table 13.2 reveals the parameters of the city's political partisanship. Clearly three-fourths (73.3%) of the African American residents of Pinpoint were registered as Democrats at the time of the survey. Of these, almost two-thirds (60%) voted a straight ticket, indicating a very strong partisan Democratic bent, typical of the African American community.[21] Independents and "other" party-affiliated voters comprised 16.7 and 6.7 percent of the population, respectively. A mere 3.3 percent were registered as Republicans, and none of the these voters claimed to be "strong" Republicans. Hence, the potential for conversion to the Republican party was there. However, table 13.2 also shows that Pinpoint's African American residents saw the Democratic rather than the Republican party as working hardest for African Americans—past, present, and future.

Table 13.3 presents the residents' evaluations of the Bush administration. Two-thirds (66.6%) of Thomas's hometown African Americans disapproved of the way in which President Bush was handling his job. More than three-fourths felt that Bush was not in touch with ordinary people like themselves, and nearly the same number (70%) felt that he did not care much about people like them.

TABLE 13.1

Demographic Characteristics of the Residents of the Pinpoint Community

Category	Number	Percentage
Education		
Grade School	3	10.0
Some High School	4	13.3
High School Graduate	8	26.7
Some College	11	36.7
College Graduate	4	13.3
	30	100.0
Income		
Less than $3,000	1	3.3
$3,000 to $14,999	2	6.7
Between $15,000-24,999	11	36.7
Between $25,000-34,999	5	16.7
$35,000 or more	5	16.7
Not Sure	3	10.0
Did Not Respond	3	10.0
	30	100.0
Gender		
Female	19	63.3
Male	11	36.7
	30	100.0
Age		
18-20	0	.0
21-24	0	.0
25-34	5	16.7
35-49	10	33.3
50-64	11	36.7
65 or over	4	13.3
Did Not Respond	0	.0
	30	100.0
Occupation		
Professional & Managerial	8	26.7
White Collar	1	3.3
Blue Collar	13	43.3
Housewife	1	3.3
Retired	6	20.0
Unemployed	1	3.3
	30	100.0
Religion		
Protestant	8	26.7
Catholic	1	3.3
Other	20	66.7
None	1	3.3
	30	100.0

SOURCE: Survey of residents of Pinpoint, Georgia: Supreme Court Justice Clarence Thomas's hometown. Conducted July 3, 1992 to February 25, 1993 by political science majors at Savannah State College.

TABLE 13.2
The Party Positions of the Residents of the Pinpoint Community

Category	Number	Percentage
Party Identification		
Strong Democrat	16	53.3
Weak Democrat	5	16.7
Independent Democrat	1	3.3
Independent	5	16.7
Weak Republican	1	3.3
Strong Republican	0	.0
Other	2	6.7
	30	100.0
Vote		
Straight Ticket	18	60.0
Different Parties	7	23.3
Do Not Know	4	13.3
Do Not Know	1	3.3
	30	100.0
Hard Work of Democrats		
Very Hard	5	16.7
Fairly Hard	7	23.3
Not Too Hard	12	40.0
Not Hard At All	3	10.0
Do Not Know	3	10.0
	30	100.0
Hard Work of Republicans		
Very Hard	2	6.7
Fairly Hard	0	.0
Not Too Hard	9	30.0
Not Hard At All	16	53.3
Do Not Know	3	10.0
	30	100.0
Party Helps Most		
Republican Party	1	3.3
Democratic Party	16	53.3
Not Much Difference	11	36.7
Do Not Know	1	3.3
No Answer	1	3.3
	30	100.0

SOURCE: Survey of residents of Pinpoint, Georgia: Supreme Court Justice Clarence Thomas's hometown. Conducted July 3, 1992 to March 10, 1993 by political science majors at Savannah State College.

Overall, these primarily Democratic partisans had a low evaluation of this Republican president.[22]

Beyond matters of demographics, partisanship, and presidential evaluation, the survey probed the Pinpoint residents' position on civil rights and discrimination to get some feel for the issues of importance to this community of African

TABLE 13.3
Presidential Evaluations by the Residents of the Pinpoint Community

Category	Number	Percentage
Bush Handling of Job		
Approve Strongly	2	6.7
Approve Not Strongly	3	10.0
Disapprove Not Strongly	7	23.3
Disapprove Strongly	13	43.3
Do Not Know	5	16.7
	30	100.0
Bush in Touch With Ordinary People		
Extremely Well	1	3.3
Quite Well	5	16.7
Not Too Well	5	16.7
Not Well At All	18	60.0
Do Not Know	1	3.3
	30	100.0
Bush Care About People		
Extremely Well	0	0.0
Quite Well	5	16.7
Not Too Well	6	20.0
Not Well At All	15	50.0
Do Not Know	4	13.3
	30	100.0

SOURCE: Survey of residents of Pinpoint, Georgia: Supreme Court Justice Clarence Thomas's hometown. Conducted July 3, 1992 to March 10, 1993 by political science majors at Savannah State College.

Americans. The results are presented in table 13.4. The majority (53.3%) of the respondents felt that civil rights leaders were pushing too slowly during the Bush presidency. Unlike President Bush and the conservative Republicans, they believed that discrimination based on race was still a major national problem. Some 80 percent, or four-fifths of the Pinpoint residents, felt this way. Nearly all (96.7%) concurred that the government should do all that it can eliminate racial discrimination. Unlike the conservatives of the era, including their own Clarence Thomas, who were clamoring for equal results, these African Americans still believed in the goal of equal opportunity.

Our survey also probed the respondents' personal familiarity and relationship with Clarence Thomas (see table 13.5). More than half of Pinpoint's African Americans (53.4 percent) claimed to know Thomas well, the majority having known him for more than seventeen years or nearly two full decades. One-third of the residents, including his mother and sister, were related to Thomas.

Did Thomas's hometown folks switch to the Republican party when he was nominated? Table 13.6 reveals the answer: Only one person, Thomas's mother, changed her partisan affiliation from the Democratic to the Republican party as

TABLE 13.4

The Position of Pinpoint Residents on Major Civil Rights Issues

Category	Number	Percentage
Push of Civil Rights Leaders		
Too Fast	1	3.3
About Right	11	36.7
Too Slow	16	53.3
Do Not Know	2	6.7
	30	100.0
Discrimination No Longer A Problem		
Agree Strongly	3	10.0
Agree Somewhat	1	3.3
Disagree Somewhat	3	10.0
Disagree Strongly	21	70.0
Do Not Know	2	6.7
	30	100.0
Society Should Do Whatever To Insure Equal Opportunity		
Agree Strongly	24	80.0
Agree Somewhat	5	16.7
Disagree Somewhat	0	.0
Disagree Strongly	0	.0
Do Not Know	1	3.3
	30	100.0

SOURCE: Survey of residents of Pinpoint, Georgia: Supreme Court Justice Clarence Thomas's hometown. Conducted July 3, 1992 to February 25, 1993 by political science majors at Savannah State College.

a response to her son's nomination and appointment to the Supreme Court. In an extensive interview, she told us why:

> When Clarence went through what he went through and I sit up there the five days and see how the Democrats did my son, I feel more like being a Republican. . . . I'm through with the Democrats. . . . Bush was the best candidate in the 1992 election . . . I voted for him in November. . . . Yes, I did.

While no other African American residents of this community switched party affiliation, 10 percent indicated that they were leaving open the possibility of conversion in the future. And, as shown in table 13.7, 20 percent revealed that although they would not become Republicans, they would vote for President Bush in the upcoming election. Thus, a fairly significant number of residents were willing to split their ticket or switch parties as a response to the President's support of one of their own.

TABLE 13.5

The Relationship of Pinpoint Residents with and to Judge Thomas

Category	Number	Percentage
Familiarity With Judge Thomas		
Extremely Well	11	35.7
Quite Well	5	16.7
Not Too Well	2	6.7
Not Well At All	6	20.0
Do Not Know	6	20.0
	30	100.0
Long Known Judge Thomas		
Less Than 1 Year	0	.0
2 - 5 Years	1	3.3
6 - 16 Years	2	6.7
17 Years Or Longer	17	56.7
Do Not Know	10	33.3
	30	100.0
Blood Relations To Judge Thomas		
Brother/Sister	1	3.3
Mother	1	3.3
Cousin	10	33.3
Not related	18	60.0
	30	100.0

SOURCE: Survey of residents of Pinpoint, Georgia: Supreme Court Justice Clarence Thomas's hometown. Conducted July 3, 1992 to February 25, 1993 by political science majors at Savannah State College.

TABLE 13.6

Number and Percentage of Party Converts and Party Stalwarts Among Pinpoint Residents

Category	Number	Percentage
Will Become a Republican		
Yes	1	3.3
No	23	76.7
Already Republican	0*	.0
Maybe	3	10.0
Do Not Know	3	10.0
	30	100.0

SOURCE: Survey of residents of Pinpoint, Georgia: Supreme Court Justice Clarence Thomas's hometown. Conducted July 3, 1992 to February 25, 1993 by political science majors at Savannah State College.

**Only one resident identified himself as a weak Republican, and even that person did not want to convert strongly to Republican as a consequence of the nomination of Judge Thomas to the Supreme Court.*

TABLE 13.7
Number and Percentage of Pinpoint Residents Who Would Vote for President Bush

Category	Number	Percentage
Vote for President Bush		
Yes	6	20.0
No	20	66.7
Maybe	3	10.0
Do Not Know	1	3.3
	30	100.0

SOURCE: Survey of residents of Pinpoint, Georgia: Supreme Court Justice Clarence Thomas's hometown. Conducted July 3, 1992 to February 25, 1993 by political science majors at Savannah State College.

Conclusions

Our analysis of the survey data revealed that there was support for our research questions. The political appointment of an African American by a Republican president had a minimal conversion impact on the residents of the community from which the appointee originated. Although several African American residents left open the possibility of a later conversion, only one person, the appointee's mother, converted, and her conversion came about not so much as a consequence of the nomination per se, but as a result of the nomination fight and the struggle by the Democrats on the Senate Committee to defeat her son's appointment. Hence, the appointment was not the only operative variable in this conversion. However, party strategists have good reason to believe in the effectiveness of political appointments as a vote-getting technique. It succeeds on at least two levels: (1) party converts and (2) new party voters. This was the case in the Pinpoint community, where, as a consequence of the President's nomination, more African American residents, while not convinced to change parties entirely, expressed their willingness to vote Republican at least in the next presidential election.

The strategy of political appointment is a means of manipulating voters in an era of contextual transformation even when the transforming party is inimical to the manipulated voter's interest. Here, the empirical data shows that, by applying this strategy, a political party can use race in a negative and demeaning way and still attract voters from the impacted community into its ranks. Of this paradoxical political reality, William Riker writes:

> It is true that people win politically because they have induced other people to join them in alliances and coalitions. But the winners induce by more than rhetorical attraction. Typically they win because they have set up the situation in such a way that other people will want to join them—

> or will feel forced by circumstances to join them—even without any persuasion at all. And this is what heresthetic is about: structuring the world so you can win.
>
> So, in both the large and the small, the manipulation of dimensions is a major part of heresthetics. This manipulation works even though those who are manipulated know they are being manipulated because, once a salient dimension is revealed, its salience exists regardless of one's attitude toward it. It may be that this is why the manipulation of dimensions is the preferred heresthetical maneuver; once performed it does it work without further exertion by the heresthetician.[23]

Presidents Reagan and Bush reintroduced the dimension of racial cleavage to American partisan politics, thereby transforming the political context. They were also able to manipulate African Americans into assisting with this transformation, partly through the tactic of political appointments. In its examination of President Clinton's political appointments, chapter 19 adds more evidence to this view and reveals that this strategy has not been monopolized by just one party. Indeed, both the major parties have used and are currently using it with regard to African American and other ethnic communities and reaping significant results, getting both converts and new voters.

14

SOUTHERN COMFORT

The Impact of David Duke's Campaigns on African American Politics

• • • • • • •

Hanes Walton, Jr. and Maxie Foster

The history of southern political demagogues is rooted in the Reconstruction and Jim Crow eras. The first era (1866–1890) gave birth to the leaders of the southern resistance, while the second era (1891–1901) provided these leaders with an atmosphere conducive to the restoration of white supremacy. It was during this second era that the most colorful, artful, entertaining, and fiery political players emerged, and the political demagogue became a staple in southern politics. Men like Ben "Pitchfork" Tillman and "Cotton" Ed Smith of South Carolina, James "The White Chieftain" Vardaman and Theodore "The Man" Bilbo of Mississippi, Tom Watson of Georgia, Jefferson Davis of Arkansas, and "Cotton" Tom Heflin of Alabama were elected to key statewide political office as a result of their "Negro-baiting" tactics. Not only did their showmanship on the stump dominate the state politics of their day, but their antics revealed to other political hopefuls for generations to come the path to political power.

A new generation of southern political demagogues emerged as the South witnessed the abolition of white primaries in the 1940s, the marches and demonstrations of the 1950s and 1960s, and the passage of civil rights legislation during the 1960s and 1970s. Governor Eugene Talmadge of Georgia was the most celebrated demagogue of the forties. "The Talmadge personality and the vividness of his race and class appeals divided the Georgia electorate into two camps."[1] Later southern politicians such as South Carolina's Strom Thurmond, Mississippi's James Eastland, Arkansas's Orval Faubus, and Alabama's George Wallace were cut from similar cloth.[2]

The marches and demonstrations led by Martin Luther King, Jr. were met by violence and naked brute force sanctioned and in some cases instigated by political demagogues calling themselves segregationists, to maintain racial inequality in their states.[3] The moral outrage and scrutiny generated by these nonviolent civil rights protests meant that outright Negro-baiting and overt segregationist stands had to be moderated and sanitized. Thus were born organizations such as the White Citizens Council in 1955.[4] Race continued to be the dominant force in the region's political culture and campaigns, even though it was camouflaged under terms such as "states' rights," "freedom of choice," "neighborhood control," "individualism," and "moderation." Its potential for partisan political gain and individual political advancement never faded completely. As one civil rights lawyer commented about the contemporary situation in Mississippi: "Although the most vicious racial demagoguery has been eliminated as a successful tactic in statewide races, it continues to appear in convert, disguised forms."[5]

V. O. Key, perhaps more so than any other political scientist, attempted to define and describe the southern political demagogue.[6] With this caveat in mind, one can better appreciate Key's efforts to describe the types of southern political leaders that emerged during the 1940s and discuss their dominant role in that region's politics. Key noted that these politicians varied significantly in both degree and kind. There were flamboyant, hilarious, rabble-rousing clowns or knaves and polished con artists as well as genuine heroes among them. Whatever their stripes or tendencies, "Negro baiting" was the most central element of their political game. As Key writes:

> The "delta" and redneck states of mind owe much for their existence to James K. Vardaman, former governor and senator. Mississippi populism never amounted to much, but the neo-populist governor, Vardaman, gave the politics of the state a spirit and a form that Theodore Bilbo carried on through the decades. Elected governor in 1902 . . . Vardaman, . . . a picturesque demagogue . . . became a popular idol. He bundled up all the populist doctrines—anti-corporations, the cause of the common man—with the advocacy of white supremacy.[7]
>
> Vardaman gave a beautiful demonstration of the uses to which the race issue can be put—by persons without scruple. His contribution to statesmanship was advocacy of repeal of the Fifteenth Amendment, an utterly hopeless proposal and for that reason an ideal campaign issue. It would last forever. The rednecks—and some delta planters—did not know that they were being humbugged and they loved it.[8]

> It is a puzzling characteristic of southern politics that candidates can at times get themselves elected by their skill in advocacy of something on which everyone is agreed. Honorable and decent men—who agree with the demagogues on the race issue—are branded by the Negro baiters as less devout communicants in the common faith.[9]

According to Key, "The 'Southern demagogue' is, nevertheless, a national institution. His numbers are few but his fame is broad. He has become the whipping boy for all his section's errors and ills—and for many of the nation's."[10]

By the early seventies, one southern political scientist, Earl Black, was suggesting that this breed and brand of political leadership was dying, at least at the gubernatorial level.[11] Black could not have foreseen the Reagan-Bush era of the 1980s and early 1990s, during which race—as an opportunistic political issue and divisive campaign tactic—would once again be reinstituted and manipulated for political gain.

As Ronald Reagan was situating himself to run for president, he made many unpublicized tours of the South, along the way advancing notions acceptable to that region. To the southern states he carried a familiar, yet subtly encoded, message.

> In Hattiesburg, Mississippi, where Theodore Biblo had carried his racist message from the piney woods to Washington, [Reagan] told them how he thought this country should be turned back again to the old tried-and-true ways that our forefathers found to be the backbone of a new nation.[12]

In Gatlenburg, Tennessee, Reagan told Republicans:

> There are a lot of people out there in our community that you and I should be talking to, and all of those people are the unsung heroes of our world. . . . [To them] we offer equal opportunity at the starting line of life, but no compulsory tie for anyone at the finishing line.[13]

Greenhaw notes:

> As [Reagan] moved around the South in those days, moving quietly but forcefully, he was really and truly a living-room candidate; he came into their meeting halls, their convention auditoriums, their hotel banquet rooms, and their panel-lined dens. He rode easily across the territory, clearing the way for another day when he would bring the campaign troops for a showdown.[14]

When Reagan ducked in and out of the one-horse towns referred to

> in Southern idiom as wide-places-in-the-road, he found no Republican organizations to speak of. But he did find sympathetic and satisfied listeners who could tell neighbors: "He's the kind of person we need in the White House."[15]

Indeed, Reagan was working the southland nearly two full decades before his 1980 presidential campaign, and he was wooing the same people that Tillman, Vardaman, Heflin, and Wallace had enlisted as voters and supporters in their day. By the time Reagan ran for president in 1980, he could count key southern leaders such as J. Strom Thurmond, Jesse Helms, Howard Baker, John Towers, Jeremiah Denton, Jerry Falwell, and J. B. Stoner among his backers. Another southerner, Lee Atwater, who would later run Bush's presidential campaign, was placed in charge of Reagan's campaign in South Carolina.[16]

With Ronald Reagan in the White House, the political context was ripe for the rebirth of the Southern political demagogue. Enter David Duke of Louisiana.

Data and Methodology

This paper explores two major research questions: (1) Can a political demagogue, in a state where race is a salient feature of the political culture, find support for his candidacy in a political context designed to advance racial cleavages for partisan gain? (If so, how much support can be generated, and at what elective level can such a candidate be successful?); and (2) What is the response of the targeted race in a situation where their political interests and rights are held in jeopardy by the emergence of such a candidate?

When Key offered his analysis of southern politicians in the 1940s, African Americans were not allowed to participate in the southern electoral process and were thus unable to respond to the antics and pronouncements of the demagogues of the day.[17] They were consigned to simply watch the passing political parade and hope for the best in the future. Therefore, the answers to these two research questions will not only provide new insights into modern-day demagoguery, but they will provide the vital missing elements of the political equations formulated by commentators like Key and used to explain the political scenarios of earlier times.

The election returns for each of David Duke's eight state races from 1988 to 1991 provide the empirical database for this analysis. In the aggregate, these data provide the general parameters and contours of Duke's political support in Louisiana. To provide an empirical rendering of the second research question data were available that enabled us to identify and isolate those parishes (counties) where African Americans comprised the dominant majority. We used voter registration records from these parishes to determine empirically the extent to which David Duke's political campaigns mobilized the electorate.

The Impact of David Duke's Campaigns on Louisiana's White Electorate

Louisiana has a history of political demagoguery, but with a distinctive twist.

> In other states there arose spokesmen for the masses who gave the people at least hope. Louisiana had no Blease or Watson or Vardaman to voice the needs and prejudices of ordinary men. It had its rabble rousers to be sure, but its annals include no outstanding popular hero acclaimed as the leader of the common cause.[18]

Key goes on to state, however, that "while Louisiana Negroes do not vote in appreciative numbers, many of them look with favor on the Kingfish [Huey Long], who is quoted as saying: 'I've never been a party to any piece of legislation calculated to hurt the Negro . . . I've always wanted to help them.' "[19] Although the Long dynasty might not have been Negro-baiting, Huey Long and his heir, Russell Long, had supporters and appointed to political office individuals who were. One, Judge Leander Perez of Plaquemines parish, did his best to maintain racial cleavages for political gain. Perez pushed laws through the state legislature that stripped African Americans of their rights and dignity.

> Like the Mississippi River gathering together all the upstream torrents into a muddy flood, Perez has gathered into one spirit all the money, lust, moon-spawned hatred for the black man and Jew and foreigner, and painful paranoiac reaction to federalism that have marked the Deep South for many years; he has gathered them from many sources, and then slopped them back upon the land. . . . He is still recorded as a rabble-rouser emeritus by deep ranks of last ditchers throughout the South. But in Louisiana his influence, where it existed, was less symbolic, more practical and much, much shadier.[20]
>
> Perez came to riches through Huey and to national infamy through the Dixiecrats, but he did not impact the full effects of his bigotry in Louisiana until the second coming of Jimmy Davis, the Singing Governor, in 1969. Davis was Perez's *tabula rosa,* on which he could scribble all sorts of insults for the federal government and the Negroes to read.[21]

Therefore, when David Duke announced his first bid for political office in 1980, he not only had a personal background of involvement with racist causes, but he announced his candidacy in a state with a similar heritage of political leadership. Moreover, he was running as a Republican in the newly reshaped Republican party headed by Ronald Reagan and George Bush.[22] But how exactly did Duke do in terms of electoral support?

Figure 14.1 reveals the level of support that Duke's race-baiting candidacy achieved in his six races for statewide office and two state representative district races. In two of the statewide contests, which occurred after Duke had won a seat in the state legislature, he captured more than 40 percent of the voters' support. When he ran for governor of Louisiana, he gained one-third of the state's electoral support in the primary and nearly 40 percent in the run-off election.

After he won a seat in the state legislature Duke received national exposure. As he rose to political power and fortune, the Republican party leadership tried to thwart him, particularly during the 1992 campaign, because of the image problem he was creating for President Bush's reelection bid, and for Lee Atwater's efforts to attract African American voters to the GOP.[23] Although the party attacked Duke, it never disavowed the race card or its use. The national party's efforts to stifle Duke simply fueled the controversy, bringing him more media attention and effectively preventing the party from taking steps to keep Duke off the ballot in the state primaries. Moreover, as Greenhaw maintains, "as far as the Deep South was concerned, [Duke] was very much a part of modern-day Republicanism in his view of the issues."[24] As the Republican party leadership learned, mere repudiation of a racist demagogue was not enough to put the racial genie back into the political bottle.

FIGURE 14.1

Percentage of the Vote for David Duke in Statewide Races in Louisiana, 1988–1992

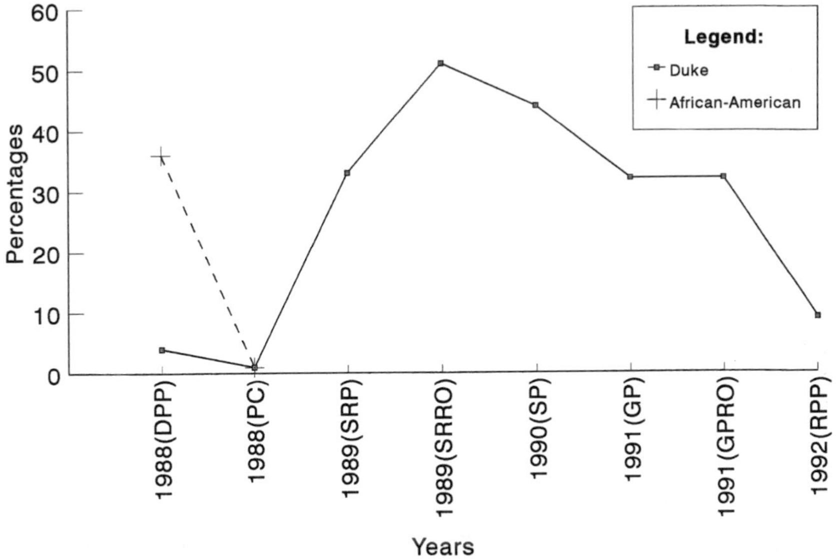

SOURCE: Louisiana Secretary of State's Office. See Appendix for details on DPP, PC, SRP, SRRO, SP, GP, SPRO, and RPP.

Duke made his poorest showing in the 1988 presidential race in his effort to run as a third-party presidential candidate on the Populist party ticket. In this race, he got a mere 1.1 percent of the vote. However, he lured away 3.7 percent of the Democratic primary vote in 1988 and 8.8 percent of the Republican primary vote in 1992. Running in both party primaries allowed Duke to gauge which party offered him the best chance at winning in subsequent state and local contests.

The dotted line in figure 14.1 reveals the strength of the African American candidates who opposed Duke in his eight election campaigns. In the 1988 Democratic presidential primary, Duke competed against the Reverend Jesse Jackson, and Jackson won the state, gaining 36 percent of the votes compared to Duke's 34 percent.

The Impact of David Duke's Campaigns on Louisiana's African American Electorate

In figure 14.2, which presents registration data for the five years from 1988 to 1992, a clear pattern can be discerned with regard to African American electoral mobilization in Louisiana. African American voter registration during this period

FIGURE 14.2

Mean African American Voter Registration in Louisiana by Political Party, 1988–1992

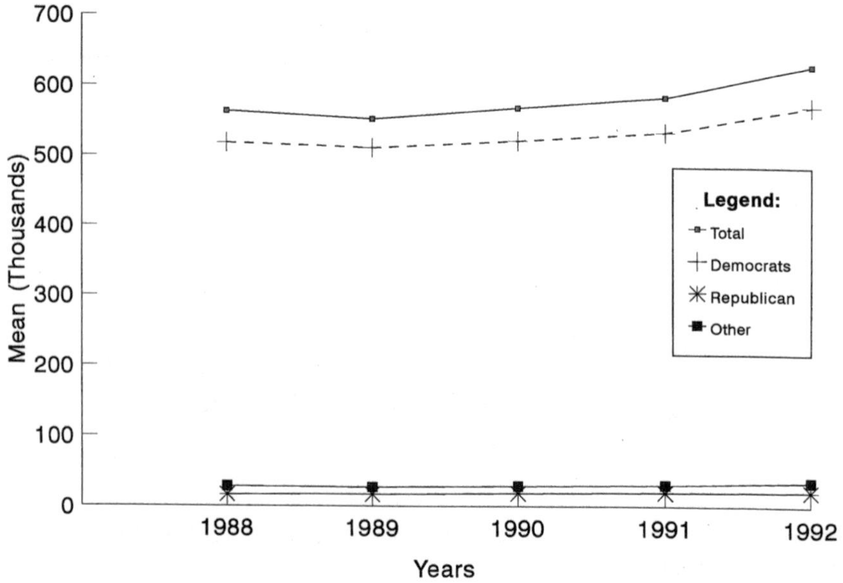

SOURCE: Louisiana Secretary of State's Office.

rose from 560,893 in 1988 to 630,066 in the early months of 1992, an increase of 11 percent. In short, nearly 70,000 additional African Americans—more than a thousand a month—registered to vote in the era of David Duke's political campaigns. Clearly the African American community mobilized to electorally resist Duke's ascendancy.

When we disaggregate the African American vote in the majority-African American parishes of East Carroll, Madison, and Orleans, we see that Reverend Jackson got significantly more votes than Duke in the 1988 Democratic primary and carried the parish by huge percentage margins. There was seemingly little support for Duke in these parishes, except in Orleans, which has a substantial white population (see table 14.1).

Table 14.2 shows the results of the 1992 Populist party vote. Duke clearly outperformed his strongest opponent, Lenora Fulani, particularly in the Orleans parish. African American voters opted not to turn to the third-party candidate in lieu of the Democratic Party candidate, Michael Dukakis.

Eventually, Duke shifted his attention away from national politics and the

TABLE 14.1

Votes for Jackson and Duke in the 1988 Democratic Presidential Primary in African American Majority Parishes

Parishes	Candidates	Votes	%
East Carroll	J. Jackson D. Duke	979 27	57.5 1.6
Madison	J. Jackson D. Duke	1,060 31	61.6 1.8
Orleans	J. Jackson D. Duke	52,036 3,013	64.2 3.7

SOURCE: "Proclamation of Election Returns: Presidential Preference Primary," *States-Times* (March 24, 1988).

TABLE 14.2

Votes for New Alliance Candidate Fulani and Populist Candidate Duke in 1988 in African American Majority Parishes

Parishes	Candidates	Votes	%
East Carroll	L. Fulani D. Duke	10 88	.3 2.5
Madison	L. Fulani D. Duke	4 123	.1 2.5
Orleans	L. Fulani D. Duke	395 1,233	.2 .7

SOURCE: "Election Proclamations: Elections for President and Vice President of the United States," *States-Times* (November 19, 1988).

Democrats to focus on a local state legislative race. This proved to be an effective strategy for him. In the district in which he chose to run, the African American electorate was small and had little political power. Table 14.3 shows that Duke, running as a Republican, defeated both the Republican and Democratic candidates in this strongly Republican district. Moderate Republicans rallied their troops for the run-off election, but their efforts were not enough to stop the Duke juggernaut. His race-baiting tactics prevailed on the local level. At this level, African American voters could make little difference.

Emboldened by this victory, Duke saw even greater political opportunities ahead. The voters at the local level were responding to his overt racial appeals. Therefore, the next year, 1990, he entered the race for the state's Senate seat. As table 14.4 shows, in the four majority African American parishes, turnout made the difference in denying Duke a seat in the United States Senate. The state's African American voters derailed the Duke campaign by generating turnout levels usually seen only in big-city African American mayoral contests.[25]

In 1991, Duke entered the state gubernatorial contest, obtaining 32 percent of the vote, enough to come in second and force a run-off in the Republican primary (see table 14.5).

TABLE 14.3

Number, Percentage, and Turnout for David Duke's 1989 State Legislative Race

Candidates	Registered Voters	Voted	Turnout	%
		Primary		
	21,297		57%	
		Republicans		
David Duke		3,995		33.1
John S. Treen		2,277		18.8
Delton Charles		2,030		16.8
Roger Villere		1,142		9.5
Ron Courtad		791		6.5
		Democrats		
Budd Ohster		1,150		9.5
Bobby Savoie		697		5.8
		Run-Off		
	21,297		78%	
David Duke		8,459		50.7
John Treen		8,232		49.3

SOURCES: *Report of the Secretary of State,* p. 8, and "Statewide Report of Registered Voters as of 12/30/88 by Parish," Department of Elections and Registration.

TABLE 14.4
Number, Percentage, and Turnout for the 1990 United States Senate Race in Louisiana's African American Parishes

Parishes	Candidates	Votes	%	Turnout
East Carroll	J. Bennett Johnston	1,865	57.8	
	David Duke	1,101	34.2	
	Nick J. Accardo	68	2.1	
	Larry Crowe	190	5.9	
		3,224		56%
Madison	J. Bennett Johnston	2,467	56.0	
	David Duke	1,649	37.4	
	Nick J. Accardo	85	1.9	
	Larry Crowe	206	4.7	
		4,407		58%
Orleans	J. Bennett Johnston	110,395	76.9	
	David Duke	30,423	21.1	
	Nick J. Accardo	1,957	1.4	
	Larry Crowe	831	.6	
		143,606		60%
St. Helena	J. Bennett Johnston	2,827	53.0	
	David Duke	2,382	44.7	
	Nick J. Accardo	67	1.3	
	Larry Crowe	53	1.0	
		5,329		68%

SOURCE: "Election Proclamation: United States Senator," *States-Times* (October 18, 1990).

Before analyzing Duke's electoral performance in the gubernatorial race, we can evaluate his performance in Louisiana's African American parishes. In two of the parishes, more African American voters turned out to vote in this election than turned out in the previous senatorial races, limiting Duke, in St. Helena parish, for example, to only one-third of the vote. Former Governor Edwin Edwards was the beneficiary of the increased African American turnout. In the run-off, African Americans increased their turnout and gave Edwards more votes in three of the four parishes. In Orleans parish, African American nearly doubled their number of primary votes, ensuring a major defeat for Duke (see table 14.6).

Duke's rising political fortunes had peaked and were beginning to be substantially checked by the African American electoral turnout. As shown in table 14.7, statewide, African Americans were defending themselves against the nation's newest political demagogue.

But Duke would not quit. By 1992, he announced that he would run for the presidency of the United States, and would seek that position under the Republican party banner. Although the national GOP blocked him from getting on the ballot in several states, he was able to get on the ballot in Louisiana and run in the Republican primaries. Due to the national outcry, the party repudiated Duke and tried a few ballot repression maneuvers. The results of that effort are

TABLE 14.5
Number, Percentage, and Turnout for the 1991 Republican Gubernatorial Primary in Louisiana

Candidates	Votes	%	Turnout
Edwin Edwards	523,195	33.8	
David Duke	491,342	31.7	
Buddy Roemer	410,690	26.5	
Clyde Hollaway	82,683	5.3	
Sam James	11,847	.8	
Ed Karst	9,663	.6	
Fred Dent	7,385	.5	
Annie L. Thompson	4,118	.3	
Jim Crowley	4,000	.3	
Albeet Powell	2,053	.1	
Ronnie Johnson	1,372	.1	
Ken Lewis	1,006	.1	
Total	1,549,354	100.0	72%

SOURCES: "Proclamation of Election Results: Governor," *Moving Advocate* (October 31, 1991) and "Statewide Report of Registered Voters as of 9/27/91 by Parish," Department of Elections and Registration.

delineated in table 14.8. Louisiana's Republicans clearly preferred Bush and Pat Buchanan to their native son. Combined, Buchanan and Duke received less than 10 percent of the vote.

The African American Republican vote alone could have doubled Duke's support, but few of these votes, if any, went to Duke. Instead, he was undercut by the very party he claimed to represent.

In the final analysis, the Duke candidacies caused greater: (1) registration in the African American community, (2) African American voter turnout, and (3) African American support for the Democratic party candidate. Overall, this meant greater mobilization of voters to register and vote Democratic, in line with what African American voters did in Georgia in the 1940s and 1950s, when they were confronted with the political demagogue Talmadge and others of his stripe.[26]

On the individual level, in 1991 one African American candidate designed his campaign materials to indicate that a vote for him was a way to defeat David Duke. This African American elected state official, Alphonso Jackson, chairman of the state house's Health and Welfare Committee, bought political ads in local African American newspapers which read: "We must Re-elect Alphonso

TABLE 14.6

Number, Percentage, and Turnout for the 1991 Republican Gubernatorial Primary in African American Parishes

Parishes	Candidate	Votes	%	Turnout
East Carroll	Edwin Edwards David Dukes Others	2,182 1,030 780 3,992	54.7 25.8 19.5	68%
Madison	Edwin Edwards David Dukes Others	2,329 1,530 1,256 5,115	45.5 29.9 24.6	67%
Orleans	Edwin Edwards David Dukes Others	85,502 21,031 50,433 156,966	54.5 13.4 32.1	64%
St. Helena	Edwin Edwards David Dukes Others	3,077 1,958 853 5,888	52.3 33.3 14.5	76%
	Total Votes	171,961		65%

SOURCES: "Proclamation of Election Results: Governor," *Moving Advocate* (October 31, 1991) and "Statewide Report of Registered Voters as of 9/27/91 by Parish," Department of Elections and Registration.

TABLE 14.7

Number, Percentage, and Turnout for the 1991 Gubernatorial General Election in African American Parishes

Parishes	Candidate	Votes	%	Turnout
East Carroll	Edwin Edwards David Dukes	3,017 1,357 4,374	69.0 31.0 100.0	75%
Madison	Edwin Edwards David Dukes	3,582 2,286 5,868	61.0 39.0 100.0	77%
Orleans	Edwin Edwards David Dukes	173,744 25,921 199,665	87.0 13.0 100.0	82%
St. Helena	Edwin Edwards David Dukes	3,700 2,448 6,148	60.2 39.8 100.0	80%
	Total Votes	216,055		81%

SOURCE: "Proclamation of Election Results: Statewide Offices," *Moving Advocate* (November 22, 1991).

TABLE 14.8
Number, Percentage, and Turnout for the 1992 Republican Presidential Primary in Louisiana

Candidates	Votes	%	Turnout
George Bush	83,744	62.0	
Pat Buchanan	36,525	27.0	
David Duke	11,955	8.8	
Pat Paulsen	1,186	.9	
Tennie Rogers	1,111	.8	
George Zimmerman	474	.4	
Thomas Fabish	114	.1	
Total	135,109	100.0	33%

SOURCES: "Proclamation of Election Results: Republican Presidential Primary," *The Advocate* (March 20, 1992) and "Statewide Report of Registered Voters as of 1/3/92 by Parish," Department of Elections and Registration.

Jackson—we must Defeat David Duke."[27] Jackson, who faced a tough reelection bid, was also defeated. Outside the state, African American civil rights leaders took notice of Duke's Republican affiliation, and they used his campaign and tactics to criticize and urge action from Republican party leaders. They also urged local leaders to respond in a forthright manner.

Conclusions

This investigation has yielded empirical support for both of the research questions. Clearly, changing the political context changes regional politics. African Americans during the Reagan-Bush era rose to meet the challenge of resurrected southern political demagoguery, combining with other forces to cause the demagogue's downfall. Yet they were not successful in blocking his efforts to attain state district office in a district where their vote had little impact. It is still possible for regional political demagogues to be reborn with some limited political success.

Appendix

1988 DPP = Democratic Party Primaries
1988 PC = Populist Party Presidential Candidate
1989 SRP = State Legislative Republican Primaries

1989 SRRO = State Republican Run-Off
1990 SP = United States Senate Primaries
1991 GP = Gubernatorial Primaries
1991 GRPO = Gubernatorial Run-Off Primaries
1992 RPP = Republican Presidential Primaries

15

AFRICAN AMERICAN REPUBLICAN CONGRESSIONAL CANDIDATES AND MONEY

The Role of the Republican Party PACs

• • • • • • •

Hanes Walton, Jr.

Maintaining or transforming the political context involves the "mother's milk of politics"[1]—money. The Reagan-Bush contextual revolution was financed by a significant infusion of political money. Political fundraising, at both the individual and the PAC (political action committee) levels, was the key factor that enabled the Republicans to attain and maintain an advantage over Democratic party candidates during the sixteen of the Reagan, Bush, and Clinton presidencies. The Republican party outspent the Democrats at every level during this era.[2] The Republicans' advantage can be attributed to the leadership of its chairman, William Brock, who served from 1977 to 1981. Brock's skillful planning and implementation strategies led to innovative fundraising techniques at both levels.

> In part this Republican advantage results from the Republican headstart. The Brock successes of the 1970s gave the Republicans an advantage in more than just the sums of money raised. It led to advantages in technology, trained personnel, the size of contributor lists, and even the reduction of fund-raising overhead. In fact, Republicans claimed their fundraising costs had dropped to a very slim 19 percent of receipts by 1980. It is, in other words, a race in which the front-runner keep improving its performance while the contender struggles not to let the gap widen.[3]

"It seems safe to say," Sorauf concluded, "that the Democratic party will not catch the Republicans in the race to the bank."[4]

To this, David Magleby and Candice Nelson add that "the Republican campaign committee began the 1980s with a tremendous fundraising advantage" that lasted well into the decade and beyond.[5] "One reality that colors all discussion," they averred, "is that the Republican party raises and spends more money than the Democratic party."[6] The Republicans' net fundraising receipts in 1980 amounted to $163 million compared to the Democrats' $30 million. In 1984, the Republicans had amassed $289 million; the Democrats only $90 million. By 1988, these figures were $191 million for the Republicans and $81 million for the Democrats. At the beginning of the 1990s, the Republicans had raised $192 million, compared to the Democrats' $104 million.[7] Thus, in every election cycle, the Reagan-Bush Republican war chest far exceeded that of the Democrats.[8]

During the 1980s, "campaign contributors also fueled the momentum toward the Republicans. Lobbyists, PACs, the feeling was everywhere. . . . Money was flowing to the GOP even more rapidly than before."[9] According to Sorauf, the corporate PACs showed an overwhelming preference for Republican candidates,[10] but the Republicans outdistanced the Democrats at the individual fundraising level, also.

> Both parties depend heavily on individual contributions, yet there are important partisan differences. Much has been said about the smaller average Republican contribution, but while the Democrats' average contribution is higher, the Republican still surpass them in the number of both small and large contributors.[11]
>
> By any measure one wants to adopt, the average individual Democratic loyalist has less disposal income than the average Republican, and that is a crucial fact in a system of campaign finance that rests ultimately on the voluntary contributions of individuals.[12]

The Republicans used their financial advantage to make them competitive in the political process. After winning the White House and gaining a majority in the Senate in 1980, they spoke openly of gaining the 26 seats necessary to win control of the House of Representatives by 1982.[13] By that year, they not only had the will and strategy to capture the House of Representatives, they had the finance muscle to do so. According to Jackson:

> In the two-year election cycle leading up to the 1980 election the NRCC [National Republican Congressional Committee] raised $26.8 million, more than double what it had achieved two years earlier. Its income was thirteen times as great as the DCCC's [Democratic Congressional Campaign Committee].[14]

Indeed, Jackson claimed, "The NRCC had so much money its biggest problem was figuring out how to spend it."[15]

The Democrats and other political players were quick to note the Republicans' potential. As Jackson related:

> Republican Rep. Guy Vander Jagt of Michigan, the Republican campaign committee chair, recalled that in 1981, the House Democrats were nicer to House Representatives than at anytime I have been there. It was real to them that they might [one day] be a minority.[16]

Both national parties have a House committee, a Senate committee and a national committee that directly or indirectly influence congressional campaigns. On the Republican side, these are the National Republican Congressional Committee (NRCC), the National Republican Senatorial Committee (NRSC), and the Republican National Committee (RNC). For the Democrats, these organizations are the Democratic Congressional Campaign Committee (DCCC), the Democratic Senatorial Campaign Committee (DSCC), and the Democratic National Committee (DNC).[17] Each committee is chaired by a Representative or Senator who is appointed or elected by the party leadership and approved by the party caucus. Committee chairmen, who are chosen because of their fundraising abilities and their capacity to recruit able and attractive candidates, are well-rewarded for their efforts.[18]

Of these congressional campaign committees, Magleby and Nelson note that they "provide financial resources in two ways: direct contributions and coordinated expenditures, which include services the party may provide or purchase for candidates such as polling, mailings, production of broadcast advertisement, or in some cases buying television or radio air time."[19] Thus, in the final analysis, "there is little difference between these (coordinated) expenditures and direct party contributions because candidates have a strong say as to how coordinated money is spent."[20] The only significant difference is that these contributions and expenditures do not have to be reported to the Federal Election Commission (FEC).

Then there is the matter of strategy. The Republican strategy to win a majority in the House of Representatives was developed long before the 1982 election and went into place as soon as the Republicans saw they had a money advantage over the Democrats.

> Republican wealth means the party can target more of the money to challengers and candidates in races for open seats. In other words, it can contribute the maximum allowed to incumbents and still have enough to fund other candidates who are competitive.[21]
>
> The Republicans' ability to raise more money than they can legally spend on behalf of individual candidates enables them to conduct generic

> national campaigns such as those used in 1980 ("Vote Republican for a Change") or in 1982 ("Stay the Course"). . . . They carefully target their resources to contests in which the money will make the greatest difference.[22]

Given the Republican party's enormous financial advantage, did the GOP use any of its financial advantage and largesse to recruit and support African American Republican congressional candidates? We have shown in earlier chapters that, via federal appointments, the GOP sought to elevate to positions of power and authority those African Americans who would assist the party in dismantling the civil rights achievements of the 1960s and 1970s. Did this extend to installing more African American Republicans in Congress?

Data and Methodology

This investigation relies upon data from the Federal Election Commission to delineate and assess the actual sums that the Republican party gave to African American Republicans who ran for congressional seats during the 1980s and 1990s. As mandated by a 1974 law, the FEC officially collects campaign disclosure forms from Senate and House electoral contests and publishes this information every two years.[23] These published reports provide information on both the major parties' contributions (donations of money or in-kind contributions of services, goods, or property to a campaign) and expenditures.[24]

Using this data, I identified and then disaggregated the campaign donations from the Republican party to African American Republican candidates running (1) against African American Democratic incumbents in the House, (2) for open House seats, and (3) for the Senate. This disaggregation allows us to isolate the amount and type of support given to each type of candidate. By isolating the open-seat category, we can determine whether the Republicans' expressed goal of targeting open seats in the House included supporting African American candidates for those seats. Isolating the senatorial races permits us to determine whether the Reagan-Bush GOP took advantage of any opportunities to advance beyond the rhetorical levels of support by backing an African American candidate (or candidates) for office in the chamber that had had but one African American member since Reconstruction.

Because the data source is the total universe and not a sampling, I relied on descriptive rather than probability statistics for this data analysis, reporting the results in tabular and graphic form where appropriate. The base year for this study is 1980, the year the Republicans captured the White House and the Senate. The endpoint is 1994, the last year for which published FEC campaign finance reports were available at the time of the study. This examination of the eight election cycles for which data are available should provide evidence of the trends in GOP support for its African American candidates during the bulk of this era of political context transformation.

African American Republican Challengers, 1980 to 1994

When the Republicans took control of the presidency and the Senate in 1980, there was but one African American Republican in Congress: Representative Melvin Evans, from the Virgin Islands. Ironically, however, Congressman Evans lost his seat in 1980 despite the Republican tidal wave and despite the $8,343 in party contributions. The Democratic challenger, Ron DeLugo, received $1,250 in party support, but he received $47,814 in total campaign contributions compared to Evans's $28,840. Evans won 47 percent of the vote, while his Democratic challenger won 53 percent.[25] After the election, President Reagan awarded Evans a small ambassadorial post.[26]

Overall, the pattern of the Republican party's funding for African American GOP candidates in 1980 was substantially lower than it had been in previous years, dating back to 1974.[27] In the three election cycles prior to 1980, African American Republican candidates had much larger campaign chests than they did in 1980. In 1978, for example, the mean campaign expenditure for Republican challengers was $12,260; for 1980, it was $7,963.

What happened after 1980? During this decade, few African American Republican candidates were recruited or sponsored by the GOP (see table 15.1). Only in 1988 did the Republicans decide to promote a substantial number of African American candidates, in about one-fourth of the contestable incumbent seats. In no year did these candidates provide any significant challenge to an African American Democratic incumbent. There were an average two Republican challengers per each congressional contest over the decade. Table 15.1 shows the exact number per election. The Republican strategy to capture the House of Representatives only minimally involved those seats occupied by African American incumbent Democrats.

As reflected in table 15.2, the mean Republican party contribution was far from substantial. Very few African American Republican candidates received even minuscule contributions from their sponsoring party. These scant contributions were significant in another way, however: none of the African American Republicans who challenged an African American Democratic incumbent and received party campaign funds won their races. In fact, the GOP-funded African American challengers met the same fate as the non-funded ones: all lost.

Turning to the open-seat category, table 15.3 reveals that the Republican party's efforts to fill open House seats with African American Republicans were uneven. Only in 1990 did one of the party's African American candidates win an open seat in the House of Representatives, regaining the single seat it had lost at the beginning of the decade.

TABLE 15.1

African American Repubican Challengers to African American Democratic Incumbents, 1980–1994

Years	Number of African American Incumbents Running for Reelection	Number of Republican Challengers	Percent of Total
1980	14	2	14
1982	19	6	32
1984*	20	4	20
1986	10	6	32
1988	22	9	41
1990	20	3	15
1992	21	1**	5
1994	36	5**	14
Mean	20	5	22

Adapted from the Federal Election Commission Final Reports on U.S. Senate and House Campaigns: 1980–1995. Calculations prepared by author.

**Two unusual realities are apparent from the 1984 data. First, the African American Republican Dale F. Harmon, who ran against Democratic incumbent Gus Savage, received a $6.00 contribution from the Republican party. Second, an Asian American Republican candidate who ran against incumbent Congressman Mervyn Dymally received no party contributions at all.*

***These are the numbers who received financial support from the party. A few got no funds at all.*

Table 15.4 depicts the level of financial support the GOP gave to African American Republican challengers in open seat House and Senate races by delineating party financial commitment in mean dollars. In the first three election cycles, this commitment to African American Republican challengers for open congressional seats was next to nothing. Beginning with 1986, the party's financial commitment to its African American candidates began to rise, until one African American Republican candidate, Gary Franks, won in Connecticut in 1990, having received the largest amount contributed by the GOP to an African American candidate for the House.[28] At the senatorial level, an African American Republican, Maurice Dawkins, got the party nomination for a Senate seat in Virginia in 1988, in part because the Democratic contender was the state's popular former governor, Charles Robb.[29] Dawkins thus got the nomination almost by default. Notwithstanding, the Republican party made a substantial expenditure on his behalf, the largest amount spent for the campaign of an African American Republican candidate during the entire era. Dawkins lost to Robb, getting only 28 percent of the total number of votes cast.[30]

TABLE 15.2

Mean Republican Party Contributions to and Expenditures for African American Republican Candidates Challenging African American Democratic Incumbents, 1980–1994

Years	Mean Major Party Contributions	Percent of Mean Total Receipts	Mean Major Party Expenditures	Percent of Mean Total Expenditures
1980	$1,054 (2)*	1	45,339 (2)	**
1982	6,704 (3)	3	25,813 (2)	7
1984	6,334 (3)	9	28,790 (2)	32
1986	1,008 (2)	4	23,046 (2)	**
1988	2,559 (2)	20	12,734 (2)	**
1990	1,340 (1)	3	42,901 (2)	**
1992	15,000 (1)	15	- 0 -	- 0 -
1994	4,651 (5)	3	17,040	12

Adapted from the Federal Election Commission Final Reports on U.S. Senate and House Campaigns, 1980–1995.

**The number in parentheses is the actual number who received contributions from Republican party PACs. Not all Republican challengers received money, and not all of the challengers were African Americans. Thus, the number in parentheses is the number that are African Americans and received money from the Republican party.*

***Represent the fact that the African American Republican challengers received* no *monies that were expended on their behalf. Hence, there were no numbers with which to calculate percentages. Put otherwise, some African American candidates received major party contributions but they did not get any party expenditures on their behalf.*

Table 15.5 indicates in actual rather than mean dollars the sums given by the GOP to African American Republican senatorial candidates in Virginia and Maryland during the 1988 elections. Both candidates (Dawkins and Keyes, respectively) ran as underdogs in contests that other Republicans chose not to run in. The GOP's expenditures on behalf of Keyes amounted to 47 percent of his total disbursements, and Keyes's overall net receipts of $684,527 was considerably larger than Dawkins's $283,095. The Republicans made a serious and substantial effort to make these two senatorial candidates competitive. Regardless, both candidates lost, Dawkins in an open seat race, and Keyes in a race against a Democratic incumbent.

Only in these two senatorial campaigns did the Republican party contribute to or expend substantial funds on its African American nominees. With African American senatorial candidates running in races white Republican candidates chose not to enter, the party had no choice but to support these nominees. In the other two categories, the party made different choices and rendered different

TABLE 15.3
Open Seats Contested by African American Republicans, 1980–1994

Years	Number of Open Seats	Number of Open Seats Challenged by African American Republicans	Percent of Total
1980	2	1	50
1982	3	0	0
1984*	0	0	0
1986	3	3	100
1988	1*	1*	100
1990	6**	4	67
1992	16	6***	38
1994	0	0	0

Adapted from the Federal Election Commission Final Reports on U.S. Senate and House Campaigns, 1980–1995. Calculations prepared by the author.
**The open seat in 1988 was a Senate seat in Virginia. There were no House seats.*
***The open seat in 1990 was in Connecticut, and there the conservative African American Republican candidate won against a liberal white Democratic incumbent.*
****This is the number that actually got financial support.*

levels of financial support, with the overall record of support being a spotty and uneven one.

White Republican Candidates versus African American Democratic Candidates: A Note

In the first decade of the Reagan-Bush era, the Republican party wound up sponsoring white candidates in predominantly African American congressional districts—districts in which the party normally would have sponsored African American challengers. In 1982, for example, in an open-seat race in Mississippi, the African American Democratic candidate, Robert Clark, faced a conservative white Republican challenger, Webb Franklin, who ran a racially divisive campaign with significant financial support from the Republican party.[31] With his superior financial resources and the use of race baiting, Franklin won the seat. In the 1986 elections in the same state, the incumbent Franklin faced a new African American Democratic challenger, Mike Espy. Again, the white Republican received superior financial support and ran the same type of incendiary campaign—and lost.[32] In 1988 Espy faced a different, well-financed white Republican challenger and won.[33]

In 1990, the Republican conservative Senator Jesse Helms of North Carolina

TABLE 15.4

Mean Republican Party Contributions to and Expenditures for African American Republican Candidates in Open Seat Congressional Races, 1980–1994

Years	Mean Major Party Contributions	Percent of Mean Total Receipts	Mean Major Party Expenditures	Percent of Mean Total Expenditures
1980	$ 1,006 (1)	26	0	0
1982	0*	0	0	0
1984	0	0	0	0
1986	5,957 (3)	11	0	0
1988	25,050 (1)	0	348,626 (1)	**
1990	30,415 (3)	6	52,453 (2)	7
1992	5,173	5	4,743	4
1994	0	0	0	0

Adapted from the Federal Election Commission Final Reports on U.S. Senate and House Campaigns, 1980–1995. Calculations prepared by the author.

**In 1982, there were three open seats. The one in New York went uncontested. The open seat in Mississippi was contested by a white Republican against an African American Democratic candidate and a similar situation prevailed in Missouri, where a white Republican ran against an African American Democratic candidate.*

***In 1988, the open seat was in the Senate and the Conservative African American Republicans had more party funds spent on their behalf than they spent in total receipts.*

was challenged by an African American Democratic hopeful, Harvey Gantt. Again, the party contributed and expended superior financial resources to save their incumbent from defeat. With his superior resources and the use of race-baiting ads, Helms won.[34]

In every instance where a white Republican challenger or incumbent faced a Democratic challenger or incumbent, the Republican party did not fail to expend superior financial resources on their behalf. In every case, white GOP candidates were given more than enough financial resources to make them competitive. This was not the case with African American Republican candidates and challengers. Apparently, race was a significant factor in determining the level of the Republican party's support for its candidates.

As table 15.6 reveals, the Republican party's major thrust in this category came in the 1988 elections; however, it declined in the very next election cycle (1990). All three African American Republican candidates who ran in 1988—Jerry Curry in Virginia, James Cummings in Indiana, and Ronald Crutcher in Ohio—received more party PAC monies than their Democratic counterparts received from that party's PACs; yet these funds were not enough to make the African American Republicans competitive. None of the three received sufficient

TABLE 15.5

Republican Party Contributions to African American Republican Senatorial Candidates, 1988 and 1992

Candidate/ State	Total Amount of Party PAC Contributions	Percent of Major Party Receipts	Total Party Expenditures	Percent of Total Disbursement
1988				
Maryland Alan Keyes	$21,645	3	$314,060	47
Virginia Maurice Dawkins	$25,050	9	$348,626	*
1992				
Maryland Alan Keyes	$17,500	2	-0-	-0-

Adapted from the Federal Election Commission Final Reports on U.S. Senate and HouseCampaigns, 1980–1992. Calculations prepared by the author.

**In this open seat for the Senate, the Republican party spent more on behalf of this conservative Republican candidate than he spent or had in receipts.*

TABLE 15.6

Mean Contributions from Republican Party PACs to African American Republican Challengers to Democratic Congressional Incumbents, 1980–1994

Years	Number of White Democrat Incumbents Challenged	Mean Major Party Contributions	Percent of Total Receipts	Mean Major Party Expenditures	Percent of Total Expenditures
1980	0				
1982	0				
1984	0				
1986	0				
1988	3	11,499	12	44,986(1)*	24
1990	1**	29,749	9	36,411	11
1992	0	0	0	0	0
1994	5***	2,691	2	113	.001

Adapted from the Federal Election Commission Federal Reports on U.S. Senate and House Campaigns, 1980–1995.

**Only one of three African American Republican challengers had major party expenditures on his behalf—Jerry Curry, running in the 2nd Congressional District in Virginia.*

***Only one African American Republican challenger appeared in 1990—J. Alphonso Brown, running in the 3rd Congressional District in Kentucky.*

****This is the number who actually got financial support.*

contributions from other supporters. Only Curry's total receipts were near the $200,000 mark, while the other two candidates received less than $50,000. Such sums did not even begin to approximate the amounts they needed to run successful campaigns. Hence, each lost, with Cummings receiving 39 percent of the vote; Curry, 35 percent; and Crutcher, 23 percent. However, white Republican candidates running against African American were funded by their party to levels that made them competitive, and led to their success (i.e., Webb Franklin).

Conclusions

The Republican party neither recruited a significant number of African American candidates to run for the positions or vacancies that became available in the House of Representatives, nor did it fund these candidates to any substantial degree. On the other hand, in the senatorial category, once African American candidates received the nomination, the party did rise to the occasion and gave them the maximum amount of funds allowable.

Of all three categories of candidates put forth by the Republican party, only one African American won: Gary Franks of Connecticut. Ultimately, the GOP came out of the 1980s right where it started, with one African American Republican in Congress. Thus, no gains, no losses. The only difference was that Evans had been elected, before the Reagan-Bush era, by a predominantly African American voting district, while Frank was elected to serve a primarily white one. In the 1994 Republican sweep of the House of Representatives another African American, J. C. Watts, was elected in a Congressional district in Oklahoma which is less than five percent African American.

Thus, if the goal of the Reagan-Bush transformation of the political context was to convert more African American congressional districts to voting for and supporting African American Republican candidates (and, through them, the conservative Republican ideology), then the transformation failed because the sole African American Republican candidate elected by the African American community lost. However, if the goal of this contextual transformation was to achieve control of the House by increasing the number of Republican representatives (and, by chance, African American Republican ones), then the party was successful, but only due to the support of the white electorate. Indeed, the GOP failed to capture the House during the Reagan-Bush era, and in 1986, due to the African American electorate, they lost the Senate as well. By 1994 and 1996 the Republicans recaptured Congress but without electing any additional African Americans.

16

AFRICAN AMERICAN FEMALE SENATORIAL CANDIDATES
Twin Assets or Double Liabilities?

• • • • • • •

Katherine Tate

A changed political context is a double-edged sword. It offers dual possibilities of political loss and gain. It can open up political opportunities as well as foreclose on them. For example, on the eve of the 1992 national elections, President Bush—although his intent was to install at the highest echelons of the American court system an African American conservative who would perpetuate the Reagan-Bush contextual revolution long after the Republican era had ended—unwittingly provided the African American community with the opportunity to realize a significant political goal. The double-edged sword of political context transformation had cut both ways, resulting in both gains and losses for the transformers.

The 1992 primary elections were exceptional for their volatility as American voters signalled their preference for political outsiders over career politicians. Not only did voter contempt for the political establishment briefly buoy the presidential campaigns of political long-shots such as Democrat Jerry Brown and Republican Patrick Buchanan, but this sentiment was also evident in the unexpected surge of voter support for the independent presidential candidacy of self-made Texas billionaire H. Ross Perot. The 1992 House elections brought 110 new faces to Congress, that body's greatest turnover since 1948. The number of women serving in the House rose from 29 to 47. In addition, more women ran for the Senate than ever before, and a significant number (eleven) won.

Several political analysts have attributed the women's victories in the 1992 elections to the emergence of a newly augmented women's vote. As concerned with the poor performance of the national economy as men, many women voters were given special cause to cast an anti-incumbency vote in 1992 given their disgust over the all-male Senate Judiciary Committee's handling of the Clarence Thomas-Anita Hill controversy. Until information was leaked to the press, the committee had failed to act on the charge made by law professor Anita F. Hill that the conservative nominee to the Supreme Court, Clarence Thomas, had sexually harassed her while he headed the Equal Employment Opportunity Commission. Several female Senate contenders, including Lynn Yeakel of Pennsylvania, maintain that outrage over the Thomas nomination hearing was a prime motivation for running in 1992. Among these candidates motivated to run by the Thomas-Hill controversy was Carol Moseley-Braun of Illinois, whose upset victory over incumbent Illinois Democratic Senator Alan Dixon, who had voted to confirm Thomas, captured significant media attention. Moseley-Braun made history by becoming the nation's first black female elected senator.

Prior to Moseley-Braun's election, no blacks and only two women were serving in the Senate. Little has been written about black women's political chances in this arena. Moseley-Braun's campaign offers a unique opportunity to ask: Was Moseley-Braun doubly handicapped as a black female candidate, or did her "double-minority" status afford her unique assets that she used to form a winning coalition and take her all the way to the United States Senate?

"All the Women Are White, All the Blacks Are Men," but Some Black Women Bravely Run for Political Office[1]

Until Carol Moseley-Braun's nomination, no black woman with major party backing had ever run for the Senate. Most major party candidates have been white men. Since 1968, a few white women and black men have been nominated (see table 16.1). Although the number of women serving in the Senate tripled after the 1992 elections, women have generally been unsuccessful in their senatorial bids. In 1984, ten women ran, but only one, Republican Nancy Kassebaum of Kansas, won a seat. In 1990, eight women ran, but only Kassebaum—the sole woman incumbent—won.

Chief among the problems limiting the electability of women as well as minorities is political incumbency. In the 1988 and 1990 elections, 85 percent and 97 percent of the incumbent Senators who sought reelection won, respectively. Most women nominated for the Senate have competed against incumbents. In 1986, however, a then-record three women ran in open-seat Senate races, and one won. Democrat Barbara Milkulski of Maryland won the seat of a retiring Republican senator in her match against the Hispanic Republican Linda Chavez, a former Reagan aide. (She thus became the first Democratic female

TABLE 16.1

Number of Women and Blacks Nominated by the Major Parties for the United States Senate

Years	Women	Blacks
1968	1 (1D, 0R)	none
1970	1 (0D, 1R)	none*
1972	2 (0D, 2R)	1 (0D, 1R)
1974	3 (2D, 1R)	1 (0D, 1R)
1976	1 (1D, 0R)	none
1978	2 (1D, 1R)	1 (0D, 1R)*
1980	5 (2D, 3R)	none
1982	3 (1D, 2R)	none
1984	10 (6D, 4R)	none
1986	6 (3D, 3R)	none
1988	2 (0D, 2R)	2 (0D, 2R)
1990	8 (2D, 6R)	1 (1D, 0R)
1992	11 (10D, 1R)	1 (1D, 0R)

* Black Independent for U.S. Senate in race.

SOURCES: Center for the American Woman and Politics, Rutgers University, and also compiled by authors as reported in the *Congressional Quarterly Weekly.*

senator not to have succeeded her husband.) In 1992 this record was tied, but all three women running for open seats emerged victorious (Carol Moseley-Braun, Barbara Boxer, and Patty Murray).

Certain general prejudices against women, which may also work against female office-seekers, persist among a minority of Americans. As Darcy, Welch, and Clark report, while only 6 percent of Americans surveyed in 1984 indicated that they would refuse to vote for a qualified woman congressional candidate nominated by their party, a much higher percentage (34 percent) still expressed the view that "Most men are better suited emotionally for politics than are most women."[2] Nevertheless, researchers have failed to find any conclusive evidence that voters actually discriminate against women candidates on the basis of their gender. Susan Carroll, a prominent researcher in this field, minimizes the importance of gender bias against women candidates.[3] Additionally, Darcy, Welch, and Clark contend that anti-female bias is offset by other voter considerations such as the candidate's party and incumbency status.

African American males running for the Senate have been even less successful than white women since women gained the right to vote. In 1988, two black candidates, both Republicans, ran for the Senate; both lost. As of 1990, only 13 blacks had ever won statewide (executive) office, and only five were then serving.[4] Like women, black senatorial candidates typically face incumbents, but in addition to this, their ability to win such races is also diminished by prejudicial voting patterns. A number of surveys have revealed that higher percentages of voters express reluctance to vote for qualified black candidates than for qualified female candidates.[5] Since half of all Senate races are hotly contested,[6] the loss of any proportion of the electorate makes it that much more difficult for black candidates to win. In addition, white Senate incumbents facing black challengers can easily use race as an issue to bolster flagging support.

Such was the situation facing the lone black senatorial candidate in 1990. In that controversial campaign, Democrat Harvey Gantt, a former mayor of North Carolina's largest city, Charlotte, lost despite strong party support and substantial funding. Gantt's white opponent, incumbent Senator Jesse Helms, a nationally known, staunchly conservative Republican, retained his seat by waging a racially charged media campaign that effectively mobilized conservative white voters. In particular, Helms aired a television commercial that showed a black getting a job through affirmative action, even though the white applicant was apparently "better qualified" and "needed the job the most." One researcher found that Helm's commercial served not so much to reduce white support for his black opponent as to convince undecided white voters to vote for Helms.[7]

In addition to being restricted to a limited universe of the white electorate because of white voters' racial biases, African American candidates in statewide contests face the additional dilemma of attempting to mobilize the African American community without alienating the white community.[8] Because black candidates lack a secure base among white voters, the failure to gain concentrated black support almost guarantees defeat. Indeed, past black-white contests suggest that African American candidates require anywhere from 85 to 95 percent of the African American vote as well as a high black turnout rate to win office. Yet a vigorous campaign for black votes can backfire, causing whites to reject the black candidate in favor of a white one. Ignoring black voters, however, is equally dangerous, since this could result in a low black turnout. For example, among the reasons why Andrew Young lost his run-off primary bid in 1990 to become Georgia's first black governor was the low turnout among African American voters. In particular, Young's efforts to de-emphasize race issues in order to pacify those whites who were concerned about his civil rights record reduced black enthusiasm for his campaign. Despite Young's extensive campaign for white votes, several pre-election surveys showed that about one-third of the white vote was totally beyond Young's reach.[9] With blacks constituting only 15 percent of the Illinois electorate, Carol Moseley-Braun faced and overcome exactly this type of racial dilemma.

Nevertheless, despite the dismal prospects for women and black candidates, the large advantage accorded to incumbents, and the negative effect of racially biased voting patterns, black women candidates may still have special advantages over their white female and black male counterparts. First, limited evidence suggests that black women are more inclined to run for political office than white women. After all, a primary reason why women are so underrepresented in the Senate is that so few women run for these seats. Although research on why women choose to run for public office is limited, it is clear that women's occupational and sex role expectations lead many women to view a political career as a less than viable option. Most of the occupations that traditionally have led men into politics, such as law and business, are also areas in which women have been underrepresented. Moreover, women are generally expected to be the primary child-care providers, a role perceived as incompatible or difficult to balance with a political career.[10] In contrast to white women, however, black women have a much longer tradition of simultaneously working and raising families. Thus, sex-role expectations may have less of a dampening effect on black women's political ambitions. Research has found that African American women tend to have higher levels of political ambition than do white women.[11] Black women delegates at a Democratic party state convention were more likely than white women delegates to express a desire to hold higher party positions and elected positions. This may be due to African American women's historical experience of participation and activism in the civil rights movement. Researchers have also suggested that resources within the African American community help African American women with political ambitions to overcome individual disadvantages such as low earning power and single-parent status. Two such resources, strong religious orientation and family background, have been identified, and their implications described, in a study by Jerry Perkins.[12] In Perkins's study, strong religious beliefs and having a politically active mother were both positively correlated to political ambition among black women.

The elections of African Americans to political office can generally be attributed to the new opportunities that opened up for African Americans as a result of the civil rights struggle and the passage of the 1965 Voting Rights Act.[13] Yet the rate of growth of female black elected officials has exceeded the rate for all black elected officials in each year since 1975. The percentage of black elected officials who are women increased from 15 percent in 1975 to 26 percent in 1990. The percentage of black mayors in 1985 who were women was 12.2 contrast to the 8.2 of white mayors who were women.[14]

Second, although black votes have been pivotal in the election of a number of white female Democratic mayors, as in Chicago and Houston, black women candidates can depend on a base of support coming from African American voters than can white women candidates. Of course, black support is never automatically handed over to every black candidate who runs for public office. Black Republicans in particular have only been able to obtain a one-quarter share of the black vote in most electoral contests. African American voters are more likely to support liberal black candidates, and turnout among blacks tends to peak in those elections involving viable black candidates.

Lastly, black women candidates may be better able to mobilize women voters across racial barriers. The "women's vote" in contrast to the "black vote," has historically been far more elusive because women, for a variety of reasons, are less likely than blacks to vote as a bloc. Indeed, the women's vote is a relatively recent phenomenon, first witnessed in the 1980 presidential election. Prior to 1980, there were only small differences (0 to 6 percent) in the proportions of women and men voting Democratic. (This gap is also substantially smaller than the racial gap that first emerged full-blown in the 1968 presidential election.[15]) The existence of a gender gap in electoral politics reflects a shift in the voting preferences of men rather than of women. As table 16.2 shows, women and men were evenly divided between Carter and Ford in the 1976 presidential election; yet, in the next four elections, fewer men voted Democratic. Thus, the gender gap emerged when men began to support GOP presidential contenders while women voters remained generally pro-Democratic in their voting behavior. Data collected by the Center for the American Woman and Politics show that, since 1982, women have also voted more consistently Democratic in congressional races than have men. Nonetheless, this gender gap would probably disappear if men returned to the Democratic fold.

That larger proportions of women than men are Democrats explains the gender gap in voting. In addition, American women's distinctive and liberal political views on foreign policy matters and social spending issues also help explain the stability of their pro-Democratic identification and voting patterns.[16] Even when controlling for party preference, women still tend to be more liberal than men. For example, research has found that female caucus participants of both major parties are consistently more liberal than the male caucus participants, with gender differences across issues most striking among activists within the Republican party.[17]

TABLE 16.2

The Gender and Racial Gaps in Presidential Elections, 1976–1992

	1976 Carter	1980 Carter	1984 Mondale	1988 Dukakis	1992 Clinton
Women	50	45	44	49	46
Men	50	36	37	41	41
Gap	+0	+9	+7	+8	+5
Blacks	83	85	90	86	82
Whites	47	36	35	40	39
Gap	+36	+49	+55	+46	+43

As reported in the *New York Times,* November 5, 1992. Data were based on surveys of 11,000 to 15,000 voters leaving 300 polling places across the country. Data for 1980, 1984, and 1988 were collected by the *New York Times*/CBS News. Data for 1992 were collected by Voter Research and Surveys. The 1976 data were based on exit polls conducted by CBS News.

At best, liberal female candidates are more likely to obtain reliable support from feminist voters, but feminists represent only a minority of female voters, estimated at from fewer than 10 percent to about one-third of the female population.[18] Although feminist organizations have become prominent financial backers of female candidates, their endorsements have not increased female support for all of their candidates. For example, although the National Organization for Women (NOW) endorsed Walter Mondale for president in 1984, ultimately his support from female caucus participants was no higher than the support he received from males.[19]

Contrasting the African American vote to the women's vote, it seems that black voters are more receptive than white women voters to the campaigns of African American women candidates. The women's vote is dependent on contextual factors that emphasize substantive, not symbolic, elements. While African American women candidates have distinct disadvantages as political newcomers insofar as they often face incumbents and racially prejudiced white electorates, in contrast to their African American male and white female counterparts, African American women candidates may be in a better position, given their stronger political ambitions and potential, to form a black and female base of support. In this paper we investigate whether or not Carol Moseley-Braun was able to make history by forging just such a special black-white female voter coalition.

Carol Moseley-Braun's Primary and General Election Campaigns and Results

Until the Thomas confirmation vote, two-term Senator Alan Dixon from Illinois seemed unbeatable. As late as October 1991 he had no declared opponents, Democrat or Republican. An established state politician since first winning office in 1950 at the age of 23, Dixon had easily won his Senate seat in an open-seat contest in 1980, and in 1986 took 65 percent of the vote against his GOP opponent, a female state representative. Dixon, however, had cast one of the pivotal votes for Thomas, who was confirmed by the narrowest Senate margin ever for a Supreme Court nominee: 52 to 48. It was precisely that vote that prompted Moseley-Braun to challenge him.

Moseley-Braun was no newcomer to politics. A native Chicagoan who attended city schools, and graduated from the University of Chicago law school, she had first been elected to the Illinois state legislature in 1978. In 1988, she left the General Assembly to run for the office of Cook County Recorder of Deeds. Her victory made her the county's highest-ranking black official.[20]

Moseley-Braun beat Dixon in the 1992 Democratic primary with 38 percent of the vote to his 35 percent. She won despite the fact that she had spent a fraction ($500,000) of what her two rivals spent and despite widespread reports of a poorly managed campaign. She won for a number of reasons: first and most importantly because the primary had been a fiercely fought, three-way race. Multimillionaire Albert Hofeld also challenged Dixon in the primary and spent $4 million of his own funds on television ads attacking Dixon as a "Washington insider," who swam "in the same dirty special-interest pool" as other Washington insiders. He also accused Dixon, who was a member of the Senate Banking Committee, of supporting the deregulation of the savings and loan industry that had led to multibillion-dollar losses. To counter, Dixon spent more than $1 million in PAC funds attacking Hofeld. He maintained that Hofeld's opposition to PACs was hypocritical since in the early 1980s Hofeld headed the Illinois Lawyers' Association, whose PAC made significant contributions to political candidates.[21] This expensive and negative campaign between Dixon and Hofeld ultimately worked against them.

Dixon was also defeated on the issues. Both Moseley-Braun and Hofeld portrayed Dixon as too conservative to represent Illinois Democrats effectively. As Moseley-Braun stated in campaign interviews, she was running to "return a true Democrat to the Senate." A strong advocate of military spending, Dixon, along with New Jersey's Senator Bill Bradley, had voted consistently for aid for the Contras of El Salvador during the Reagan-Bush years. In 1991, he voted with President Bush 58 percent of the time. Dixon worked hard to deflect attention from his conservative voting record by publicizing the fact that he was one of ten Senate cosponsors of the "play-or-pay" health care proposal. He was aided by fellow Illinois Senator Paul Simon's endorsement of him over Moseley-Braun, for Moseley-Braun was a longtime ally of Simon and had cochaired Simon's 1990 reelection campaign.

Ultimately, however, Dixon lost because he was an incumbent seeking reelection in an anti-incumbent political environment. Illinois incumbents fared badly in the March primary. Along with Dixon, two other incumbents, Representatives Charles Hayes and Gus Savage, were defeated.[22]

Although Moseley-Braun had feminist anger against Dixon working for her, women's groups did not climb aboard until very late. Emily's List, a group that raises money for female Democratic candidates, was convinced that Moseley-Braun had little chance of winning; the organization sent her $5,000 only days before the primary. The Women's Campaign Fund sent $5,000 the day after she defeated Dixon, while the National Women's Political Caucus pledged to mail a fundraising solicitation to its members. Prominent feminist Gloria Steinem did campaign for her during the primary contest; however Moseley-Braun's support among women was modest. Exit polls revealed that Moseley-Braun received 40 percent of the women's vote against 35 percent of the men's vote. However, she received 62 percent of the vote of white suburban women who felt that Thomas should not have been confirmed, although at the time, a large majority of Americans thought Thomas should have been confirmed.

By contrast, Moseley-Braun's support among African Americans was much more solid. She received 85 percent of the black vote, which had surged to larger-than-expected numbers for the primary.[23]

Overall, Moseley-Braun received 51 percent of the vote in Chicago, 39 percent in the six-county suburbs, and 20 percent downstate. In some downstate counties, she received less than 10 percent of the vote. The numbers illustrate the classic dilemma that Moseley-Braun faced as a black candidate: how to hang on to her core of black voters as well as win over many conservative downstate whites.

Moseley-Braun's victory in the Illinois Democratic primary on March 17, 1992, surprised everyone, especially the GOP. Expecting to challenge Dixon, the Republicans had not mustered any high-profile Republican politicians to run. Their candidate, Richard Williamson, a former Reagan-Bush appointee who had run unopposed in the Republican primary, was totally unknown to those outside the state GOP's inner circle. In interviews conducted immediately after the primary, he stated his intention to portray Moseley-Braun as another "tax-and-spend" liberal Democrat.

Until the Medicaid scandal become public, Moseley-Braun's victory in November seemed certain. Despite persistent rumors that her campaign was internally disorganized, polls indicated that she led Williamson by a 2-to-1 margin. She had raised more money than her opponents, reportedly $5 million. Compared to Williamson, Moseley-Braun was a far more dynamic, articulate, and experienced grassroots campaigner, and challenger quality was an important factor in this race. In general, high-quality challengers are defined as those having prior officeholding experience. Researchers have found that high-quality Senate challengers receive more votes than low-quality (or inexperienced) challengers.[24] Williamson, who had never before been elected to public office, thus represented a weak opponent. Moreover, while Illinois had voted Republican in the presidential elections in 1976, 1980, 1984, and 1988, the state was trending Democratic.

Indeed, Moseley-Braun's campaign represented a textbook example of successful Senate bids that virtually guaranteed victory. In general, presidential popularity and the state of the economy are related to Senate election outcomes,[25] and she was fortunate to run for the Senate at the time when the incumbent Republican president's popularity was at an all-time low. Although public evaluations of the health of the economy were strongly negative, Illinoisans apparently were not hit as hard by the economic downturn in 1992 as were residents of other states. However, apprehension about their economic future was strong. Election polls conducted in mid-October showed Bush's Democratic challenger beating him by a comfortable 13-point margin; in the event, registered voters in Illinois favored Clinton by a 19-point margin.

The Medicaid scandal concerned the $28,750 Moseley-Braun's 71-year-old mother received in royalties from the sale of timber rights on family-owned property in Alabama. Moseley-Braun's mother lived in a nursing home, having suffered a stroke and two heart attacks, and received Medicaid. Under the Medicaid program, such windfalls should be applied toward the cost of the recipient's medical care. Instead, the mother distributed the money to her three children, including $10,000 which was given to Moseley-Braun. Moseley-Braun contended that the money was the repayment of a loan made to her mother to pay for her brother's funeral. Moseley-Braun's mother also contended that she had reported the windfall to the Illinois Department of Public Aid, although officials at the agency had no record of having been notified.[26] The failure to have reported the windfall constituted possible fraud. In the end, the state agency dropped its investigation of Mrs. Mosely, although Moseley-Braun promised to repay the state agency any money it was due from her mother.

The scandal was potentially devastating for Moseley-Braun's campaign for many reasons, particularly because it served to invoke racial stereotypes of blacks as welfare defrauders. While her lead narrowed as a result of the publicity over the scandal, an October 12–13, 1992, *New York Times*/CBS telephone survey of registered voters in Illinois showed Moseley-Braun still ahead of Williamson by a 19-point margin. Nevertheless, 43 percent of those surveyed indicated that Moseley-Braun's management of her mother's finances "raised doubts about her honesty and integrity."

As Sam Popkin argues, voters rely heavily on personal information about candidates to judge them because it is easier to "take personal data and fill in the political facts and policies than to start with political facts and fill in the personal data." This heavy reliance on personal data explains what Popkin calls the "Gresham's law of political information:"

> personal information can drive more relevant political information out of consideration . . . a small amount of personal information can dominate a large amount of historical information about a past record . . . . Just as bad money drives good money out of circulation.[27]

The scandal was less damaging than it might have been to Moseley-Braun because it emerged in the last few months of the campaign. Had it been made public in the beginning, when little contrary information would have been available regarding Moseley-Braun's record and integrity, the GOP could have packaged the whole affair into a tidy, but devastating, racially divisive weapon. And Moseley-Braun probably would have lost.

Yet Carol Moseley-Braun won the Illinois Senate seat on November 3, 1992, taking 53 percent of the vote compared to Williamson's 43 percent (see table 16.3). (The remaining votes were spread among the independent candidates.) Although she lost the ring of counties surrounding the Chicago area to her Republican opponent, Moseley-Braun received 76 percent of the Chicago vote and 53 percent of the downstate vote (excluding returns for minor candidates), which represented 21 percent and 39 percent of the total vote, respectively.

TABLE 16.3

Breakdown of 1992 Senate and Presidential Vote in Illinois by Region

	Senate		Presidential		
	Braun	Williamson	Clinton	Bush	Perot
Statewide	55%	45%	48%	34%	17%
Chicago	76	24	72	18	7
Cook Suburbs	49	51	44	39	17
Du Page	40	60	31	48	21
Kane	45	55	35	44	21
Lake	45	55	37	44	19
McHenry	40	60	28	47	25
Will	46	54	42	35	23
Downstate	53	47	45.5	36	18.5

Calculated from unofficial results as reported in the *Chicago Tribune,* November 5, 1992. Vote totals for minor candidates (not printed) were necessarily excluded in the calculations. Results are shown for Cook County (Chicago and its suburbs) and for five northeastern counties that surround Cook County; the downstate region includes all other counties in Illinois.

Moseley-Braun was able to win by drawing on her African American base of support in Chicago and white base of support downstate.

In general, Senate elections are seen as voter referendums on a president's performance in office. As shown in table 16.3, comparing the Senate election results to the presidential vote in Illinois, it appears that Moseley-Braun benefitted more from the anti-Bush vote than from the pro-Clinton drive, as Clinton's support was not exceptionally strong except in Chicago. Perot supporters seemingly divided their votes evenly between Moseley-Braun and Williamson.

The Gender, Racial, and Gender-Racial Dynamics of the 1992 Illinois Senate Race

A profile of Carol Moseley-Braun's supporters is presented in table 16.4. Moseley-Braun benefited significantly from the women's vote and the African American vote. Fifty-eight percent of all women voters voted for Moseley-Braun. In contrast, only 49 percent of the men interviewed in the exit polls claimed to have voted for Moseley-Braun. This represents a 9-point gender gap, almost twice the 5-point difference between women and men voters in the presidential election. This larger gender gap in the senatorial contest undoubtedly was heightened because of Moseley-Braun's campaign focus on the Thomas hearings. Although the majority of women did not, at the time, believe Hill's charges of sexual harassment were true,[28] the hearings raised concern among women about their absence from the Senate judiciary committee and their tiny numbers (two) in the Senate as a whole.

Moseley-Braun won 95 percent of the African American vote. Indeed, in some black majority wards in Chicago, she obtained 99 percent of the vote, a level comparable to Harold Washington's support in his 1983 bid for mayor. She narrowly lost the white vote to Williamson, receiving 49 percent to his 51 percent. However, very little racially polarized voting occurred in this election. First, there was very little crossover voting along party lines: 86 percent of the Democrats voted Democratic for an African American nominee. This was quite in contrast to the 1983 Chicago mayoral election, when large percentages of life-long white Democrats voted Republican to block the election of the city's first black mayor. Surprisingly, party crossover voting was somewhat higher among Republicans in the 1992 senate election than among Democrats, suggesting that some Republican women may have crossed party lines to support Moseley-Braun's historic bid. Moseley-Braun actually won a larger share of the white vote than did the last four white male Democratic presidential contenders (see table 16.4).

TABLE 16.4

Demographic Comparison of Braun and Williamson Supporters

	Braun	Williamson
Democrats	86	14
Republicans	18	82
Other/Independents	58	42
Men	49	51
Women	58	42
Blacks	95	5
Whites	48	52
Age: 18–29	61	39
30–44	55	45
45–59	54	46
60+	50	50
Income: $0–15,000	71	29
$15–30,000	64	36
$30–50,000	56	44
$50–75,000	44	56
Over $75,000	49	51

SOURCE: Voter research and surveys as reported in the *Chicago Tribune,* November 5, 1992.

In an important article analyzing Douglas Wilder's successful bid in Virginia to become the country's first black governor, Charles Jones and Michael Clemons present a model of racial crossover voting that purports to explain black electoral success in majority white districts.[29] Two factors they identify in their model as vital to black electoral success in white districts—a candidate's office-holding experience and strong party support—could be applied to electoral success more generally. Two other factors identified in their model related especially to African Americans. The first of these is that, in order to win in a white majority area, black candidates must adopt a "deracialized approach" in campaigning. This approach is defined by Jones and Clemons as "conducting a campaign in such a way as to diffuse the polarizing effects of the race factor in an election."[30] To utilize this approach, African American candidates must stick to the issues, avoid making overt racial appeals to black voters, and adopt a "nonthreatening" political style. Indeed, Moseley-Braun did focus on the issues. She also campaigned on the theme of change, highlighting the need for more female, as opposed to black, representation in the Senate. She spent a larger proportion of her time campaigning for downstate votes than for African American votes, so much so that some black activists were quoted as predicting a low turnout among blacks since Moseley-Braun was taking the black vote "for granted."[31] However, given her vote margins and high turnout among African American voters in the general election, Moseley-Braun obviously overcame the dilemmas of simultaneously courting both black and white votes. Overall, Moseley-Braun displayed more skill than Wilder in developing a racially neutral campaign. Her margin of victory was substantially higher than Wilder's, who won by the slimmest of margins, 7,000 votes out of the 1.7 million cast.

Many African American office-seekers in white majority districts have found it difficult to adopt the nonracial approach advocated by Jones and Clemons because the political environments into which they enter are so highly racialized. Although this is certainly a matter that deserves greater research, political contests involving African American candidates can become racialized independent of the African American candidate's strategic campaign behavior. For example, prior to his election as New York City's first black mayor in 1989, David Dinkins's political style could hardly be characterized as racially threatening. However, enmeshed in the racialized climate brought about by the Tawana Brawley hoax, the murder of a black teenager Yusef Hawkins in the white section of Brooklyn, and the Central Park rape of a white woman by black and Latino teenagers, Dinkins could hardly avoid racial issues. Outgoing Mayor Koch also had contributed to the worsening race relations in the city through his caustic opposition to Jesse Jackson's 1988 candidacy.[32] The slim margin of Dinkins's victory implies that a minority of whites simply refused to vote for him as a consequence. For the same reason, black North Carolina senatorial candidate Harvey Gantt, widely viewed as a racial moderate, cannot be blamed for the injection of race into his campaign. That was achieved through his opponent Jesse Helms's wily decision to air television commercials that harangued against affirmative action. Through her careful avoidance of racial issues, Moseley-Braun was able to win substantial support from white voters.[33]

The second factor related to African American electoral success in Jones and Clemons's model is what they call the "racial ombudsman" factor. In this regard, they maintain that the media is crucial to African American success in majority white districts. As racial ombudsman, the media acts to prevent the successful exploitation of race and racial issues in black versus white political contests.[34] However, Jones and Clemons greatly overstate the ability of the media, and of African American candidates themselves, to control the race factor in black versus white campaigns. Furthermore, while African American men suffer from pernicious media stereotypes that depict them as violent, dangerous, and irresponsible, equally negative stereotypes about African American women as single parents, lazy, and welfare-dependent also exist and persist to their detriment.

The final element in Jones and Clemons's model they label the "wild card" factor. This component involves the emergence of an unanticipated issue or event in the political campaign. In Doug Wilder's campaign, for instance, the Supreme Court's 1989 decision in *Webster v. Reproductive Health Services* served as the catalyst that mobilized the pro-choice activists in Virginia who backed Wilder. Correspondingly, in the Illinois Senate race, the wild card was the Thomas-Hill drama. Moseley-Braun most likely would not have challenged Dixon had it not been for his vote for Thomas, nor would she have been as successful in mobilizing female voters.

One additional element, not formally recognized by Jones and Clemons, which probably contributed to Moseley-Braun's as well as Wilder's success, is that these two candidates sought higher office having previously won positions in white majority districts. When seeking statewide positions, black politicians representing black majority districts are at a greater disadvantage than white politicians or blacks representing white majority areas. Moseley-Braun was able to build a biracial coalition to win her Senate seat because her last campaign netted her the position of Cook County Recorder of Deeds. She might not have been able to win as many white votes campaigning for the Senate had she attempted to do so as the elected state representative of a predominantly black southside Chicago district. Such African American officeholders are easier to stereotype as being out of the mainstream, too liberal, and too race-oriented to represent whites adequately.

In the 1992 Illinois Senate contest, then, was the racial factor overcome because white voters and especially white women voters are more willing to support an African American female's bid for prestigious, statewide position as opposed to an African American male candidate? This one case does not provide conclusive evidence of this contention. Nevertheless, such a theory has gained credibility in light of Moseley-Braun's victory. In the *Chicago Tribune,* for example, one reporter wrote, "Braun's ease in attracting voters across racial lines is probably due to the fact that she is a woman and is viewed as less threatening than Washington or Jackson, prominent leaders of the black political empowerment movement in Chicago."[35] Yet Moseley-Braun was irrefutably active in the black community. As a member of the Illinois Assembly, she had served as floor leader for the agenda of Chicago's African American mayor, Harold Washington. She also refused to repudiate Jesse Jackson or Louis Farrakhan during the campaign. But she was careful not to alienate whites, having endorsing both Richard Daley, who is white, and Timothy Evans, an independent black mayoral candidate of the Harold Washington party, in 1987.

African American women candidates are likely to be at a disadvantage to African American male candidates in contests for state or national positions. As women, they remain seriously underrepresented in government, and are therefore less poised to seek the highest, most desirable posts. It is important to remember that Carol Moseley-Braun's historic accomplishment, while it broke new political ground for African American women, did not make her the first black since Reconstruction elected to the Senate. That honor belongs to Edward Brooke of Massachusetts, elected in 1966. Mosely-Braun's success cannot simply be attributed to her gender, but to the political environment in the aftermath of the Thomas confirmation hearings that made gender politcally relevant. Given Moseley-Braun's campaign success in the 1992 elections, is it possible that other African American women, such as Maxine Waters of Los Angeles, could also stage a successful bid for the Senate? Success for black women will depend upon a host of factors, including whether the seat is an open one, the popularity and party of the sitting President, and the candidates' ability to construct a biracial or multi-racial coalition.

Biracial Coalitions and the Prospects for a Black and Female Voters' Alliance

As Jones and Clemons contend, biracial coalitions are absolutely necessary if more black candidates are to win statewide elective offices. Yet, while a growing number of analysts have focused on the prospects of building black-white electoral coalitions[36] and, to a lesser extent, black-Latino coalitions,[37] few, if any, have discussed the prospects for the emergence of a voting coalition of blacks and women.

Throughout American political history, the race factor has made it difficult for blacks to build a stable black-white coalition. At times, blacks have sought to create a minority voters' alliance, as Jesse Jackson did in his 1984 and 1988 bids for president. While African Americans have successfully combined their voting strength with that of Hispanics to elect black mayors in such cities as Chicago and New York, these minority coalitions tend to be fragile and are rarely sustainable after the election. Blacks and Latinos in particular share a number of political concerns, including improving the public school system and reducing the unemployment rate. However, political discord between the two groups has often centered around questions of leadership. Moreover, the redistricting efforts taking place today has intensified such conflict between the two groups in areas such as New York city and Texas, where black and Hispanic leaders clash over the dilution of the voting power of Latinos in efforts to create new black majority districts.

The women's vote may thus be a crucial factor in the future election of blacks to statewide office, just as it was a crucial factor in the election of Doug Wilder and Carol Moseley-Braun. As Jones and Clemons have shown, a gender gap did not emerge in Wilder's 1985 election as lieutenant governor, but it did account for his 1989 victory.[38] Survey research has revealed that, on the issues, black leaders and feminist leaders have the most in common.[39] Still, mutual mistrust persists between feminists and blacks, stemming primarily from white women's participation in the larger system of racial oppression. An additional barrier is the sexism of prominent black political, civil rights, and Black Power advocates.

In order to capitalize effectively on their mutual political interests, a number of transformations have yet to occur before a viable African American and women voters' coalition can be realized. First, feminist organizations must establish a better record of supporting black liberal candidates; historically, these organizations have been weak and reluctant supporters of African Americans, either male or female, running for political office. For example, when long-shot candidate Shirley Chisholm, the African American congresswoman from New York, ran for president in 1972, the National Organization for Women (NOW), chose not to endorse her. NOW leaders gave several reasons for its non-support of Chisholm. They claimed that Chisholm, by her own admission, was not a serious president candidate. Additionally, they maintained, NOW, founded in 1966, should remain nonpartisan and refrain from endorsing presidential candidates. In 1976, however, the organization endorsed Jimmy Carter's presidential bid, and in 1984, it endorsed Walter Mondale.[40] NOW virtually ignored the candidacy of Jesse Jackson, the African American majority preferred candidate, who ran in both 1984 and 1988.

Second, if blacks are to benefit from such an alliance, feminists must become skilled at delivering their vote.[41] Part of the difficulty in the formation of a powerful women's vote is that many women view the concept of feminism negatively and in particular, see feminist organizations as too elitist. Another problem is that feminists tend to be single-issue voters. As such, feminists have sometimes supported candidates whose records are too conservative to generate significant African American support.[42] Nonetheless, African American candidates for political office can strengthen their share of the women's vote by making more women aware of the issues that are simultaneously of direct relevance to them and to African Americans, such as affirmative action.

Finally, African American politicians and civil rights leaders, most of whom are men, have for too long been silent about women's issues that could benefit African American women, and therefore, the African American community. A fundamental change must involve the recognition by civil rights organizations that "black progress and progress for women are inextricably linked in contemporary American politics, and that each group suffers when it fails to grasp the dimensions of the other's struggle."[43] Both groups clearly benefited in 1985 when civil rights and women's organizations lobbied successfully to block the appointment of ultra-conservative Robert Bork to the Supreme Court. In Judge Thomas's confirmation hearings, however, black civil rights activists, mostly men, not only kept silent regarding Anita Hill's rights in this matter but maintained their silence on the larger issue of sex discrimination. Although a few black organizations ultimately opposed Thomas's appointment,[44] the silence among black leaders during the Thomas-Hill confrontation probably helped Thomas win confirmation. Subsequently, because Thomas's decisions as an associate justice of the Supreme Court have already conflicted with the black community's liberal interests, the issue of forging a stable coalition between feminists and blacks deserves greater attention than it has received thus far.

Ethel Klein argues that the "women's vote reflects a difference in men's and women's perception of what is best for the country and what is best for women."[45] Traditionally, at least since the New Deal era, the Democrats have offered a vision that best captures what many women feel is best for the country. Candidates hoping to benefit from the burgeoning women's vote, however, must emphasize a vision that addresses the special concerns of women as well. African American leaders and voters must also change their political strategies if they wish to reap the benefits of an African American and women voters' alliance.

Postscript

Halfway into her first six-year term as senator, Carol Moseley-Braun has self-consciously embarked upon a course toward building a personal base of power within the Senate. A significant step in that direction was securing a position on the Senate Finance Committee, which writes tax laws and is also the source of legislation for Social Security, welfare, Medicaid, and Medicare. Abandoning her post on the Senate Judiciary Committee, Moseley-Braun had lobbied hard to win this prized position, becoming the first black and first Democratic female to serve on it. She has also signalled her intention to remain politically independent, if not decidedly pro-business, voting along with the majority of conservative members of Congress for the North American Free Trade Agreement (NAFTA), the General Agreement of Tariffs and Trade (GATT), and the centerpiece of the Republican party's Contract with America, the balanced-budget amendment. Her votes on these key pieces of legislation indicate that Senator

Moseley-Braun will not be easily typecast as the representative of "women" or as the representative of "blacks." She will remain her own person, a strategy that may sit well with some feminists,[46] perhaps, but will likely invite mounting criticism from liberal blacks who desire more from their representatives in government.

Moseley-Braun's effort toward accumulating personal power and political independence may be a reflection of her own political philosophy, or it may stem from the political realities of serving as one of the Senate's few female members and its only black member. The 1994 elections did not break new and substantial ground for women as did the 1992 elections. The Senate gained one woman, Republican Olympia Snowe of Maine, while the number of women in the House remained constant at forty-seven. Most significant about 1994 were the gains of the Republicans, who now dominate in the House and Senate. There is no Senate caucus for women nor one for blacks. Moseley-Braun's strategy of adopting to the norms and procedures of the Senate is no different than that of other newcomers, especially women.[47] The early evidence suggests that she intends to master the game.

Senator Moseley-Braun received considerable media attention for her victory over Senator Jesse Helms in blocking legislation to confer national legitimacy to a symbol of the confederacy by giving a patent to the Confederate flag. Recently, Senator Moseley-Braun introduced a welfare reform measure whose key features include job creation in poor communities, improved work incentives, and state flexibility—the last two features sit well in principle with the conservative mood of the electorate and of Congress. In what may be a pragmatic response to the political realities of the day, Moseley-Braun's legislative record may not meet the high expectations of women and of blacks who celebrated her election as pathbreaking and historic. Although integrating the Senate and other white male-dominated legislative bodies remains an important goal of America's underrepresented political minorities, and especially women, successful integration will likely only illustrate more starkly the inherent limits of such representation.

17

AFRICAN AMERICANS, H. ROSS PEROT, AND IMAGE POLITICS

The Nature of African American Third-Party Politics

• • • • • • •

Hanes Walton, Jr.

Occasionally, in the midst of political contextual transformation, a new party alternative is born.[1] This occurred during the Bush administration in the 1992 presidential election, when Texas billionaire H. Ross Perot launched a two-stage campaign for president on his own third-party ticket.[2] His independent candidacy was unique in the history of alternative (or third) parties in the United States, most significantly because its financial resources were comparable to those of the major parties. Perot bankrolled his campaign to the tune of $73 million, nearly all of it his own.[3] Moreover, because he did not apply for federal matching funds for his campaign, he was not bound by Federal Election Committee (FEC) campaign spending limits.

Generally, however, Perot's United We Stand, America movement fits the overall pattern of third-party politics in twentieth-century America.[4] As Steven Rosenstone, the preeminent scholar on third parties, has noted:

> The nineteenth-century pattern of third party development [in which] parties formed, then picked their candidates, did not persist into the twentieth century. Candidates began to emerge before the movements, and third party politics began to revolve around individuals instead of parties.[5]
>
> The most prominent [third-party] movements of the 1990s . . . are all

> more accurately labeled independent campaigns than political parties. None had any real organization distinct from the candidate's own following, and for most of them the "party" would not have existed without the candidate.[6]
>
> Technological and political changes over the last century have lessened the need for political parties and have made it possible for both major and minor party candidates to run without the aid of a preexisting organization.[7]

Thus with "little more than a computer, telephone, a postage meter . . . a consultant, . . . direct mail, [and] polls to gauge the pulse of the electorate," any candidate can create a grass roots organization to support a third-party movement.[8] "The technological and political change that allowed Jimmy Carter to win the presidency also allowed men like George Wallace and John Anderson to make relatively successful independent challenges without preexisting organization."[9]

The first stage of Perot's campaign was from February to July; the second stage began in October and ran until the November general election. On October 1, 1992, one month before the election, Perot, who had flirted with an independent candidacy since February and formally abandoned the race on July 16, officially re-entered the race.[10] After October, the presidential campaign became a three-way race among George Bush, Bill Clinton, and H. Ross Perot.

Prior to Perot's candidacy, it appeared that African Americans were limited in their choices to their perennial support for the Democratic party. Beginning with Barry Goldwater's 1964 presidential bid and continuing through the Reagan-Bush era, the Republican party had become one of the least attractive political alternatives for African Americans. Thus, United We Stand, America offered African Americans a potential new party home.

African Americans have a history of involvement with a wide variety of independent political parties on both the left and the right.[11] Primarily this involvement has been viewed as a means of registering dissatisfaction and frustration with the political, economic, and social discrimination of American society.[12] African Americans have also launched their own political parties at various points.[13] Yet the strongest measure of African Americans involvement has been in progressive independent parties.[14]

Ross Perot's quest was not for the small number of persistent third-party voters in the African American community; rather, his campaign sought the large numbers of unhappy mainstream African American voters who might be converted to his movement. Before such a political shift could become a reality, however, this new movement had to address the critical factors related to African American third-party voting. These factors are (1) a party's position on the issues critical to the African American community, and (2) the image a party holds of African Americans.[15] How well a party addresses these two factors determines the extent to which it can capture mainstream African American voters.

This paper focuses on the image variable. This factor entered American politics with the establishment of the National Association for the Advancement of Colored People (NAACP) in 1910. Born in the era of Jim Crow, the NAACP fought diligently to counter the demeaning images of African Americans promulgated by demagogues who built their political careers upon racial divisive doctrines such as white supremacy and segregation.[16] In its early years, under the guidance of W. E. B. DuBois, the NAACP put a great deal of emphasis on the creation and maintenance of a positive image of African Americans. Politically, it supported those candidates and elected officials who portrayed and related to African Americans positively, and vigorously rallied African American voters to defeat or remove from office those who made public pejorative remarks about members of the African American community. Perhaps the best-known example of the NAACP's image-building politics was the celebrated defeat of Judge John J. Parker's nomination to the Supreme Court in 1930.[17] Gradually, as a result of the NAACP's and other groups' efforts, the national political parties and their candidates began to recognize the importance of treating African American voters with a modicum of respect and decency.

African American leaders of subsequent decades continued to pressure the major political parties to improve their image with African Americans. Over the years, mainstream African American voters came to be concerned not only with certain issues of concern to their group, but also with the image held of African Americans and the way they were treated and addressed by public officials. Image became a determining variable in their political behavior. When President Gerald Ford's Secretary of Agriculture, Earl Butz, made a demeaning public joke about African Americans, he was forced to resign to appease incensed civil rights leaders. The same happened to notable television commentators and sports announcers who made derogatory and racist remarks about African Americans on the air. Democratic presidential candidate Jimmy Carter, to reassure African American voters that he could be trusted, had to make a quick trip to Atlanta to get the support of the King family after making ambiguous remarks about "ethnic purity" in an interview.[18] The importance of image in African American political behavior was further increased during the Reagan-Bush era with the Jesse Jackson campaigns and Bush's notorious Willie Horton ads.

Data and Methodology

The term "mainstream African American voters" is used to designate those African Americans who traditionally vote for one or the other of the two major parties' candidates; in lieu of a suitable candidate from either of the major parties, these voters typically sit out an election rather than vote for an independent candidate.[19] Hence they are rarely open to conversion. By contrast, traditional African American third-party voters are those who can be driven by ideological realities to support various independent parties' candidates because of their political and economic stances on issues that are pertinent to various segments of the African American community.

It was the former group, the mainstream African American voters, that Perot was after in 1992. These were his potential converts if the issue and image factors could be surmounted. Using the contextual analysis approach, I will explore the extant literature on the 1992 presidential campaign to determine the existence and influence of the issue variable. This literature, along with my interviews with two African American Perot operatives, provide the data source for this investigation.

African American Image, Third Parties, and the Reagan-Bush Era: The Jesse Jackson Candidacies

One of the main reasons Jesse Jackson ran for president in 1984 and 1988 was because he wanted the Democratic party to stop taking African American voters for granted. African American voters, Jackson maintained, wanted respect.

> Some support for Jackson was based on group identification and pride, sentiments his critics dismiss as emotional and symbolic rather than strictly political. But much of politics is symbolic, and by no means trivial.[20]

Historically, image has been a very real part of African Americans' symbolic political needs. Some of the African American voters who supported Jackson in the Democratic party primaries in 1992 were willing to following him into an independent third party movement after he lost the nomination.

Table 17.1, taken from the National Black Election Study (NBES) survey data, breaks down African American support for an independent Jackson presidential bid. Of the total sample, 52.7 percent of the respondents indicated they would vote for Jackson if he ran as an independent; 31.5 indicated support for Mondale in such a scenario, and 5.0 stated they would vote for Reagan. More women than men, more southerners than northerners, more young people than old, more higher-educated voters than less-educated voters, and more lower-income groups than higher-income ones, stated they would be willing to follow Jackson into a third political party.

As table 17.2 reveals, approximately 25 percent of African Americans polled in the NBES sample either approved or strongly approved of the formation of an independent African American political party. While these voters constituted a potential block of third-party voters for Jackson in 1984 and 1988, many of them also indicated that they really wanted the Democratic party to win back the presidency. Thus, as Gurin, Hatchett, and Jackson contend, while African

TABLE 17.1

Support for Jackson as an Independent Candidate, 1984

	Jackson	Mondale	Reagan	Don't Know	Total
Total Sample	52.7	31.5	5.0	10.8	100.0
Gender*					
Men	52.6	31.0	8.2	8.2	100.0
Women	52.8	31.8	3.0	12.4	100.0
Region X Urbanicity*					
South: Rural	56.3	27.1	4.5	12.1	100.0
South: Small City	59.0	26.7	7.6	6.8	100.0
South: Large City/Suburb	47.8	38.9	5.2	8.1	100.0
NonSouth: Rural	55.6	25.4	6.3	12.7	100.0
NonSouth: Small City	56.4	31.3	2.2	10.1	100.0
NonSouth: Large City/Suburb	45.3	35.5	4.8	14.5	100.0
Age**					
17-24	59.4	29.1	6.8	4.6	100.0
25-34	58.5	28.3	6.3	7.0	100.0
35-54	49.1	34.3	4.8	11.9	100.0
55-91	44.6	34.2	1.4	19.7	100.0
Education**					
Some High School	48.8	29.8	3.6	17.8	100.0
High School Graduate	53.7	33.1	5.8	7.4	100.0
Some College	54.4	34.1	6.8	4.8	100.0
College Graduate	56.1	25.6	3.3	15.0	100.0
Total Household Income*					
$0-9,999	50.0	29.5	5.8	14.7	100.0
$10,000-19,999	55.5	33.8	3.1	7.6	100.0
$20,000-29,999	57.3	31.8	5.0	5.9	100.0
$30,000+	51.2	35.5	6.7	6.7	100.0

Support for Black Party, 1984

	Yes Very Strongly	Yes Fairly Strongly	Yes Not Too Strongly	Yes Not Strongly At All	No Not Strongly At All	No Not Too Strongly	No Fairly Strongly	No Very Strongly	Don't Know	Total
Total Sample	15.0	7.9	1.3	0.6	4.4	10.4	15.7	41.0	3.6	100.0
Gender**										
Men	14.8	7.1	1.2	0.2	2.6	10.1	15.6	47.4	1.0	100.0
Women	15.1	8.4	1.4	0.9	5.7	10.7	15.8	36.8	5.3	100.0
Region X Urbanicity**										
South: Rural	20.1	6.2	2.8	2.2	5.3	13.9	13.3	31.0	5.3	100.0
South: Small City	13.5	6.3	0.0	0.0	5.3	13.0	15.5	43.0	3.4	100.0
South: Large City/Suburb	13.7	5.4	3.4	0.5	4.9	12.2	13.2	43.9	2.9	100.0
NonSouth: Rural	14.9	6.4	0.0	0.0	0.0	6.4	12.8	59.6	0.0	100.0
NonSouth: Small City	6.5	19.6	0.0	0.0	2.6	7.8	28.1	30.7	4.6	100.0
NonSouth: Large City/Suburb	15.5	7.5	0.3	0.0	4.0	5.3	13.0	51.6	2.8	100.0
Age**										
17-24	19.2	12.5	2.0	0.0	2.7	11.8	21.6	29.4	0.8	100.0
25-34	16.8	10.6	1.1	0.0	3.1	12.8	20.7	33.2	1.7	100.0
35-54	8.1	5.7	1.8	0.0	5.7	8.9	14.3	51.8	3.6	100.0
55-91	18.9	2.5	0.4	2.9	6.2	7.6	6.5	46.5	8.4	100.0
Education**										
Some High School	21.3	7.2	1.4	2.3	4.6	10.1	10.4	34.3	8.4	100.0
High School Graduate	17.6	4.9	2.4	0.0	4.3	13.8	18.2	38.2	0.5	100.0
Some College	10.1	11.6	0.3	0.0	5.4	11.0	19.9	39.6	2.1	100.0
College Graduate	6.0	8.7	0.9	0.0	3.2	5.0	13.3	59.2	3.7	100.0
Total Household Income**										
$0-9,999	22.0	7.1	3.4	1.6	5.3	9.0	13.4	31.1	7.1	100.0
$10,000-19,999	16.0	11.5	0.3	0.0	3.7	11.5	16.0	38.7	2.3	100.0
$20,000-29,999	15.4	6.8	1.8	0.0	6.8	9.0	19.0	41.2	0.0	100.0
$30,000+	5.6	4.5	0.4	0.0	3.0	7.9	16.5	60.2	1.9	100.0

SOURCE: Katherine Tate et al., *The 1984 National Black Election Study Sourcebook* (Ann Arbor: Program for Research on Black Americans/Institute for Social Research/University of Michigan, February, 1988), Table 14.5.

American Democratic voters "seemed ready to act independently within the party but not to defect," their voting behavior "confined their loyalty" to the Democratic party.[21] Gurin's remark notwithstanding, not all African American Democratic voters wanted the party to win again.

When the 1992 election offered an independent candidate and party in the person of H. Ross Perot, the question was simple: How many of these potential mainstream African American voters who had expressed a desire to defect from the Democratic party in the 1984 and 1988 campaigns would convert to the Perot movement?

H. Ross Perot, the NAACP, and the African American Voter: The Influence of Image Politics on a Third-Party Movement

On July 11, one day before the NAACP's 83rd Convention was officially scheduled to open in the Nashville Convention Center, two of the three presidential contenders, Democratic Governor Bill Clinton and independent candidate H. Ross Perot, arrived to speak to the NAACP conventioneers.

> Perot came ill-prepared for the occasion. He said he had no speech writer—and that quickly became apparent. No speech writer in his or her right mind would have given him some of the phrases he chose to utter or the anecdotes he chose to share with his media.[22]
>
> What got [Perot] into trouble was the use of the terms "you people" and "your people": . . . anyone with a modicum of understanding of the black psyche would know those terms are deadly poison. Whenever they are used, the hackles of black people rise. They instinctively feel they are being set aside as something not quite up to standard and lumped together as if they are a monolithic entity.[23]

But Perot, failing to understanding the negative and historical impact of those phases, continued. In his speech, Perot "reached back into his boyhood days to recall how his father and mother had been charitable to the black poor, because 'they are people too, and they have to live.' "[24]

> Perot did not mean to be insulting and that's the tragedy of it all. As soon as the words were out of his mouth, and the audience gasped, we knew that the media would play it up all cross the country. It was like throwing fresh meat to a school of hungry sharks. Lost were his pleas for an end to race hate and jobs for the jobless.[25]

Although, according to Williams, "the press was probably unfair in the way it overplayed the incident [and] political reporters stopped caring about such matters years ago,"[26] the result of Perot's faux pas was that

> from that point on, Perot, who was already coming under closer scrutiny by the media, began to lose more and more of his Teflon coating, and his qualifications for such a high office were increasingly questioned. No story was written about him without a reference to the NAACP misstep.[27]

Five days later, Perot ended the first stage of his campaign and withdrew from the presidential race.[28]

After Perot's speech, several African American leaders stepped forward to criticize it. As Willie Clark, president of the NAACP branch in San Bernadino, California, told the *New York Times,* Perot's use of the phrase "you people" "reflected how culturally out of touch he was with his audience. . . . It was like waving a red flag in front of a bull." Clark noted that the phrase was one that "white folks have used when they don't want to call us 'nigger,' but they don't want to treat [us] like an equal." Other African American leaders called the speech "insensitive" and "uninformed." Clearly they perceived this matter as an image problem for Perot.

Prior to his ill-fated remarks, the Joint Center for Political Studies, an African American think tank, found in its national poll that 14 percent of African Americans favored Perot.[29] A survey of 3,500 voting-age African Americans conducted by the Times-Mirror Center for the People and the Press indicated that 30 percent of African American voters under the age of 30 supported Perot.[30] After the NAACP convention, however, the budding African American interest and enthusiasm for Perot's candidacy dropped off significantly. Consequently, upon Perot's reentry into the campaign, African Americans did not rally to his second-stage campaign; and on election day, he received roughly 7 percent of the African American vote.[31] This was clearly a drop from the pre-election polls data. Perot's image problems with African American voters had apparently not been resolved. The damage from the speech had not been repaired.

Regardless, the vote Perot did receive from the African American community was greater than that given to any other independent party candidate in recent years. Perot bested the New Alliance party, headed by an African American woman, Lenora Fulani.

H. Ross Perot's African American Political Activists: The Reverend Calvin Butts and Dr. Phyllis Mack

On February 20, 1992, during Cable News Network's "Larry King Live" show, H. Ross Perot officially announced his bid for the presidency. Late as it was in the election season, most notable African American leaders, organization heads, and political operatives had already pledged their commitment to one of the several Democratic contenders. Perot's options for endorsement within the African American community were thus extremely limited.

Notwithstanding, a few African American religious leaders were among the uncommitted. To maximize their clout and leverage with the major party contenders, African American churchmen traditionally have waited until presidential campaigns reach their respective states before committing the support of their congregations and denominations. Perot's tactic was to choose one leader from this pool of potential supporters, one from a large state with a large number of African American voters. Jimmy Carter had used this same tactic, to some success, in the South. Perot, however, sought out the endorsement of an African American church leader in a northern state, and he planned to announce this support just before his speech to the NAACP convention.

The Perot campaign approached Reverend Calvin O. Butts, III, pastor of the Abyssinia Baptist Church in Harlem, a position once held by the late Congressman Adam Clayton Powell. Reverend Butts agreed to meet with Perot and hear his views before deciding whether or not to give him an endorsement. At that meeting, according to Butts, Perot told him about his "plan for economic development of the inner cities, job programs for the people in these impacted areas, [and] support for civil rights."[32] When former congresswoman and presidential candidate Shirley Chisholm joined the two men at this meeting, Butts recalled, "Perot talked about the possibility of putting an African American woman on the ticket as a vice presidential running mate."[33] Indeed, Perot promised everything an African American leader wanted to hear, and Butts was impressed—so much so that, when Perot informed him that he was going to take his message to the NAACP convention in a few days, Butts offered to write Perot a speech for that gathering. The speech would later be ignored.

Butts endorsed Perot after their meeting. *New York Times* as saying: "Perot is someone I think can win. It's a calculated risk on my part, but one I'm willing to take."[34] Butts was made co-chair of the New York party committee of United We Stand, America just before the NAACP convention.

Within three days of his endorsement of Perot, Butts was severely criticized by Congressman Charles Rangel of Harlem and others in the Harlem community.[35] Congressman Rangel censured Perot's remarks at the NAACP convention, claiming that they revealed the candidate as one unable to accept African Americans as equals. Reverend Butts strongly denounced Rangel, noting that the "social and economic conditions in Harlem had declined substantially during Mr. Rangel's tenure in Congress compared with that of the late Adam Clayton Powell, [whom] Mr. Rangel defeated to win the Congressional seat."[36] Butts claimed that Perot represented "a viable alternative for black voters because he would be a staunch defender and enforcer of civil rights."[37] Regardless, Butts faced mounting criticism, even from his own parishioners and colleagues, who felt that he had been "premature in endorsing Mr. Perot before seeing his political platform."[38]

Receiving no support from Perot, who dropped out of the race shortly thereafter, Reverend Butts quickly relented. He withdrew his endorsement of Perot and endorsed instead African American educator Ron D. Daniels, who was running as an independent candidate. In making the Daniels endorsement, Reverend Butts claimed: "I don't believe that Bill Clinton is going to be any better than George Bush. . . . The Republicans have ignored people of African descent. The Democrats have taken us for granted."[39]

Thus Perot lost one African American leader by the end of stage one of his campaign. Dr. Phyllis Mack, an African American dentist in Savannah, Georgia, has long been active in Savannah's African American community, searching for solutions to that community's egregious problems for more than a decade. She is committed, fearless, and confrontational. In the fray in every local election, she has been a candidate for local office as well as a strong supporter of other African American and white candidates who have a progressive platform.

In the 1992 presidential race, Dr. Mack began following H. Ross Perot's campaign closely. In her words, she "liked what he was saying about jobs, ethics in government, keeping people working and making them happier, their families stronger, and having people willing to participate in politics."[40] She also liked Perot's ideas about "a complete change in the way government and politics is done—an overhaul, and that people have the power to cause change. You didn't need a leader, you can do it on your own. You can determine what you need from your government."[41] Perot's ideas "of change and empowering people" were what recruited her to join his movement in the first stage of the campaign.

Mack used her dental office as a site for the petition drive to get Perot on the ballot in Georgia. Dr. Mack "would encourage people who asked questions to think positively about the Perot message of change. . . . I wanted George Bush out of there. And Perot, I thought, would clearly help that effort."[42]

Then came Perot's withdrawal from the race. "It was," Mack said, "the way that he did it. He violated his own principle of including people in the process."[43] Yet, as she saw it, Perot "was being pulled into the system and its old way of doing business, and he must have felt that he could be more of an influence on the outside. That's why be quit."[44]

When Perot re-entered the campaign in October, "he was really a threat to Clinton and Bush, and their campaign had degenerated into mud-slinging and a bitter battle. And the crucial issue of change was being neglected."[45] But Perot, she believed, had re-entered the race merely to "save face, but it was too late. And this made him appear wishy-washy."[46] By this point, Dr. Mack had moved on to support another candidate.

Thus, the transformed political context made two African American political activists open to recruitment by an alternative political phenomenon. While one was recruited on a personal basis, the other was recruited by the message of change. Both exited the independent candidate's organization well before the elections. Community criticisms and the failure of the candidate to live up to his promises caused one leader to leave, and the candidate's failure to live up to his principles forced the other leader out of the campaign. Both leaders moved on to new alliances.

In addition, both Butts and Mack noted Perot's failure to more adequately address his image problem in the African American community. However, they did not view that aspect as being as important as the candidate's sticking to his political promises. Thus, for these two political leaders of the African American mainstream vote, Perot's "image" problem, while not fatal, was at least important.

Overall, Perot captured 7 percent of the African American vote. As table 17.3 reveals, among African American voters in the 1992 election, more men than women supported Perot, and more younger rather than older persons supported him. He also received more support from African Americans in the East and West than in the Midwest and South, and more in California than New York.

While Perot won the largest vote for an independent candidate in the history

TABLE 17.3

1992 African American Vote for H. Ross Perot

The Categories of the African American Electorate	Perot	Clinton	Bush
Totals			
African-Americans	7	82	11
Demographics			
Gender			
Men	9	77	15
Women	5	86	9
Age			
18-29 year old	8	83	9
30-44 year old	8	81	11
45-59 year old	6	79	15
60 and older	4	89	7
Partisanship			
Democrats	4	92	5
Republicans	NA	NA	NA
Region			
East	8	79	14
Midwest	5	86	9
South	6	82	12
West	11	83	7
States			
New York	6	86	8
California	8	83	9

Adapted from "The 1992 Elections: Portrait of the Electorate," *New York Times,* November 5, 1992.

of African American third-party voting, his support among African Americans might have been even larger had he resolved his "image" problem more effectively.

Conclusions

The image factor in African American politics was very much a part of this independent party's efforts to attract a portion of the mainstream African American constituency from the major parties. Although candidate Ross Perot handled the matter of image in a questionable and unsettled way, there was still enough dissatisfaction among African American voters with the major parties that they supported a third party at levels unprecedented in the history of American politics.

This effort confirms the reality that in addition to the issues, an independent party movement must pay careful attention to certain cultural factors at work within the African American community if it hopes to lure their votes away from the major parties. Failure to understand these cultural realities may diminish, if not destroy, a party's chances of making inroads into this community.

In the 1996 presidential campaign, Perot's renamed Reform party needed to run a different candidate or seriously address the cultural factor of "image" if it is to win over more than 7% of mainstream African American voters. He did not. His support fell to 4% of mainstream African American voters.

Crossover - Black Politicians who tries to broaden his contituency so he is

18

AN AFRICAN AMERICAN PRESIDENTIAL CANDIDATE

The Failed Presidential Campaign of Governor L. Douglas Wilder

• • • • • • •

Paula D. McClain and Steven C. Tauber

Political context involves political innovations on the part of both the transformers and those whose political context is being transformed. The twelve years of the Reagan and Bush administrations witnessed the implementation of many dramatic and creative political innovations aimed at altering the American political landscape. While Richard Nixon's 1968 presidential campaign is remembered for his use of racial "code words,"[1] Ronald Reagan and George Bush were far less subtle in their appeals to racial fears. Reagan's use of the fictitious "welfare queen" stereotype conjured up the image of massive numbers of black welfare cheats living at the expense of hard-working whites. George Bush's use of the Willie Horton campaign ads was a blatant attempt to tap the latent, and in some cases, active, racism of a segment of the white electorate. Given the rightward shift in the national as well as state political arenas during these neoconservative Republican administrations, the urgency of the need for adjustment and innovation in political strategizing was not lost on African American politicians. This was especially the case with Governor L. Douglas Wilder of Virginia, the first African American elected governor in United States history, who, shortly after assuming the governor's office in 1989, embarked on a short-lived quest for the 1992 Democratic presidential nomination.

To better understand the events surrounding Wilder's aborted attempt for the presidency, this chapter examines his innovative efforts to "deracialize" the political landscape in the 1985 and 1989 Virginia election campaigns. It will also explore the relationship of Virginia's political culture and political context to Wilder's national strategy.

Data and Methodology

The concept of deracialization is the organizing principle for the analysis in this chapter. The theoretical section is drawn from the extant literature on the concept of deracialization. The analysis of Wilder's 1985 and 1989 Virginia campaigns are drawn from studies of and voting returns from those campaigns. The 1992 campaign analysis is based on a content analysis of newspaper articles from the *Washington Post* and *New York Times* from March 1991 to January 1992.

Deracialization

The most appropriate construct within which to understand the Wilder phenomenon is the concept of deracialization. The originator of the term, Charles V. Hamilton,[2] initially intended the concept as a strategy by which the Democrats could regain some of the ground they had lost to the Republicans during the 1972 presidential elections.[3] Hamilton "advised the Democrats to pursue a deracialized electoral strategy, thereby denying their Republican opponents the opportunity of using race as a polarizing issue."[4] Essentially, Hamilton was exhorting the Democratic party to emphasize those issues that had broad appeal to the electorate across racial lines.

> I suggested that there were certain clear political advantages to be derived from emphasizing issues that lent themselves to what I called "de-racialist solutions." By this I meant that certain issues, such as full employment, a meaningful national health insurance law, and a sound income-maintenance program, would (or at least ought to) appeal to broad segments of the electorate across racial lines.[5]

Deracialization, as originally conceived, is best understood as a strategy by which African Americans can maximize their interests in the political arena. However, Hamilton argued that it does not apply to all issues, and particularly not to racial zero-sum issues such as busing and affirmative action.[6] Rather, deracialized politics emphasizes issues that appeal to both whites and blacks. A deracialized political strategy is one that would allow the Democrats to gain the support of both races, or at least not lose the support of whites. Hamilton intended the Democrats to continue to emphasize progressive, yet broad based issues.

Some aspects of Hamilton's conceptualization of deracialization have been echoed by Martin Kilson's notion of the transethnic imperative.[7] Kilson attempts to broaden Hamilton's concept to fashion a framework for African American politicians, especially those representing largely white constituencies.

> In the years ahead, what I call a transethnic imperative will increasingly inform black American life in general and its politics in particular. The goal of such an imperative would be to intertwine the leadership of black and white sociopolitical institutions. . . . The initial focus of an emergent black transethnic politics must be to transform black elected officials into politicians elected by multi-ethnic votes, not simply black votes.[8]

Moreover, Kilson, unlike Hamilton, stresses the fact that these transethnic politicians need to be pragmatic, or "technocratic." They must emphasize their skill and efficiency in order to allay the fears of white voters, attract funds and volunteers from white voters, and still manage to appear to be loyal to black concerns.[9]

Unlike Hamilton's deracialization strategy, the transethnic imperative is symmetrical: white politicians who represent black constituencies should be included within the latter concept. The two concepts are similar in that the transethnic imperative also presumes a progressive streak. Kilson expects the link between minority politicians and white voters to consist of progressive, inclusive, and egalitarian themes. Therefore, he views Jesse Jackson, with his vision of uniting racial minorities with white ethnics, as the quintessential transethnic politician.[10]

While obvious distinctions may be drawn between Hamilton's deracialization and Kilson's transethnic imperative, the two concepts share one important component: they both envision the African American "crossover politician" as adhering to a progressive brand of politics. Both Hamilton and Kilson argue that African American politicians must shift from stressing themes that only appeal to their race; yet neither suggest that African American politics or politicians move to a more moderate or conservative political posture.

More recently, the conceptualization of deracialization, or crossover politics, has abandoned its liberal approach in exchange for a more conservative or moderate approach as a direct consequence of the rightward shift in the political arena during the Reagan and Bush administrations. According to McCormick and Jones, deracialization in the transformed political arena is the process of

> conducting a campaign in a stylistic fashion that defuses the polarizing effects of race by avoiding explicit reference to race-specific issues, while at the same time emphasizing those issues that are perceived as racially transcendent, thus mobilizing a broad segment of the electorate for purposes of capturing and maintaining public office.[11]

The vast majority of the research thus far on deracialization and its salience for American politics has been in urban politics.[12] While some research demonstrates that deracialization may encompass progressive themes[13], deracialized strategies have been found most often to employ conservative themes generated to appeal to conservative constituencies. It is under the latter, more conservative understanding of deracialization that Doug Wilder's political campaigns must be analyzed. Why was Wilder able to successfully employ a deracialized strategy during his 1985 and 1989 Virginia races, but unsuccessful in employing that strategy in his aborted bid for the 1992 Democratic presidential nomination?

The Virginia Context

To better understand the significance of the deracialization hypothesis to Doug Wilder's political career, one must first understand the constituencies that Wilder represented and the political context in which he ran his political campaigns. During the colonial period, Virginia's economy was chiefly agricultural. This sector produced a small, aristocratic, and landed gentry class, whose members included key figures in the American Revolution and the framing of the Constitution, such as George Washington, Thomas Jefferson, James Madison, and John Randolph. As the nineteenth century proceeded, Virginia lagged behind the rest of the nation in industrialization, but the landed gentry were determined to defend the dying institution of slavery, which undergirded their privileged way of life. With the Civil War, much of which was fought on Virginia soil, Virginia's economy was ravaged, and the state's elite continued to fight vigorously against the rising tide of progress.

By the twentieth century, this tradition was represented by the Byrd political machine. The dynasty of Democrats Harry Byrd, Sr. and Harry Byrd, Jr. perpetuated the ultra-conservative tradition of Virginia's landed gentry as they and their operatives fought both FDR's New Deal liberalism and, more significantly, racial integration. The Byrd machine's hold over Virginia's state government was broken with the election of Charles Robb, a Democratic moderate, to the governorship in 1981. Despite Robb's election, Virginia remained an extremely conservative state. Nine out of ten of its congresspersons were Republicans in 1981, and, as they had since 1952 (with the exception of 1964), Virginians continued to vote Republican in presidential elections. It is against this conservative backdrop that L. Douglas Wilder decided to run for statewide office in 1985.[14]

Wilder's 1985 and 1989 Campaigns

Doug Wilder was elected to the state Senate from Richmond in 1969, the first African American elected to that body. Using a combination of combative personal style coupled with centrist politics, he developed a favorable relationship with Virginia's conservative Democratic leadership.[15] As a result, Wilder enjoyed a number of legislative and political successes. For example, he engineered the compromise that created a Martin Luther King, Jr./Robert E. Lee/Stonewall Jackson state holiday, and he greatly increased the state's minority-owned business procurement. In 1982, he forced out of the race a Byrd protege who sought the Democratic nomination for the United States Senate by threatening to run as an independent.[16] By 1984, Wilder was considered a major player in the Virginia Senate, having risen to chair several prominent and powerful committees.

Wilder decided to run for Lieutenant Governor[17] in 1985 after receiving the endorsement of A. L. Philpott, the powerful Speaker of the Virginia House of Delegates. He ran as the sole contender for the Democratic nomination. It was during this campaign that Wilder first employed a conservative, deracialized strategy. He hired Paul Goldman, a centrist, political consultant, as his chief adviser.[18] He then embarked upon a 3,700 trek across the state to introduce himself to the people.[19] During the campaign, Wilder purposely did not bring up any issues that called attention to his race; moreover, he stressed a Reaganesque commitment to fiscal conservatism (cutting spending without raising taxes) and law and order.[20] Consequently, in many parts of the state, even those with long histories of racism and black disenfranchisement, Wilder was able to make a favorable impression on the conservative, predominantly white Virginia populace. Wilder won the lieutenant governorship with 51.8 percent of the total vote, 97 percent of the black vote and 46 percent of the white vote.[21]

In view of his successful election as Lieutenant Governor, Wilder decided to enter the 1989 gubernatorial race. Again employing the services of Paul Goldman, he developed further his deracialization strategy.[22] He continued to de-emphasize race and stress his low-tax and pro-spending-cuts positions. Yet he counted on his race and the historic nature of his campaign to bring African American voters to the polls.[23] Moreover, like David Dinkins of New York city, Wilder purposely distanced himself from Jesse Jackson. After the 1988 presidential election, Jackson had positioned himself as the leader of the left wing of the Democratic party. By distancing himself from Jackson, Wilder was able to portray himself as a true centrist to the citizens of Virginia.[24]

In both statewide races, Wilder's deracialized strategy was similar to the current conceptualization, which consists of abandoning the liberal/progressive electoral strategy for a more conservative or moderate approach. However, one aspect of Wilder's gubernatorial campaign did employ Hamilton's version of deracialization. In July 1989, the United States Supreme Court ruled in *Webster v. Reproductive Health Services* (109 S.Ct. 3040) that states have more freedom to regulate abortion, thereby making states major actors in the abortion battle. When Wilder's opponent Marshall Coleman took the position that abortions should be illegal, Wilder emphasized a pro-choice position that was particularly salient in the northern Virginia suburbs and with younger female voters. Consequently, Wilder's progressive stance on a racially neutral issue suggests that his deracialized campaign was not completely conservative. In the end, Wilder won the race by a mere 6,741 votes, receiving a total of slightly more than 50 percent, 41 percent of the white vote, and 96 percent of the black vote.[25]

Wilder's Run for the Presidency

With only one announced Democratic candidate, Paul Tsongas, and President Bush's popularity at an all-time high after the Gulf War, Governor Wilder in March 1991 formed an exploratory committee to examine the feasibility of his running for the presidency.[26] It was Wilder's intention to run his presidential campaign in a manner similar to his two previous statewide races; he would deemphasize race and emphasize fiscal conservatism and law and order. At the time Wilder formed his exploratory committee, the question of whether Jesse Jackson would enter the race was as yet unanswered. Even though the contrast between the two politicians was striking, Jackson, if he decided to run, would take votes away from Wilder. As Democratic party consultant Raymond Strother said, whereas Jackson was a "black candidate, [Wilder was] a candidate who happens to be black."[27]

Jackson's political base was the left or progressive wing of the Democratic party,[28] while Wilder expressed a far more moderate, even conservative brand of politics. In an interview in the conservative journal *Policy Review,*[29] Wilder stressed his accomplishment of balancing the state budget without raising taxes.

> When I said in my campaign that I saw no need to raise taxes, I was looking at revenue projections based on expectations of a robust Virginia economy. Then, when I came into office, I was advised that there was a shortfall from these projections. I didn't consider new taxes, though, because there were areas of unnecessary spending that could be cut. Having been involved in state government for twenty years, I knew there was fat.[30]

In addition to expressing a conservative view on fiscal matters, he advocated more conservative views on law and order. He also expressed his opposition to stringent and "arbitrary" racial hiring quotas such as those in effect in the capital city of Richmond.[31] The only racial issue that Wilder stressed in this interview was his harsh criticism of President Bush's veto of the 1990 Civil Rights Act. Wilder argued that the Act was not a quota bill, and challenged Bush to give him the opportunity to teach him about "real" racial quotas.[32] While one could argue that this represented a racial campaign issue, the fact that this legislation had by then passed both houses of Congress made it more a bipartisan rather than a racially divisive issue.

Wilder took his conservative, deracialized campaign to New Hampshire on an exploratory trip during the summer of 1991 with the campaign slogan: "Put America First." Under his plan, Wilder would cut $50 billion in waste and needless middle-class entitlements and use the savings for a $35 billion middle-class tax cut and a $15 billion grant to state and local government projects.[33] Wilder formally announced his candidacy for the Democratic nomination and pushed forward his conservative deracialized electoral strategy. However, he quickly encountered difficulties.

Deracialization Abandoned

Wilder's presidential campaign troubles began before his campaign formally got underway. During the spring and summer of 1991, Governor Wilder made several public misstatements that served to undercut his viability as a presidential candidate. His first blunder was his response to the well-publicized drug raid on several University of Virginia fraternities. Governor Wilder publicly considered mandatory drug testing for all of Virginia's state college and university students, angering many civil libertarian groups and individuals.[34] Secondly, reacting to President Bush's nomination of Clarence Thomas to the Supreme Court, Wilder commented that Thomas's Roman Catholic religious background required that he face a stricter standard of questioning on abortion,[35] greatly angered many Catholics, even pro-choice Catholics.[36] Shortly thereafter, Wilder, appearing on the Public Broadcasting System (PBS) television program "American Interests," strongly implied that the United States should employ the CIA to remove Iraqi leader Sadaam Hussein, even if that meant assassinating him. Wilder retracted this statement moments later.[37]

In addition to these blunders, Wilder engaged in two well-publicized, bitter feuds that further decreased his viability as a presidential candidate. Governor Wilder and Senator Charles Robb had been feuding for several years, but during the summer of 1991 their personal and political problems overflowed into the public arena. Wilder was overheard in a telephone conversation ordering a state police probe of Senator Robb, but when asked, he told reporters he had nothing to do with the investigation of the Senator.[38] Once again, Wilder had to apologize, this time on national television in an appearance on *Meet the Press,* for misleading the press by denying his involvement in the investigation.[39]

Governor Wilder's second public feud was with another political rival: Jesse Jackson. While part of his initial deracialized electoral strategy in Virginia had been to distance himself from the more liberal Jackson, Wilder clearly realized that he would need Jackson's support to win a national campaign. However, Wilder's combative style and his earlier distancing himself from Jackson did not endear him to Jackson. The fight between the two arose from Wilder's 1989 gubernatorial pledge to eliminate the funding disparity between Virginia's rich and poor school districts; a promise, by Wilder's own admission, he was unable to keep. In September 1991, Jackson visited several of Virginia's poorest school districts and chided Wilder for not keeping his promise. Wilder responded by alleging that Jackson was purposely trying to embarrass him and sabotage his presidential campaign.[40] Although the two met in an attempt to ameliorate their differences,[41] three months later Wilder again accused Jackson of sabotaging his campaign.[42]

As Larry Sabato, a University of Virginia political scientist, said of Wilder's two public apologies (his misleading reporters about the Robb investigation and his Clarence Thomas comment), "Not only is [Wilder] hurting his credibility, I think that he is not ready for prime time."[43] Moreover, Wilder encountered difficulty raising money for his presidential bid.[44] By the autumn of 1991, Wilder's polling numbers were not encouraging. He was last in the field of six Democratic candidates in the New Hampshire primary, and his rallies were attracting few supporters. The only good news Wilder received early in the campaign was the endorsement of an obscure Republican senator who had backed Pat Robertson in 1988.[45] Wilder was also having problems back home in Virginia. His frequent absences from the state, 111 days in 1991, many of which were presidential campaign trips, were being roundly criticized, and a survey by Virginia Democratic party leaders revealed that Arkansas governor Bill Clinton was leading Wilder among party regulars.[46]

The final blow to Wilder's aspirations was his poor showings in the televised Democratic debates. In an early November 1991 debate with Bill Clinton and Paul Tsongas, Wilder appeared to be "too combative,"[47] and the reviews of his performance in the December debate were uniformly unfavorable.[48] It was becoming clear that Wilder's presidential campaign was finished unless he could generate support for his lagging effort.

Jesse Jackson's declining to enter the 1992 presidential contest had opened a window of opportunity for another candidate to court African American support. Wilder viewed himself as the natural inheritor of Jackson's constituency; yet, in order to appeal to this block of voters he would have to change his positions on some key issues. This, however, entailed a purposeful shift in constituency focus from conservative Virginia whites to a nationally diffuse black electorate. Therefore, Wilder abandoned his carefully developed and nurtured conservative, deracialized strategy in favor of more liberal and racially oriented themes.

He hired a former Jackson 1988 campaign official as his campaign manager and began to stress more liberal and racially oriented themes.[49] In a speech to the AFL-CIO, Wilder accused President Bush and the Republicans of "conducting a decade of code-word politics."[50] In Dubuque, Iowa, a city then recently torn by racially motivated cross burnings, Wilder blamed the Republicans for creating a climate where racism could flourish. He also lambasted his Democratic opponents (particularly his chief rival, fellow moderate southern governor Bill Clinton) for distancing themselves from labor and minorities.[51] Immediately after that speech, Wilder flew to Selma, Alabama, and repeated the same themes, blaming Reagan's welfare queen illustration and Bush's use of Willie Horton as contributing to the environment of intolerance.[52] He also went to Arkansas, where he accused Clinton on his home turf of working against the concerns of minorities.[53] While one could argue about the extent to which these pronouncements actually emphasized racial issues, for Wilder, who had previously prided himself in downplaying race, they represented a switch in strategy.

In addition to emphasizing race, Wilder began to sound more liberal themes. In an attempt to counter Clinton's rising popularity, Wilder characterized the Arkansas governor as representing the "Reagan/Bush wing of the Democratic party," and called Clinton and other members of the moderate-to-conservative Democratic Leadership Council (DLC), a Clinton creation, "the Democrats of the leisure class."[54] Previously, the DLC had been an organization with which Wilder was usually in agreement. Moreover, Wilder borrowed this particular characterization from his rival Jesse Jackson. Although Wilder claimed that the statement was a joke, the underlying premise of the statement further signaled the leftward shift in Wilder's strategy.[55]

Ultimately, Wilder's altered strategy, and his belated efforts to build a nationwide constituency among the African American electorate, were unsuccessful. Citing pressing concerns in Virginia, Wilder shocked many of his close supporters and announced his intention to withdraw from the race during his State of the Commonwealth address on January 8, 1992.[56] Although Wilder eloquently cited the state's economic problems and the difficulty of administering the state and conducting a national campaign as his reasons for withdrawing, it was clear that his presidential campaign was faltering. At the national level, Wilder was unable to pull together a similar coalition of blacks and moderate whites as he had in his 1989 gubernatorial race, and his missteps made it difficult for him to raise money.[57] Others suggested that Wilder's debate and campaign appearances were marked more by slogans than by substance.[58]

Conclusions

Political context is a major determinant of the effectiveness of the strategy of deracialization in political campaigning. While several African American politicians (most notably Gary Franks of Connecticut and J. C. Watts of Oklahoma) innovatively accommodated their electoral strategies to conform to the conservative political context of the Reagan-Bush era, they met with limited success. In Doug Wilder's case, deracialization proved a successful electoral strategy at the state level, but it clearly did not translate into success in a national presidential campaign. In order to be competitive in the Democratic presidential primaries, Wilder realized that he needed first to begin with a national electoral base, and then build upon that base. Presumably, Wilder should have been the natural recipient of Jesse Jackson's electoral base when Jackson declined to run in 1992; yet, Wilder's carefully crafted image as a political conservative and his resultant conservative policy pronouncements placed him at odds with this diverse and diffuse national constituency. Hence, in an effort to improve his standings, he abandoned deracialization as an electoral strategy.

Wilder's dramatic mid-campaign strategic shift highlights the political costs associated with his latter approach. Indeed, the turnabout from a conservative, deracialized political persona to a progressive, racially oriented one was a difficult shift for Wilder to achieve. It was also a shift that clearly failed. Yet, after analyzing the campaign, one could effectively argue that if Wilder had initially adopted a deracialized strategy more in keeping with Hamilton's progressive definition, the transition might have been more successful. On the other hand, he might not have won the governor's office in the heart of the Old Confederacy if he had.

PART 7

DECISIONS

During the Reagan-Bush years, the transformation of the political context so as to disadvantage African Americans involved all of the major decision making bodies in the American political system in these context-altering initiatives, which came in the form of rhetoric and leadership, executive orders, Supreme Court decisions, program reductions, budget cutbacks, and changes in federal rules and regulations.

One of President Reagan's chief thrusts was to weaken and disable the civil rights and equal employment opportunities and protections that had been initiated by earlier Democratic administrations. He turned to the court system, traditionally viewed by African Americans as the last bastion of relief for civil rights issues, to facilitate his plans. Reagan and Bush nominated, and Congress subsequently confirmed, several conservative justices to the Supreme Court. During Reagan's first term, the newly configured Supreme Court's decision in *Grove City College v. Bell* effectively narrowed the reach and scope of the 1964 Civil Rights Act—a Reagan imperative. Congress responded with the Civil Rights Restoration Act of 1987, which Reagan vetoed. Congress later overrode the President's veto, and the law negating the Court's decision went into effect.

During Bush's term, five key Supreme Court decisions in 1989 led to the weakening of title VII of the federal equal employment opportunity law. Once again, Congress respond with the Civil Rights Restoration Act of 1991. Although the bill passed both the Senate and the House, Bush vetoed it. At the next legislative session, Republican Senator John Danforth, one of Supreme Court nominee Clarence Thomas's key backers, worked out numerous compromises and replaced the original bill with a weakened version.[1] Both chambers adopted the compromise bill, and Bush signed P. L. 102–166 into law in the aftermath of Thomas's controversial confirmation hearings.[2]

Thus, while Reagan did not prevail in using the courts to erode African Americans' traditional (since the 1960s) civil rights and equal employment protections, Bush did.

Both Presidents Reagan and Bush, under the guise of seeking to reduce the involvement of the federal bureaucracy in citizens' affairs, invoked the power of the executive order to diminish regulatory and enforcement support for African Americans' civil rights.

> Apart from budget reduction, the Reagan administration relied on two other means to control regulatory expansion: a rather single minded pattern of appointments and a new system for screening agency rules at the Office of Management and Budget [OMB]. Neither required as much cooperation from Congress and in this sense facilitated more central control.[3]

Reagan moved aggressively to undermine civil rights via the regulatory route. He issued two executive orders to reduce the civil rights regulatory reach of the federal government. In 1981, he issued Executive Order 12291, which required that all proposed "major" changes to federal regulations be subjected to a cost-benefit analysis before the rules could be implemented and enforced.[4] Four days into his second term, on January 4, 1985, Reagan issued Executive Order 12498. Under this new order, federal agencies were annually required to establish a regulatory agenda which is subject to OMB review.[5]

> Thus, with these two Orders, President Reagan gave OMB the right to review and to control agency rule making from initial formulation to final promulgation. . . . OMB is no longer a mere pressure group in the civil rights regulating process; it now determines how the rules and regulations covering civil rights compliance can be enforced.[6]

After 1985, fewer and fewer regulatory rules were proposed to address the crisis in enforcement that faced the nation's civil rights implementation agencies.[7] A recent study by Willie Johnson, Roosevelt Green, and Kenneth Jordan reports similar reductions in regulatory activity in the area of civil rights during the Bush administration.[8] Bush maintained and completed the shift that began in the Reagan era "to avoid carrying out the law of the land with regard to civil rights."[9] Unless President Clinton issues his own executive orders to the contrary or directs his OMB director to relax the Reagan-ordered scrutinies, neither of which actions have yet taken place, the situation will remain the same. As of 1996, Clinton has not issued any executive orders to supplant or replace those of the Reagan-Bush era.

Presidents Reagan and Bush placed numerous conservative Republican African American judges in the federal court system at all levels, from the District Appellate Court to the Supreme Court. Judge Theodore R. Newman, Jr., chief judge of the District of Columbia Court of Appeals, offered the following description of his judicial bent:

> if Edmund Burke is a symbol of conservatism, I will argue that I am a true conservative. Burke's philosophy, simply put, is that government ought to stay out of the individual's private life. In this day and age, conservatives want to keep government out of people's economic affairs, we are quite willing to permit governmental intrusion into the bedroom. My conservatism, however, extends to the latter as well. . . . I've always had a keen interest in the rights of the individual. In terms of the relationship of the individual to the state—in terms of the law—I am an Edmund Burke conservative.[10]

African American novelist and poet Maya Angelou cogently sums up African Americans' larger concerns:

> Judge [Clarence] Thomas, chosen by President Bush, has demonstrated that he is as conservative as the President and the administration, else he would not have been selected. The African American savants know that, and we know as well, that if efforts to scuttle his appointment are successful, another conservative possibly more harmful, . . . will be seated firmly on the bench till death or decision rules otherwise.[11]

However, Reagan's and Bush's initiatives in the judicial arena did not always prevail. For example, on June 20, 1991, in the midst of the Bush presidency, the Supreme Court ruled that "elections for judges are covered by the federal Voting Rights Act." In two cases, one challenging the electoral districts for the Louisiana Supreme Court and another involving trial courts in ten counties in Texas, the Court ruled in favor of minorities. The twin 6-to-3 rulings reinstated lawsuits brought in the lower federal courts by black and Hispanic voters. The lawsuits had been dismissed the year before on the basis of a ruling by the United States Court of Appeals for the Fifth Circuit, which claimed that the Voting Rights Act did not apply to judicial elections. That court, which sits in New Orleans and covers Texas, Louisiana, and Mississippi, ruled that the law applies only to elections for executive and legislative offices.[12] The Supreme Court determined that judicial electoral contests, like all other elections, had to be free of racial bias and discrimination.

Four years previously, on April 1, 1987, the federal district court of the

Southern District of Mississippi, ruled that "in the 5th, 7th, 9th, and 11th Chancey Court districts; the 4th, 7th, and 11th Circuit Court Districts; and the Hands County Court district," African Americans were entitled to single-member districts with populations sufficient to have African Americans elected as judges.[13] This ruling eliminated at-large, numbered-post election methods and multimember districts that diluted African American voting rights. This unexpected decision enabled African Americans in Mississippi to elect more of their own kind to the judicial branch of government in their state, something that the conservatives, with a conservative majority on the courts, had hoped would not happen.

In another case, in 1988 in Georgia, *Brooks v. State Board of Elections,* an African American state legislator sued the state and its governor for their failure to increase the number of African American judges. After many sessions and in light of the Supreme Court's rulings, Georgia officials eventually settled out of court. State Representative Tyrone Brooks, who spearheaded the effort, noted the following:

> The African-American plaintiffs in *Brooks v. State Board of Elections* and state officials signed an historic agreement today in the office of Governor Zell Miller providing for a new method of selecting state court, superior court and appellate court judges in Georgia. Among the key features is that there will be not less than 25 black superior court judges by December 31, 1994, and an additional five new black superior or state court judges. Including the three sitting black state court judges and the three sitting black appellate court judges, that will bring the total of black judges to a minimum of 36 by December 31, 1994.
>
> The black community will have substantial input into the selection of these judges, by having one of the plaintiffs and one of plaintiff's counsel sitting members of the Judicial Nominating Commission which makes the recommendation to the Governor of persons to be appointed to judgeships.
>
> All judges will be subject to retention elections—meaning that the voters can vote YES or NO on whether [the judges] continue in office. This system is known generally as the "Missouri Plan." In the event black judges lose these retention elections, the special JNC described above would nominate their replacement.
>
> The state would be permanently barred from discriminating on the basis of race in nominations or appointments and would remain subject to the jurisdiction of the court until such time as it achieved a "racially diverse judiciary which is reasonably representative of the population of the state."[14]

This was an unexpected victory for African Americans because the Reagan-Bush administrations had put a conservative majority on the Supreme Court and the movement to curtail the expansion of civil rights and liberties for blacks and other minorities was under way. When the Court ruled otherwise in this case, the state of Georgia chose to settle out of court. Overall, Texas, Louisiana, and Mississippi, stand to gain more African American and Hispanic judges in years to come.

In another case, President Bush's Justice Department, under Attorney General Dick Thornburgh, and its civil rights division filed suit against Brooks County, Georgia.

> This action was brought by the United States alleging that defendants have engaged in a pattern of discrimination on the basis of race in the election, employment, and assignment of black persons to serve as poll officers.[15]
>
> The total population in Brooks County is 44 percent black. . . . For seven elections in Brooks County, from 1986 through 1988, only 29 or 8.6 percent of the 334 appointees to serve as poll officers have been black. . . . During the July 17, 1990 primary election, only five of the county's 47 poll officers (9.9 percent) were blacks: black persons in Brooks County have been underrepresented as poll officers in comparison to their numbers as county residents and registered voters.[16]

In fact, the Justice Department reported, while "the total number of persons appointed as poll officers at each election has varied between 45 and 53 persons; black persons have never constituted more than five of the officers."[17] To stop the suit, the county entered into a consent decree to stop discrimination against African Americans as poll officers.[18] Thus, once again, the political context had changed in African Americans' favor, with the help of the Justice Department, despite the President's wishes for the contrary.

One of the unintended consequences of this contextual transformation was the reestablishment within the Democratic party of a new and dominant southern wing. The strength of the former Democratic southern wing, the Dixiecrats, had dissipated with the rise of the Goldwater, Nixon, and Reagan factions within the Republican party. In 1985, in the aftermath of Jesse Jackson's 1984 presidential bid, a new wave of Democratic politicians, "predominantly from the South and West, including several who want the party to moderate its position and shed its image as a bastion of liberal special interest,"[19] emerged to launch the Democratic Leadership Council (DLC). They were led by the then-governor of Arkansas, Bill Clinton.

The members of the DLC, according to a statement released at the group's founding convention in March 1985, "have set their sights to recapture the loyalty of elected Democrats who have shown identification with the national party and see it as the captive of 'special interest' groups."[20] Senator Sam Nunn of Georgia stated: "The perception is that the party had moved away from mainstream America. . . . We are going to try to move the party—both in substance and in perception—back into the mainstream of American political life."[21] The DLC "contrasted itself to the Democratic party by focusing on [its members'] greater willingness to use military force, limit social spending, vigorously attack welfare, lessen [the party's] commitments to civil rights, support a fast track trade agreement with Mexico and school choice"[22]—much of which echoed the Republican party's southern platform.

African American founding members included William H. Gray, III, who did not attend the convention, and former congresswoman Barbara Jordan, who gave a speech to the attendees. Lieutenant Governor L. Douglas Wilder of Virginia was invited and attended. Jesse Jackson was not invited to participate.

After its founding convention, the DLC moved quickly to change party procedures and rules for the next election campaign.[23] Shortly after the Democrats' loss in 1988, news leaked that the party had commissioned a secret report, which concluded, among other things, that in order "to get the white votes needed to win the presidency," the Democrats "must quit emphasizing the 'economic and social underclass.' "[24] The report further noted that "middle class whites feel threatened by Affirmative Action," and that the party's strategy "for attracting minority votes must transcend an emphasis upon blacks."[25]

The conclusions reached in the Democratic party's secret report support the following contention voiced by Matthew Holden, Jr.:

> No President has yet come to office free of a past in which he himself did not benefit, at some stage, from the social power of white hostility and the desire to maintain white supremacy. . . . Some prior implications in the heritage of white supremacy had been part of the progress to the presidency for each of [nine] members after Roosevelt. None has been a mere innocent bystander.[26]

Given this legacy, it is not surprising that Clinton's efforts to appeal to the white middle class gave him a victory in 1992.

The DLC has succeeded not only in moving the Democratic party back to the political right but in undercutting the liberal and African American wings of the party.[27] Moreover, it found and exploited a fundamental weakness in the Republican party's southern strategy: the Republicans had won the South on the basis of racially divisive appeals to white voters, not by running southern Republican candidates. The DLC broke the Republicans' grip on that region by running not one but two native sons of the South in a national election, decisively winning four out of eleven southern states in 1992.

This unintended consequence of the Republicans' context-changing efforts put the Bush administration out of office and brought the Reagan-Bush era to an end. But not before these conservative Republican administrations had so heightened the racial cleavages in the nation's social fabric that the Democratic presidential candidate remained virtually silent about the issue of civil rights during his entire campaign. The Reagan-Bush Republicans may have lost the election, but they succeeded in constraining the political discourse of the Democrats. Moreover, their legacy lingers in the form of the political appointees and regulatory initiatives they left behind, potentially ready to transform the political context once more.

Although conservative African American judges on the Supreme Court and the Federal District courts have been most aggressive in helping to transform the political context for African Americans in a negative manner in terms of civil rights, they have also been strong proponents of anti-crime policies.[28] Conservative federal district court Judge Henry Bromwell bluntly calls for "stricter enforcement of criminal laws" and criticizes black leaders for "not fully" addressing the problem of crime in the black community.[29] The federal court system has been most active in transformating the political context in civil rights policy and most especially in incarceration policy. In many ways, the conservative court system has made public policy for the African American community by instituting incarceration policy—jail sentencing—and de-emphasizing civil rights policy.

In watching this transition in the Court's policy making efforts, an African American jurist tells of repeated clashes with prosecutors who seek prison for nonviolent black offenders and probation for violent white offenders on the claim that whites from good neighborhoods and homes are better candidates for leniency.[30]

Yet the courts are not the only decision-making agencies impacting the political context. Therefore this section discussed the presidency and Congress. The paper on the presidency look at a Democratic decision-maker while the essay on Congress explores Republican decision-makers. By focusing upon these two branches of government, the reader is given some sense of how each branch can facilitate the transformation of political context in a negative, positive, or neutral manner for African Americans.

Before we closed our discussion here, a few insights can be made about the Republican capture and control of the federal bureaucracy.

It was a three step process. The first step involving centralizing and then reducing federal regulatory rule-making. The second was to cut the budgets and the staff of these agencies. And finally, to put conservative personnel (African American and whites) in control of these agencies.

On January 4, 1985, Executive Order 12498 was issued by the Reagan White House. Under this new order, agencies each year are required to establish a regulatory agenda which is subject to review by OMB. This centralized all regulating rule-making inside the White House. Any rules complated by the federal bureaucracy on racial discrimination or civil rights can be rejected by OMB. Needless to say, by the end of the Reagan presidency, the federal bureaucracy issued few regulations to protect, advance and enhance civil rights.

The same reality has prevailed in terms of presidential budgetary policy.

Federal civil rights budgets began to disappear in Reagan administration budget documents. The Clinton administration has not reversed this policy stance of the presidency.

Finally, there is the matter of personnel. Joel Aberbach and Bert Rockman in their pioneering empirical study on "The Political Views of U.S. Senior Federal Executives, 1970–1992" found that upon taking office, Reagan and his advisors "devised a systematic recruitment and selection effort to populate the appointive positions in the executive branch (Bureaucracy) with people committed to carry out the tenets of Reaganism."[31] James Pfiffner notes: "Presidential candidates in the United States have increasingly come to office distrusting the bureaucracy."[32] Hence "the federal bureaucracy" became a political target during the period of the Reagan-Bush presidencies.[33]

Reagan left "no one confused about what he wanted, which in terms of the role of government was less except for defense, intelligence, and law enforcement."[34] And this ideological position lead to a strategy of "appointing presidential 'loyalists' who had no independent standing and therefore could be manipulated at will to high level positions in federal departments and agencies."[35] When the Bush administration came into office it would maintain the Reagan administration's bureaucratic strategies "but moderate them and be more inclusive."[36]

> Career executives also were more conservative during both the Reagan and Bush periods than during the Nixon years [and] Republican control of the White House was accompanied by both increased controls over the ability of civil rights to gain support from possible allies outside of the executive [such as members of Congress and interest groups] and budgetary limitations that have constricted program initiatives and resources.[37]

"The agencies that are in charge of social services were one of the areas that the Reagan [and Bush] Administration targeted when it [they] came into office," for personnel shifts and changes.[38]

The Clinton administration, being a centrist one and therefore seeking moderation, did not have a personnel policy to confront the conservative personnel legacy left by his Republican presidential successors. Hence, the rightward shift of the personnel in social service federal bureaucracies in order to alter the political context for African Americans have not been effectively constrained by the Clinton administration.[39] Henry Foster was never confirmed as Surgeon General, Jocelyn Elders was fired as Surgeon General, and Lani Guinier had her nomination to the Justice Department withdrawn. Each time the action was a result of a Republican ooutcry. Even in the eyes of his supporters, Clinton has waffled on replacing the conservative personnel of a previous administration.

19

AFRICAN AMERICANS AND THE CLINTON PRESIDENCY

Political Appointments as Social Justice

Hanes Walton, Jr.

The coalitions President Reagan had built to attain the presidency in 1980 fell apart in 1992 during President Bush's reelection campaign, and the 12-year reign of the conservative Republican forces came to an abrupt and unexpected end. However, the end of this era did not mean an automatic end to the political contextual changes Reagan and Bush had wrought. The transformed political geography was still very much in place when President-elect Clinton took office in January 1993.[1] Just as some vestiges of segregation remained in place after the contextual revolution of the 1960s and 1970s,[2] aspects of Reagan-Bush politics, although temporarily submerged for now, may very well prevail long into the Clinton age.

Contextual transformers at the presidential level not only leave behind an altered political landscape, they also leave behind their operatives, particularly in the federal bureaucracy and courts, to say nothing of like-minded individuals in Congress who will seek to maintain and protect as much of their former leaders' transformed political context as possible. They know that they will be back one day, maybe even in four years. That is why it is essential for any incoming administration to develop and implement a plan to dismantle the old political context and shape a new political landscape.

Data and Methodology

The research questions to be explored in this paper are: Did the Clinton administration have such a plan? What techniques and methods did it plan to use? How was this plan operationalized? Most importantly, what role, if any, did African Americans play in this process? An internal role or one external to the new administration, or a bit of both? Overall, exactly how much of the Reagan-Bush context remains and how much has been removed by the new administration?

To explore these questions, I will present a content analysis of President Clinton's major civil rights speeches as well as his political speeches to major civil rights organizations and groups during the campaign and since his election. Such an analysis should provide some insights into the administration's political intent as well as political plans in regard to those issues that his predecessors failed to address, namely, issues of vital concern to African Americans. I will also analyze the role and influence, as well as the political backgrounds, of those African American political operatives and leaders active at the 1992 Democratic National Convention, on the transition team, and within the Clinton administration.

The data base consists of (1) the words and deeds of the Clinton administration in its transition and initial stages (i.e., political speeches and appointments); (2) data on the institutional and positional power of key African American political players in the Democratic party and the new administration, and on their accountability to the African American community; and (3) assessments of the ability and inclination of President Clinton's African American political appointees to dismantle the legacy of the Reagan-Bush years and construct a new political landscape.

Content analysis is supplemented by logical models, analytical procedures, and factual data. All of these tools will be employed in an effort to forecast the behavior of Clinton administration with regard to dismantling the old and building a new political context.

President Clinton's Philosophy of Political Partisanship

Beyond an analysis of the political rhetoric he espoused during the 1992 campaign and the promises he made to various constituency elements within the Democratic party's electoral coalition, an understanding of Bill Clinton's partisanship goes a long way toward explaining and predicting his presidential political behavior toward the African American community. Indeed, President Clinton has a clear-cut, basic core of beliefs and values about what his party, as an instrument of governance, should do. This philosophy was significantly shaped by the outcome of the 1984 presidential election.

Shortly after that election, the Democratic Leadership Council (DLC) was created, with Clinton at its head, to mobilize the centrist wing of the Democratic party. Jesse Jackson and his supporters constituted the left wing of the party, while its right-wing contingent (the Dixiecrats) had all but dissipated with the death, retirement, or desertion (such as that of Strom Thurmond of South Carolina) to the Republican party of its most active members. Figure 19.1 illustrates the various alignments of the ideological wings of the Democratic party from 1932 to 1996.

The DLC was not able to wrestle the presidential nomination from party liberals in 1988, however, and Democratic nominee Michael S. Dukakis carried just ten states. But while Dukakis disappointed those who sensed a chance for victory after two terms of Ronald Reagan, the 1988 results included signs of recovery.[3]

Iowa and Oregon went Democratic in 1988 for the first time since 1964; Washington for the first time since 1968. Furthermore, Dukakis came within five points of capturing a half dozen other states including California, Illinois, Pennsylvania, Maryland, and Missouri.[4] In the eyes of some, this indicated that the political geography was gradually being altered.

After Reverend Jesse Jackson lost in the primaries and Dukakis lost in the general election, the African American wing and the left wing of the Democratic party attempted to jointly refashion the Democratic National Committee (DNC) and party apparatus. As consolation, Dukakis appointed Jackson's campaign manager, Ron Brown, as the new chair of the DNC. Nonetheless, the Jackson movement failed to institutionalize itself into the national organization except symbolically. Jackson and his African American contingent could not completely restructure the party in their image, nor was their compromise party chair completely beholden to them. On the other hand, the liberal wing was having a difficult time maintaining its stronghold over the party apparatus. The Reagan landslide of 1980 had swept from office some eight to ten major Democratic liberals including senators Frank Church of Iowa and Bruce Bayh of Indiana.[5] Clearly, both the left wing's traditional hegemony in Democratic party affairs and the insurgent African American wing's claims to leadership were simultaneously diminishing.

By contrast, the newly reemerging southern wing of the party had officeholders and influence aplenty—governors and senators, key figures in the party apparatus, and, most importantly, members of the DLC. Among them was their leader: the Democratic governor of Arkansas, Bill Clinton. The liberal and the African American wings of the party had given symbolic recognition to this ascending wing in 1988, when Dukakis allowed Clinton the privilege of nominating him at the 1988 convention with a 35-minute speech that was so uninteresting to the restive crowd that the largest cheer came when Clinton said, "and in closing . . . ." Notwithstanding, between 1988 and 1992, the DLC contingent

FIGURE 19.1

The Rise, Fall, and Resurgence of Political Wings in the Democratic Party, 1932–1992

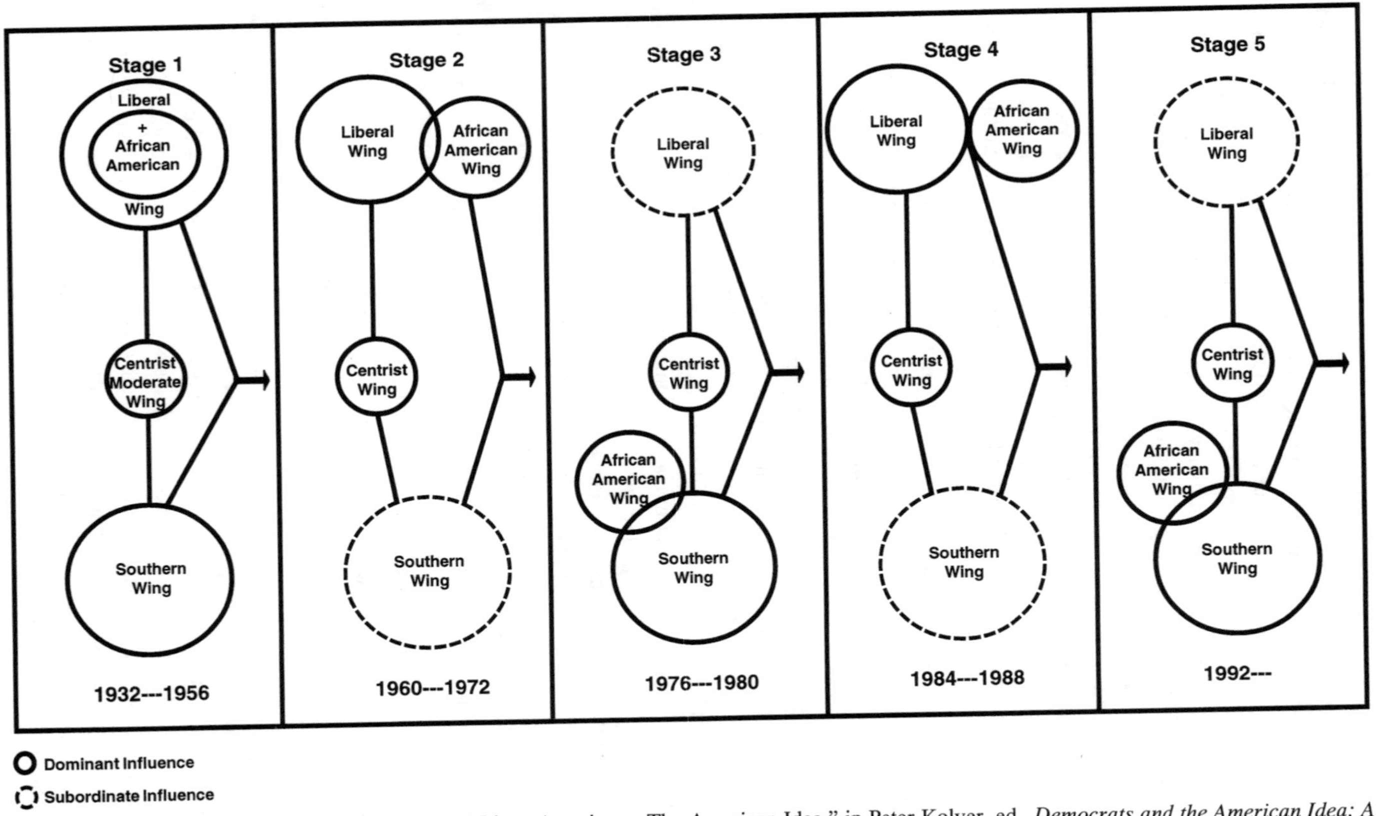

Adapted from Hanes Walton Jr., "Democrats and African Americans: The American Idea," in Peter Kolver, ed., *Democrats and the American Idea: A Bicentennial Appraisal* (Washington, D.C.: Center for National Policy Press, 1992), 343.

made impressive inroads into the national party apparatus. Their movement to capture the party leadership was aided by a crucial misstep by DNC chairman Ron Brown.

Early in his tenure, national committee chairman Brown made a very conspicuous attempt to shift the leadership of the national organization and party apparatus to the liberal heir-apparent, Governor Mario Cuomo of New York. Not only were the two good friends (Cuomo was one of Brown's professors in law school),[6] but Brown was also seeking to repay his debt to the liberal wing. Brown's open overtures failed to secure the leadership position for Cuomo and left him open to entreaties from the DLC. Therefore, as the Clinton campaign gained increasing support in the 1992 party primaries, the DNC's attachment to his candidacy increased. During the primaries, Brown made it repeatedly and emphatically clear that the party leaders wanted a consensus candidate early on—"so as to prepare for President Bush in the fall."[7] Even before the DNC began its critical shift toward the Clinton candidacy, Brown's former law firm began fundraising for the candidate all around the country as well as introducing Clinton to key political figures and potential supporters.[8]

The southern wing was gradually displacing the liberal and the African American wings of the Democratic party in terms of power and influence in the national party apparatus. By the time the 1992 national convention took place, this erosion of power was complete. True, some liberal white Democrats were given key roles at the convention.[9] And while the liberals virtually surrendered to the DLC, even if only temporarily, the African American wing put up a limited and sporadic show of resistance. Their inability or refusal to take the leadership initiative left the field wide open for the Clinton-led southern wing.

In retrospect, from where could an African American political leveraging effort have emerged within the Democratic party? From Jesse Jackson and the African American delegates to the national convention. Indeed, such a movement could have started during the primaries, with the implementation by African American Democrats of new political strategies early in the campaign. Strategies like running favorite-son candidates and insurgent movements could have been attached to a symbolic Jackson candidacy or that of Ron Daniels, the independent, third-party African American candidate. Democratic African American elected officials could have fashioned themselves into a caucus and created a formally organized bargaining group at the convention. (They had tried this latter approach in earlier years,[10] but it failed even to coalesce in 1992.)

In only one state, Ohio, did African American Democrats run a favorite son candidate. Representative Louis Stokes, the dean of Ohio's 178-member delegation and the state's only African American congressperson, sought and captured some delegates. According to the executive director of the Ohio Democratic party, "vigorous efforts" by African American and labor groups enabled Stokes to capture 3 delegates.[11]

Earlier in the campaign, Clinton had trouble wooing one of Ohio's most prominent African American Democrats, Cleveland mayor Michael R. White, who criticized Clinton "for failing to address the problems of cities and minorities."[12] However, White later endorsed Clinton and his early reservation did not appear to hamper Clinton's appeal among Ohio's African American Democrats. At the convention, 21 of the 29 pledged black delegates from Ohio, including White, were committed to Clinton.[13] Stokes, who ran as a favorite son in his district during the primaries, won three delegates.[14]

Other African American delegates such as Baltimore Representative and Congressional Black Caucus leader Kweisi Mfume, May Louise (a political activist and 1988 Jackson delegate from Massachusetts), New York city Mayor David Dinkins, and Virginia governor L. Douglas Wilder employed the uncommitted strategy. Jackson did not use this delegate base or his unannounced status to leverage the power of the African American wing within the party. The one place in which Jackson might have had enough leverage to stage such a revolt was in his own state of Illinois.[15] However, the Illinois delegation of 1992 was not as racially divided as it had been at the Atlanta convention in 1988.[16] Clinton had lined up early support from a number of leading African American Democratic figures in the state. Of the 33 pledged African American delegates from Illinois, 25 were for Clinton.[17]

Clinton's pre-convention strategy to capture African American delegates was twofold: first, he sought to move into the vacuum created by the inaction of Jackson and his followers. Secondly, Clinton courted those African Americans who had been allied with the other Democratic candidates whom he defeated in the primaries. As Phil Duncan recalls, "as Clinton's rivals fell, he was attentive about counting their minority backers. Detroit Mayor Coleman A. Young, who had supported Harkin, moved to Clinton, as did Joel Ferguson, a former supporter of Nebraska Senator Bob Kerry who ran Jackson's 1988 Michigan campaign."[18] These strategies ensured minimal resistance at the national convention. It also gave leading nominee Clinton the opportunity to shift gears and put his centrist partisan philosophy into reality.

Clinton's Politics of Dominance at the Democratic National Convention

Garnering enough delegates to secure the nomination on the first ballot yielded visible dividends for Clinton. His designees enjoyed clear majorities in all the committees that assembled the elements of the convention, namely the platform, rules, and credentials committees.[19] For the three keynote speakers at the convention, Clinton chose Democrats who were riveted to the DLC philosophy of moderation and centrism: Senator Bill Bradley of New Jersey, a critic of both liberals and conservatives;[20] Governor Zell Miller of Georgia, who had informed the national committee's southern caucus in June 1991 that "social liberalism had became the Democratic party's Achilles' heel";[21] and former Representative Barbara Jordan of Texas, an African American veteran of previous conventions who was an early supporter of the DLC.[22]

Clinton took firm control of the party's platform. According to Jeffrey Katz, the platform draft was largely written for the Clinton campaign by John D. Holman, a Washington lawyer who worked on the presidential campaigns of George McGovern, Jimmy Carter, and Gary Hart.[23] Overall, Katz asserts, the draft, which leaned heavily on the moderate ideas pushed by the DLC, rejected both Republican conservatism and traditional Democratic liberalism, to form a "third wing." The platform included an emphasis on the importance of economic expansion as well as pledges to uphold law and order and support the right of states to enact death penalty statutes.[24] While it expressed a commitment to civil rights, the issue was clearly a low priority, listed next to last in the "opportunity" section of the platform document.[25] Having subdued the African American wing of the party, Clinton, who had earlier in the campaign told the NAACP that he wanted to "make economic empowerment opportunity the civil rights issue of the 1990s,"[26] successfully prevented civil rights from becoming a major issue at the convention.

The Politics of Transition: African Americans and President-Elect Clinton

During the 1992 presidential campaign, African American Democratic politicians lacked a specific, unified agenda of their own. They became non-players in the post-election period. During the campaign, Clinton had taken the initiative to redefine the relationship between African Americans and the Democratic Party. After winning the presidency, Clinton sought, without any sustained resistance, to define who the new African American political leaders would be. As the key African American on his transition team, Clinton chose Vernon Jordan, who had been out of the national political scene for nearly two decades. Jordan, the former head of the Voter Education Project and the United Negro College Fund, had long been in the moderate group of civil rights leaders.[27] His last political utterances were heard during the Carter administration when he criticized Carter's lack of a proactive stance on issues of vital importance to African Americans, only to be roundly criticized by the King family and Andrew Young (then Carter's UN ambassador) for his comments.[28] After this, Jordan fell from the national spotlight.

Besides Jordan, who served as co-chairman of Clinton's transition team, there were no African Americans among the president-elect's inner circle. In the past, Democrats victors had selected some African American insiders. For Carter, it was Andrew Young; for Johnson, it was Hobart Taylor. Franklin D. Roosevelt, who started the practice, had some inner-circle African American participants, even if they were only symbolic appointments. Clinton not only did not appoint any African Americans as policy advisors, but to spearhead his domestic policy agenda he selected Al Fromm, the executive director of the DLC.[29]

President Clinton's African American Political Appointees

Thus, having little influence upon the policy formulation activities of the incoming administration, all that African Americans could hope for from the transition team was political appointments. With all due credit to Jordan in his role as the team's co-chair, of the 14 cabinet slots, African Americans were named to four: (1) Veterans Affairs (Jesse Brown), (2) Commerce (Ronald Brown), (3) Agriculture (Mike Espy), and (4) Energy (Hazel O'Leary).[30] Beyond these major cabinet appointees, Clinton appointed several African Americans to subcabinet positions. Law professor Drew Days was appointed to the Solicitor General's position and Arkansas physician Jocelyn Elders was appointed Surgeon General. None of these individuals had been major players in the civil rights struggle of the 1950s and 1960s, nor had they been involved in either the insurgent liberal or African American wings of the Democratic party. Nor was there, as in the past, any ground swell of support for these appointees from the African American community. They were clearly Clinton's choices.

Clinton has named more African Americans as political appointees than any other president in history. This is indeed important in that it gives the African American community a degree of political visibility at the national level that it has never had before. But what is the potential of these appointees in removing the vestiges of the Reagan-Bush legacy?

A second question is, how closely do these appointees' new positions match the needs of the African American community? The answer is, not well. In the aftermath of the Reagan-Bush era and the context that those conservative Republican administrations established, the African American community's needs loomed large in the areas of unemployment and jobs training, housing, civil rights enforcement, political empowerment, health care, urban renewal, education, legal rights, and economic progress. The failure of Clinton's transition team to take these needs into consideration with regards to appointing African Americans in the new administration simply means that, once again, political appointments are being used as a substitute for social justice. With so many African American appointees in the Clinton administration, it becomes difficult for African American spokespersons like Jesse Jackson to launch major criticisms of the President. Ultimately, the appointment of significant numbers of African Americans to high-level political positions has the potential of maintaining African Americans as part of the DLC-led Democratic political coalition.

The Clinton administration's political appointments of African Americans has not been without controversy, however. In May 1993, President Clinton nominated an African American woman, law professor Lani Guinier, as assistant Attorney General for civil rights at the Justice Department.[31] The nomination set off a firestorm of protest, first from the Republicans and from right-wing conservatives generally, who, on the basis of Guinier's law review articles on the subject, feared that she would push too hard to enforce civil rights; then from traditional Democratic liberals such as Senator Edward Kennedy; and finally from some African American conservatives. The wave of shrill voices continued to grow despite Guinier's outstanding legal credentials and experience (she had formerly been employed by the civil rights division of the Justice Department and was familiar with its operations and programs). President Clinton waffled under the barrage of criticism, claiming that he had not read Guinier's legal writings, and withdrew Guinier's nomination even before she had a chance to explain her views to the Senate Judiciary Committee. This set off another wave of criticism, from the African American community. The President promised to meet with the Congressional Black Caucus (CBC) to get their input for a new nominee. However, the CBC refused to meet with Clinton, citing his withdrawal of the Guinier nomination as evidence that the new administration's commitment to civil rights was insincere. As one observer wrote, "The nomination of Ms. Guinier . . . represents the Clinton administration's most pointed effort yet to change the character of the Government's approach to civil rights issues."[32]

Clinton's failure to expend his political capital on this nominee and this issue sent a signal to his cabinet and sub-cabinet-level appointees: that, at best, the President had a minimal-to-modest, if not negligible, civil rights agenda; and that they should not push too hard within their respective agencies to achieve social justice for African Americans and other oppressed minorities.

The federal bureaucracy's hand was stayed in undoing the legacy of the Reagan-Bush years. Moreover, this episode, further signalled to the country and the Democratic Party that the party's position on civil rights and social justice would be closer to that of the outgoing Republican presidencies than the Kennedy or Johnson administrations. But this was only one incident indicating President Clinton's position; a second example came nearly a week later.

In the aftermath of the Guinier debacle, even before it subsided, Clinton nominated a political moderate, Ruth Bader Ginsburg, to the Supreme Court, on whose bench already sat seven conservatives.[33] This told African Americans that political appointments would be the only type of political pay-off they could expect in return for their electoral support.

Clinton's nominee to replace her, Henry Foster, immediately came under fire from the Republican party and, despite objections from the Congressional Black Caucus, Foster was never confirmed. The Republicans had learned from the Guinier affair that if they painted an African American nominee as extreme, even if this were not the case, Clinton would not support his own nominee. Clinton had in effect given the Republicans a veto over his nominees.

Problems and Prospects

While transforming the political context, the Reagan-Bush Republicans influenced the Democratic party, its leadership, and its first president in nearly two decades. At the national level, the Democratic party has moved to the right of center. Its present dominant wing is the southern wing, which has reconstituted itself as the moderate and centrist wing. Civil rights became a lost issue; for the moment, economic issues have transcended racial ones—even in the aftermath of the Los Angeles riots, an urban explosion brought about by racially motivated violence.

Appointments cannot in themselves alter or restore the political context. A bold and creative new strategy is necessary to erode and eventually demolish the entrenched opposition to civil rights and social justice engendered during the Reagan-Bush years. However, the Clinton administration has yet to announce plans for such a strategy, even at the federal level. The political context thus stands intact, as it was inherited from the preceding generation of contextual transformers. As the Clinton administration headed for the 1996 elections, the President had not moved much beyond a political appointment strategy. And during this first term he never charged his political appointees to firmly support civil rights laws. In fact, as the Supreme Court and political critics eroded these laws and remedies during his first term, his African American appointees remained silent.

20

AFRICAN AMERICANS AND THE RESURGENT REPUBLICAN CONGRESS

The Duality of Transformation

Hanes Walton, Jr., Roosevelt Green, Jr., Ronald D. Clark

Efforts to transform the political context encompass both the capture and loss of national and state institutional bases of power. In the 1994 elections, for example, the Republican party gained control of the House of Representatives for the first time in forty years and the Senate for the first time in nine years. The Democrats lost control of both houses of Congress, ten state governments, and many local jurisdictions in 1994. These significant defeats left that party in charge of only one of the national institutional power bases: the presidency.

In his four years as president, Bill Clinton had been attempting to undo the transformed political context that had been wrought by the Reagan and Bush administrations. However, this task was proving itself even more difficult because the context was also being sustained by a conservative Supreme Court[1] and federal bureaucracy[2] rife with Reagan-Bush appointees. Then came the 1994 elections, and the swelling GOP tide brought President Clinton face to face with a new, aggressively conservative Republican Congress hellbent on transforming the political context even further. No longer able to focus largely on rolling back the policies and rulings of his Republican predecessors, Clinton would find himself on the defensive, trying to maintain the Democratic party agenda in the face of a renewed Republican majority fueled by the Contract with America.

Ultimately, these gains and losses mean that the powers to direct national legislation and public policy would shift from the Democrats into the hands of the Republican party. They also meant that, given the transformed political context, the Democrats, not the Republicans, would be forced to play the role of political critics and gadflies—for at least two years if not beyond.

Many of the political context transforming efforts undertaken in the early phases of the Reagan-Bush era revolved around the issue of race. The bulk of these efforts targeted the policies developed and implemented during the 1960s and 1970s to ameliorate racial discrimination and racial inequality in America. In the aftermath of the 1994 elections, GOP partisan politicians resumed the quest begun during the Reagan and Bush administrations, namely, that of rolling back the advances made by African Americans and other racial and ethnic minorities during the civil rights era. Masking their race-baiting agenda in a larger and much broader populist one in order to give the appearance that their thrust was not really based upon race, the new Republican congressional majority pounced vigorously upon unresolved issues from that era such as affirmative action.

This brings us to the central research question here: Given the intense political rivalry and competition that ensued as a result of this Republican resurgence, what has happened to the African American political context? More specifically, what role has the Republican-led 104th Congress played in further transforming the African American political context?

Data and Methodology

To explore and capture the essence of this research question Congress must be approached as an institution whose African American members share and participate in both its formal and informal bases of power[3] as well as a legislative or lawmaking body.

Because the Republican congressional resurgence can be marked by a single event in time, one must address the continuum of events that occurred both before and after the 1994 elections. Political scientists have developed a methodology known as the interrupted time-series approach to describe and explain the factors leading to and evolving from a major political event and to determine its impact. E. Terrence Jones has stated that this involves comparing "the preinterruption dependent variable trend with the postinterruption trend."[4] However, the interrupted time-series methodology is not without its limitations. As Jones notes, "Although it provides clear-cut evidence on time order and when their is only one independent variable, adequate co-variation, it has other limitations. It typically does not eliminate all other possible alternates and spurious causes."[5] Jones goes on to point out that one of the ways to overcome this limitation is to "use secondary evidence to determine the likelihood that the independent variable occurred before the [change in the] dependent variable."[6] This, we plan to do.

In the following analysis, the institutional dependent variables are (1) the number of African American committee and subcommittee chairs in the congressional session prior to the 104th Congress, and (2) the status of the Congressional Black Caucus (hereafter referred to as the CBC) before (preinterruption) and after (postinterruption) the Republican takeover of Congress in 1994. The legislative dependent variables are the types of legislation enacted before and after Republican control. Beyond these primary dependent variables, this study shall probe several other minor variables as well.

To effectuate our interrupted time series design, before and after data were gathered on African American (1) congressional partisanship, (2) formal and informal power in Congress, (3) African American party and policy positions, (3) legislative voting patterns, and (4) bill passage ratios. This is the primary data for the institutional analyses. Data for the legislative analysis entails a look at (1) categories and types of legislative enactments, (2) budget recessions and reductions, and (3) veto overrides proposed and supported before and after the Republican resurgence.

Institutional Analysis

Since World War II, the traditional approach to describing the African American presence in Congress has been to explain it from the standpoint of it informal power base, namely, the Congressional Black Caucus (CBC).[7] In point of fact, the preponderance of academic and scholarly literature on the subject highlights the nature, scope, and significance of the CBC.[8] However, as the conservative Reagan and Bush administrations began the process of transforming the African American political context, the focus of the literature shifted noticeably. Issues related to the redistricting of African American congressional districts took precedence, and doubts were raised in the literature about whether African Americans should be united by a congressional caucus. This preposterous focus was widely disseminated by numerous conservative scholarly advocates, law professors, and media pundits.[9]

After the 1984 elections, Aaron Wildavsky stated: "The decisive movement of blacks into the Democratic party . . . is not only bad for democracy, it is also a barrier to the potential emergence of a Republican majority able to capture not only the presidency but also both houses of Congress."[10] Notwithstanding, a decade later, with African Americans even more fully entrenched in the Democratic party, the Republicans captured both houses of Congress. Both then and now, declarations such as Wildavsky's above remain ludicrous, for they blame, without evidence, the Republicans' prior organizational failure on the African American electorate. Indeed, the record shows that the Republican party regained control of the Congress in 1994 not only by opposing African American public policy needs and concerns but without the support of the African American electorate. To further illuminate this point, and to get a better sense of the scope of the 1994 Republican congressional resurgence, we begin our analysis with a look at African American partisanship in Congress both before and during that body's 104th session.

Table 20.1 reveals that the number of African American Republican congresspersons increased by only one in 1994 with the election of former college football star J. C. Watts from Oklahoma. Noting that both Watts and Gary Franks of Connecticut, the other African American Republican member of the House, represent majority white districts, Sam Fulwood claims that their electoral victories illustrate "the willingness of whites to vote for blacks with conservative values."[11] No African American Democratic congressional candidate lost to a Republican challenger. None of the predominantly African American congressional districts switched to an African American nominee from the resurgent Republican party; this was the case in a predominantly white district. Moreover, the election of the two new Democratic African Americans to the House, Chaka Fattah of Pennsylvania and Shelia Jackson Lee of Texas, can be attributed to intradistrict politics rather than to the reapportionment that made many new electoral seats available to African Americans after 1990.[12]

The Republican capture of majority control in the House of Representatives in 1994 further diminished African Americans' institutional power base in Con-

TABLE 20.1

Number and Percentage of African American Partisans in the 103rd and 104th Congresses

103rd Congress Number (Before)		104th Congress Number (After)		Change
House of Representatives		**House of Representative**		
1. Democrats	37	1. Democrats	37	0
2. Republicans	1	2. Republicans	2	+1
Total	**38**	**Total**	**39**	
Senate		**Senate**		
1. Democrats	1	1. Democrats	1	0
2. Republicans	0	2. Republicans	0	0
Total	**1**	**Total**	**1**	+1
Grand Total	**39**	**Grand Total**	**40***	

Adapted from *Congressional Quarterly Weekly Report* (November 12, 1994), 10; see also "Black Caucus Grows, Moves Toward Center," *Congressional Quarterly Almanac* 48 (1993): 18–20.

**This listing does not include an African American independent Congressman from the Virgin Islands. If he were included, the total number would be 41.*

gress. As table 20.2 shows, three African American Democrats lost their position as chairs of full committees, as did seventeen African American Democratic subcommittee chairpersons. Although white freshman Republicans reaped several of the subcommittee chairmanships formerly held by black House Democrats, none of these positions were transferred to the African American Republican representatives.

For example, in the 104th Congress, chairmanship of the District of Columbia Subcommittee, stripped from senior African American Representative Julian Dixon of California, was handed over to freshman Thomas M. Davis, III, who represents a Virginia suburb of the District. The chairman of the full committee, William F. Clinger (R-PA), "skipped seniority for [the] freshman at the bequest of Gingrich."[13] Not only did Speaker of the House Newt Gingrich overlook the freshman African American congressman J. C. Watts for any subcommittee position, he also bypassed Gary Franks, elected to the House in 1990, had as much seniority as most of his Republican peers.[14] Franks does not chair a single full committee, nor any of the subcommittees.[15]

The matter of committee assignments is critical to this discussion of African American institution power at the congressional level.

> On the national and state levels, blacks are appointed to minor and moderate committees limiting their legislative clout . . . The budget is also a tool [and] keeping blacks off the Finance Committee obviously has an impact on their performance.[16]

As Robert Smith writes: "In the House, political scientists and members alike generally agree that Ways and Means, Rules, and Appropriation are the more powerful and important."[17] However, upon the Republican capture of the House of Representatives, House Speaker Newt Gingrich removed all of the blacks from the Ways and Means, Rules, and Appropriation committees, and he did not replace them with African American Republicans.

The Republican resurgence may have carried one additional African American into Congress, but it swept out of institutional power all of the African American Democrats. To make matters worse, the white Republicans have not shared any of their newfound power with their African American freshman or senior representative peers. The net result: at the congressional level, all African American partisans, despite the rhetoric of African American Republicans to the contrary, have lost power. Whereas the House unit charged with oversight of the predominantly black District of Columbia was previously a full committee chaired by an African American, the Republicans reduced its status to that of a subcommittee and transferred its chairmanship to a white freshman Republican. The contextual revolution in the House of Representatives has remained true to the old southern tradition that insists upon placing leadership in white hands.

TABLE 20.2

Number and Percentage of African American Committee and Subcommittee Chairs, 103rd and 104th Congresses

103rd Congress Number Percentage (Before)		104th Congress Number Percentage (After)		Loss
Full Committee Chairs				
Armed Service	R. Dellums			
Government Operations	J. Conyers			
Post Office & Civil Service	W. Clay			
Total 3	(15%)	0	0	3
Subcommittee Chairs				
Military Acquisitions	R. Dellums			
District of Columbia	J. Dixon			
Judiciary & Education	E. Norton			
Compensation & Employee Benefits	E. Norton			
Commerce, Consumer Protection & Competitions	C. Collins			
Minority Enterprise, Finance & Urban Development	K. Mfume			
Legislation & National Secretary	J. Conyers			
Postal Operations & Services	B. Collins			
Libraries & Memorials	W. Clay			
Oversight & Investigations	W. Clay			
Government Operations & Metropolitan Affairs	A. Wheat			
Government Oversight, Investigation & Resolution of Failed Financial Institution	F. Flake			

Human Resources & Intergovernmental Relations	E. Towns			
Select Education & Civil Rights	Owens			
Select Preview Measures	C. Rangel			
VA, HUD, & Independent Agencies	Stokes			
Human Resources	H. Ford			
Total 17	(85%)	0	0	17

Adapted from David Bostis, "The 1994 Mid-term Elections: A Profile of African American Candidates and Voters," (Washington, D.C.: Joint Center for Political and Economic Studies, 1994), 7. See also his *The Congressional Black Caucus in the 103rd Congress* (Washington, D.C.: Joint Center for Political and Economic Studies, 1994), 91–101.

African American Congressional Committee Staffers

The chairs of congressional committees are allowed to select their own staff members to assist them in gathering data, doing analyses, interpreting findings, and making recommendations about how those findings should inform congressional hearings, bills, and investigative reports. These staffers also do background work on previous legislation, investigations, and hearings so as to provide the chair with a comprehensive context for assessing current congressional affairs. Staffers become important, and at times crucial, to the congressional process: one scholar has dubbed them the "unelected representatives."[18]

As the majority party in Congress after the 1994 elections, the new Republican chairpersons swiftly replaced the existing committee staffs with staffers of their own choosing. How did the African Americans who were previously members of these committee staffs fare in the 104th Congress's transition from Democratic to Republican leadership? To date, little has been written about this group of African Americans in Congress; thus, little is widely known about the nature, scope, and significance of their institutional power.

According to Lucius Barker and Mack Jones, the first study of African American committee staffers appeared in 1979.[19] Blacks and other minorities constituted only about five percent of these staffs, or 85 out 1,669 staffers, at the time. Barker and Jones further point out that "the few blacks who are on committee staffs are often selected by black members who serve on these committees."[20] The picture for African American staff personnel in the 535 congressional offices was not much better. As Barker and Jones note, "blacks are clustered in the lower prestige and salaried jobs. Almost one-half (49 percent) of all blacks in members' offices are in (clerical) positions, with 75 percent clustered in the bottom three categories."[21]

A 1991 study was undertaken by African American congressional staffers themselves. In a survey of staffing patterns in both houses of Congress, this study found that blacks held "only about 300 or 3.7 percent of the 8,200 power jobs that influenced legislation and political decisions."[22] In the House of Representatives, blacks held about 240, or 4.4 percent, of the 5,500 most important staff jobs; in the Senate, blacks held 68, or 2.5 percent, of the 2,700 important positions. Of these blacks, however, more than half worked for the 26 African American members of the House.[23]

In addition to these two studies, there was congressional testimony given by the chair of the Senate Black Legislative Staff Caucus (SBLSC), Ms. Jackie Parker, on September 14, 1989 to a Senate Committee on Governmental Affairs hearing.[24] This hearing was held on two Senate bills—S. 272 and S. 1165—that sought to apply the civil rights legislation of the 1960s and 1970s to Congress itself. Although this legislation was applicable to the country as a whole, Congress itself was exempt. The consequences of this exemption was a significant underrepresentation of African American staffers in both houses of Congress. Ms. Parker told the hearing:

> There are no black administrative assistants and only one committee staff director out of a total of 26; one deputy committee staff director, three subcommittee hearings out of 95, and one legislative director, deputy press secretary, on the personal staffs of the 100 members of the Senate, and none on the 121 full committee and subcommittees. It is sad that this is the highest number of black policy advisors in the history of the U.S. Senate.[25]

In their reconfiguration of these institutions, the Republicans not only made no efforts to rectify this matter of underrepresentation, but this institutional power base of African American congressional staffers underwent a major transformation. In short, most of these people disappeared. All of the African Americans who held power positions as senior staff members or as legislative and administrative assistants in the 103rd Congress were replaced in the 104th.[26]

The Congressional Black Caucus: African America's Informal Power Base

If the Republican resurgence in the 104th Congress eliminated the formal bases of power for both African American Democratic and Republican partisans in the House of Representatives, it likewise removed much of their informal power base as well. Since its formation in 1970 in the wake of the deaths of Malcolm X and Martin Luther King, Jr., the CBC has provided national leadership on issues of importance to African American communities across the land. Most importantly, it has served as a medium for African American legislators to come together to "take official positions [on national issues], coordinate their members' votes on certain bills, and use their numbers to extract concessions on legislation."[27] As one of 28 legislative service organizations officially certified by the House Administration Committee, the CBC was entitled to "office space and equipment, and members [were] permitted to contribute from their office funds to pay for hiring staff and caucus activities."[28] Its members later created the Congressional Black Caucus Foundation to solicit corporate contributions to pay for scholarships, policy forums, and other activities sponsored by the CBC. All of this vanished in the wake of the Republican takeover of the House of Representatives.

Just prior to the 1994 elections, the CBC chose Donald Payne as its chairman. Payne was willing to work with the GOP:[29] "The Caucus, in general, felt that during this next year it's better to have a strong negotiator, a person that can compromise, one [who] can move the organization through these troubled times."[30] Payne met with Speaker-to-be Gingrich to search for common ground between African American legislators and the resurgent Republicans and to argue for the maintenance of the congressional caucuses, specifically the CBC. This meeting and the objections of the African American members of the CBC came to naught. Speaker Gingrich and his partisans enacted legislation eliminating these caucuses as part of the ten-item set of legislative proposals that they promised to bring to the floor of the House for a vote within one hundred days of the start of the session. That was the Contract with America.

"The most sweeping action taken by the Republicans [after the 1994 elections] was the decision to eliminate congressional funding for member caucuses." By so doing, outgoing CBC chairman Kweisi Mfume (D-MD) claimed the Republicans were "attempting to 'disempower' minorities who disagree with them on many issues."[31] Without office space, staff, or monies for salaries and operations, African Americans' informal power base in Congress, if not specifically targeted by the Republicans for destruction, was all but decimated. However, as incoming CBC chairman Donald Payne (D-NJ) asserts, the CBC has survived, albeit in "a reconfigured form," and African American elected representatives "are more determined than ever to be the moral voice and conscious of Congress."

A Legislative Analysis

Beyond the matter of the CBC's institutional power in Congress, there is the question of the effect of the Republican resurgence on African American efficacy in the main congressional function: the passage of legislation. A closer look at the Contract with America is critical to this discussion.

Announced at a September 27, 1994, news conference, the Contract was signed by over three hundred Republicans, 170 newly elected members and 160 incumbents.[32] Of the ten conservative legislative priorities listed in this document, several spoke directly and in a very negative way to the legislative priorities of African American Democratic congresspersons and the needs of the African American community.

An earlier analysis of legislative sponsorship patterns reveals that, prior to the advent of the Republican majority in the 104th Congress, African American legislators were "concerned with traditional civil rights issues, but also with 'class' legislation of importance to low-income persons and the educationally disadvantaged."[33] Marguerite Ross Barnett writes that, even in its formative years, the CBC focused on social welfare matters such as saving the Office of Economic Opportunity (OEO), assisting the District of Columbia government and fighting "inflation, recession, and unemployment."[34] As Robert Smith adds: "That blacks constitute perhaps the most liberal voting bloc in the House is an important . . . finding given that the black population is the most liberal of the major United States population groups."[35]

The resurgence of the southern-led, conservative wing of the Republican Party in the House not only forced the CBC onto the defensive, but the Contract with America upended and upstaged the African American congressional agenda. True, African American Democrats were not prevented from introducing social welfare legislation. But Speaker Gingrich relegated all legislative concerns other than those listed in the Contract to low-priority status.

"For nearly 100 days that came to a close April 7th, Republicans displayed an almost lock-stip unity in pushing their 'Contract with America' through the House."[36] In the end, despite political wangling, countless powerful and moving speeches, and numerous defiance votes, nine of the ten legislative priorities listed in the Contract with America passed the House, including a balanced-budget amendment, changes to presidential line-item veto powers, welfare reform, a crime package, tax cuts, and a curb on unfunded mandates. Changes in the way the House operates, detailed in the preface to the Contract, were also adopted.[37] Only the Republicans' term-limits initiative failed to pass when several GOP representatives defected from the party line to oppose it. At the time of writing, of the Contract items, the President has signed into law a crime bill, the line item veto, a bill barring unfunded mandates, and welfare reform.

For the most part, African American congressional Democrats opposed the conservative Republican legislative agenda.

> Black members of Congress cannot afford to abandon their agenda for improving the social, economic, and political lot of 32 million black Americans. Despite the vigorous attacks on the concept of Affirmative Action from numerous and powerful quarters, we must continue to promote set-asides in government contracts based on race; favor scholarships

> for economically and educationally disadvantaged black students; support on-the-job training for minorities, and insist on goals and timetables for placing blacks on a par with the larger society in every aspect.[38]

In the end, however, given the Republicans' numerical majority and partisan solidarity, African American Democrats could neither advance their constituents' legislative priorities nor block the conservative agenda from succeeding. Upon review of the performance of African American congresspersons in the Republican-controlled 104th Congress, James Steels has noted that:

> one cannot not be disturbed by the slowness with which the CBC has reacted to the sea change that has taken place in U.S. politics.
>
> Now that they are in charge, the Republicans are delivering a blistering combination of head and body shots to Blacks in Congress, and to consideration of African American interests in congressional policy outcomes. So far, the CBC has staggered in desperation toward a neutral corner without throwing so much as a counterpunch.[39]

As another observer states:

> In the 104th Congress, black members will no longer chair committees or subcommittees. Indeed, the very existence of the CBC is threatened, [and] Representative [J. C.] Watts and [Gary] Franks can now form a right-wing bloc that will further polarize the CBC.[40]

Thus, the African American community has watched as their representatives, the largest number of African Americans ever sitting in Congress at one time, were reduced to near powerlessness in the first one hundred days of the 104th Congress.

The Republicans next turned to the federal budget, promising to reduce or abolish numerous social programs as well as several governmental bureaucracies.[41] Virtually every legislative social policy initiative that has ever assisted the African American community was targeted for cutbacks and elimination.[42] African American Democrats stepped forward to prevent some of the proposed budget cuts from being as severe as the Republicans wanted. In one such instance, as CBC Chairman Payne recalls:

> The Chairman of the Senate Appropriations Subcommittee on Foreign Operations McConnell had proposed a $110 million recession cut in the currently approved 1995 Budget of $900 million. With help of both Republicans and Democratic friends, we [members of the CBC] were able to forstall this entire cut.[43]

The strenuous efforts of the CBC notwithstanding, it was Senate action that kept cuts to social safety net programs from being truly deep. Had the Senate been willing to cut these programs, many of the constituents represented by the African American Democrats in the House would have sustained even more significant losses to these programs. Table 20.3 shows the difference in the size of the initial proposed cuts recommended by the House and the Senate.

The Republican legislative transformation of the political context amounts to a full-scale offensive against African American political empowerment. As the Republican threatened, made, or attempted to make cut after cut in vital social programs, African American Democratic legislators found themselves repeatedly on the defensive. Despite their increased numbers, at the legislative level they were simply overrun.

African American Political Appointments in the Midst of the Republican Resurgence

In addition to its legislative and investigative powers, Congress also has appointive power, as presidential nominees must gain the approval of the Senate before they are confirmed in their positions.

The Republicans extended their nominations strategy even further into the Clinton administration when they forced the President to fire his African American Surgeon General Joycelyn Elders for suggesting a contraceptive policy that enraged and embarrassed conservative Republicans. Although calls for Elders's resignation were spearheaded by Democratic congressmen via their organization, the Democratic Leadership Council, conservative Republican congresspeople quickly joined the fray, forcing the President to abandon one of his own subcabinet appointees. Again, this was while the Republicans were still the minority party in Congress.

The question now: Will the Republican-controlled 104th Congress continue to push the nomination and appointments strategy for African American developed during the Reagan and Bush presidencies? Currently, Speaker of the House Gingrich has gone on record as opposing the nomination of Foster to replace Elders in the Surgeon General's spot. Other Republican House members have signal their opposition as well. Strong Republican opposition to Foster has also surfaced in the Senate.

To counteract this Republican opposition, members of the CBC have gone to the President and urged that he support this nominee completely and fully. They have let it be known that the African American community will be watching, and that abandonment of this African American nominee will send a negative signal to the African American electorate in 1996. The Republicans, on the other hand, have nothing to lose. Attacking Dr. Foster, even if they eventually confirm him, will not only play well with their constituents, but will extend the Reagan-Bush legacy of introducing racial cleavages for partisan gain.

Conclusions

The present case study of African American congressional representatives in the Republican-dominated 104th Congress offers several propositions that can be empirically tested. The first of these is that the resurgence of Republican control in Congress has diminished African Americans' institutional power, both formally and informally, at the congressional level. Secondly, in a political context in which race is used by the Republicans as a wedge issue for partisan gain, African American congresspersons of both parties are denied even more of their institutional power. African American congresspersons are thus relegated to a defensive position, and retreat and compromise will form the basis of their efforts.

The third testable proposition emerging from this case study is that because the legislative priorities of African American congresspersons have been stalled at the introductory level in the 104th Congress, legislation as well as budgetary action inimical to African Americans can be passed. The fourth testable proposition is that the resurgent Republican congressional majority has led to the displacement of African American congressional staffers and their replacement with conservative white staffers. The fifth and last proposition is that African American congresspersons have been forced to back African American nominees who have a conservative bent.

Overall, the resurgent Republican majority in the 104th Congress has transformed the political context of that body at the institutional, public policy, and appointment levels. Although African American congresspersons have played and can play a significant role in resisting these transformative efforts, it is a greatly diminished one as a minority within a minority.

PART 8

POLICY

When the political context is transformed to disadvantage African Americans, as it was during the Reagan-Bush years, the political agenda is redefined for both political leaders and their constituents. Additionally, the course of action of the nation's political parties and interest groups is recharted. These are expected results. Does transformation of the political context lead to changes in areas besides civil rights, regulations, and legal policy? Is economic policy affected? Is domestic policy affected? Is foreign policy affected?

In this section, we will examine federal financial support for the nation's major urban areas during the Reagan-Bush and Clinton years. Prior to these conservative Republican administrations, the amount of federal assistance directed toward urban areas had been gradually increasing. One of the techniques by which this assistance was extended to the cities was the policy of revenue sharing, a procedure developed during the Nixon administration to return money to the state and local governments based on a percentage of the funds these entities annually contributed to the federal treasury. Nixon initiated revenue sharing to appease his southern constituency and provide a means for southern local governments to circumvent desegregation measures. In 1986, President Reagan abolished this policy. An African American political scientist, Wilbur Rich, describes the context in which this decision was made:

> In the early 1970s many felt that the prospects for revitalizing American cities were very good; but . . . in 1980 with the election of Ronald Reagan, the conservative Republican, anti-city sentiments were unleashed. It was almost as if cities, and particularly the inner-city residents, had become targets of economic retribution. Programs designed to reverse urban decline were labeled wasteful. . . . The partial withdrawal from cities by the federal government during the decade further divided residents along racial, class, and ethnic lines.[1]
>
> The newly elected president had run on a platform of fiscal restraint and decreasing social programs. . . . There was no reason to believe that the new president could not carry out his threats to dry up most CETA funds, revenue sharing, and economic development monies.[2]

Since "only 25 percent of [most] city budgets was covered by revenues from taxes, fees, and interests," the remaining 75 percent had to come from grants-in-aid from the state and federal governments.

Reagan's and Bush's urban economic policies were also motivated by politics. Urbanites were the Democratic party's electoral bastions in presidential elections; suburban voters were the Republican party's stronghold. By withdrawing federal funds from the cities and redeploying them to the suburbs, the Republicans helped their political allies and crippled their political foes. City budgets were strained as their revenues were cut. With the retrenchment and redistribution of federal funds away from the cities to the suburbs the nation's African American big-city mayors and other municipal officials who had risen to prominence during the 1970s were forced to become what Michael Lipsky has called "street-level bureaucrats."[3] That is, they had to become more than just mayors and public policy implementers; they had to become case workers and grass roots providers of constituent service. They had to make public policy on the run, on a day-to-day basis. They had to reach out to their constituents in a very personal way. Unfortunately, several African American elected officials did not see or care to see themselves in this new role. Many, such as Mayor Richard Hatcher of Gary, Indiana,[4] found themselves out of a job. Others accepted the challenge and adapted accordingly.

Chatham County Commissioner Deanie Frazier describes the dilemma of black elected officials during the Reagan-Bush years:

> Traditionally, Black elected officials cut red tape, if they were politically astute, for people in their district. Today, that is simply not enough. You must be involved in peoples' day-to-day lives. You must provide for their immediate needs, not just their material concerns, but their emotional ones, things that affect their families and them.
>
> When the Reagan administration cut jobs and cut benefits, the blighted

> neighborhoods of the inner cities were thrown into a crisis of unbelievable proportions because to adjust to these cuts, people turned to the underground economy for employment and daily sustenance. The drug culture bred kingpins and activists and these folks found a market making the culture heavily concentrated in the African American community. This is so because blacks were distributors, sellers, and users. Thus, the consequences were severe and nightmarish. For instance, one drug addict touched at least five people and therefore nearly every family was involved in some way. The entire neighborhood becomes tainted. Families are emotionally hurt and drained and they need help. Cutting red tape, in this type of situation, is simply not enough.
>
> As soon as someone is caught and sent to jail, I get calls to go to court, to speak to the Judge, to the Sheriff, and other parts of the criminal justice system to assist the families and to help them get (1) bond, (2) lawyers, (3) help at the court, (4) treatment, and (5) some rehabilitation. I am the only African American official at court with this constituency on Monday morning.
>
> But this isn't all. The cut in jobs and benefits leave people unable to pay light bills, water bills, get their hair fixed, or someone to babysit while they go to look for another job. All of these things must be done. And these things involved much more than cutting red tape. The new role for African American elected officials, either in the Mayor's office or elsewhere is to become public policy makers on the spot. Passing laws in a transformed political context is simply not enough. African American elected officials must become substitutes for the lack of national, state, county and local public policies.[5]

Beyond the pioneering response of some African American elected officials to the crises in the inner cities, the African American communities themselves were also gearing up to act at the grass roots level.[6] This was an unintended consequence of the transformative process.

According to James Jennings, a "new black political activism, more militant in style and substance than traditional electoral activism in [the] community" emerged in the wake of the urban economic crises of the Reagan-Bush years.[7] Advocates of this self-help, empowerment ethic viewed power sharing or community control as their goal; they sought to "rearrange social and economic systems to enhance the position of the poor and the working class and promote neighborhood interests."[8] Such activism has a long history in the African American community. Jennings refers to one study which reports that the self-help tradition "is so embedded in the black heritage as to be virtually synonymous with it."[9] However, the re-emergence of self-help activism during the Reagan-Bush years was partly due to the "explosive growth of an impoverished black lumpenproletariat in the last twenty years, concurrent with a rightward drift of American society and a marked deterioration in living conditions for poor and working-class sectors in the black community."[10]

Domestic policy is not the only policy issue caught up in a contextual transformation. There are foreign policy matters. The African American community has never been solely concerned with domestic issues. Foreign policy issues have been, at times, equally critical to the community.

Robert Smith and Richard Seltzer found in their recent study that: "overall, then, liberalism in the black community in . . . foreign policy . . . appears to be a characteristic of the political culture that distinguishes mainstream black Americans from the white mainstream."[11] African American foreign policy leaders and activists act from a solid base inside the community in promoting and advocating foreign policy stances. And the need for such promotion and advocacy did arise during the Reagan-Bush-Clinton eras on such issues as South African apartheid and refugee policy. The second paper in this section addresses foreign policy during a period of contextual transformation.

21

AFRICAN AMERICAN MAYORS AND NATIONAL URBAN POLICY

The Fiscal Politics of Urban Federalism

• • • • • • •

Hanes Walton, Jr. and Marion E. Orr

"This country is known by its cities: those amazing aggregations of people and housing, offices, and factories, which constitute the heart of our civilization, the nerve center of our collective being."[1] Yet, "the problems of the city and of institutional racism are clearly intertwined.[2] . . . If the crisis we face in the city is to be dealt with, the problem of the [African American urban] ghetto must be solved first."[3]

The crisis of the cities emerged as a prominent national issue just as the civil rights era was coming to an end and just prior to the period of African American political control of urban areas.

> Black politicians are coming to power at a time when the central city is falling apart. They are assuming positions that are losing power in view of the rising need for federal assistance to cities and states. They are coming to power just as the urban crisis is peaking [and they are] expected to devise solutions and solve problems that will avert the impending crisis.[4]
>
> Black politicians in city administration will find that . . . continued concentration of poverty and unemployment puts an enormous strain on the city budgets with the result that there will not be sufficient funds to pay for welfare programs, housing programs, improved schools, union pay rates, control of violence and juvenile delinquency.[5]

Indeed, African Americans became power-holders in the promised land, but their power base was in the nation's most crisis-burdened urban areas.

> Most of these minority office holders have . . . faced an astonishingly parallel set of problems. A fiscal crisis in government, a set of rigid state institutions, a weak and fragmented power system all of which work to prevent [African American] mayors from running the city. Moreover, these factors, coupled with a continuing lack of support from state and federal governments as the U.S. political system turns increasingly conservative, prevent these mayors from instituting badly needed reforms in the program and management structures of their governments. Issues that command constant attention include poor-quality services, police system excesses, deteriorating physical infrastructure, and obsolescent management institutions, . . . demands and pressures from poor constituents, regional economic interests, and public labor.[6]

The presence of African American mayors, in and of itself, has not been enough to ameliorate the urban crisis.

> Perhaps there was an additional naive assumption that all that was needed was to elect a few powerful and talented black mayors, appoint some black police chiefs and heads of school districts, and by all means register and vote. Surely, this process of playing by the rules would lead to improvement, not decline in status.[7]

This simply did not happen. "Putting a black or liberal in local office," Carmichael and Hamilton assert, "is another step, but by no means the final step."[8] In most cases, however, it has been the first and the final step. In the majority of the nation's economically burdened, crime-ridden, and drug-impacted cities that have been or are still led by African American mayors—New York, Newark, Washington D.C., Atlanta, Los Angeles, Philadelphia, Chicago, Detroit, Charlotte—the crisis continues unabated. The Los Angeles riots revealed that.[9] And some of these cities are in their second and third round of African American mayoral rule.

The resistance of the urban crisis to solutions has led to some interesting theorizing about the source of the problem. Some analysts place the blame squarely at the feet of African American mayoral leadership.[10] Others have cast aspersion on the types of behind-the-scenes coalitions that run African American-led cities, noting that these coalitions essentially represent the interests of the traditional ruling elites and do not include poor and disadvantaged urban dwellers.[11] Still others suggest that African American mayors have begun inner-city redevelopment projects with the wrong people (i.e., downtown business interests).[12]

One school of thought argues that big city governments have been disempowered by the district- or county-wide boards and commissions that rule many of the metropolitan areas, and that such suburb-favoring governing bodies have far more power than the electoral coalitions that run the cities. In this view, city halls in urban areas are little more than facades.[13] Another theory posits that urban governments, caught as they are in the middle of traditional inter-ethnic and intra-ethnic rivalries, are rendered nearly impotent in the face of such conflicts.[14] Others claim that it is not the lack of power, resources, or neighborly cooperation nor the nature of the governing coalition that fuels the crisis in the cities, but rather the culture of poverty associated with those entrapped in the cities' innermost cores.[15]

Because these approaches focus solely upon the players in the urban political arena, they represent little more than microanalytical views and are subsequently far from complete. Analysis of the evolution and impact of urban federalism is a crucial part of any theoretical formulation about the urban crisis.

> Federal involvement in urban affairs extends to many . . . areas. . . . Urban renewal and urban freeway systems resulted directly from federal activity. Urban welfare programs, criminal justice programs, and health care programs are heavily financed by the federal government. So extensive has the federal involvement become and so far reaching have been the changes in the nature of its involvement that the changing federal role in urban affairs requires . . . detailed explanation.[16]

Harrigan identifies five broad changes in the federal role during the modern period:

> First was the invention of the grant-in-aid as a device for urban problem solving. This device saw its greatest expansion in the 1930s and 1960s. Second were the grand designs of the Lyndon Johnson presidency: the waging of the War on Poverty and the creation of the Great Society. Third were the Nixon administration proposals of revenue sharing and grant consolidation, as well as the attempts to reorient federal domestic programs away from big-city Democratic officials favored under Johnson's Great Society and toward more Republican-oriented officials in suburbs, small towns, and state governments. Fourth was the attempt of the Carter administration to articulate a coherent national urban policy that could guide the hundreds of specific programs the federal government promotes in urban areas. Fifth were the efforts of the Reagan and Bush administrations to reduce the federal urban role through initiatives such as New Federalism, budget reductions, and regulatory cutbacks.[17]

Most importantly, Harrigan notes, the contributions of each president to shaping the federal urban role did not always disappear once they left the White House.[18]

During the Reagan-Bush era, urban federalism was characterized by significant and sustained decline in the federal budgetary contribution to urban areas. The resulting financial shortfalls had to be made up by the municipalities themselves, and the responsibility for covering these deficits fell upon the shoulders of local government officials. Mayoral leadership had to do what the federal government refused to do. Thus big-city mayors became national policy makers at the local level.

African American mayors have long been familiar with such a role. For several years during the post-civil rights era, in the absence of a comprehensive federal urban policy, African American mayors were heralded as national figures and deemed the cure-all for the nation's urban ills. Somehow, it was hoped, they would be able to make the difference.

The elimination of revenue-sharing dollars to the cities exacerbated the urban crisis, especially in the nation's African American-governed cities. The three questions examined in this paper are:

(1) Did the Reagan or Bush administrations develop any programs to address forthrightly the urban crisis facing African American big-city mayors?

(2) Did these programs abate or exacerbate the urban crisis?

(3) How did these administrations use the federal budget to influence urban federal policies and programs?

DATA AND METHODOLOGY

The Census Bureau's *City Government Finances* provides an invaluable data source for such an analysis as it delineates the revenues provided to the nation's cities from both the federal government directly and from general revenue-sharing funds.[19] We examined these data for the decade from fiscal year 1979 to 1988 with the goal of uncovering any trends in federal funding to urban municipalities during the two Reagan administrations. Further, we compared federal funding in cities with African American mayors in different regions of the country to determine if the regionalism of these two conservative Republican administrations might have affected urban federalism during this decade. Macro-analysis of the urban scene will permit us to see, first of all, how much or how little a national role African American mayors played during this period of Republican-led political context transformation. Additionally, it will permit us to discern the role and significance of the other political players involved.

The ten cities in this analysis are, in the South, Atlanta, Birmingham, and New Orleans; in the Midwest, Detroit and Gary; in the West, Oakland and Los Angeles; and in the East, Newark, Hartford, and Baltimore.

The Budgetary Force of Urban Federalism

Table 21.1 reveals the mean federal dollars allotted to cities with African American mayors from 1979 through the decade of the 1980s. This table shows that in 1979–80, the cities of the Midwest, West, and East received the largest amount of federal fiscal support, while the southern cities received the least assistance. During Reagan's first term the eastern cities experienced a substantial cut in their federal fiscal support, while the cities of the Midwest and West realized a slight increase. The level of support for the southern cities remained constant during Reagan's first term; during his second term, when cities in other regions of the country were experiencing huge losses of federal revenue-sharing dollars, the decrease in financial support in the southern cities was far less drastic.

This trend should come as no surprise when one recalls that the Reagan Republicans sought to woo the South and incorporate it into a winning electoral coalition. An unwitting side benefit was that southern cities led by African American mayors reaped some of the benefits of this attention. The Midwest was initially spared. Later, it too would feel the impact of the budget cuts of the Reagan era, as would African American mayors in this region.

Another trend becomes obvious upon examining the data for fiscal year 1986. In that year, President Reagan, in his second term, eliminated the federal

TABLE 21.1
Mean Federal Dollars to Cities with African American Mayors by Region, 1979–1989 (in thousands)

Years	Region			
	Midwest	West	South	East
1979-80	$164,764	$184,319	$83,205	$102,844
1980-81	272,405	191,239	77,340	104,338
1981-82	223,712	171,045	67,755	69,431
1982-83	215,608	166,857	77,789	67,574
1983-84	105,763	167,826	71,485	68,913
1984-85	108,740	152,747	73,244	55,590
1985-86	100,932	134,999	64,390	69,233
1986-87	76,398	64,977	43,546	50,553
1987-88	48,393	49,662	39,888	59,885
1988-89	58,226	61,831	41,921	50,454

Adapted from U.S. Census, *City Government Finance: 1979–1989* (Washington, D.C.: Government Printing Office).

revenue-sharing program. While all regions suffered, the Midwest and West were hit the hardest. In the West, for example, federal assistance plunged from approximately $135 million in 1985 to about $65 million in 1986, representing an enormous decrease in city services and outreach efforts.

Figure 21.1 reveals the mean percent of the total amount of federal financial assistance to the cities that was attributed to revenue-sharing funds during the bulk of the decade. At the onset, in each of the four regions, mean general revenue sharing in all regions was below 20 percent of total federal aid to urban areas. The abrupt loss of these millions of dollars, nearly one-fifth of the cities' financial support, took its toll in human suffering and hardship for the nation's African American mayors and their constituencies. By the beginning of the Bush administration all of the regions had seen a drop in their budgets in terms of federal dollars.

Figure 21.2 reveals the mean percentage of the total budget of the ten African American-led cities under question that was provided by the federal government. The most readily discernible trend revealed by these data is that federal financial assistance in urban areas in all regions of the country dropped steadily from 1979 until 1986 (and the elimination of revenue-sharing), when the funding level took a sharp plunge from which it has yet to recover.

FIGURE 21.1

General Revenue Sharing as a Mean Percentage of Total Federal Financial Assistance to Cities with African American Mayors, by Region

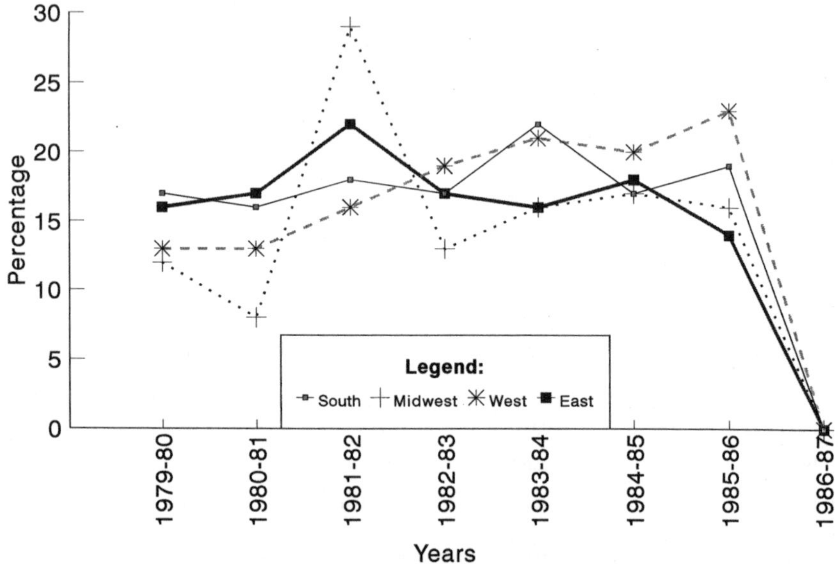

Adapted from U.S. Census, City Government Finances: 1979–89 (Washington, D.C.: Government Printing Office, 1979–89). Calculations prepared by authors.

FIGURE 21.2

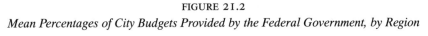

Mean Percentages of City Budgets Provided by the Federal Government, by Region

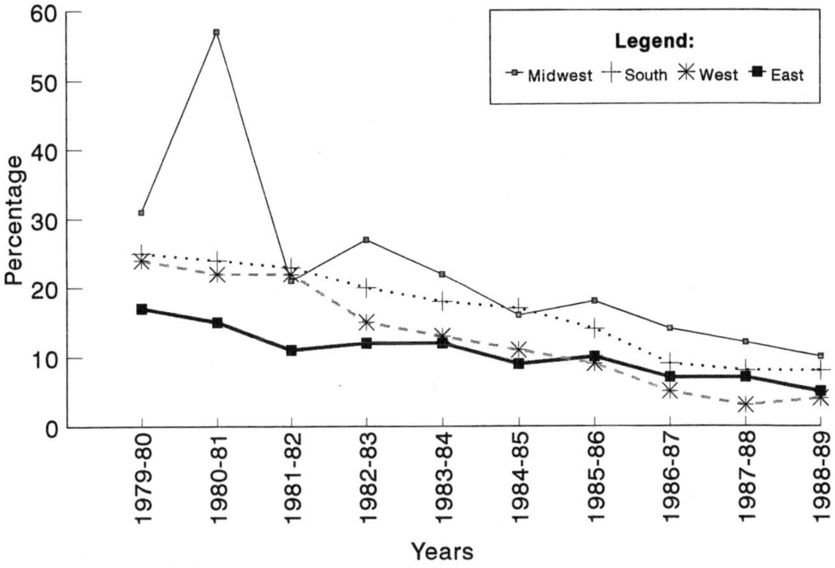

Adapted from U.S. Census, City Government Finances: 1979–89 (Washington, D.C.: Government Printing Office, 1979–89). Calculations prepared by authors. For each year we used the "General Revenue Totals" instead of the "Total Revenue" for our calculations.

Paul Peterson has claimed that federal dollars have no impact on cities; that it is the cities' own fiscal capacity that counts. According to Peterson, "Federal aid is strongly associated with welfare and highway expenditures locally. The causal direction of this relationship is not easily discerned."[20] After running a correlational analysis to determine the influence of federal aid an local expenditures, and having obtained all positive and some significant coefficients under federal aid, Peterson tries to explain away his findings. He posits that "these correlations are not my primary consideration: [the data analysis] reveals that the federal impact on these relationships is minimal."[21] This conclusion is false and misleading, based as it is on a flawed model.

The Impact of Reagan Era Urban Federalism on African American Urban Policy

With each successive presidential administration developing and emphasizing its own urban policy, African American mayors find themselves entangled in a complicated implementation nightmare. Local concerns and priorities are often put on hold, forgotten about, or abandoned in midstream. There has been little continuity, constant turmoil, and precious little forward motion in national urban policy. A scholar of the urban crisis concludes, in analyzing the impact of this continually fluctuating federal urban policy on one city (Newark, New Jersey) and its African American mayor (Kenneth Gibson):

> Finally, there was the roller coaster of federal policy changes. Plans patiently evolved during the first part of Gibson's administration in housing, economic development, and transportation had to be abruptly shelved following federal policy changes. Much of the optimism and momentum generated over rebuilding was subsequently lost. Then, following a second administration change, three additional years had to be spent updating and redeveloping plans for yet another effort. Finally, in 1981, the city was forced once again to readjust, wind down, face yet another four-year moratorium and change. The impacts on building confidence, gaining commitments, and mobilizing support promise once again to be devastating.[22]

Urban federalism (under Reagan and later Bush) came to mean not only changes in urban policy but also sharp budgetary reductions in federal aid to cities. The resources available to African American managers to solve their cities' crises became less and less sufficient. The resulting transformation of the urban setting—primarily via the elimination of the federal revenue-sharing program—corresponded with the Reagan administrations' overall design to shrink the role of the national government, with the nation's cities, especially its African American-led ones (Democratic strongholds), footing the bill.

In 1992, Bill Clinton ran and won as a centrist candidate lacking the old liberal Democratic response and concerns for the nation's urban ills. African American mayors of large cities who helped him win their respective states, waited for his policy responses.

President Clinton's urban policy initiative is called urban empowerment zones. The initiative is similar to the enterprise zone proposal developed by Jack Kemp as secretary of Housing and Urban Development in the Bush administration.[23] Kemp's enthusiasm for the enterprise zone concept was never shared by President Bush, and Congress never approved it. During the 1992 campaign, Clinton came out for enterprise zones. Under the Clinton administration's urban empowerment zone, cities and rural areas will receive block grants to implement ten-year development plans. In addition, businesses located in the designated zones will be eligible for federal tax credits for expanding their activities and hiring residents of the area. For example, the program provides wage credits of up to $3,000 for those businesses that employ a resident of the zone. Congress earmarked $3.5 billion for these purposes. The legislation allowed the federal government to designate up to nine empowerment zones (six urban and three rural) and 95 enterprise communities. Cities were to submit comprehensive revitalization plans to federal officials who would then decide the winners.

In December 1994, the Clinton administration announced the winners. The six urban areas designated as empowerment zones were Atlanta, Baltimore, Chicago, Detroit, New York, and Philadelphia-Camden. All of these cities have substantial black populations (Atlanta, Baltimore, and Detroit have black majorities). Baltimore's African American mayor, Kurt Schmoke, upon hearing the announcement, said: "I'm really excited. This is really a big victory for our community."[24] The designation of additional federal largesse came four days prior to Christmas. As the head of one neighborhood association in Baltimore put it: "We are recipients of God's Christmas present. We've had many dreams. We've had many plans that have died or suffered an early death or lived an anemic life because of lack of funds. Now we can go to work."[25]

When we examine the regional distribution of the empowerment zone funds, the following pattern emerges. The urban areas in the South were provided $106 million: Atlanta received $100 million; Birmingham and New Orleans received $3 million a piece. Detroit, in the Midwest, received $100 million. With Los Angeles getting $100 million and Oakland $25 million, cities in the West received a total of $125 million. Eastern cities were awarded $103 million ($100 mission to Baltimore; Newark was awarded $3 million). Two of our ten African American-led cities, Gary and Hartford, received nothing.Figure 21.3 reveals the regional differences in this new presidential policy initiative to assist urban areas.

Each major city in each region got the same amount of money despite their different urban ills. For example in 1992, Los Angeles experienced a major urban riot and the concomitant problems of community and personal losses associated with such an event; yet this city received as much as Detroit, which did not experience such a catastrophe.[26]

The other cities in each region got either nothing or next to nothing. Two of the cities got nothing, only one, Oakland, got 25 million. Clearly, need was not the determining factor. And when one reads the announcement and supporting documents given for this Urban Empowerment Zone, no rationale is provided.

The other curious reality is that the monies for the urban policy initiative came from two cabinet departments headed up by ethnic and racial political officials. Henry Cisneros, Clinton's HUD secretary, is a former mayor of San Antonio, Texas. He was one of the first big-city Mexican American mayors. The Department of Agriculture was also involved in the empowerment zone program. Michael Espy was Clinton's first Secretary of Agriculture before he resigned in 1995. Espy was the first African American congressman elected from Mississippi since Reconstruction. Cisneros and Espy were key players in the empowerment zone program.

Another possible explanation for this urban policy initiative is its closeness to an election year and the fact that African American political operatives had

FIGURE 21.3

Federal Grants to Cities with African American Mayors During the Clinton Administration, by Region

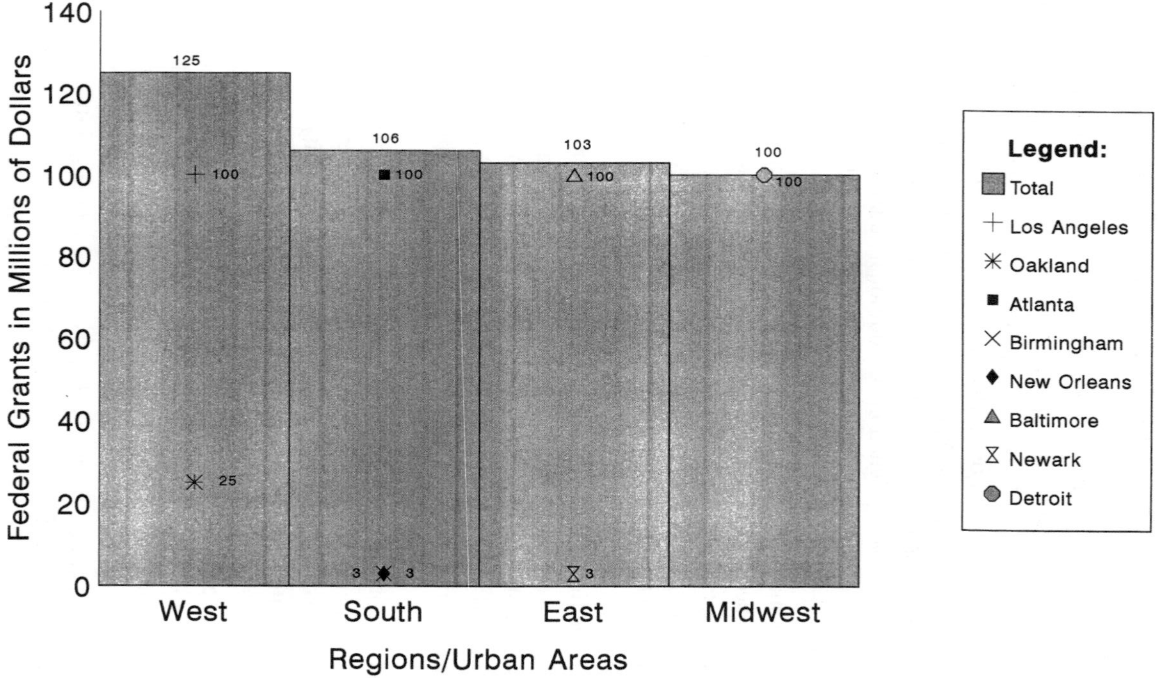

Adapted from data from Department of Agriculture and Housing and Urban Development, 1995.

played a major role in President Clinton's election. For example, Mayor Schmoke in Baltimore was one of Clinton's earliest black supporters in 1992. Schmoke's chief political strategist and advisor, a black attorney and law professor, Larry Gibson, was Clinton's top campaign operative in Maryland. Not only did Clinton win in Maryland, but among Maryland's 24 jurisdictions, Baltimore city provided candidate Clinton with the largest margin of victory in terms of the percentage of total vote received—76 percent.

Did the Clinton urban initiative address the losses that came with the termination in 1986 of the general revenue sharing program? Clinton's initiative seems no more than a token effort. These new monies are simply gifts rather than well thought out plans.

The overriding concern here is whether or not President Clinton's initiative is enough to reverse the effects of the Reagan-Bush contextual transformation. At this writing, that does not appear to be happening. Indeed, former HUD Secretary Kemp, an early supporter of the empowerment zone concept, criticized the Clinton approach for having "taken what was essentially a wonderful idea to jump-start inner city economies and turned it into a rather timid, pale version. It's the very same trickle-down idea of which they are so critical."[27] Kemp's criticism of the Democratic administration could be expected. But Lemann, in his insightful article on previous federal efforts to "jump-start" ghetto communities, quoted administration officials and Democratic members of Congress who expressed only modest expectations about the ability of empowerment zones to revitalize distressed urban areas. According to Lemann, "administration officials predict that perhaps one of the six zones could end up a visible economic success, while the rest can only hope to be somewhat safer and less deteriorated-looking."[28]

In short, a single infusion of token financial assistance means that the contextual transformation continues, with some minor modification.

22

AFRICAN AMERICAN FOREIGN POLICY
From Decolonization to Democracy

• • • • • • •

Hanes Walton, Jr.

The context variable is operative in both the domestic and foreign realms of the American political experience. Therefore, the domestic roots of United States foreign policy toward Africa and the people and nations of the African diaspora[1] lie in part in the political interests and concerns of those Americans of African descent. An understanding of this interconnectedness and relationship is crucial.[2]

African Americans have long been active in international affairs.[3] Throughout U.S. history, they have banded together to form organizations and launch movements in an effort to shape or refashion America's approach to Africa and other regions of the world in which people of color predominate. A handful of African Americans within the foreign policy establishment have also labored diligently for this cause. More often than not, however, African Americans have been neither "influential, consistent, systematic, [nor] powerful" actors in the foreign policy theater.[4]

The Reagan-Bush era provides an important timeframe for assessing African American involvement in foreign policy. The foreign policy approach of these two Republican presidents, as well as that of their Democratic successor, toward the nations and people of Africa and the Caribbean was and is clearly consistent with their domestic policies and their philosophies about race and race relations.

The Data and Methodology

The basic research contention of this paper is that the transformation in U.S. African and Caribbean foreign policy begun during the Reagan and Bush administrations so engaged the African American community and its political leadership that these forces rallied to play a pivotal role in reshaping that policy. Their efforts culminated in the achievement of two longstanding African American foreign policy goals: the end of colonialism in southern Africa and of autocratic rule in Haiti. Empirical support can be found in evidence from three sources: data on American and Soviet policies toward Africa and the Caribbean since 1980 up to the present; data on the Congressional Black Caucus members' support for the Comprehensive Anti-Apartheid Act of 1986 and for U.S. intervention in the 1994 Haitian political and refugee crisis; and data on the activity of African American foreign policy lobbying organizations such as TransAfrica and the Free South Africa Movement. This analysis yields findings on the executive branch, the legislative branch, and the private sector.

The techniques employed in appraising these findings include content analysis of official governmental documents, legislative roll-call analysis, and review of the academic literature. This study also employs a data-sequencing approach. The variable analysis begins with an investigation of the superpowers' foreign policy stances in Africa and the Caribbean. It then examines the specific policies of the administrations of Reagan, Bush, and Clinton. It then explores how these policies activated and motivated individuals and organizations within the African American community. Lastly, it describes the nature of the resultant foreign policy. It is hoped that these inquiries will lead to the shaping of additional testable propositions by which the influence of the context variable on the African American political experience can be ascertained.

Cold War Foreign Policies Toward Africa and the Caribbean

Africa and most of the African diaspora were peripheral to the foreign interests of the United States and the Soviet Union prior to and during the Cold War era, and they remain so.[5] Essentially, what led the two superpowers into conflicts in these areas of the globe was their larger conflict with each other.[6]

> For decades following the end of colonialism, African nations could leverage support from the superpowers as pawns in the Cold War. Preventing communism from taking root in the continent was the driving force behind U.S. policy.[7]

Such sentiments are echoed in the following comments from an African American scholar:

> For an administration [Nixon's] that has placed Africa at the bottom of its priorities; for an administration that has not only had a devious policy, as finally revealed in National Security Study Memorandum 309 (NSSSM-39), of actual support of the status quo and hence the minority regimes in Africa, but has had the conviction that the white regimes are here to stay;[8] [the United States also] supported the status quo in its private dealings.[9]

Indeed, the American approach toward Africa has been decidedly hypocritical for some time. Such distancing and duplicity have long characterized the nation's foreign policy behavior toward Africa.[10] The State Department did not have an African desk until the advent of the Kennedy administration.[11]

While segregation was the social system with which African Americans had to contend on the domestic scene, its counterpart in the foreign sphere—colonialism—was what shaped African American political efforts in the foreign policy area. Primarily as non-state actors working outside the foreign policy-making apparatus, African Americans have tried repeatedly to make the U.S. confront and help to eliminate the race-base system of colonialism throughout the world, especially in Africa and the Caribbean. They tried after World War I, as the League of Nations was being formed.[12] They tried once again after World War II, as another major international organization, the United Nations, was launched, but to no avail. By the onset of the Cold War, African Americans were still trying to shift America's foreign policy into a meaningful anti-colonialistic stance.

The initial days of the Cold War in the 1940s saw one of the handful of African American foreign policy insiders, Ralph Bunche, working at the State Department. Before the decade ended, Bunche would be at the United Nations struggling to fashion an international anti-colonialism policy. One participant-observer, Laurence Finkelstein, notes that he "wrote and spoke about colonialism quite a lot," and that his views reflected "the liberal, anticolonial sentiment of the times."[13]

> Bunche's impact was limited by the fact that he arrived late on the State Department scene and was hierarchically situated where little leverage was normally available to him. . . . His potential influence was circumscribed also by the fact that, for the most part, the outline of U.S. policy on post-war colonial arrangements had been fixed long before he turned up.[14]

Despite these obstacles, Finkelstein concludes that Bunche's ability "to convert policy objections into realized programs . . . was exceptional."[15]

Herschelle Challenor is even more commendatory about Bunche's work at the United Nations, noting that his "most direct contribution to the decolonization process is embodied in his involvement in the shaping of the United Nations organization into an instrument for change in the colonial world."

> As perceptive thinker, accomplished technician, and superb negotiator, [Bunche] was a catalyst for change. He was both a source of knowledge about the colonial condition and of know-how about what should be done to ameliorate its inequities.[16]

Finkelstein adds: "Bunche had different kinds of opportunities to influence events. He seized on them with great manipulative dexterity and a keep sense for what may be called situational leverage."[17]

The legacy Ralph Bunche left African American diplomats, foreign service bureaucrats, and an attentive African American public was the basic structure of a foreign policy toward Africa and the third world, namely, one of decolonization. Another part of his legacy was a set of strategies and tactics for implementing this stance from inside the foreign policy bureaucracy. Nonetheless, Bunche's Nobel Peace Prize in 1950 recognized his contributions to international foreign policy making much more than his decolonization strategies.

Bunche neither enlisted nor trained a cadre of African American diplomats and foreign service officers in support of his decolonization initiative, nor did it capture the imagination of the ever-attentive African American masses. Moreover, he did not become involved in the civil rights movement until late,[18] and when he did, leaders in that movement such as Malcolm X and Congressman Adam Clayton Powell dubbed him an "international Uncle Tom."[19] Hence, decolonization as an African American foreign policy stance had to await additional socializing forces, individuals, organizations, and events before it could move to the foreground of that community's attention.

Bunche planted the seed for later organized efforts by African Americans. Only later would selected individuals both inside and outside the foreign policy apparatus attempt to emulate Bunche's strategy and embrace his decolonization foreign policy stance. Among them was an African American attorney named Goler Teal Butcher. In her role as a staff member of the State Department's legal unit, as Counsel to the House Subcommittee on Africa, as Assistant Administrator for African Affairs at the Agency for International Development (AID), and as a private attorney, Butcher, from 1953 to 1988, waged a major struggle to make decolonization an African American foreign policy goal. One of her supporters and coworkers contends: "[James] Baldwin did not get the chance to write about this black woman who confronted the wrong values and bad laws of the *world community* as they threatened black people and all people's human rights." When Butcher threatened "to show other starting points, white-shoe lawyers [responded] with all of the litigational opposition, bureaucratic undercutting, and subtle destruction that they throw against their worse professional enemies."[20]

Like Bunche, Butcher steadfastly maintained the importance of decolonization. However, in her view, the fact that African Americans had not thrust themselves into the foreign policy-making arena was all the more reason for well-situated African American individuals to promote and push decolonization as a policy. As she noted:

> Black Americans are beginning to identify with the black world, but we have not yet had the complete transition of seeing to it that the makers of foreign policy have this interest reflected as one of their concerns [and] we're not doing what the Poles do and the East Europeans do, but we are beginning to see the connection between ourselves, our fate, and Africa, and what happens to Africa.[21]

Another major player in the foreign policy apparatus who promoted decolonization was the first United States African American ambassador to the United Nations, Andrew Young. In 1977, former Congressman Young became U.N. Ambassador and an outspoken critic of human relations in South Africa. Young's attacks on racism and vigorous support of third world nations led to enormous criticism and cries for his removal.[22]

Like Butcher, Young was appointed to his position by President Jimmy Carter, who made human rights a priority for American foreign policy. Carter's stance helped the decolonization cause and marked a commonality of interest between government officials and non-state actors. As Butcher notes:

> A very, very important point when black people talk about U.S. policy toward Africa [is that] if we are going to succeed in getting the kind of policy that we would like to see toward Africa, we have to put it in terms of U.S. interest . . . bold, practical, hard, realistic interest.[23]

During the Carter administration, African American diplomats and bureaucrats tried to bring America's Cold War foreign policy of anticommunism into congruence with the foreign policy interest and concerns of the African American community. They were joined by sundry grassroots movements as well as by organizations like the Congressional Black Caucus and TransAfrica, a pro-African and Caribbean foreign policy group headed by African American political leaders and grassroots organizers.[24] African Americans started to have an influence on policy toward Africa.[25]

The Reagan presidency would transform the Carter-era political context generally, and its foreign policy subcontext specifically, and put the two interests in conflict once again.

Reagan's Africa Policy: "Constructive Engagement" with Nuclear Assistance

The Reagan administration's foreign policy toward South Africa was dubbed constructive engagement. According to its developer, Reagan's Assistant Secretary of State Chester Crocker, this policy,

> contended that Washington could do more to encourage change by showing great patience, understanding and willingness to help Pretoria shed its pariah image world wide ... It was wrong to hector the white-minority government publicly about its racial policies. A greater effort should be made ... to understand the fears and needs of the Afrikaners who rule South Africa and "engage them constructively."[26]

Another source describes the policy as follows:

> As envisioned by Crocker, the policy was to apply to all of southern Africa and was to include friendly persuasion not only toward racial reform in South Africa but also toward settlement of longstanding disputes involving South Africa and the neighboring countries of Angola, Mozambique, and Namibia.[27]

Although Crocker drafted and got Reagan's approval for the policy, Reagan himself "devoted no speeches to and made no comments about South Africa until late 1984, when the movement toward sanctions was beginning to build."[28] Even when it became clear that talking to the white South Africans failed to stem the escalating harshness of the apartheid system, and despite actions by the South African government that threatened "to jeopardize U.S. diplomatic objectives in the region," President Reagan continued this policy.[29]

The Reagan administration's policy of constructive engagement would have done far more than merely transform the decolonization initiative and render it ineffective. It would also have permitted the South African government greater access to nuclear weapons to employ against the communist and procommunist states along its borders and possibly internally against elements of the South African black liberation movement.[30] Indeed, one scholarly observer has dubbed it "Constructive Nuclear Engagement."[31]

A member of the Congressional Black Caucus, John Conyers (D-MI), introduced H.R. 1460 in 1985, which stated that "cooperation of any kind provided for in the Atomic Energy Act of 1954 is hereby prohibited with respect to the Republic of South Africa." H.R. 1460 and its Senate counterpart, S. 995, would have placed legal prohibitions on any nuclear relationship between the United States and South Africa. However, faced with the passage of such strong anti-apartheid legislation from both the House and the Senate, Reagan chose instead to issue an executive order that continued "only mild sanctions" against South Africa and restored nearly all the prohibitions against nuclear cooperation set forth in the congressional legislation.[32]

Reagan's constructive engagement policy toward South Africa challenged African American foreign policy desires by giving the whites the upper hand in deciding the tenor and tempo of decolonization there. Indeed, it permitted the colonizers the option of not even carrying out decolonization, and, far worse, it provided the colonizers with a potential nuclear capacity to subdue their neighbors and any other threat from within.

Defenders of constructive engagement argued that the nuclear assistance component of that policy was a way to check and deal with the superpower conflict in the region. According to one, "South Africa, an avowedly anti-communist state, is evidently upset by a vision of the future of the region with the Marxist states sharing its borders."[33] Another indicated:

> The Soviet Union has invested substantially in the outcome of political struggles in both Angola and Mozambique, as indicated by arms sale data. Furthermore, their support of the liberation movements in Namibia and South Africa has also been important to the ability of Africans to prosecute the war. [The two superpowers are] on opposite sides of the strategies for achieving political settlements in the region, especially in territories such as Angola, Mozambique, South Africa, Zimbabwe, and Namibia.[34]

Assistant Secretary Crocker sent a memorandum to Secretary of State Alexander Haig declaring that "South Africa was being threatened by the U.S.S.R. and its associates."[35] The defenders of constructive engagement found themselves caught in a loop—the situation dictated the policy and the policy dictated the situational response. What was lost in all of this was any realization of the devastating effects of apartheid on its victims.

Premier Gorbachev had different perspectives about, and therefore different responses to, American foreign policy in southern Africa, and, like his predecessors, did not see it as being worthy of a superpower conflict.[36] According to Ted Hopf,

> Gorbachev learned from Soviet victories in Angola, Ethiopia, and Afghanistan that revolutionary gains in the Third World came with a high price for Soviet foreign policy in general. [This perception] allowed him to abandon longtime Soviet commitments to the victories of national liberation movements around the globe.[37]

With such a strategy of "constructive Soviet behavior in regional conflicts, Gorbachev expected to be able to remove one of the conditions that motivated

American deterrent strategy."[38] Thus, nuclear conflict between the superpowers in the periphery was greatly diminished.

Eventually, however, Reagan's African foreign policy faltered. Even his own advisory panel on South Africa, comprised of distinguished citizens and co-chaired by well-known African American Republican William T. Coleman, concluded "that the U.S. policy of 'constructive engagement' failed to achieve its original objectives."[39] Apartheid in South Africa was more entrenched than ever before. Yet, not only did President Reagan refuse to acknowledge the inadequacies of the policy, he vetoed the Comprehensive Anti-Apartheid Act of 1986.[40] Congress overrode Reagan's veto with 75% of the Republicans voting for the override. Throughout the remainder of his term, Reagan bitterly opposed implementing congressional sanctions against South Africa.

The Refugee and Political Asylum Policies of Presidents Bush and Clinton: The Case of Haiti

The Cold War, in all of its phases, rarely disturbed the racial preferences inherent in the nation's immigration laws and policies. Nor did the decolonization movement: other concerns simply took precedence,[41] until the Reagan-Bush era.

Many scholars have suggested that U.S. immigration policies send messages of exclusion to African Americans.[42] Indeed, a long line of racially restrictive laws traces the history of U.S. immigration policy. In the earliest days of the Union, the Nationality Act of 1790 limited naturalization to free white persons and specifically excluded persons of African and Native American descent. By 1870, when Congress extended naturalization rights to African immigrants seeking to become American citizens, black newcomers were still not widely accepted in the United States. This situation did not change appreciably with the passage of the landmark Immigration Act of 1924, which established a quota system based on estimates of the composition of the national origins of the population in 1920. In 1965, the quota system was repealed in favor of a family-unification system of categories. Contemporary legislation includes the Immigration Reform and Control Act of 1986 and other naturalization policies enacted during the 1990s. However, these policies continue to restrict immigration generally and place significant restraints upon people of color who would enter from the poverty-stricken nations of the third world specifically. U.S. policy with regard to refugees and political asylum is an offshoot and related matter.

> Prior to 1980, refugees were admitted on an ad hoc basis, largely in response to foreign policy considerations. Citizens of countries hostile to the United States were routinely approved, while citizens of friendly countries were rejected.[43]

In 1980, Congress passed legislation that brought refugee policy into compliance with international protocols and thereby removed some of the ideological barriers that had restricted the admission of refugees from third world nations. While Baker-Kelly notes that "in theory, under [the Refugee Act of 1980], individual humanitarian concerns outweigh nationalistic ideological prejudices," she also contends that, in practice, "preferential treatment creeps into the determination of refugee status through several loopholes, particularly since 'special humanitarian concern to the U.S.' has never been defined."[44] Using just such a loophole during the Haitian refugee crisis during the Bush administration "justified repatriating Haitians by terming them 'economic' rather than 'political' refugees."[45] This policy was maintained under the succeeding administration until President Clinton was confronted by an organized front of African American foreign policy elites from the Congressional Black Caucus and TransAfrica.

> To many African Americans, the Coast Guard's interdiction and forced reversal of boats carrying Haitian refugees is a racist act directed at people of African descent . . . This perception of racism in the application of U.S. immigration policies were reinforced by the contrasting news of planeloads and boat loads of Cuban refugees being warmly received just miles down the coast in Florida.[46]
>
> Comparisons to other refugee groups suggest that the treatment of Haitians is perhaps not just ideologically, but racially, motivated. For example, although the United States has an embargo against both Cuba and Haiti, Cubans are allowed to reach U.S. shores while Haitians are interdicted at sea. Under the Cuban Adjustment Act, Cubans are almost routinely granted asylum because they are Cuban, but Haitians are regularly turned away because they are Haitians.[47]

By ushering into the nation's refugee policy a race-based and dualistic approach toward Haiti and Cuba, President Bush further transformed the political context for African Americans. African American foreign policy elites saw the familiar specter of racism and racial bias within these disparities in the formulation and application of U.S. refugee policy. As a consequence of both this perception and these practices, they were motivated to confront this remnant of the Cold War head-on.

Lucius Barker and Mack Jones recall that during his 1992 presidential campaign, Bill Clinton promised to "admit Haitian refugees and do away with the more 'inhumane' restrictive Haitian immigration policy of the Bush Administration."[48] As president, however, Clinton "decided not only to essentially follow the more restrictive Bush immigration policy, but also acted to successfully defend that policy in the Supreme Court."[49]

The Evolution of African American Foreign Policy from Decolonization to Democracy

Pearl T. Robinson writes, "the forces of imperialism and colonialism have not succeeded in preempting the capacity of [persons of African descent] to play a role in shaping their own destiny."[50] Robinson's sentiments are echoed by former African American statesman Elliott P. Skinner. "Thanks to the relative successes [of] the Civil Rights Movement, the Negritude Movement, . . . and the rise of the Third World, the racism that DuBois labeled as the problem of the twentieth century is radically being eliminated."[51] He concludes, however, that black intellectuals, "like all other intellectuals," must now "deal with the problems of the emerging global civilization."[52]

In November 1984, shortly after Reagan won reelection to a second term, Bishop Desmond Tutu was visiting in the United States on his way to accept the Nobel Peace Prize.[53] Demonstrations at the South African embassy against the jailing of many black South African labor leaders were organized by the Free South Africa Movement, an activist group spearheaded by District of Columbia congressional delegate Walter E. Fauntroy, and Randall Robinson, the executive director of TransAfrica. Both men allowed themselves to be arrested and jailed for their involvement in this protest. They were later released, only to continue to organize and participate in a continuing string of similar protests and arrests. They were soon joined by other African American leaders, members of the Congressional Black Caucus, religious leaders, labor unionists, state and local political activists, and common folk. Their efforts also gained substantial white support, even among conservatives, and similar protests were organized at South African consulates around the country.

Nearly overnight, the Free South African Movement became a major political force, partly due to the timing of its protests and partly to the celebrities who became involved in them. Congressman Julian Dixon (D-CA) noted that, because the protests occurred during the lull between the election and Congress convening, "the press really picked this up." In addition, the list of those who allowed themselves to be arrested included Professor Goler Butcher, who was among the first to be arrested; Ramsey Clark, Attorney General in the Johnson administration; Father Robert Drinan, a professor of law at Georgetown Law Center; George Dalley, the former deputy campaign manager for Walter Mondale; John Krammer, associate dean of the Georgetown Law Center; National Bar Association president Arthenia Joyner; Mississippi civil rights attorney Victor McTeer; and Gay Johnson McDougall, director of the Southern Africa Project. Eighteen members of Congress were arrested, including Lowell Weicker, who became the first American senator to be arrested for civil disobedience while in office.[54] Among the others were Senator Ted Kennedy and former Congressional Black Caucus chairman Representative Mervyn Dymally.

The involvement of celebrities meant that the news media enhanced their coverage of the protests. The Free South Africa Movement not only gained exposure, momentum, and clout, but it started to expand its focus.

> One of the strategic tactics of the Free South Africa Movement was to encourage black and white Americans to boycott American businesses which did business either with the South African government or in South Africa. The Shell Oil Company was the first target.[55]

These efforts fueled a larger anti-apartheid movement.[56] The Free South Africa Movement socialized and mobilized both the African American community and the American community at large. Professor Smith comments that this movement

> was unique in American history . . . because it gave average black and white citizens an opportunity to help create and shape the analysis of U.S. foreign policy in Africa and South Africa in particular.[57]
>
> [It] provided an opportunity for people to march against the apartheid regime, to put political pressure on the United States foreign policy in South Africa, and to exert economic pressure on domestic corporations doing business in South Africa.[58]

The movement "brought the term 'apartheid' and its meaning into every home in the nation when televised accounts of the protest aired."[59] Just as the civil rights movement had forced legal segregation off the American landscape, the Free South Africa Movement pushed the Reagan-Bush strategy of constructive engagement out of the foreign policy picture. African American foreign policy leaders and energized black citizens confronted and finally helped to defeat the forces of apartheid.

Not only did this African American foreign policy initiative include a full-fledged protest strategy against constructive engagement, it also included a major legislative strategy.

On May 21, 1986, Congressional Black Caucus and House Foreign Affairs Committee member Congressman William Gray (D-PA) put forth House bill H.R. 4868, which leveled sanctions against South Africa in the form of disinvestment, import and export restrictions, and the banning of landing rights in the United States to South African airlines.[60] Congressman Ronald Dellums (D-CA) considered Gray's bill mild and offered his own stronger measure, which failed. By June 13, Gray's bill was out of the Foreign Affairs Committee; by June 16, it had cleared the House Ways and Means Committee. Three days later, H.R. 4868 passed the House by a vote of 286 to 127. When it was introduced to the Senate, it was amended, yet approved, by an 84-to-14 vote on August 15 and sent back to the House for a final vote. House members passed the legislation in its final form as the Comprehensive Anti-Apartheid Act on September 12.

When the bill reached President Reagan's desk on September 26, he promptly vetoed it. In his veto message, Reagan declared:

> Disrupting the South African economy and creating more unemployment will only fuel the tragic cycle of violence and repression that has gripped that troubled country. . . . It will not improve prospects for negotiations. . . . That is why sweeping punitive sanctions are the wrong course to follow, . . . increased American and western investment . . . is the right course to pursue.[61]

The House was not persuaded and voted to override the president's veto on September 29. Reagan wrote letters to House majority leader Thomas O'Neill, Jr. (D-MA) and Senate majority leader Robert Dole (R-KS) outlining the terms and conditions of an executive order on South Africa that he proposed to issue if the House and Senate agreed not to override his veto.[62] In that letter he stated that "Sanctions, in and of themselves, do not add up to a policy for South Africa and the Southern African region. . . . South Africans continue to search for solutions. Their true friends should help in this search."[63]

The next day, to sweeten his offer, Reagan named Edward Perkins, an African American senior foreign service officer, as the new U.S. ambassador to Pretoria. However, many in the Senate, even those in the Republican majority, saw Reagan's overtures as yet another series of symbolic gestures and stood poised to override the veto. Members of Reagan's own party, including Senator Richard Lugar (R-IN), chair of the Senate Subcommittee on Africa, could not persuade him to make a strong anti-apartheid speech. On October 2, the Senate voted to override the president's veto and the Comprehensive Anti-Apartheid Act became Public Law 99–440. This congressional action marked the first override of a presidential veto on a majority foreign policy issue since 1973. Congress had never before repudiated Reagan so decisively. In both the final vote and the veto override, Reagan's own party deserted him.

Table 22.1 provides the empirical evidence for African Americans' legislative support for Public Law 99–440, as well as a record of other members' voting on this matter. The left-hand side of this table notes the proportions and numbers of party groups and subgroups within the House of Representatives that voted to pass this piece of legislation. African American Democrats in the House voted solidly in favor of the Act, followed in support by northern and southern Democrats. While nearly all of the Democratic members of Congress voted for the legislation, only a little over one-fourth of Republican members backed it.

The voting pattern of the Senate (shown on the right-hand side of the table) was partially reversed in terms of partisanship. All segments of the Democratic

TABLE 22.1

Party Support Ratios for the 1986 Comprehensive Anti-Apartheid Act, Passage and Veto Override

Total Party Categories	Proportion of Yes Votes	Proportion of No Votes	Total Number of Votes	Proportion of Yes Votes	Proportion of No Votes	Total Number of Votes
House Passage 1986 Act				**Senate Passage 1986 Act**		
Total Votes	69	31	413	86	14	98
Republican Votes	28	72	171	73	27	51
Democratic Votes	98	2	242	100	0	47
Northern Democrats	99	1	167	100	0	33
Southern Democrats	94	6	77	100	0	14
African American Democrats	100	0	18	*	*	*
House Veto Override 1986 Act				**Senate Veto Override 1986 Act**		
Total Votes	79	21	396	79	21	99
Republican Votes	51	49	160	60	40	52
Democratic Votes	98	2	236	100	0	47
Northern Democrats	100	0	163	100	0	33
Southern Democrats	95	5	73	100	0	14
African American Democrats	100	0	18	*	*	*

Compiled from data in *The Congressional Quarterly Almanac* (Washington, D.C.: Congressional Quarterly), 50-H. For the Senate data, see pp. 110-S and 10-E.

**No African American was in the Senate in the 99th Congress.*

party gave the measure full and complete support while nearly three-fourths of the Republican majority in the Senate followed suit. There was very little opposition to the measure in the Senate, even from the Republican party.

That the African American Democratic legislative leadership was able to pull both the northern and southern wings of their party toward their goal was a rarity because on other pieces of legislation, white southern Democrats and African American Democrats have significantly opposed each other.[64] Beyond the partisan support for the Comprehensive Anti-Apartheid Act that African American Democrats garnered in the House of Representatives, similar and even stronger support was rallied in the Senate, despite the lack of any African American presence in that body.

In the final analysis, the Free South Africa Movement, as a segment of the African American foreign policy leadership, achieved overwhelming success. Nor only did it generate a mass protest movement as a lobbying device, it eventually created a legislative movement in both houses of Congress and won bipartisan congressional support for the African American anti-apartheid initiative. With this success, the Reagan policy of constructive engagement met its demise, and a significant phase in the history of African American foreign policy maneuvering came to an end.

The eradication of apartheid in South Africa and the end of constructive engagement set the stage for the next phase of African American foreign policy: a shifting of political gears to focus on dismantling America's racist refugee policies toward Haiti specifically and support for the advancement of democracy in Africa and the Third World generally. Toward these ends, African American foreign policy leaders once again employed the tactic of public protest.

In 1994, a coup, led by military forces loyal to the former Duvalier dictatorship, overthrew the first-ever democratically elected Haitian civilian government of newly elected President Jean-Bertrand Artistide. The repressive policies of the Haitian military had set into motion the mass exodus of immigrants from that nation to the United States. President Aristide was granted political asylum. However, the majority of Haitians, most of whom set out for America via boat, were rebuffed en masse by U.S. immigration officials and forced back to the American base at Guantanamo, Cuba or to their homeland, where many faced retribution at the hands of soldiers and militiamen as well as starvation and poverty. On March 27, 1994, TransAfrica's Randall Robinson embarked upon a 27-day fast to protest the Clinton administration's policy of summary repatriation of Haitians fleeing their country's dictatorship. When a famished and debilitated Robinson had to be hospitalized to monitor his weakened condition, members of the Congressional Black Caucus called an urgent meeting to discuss the Haitian political crisis with President Clinton, who shortly thereafter shifted the nation's policies with regard to Haitian and Cuban refugees. The administration in September 1994 ended Cubans' automatic right of asylum in the U.S.

Now almost all rafters are sent back to Cuba. Cubans who wish to leave normally are allowed in at the rate of 20,000 a year.

The Congressional Black Caucus and TransAfrica also insisted on active American support for the government of President Artistide. To this demand, President Clinton responded by sending American armed forces to Haiti to restore the deposed Artistide to power and initiate democratic processes in that former dictatorship.

On March 17, 1995, with the democratization of South Africa and the Haitian success, Randall Robinson called a news conference to announce a nationwide campaign against Nigeria's military dictatorship, which had recently overthrown the democratically elected government.[65] Supported once again by numerous public personalities and celebrities, Robinson accused the Nigerian military leaders of human rights abuses, and of squandering the nation's oil revenues, participating in international drug smuggling and money laundering schemes, suppressing any opposition, and generally inhibiting both democracy and economic improvements.[66] He called for the Clinton administration to institute economic sanctions against Nigeria as a means of inducing its military leaders to move toward democracy.

Of this effort on the part of an African American foreign policy lobby group, one newspaper observed that it marked "the first time [a black group] has undertaken a major effort against a black African government. The overdue action against Nigeria signals TransAfrica's willingness to oppose corruption regardless of ethnicity."[67] Another source proclaimed that "It is highly unusual, probably unprecedented, for American blacks to speak out so loudly about the abuses of a black African regime. It is a major step, a triumph of outrage over a deeply embedded . . . sense of collective mortification."[68] Still another noted: "TransAfrica has been . . . critical of the more outrageous black African regime such as Zaire under Mobutu Sese Seko or Ethiopia under Mengistu Haile Marian. But it had never actively sought their overthrow."[69]

In this new policy stance, African American foreign policy leaders have connected themselves for the first time to efforts aimed at bringing down a dictatorship in black Africa. However, the absence of democratic rule on the African continent is also an unresolved aspect of the African American foreign policy focus on decolonization. In their zeal to hurry the collapse of apartheid and European colonialism in Africa, African Americans had previously often overlooked some of the sins of African and Caribbean leaders. One critic of this tendency notes that several nations that "violated their citizens' human rights but happened to be governed by blacks were given a free pass from criticism by groups like TransAfrica."[70]

The struggle to fix the Clinton administration's refugee policy became the transformational watershed for fixing African American foreign policy and moving its focus from decolonization to democracy. Spreading democracy, not merely preventing communism, is currently the dominant thrust of that movement, and a new congruence is under way. This is indeed a fitting end to Cold War diplomacy and a chance to reconcile the foreign policy interests of the African American community and American society at large.

Conclusion: Testable Propositions

The Reagan-Bush and early Clinton administration policy tools that were designed to transform African American foreign policy forced a transformation that was vastly different from the transformation that was intended. Reagan's policy of constructive engagement with nuclear assistance was supposed to shift the African American foreign policy focus from an insistence on democratization to one in which the initiative and power remained in the hands of the white minority. In the end, Reagan's policies led to the success of African American foreign policy initiatives, and the reins of power in South Africa were transferred to the formerly colonized.

On the other hand, Bush's and later Clinton's apparently race-based refugee policies forced African Americans to formulate a new policy strategy.

This analysis offers some testable propositions about African American involvement in foreign policy making. The first of these is that the development of influence in the foreign policy arena involves the rise of strong protest organizations and groups or the remobilization of older protest organizations and groups around a new foreign policy thrust. A second testable proposition is that African Americans have taken legislative action to commit the nation to the pursuit of their foreign policy initiatives in Africa and the African diaspora. A third testable proposition is that efforts in support of African American foreign policy initiatives have necessarily involved the executive branch of government. The fourth proposition relates to the fact that African American leaders and citizens have switched strategies, tactics, and finally policies in order to affect the long-range foreign policy goals and objectives sought by their community.

We have also learned from this analysis that, in an era of African American political context transformation, Republican and Democratic administrations alike seek to change the foreign policy stances of African Americans. Such efforts have met with a mixture of success and failure. However, they can be empirically assessed, both in terms of the extent of the transformation desired and the opposition to that transformation lodged by those communities that are targeted for change.

PART 9

PROSPECTS

Racism is a part of the political as well as the cultural context of America. It is thus a potential variable in the analysis of the political scene. The race factor is powerful enough to transform the American political context at both the individual and the mass levels. When it is introduced for partisan purposes it can and often does succeed in transforming the political context in the cultural, constitutional, methodological, organizational, participatory, decision making, policy, and opinion arenas.

True, there are setbacks and weaknesses to using this tactic. The African American electorate has been somewhat successful at blocking politicians who use race-baiting for partisan purposes from achieving political success. Under certain conditions, however, particularly at the presidential level, African Americans have proven to be of insufficient strength to stop candidates who elect to employ racially divisive and polarizing means.

Yet, it matters not so much that a specific factor in American life can cause the transformation of the political context—although that is important—as it matters who decides to use this factor to precipitate the transformation in the first place. As Rosenstone and Hansen note, once citizens are mobilized around this contextual variable or other "especially salient issues," the transformation will begin.[1]

FIGURE P.1

Conceptual Schema of the Reagan-Bush Transformation Efforts

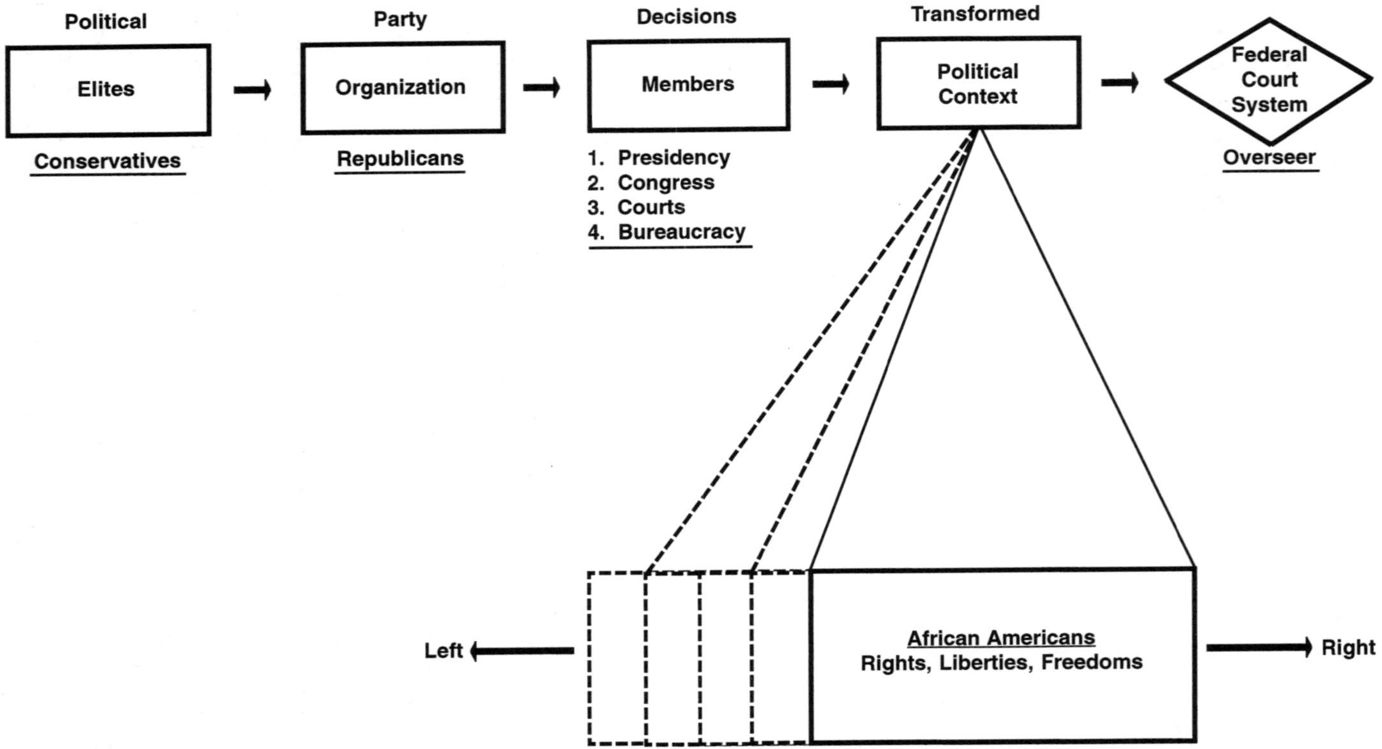

During the Reagan-Bush era, African Americans learned once more that political majorities can shift the political context by mobilizing around the issue of race, and that such a shift most often results in the loss of rights, liberties, and freedoms for African Americans. It took seventy years, from 1895 to 1965, to finally change the political context in African Americans' favor. In twelve years, the Reagan-Bush presidencies nearly undid the political context of the preceding era and, in fact, severely restricted it.

Figure P1 illustrates how a group of conservative political elites, using the Republican party as their vehicle, divisively mobilized Americans around the issue of race and captured control of some of the nation's chief decision-making bodies

Another important aspect of the transformation of the political context for African Americans is its destabilizing nature. African Americans are never quite sure where they stand politically, never quite at rest. They are thus forced to raise over and over again the age-old questions: What will it take to achieve political, social, and economic parity? How long will it take? Will we ever get there? In a political environment of sporadic contextual shifts, the past is never completely destroyed. The problems of the past, mingled as they are with a host of new problems, remain quite unsolved.

But what of the future? At best, the Clinton administration holds out a promise of contextual change, but it is a promise that has hedged its bets. It is an administration bent, it claims, on achieving justice for African Americans and other people of color and women by not criticizing the injustices or the unfairness of the previous Republican presidential administrations. This rationale is suspect, however, and one can only conclude that, by their silence, the Democrats are actually in search of a new electoral coalition. Because of this, the political context might very easily swing back in the direction of that of the Reagan-Bush era. How far, no one knows. For the sake of another election majority, the Democrats, led by Clinton, might choose to maintain a stationary position on African Americans' civil rights and liberties. If they do, then the promise of this administration will pass away unfulfilled, and the Clinton presidency will be remembered as but a transitional stage between the end of the Reagan-Bush political context revolution and the future contextual revolutions that the unresolved matters of the past will soon demand.

Moreover, the reader must recognize that a transformed political context involved both the expansion as well as the contraction of African American political empowerment. The Reagan-Bush presidencies sought a very active federal judiciary, federal bureaucracy, Congress, and Presidency, which would limit the rights, liberties, and freedoms of African Americans.

If the Reagan-Bush presidencies wanted an activist federal government to create a negative reality, they also wanted an activist government to create a positive reality. They sought an activist government and partisan leadership to create African American political empowerment, only if it would enhance the Republican advantage in the political system. The search for African American conservative leaders, beginning with the Fairmont conference, and the use of political patronage to increase the number of these right wing ideologues is the obvious development of an activist government, to build over time a conservative Republican African American political base and constituency. But in the final analysis, this type of Republican led African American empowerment could only take place if it advances the Republican agenda and its political fortunes.

African American political leaders worked during this era of context transformation to affect the political context so as to expand their political power and political reach. For example, California Congressman Mervyn Dymally retired from Congress in 1992 and formed the California Water Caucus and a nonprofit water policy group, The Robert Smith Water Institute.[2]

Five months before the 1994 elections the Institute sponsored eight candidates for positions on the West and Central Basin Municipal Water Districts. "The agencies store and distribute water for more than 20 communities stretching from Malibi to Long Beach and inland to East Los Angeles and Pico Rivera." By all accounts, these Water District elections are "typically sleepy affairs in little known districts," "sedate affairs," yet these water boards "control multimillion dollar budgets in virtual obscurity."[3] For instance, "The West and Central districts collectively spend about $10 million a month on construction programs in urban communities that are home to large numbers of Latinos, African Americans, and Asian Americans," that are looking for jobs and employment. These boards, which are dominated almost exclusively by whites,[4] "also deal with the structure of water rates," which critics charge "fall unfairly on poor and urban communities."[5]

In mobilizing the African American community to expand their political reach in this area, Congressman Dymally stressed the following reality: "The fact of the matter is that water more than any other resource affects our daily lives and yet minorities in general and African Americans in particular, have no say in the political decisions or the economic benefits of water resources."[6]

In the 1994 local elections, five of the Institute's eight candidates won seats on three of the water boards.[7] "A coalition of minority candidates has captured seats on three obscure but powerful water boards, giving the challengers a foothold in an industry that for years had been the domain of whites."[8] Therefore, at the very moment that the Republicans captured Congress, African Americans were expanding their political power and reach on a different level.

An African American political entrepreneur like Congressman Dymally was well suited to lead this contextual transformation for the African American community. He had been a California Assemblyman, a State Senator, and Lieutenant Governor. As State Senator, he served as vice-chairman of the Water Resources Committee. Throughout his career, he has been a trailblazer. This recent effort continued that tradition.

In sum, African American empowerment will continue to find novel responses to context transformation.

23

AFRICAN AMERICANS, POLITICAL CONTEXT, AND THE CLINTON PRESIDENCY

The Legacy of the Past in the Future

• • • • • • •

Hanes Walton, Jr. and William O. Generett, Jr.

The importance of political context as a determining and dominant variable in African American political behavior has, for the most part, gone unacknowledged. In the 1960s and 1970s, it was considered to be essentially a southern regional phenomenon. The purpose of this volume has been to reintroduce political context as an analytical variable in African American politics and to reveal its implications and manifestations at the national, state, and local levels. The Republican-led transformation of the political context for African Americans was formally set into motion at the December 1980 Fairmont conference, held less than a month after Ronald Reagan was first elected president.[1] The political environment in which African Americans operated began to shift in a direction that was fashioned by the conservative agenda of the Republican party. At that point, the movement to redefine and reshape the liberal policies and programs of the Kennedy and Johnson years began in earnest, led by a conservative presidency bent on disadvantaging African Americans and dismantling the achievements of the civil rights era. This was a political context crafted by those who were opposed to African Americans' advancement in society. At its best, this contextual transformation was contemporary paternalism with a mission—and that mission, strangely enough, was dictated by the southern wing of the Democratic party,[2] which became the decisive force in the Republican electoral coalition that captured the White House. That wing would play a central role in the Democrats' recapture of the White House in 1992,[3] and in the Republican recapture of both houses of Congress in the 1994 midterm election.

During the 1950s, 1960s, and 1970s, Reagan transversed the South, stomping first in the small towns, later in that region's large cities, making countless speeches and endearing himself to this electorate. Utilizing racial code words and direct pitches, Reagan brought himself into line with the conservativism and racism of the white South. Reagan's warm words gained him many admirers in this pre-presidential season.

> And the end result of these three decades of wooing and planting the seeds of friendship paid off in the 1980 election, when this Republican hopeful beat another southerner in his own region, to his chagrin and dismay. President Carter lost the region, to a non-southerner. A southerner who had African American support lost the region to one who disdained and denied and denounced African Americans themselves and their support.[4]

The last contextual revolution prior to the arrival of the Reagan-Bush era was that of the civil rights era, which, by the early 1970s, had more or less collapsed.[5] The Reagan-Bush era unravelled the gains of the civil rights era and transformed once more the context in which African Americans conducted their political affairs. By reintroducing racial cleavages for partisan gain, the Reagan-Bush Republicans turned the anger, resentment, and frustration of whites to their own partisan advantage.

African Americans' efforts to attain their civil rights were reconstrued as a zero-sum game in which whites were the losers. Problems in the nation's African American-governed urban areas became acute, and the hard-fought constitutional attainments of the preceding decades were put into jeopardy. Forward motion on the unfinished agenda of the civil rights movement was stalled while African Americans and their civil rights allies engaged in damage control to maintain some degree of stability. The Republicans' conservative politics were promoted, with conservative African American operatives being recruited and appointed.

Contextual transformation in the political arena is a multi-phased process. First, a desire to transform the political context must be evident, along with a strategy. Second, that desire and strategy must become institutionalized. During the Reagan-Bush and Clinton years, the Republican party became the organizational vehicle for the conservative reshaping of the political context.

The South was crucial to the presidential victories of Reagan and Bush. Of the eleven southern states, Carter carried only Georgia in 1980. In 1992, Clinton and Gore carried their respective states of Arkansas and Tennessee, plus Georgia. In the 1994 congressional election, a majority of southern Democrats voted the straight Republican ticket. For the first time since Reconstruction, the majority of southern governors, representatives, and senators were Republican. In addition, elected Democrats who later switched to the Republican party placed the Tennessee and Florida state senates and the South Carolina and North Carolina state house in Republican control.

The Reagan-Bush contextual revolution changed the nature of both their competitors and partisan competition in the political process generally. The transformation of the political context not only had an impact on the Republican party, the federal government, and the Congress, it likewise forced a shift in the Democratic party. Prior to the Republican-led contextual revolution, the Democratic party had been a force in assisting African Americans in getting their long-delayed constitutional rights. During the Reagan-Bush years, the Democratic party leadership gradually moved away from its traditional commitment to civil rights and affirmative action. The Reagan-Bush years witnessed rise of the conservative Democratic Leadership Council within the Democratic party, impelled the resurgence of the southern wing in the party, and inadvertently propelled Bill Clinton to the presidency. Moreover, the altered political context fostered the reemergence of the southern demagogue and led African American politicians to attempt deracialized candidacies at the presidential level. It also made it easier for mainstream African American voters to consider third-party candidates in lieu of their traditional affinity for Democratic party candidates.

Transformers of the political context must ensure that the changes they effect outlive them. Presidents Reagan and Bush installed numerous conservative justices in the federal court system whose decisions will continue to influence the political context for decades to come. They also appointed conservative bureaucrats to key federal agencies whose activities critically impacted on the African American community. Additionally, through executive orders, they changed federal policy such that implementation or enforcement of civil rights and affirmative action initiatives has become an arduous ordeal.

The papers in this volume have described this contextual transformation as well as the sundry ways in which the African American community responded to it. African Americans met with both successes and failures during the Reagan-Bush and Clinton eras. Fortunately, African Americans are no strangers to fitful political surroundings. Most often, they have had to struggle against the prevailing political context and its concomitant thrusts to define and structure African American political participation. Yet, without concerted effort on the part of the Clinton administration and the Democratic party, the forward movement of this Republican-led transformation will continue. The implications of this cannot be overstated. Without presidential-level action, the political context of the present, and possibly the future, will continue to include the problems of racial divisiveness, constitutional inequality, and urban decay.

The Clinton administration can elect to prevent the legacy of the Reagan-Bush years from flowing into the future, or it can ignore the implications of this legacy and do nothing. This is its challenge and its potential. The initial steps are not completely promising.

Finally, a closing word about theory building around the political context variable and race. At the conceptual level, the weight of these case studies is that it is bidirectional. Influence can flow in both directions. African Americans as well as whites can transform the political context.

At the level of theory building, each of the papers presented here offer in either a formal or informal manner some testable propositions which can in the future be used to make empirical estimations and provide the base for theory testing. This study lays the foundation, as well as providing perspectives on how Republican and Democratic leaders can effectuate and react to contextual change and transformation.

Upon Our Body Politic

The
African American
Body politic
Can ill afford
Setting its collective clockwork
Upon
The sometimey conscience
Of outer America's "goodwill"

Powerbase buildings' First Rule
Is *Weakness Can Kill*
Regardless
Of affiliations
Achievements and aspirations

Ours still, is a climb uphill
Our
Body politic.
Has arguably come a long way
With many burning sands.
To go

But its candidates, mandates, leadership
Of cities, departments, and states
In this
Rookies' game so touch and go

MUST
Have a Black nation
Of competent, networked voters in the know
In
Order to have a President
Or
Any other such representative
of the Electorial Process' promise
of legislated liberation

'Else
Still too slowly
We march
Toward our dreamt, deferred
Destination

Nadra

REPRESENTATION

Politics . . .
An
Aggressive art
of the possible:
Votes
Values, victory
Managing
Moods, masses, money
Means
Representation
That ultimately,
Whether we're
Democrat, Independent
Republican,
NEVER neglects advancing
African-Americans!

—NADRA

NOTES

PREFACE

1. Jack Bass, *Taming the Storm: The Life and Times of Judge Frank M. Johnson, Jr. and the South's Fight Over Civil Rights* (New York: Anchor Books, 1993), 469.

2. Patricia Grace Smith, "Judge Johnson Stood for Fairness and Justice," *Sunday Montgomery Advertiser* 21 July 1990.

3. Patricia Grace Smith and Clive O. Callender, "The Anatomy of a Black Community-Based Transplant Education Program: A Model for Community Empowerment," in Annette Dala and Sarah Goering (eds.), *"It Just 'Ain't' Fair:" The Ethics of Health Care for African Americans* (Connecticut: Praeger, 1994), 234–43.

4. See Hanes Walton, Jr., Leslie Burl McLemore, and C. Vernon Gray, "The Problem of Preconceived Perceptions in Black Urban Politics: The Harold Gosnell, James Q. Wilson Legacy," *National Political Science Review* 3 (1992): 217–29.

5. See Robert Brisbane, Jr., *The Black Vanguard* (Valley Forge: Judson Press, 1970) and his *Black Activism* (Valley Forge: Judson Press, 1974).

6. Tobe Johnson, *Metropolitan Government: A Black Analytical Perspective* (Washington, D.C.: Joint Center for Political Studies, 1972) and his "Review of the Politics of the Southern Negro by Harry Holloway," *American Political Science Review* 64 (March, 1970): 196–97.

PROLOGUE

1. Charles Prysby, "Attitudes of Southern Democratic Party Activists Toward Jesse Jackson: The Effect of the Local Context," *Journal of Politics* 51 (1989): 305–18.

2. Michael Giles and Melanie Buckner, "David Duke and Black Threat: An Old Hypothesis Revisited," *Journal of Politics* 55 (1993): 702–713.

3. Ibid., 711.

4. Earl Black, "The Militant Segregationist Vote in the Post-Brown South: A Comparative Analysis," *Social Science Quarterly* 54 (1973): 67.

5. Thomas Carsey, "The Contextual Effects of Race on White Voter Behavior: The 1989 New York City Mayoral Election," *Journal of Politics* 57 (1995): 221–28.

6. Black, 66.

7. Giles and Buckner, 705.

8. Prysby, 309.

9. Ibid., 306.

10. Black, 69.

11. Prysby, 312.

12. Gerald C. Wright, Jr., "Contextual Models of Electoral Behavior: The Southern Wallace Vote," *American Political Science Review* 71 (1977): 497–508.

13. Rufus Browning, Dale Rogers Marshall, and David Tabb, *Racial Politics in American Cities* (New York: Longman, 1993), 3–30.

1. OVERVIEW

1. Mack Jones, "Political Science and the Black Political Experience: Issues in Epistemology and Relevance," *National Political Science Review* 3 (1992): 25–39.

2. Lenneal J. Henderson, Jr., (ed.), *Black Political Life in the United States* (San Francisco: Chandler, 1972), xiii.

3. Jones, 32, 36.

4. Hanes Walton, Jr., Cheryl Miller, Joseph P. MacCornick, II, "Race and Political Science: The Dual Traditions of Race Relations Politics and African American Politics," in James Farr, John Drizzek, and Stephen Leonard (eds.), *Political Science in History: Research Programs and Political Traditions* (New York: Cambridge Press, 1995): 145–174; Hanes Walton, Jr. and Joseph P. MacCornick, II, "The Study of African American Politics as Social Danger: Clues From the Disciplinary Journals," *National Political Science Review* 6 (1996).

5. John Hope Franklin and Glenna Rae McNeil, *African Americans and the Living Constitution* (Washington, D.C: Smithsonian Institution, 1995), xiv, 3.

6. Regina Freer, "Black-Korean Conflict," in Mark Baldassare (ed.), *The Los Angeles Riots: Lesson for the Urban Future* (Boulder: Westview Press, 1994), 175–204.

7. Hanes Walton, Jr., *Invisible Politics: Black Political Behavior* (Albany: State University of New York Press, 1985), chap. 3.

8. See Hanes Walton, Jr., *Black Politics: A Theoretical and Structural Analysis* (Philadelphia: J. B. Lippincott, 1972) for a review of the literature on African American Democrats. The current literature includes Hulan E. Jack, *Fifty Years A Democrat: The Autobiography of Hulan E. Jack* (New York: The New Benjamin Franklin House, 1982); Nancy Weiss, *Farewell to the Party of Lincoln: Black Politics in the Age of FDR* (Princeton: Princeton University Press, 1983); and Hanes Walton, Jr., "Democrats and African Americans: The American Idea," in Peter Kolver (ed.), *Democrats and the American Idea: A Bicentennial Appraisal* (Washington, D.C.: Center for National Policy Press, 1982), 333–48.

9. See Tali Mendelberg, "The Politics of Racial Ambiguity: Origins and Consequences of

Implicit Racial Appeals," (Ph.D. diss., University of Michigan, Ann Arbor, 1994). See also David Henderson, "Campaigning in Code," *Washington Post* 1 July 1990.

10. Hanes Walton, Jr., "Black Political Payoff: Used and Unused Strategies," *Political Science Review* 20 (July-September, 1981): 287–98.

PART I. DEFINITION

1. Walton, *Invisible Politics,* chap. 1.

2. THE POLITICAL CONTEXT VARIABLE: THE TRANSFORMATION POLITICS OF THE REAGAN, BUSH, AND CLINTON PRESIDENCIES

1. Robert Huckfeldt and John Sprague, "Citizens, Contexts, and Politics," in Ada Finifter (ed.), *Political Science: The State of the Discipline II* (Washington, DC: American Political Science Association, 1993), 282.

2. Lester Milbrath, *Political Participation* (Chicago: Rand McNally, 1965), 36.

3. Lester Milbrath and M. L. Gael, *Political Participation* 2d ed. (Chicago: Rand McNally, 1977), 123.

4. Huckfeldt and Sprague, 289.

5. Ibid.

6. John W. Books and Charles Prysby, *Political Behavior and the Local Context* (New York: Praeger, 1991), 151.

7. Books and Prysby, 151.

8. Ibid.

9. Ibid., 26.

10. Thomas M. Carsey, "The Contextual Effects of Race on White Voters' Behavior: The 1989 New York City Mayoral Election," *Journal of Politics* 57 (February 1995): 221.

11. Ibid.

12. Ibid., 223.

13. V. O. Key, Jr., *Southern Politics* (New York: Vintage Books, 1949), 5–12.

14. Carsey, 228.

15. Books and Prysby, 26. See also Wright, "Contextual Models of Electoral Behavior" and his "Community Structure and Voting in the South," *Public Opinion Quarterly* 40 (Summer 1976): 201–215.

16. William Keech, *The Impact of Negro Voting: The Role of the Vote in the Quest for Equality* (Chicago: Rand McNally, 1968), 1–23.

17. Books and Prysby, 27. See also Donald Matthews and James Prothro, *Negroes and the New Southern Politics* (New York: Harcourt, Brace, and World, 1966).

18. Ibid. See also Prysby, "Attitudes of Southern Democratic Party Activists Toward Jesse Jackson," 305–18.

19. Michael Giles and Kaenan Hertz, "Racial Threat and Partisan Identification," *American Political Science Review* 88 (June 1994): 317.

20. Jones, "Political Science and the Black Political Experience," 29.

21. Ibid., 31.

22. Robert Huckfeldt, *Politics in Context: Assumption and Conflict in Urban Neighborhoods* (New York: Agathan Press, 1986), 11.

23. Lawrence Bobo and Franklin Gilliam, Jr., "Race, Sociopolitical Participation, and Black Empowerment, "*American Political Science Review* 84 (June 1990): 377–94.

24. Cathy Cohen and Michael Dawson, "Neighborhood Poverty and African American Politics," *American Political Science Review* 87 (June 1993): 286–302.

25. Huckfeldt, 11.

26. Ibid.

27. Christopher Achen and W. Phillip Shively, *Cross-level Inference* (Chicago: University of Chicago Press, 1995), 7.

28. See Courtney Brown, *Serpents in the Sand: Essays on the Nonlinear Nature of Politics and Human Destiny* (Ann Arbor: University of Michigan Press, 1995), 5.

29. Ibid., 219–33. See also John Sprague, "Is There a Micro-Theory Consistent with Contextual Analysis?" In Elinor Ostron (ed.), *Strategies of Political Inquiry* (California: Sage, 1982); and his "On Warren Miller's Longest Footnote: The Vote in Context" in M. Kent Jennings and Thomas Mann (eds.), *Elections at Home and Abroad: Essays in Honor of Warren and Miller* (Ann Arbor: University of Michigan of Press, 1994), 202–34.

30. V. O. Key, Jr., *Southern Politics in State and Nation,* new edition (Knoxville: University of Tennessee Press, 1972). The chapter on suffrage is profound in its revelations about how white minority action changed the political context for African Americans.

31. See C. Vann Woodward, *The Strange Career of Jim Crow* 3rd rev. ed. (New York: Oxford University Press, 1974), 3–85.

32. Ibid.

33. V. O. Key, Jr. and Frank Munger, "Social Determinism and Electoral Decision: The Case of Indiana," in Eugene Burdick and Arthur Brodbeck (eds.), *American Voting Behavior* (Glencoe: Free Press, 1959), 295.

34. On the Free Men of Color see Walton, *Black Politics,* chap. 2.

35. Ibid., pp. 17–28.

36. Phyllis Field, *The Politics of Race in New York: The Struggle for Black Suffrage in the Civil War Era* (Ithaca: Cornell University Press, 1982), 19.

37. Donald G. Nieman, *Promises to Keep: African Americans and the Constitutional Order, 1776 to Present* (New York: Oxford University Press, 1991), 28.

38. Ibid., 20.

39. Ibid., 44–49.

40. Richard Valelly and Jeffrey Tulis, "On the Study of Race and Politics," *CLIO* 3 (Fall and Winter 1992/93): 4.

41. Judith Skhlar, "Redeeming American Political Theory," *American Political Science Review* 85 (March 1991): 3.

42. Ibid., 4.

43. John Hope Franklin, "Race and the Constitution in the Nineteenth Century," in Franklin and McNeil (eds.), *African Americans and the Living Constitution,* 22–23.

44. Ibid., 28.

45. John Hope Franklin, "The Moral Legacy of the Founding Fathers," reprinted in his *Race and History: Selected Essays 1938–1988* (Baton Rouge: Louisiana State University Press, 1990), 153–62.

46. Nieman, *Promises to Keep,* 9.

47. Gary Wills, *Lincoln at Gettysburg: The Words that Remade America* (New York: Touchstone Book, 1992), 147.

48. Ibid.

49. Ibid., 146.

50. For the states' right argument see Barry Goldwater, *The Conscience of a Conservative* (Kentucky: Victor Publishing, 1960), 24–37. On his feelings about focusing on race as a tool of political cleavage and polarization in the 1964 election see *With No Apologies: The Personal and Political Memoirs of Senator Barry M. Goldwater* (New York: Morrow, 1979), 180–181, 185.

51. Kevin Phillips, *The Emerging Republican Majority* (New York: Anchor Books, 1970).

52. Wayne Greenshaw, *Elephants in the Cottonfields: Ronald Reagan and the New Republican South* (New York: MacMillan, 1982), 62–69. See also John Saloma, *Ominous Politics: The New Conservative Labyrinth* (New York: Hill and Wang, 1984), and Peter Steinfels, *The Neo-Conservatives* (New York: Simon and Schuster, 1979).

53. Ibid.

54. Steven Lawson, *Running for Freedom: Civil Rights and Black Politics in America Since 1945* (Philadelphia: Temple University Press, 1991), 294.

55. William Schneider, "The November 4 Vote for President: What Did It Mean?" in Austin Ranney (ed.), *The American Elections of 1980* (Washington, DC: American Enterprise Institute, 1981), 261.

56. Ibid., 259.

57. Walter Dean Burnham, "The Reagan Heritage," in Gerald Pomper (ed.), *The Election of 1988: Reports and Interpretations* (New Jersey: Chatham House, 1989), 11.

58. Ibid., 12.

59. Ibid.

60. Shull, *The President and Civil Rights Policy* (New York: Greenwood, 1989), 196–7.

61. Lawson, *Running for Freedom,* 239.

62. Kathleen Hall Jamieson, *Dirty Politics* (New York: Oxford University Press, 1993), 134.

63. Hanes Walton, Jr., Roosevelt Green, Jr., Willie E. Johnson, and Kenneth Jordan, "The Civil Rights Regulatory Agenda of the Bush Administration," *The Urban League Review* 14 (Summer 1990): 7–15.

64. Ibid. Also Cheryl Miller and Hanes Walton, Jr., "Congressional Support of Civil Rights Public Policy: From Bipartisan to Partisan Convergence," *Congress and the Presidency* 21 (Spring 1994): 11–28.

65. W. Avon Drake and Robert Holsworth, "Electoral Politics, Affirmative Action, and the Supreme Court: The Case of Richmond v. Croson," *National Political Science Review* 2 (1990): 65–91.

66. Miller and Walton, "Congressional Support of Civil Rights Public Policy," 11–18.

67. Frank Parker, *Black Votes Count: Political Empowerment in Mississippi after 1965* (Chapel Hill: University of North Carolina Press, 1990), 185.

68. Walton, *When the Marching Stopped,* 170–74.

69. Ibid.

70. Ibid., 142–3.

71. Jeffrey Elliot, *Black Voices in American Politics* (New York: Harcourt, Brace, and Jovanovich, 1988), 14–144.

72. 73. Walton, Green, Johnson, and Jordan, "The Civil Rights Regulatory Agenda of the Bush Administration," 7–15.

73. William Rasberry, "A Double Disaster for EEOC," *Washington Post* 18 November 1991. And J. Clay Smith, Jr., "A Black Lawyer's Response to the Fairmont Papers," *Howard Law Journal* 7 (1983), pp. 195–225.

74. Saloma, *Ominous Politics,* 137.

75. Linda S. Lichter, "Who Speaks for Black America," *Public Opinion* 8: 47–70, and "Notes and Comments: The Talk of the Town," *The New Yorker* 1 August 1991, 21–22.

76. Harold M. Rose and Paula D. McClain, *Race, Place, and Risk: Black Homicide in Urban America* (Albany: State University of New York, 1990), 18–66.

77. Alan Simpson, "Atwater's Election as Howard University Trustee Sparks Dissension," *Washington Post* 23 February 1989.

78. Georgia A. Persons, "The Election of Gary Franks and the Ascendancy of the New Black Conservatives," in Georgia A. Persons, ed., *Dilemmas of Black Politics: Issues of Leadership and Strategy* (New York: HarperCollins, 1993), 194–208.

79. Smith, "A Black Lawyer's Response to the Fairmont Papers," 195–225.

80. Hanes Walton, Jr. and Daniel Brantley, "Black Southern Politics: A Look at the Tradition and the Future," in Hanes Walton, Jr., *Black Politics and Black Political Behavior: A Linkage Analysis* (Connecticut: Praeger, 1994), 296–7.

81. Ibid., 296. See also Hanes Walton, Jr., *The Native Son Presidential Candidate: The Carter Vote in Georgia* (New York: Praeger, 1992).

82. Lucius Barker and Mark Jones, *African Americans and the American Political System* 3rd ed. (Englewood Cliffs, New Jersey: Prentice-Hall, 1994), 347.

PART 2. METHODOLOGY

1. Achen and Shively, *Cross-Level Influence*, 219.

2. Ibid., 219–220.

3. Donald R. Matthews, "Political Science Research on Race Relations," in Irwin Katz and Patricia Gurin (eds.), *Race and the Social Sciences* (New York: Basic Books, 1969), 116.

4. Walton, Miller, and McCornick, "Race and Political Science," 145–74.

5. Walton and McCornick, "The Study of African American Politics as Social Danger," *National Political Science Review* 6 (1996).

6. Ibid.

7. See Donald Strong, "The Poll Tax: The Case of Texas," *American Political Science Review* 38 (August 1944): 693–709 and his "Rise of Negro Voting in Texas," *American Political Science Review* 42 (June 1948): 510–22. O. Douglas Weeks, "The White Primary," *American Political Science Review* 42 (June 1948): 500–509; Lester M. Salamon and Stephen Van Evera, "Fear, Apathy, and Discrimination: A Test of Three Explorations of Political Participation," *American Political Science Review* 67 (December 1973): 1288–1306, and Harold F. Gosnell, "Political Meetings in Chicago's Black Belt," *American Political Science Review* 28 (April 1934): 254–8.

8. African American historians have provided valuable clues into how the white dominated context have shaped African American political behavior. See Rayford Logan (ed.), *The Attitudes of the Southern White Press Toward Negro Suffrage, 1932–1940* (Washington, DC: Washington Foundation Publishers, 1940) and R. Grann Lloyd, *White Supremacy in the United States* (Washington, DC: Public Affairs Press, 1952).

9. Walton, *Invisible Politics*, 14–19.

10. Michael Dawson and Ernest Wilson, III, "Paradigms and Paradoxes: Political Science and African-American Politics" in William Crotty (ed.), *Political Science: Looking to the Future* vol. 1, (Illinois: Northwestern University Press, 1991), 198.

11. Donald Tryman, *Afro-American Mass Political Integration* (Washington, D.C.: University Press of America, 1982), 12–91.

12. Ibid.

13. Hanes Walton, Jr., Leslie McLemore, and and C. Vernon Gray, "Black Politics: The View from the Readers," *American Politics Quarterly* 1 (1973): 43–50.

14. Jones, "Political Science and the Black Political Experience," 36. Hanes Walton, Jr., "Black Political Thought: The Problem of Characterization," *Journal of Black Studies,* (Third Quarter 1970): 214–218. See also, Stuart Alan Clarke, "Liberalism and Black Political Thought," *National Political Science Review* 1 (1989): 5–14.

15. Smith, "A Black Lawyer's Response to the Fairmont Papers," 195–225.

16. Jones, 35.

17. Ibid., 34–35.

18. Ibid., 35.

19. Edward Carmines and James Stimson, *Issue Evolution: Race and the Transformation of American Politics* (Princeton: Princeton University Press, 1989), 44, 45. See Samuel DuBois

Cook, "Political Movements and Organizations," *Journal of Politics* (February 1964): 130–153.

20. Lisio, *Hoover, Blacks, and Lily-Whites,* xviii.

3. AFRICAN AMERICAN POLITICS: A CASE STUDY METHODOLOGICAL APPROACH

1. Robert K. Yin, *Case Study Research: Design and Methods* rev. ed. (Newbury Park: Sage Publications, 1989), 23.

2. Ibid., 20.

3. Ibid., 21.

4. For an analysis of another contextual revolution see Bess Beatty, *A Revolution Gone Backward: The Black Response to National Politics 1876–1896* (Connecticut: Greenwood Press, 1987).

5. See Matthews and Prothro, *Negroes and the New Southern Politics,* for the use of single case studies and the aggregation of their findings in an empirical and quantitative manner; see Harry Holloway, *The Politics of the Southern Negro: From Exclusion to Big City Organizations* (New York: Random House, 1969), for the use of single case studies and the aggregation of his findings in an qualitative manner. Neither book views the political context revolution as such, yet each work seeks to analyze the influence and impact of the local context.

6. See Alfred A. Moss, Jr., *The American Negro Academy: Voice of the Talented Tenth* (Baton Rouge: Louisiana State University Press, 1981), 1.

7. For a comprehensive and systematic bibliography of both the monographs and papers see *The American Negro Academy,* 308–10.

8. Ibid., 2.

9. These pioneering case studies in African American politics cry out for serious scholarly analysis. For the entire collection see Ernest Kaiser, (ed.), *The American Negro Academy: Occassional Papers 1–22* (New York: Arno Press and the New York Times, 1969).

10. See W. E. B. DuBois, (ed.), *Atlanta University Publications* Vol. 1–111 (New York: Octagon Books, 1968).

11. Luther P. Jackson, "Race and Suffrage in the South Since 1940," *New South* (June/July 1940); and Margaret Price, *The Negro Voter in the South* (Atlanta: Southern Regional Council, 1957); and her *The Negro and the Ballot in the South* (Atlanta: Southern Regional Council, 1959).

12. One well known case study was Charles V. Hamilton, *Minority Politics in Black Belt Alabama* (New York: McGraw-Hill, 1962). The other case studies in this series are: Allan Sindler, *Negro Protest and Local Politics in Durham, N.C.* (New York: McGraw-Hill, 1965); G. James Fleming, *An All-Negro Ticket in Baltimore* (New York: Holt, Rinehart, and Winston, 1969); William E. Wright, *Memphis Politics: A Study in Racial Bloc Voting* (New York: McGraw-Hill, 1960); Edward L. Pinney and Robert S. Friedman, *Political Leadership and the School Desegretation Crisis in Louisiana* (New York: McGraw-Hill, 1963); David Haygood, *The Purge that Failed: Tammy v. Powell* (New York: McGraw-Hill, 1960); and Jack L. Walker, *Sit-ins in Atlanta* (New York: McGraw-Hill, 1963).

13. See Janet Wells, "43 Blacks Win Elections in Three Southern States," *VEP News* (May 1969): 1–10.

14. See John Dean, *The Making of a Black Mayor* (Washington, D.C: Joint Center for Political Studies, 1973), 1.

15. Chandler Davidson, (ed.), *Minority Vote Dilution* (Washington, D.C.: Howard University Press, 1984). Thomas E. Cavaunagh and Lorin S. Foster, *Jesse Jackson's Campaign: The Primaries and Caucuses* (Washington, D.C.: Joint Center for Political Studies, 1984).

16. John Hope Franklin and Eleanor Holmes Norton, *Black Initiative and Governmental Responsibility* (Washington, D.C.: Joint Center for Political Studies, 1987).

17. Allan Sindler, *Negro Protest and Local Politics in Durham, D.C.* (New York: McGraw-Hill, 1965), ii. All the studies bore this statement.

18. Ibid.

19. Ibid.

20. G. James Fleming, *An All-Negro Ticket in Baltimore* (New York: Holt, Rinehart and Winston, 1960).

21. Sindler, *Negro Protest and Local Politics,* 1.

22. Charles V. Hamilton, *The Bench and the Ballot: Southern Federal Judges and Black Votes* (New York: Oxford University Press, 1973). Donald Strong, *Negroes, Ballots, and Judges: National Voting Rights Legislation in the Federal Courts* (Alabama: University of Alabama Press, 1958).

23. Aldon Morris, *The Origins of the Civil Rights Movement: Black Communities Organizing for Change* (New York: Free Press, 1984).

24. Charles Eagles, (ed.), *The Civil Rights Movement in America* (Jackson: University Press of Mississippi, 1986).

25. Clayborne Carson, *In Struggle: SNCC and the Black Awakening of the 1960s* (Cambridge: Harvard University Press, 1981).

26. Pinney and Friedman, *Political Leadership,* 31–32.

27. Sindler, *Negro Protest and Local Politics,* 22–26, and Walker, *Sit-ins in Atlanta,* 11–19.

28. Hamilton, *Minority Politics in Black Belt Alabama,* 4–28.

29. Fleming, *An All-Negro Ticket in Baltimore,* 2–14. See also his *Baltimore's Failure to Elect a Black Mayor in 1971* (Washington, D.C.: Joint Center for Political Studies, 1972).

30. Wright, *Memphis Politics,* 1.

31. Ibid., 1–2.

32. Walton, McLemore, Gray, "Black Politics," 203.

4. AFRICAN AMERICAN RACE RELATIONS POLITICS: THE FAILURE OF EMPIRICAL METHODOLOGY

1. See Samuel Dubois Cook, "Introduction: The American Liberal Democratic Tradition: The Black Revolution and Martin Luther King, Jr," in Hanes Walton, Jr., *The Political Philosophy of Martin Luther King, Jr.* (Connecticut: Greenwood Press, 1971), xxiv–xxv.

2. Ibid., xxvii.

3. Institute for Contemporary Studies, *The Fairmont Papers: Black Alternatives Conference* (San Francisco: Institute for Contemporary Studies, 1981), xi, 159–62.

4. Ibid., xii.

5. Ibid., 160.

6. Lichter, "Who Speaks for Black America," 47–70.

7. Patricia Gurin, Shirley Hatchett, James S. Jackson, *Hope and Independence: Blacks' Response to Electoral and Party Politics* (New York: Russell Sage, 1989), 262 n9.

8. Saloma, *Ominous Politics,* 64–89.

9. See Richard Morgan, *Disabling America: The "Rights" Industry in Our Time* (New York: Basic Books, 1984), 3.

10. Ibid.

11. Nathan Glazer, *The Limits of Social Policy* (New York: Basic Books, 1988) 3–74.

12. Charles Murray, *Losing Ground: American Social Policy, 1950–1980* (New York: Basic Books, 1984).

13. Parker, *Black Votes Count,* 11–13.

14. Abigail Thernstrom, *Whose Votes Count: Affirmative Action and Minority Voting Rights* (New York: Harvard University Press, 1987).

15. Abigail Thernstrom, "The Odd Evolution of the Voting Rights Act" *Public Interest* (Spring 1979): 49–76.

16. Robert Hucksfeld and Carol Kohfeld, *Race and the Decline of Class in American Politics* (Urbana: University of Illinois Press, 1989), and Edward Carmines and Janes Stevenson, *Issue Evolution* (Princeton: Princeton University Press, 1989). The argument was first floated in Robert Weissberg, "The Democratic Party and the Conflict over Racial Policy," in Benjamin Ginsberg and Alan Stone (eds.), *Do Elections Matter?* (New York: M. E. Sharpe, 1986), 204–20.

17. Hanes Walton, Jr., "Race Relations Courses in Negro Colleges," *The Negro Educational Review* 19 (October 1965): 123–32.

18. Walton, Miller, and McCornick, "Race and Political Science," 145–74.

19. Ibid.

20. Ibid.

21. For the premier work on race relations politics see Gunnar Mydral, *An American Dilemma* (New York: Harper and Row, 1944).

22. For an initial example of using traditional methodologies to deny African American their constitutional right to vote, see John C. Rose, "Negro Suffrage: The Constitutional Point of View," *American Political Science Review* (November 1906): 17–43.

23. See Walton, *Invisible Politics,* chap. 1.

24. Thomas Pettigrew and Denise Alston, *Tom Bradley's Campaigns for Governor: The Dilemma of Race and Politics* (Washington, D.C.: Joint Center for Political Studies, 1988).

25. Charles Henry, "Racial Factors in the 1982 California Gubernatorial Campaign: Why Bradley Lost," in Michael B. Preston, Lenneal J. Henderson, Jr., Paul Puryear, (eds.), *The New Black Politics: The Search for Political Power* 2d ed. (New York: Longman, 1987), 76–94.

26. Ibid., 76. Henry argues the role of race as the determining variable and makes a strong case in his analysis of the Democratic crossover vote. See 84–90. See also, "Tom Bradley's Defeat: The Impact of Racial Symbols on Political Campaigns," *The Black Scholar* (Fall 1982): 32–45.

27. Ibid., 76.

28. Asher Arian, Arthur S. Goldberg, John Mollenkopf, and Edward Rogowsky, *Changing New York City Politics* (New York: Rutledge, 1991), ix.

29. Ibid., xi.

30. Ibid., xii.

31. Ibid., 82.

32. Ibid., 192.

33. Ibid., 134.

34. Ibid., 186–196.

35. See Lucius J. Barker, *Our Time Has Come: A Delegate's Diary of Jesse Jackson's 1984 Presidential Campaign* (Urbana: University of Illinois Press, 1988), and *Blacks and the 1988 Democratic Convention* (Washington, D.C.: Joint Center for Political Studies, 1988).

36. T. H. Landess and R. M. Quinn, *Jesse Jackson and the Politics of Race* (Ottawa, IL: Jameson Books, 1985).

37. Bob Farr and Nancy Skelton, *Thunder in America: The Improbable Presidential Campaign of Jesse Jackson* (Texas: Texas Monthly Press, 1986).

38. Sheila D. Collins, *The Rainbow Challenge: The Jackson Campaign and the Future of U.S. Politics* (New York: Monthly Review Press, 1986).

39. Adolph L. Reed, Jr., *The Jesse Jackson Phenomenon* (New York: Yale University Press, 1985).

40. Huckfeld and Kohfeld, *Race and the Decline of Class,* x.

41. Robert Weissberg, "The Democratic Party and the Conflict over Racial Policy," in Benjamin Ginsberg and Alan Stone (eds.), *Do Elections Matter?* 2d ed. (New York: M. E. Sharpe, 1991). This paper also appears in the first edition published in 1986.

42. Ibid. See also Lorenzo Morris (ed.), *The Social and Political Implications of the 1984 Jesse Jackson Presidential Campaign* (New York: Praeger, 1989) and Ronald W. Walters and Lucius Barker, (eds.), *Jesse Jackson's 1984 Presidential Campaign* (Urbana: University of Illinois Press, 1989).

43. Ibid. and Weissberg, "The Democratic Party," 150–70.

44. Ibid., 1, 2.

45. Ibid., 128.

46. Ibid., 139.

47. On this technique of merely asserting rather than building the argument on empirical data, see ibid., x-xi. See also Hanes Walton, Jr., "Review of Race and the Decline of Class in American Politics," in *Journal of American History* (December 1990): 1097–8. For an excellent critique see Adolph Reed, Jr., "Race and the Disruption of the New Deal Coalition: Book Review," *Urban Affairs Quarterly* (December 1991): 326–33. And Adolph Reed, Jr. and Julian Bond, "Equality: Why We Can't Wait," *The Nation* (9 December 1991): 733–737.

47. For a review of these books see Hanes Walton, Jr. and Daniel Brantley, "Black Southern Politics: A Look at the Tradition and the Future" in Walton (ed.), *Black Politics and Black Political Behavior: A Linkage Analysis* (Connecticut: Praeger, 1994), 283–5.

48. Chandler Davidson, "The Voting Rights Act: A Brief History," in Bernard Grofman and Chandler Davidson, (eds.), *Controversies in Minority Voting: The Voting Rights Act in Perspective,* (Washington, D.C.: Brookings Institution, 1990), 21. See also *South Carolina v. Katzenbach,* 383 U.S. 301 (1966).

49. Grofman and Davidson, *Controversies in Minority Voting,* 1.

50. Ibid., 2.

51. Davidson, "The Voting Rights Act," 39.

52. Ibid.

53. Thermstrom, *Whose Votes Count,* 204–312.

54. See Pamela S. Karlan and Peyton McCrary, "Book Review: Without Fear and Without Research: Abigail Thernstrom on the Voting Rights Act," *Journal of Law and Politics* 4 (Spring 1988): 751–77. For another critique, see J. Morgan Kousser, "The Voting Rights Act and the Two Reconstructions," *Journal of Law and Politics* 4 (Spring 1988): 160–76.

55. Hugh Davis Graham, "Voting Rights and the American Regulatory State," *Journal of Law and Politics* 4 (Spring 1988): 177–96.

56. See Richard Engstrom and Michael McDonald, "Quantitative Evidence in Vote Dilution Litigation: Political Participation and Polarized Voting," *Urban Lawyer* 17 (Summer 1985): 371–77 and their "Quantitative Evidence in Vote Dilution Litigation, Part II: Minority Coalition and Multivariate Analysis," *Urban Lawyer* 19 (Winter 1987): 65–75. For the opposite argument, see John K. Wildgen, "Adding Thornburg to the Thicket: The Ecological Fallacy and Parameter Control in Vote Dilution Cases," *Urban Lawyer* 20 (Winter 1988): 155–73. For a rejoinder, see Richard Engstrom and Michael McDonald, "Definitions, Measurements, and Statistics: Weeding Wildgen's Thicket," *Urban Lawyer* 20 (Winter 1988): 174–91.

57. Parker, *Black Votes Count.*

58. Graham, "Voting Rights."

59. Thomas Sowell, *Civil Rights: Rhetoric or Reality* (New York: Morrow, 1984).

60. Murray, *Losing Ground.*

61. Hugh Davis Graham, *The Civil Rights Era: Origins and Development of National Policy, 1960–1972* (New York: Oxford University Press, 1990), 123–367.

62. Ibid.

63. Ibid.

64. For new procedures and techniques, see Gary King, *Unifying Political Methodology:*

The Likelihood Theory of Statistical Inference (Cambridge: Cambridge University Press, 1989). And for a field that is usually not covered, see Gary King and Lynn Ragsdale, *The Elusive Executive: Discovering Statistical Patterns in the Presidency* (Washington D.C.: Congressional Quarterly Press, 1988).

PART 3. CONSTITUTIONALISM

1. Barbara Luck Graham, "Executive Authority, Constitutional Interpretation, and Civil Rights," *National Political Science Review* 1 (1989): 114–20. In the same volume, see William J. Daniels, "The Constitution, The Supreme Court, and Racism: Compromises on the Way to Democracy," 126–30, and Twiley Barker and Michael Combs, "Civil Rights and Liberties in the First Term of the Rehnquist Court: The Quest for Doctrine and Votes," 31–57.

2. Ibid.

3. Ibid. See also, Michael Combs and John Gruhl, (eds.), *Affirmative Action: Theory and Analysis and Prospects* (North Carolina: McFarland, 1986).

4. Edwin Meese, III, "A Jurisprudence of Original Intention," in Robert DiClerico and Allan Hammock (eds.), *Points of View: Readings in American Government and Politics* 5th ed. (New York: McGraw-Hill, 1992), 262.

5. Ibid., 265.

6. Irving Kaufman, "What Did the Founding Fathers Intend?" in *Points of View,* 267.

7. Ibid., 266.

8. Matthew Holden, Jr., "Race and Constitutional Change in the Twentieth Century: The Role of the Executives," in Franklin and McNeil (eds.), *African American*s and the Living Constitution, 118–99. See also Irvin Washington (ed.), *Black Judges on Justice* (New York: The New Press, 1995).

9. Ibid, 118.

10. Nieman, *Promises To Keep,* 65–91.

11. Walton, *Black Politics,* 175.

12. Ibid.

13. Drake and Holsworth, *op. cit.,* 74–84.

14. Graham, "Executive Authority," 116.

15. Ibid.

16. Mailgram from J. Clay Smith, Jr., July 10, 1985, pp. 1–2. Copy in author's possession.

17. See Abigail Thernstrom, *Whose Votes Count* and Hugh Davis Graham, "Voting Rights and the American Regulatory State," in Grofman and Davidson, *Controversies in Minority Voting,* 177–96.

18. For a critique of these limited theories of legislative representation see Lani Guinier, *The Tyranny of the Majority* (New York: Free Press, 1993).

19. Mailgram, and see also letter, J. Clay Smith, Jr. to Jay A. Parker, President Lincoln Institute for Research and Education (August 30, 1985), 1. The author would like to thank Professor Clay Smith for the correspondence and the mailgram.

20. Ibid.

21. Ibid.

5. AFRICAN AMERICAN POLITICS AND THE CONSTITUTION: NEOCONSERVATIVE, NEOLIBERAL, AND AFRICAN AMERICAN CONSERVATIVE THEORIES OF CONSTITUTIONAL INEQUALITY

1. Roy L. Brooks, *Rethinking the American Race Problem* (Berkeley: University of California Press, 1990), 150–173.

2. Kenneth Prewitt, *Institutional Racism in America* (Englewood Cliffs, NJ: Prentice Hall, 1970), 24, 50, 81, 110, 117.

3. On the neoconservatives see Steinfels, *The Neo-Conservatives* and Saloma, *Ominous Politics.* On the neoliberals, see Randall Rothenberg, *The Neoliberals: Creation of the New American Politics* (New York: Simon and Schuster, 1984). On the African American conservatives, see Lee Daniels, "The New Black Conservatives," *New York Times* Magazine (4 October 1981), 20–24 and Hanes Walton, Jr., *When the Marching Stopped,* 170–74. For a historical overview see Hanes Walton, Jr., "Blacks and Conservative Political Movements," in Henderson, *Black Political Life,* 56–65.

4. Ibid.

5. Nathan Glazer, *Affirmative Discrimination: Ethnic Inequality and Public Policy* (New York: Basic Books, 1975), 23–131.

6. Ibid., 4–5.

7. Ibid., 31.

8. Ibid., 67–68.

9. Ibid., 197.

10. Ibid., 196.

11. Ibid.

12. Thernstrom, *Whose Votes Count,* 204–319.

13. See Walton, *When the Marching Stopped,* 122–175.

14. Graham, *The Civil Rights Era,* 370.

15. Ibid., 461.

16. Ibid., 370.

17. Ibid.

18. Ibid., 189.

19. Ibid., 235.

20. Graham, "Voting Rights," in Grofman and Davidson, *Controversies in Minority Voting,* 184, 188.

21. Ibid., 188.

22. Ibid.

23. Alex Willingham, "Voting Policy and Voter Participation: The Legacy of the 1980s" *Trotter Review* (Fall 1992): 25.

24. Sowell, *Civil Rights,* 15.

25. Ibid., 16.

26. Ibid., 16.

27. Ibid., 16–35.

28. Ibid., 73.

29. Ibid., 86.

30. Ibid., 90.

31. Ibid., 118.

32. Ibid., 90.

33. Ibid., 14.

PART 4. CULTURE

1. Heinz Eulau, *The Behavioral Persuasion in Politics* (New York: Random House, 1963), 75.

2. Ibid., 73.

3. Nieman, *Promises to Keep,* 110–13.

4. Institute for Contemporary Studies, *The Fairmont Papers,* 18.

5. Aaron Wildavsky, "Choosing Preferences by Constructing Institutions: A Cultural Theory of Preference Formation," in Arthur Asa Berger (ed.), *Political Culture and Public Opinion* (New Brunswick: Transaction Publishers, 1989), 42 n10. Also see his "Industrial Politics in American Political Cultures," in Charles E. Barfield and William A. Schambra, (eds.), *The Politics of Industrial Policy* (Washington, DC: American Enterprise Institute, 1986).

6. Ibid., and 34–35.

7. Ibid., 42.

8. Ibid.

9. Ibid.

10. Walton, *Invisible Politics,* 27–28.

11. Ibid.

12. Richard Allen, Michael C. Dawson, Ronald Brown, "A Schema-Based Approach to Modeling an African-American Racial Belief-System," *American Political Science Review* 42 (June 1989): 420–42. And their "Racial Belief Systems, Religious Guidance, and African-American Political Participation," in *National Political Science Review* 2 (1990): 22–44.

13. Robert C. Smith and Richard Seltzer, *Race, Class, and Culture: A Study in Afro-American Mass Opinion* (Albany: State University of New York Press, 1992).

14. William E. Cross, Jr., *Shades of Black: Diversity in African-American Identity* (Philadelphia: Temple University Press, 1991), 93.

15. Ibid., 121.

16. Ibid.

17. Ibid., 154.

18. Ibid., 152.

19. Ibid.

20. See Martin Kilson, "The Black Experience at Harvard," *New York Times* Magazine (2 September 1973) and his "Political Studies of American Negroes in the Twentieth Century," in Martin Kilson and Robert I. Rothberg (eds.), *The African Dream: Interpretive Essays* (Cambridge: Harvard University Press, 1976), 459–84. In that article he claimed: "This politicization of black ethnicity had eluded both the client and civil rights leadership in the years between the two world wars because of the typical Negro's lack of a positive self-image."

6. AFRICAN AMERICAN POLITICAL CULTURE: THE MORAL VOICE AND PERSPECTIVE IN THE RECENT URBAN RIOTS

1. Lawrence D. Bobo, James J. Johnson, Jr., Melvin L. Oliver, James Sidanium, Camille Zubrinsky, "Public Opinion Before and After a Spring of Discontent: A Preliminary Report on the 1992 Los Angeles County Social Survey," (Los Angeles: UCLA Center for the Study of Urban Poverty Occassional Working Paper, vol. 3, no. 1 (September 1992), 3. The author thanks Professor Michael Dawson, Department of Political Science, University of Chicago, for a copy of the paper.

2. James C. Scott, *Domination and the Art of Resistance: Hidden Transcripts* (New Haven: Yale University Press, 1990), 1–44.

3. For the political science literature, see Abraham N. Miller, Louis H. Bolce, and Mark Hallingan, "The J-Curve Theory and the Black Urban Riots: An Empirical Test of Progressive Relative Depriviation Theory," *American Political Science Review* 71 (September 1977): 964–82; Manus Midlarsky, "Analyzing Diffusion and Contagion Effects: The Urban Disorder of the 1960s," *American Political Science Review* 72 (December 1978): 1996–1008; Joel Lieske, "The Conditions of Racial Violence in American Cities: A Developmental Synthesis," *American Political Science Review* 72 (December 1978): 1324–40; Robert Fogelson, "White on Black: A Critique of the McCone Commission Report on the Los Angeles Political Riots,"

Political Science Quarterly (September 1967): 337–67 and his "From Resentment to Confrontation: The Police, the Negro, and the Outbreak of the Nineteen-Sixties Riots," *Political Science Quarterly,* (June 1960): 217–47.

4. Michael Lipsky, "Protest as a Political Resource," *American Political Science Review* 62 (December 1968): 1114–58 and his *Protest in City Politics* (Chicago: Rand McNally, 1969).

5. James Button, *Black Violence: Political Impact of the 1960s Riots* (Princeton: Princeton University Press, 1978). For an opposing point of view see Bruce Porter and Marvin Dunn, *The Miami Riot of 1980: Crossing the Bounds* (Lexington, Mass: Lexington Books, 1984).

6. Ibid., 161, 160.

7. Ibid., 161.

8. Walton, Miller, and McCormick, "Race and Political Science," 145–74.

9. For such a study, see Smith and Seltzer, *Race, Class, and Culture* p. 1–20; for other studies on political attitudes, see Howard Schuman and Shirley Hatchett, *Black Racial Attitudes: Trends and Complexities* (Ann Arbor: University of Michigan, 1974); Howard Schuman, Charlotte C. Steeh, and Laurence Bobo, *Racial Attitudes in America: Trends and Interpretations* (Cambridge: Harvard University Press, 1988), and Richard Apostel, et. al., *The Anatomy of Racial Attitudes* (Berkeley: University of California Press, 1983).

10. Ibid., 1–20.

11. Allen, Dawson, and Brown, "A Schema-Based Approach," 420–42.

12. For such misguided approaches, see James R. Kluggel and Eliot Smith, *Beliefs About Inequality* (New York: Aldine deGruyter, 1986), and Lee Sigelman and Susan Welch, *Black Americans' Views of Racial Inequality: The Dream Deferred* (New York: Cambridge University Press, 1991).

13. Sigelman and Welch, *Black Americans' Views,* 10–164.

14. Bobo, Johnson, Oliver, Sidanium, Zubrinsky, "Public Opinion," 1.

15. Ibid.

16. Joint Center for Political and Economic Studies, "HBO/Joint Center Poll: Summary of Findings," (Washington, DC: Joint Center for Political and Economic Studies, 8 July 1982).

17. Ibid.

18. See Herbert Hyman, *Secondary Analysis of Sample Surveys: Principles, Procedures, and Potentialities* (New York: John Wiley, 1972), and K. Jill Kiecolt and Laura E. Nathan, *Secondary Analysis of Survey Data* (Beverly Hills: Sage, 1985). Jean Converse, *Survey Research in the United States: Roots and Emergence* (Berkeley: University of California Press, 1987).

19. Joint Center for Political and Economic Studies, "HBO/Joint Center Poll," 3.

20. Converse, *Survey Research in the United States.*

21. Bobo, Johnson, Oliver, Sidanium, Zubrinsky, "Public Opinion," 7.

22. Ibid., 8.

23. Ibid., 6.

24. Ibid., 8.

25. Ibid., 7.

26. Cross, *Shades of Black.*

27. Thomas E. McCollough, *The Moral Imagination and Public Life: Raising the Ethical Question* (New Jersey: Chatham House, 1991), 6–7.

28. Charles Henry, *Culture and African American Politics* (Bloomington: Indiana University Press, 1990), 61.

29. Ibid., 62.

30. David Howard-Pitney, *The Afro-American Jeremiad: Appeals for Justice in America* (Philadelphia: Temple University Press, 1990), 187.

31. McCollough, *The Moral Imagination and Public Life,* 55–56.

32. Glenn Tinder, *Political Thinking: The Perennial Questions* 5th ed. (New York: HarperCollins, 1991), 185.

33. Scott, *Domination and the Art of Resistance,* 4.

34. Ibid., 8.

35. Ibid., 6.

PART 5. SOCIALIZATION

1. Walton, *Invisible Politics,* 47–50.

2. Laura Reese and Ronald Brown, "The Effects of Religious Messages on Racial Identity and System Blame Among African Americans," *Journal of Politics* 57 (February 1995): 38.

3. Ibid., 24–43.

4. Samuel DuBois Cook, "Introduction: The Politics of the Success of Failure," in Hanes Walton, Jr., *Black Political Parties: An Historical and Political Analysis* (New York: Free Press, 1972), 3.

5. Books and Prysby, *Political Behavior and the Local Context,* 12.

6. Ibid.

7. AFRICAN AMERICAN POLITICAL SOCIALIZATION: THE PROTEST RESIGNATIONS OF COUNCILPERSONS JEROME WOODY AND RENE BAKER

1. See Walton, *Invisible Politics,* 43–53. For a look at the concept of political socialization, see Herbert Hyman, *Political Socialization* (New York: Free Press, 1959) and M. Kent Jennings, *Generations and Politics* (Princeton: Princeton University Press, 1981). For a look at another subcultural community see F. Chris Garcia, *Political Socialization of Chicano Children* (New York: Praeger, 1973).

2. Ibid., 47.

3. Ibid.

4. Aldon Morris, Shirley Hatchett, and Ronald Brown, "The Civil Rights Movement and Black Political Socialization" in R. S. Sigel (ed.), *Political Learning in Adulthood* (Chicago: University of Chicago Press, 1989), 273.

5. Ibid., 176.

6. Ibid., 277.

7. Ibid., 278, 279.

8. Ibid., 282.

9. Ibid., 284.

10. Ibid., 300.

11. See Hanes Walton, Jr., "Review: W. E. B. DuBois, Biography of a Race 1868–1919," *Journal of Negro Education* 63 (Fall 1994): 675–76.

12. Gilbert Ware, *William Hastie: Grace Under Pressure* (New York: Oxford University Press, 1984). For a pioneering discussion of Judge Hastie's protest resignation see Matthew Holden, Jr., "Race and Constitutional Change in the Twentieth Century," in Franklin and McNeil (eds.), *African Americans and the Living Constitution,* 134–5.

13. Jean Satterthwaite, "Unhappy with Committee Assignment: Woody Says he will Resign Council," *Claxton Enterprise,* 7 February 1985 and "Baker Resigns City Council Seat; Members Vote 5–1 to Accept Councilwoman, Decision, Call Election," *Claxton Enterprise,* 13 February 1992. Laura Milner, "Woman Quits Claxton City Council Post: Baker Levels Charges of Racism Against Mayor, Councilmen," *Savannah Morning News and Evening Press,* 6

February 1992. While the Savannah paper is a daily, with a morning and evening edition, the *Claxton Enterprise* is a weekly which comes out every Thursday and averages about 8 to 12 pages. The *Enterprise* gives very limited coverage to the African American community.

14. We chose the starting date of 1979 for our content analysis of the *Claxton Enterprise* because this was just prior to the beginning of the Reagan-Bush era. It also coincided with the first serious electoral challenge that the incumbent mayor had faced since he was first elected to office in 1969. Mitchell Peace, "Councilman Challenges Mayor," *Claxton Enterprise,* 8 November 1979.

15. "Group to File County Reapportionment Suit: Evans County, Claxton, Hagan Named in Action Charging Racial Discrimination," *Claxton Enterprise,* 4 August 1983; "Board of Education Members Named in Reapportionment Suit," *Claxton Enterprise,* 11 August 1983; Mitchell Peace, "Reapportionment Suit Update: County Commissioners, City Official Huddle with Attorneys To Map Courses of Action," *Claxton Enterprise,* 8 September 1983; Peace, "City Gets Group's Redistricting Proposal," *Claxton Enterprise,* 29 September 1983; Mitchell Peace, "Redistricting Plan Rejected; Clerk Calls Council Elections," *Claxton Enterprise,* 3 November 1983. Also see the suit that evolved as a result of the litigation: *Concerned Citizens for Better Government for Evans County vs. DeLoach,* No. CU3–343 (S.D. Ga., 13 January 1984). See also *Woody v. Evans County Board of Commissioners* No. CU692–073 (S.D. Ga., 7 December 1992).

16. See V. O. Key, Jr., *Southern Politics* (New York: Vintage Books, 1949).

17. Mitchell Peace, "City Borrows $126,000 to Pay Creditors," *Claxton Enterprise,* 2 August 1979. The council meeting revealed that the city needed $150,000, but the bank lent only $126,000.

18. "Behind on Payments: Claxton Still in Debt After Discussion," *Claxton Enterprise,* 18 September 1980.

19. "Seems Like Old Times: Claxton Gaining on City Debt," *Claxton Enterprise,* 9 April 1981.

20. "Audit Explained to Council," *Claxton Enterprise,* 24 February 1983.

21. Dal Cannady, "Council Delays Committees, Appointees," *Claxton Enterprise,* 9 January 1992; and Donna D'Ambrosio, "City Council Hears Proposal for 1993 Fiscal Budget," *Claxton Enterprise,* 5 June 1993.

22. D'Ambrosio, "City Council Hears Proposal."

23. Mitchell Peace, "Grand Jury Action Not Expected on GBI's Probe of City Voting," *Claxton Enterprise,* 13 December 1979.

24. "DA Asks for Full Inquiry into Claxton City Voting," *Claxton Enterprise,* 27 December 1979. See also "GBI Probe Ends: Results Not Known," *Claxton Enterprise,* 17 January 1980.

25. Donna D'Ambrosio, "City Council Learns City Elections Fairly Conducted," *Claxton Enterprise,* 6 June 1992.

26. Mitchell Peace, "Report Critical of City's Recent Grant Application," *Claxton Enterprise,* 4 June 1987. See also "State Nixes Block Grant for Claxton," *Claxton Enterprise,* 23 April 1987.

27. Monty Cagle, "Will Annexation End Claxton's Stagnation," *Claxton Enterprise,* 19 March 1981. See also "Evans Blacks Concerned about Possible Annexation," *Claxton Enterprise,* 30 April 1981.

28. Misty McPherson, "Problems Apparent within City Council," *Claxton Enterprise,* 6 August 1992.

29. "Royal Protests Remarks on Attendance Record," *Claxton Enterprise,* 5 February 1992, and "Two Council Members Air Complaint about Committee Post Assignments," *Claxton Enterprise,* 30 January 1992. See also Scott Denham, "Tempers Flare at Monday City Council Meeting," *Claxton Enterprise,* 23 March 1989.

30. Mitchell Peace, "Mayor's Vote Gives OK to Councilman's Contract," *Claxton Enter-*

prise, 20 July 1989 and his "Claxton Council Members Overturn Mayor's Decision on Goode St. Work," *Claxton Enterprise,* 27 July 1989.

31. "Klan Seeking Parade Permit; City Council Tables," *Claxton Enterprise,* 21 June 1984; "Klan's Claxton Visit Uneventful," *Claxton Enterprise,* 5 July 1984.

32. Interview with Mayor Perry DeLoach, Claxton, Georgia, 3 February 1995.

33. Ibid.

34. Tom Watson, "Blacks Say Racism is a Claxton Tradition," *USA Today,* 7 December 1994.

35. Monty Cagle, "Claxton City Council, Housing Authority Vow to Find New Low Rent Project Site," *Claxton Enterprise,* 17 April 1980. See also "City No Longer Eligible for UDAG Funds," *Claxton Enterprise,* 1 May 1980; Monty Cagle, "Financial Discussion Bows To Housing Project Argument," *Claxton Enterprise,* 1980; Monty Cagle, "Court Rules in Favor of Housing Authority," *Claxton Enterprise,* 26 June 1980; Monty Cagle, "Council Moves to Block Housing with Rezoning Request," *Claxton Enterprise,* 26 June 1980; "Claxton Could Lose Federal Funds," *Claxton Enterprise,* 24 April 1980; "Claxton to Lose UDAG Eligibility?" *Claxton Enterprise,* 24 April 1980.

36. "Building Permit Utilities at Issue: Housing Authority Takes City to Court," *Claxton Enterprise,* 31 July 1980.

37. "Housing Authority Wins Back Permit," *Claxton Enterprise,* 21 August 1980. "Council Votes to Appeal Building Permit Verdict," *Claxton Enterprise,* 11 September 1980.

38. "Blacks Say Council Action 'Slanderous'," *Claxton Enterprise,* 8 November 1980; "Suits Cost City over $5,000," *Claxton Enterprise,* 11 September 1980.

39. "City's Redistricting Plan May be in Trouble," *Claxton Enterprise,* 29 September 1983; Mitchell Peace, "Redistricting Plan Rejected: Clerk Calls Council Elections," *Claxton Enterprise,* 3 November 1983.

40. "Consideration Sought for Original Plan: City Files Response to Redistricting," *Claxton Enterprise,* 23 November 1983.

41. "City Expects Settlement on Redistricting Proposal," *Claxton Enterprise,* 19 July 1984.

42. "Woody 'Forces' Vote on Question: Council Rejects MLK Holiday Request," *Claxton Enterprise,* 10 April 1986.

43. "Editorial: Poor Judgement?," *Claxton Enterprise,* 10 April 1986.

44. "City Rejects Request for MLK Drive: Petitions Seek Change in Name of Church Street," *Claxton Enterprise,* 5 March 1992. See also Misty McPherson, "Controversy Surrounds Renaming of Long Street in Honor of Late Martin Luther King," *Claxton Enterprise,* 30 July 1992. Laura Milner, "Claxton Faces New Dispute on King Name," *Savannah Morning News and Evening Press,* 10 March 1992.

45. Ibid.

46. Interview with Councilman Jerome Woody, Claxton, Georgia, 6 February 1995.

47. Satterthwaite, "Unhappy with Committee Assignments," *Claxton Enterprise,* 7 February 1985 and "Two Council Members Air Complaint," *Claxton Enterprise,* 30 January 1992.

48. Tom Zoellner, "Claxton Town Clerk Given New Powers: Some on Council Protest Vote in Suprise Resolution," *Savannah Morning News Evening Press,* 7 February 1995.

49. "Two Council Members Air Complaint," *Claxton Enterprise,* 30 January 1992.

50. Ibid.

51. Section B of Article II of the Claxton City Charter says: "Ordinances shall be proposed and read at a regular meeting of the Council and shall not be passed until the next regular meeting."

52. In Thunderbolt and Athens, Georgia, similar tactics were employed. See Walton, *Invisible Politics,* 193–208.

53. "Royal Protests Remark on Attendance Record," *Claxton Enterprise,* 6 February 1992; Misty McPherson, "Problem Apparent Within City Council," *Claxton Enterprise,* 5 August

1992; Scott Denham, "Tempers Flare at Monday City Council Meeting," *Claxton Enterprise*, 23 March 1989.

54. For the Andrew Young cartoon see *Claxton Enterprise*, 4 May 1989. It suggested that Young was always out of town. The Jesse Jackson cartoon suggested that he was controlling the Democratic party. For additional Jackson cartoons see the *Claxton Enterprise* of 24 March 1988, 31 March 1988, and 21 July 1988.

55. Bobby Beecher, "President Bush Will Feel Patrick Buchanan's Heat," *Claxton Enterprise*, 19 December 1991.

56. See Bobby Beecher, "Black-on-Black Violence is Hard to Understand," *Claxton Enterprise*, 25 December 1991; his "Uncle Sam Too Black for Racial Discord," *Claxton Enterprise*, 27 February 1992; his "Justice Department's Action is Another Slap in the Face," *Claxton Enterprise*, 26 March 1992; his "Georgia Raped During Reapportionment," *Claxton Enterprise*, 9 April 1992; his "America Needs God—Not Government," *Claxton Enterprise*, 14 May 1992; his "Presidential Candidate Clinton," *Claxton Enterprise*, 2 July 1992; his "A Clinton Supreme Court is Reason Enough to Vote For Bush," *Claxton Enterprise*, 13 August 1992; his "Coerced Integration Has Hurt More Than Helped Race Relations," *Claxton Enterprise*, 20 August 1992; and his "Blacks Need New Leadership," *Claxton Enterprise*, 11 March 1993.

57. "Banquet Features CSRA's First Elected Black Mayor," *Claxton Enterprise*, 18 March 1982. When we interviewed Councilman Woody, he was in the process of arranging a similar event in observance of Black History Month and was experiencing difficulty with the *Claxton Enterprise* to adequately publicize the event.

58. "Rev. Jackson's Wife Visits Claxton," *Claxton Enterprise*, 15 March 1984.

59. Richard Sellers, "Candidates Absent at Voters' Seminar," *Claxton Enterprise*, 1 December 1983.

60. "Vote Drive Sponsored by Black Groups," *Claxton Enterprise*, 26 April 1982; "Group to File County Reapportionment Suit," *Claxton Enterprise*, 4 August 1983.

61. "NAACP, School Systems Going to Court September 12," *Claxton Enterprise*, 23 June 1983; "Board of Education Members Named in Reapportionment Suit," *Claxton Enterprise*, 1 September 1983; "Evans School System in Court in Savannah," *Claxton Enterprise*, 10 November 1983; Richard Sellers, "Judge Now to Decide on Evidence: NAACP School Discrimination Suit Drawing to a Close," *Claxton Enterprise*, 19 January 1984; Richard Sellers, "Board Gets Settlement Proposal From 'Concerned Citizens' Group," *Claxton Enterprise*, 8 March 1984; "Court Rules Evans School System, Others Did Not Discriminate Against Black Kids," *Claxton Enterprise*, 5 July 1984; "School System Responds to NAACP Survey," *Claxton Enterprise*, 9 January 1986; "NAACP Wants More Black Teachers Hired: Dual Queens, Official Custom Abolished," *Claxton Enterprise*, 10 April 1986; Mitchell Peace, "NAACP Charges School System 'Re-segregating' Classes Here," *Claxton Enterprise*, 15 June 1989.

62. "Judge Signs Claxton's Redistricting Plan," *Claxton Enterprise*, 8 August 1984. See also *Woody v. Evans County Board of Commission.*

63. "City Preparing for Election at City Hall," *Claxton Enterprise*, 23 August 1984; "Freeport, Five City Council Post on December Ballot," *Claxton Enterprise*, 21 November 1984; Jean Sattherwaite, "Claxton Voters Get Ready for December City Elections," *Claxton Enterprise*, 29 November 1984; "City Ready for Elections," *Claxton Enterprise*, 6 December 1984; and "City Gives Big 'Yes' To Freeport: Woody, Harper Win Only Contested Race," *Claxton Enterprise*, 13 December 1984.

64. "Renee Baker Defeats Mary Lee Harper in City Election: Others Return to Office Without Opposition," *Claxton Enterprise*, 12 December 1985. For more on Ms. Baker see "Renee Baker Graduate from UGA Bank Operations School," *Claxton Enterprise*, 5 November 1987.

65. "Six Candidates Now Qualified for City Council Elections," *Claxton Enterprise,* 6 November 1986; "City Voters to Elect Four Council Members December 4," *Claxton Enterprise,* 27 November 1986; "Woody Defeated, Incumbents Win," *Claxton Enterprise,* 11 December 1986; "Councilman Recognized," *Claxton Enterprise,* 18 December 1986.

66. Satterthwaite, "Unhappy with Committee Assignments."

67. Ibid.

68. Ibid.

69. Interview with former Councilwoman Renee Baker, Claxton, Georgia, 5 February 1995.

70. "Baker Resigns City Council Seat; Members Vote 5–1 to Accept Councilwoman Decision, Call Elections," *Claxton Enterprise,* 13 February 1992 and "Plans Okayed for Election on March 19," *Claxton Enterprise,* 13 February 1992. Laura Milner, "Woman Quit Claxton City Council Position," *Savannah Morning News* and *Evening Press,* 6 February 1992.

71. See Robert Sherrill, *Gothic Politics in the Deep South: Stars of the New Confederacy* (New York: Grossman, 1968).

72. The City Charter of Claxton, Georgia, page CH-3. The City Clerk provided us with a xeroxed copy.

73. Interview with former Councilwoman Renee Baker, Claxton, Georgia, 5 February 1995.

74. Misty McPherson, "Problems Apparent within City Council," *Claxton Enterprise,* 5 August 1992.

75. Ibid.

76. Hanes Walton, Jr., "The Political Use of Absentee Ballots in a Rural Black Belt County: Dr. Merolyn Stewart-Gaulden's Election Campaign for Taliaferro County School Superintendent," in his *Black Politics and Black Political Behavior,* 178–87. For profound insights into African American politics in another small rural backwater township in Mississippi see Minion K. C. Morrison, *Black Political Mobilization: Leadership, Power, and Mass Behavior* (Albany: State University of New York Press, 1987).

77. Walton, *The Native Son Presidential Candidate,* 121–60.

78. Another pertinent example of protest resignation by an African American woman is that of Ruby Martin in the first Nixon administration. When Nixon won in 1968, Martin was director of the office of civil rights in the office of education in Health, Education, and Welfare (HEW). With Nixon's appointment of Robert Finch as head of HEW came a slowdown in desegregation enforcement. Although Martin resisted the new approach, she eventually resigned in protest, saying she could be more effective on the outside, where she staged protest demonstrations at the Justice Department and wrote exposés for the Washington Think Tank. See Leon Panetta and Peter Gall, *Bring Us Together: The Nixon Team and the Civil Rights Retreat* (Philadelphia: J. B. Lippincott, 1984), 81.

PART 6. PARTICIPATION

1. Lawson, *Running for Freedom,* 207, 208, 209.

2. Lorn Foster, (ed.), *The Voting Rights Act: Consequences and Implications* (New York: Praeger Publishers, 1985). Dianne Pinderhughes, "Legal Strategies for Voting Rights: Political Science and the Law," *Howard Law Journal* 28 (1985): 515–40. Bernard Grofman and Chandler Davidson, (eds.), *Controversies in Minority Voting: The Voting Rights Act in Perspective* (Washington, DC: Brookings Institution, 1992).

3. Lawson, *Running for Freedom,* 289.

4. Ibid., 247.

5. Ronald Smothers, "Blacks Say G.O.P. Ballot Challengers Use Tactics to Harass Minority Voters," *New York Times,* 25 October 1992.

6. Langhlin McDonald, "The 1982 Amendments of Section 2 and Minority Representation" in Grofman and Davidson, *Controversies in Minority Voting,* 66–84. And his "The Quiet Revolution in Minority Voting Rights," *Vanderbilt Law Review* 51 (Fall 1983): 1249–97. Frank Parker, "The 'Result' Test of Section 2 of the Voting Rights Act: Abandoning the Intent Standard," *Virginia Law Review* (May 1983): 715–74. Chandler Davidson, *Minority Vote Dilution* (Washington, DC: Howard University Press, 1984).

7. Denton L. Watson, *Lion in the Lobby: Clarence Mitchell, Jr.'s Struggle for the Passage of Civil Rights Laws* (New York: William Morrow, 1990), 29–221.

8. Walton, *When the Marching Stopped,* 122–75.

9. Institute for Contemporary Studies, *The Fairmont Papers,* 27.

10. Ibid., 141.

11. "Cornelius Alive and Well, Ready to Kill Food Stamps," *Jet,* 22 March 1982. See also, "Hundred Protest Closing of Agency to Aid Needy," *Jet,* 22 October 1981.

12. "Food Stamp Administration Aide Named to Head of Department of Agriculture," *Jet,* 7 February 1983.

13. "Campbell Savin in as Assistant Commerce Secretary," *Jet,* 25 January 1982.

14. "EEOC Contender Shot During Ohio Bank Robbery," *Jet,* 22 January 1982.

15. Key, *Southern Politics* new ed., 315–16.

16. Steven J. Rosenstone and John Mark Hansen, *Mobilization, Participation, and Democracy in America,* (New York: Macmillan, 1993), 100.

17. Lucius Barker, *Our Time Has Come*; Lucius Barker and Ronald Walters (eds.), *Jesse Jackson's 1984 Presidential Campaign* (Urbana: University of Illinois Press, 1989); Morris, *The Social and Political Implications of the 1984 Jesse Jackson Presidential Campaign*; and Charles P. Henry, *Jesse Jackson: The Search for Common Ground* (California: The Black Scholar Press, 1991).

18. Rosenstone and Hansen, *Mobilization,* 101.

19. Marcia Coyle, "The Court's New View: Color Blind? Rulings put Heavy Burden on Racial Classifications," *The National Law Journal* (July 10, 1995), A21.

8. AFRICAN AMERICAN POLITICAL OPINION: VOLATILITY IN THE REAGAN-BUSH ERA

The author would like to thank Ron Brown, Alice Furumoto, Paul Gomberg, Lynn Sanders, the participants of the African American workshop at the University of Chicago, the participants in the Benton Fellowship Program in Broadcast Journalism, and the student and faculty participants in the Arts and Science Forum Series Lectures for constructive comments.

1. Toni Morrison, "Introduction," *Race-ing Justice, Engenderder-ing Power: Essays on Anita Hill, Clarence Thomas, and the Construction of Social Reality* (New York: Pantheon Books, 1992).

2. Ibid.

3. See Morrison, *Race-ing Justice* and Robert Chrisman and Robert Allen, *Court of Appeal: The Black Community Speaks Out on the Racial and Sexual Politics of Thomas vs Hill* (New York: Ballantine, 1992) for a sampling on the wide range of interpretations and opinions on the hearings.

4. Bobo, Johnson, Oliver, Sidanium, Zubrinsky, "Public Opinion."

5. Dawson and Wilson, "Paradigms and Paradoxes," 189–234.

6. Lucius J. Barker and Ronald W. Walters, "Jesse Jackson's Candidacy in Political-Social Perspective: A Contextual Analysis," in *Jesse Jackson's 1984 Presidential Campaign,* 3–34.

7. Michael C. Dawson, *Behind the Mule: Race and Class in African American Politics* (Princeton: Princeton University Press, 1993).

8. Paula Giddings, *When and Where I Enter: The Impact of Black Women on Race and Sex in America* (New York: William Morrow and Company, 1984).

9. For an extensive discussion of this model see Dawson, *Behind the Mule.*

10. This heuristic should in principle be applicable to other groups. For example, in many historical periods and places, identity as a Jew could well be imagined to dominate all other social identities. The historical context of the development of any given group would shape how the heuristic is manifested. In the France of the 1980s, North Africans' identity and political struggles were tied to their belief in Islam. African Americans' racial identity, I argue, has been tied to their subordinate economic status.

11. Robert A. Dahl, *Who Governs?* (New Haven: Yale University Press, 1961).

12. William J. Wilson, *The Truly Disadvantaged: The Inner City, The Underclass, and Public Policy* (Chicago: University of Chicago Press, 1987).

13. Cohen and Dawson, "Neighborhood Poverty and African-American Politics," 286–302.

14. Douglas S. Massey and Nancy A. Denton, "Residential Segregation of Blacks, Hispanics, and Asians by Socioeconomic Status and Generation," *Social Science Quarterly,* 69 (1988): 797–817.

15. See Cohen and Dawson, "Neighborhood Poverty and African-American Politics," for an analysis which shows the effects of high levels of neighborhood poverty on micro-level black politics. African Americans who live in the most devastated neighborhoods are more likely to reject alliances with social classes (such as the working class) and institutions that other African Americans, even African Americans who live in moderately impoverished neighborhoods, embrace.

16. Daniel Kahneman and Amos Tversky, "The Simulation Heuristic," in Daniel Kahneman, Paul Slovic, and Amos Tversky (eds.), *Judgement Under Uncertainty: Heuristics and Biases* (New York: Cambridge University Press, 1982), 190–200.

17. Shelley B. Taylor, "The Availability Bias in Social Perception and Interaction," in Kahneman, Slovic, and Tversky, *Judgement Under Uncertainty,* 214–228.

18. Allen, Dawson, and Brown, "A Schema-Based Approach," 421–41.

19. Dawson, *Behind the Mule.*

20. Ibid. Gurin, Hatchett, and Jackson, *Hope and Independence.*

21. A simultaneous equation model was built which took into account the reciprocal "causation" of linked fate and the assessment of the relative economic status. This model was estimated using a three stage least squares estimator. The table of results from which these inferences are drawn are available from the author on request.

22. Edward Carmines and James Stimson, *Issue Evolution: Race and the Transformation of American Politics* (Princeton: Princeton Univeristy Press, 1989).

23. Dawson, *Behind the Mule,* 169.

24. Ibid.

25. Martin Luther King, Jr., *Where Do We Go From Here: Chaos or Community?* (Boston: Beacon Hill, 1967).

26. Ibid., 188.

27. Ibid., 144.

28. A probit estimator was used to estimate the probability of support for a black political party. Similar analyses using either ordinary least squares or probit estimators were also used to test the effect of economic status and several other factors on support for indicators of black nationalism, racial policies, and economic redistribution. The analyses were complicated by

several factors including selection bias. Appropriate corrections were made to provide unbiased estimates of the parameters. The series of analyses is available from the author on request.

29. Cohen and Dawson, "Neighborhood Poverty and African-American Politics," 286–302.

30. Ibid.

31. As in our work on black presidential approval we tested both the level of black unemployment and the difference between black and white unemployment as predictors. Once again, the difference between black and white levels of unemployment proves to be the better predictor. For a theoretical explanation of why this might be the case see chapters 3 and 7 in Dawson, *Behind the Mule.*

32. Joleen Kirschenman and Kathryn M. Neckerman, "We'd Love to Hire Them, But . . . : The Meaning of Race for Employers," in Christopher Jencks and Paul E. Peterson (eds.), *The Urban Underclass* (Washington, D.C.: The Brookings Institution, 1991), 203–32.

33. Louis Bolce and Gerald de Maio, "The 1992 Republican 'Tent': No Blacks Walked In," *Political Science Quarterly* 108(2): 255–70.

34. The estimates were derived using ordinary least squares regression. Since the lag of the dependent variable was used as a predictor, the first observation is not used. Consequently, there are 123 observations in this analysis. Details of the estimation process and a rationale for inclusion of the non-Reagan/Bush variables can be found in the work of Dawson and Brown (Robert) on differences in black and white macropartisanship. We performed some of the exogeneity tests suggests by Michael MacKuen, Robert Erikson, and James Stimson, "Macropartisanship," *American Political Science Review* 83 (December 1989): 1125–42. Our preliminary results, similar to theirs, suggest that while presidential approval is a "cause" of identification over time, the reciprocal relationship does not hold. Comparisons of the results from black and white macropartisanship demonstrate, as does our work on presidential approval, significant structural differences between races in what is important in influencing public opinion over time.

35. MacKuen, Erikson, and Stimson, "Macropartisanship."

36. Bobo, Johnson, Oliver, Sidanium, Zubrinsky, "Public Opinion."

37. Dawson, *Behind the Mule.*

38. Ibid.

9. AFRICAN AMERICAN PRESSURE GROUP POLITICS: THE REFORMULATION OF A REPLY BRIEF TO THE SUPREME COURT BY J. CLAY SMITH, JR., ROBERT GOODWIN, AND ELIAS BLAKE

1. Lerone Bennett, *Confrontation: Black and White* (Chicago: Johnson Publishing, 1965).

2. See Walton, "The Political Use of Absentee Ballots in a Rural Black Belt County."

3. Meeting with Hazel Mingo, acting director of White House Initiatives on Black College and Universities, at GSA building, 2 June 1993. Also at this meeting was Professor Marion Orr, visiting scholar at the Brookings Institution, now a professor at Duke University. Letter, Hazel Mingo to Hanes Walton, Jr., 15 July 1992.

4. Ibid.

5. Ibid.

6. Telephone interview, Elias Blake with Hanes Walton, Jr., (10 June 1992).

7. Ralph Bunche, "A Critical Analysis of the Tactics and Programs of Minority Groups," *Journal of Negro Education* 4 (July 1935), "Programs of Organizations Devoted to Improvement of the Status of the American Negro," *Journal of Negro Education* 8 (October 1939), and his "The Negro in the Political Life of the United States, *Journal of Negro Education* 10 (July 1941). An extended version of his thoughts on African American pressure groups can be found in his memorandum, "Ideologies, Tactics, and Achievements of Negro Betterment and

Interracial Organization" (Schomburg Library of the New York Public Library, microfilm, 1940).

8. See Peter Odegard, *Pressure Politics: The Story of the Anti-Saloon League* (New York: Columbia University Press, 1928), and Arthur F. Bentley, *The Process of Government* (San Antonio: Principia Press, 1949).

9. For a review of these works, see Hanes Walton, Jr., Leslie McLemore, and C. Vernon Gray, "The Pioneering Books on Black Politics and the Political Science Community, 1903–1965," *National Political Science Review* 2 (1990): 201.

10. See Nancy T. Weiss, "The Negro and the New Freedom: Fighting Wilsonian Segregation," *Political Science Quarterly* 89 (Winter 1974/75): 751–76 and her "Creative Tensions in the Leadership of the Civil Rights Movement," in Charles W. Eagles (ed.), *The Civil Rights Movement in America* (Jackson: University Press of Mississippi, 1986), 39–55. Some who criticized this approach used it themselves: see David Garrow, "Commentary," in Eagles, 55–64 and his *Bearing the Cross: Martin Luther King, Jr. and the Southern Christian Leadership Conference, 1955–1968* (New York: William Morrow, 1986).

11. Harry A. Bailey, Jr., "Negro Interest Group Strategies," in Lenneal J. Henderson, Jr. (ed.), *Black Political Life in the United States* (San Francisco: Chandler, 1972), 170.

12. See Aldon Morris, *The Origins of the Civil Rights Movement: Black Communities Organizing for Change* (New York: Free Press, 1984).

13. See Dianne M. Pinderhughes, "The Role of African American Political Organizations in the Mobilization of Voters," in Ralph Gomes and Linda Faye Williams, (eds.), *From Exclusion to Inclusion: The Long Struggle for African American Political Power* (Connecticut: Greenwood Press, 1992), 35–52.

14. See Hanes Walton, Jr., "Black Interest Group Behavior," unpublished manuscript.

15. Ibid.

16. James Jennings, *The Politics of Black Empowerment: The Transformation of Black Activism in Urban America* (Detroit: Wayne State University Press, 1992).

17. Paul Light, *The President's Agenda: Domestic Policy Choices from Kennedy to Carter* (Baltimore: John Hopkins University Press, 1985), 88.

18. Ibid., 94.

19. Ibid.

20. C. Van Woodard, *The Origins of the New South, 1877–1913,* (Baton Rouge: Louisiana State University Press, 1951), chap. 12.

21. U.S. v. Fordice, No. 90–1205, and Ayers, et al. v. Fordice, No. 90–6588, 1.

22. Ibid., 5–6.

23. Ibid., 7.

24. Ibid.

25. Ibid., 7–8.

26. Interview with J. Clay Smith, Washington, DC, 1 June 1992. For more on this race-neutral argument see chapter 4.

27. U.S. v. Fordice, 9.

28. Ibid., 10.

29. Ibid., 9.

30. Ibid., 13.

31. Ibid., 24.

32. Ibid.

33. Presidential Documents: Executive Order 12577 of April 28, 1989: "Historically Black Colleges and Universities," Federal Register 52 (2 May 1989), 18869–71.

34. Pomper, *The Election of 1988* and James Ceaser and Andrew Bush, *Upside Down, Inside Out: The 1992 Elections and American Politics* (Maryland: Rowman and Littlefield, 1993).

34. Walter Dean Burnham, "The Legacy of George Bush: Travails of an Understudy" in Pomper, *The Election of 1988,* 1–38 and Ruth Marcus, "The Shifting Sands of George Bush's Civil Rights Position," *Washington Post National Weekly* 24–30 (August 1992): 8–9.

35. Smith memorandum and author's telephone interview with Dr. Elias Blake, 10 June 1992.

36. Ibid.

37. Ibid and Dr. Blake telephone interview.

38. Ibid.

39. Smith memorandum.

40. Ibid.

41. Letter from Dr. James E. Cheek to President George W. Bush, 26 June 1991.

42. David Johnston, "In Justice Department of the 90s Focus Shifts from Rights," *New York Times,* 26 March 1991.

43. "The Court Still Haggling Over Rights, *New York Times,* 16 June 1989; William Raspberry, "The Shame of the Supreme Court," *Washington Post,* 17 June 1989.

44. "President Nominates Judge Clarence Thomas for Supreme Court Seat," *The Third Branch,* 1 July 1992.

45. Nelson Lund to James E. Cheek, 2 August 1992. See also Robert Goodwin interview, 1 June 1992. Dr. Blake's memorandum to Dr. William Harvey, 10 July 1991 discussed Professor Smith's concerns about the objectionable language in the recently filed brief of the Department of Justice. "This is a devastating and aggressive attack on all institutional funding that compensates for past discriminatory funding which deprives the students of equal protection. The Justice Department in effect says that those who freely choose a predominantly Black college are beyond the reach of the equal protection clause of the Constitution. They are not entitled to equal education. It is an incredible piece of logic created out of their own convictions . . . The writers of this brief are enemies of the advancement of Blacks in higher education in the South, whether out of ignorance or malicious intent."

46. Dr. Arthur E. Thomas, *Statement to the President's Advisory Board on Historically Black Colleges and Universities,* 9 September 1991, original emphasis.

47. Quoted in Smith memorandum.

48. Interview, Robert Goodwin with Hanes Walton, Jr., in his office at the Points of Lights Foundation, 1 June 1992.

49. Robert K. Goodwin, "Memorandum to File," copy in author's possession.

50. Ibid. Another account of this meeting appeared in Joye Mercer, "Bush Administration to Take Second Look at Its Position in Landmark Mississippi Case," *Black Issues in Higher Education,* 26 September 1991, 43–58. See also Smith memo. Here Smith describes how he was invited to the meeting.

51. Letter from James E. Cheek to the Honorable C. Boyden Gray, September 13, 1991.

52. Department of Justice Brief, pp. 32–33, 41.

53. Smith memorandum, 20.

54. Ibid.

55. Letter from James E. Cheek to C. Boyden Gray, 13 September 1991.

56. Letter from Samuel L. Myers to C. Boyden Gray, 26 September 1991.

57. Goodwin Memo to file, 1.

58. See Maureen David, "President Orders Aide to Review New Minority Scholarship Policy," *New York Times,* 18 December 1990. See B. Denise Hawkins, "Enrollment of HBCUs Experience an Influx of White Students," *Black Issues in Higher Education,* 22 August 1992, 9.

59. Goodwin Memo to file, 1.

60. Letter from James E. Cheek to Louis W. Sullivan, 2 October 1991. For Secretary

Sullivan's position, see Louis W. Sullivan, "Alma Maters that Matter: The Unique Mission of Historically Black Colleges and Universities," *The Hilltop,* 13 September 1991.

61. Letter from James E. Cheek to C. Boyden Gray, 5 October 1991.

62. Ibid.

63. Ibid.

64. Richard L. Burke, "Thomas's Accuser Assails Handling Her Complaint," *New York Times,* 8 October 1991. And Sharon LaFraniere, "It is an Unpleasant Issue," *Washington Post,* 8 October 1991.

65. Interview, J. Clay Smith, Jr. with Walton, Washington, DC, 1 June 1992. See Patricia Meiso, "Panel Accused of Bias Against Black Colleges," *Baltimore Sun,* 13 October 1991 and "Plan to Improve MD's Black Institutions Clears First Huddle," *Washington Post,* 20 November 1991.

66. Juan Williams, "The Continuing Education of Franklyn Jenifer," *Washington Post* Magazine, 20 September 1992.

67. Ibid.

68. Aaron Epstein and Karen Warren, "2nd Woman Implicates Thomas," *Philadelphia Inquirer,* 11 October 1991; Carl Caldwell, "Spector of Denial May Do Thomas In," *New York Daily News,* 11 October 1991; and Jill Abramson, "Thomas Down Play in a Congress Teeming with Sex and Harrassment," *Wall Street Journal,* 11 October 1991.

69. J. Clay Smith Jr. interview.

70. Brief of the *State of Mississippi United States v. Mabus,* 21, n22: "Even the Government, at long last, seems to recognize the futility of 'enhancement' as a desegregative tool, See Brief for the United States at 32."

71. For the activity that took place on October 8, see Goodwin Memo to file, 11–15.

72. Smith memorandum, 28–29.

73. Professor Smith's recollection is reinforced by the *Washington Times:* "The Justice Department, obeying a direct order from President Bush, did an about-face from its earlier position in a Supreme Court desegregation case that blacks said threatened the existence of historically Black colleges, the White House confirmed yesterday." Carol Innerst, "Bush Orders Switch on Black College Aid," *Washington Times,* 23 October 1991. See also Linda Greenhouse, "Bush Reverses U.S. Stance Against Black College Aid," *New York Times,* 22 October 1992 and Ruth Marcus, "Bush Shifts Stand on Aid to Black Colleges," *Washington Post,* 23 October 1991.

74. The language quoted appears in Justice Department Reply Brief 15–15, filed October 9, 1992. See "NBA Argues for Black Colleges Before the U.S. Supreme Court," *National Bar Association Magazine* 6 (July 1992), which "credits the turn around of the [brief of the Department of Justice] in large measure to the efforts of NBA Counsel J. Clay Smith, Jr., who negotiated the final language of the Reply Brief."

75. R. W. Apple, Jr., "Senate Confirms Thomas, 52–48, Ending Week of Bitter Battle: 'Time for Healing,' Judge Says," *New York Times,* 15 October 1991. Aaron Epstein, "Thomas Survives Controversy, Wins Senate Confirmation, 52–48, Bush Nominee Carries Closest Vote Since 1888," *Philadelphia Inquirer,* 15 October 1991.

76. Goldie Blumenstyk, "Justice Department Affirms Federal Backing for Black Colleges," *The Chronicle of Higher Education,* 15 October 1991. Joyce Mercer, "Justice Department Changes Position in Landmark Desegregation Case to be Heard by Supreme Court," *Black Issues in Higher Education,* 24 October 1991.

77. Memorandum from Robert K. Goodwin, October 11, 1991.

78. Ruth Marcus, "What Does Bush Really Believe," *Washington Post,* 18 August 1992. In 1992, President Bush signed into law the "Higher Education Amendments of 1992," which included capital financing provision of $375 million for HBCU's "in a way that could never

be realized under existing programs," according to William Gray, President of the United Negro College Fund. "UNCF CEO William Gray Praises President Bush for $375 Million Education Bill," *Jet,* 10 August 1992.

79. H. R. Mahood, *Interest Group Politics in America: A New Intensity* (Englewood Cliffs, NJ: Prentice Hall, 1990), 144.

80. Ibid., 145.

81. Timothy J. O'Neill, *Bakke and the Politics of Equality: Friends and Foes in the Classroom of Litigation* (Connecticut: Wesleyan University Press, 1985), 3.

82. Robert Goodwin interview, 1 June 1992.

83. Mahood, *Interest Group Politics in America,* 135.

84. Ibid, 136.

85. Lynne Duke, "Key Official on Black Colleges Fired," *Washington Post,* 14 February 1992.

86. Joyce Mercer, "Some Black College Chiefs Angered Over Goodwin Firing," *Black Issues in Higher Education,* 27 February 1992.

87. United States v. Fordice, 112 Supreme Court 272 (1992).

88. J. Clay Smith, Jr., "Historically Black Colleges and Universities are Justified," paper before National Association for Equal Opportunity in Higher Education (NAFEO) Seminar, August 4, 1992, Hilton Head Island, SC, and published under the same title without footnotes in *Black Issues in Higher Education* 9 (27 August 1992): 70. See Linda Greenhouse, "Court, 8–1, Faults Mississippi on Bias in College System," *New York Times,* 27 June 1992; Aaron Epstein, "Mississippi's Segregated Colleges Unlawful, Supreme Court Says," *Philadelphia Inquirer,* 27 June 1992.

89. J. Clay Smith, Jr., "Historically Black Colleges and Universities are Justified," 1.

90. Smith memorandum.

91. Sonya Ross, "Black Colleges on a Limb: Court Decision Leaves Uncertainty Over Future," *Savannah Morning News,* 6 July 1992; Lynne Duke, "Integration Agreements Could Be Reexamined: Fate of Historically Black College Muddled," *Washington Post* 27 June 1992 Joyce Mercer, "Republican Lawyer is Administration's Choice to Head White House Effort on Black Colleges," *Chronicle of Higher Education,* 6 June 1992; "NBA Argues for Black Colleges Before the U.S. Supreme Court," *National Bar Association Magazine* 5 (July 1992): 10. The author would like to thank Professor Cheryl Miller for these last three.

10. AN AFRICAN AMERICAN GRASS ROOTS POLITICAL CAMPAIGN: CAMPAIGN MANAGER RICHARD SMILEY AND CANDIDATE BARBARA J. MOBLEY

1. Shirley Chisholm, *The Good Fight* (New York: Harper and Row, 1973); Morris, *The Social and Political Implications of the 1984 Jesse Jackson Presidential Campaign*; Walters and Barker, *Jesse Jackson's 1984 Presidential Campaign,* and Elizabeth Colton, *The Jackson Phenomenon* (New York: Doubleday, 1989).

2. Mary Coleman and Leslie B. McLemore, "Continuity and Change: The Power of Traditionalism in Biracial Politics in Mississippi's Second Congressional District," in Preston, Henderson, and Puryear, *The New Black Politics,* 45–58. Persons, "The Election of Gary Franks," 194–208.

3. Henry, "Racial Factors in the 1982 California Gubernatorial Campaign"; Charles Jones and Michael Clemmons, "A Model of Racial Crossover Voting: An Assessment of the Wilder Victory," in Persons, *Dilemmas of Black Politics,* 128–46; and Marilyn Davis and Alex Willingham, "Andrew Young and the Georgia State Elections of 1990," in Persons, *Dilemmas of Black Politics,* 147–75.

4. Georgia Persons, "Black Mayoralties and the New Black Politics: From Insurgency to

Racial Reconciliation," in her *Dilemmas of Black Politics,* 38–65. And part three in Preston, Henderson, and Puryear, *The New Black Politics,* 137–290; MFanya Tryman, "Black Mayoralty Campaigns: 'Running the Race,' "*Phylon* (December 1974): 346–58; L. H. Whittmore, *Together: A Reporter's Journey into the New Black Politics* (New York: William Morrow, 1971).

5. Julian Bond, *Black Candidate: Southern Campaign Experiences* (Atlanta: Southern Regional Council, 1969), iii.

6. Ibid., iii, iv.

7. Ibid., 47.

8. Interview with Richard Smiley, Decatur, Georgia, 13 November 1992.

9. For a discussion of the march see Garrow, *Bearing the Cross,* 357–430.

10. Thomas E. Ball, *Julian Bond vs. John Lewis: On the Campaign Trail with John Lewis and Julian Bond* (Atlanta: HBCCC, 1988). This is the only book length analysis of this key election.

11. Transcript of the Smiley interview, 9–10.

12. Ball, *Julian Bond vs. John Lewis,* 119–26.

13. Transcript of the Smiley interview, 14.

14. Rhonda Cook, "Redding Changes Tune, Pleads Guilty in Extortion Case," *Atlanta Journal/Constitution,* 20 August 1992.

15. Rhonda Cook, "Redding Mulls Pleading Guilty to Taking Cash," *Atlanta Journal/Constitution,* 15 August 1992.

16. Ibid.

17. David T. Canon, *Actors, Athletes, and Astronauts: Political Amateurs in the United States Congress* (Chicago: University of Chicago Press, 1990), xiii.

18. Ibid., 6. Pauline Stone, "Ambition Theory and the Black Politician," in *Western Political Quarterly* 32 (March 1980): 94–107.

19. Interview with Barbara J. Mobley, Decatur, Georgia, 14 November 1992.

20. Ibid. The other political neophyte in the race chose her well known father, a veteran of numerous city, state, and county political campaigns.

21. Ibid. 2.

22. Ibid., 2–3.

23. Transcript of the Smiley interview, 16.

24. Ibid., 17–18. Also see David Garrow, *Protest at Selma: Martin Luther King, Jr., and the Voting Rights Act of 1965* (New Haven: Yale University Press, 1978).

25. Ibid., 18.

26. Transcript of the Mobley interview, 4–5.

27. Canon, *Actors, Athletes, and Astronauts,* 3.

28. Ibid.

29. Transcript of the Smiley interview, 18.

30. Transcript of the Mobley interview, 6.

31. Transcript of the Smiley interview, 19.

32. Ibid., 20.

33. Transcript of the Mobley interview, 11.

34. Ibid.

35. Ibid.

36. Transcript of the Smiley interview, 45.

37. Ibid.

38. Ibid., 24.

39. Ibid.

40. Ibid., 25–26.

41. Transcript of the Mobley interview, 7–8.

11. THE AFRICAN AMERICAN REPUBLICAN VOTE IN A SOUTHERN MAYORAL ELECTION

I would like to give credit to Jennifer Parham and Arlene Chalwell.

1. Kay Williams Graves, "New Mayor, Old Problems," *Georgia Trend* (November 1992): 50–53.

2. For a discussion of African American voting in the 1930s see Paul Lewinson, *Race, Class, and Party: A History of Negro Suffrage in the South* (New York: Russell and Russell, 1963). For a discussion of African American voting in the 1940s see Ralph Bunche, *The Political Status of the Negro in the Age of FDR* Dewey Grantham (ed.) (Chicago: University of Chicago Press, 1943).

3. See Keech, *The Impact of Negro Voting.*

4. Walton, *Invisible Politics,* 184–85.

5. Interview with Mayor John P. Rousaksis, Savannah, Georgia, 29 December 1991.

6. Ibid.

7. Interview with Enoch Mathis in Savannah, Georgia, June 1989.

8. Ibid.

9. Quoted in Walton, *When the Marching Stopped,* 140. See also Eddie Fleming, "Anderson's Savannah Expose called Lies," Savannah *Morning News,* 14 November 1975; Jack Anderson, "Did Bell Influence Savannah Annexation," Savannah *Morning News,* 14 November 1975; "Jack Anderson Defends his Column," Savannah *Morning News,* 14 November 1975; Jack Anderson, "The Savannah Story: Corrections," Savannah *Morning News,* 27 November 1978.

10. Arian, Goldberg, Mollenkopf, and Rogowsky, *Changing New York City Politics,* 68.

11. Walton, *The Native Son Presidential Candidate,* 132–42.

12. See Morris, *The Social and Political Implication of the 1984 Jesse Jackson Presidential Campaign*; Walters and Barker, (eds.), *Jesse Jackson's 1984 Presidential Campaign,* and Barker, *Our Time Has Come.*

13. Interview with Otis Johnson, 28 December 1991.

14. Interview with Alderman John P. Rousakis, 29 December 1991.

15. Data prepared by the Chatham County Savannah Metropolitan Planning Commission for 1990. A copy was made available by Ms. Allyne Tosca Owens-Harris. Such registration data by race and district was not available for 1980 or 1970. Only population data was available for 1980.

16. Interview with Mayor Rousakis.

17. Graves, "New Mayor, Old Problems," 50–53.

18. Henry Lee Moon, *Balance of Power: The Negro Vote* (New York: Doubleday, 1948).

19. Interview with Clarence Martin, Savannah, Georgia, 9 March 1993.

12. AFRICAN AMERICAN REPUBLICAN PARTISANSHIP: ALIGNMENT AND DEALIGNMENT

1. For the pioneering work, see A. Campbell, P. Converse, W. E. Miller, and D. Stokes, *The American Voter* (New York: Wiley, 1960). Richard Niemi and Herbert Weisberg (eds.), *Controversies in American Voting Behavior* (San Franciso: W. H. Freeman, 1976).

2. Gurin, Hatchett, and Jackson, *Hope and Independence,* 54–56.

3. Walton, *Invisible Politics,* 131–66.

4. Gurin, Hatchett, and Jackson, *Hope and Independence,* 49.

5. Ibid., 51–52.

6. See Colin Campbell, S. J. Rockman, and Bert Rockman (eds.), *The Bush Presidency: First Appraisals* (New Jersey: Chatham House, 1991).

7. Institute for Contemporary Studies, *The Fairmont Papers,* 159–62.

8. Simpson, "Atwater's Election as Howard University Trustee." Diane Pinderhughes, "Political Choices: A Realignment in Partisanship Among the Black Voters," in J. D. Williams (ed.), *The State of Black Americans* (New York: Urban League, 1985), 85. See also Colbert I. King, "The Dilemma of Black Republicans," *Washington Post,* 22 September 1992.

9. Ibid.

10. Smith, "A Black Lawyer's Response to the Fairmont Papers," 221–3. For an analysis of how African Americans were recruited to the party during William Brock's term as chairman of the Republican Party, see Pearl T. Robinson, "Whither the Future of Blacks in the Republican Party?" *Political Science Quarterly* 97 (Summer 1982): 207–31.

11. Interview with Michael Pratt, Savannah, Georgia, 2 May 1995.

12. Ibid.

13. The white Democratic candidate had run in previous elections as a Republican but switched in this election, won the Democratic primary, and then the general election.

14. Interview with Michael Pratt.

15. Telephone interview with former Bryan County Commissioner Richard Riley, 15 July 1995.

16. Mack Mattingly became Georgia's first Republican Senator in 1980 when he defeated long time Democratic Senator Herman Talmadge, who was under investigation.

17. Walton, *The Native Son Presidential Candidate.*

18. Ibid.

19. Robert Pear, "Judge Tells U.S. to Make Political Parties Comply with Rights Law," *New York Times,* 8 April 1992.

20. Ibid.

21. Ibid.

22. See Walton, *When the Marching Stopped,* 143–216.

23. For an analysis of actual party voting from exit poll data, see Louis Bolic, Gerald DeMaio, and Douglas Muzzio, "Blacks and the Republican Party: The 20 Percent Solution," *Political Science Quarterly* 107 (Spring 1992): 63–79, and their "The 1992 Republican Tent: No Blacks Walked In," *Political Science Quarterly* 108 (Spring 1993): 255–70.

24. Frank J. Sorauf and Paul Allen Breck, *Party Politics in America* 6th ed., (Boston: Scott Foresman, Little Brown, 1988), 113–31.

25. See Hugh D. Price, *The Negro and Southern Politics: A Chapter of Florida History* (New York: New York University Press, 1957), 112.

26. Key, *Southern Politics,* 85, 82.

27. Price, *The Negro and Southern Politics,* 112.

28. Helen Jacobstein, *The Segregation Factor in the Florida Democratic Gubernatorial Primary of 1956* (Gainesville: University of Florida Press, 1972), 60–61.

29. Ibid.

30. Ibid.

31. Ibid.

32. Annie Mary Hartsfield and Elston E. Roady, *Florida Votes* rev. ed. (Tallahassee: Florida State University Institute for Social Research, 1972), 34.

33. U.S. Commission on Civil Rights, *Political Participation* (Washington, D.C: Government Printing Office, 1968).

34. Hartsfield and Roady, *Florida Votes,* 20.

35. Ibid.

36. Ibid.

13. AFRICAN AMERICAN POLITICAL PARTY CONVERSION: THE IMPACT OF THE CLARENCE THOMAS NOMINATION ON THE PARTY PARTISANSHIP OF THE RESIDENTS OF HIS HOMETOWN

The author wishes to give credit to Jennifer Parham and Arlene Chalwell.

1. See Bruce A. Campbell and Richard J. Trilling (eds.), *Realignment in American Politics: Toward a Theory* (Austin: University of Texas Press, 1980). Byron E. Shafer (ed.), *The End of Realignment? Interpreting American Electoral Eras* (Madison: University of Wisconsin Press, 1991). Walton, "Black Presidential Participation and Critical Election Theory," in Morris (ed.), *The Social and Political Implications of the 1984 Jesse Jackson Presidential Campaign,* 49–62.

2. Richard Valelley and James Morone, "On the Study of Race and Politics," *CLIO* (Winter, 1992/93), 4–5.

3. Lawrence Grossman, "Democrats and Blacks in the Gilded Age," in Peter Kowler (ed.), *Democrats and the American Idea* (Washington, D.C.: Center for National Policy Press, 1992), 139.

4. Ibid., 140.

5. Walton, *Black Politics,* 111.

6. Grossman, "Democrats and Blacks in the Gilded Age," 143.

7. Ibid.

8. Ibid.

9. Walton, "The Democrats and African Americans," 337–8.

10. Walton, "Black Presidential Participation," 49.

11. For extensive coverage of the literature and the debate about the conversion mobilization hypothesis, see Gerald H. Gamm, *The Making of New Deal Democrats: Voting Behavior and Realignment in Boston, 1920–1940* (Chicago: University of Chicago Press, 1986), 3–27.

12. Ibid.

13. Ibid., 94. See also Kristi Andersen, *The Creation of a Democratic Majority, 1928–1936* (Chicago: University of Chicago Press, 1979).

14. Ibid.

15. Hanes Walton, Jr., *Black Republicans: The Politics of the Black and Tans* (New Jersey: Scarecrow Press, 1975), 21. Also his "Black Politics Payoff: Used and Unused Strategies," *Political Science Review* (July-September, 1981): 288–297.

16. Grossman, "Democrats and Blacks in the Gilded Age," 140.

17. Marcus Holland and Patrick Armstrong, "Mother Trusting in the Lord to Put Son on Supreme Court," *Savannah Evening Press,* October 15, 1991, p. 1. See also Lee R. Haven, "In Pinpoint, Nothing But Support," *Savannah Morning News,* October 9, 1991, p. 1 and "Thomas' Supporters Rally in Hometown of Pinpoint," *Savannah Morning News,* October 14, 1991, p. 1.

18. For construction of earlier surveys, see Hanes Walton, Jr. and Clarence Martin, "The Black Electorate and the Maddox Administration," *Negro Educational Review* (April 1971): 112–14. See Walton, *Invisible Politics,* 306–15, for a copy of the questionnaire. The former was a state questionnaire and the latter was a national questionnaire.

19. Katherine Tate, Ronald Brown, Shirley J. Hatchett, and James Jackson, *1984 National Black Election Study Sourcebook* (Ann Arbor: The Institute for Social Research, University of Michigan, 1988).

20. We attempted two additional interviews but the subjects could not complete them, and the incomplete surveys were dropped from the total.

21. Walton, *Invisible Politics,* 122–24, 140–47.

22. For the low evaluations that African Americans have given Republican Presidents over

time, see George C. Edward, III with Alex M. Gallup, *Presidential Approval: A Sourcebook* (Baltimore: John Hopkins University Press, 1990), 12–113.

23. William H. Riker, *The Art of Political Manipulation* (New Haven: Yale University Press, 1986), ix.

14. SOUTHERN COMFORT: THE IMPACT OF DAVID DUKE'S CAMPAIGNS ON AFRICAN AMERICAN POLITICS

1. Key, *Southern Politics,* 106–7.

2. Sherrill, *Gothic Politics in the Deep South.* Earl Black, *Southern Governors and Civil Rights: Racial Segregation as a Campaign Issue in the Second Reconstruction* (Cambridge: Harvard University Press, 1976).

3. Hanes Walton, Jr., *The Political Philosophy of Martin Luther King, Jr.* (Connecticut: Greenwood Press, 1971).

4. Neil McMillen, *The Citizens' Council: Organized Resistance to the Second Reconstruction, 1954–1964* (Urbana: University of Illinois Press, 1971) and Numan V. Bartley, *The Rise of Massive Persistance* (Baton Rouge: Louisiana State University Press, 1969).

5. Parker, *Black Votes Count,* 200.

6. Philip E. Converse, "V. O. Key, Jr., and the Study of Public Opinion," in Milton C. Cummings, Jr., (ed.), *V. O. Key, Jr. and the Study of American Politics* (Washington, DC: American Political Science Association, 1988), 39.

7. Key, *Southern Politics,* 232.

8. Ibid.

9. Ibid., 233.

10. Ibid., 243.

11. Black, *Southern Governors and Civil Rights,* 7–91.

12. Greenshaw, *Elephants in the Cottonfields,* 9.

13. Ibid.

14. Ibid.

15. Ibid., pp. 13–14.

16. Ibid., 14.

17. Key, *Southern Politics,* 159–60.

18. Quoted in Key, *Southern Politics,* 165 n15.

19. Ibid.

20. Sherrill, *Gothic Politics in the South,* 7.

21. Ibid., 8.

22. Greenshaw, *Elephants in the Cottonfields,* 183–88, provides a detailed description of Duke and his rise in Louisiana politics. See also Douglas Rose (ed.), *The Emergence of David Duke and the Politics of Race* (Chapel Hill: University of North Carolina Press, 1992).

23. Simpson, "Atwater's Election as Howard University Trustee."

24. Greenshaw, *Elephants in the Cottonfields,* 184.

The Native Son Presidential Candidate, 101–30.

25. Wilbur Rich, *Coleman Young and Detroit Politics: From Social Activist to Power Broker* (Detroit: Wayne State University Press, 1989), 91–125. Persons, "Black Mayoralties and the New Black Politics," 8–65.

26. Walton, *The Native Son Presidential Candidate,* 1–34.

27. "If David Duke is Governor—You Need Alphonse Jackson" (advertisement) *The Shreveport Sun,* 14 November 1991; "We Must Re-elect Alphonse Jackson—We Must Defeat David Duke" (advertisement) *The Shreveport Sun,* 14 November 1991. Bill Bowen, "Mitchell Ousts Jackson to End 20 Year Reign," *The Shreveport Times,* 17 November 1991.

15. AFRICAN AMERICAN REPUBLICAN CONGRESSIONAL CANDIDATES AND MONEY: THE ROLE OF THE REPUBLICAN PARTY PACS

1. Frank J. Sorauf, *Money in American Elections* (Boston: Scott, Foresman, 1988), 4–5.
2. Ibid., 149–50.
3. Ibid.
4. Ibid., 151.
5. David Magleby and Candice J. Nelson, *The Money Chase: Congressional Campaign Reform* (Washington, DC: Brookings Institution, 1990), 98.
6. Ibid.
7. Sorauf, *Money in American Elections,* 131.
8. Gary C. Jacobson, "The Republican Advantage in Campaign Finance," in John E. Chubb and Paul Peterson (eds.), *The New Directions in American Politics* (Washington, DC: Brookings Institution, 1985), 143–173 and his *Money in Congressional Elections* (New Haven: Yale University Press, 1980).
9. Brooks Jackson, *Honest Graft: Big Money and the American Political Process* 2d ed. (Washington, DC: Farragut, 1990), 61.
10. Sorauf, *Money in American Elections,* 101.
11. Magleby and Nelson, *The Money Chase,* 111.
12. Ibid.
13. Jackson, *Honest Graft,* 60–61.
14. Ibid., 54.
15. Ibid.
16. Ibid., 61.
17. Magleby and Nelson, *The Money Chase,* 100.
18. Ibid.
19. Ibid., 103.
20. Ibid.
21. Ibid., 113.
22. Ibid., 119.
23. Federal Election Commission, *FEC Reports on Financial Activity 1979–1980, Final Report: U.S. Senate and House Campaigns* (Washington, DC: Federal Election Commission, 1982), xvi.
24. Ibid., 437–42.
25. See Charles Henry, "Money, Law, and Black Congressional Candidates," *Urban League Review* 8 (Summer 1984): 87–103.
26. Walton, *Invisible Politics,* 157.
27. Ibid.
28. Persons, "The Election of Gary Franks," 194–208.
29. Federal Election Commission, *FEC Reports on Financial Activity, 1989–1990: Final Report: U.S. Senate and House Campaigns,* (Washington, DC: Federal Election Commission, 1991), 315–18.
30. Ibid.
31. See Melany Nelson, *Even Mississippi* (Alabama: University of Alabama Press, 1989). Also see Coleman and McLemore, "Continuity and Change," 45–58.
32. Federal Election Commission, *FEC Reports on Financial Activity 1985–1986: Final Report: U.S. Senate and House Campaigns,* 233–4.
33. Ibid., 223–6.
34. Zaphon Wilson, "Gantt Versus Helms: Deracialization Confronts Southern Traditionalism" in Persons, *Dilemmas of Black Politics,* 176–93. And *FEC Reports on Financial Activity 1989–1990: Final Report: U.S. Senate and House Campaigns,* 224–6.

16. AFRICAN AMERICAN FEMALE SENATORIAL CANDIDATES: TWIN ASSETS OR DOUBLE LIABILITIES?

The author wishes to thank Ray Joseph, Jr., at Harvard University for his superb research assistance. Data for this paper were also made available by the Center for the American Woman and Politics (CAWP), Eagleton Institute of Politics, Rutgers University.

1. The inspiration for this subtitle comes from *Black Women's Studies: All the Women are White, All the Men are Black, But Some of Us are Brave,* edited by Gloria T. Hull, Patricia Bell Scott, and Barbara Smith (Old Westbury, NY: Feminist Press, 1982).

2. Robert Darcy, Susan Welch, and Janet Clark, *Women, Elections, and Representation* (New York: Longman Press, 1987), 69–70.

3. Susan J. Carroll, *Women as Candidates in American Politics* (Bloomington: Indiana University Press, 1985), 103–4.

4. Linda Williams, "White and Black Perceptions of the Electability of Black Politics Candidates," *National Political Science Review* 2 (1990): 45–64.

5. Mark C. Westlye, "Competitiveness of Senate Seats and Voting Behavior in Senate Elections," *American Journal of Political Science* 27 (May 1983): 253–83.

6. Davis and Willingham, "Andrew Young and the Georgia State Elections of 1990," 176.

7. Mack McCorkle, "Gantt versus Helms: Toward the New Progressive Era?" *Reconstruction* 1(3): 8–24.

8. Pettigrew and Alston, *Tom Bradley's Campaigns for Governor,* 83.

9. Davis and Willingham, "Andrew Young and the Georgia State Elections of 1990," 162.

10. Darcy, Welch, and Clark, *Women, Elections, and Representation,* 152.

11. R. Darcy and Charles D. Hadley, "Black Women in Politics: The Puzzle of Success," *Social Science Quarterly* 69 (1988): 629–45.

12. Jerry Perkins, "Political Ambition among Black and White Women: An Intragender Test of the Socialization Model," *Women & Politics* vol 6 (1966), 27–40.

13. Darcy and Hadley, "Black Women in Politics," 629–31.

14. Katherine Tate, *From Protest to Politics: The New Black Voters in American Elections,* (Cambridge: Harvard University Press, 1993), chap. 6. See also Carmines and Stimson, *Issue Evolution.*

15. Robert Y. Shapiro and Harpreet Mahajan, "Gender Differences in Policy Preferences: A Sumary of Trends from the 1960s," *Public Opinion Quarterly* 50 (1986): 42–61. See also Martin Gilens, "Gender and Support for Reagan: A Comprehensive Model of Presidential Approval," *American Journal of Political Science* 32 (1988): 19–49.

16. Ronald B. Rappoport, Walter J. Stone, and Alan I. Abramowitz, "Do Endorsements Matter: Group Influence in the 1984 Democratic Caucuses," *American Political Science Review* 85 (1991): 193–203.

17. Jane Mansbridge and Katherine Tate, "Race Trumps Gender: The Thomas Nomination in the Black Community," *PS: Political Science and Politics* 25 (1992): 488–92.

18. Rappoport, Stone, and Abramowitz, "Do Endorsements Matter?"

19. Ibid.

20. The county recorder of deeds oversees 300 employees and manages a budget of $8 million.

21. *Congressional Quarterly,* 29 February 1992, 42.

22. Democrat Dan Rostenkowski and Republican Philip M. Crane won with less than three-fifths of the vote in their bids for renomination.

23. Black voter participation in the Illinois primary was still reported to have been lower in 1992 than in 1988 and 1984. Only 19% of those who left polling places in the Illinois primary were Black in contrast to 28% four years prior. *New York Times,* 19 March 1992.

24. David Ian Lublin, "Quality, Not Quantity: Strategic Politicians in U.S. Senate Elections,

1952–1990," paper under review. Also see Alan I. Abramowitz, "Explaining Senate Outcomes," *American Poltiical Science Review,* 32 (1988): 385–403.

25. Peverill Squire, "Challengers in U.S. Senate Elections," *Legislative Studies Quarterly* 14 (1989): 531–47. Abramowitz, "Explaining Senate Outcomes."

26. *New York Times,* 11 October 1992.

27. Samuel Popkin, *The Reasoning Voter: Communications and Persuasions in Presidential Campaigns* (Chicago: University of Chicago Press, 1991) 33–47.

28. Mansbridge and Tate, "Race Trumps Gender."

29. Jones and Clemons, "A Model of Racial Crossover Voting."

30. Ibid., 133.

31. Ibid., 131–132.

32. John H. Mollenkopf, "New York: The Great Anomaly," in Browning, Marshall, and Tabb, *Racial Politics in American Cities.*

33. Thomas Hardy, "Braun Rode Colorblind Coalition," *Chicago Tribune,* 8 November 1992.

34. Browning, Marshall, and Tabb, *Racial Politics in American Cities.*

35. Jones and Clemons, "A Model of Racial Crossover Voting," 142.

36. Sidney Verba and Gary Orren, *Equality in America: The View from the Top* (Cambridge: Harvard University Press, 1985).

37. Armando Guterriez, "The Jackson Campaign in the Hispanic Community: Problems and Prospects for a Black-Brown Coalition," in Barker and Walters, *Jesse Jackson's 1984 Presidential Campaign.*

38. Jones and Clemons, "A Model of Racial Crossover Voting," 142.

39. Rappoport, Stone, and Abramowitz, "Do Endorsements Matter," 195.

40. Jane Mansbridge, *Why We Lost the ERA* (Chicago: University of Chicago Press, 1986).

41. For example, in the 1990 governor's race in Massachusetts, many feminists (as did a number of blacks) refused to support the Democratic candidate, John Silber, who alienated feminists and working mothers by expresing his view that sending small children to group daycare centers was a form of child abuse. William Weld, his pro-choice, Republican opponent, won, and has presided over major cutbacks in state funding for social services, including programs that provide low-income families, mostly female-headed, with subsidized or free child-care.

42. Mansbridge, *Why We Lost the ERA.*

43. Quoted ibid.

44. Mansbridge and Tate, "Race Trumps Gender."

45. Ethel Klein, *Gender Politics* (Cambridge: Harvard University Press, 1985), 164.

46. Dianne Pinderhughes, "Divisions in the Civil Rights Community," *PS: Political Science and Politics* 25 (1992): 485–87.

47. Ibid.

17. AFRICAN AMERICANS, H. ROSS PEROT, AND IMAGE POLITICS: THE NATURE OF AFRICAN AMERICAN THIRD-PARTY POLITICS

1. See Hanes Walton, Jr., *The Negro in Third Party Politics* (Philadelphia: Dorrance, 1959), Daniel Mazmanian, *Third Parties in Presidential Elections* (Washington, DC: Brookings Institution, 1974), and Frank Smallwood, *The Other Candidates: Third Parties in Presidential Elections* (Hanover: University Press of New England, 1983).

2. The concept of a two-stage campaign arose during discussions with my colleague Steven J. Rosenstone at the University of Michigan, in the aftermath of the 1992 elections. Professor Rosenstone is an authority on third parties.

3. Ronald D. Elving, "Return of Perot, Debates Energize Final Weeks," *Congressional Quarerly Weekly Report* 50 (3 October 1992): 3086.

4. See Steven J. Rosenstone, Roy L. Behr, and Edward H. Lazarus, *Third Parties in America: Citizen Response to Major Party Failure* (Princeton: Princeton University Press, 1984), 80.

5. Ibid.

6. Ibid., 81.

7. Ibid., 120.

8. Ibid., 121.

9. Ibid.

10. Elving, "Return of Perot," 3086.

11. Walton, *The Negro in Third Party Politics,* 110–24.

12. For a discussion of the role that discrimination plays in the creation and evolution of African American third parties see, Leslie McLemore, "Mississippi Freedom Democratic Party," *Black Politicians* 3 (October 1971): 19–23.

13. Walton, *Black Political Parties,* chap. 1.

14. Walton, *Invisible Politics,* 174–82.

15. Walton, *Black Politics,* 121–38.

16. C. Van Woodard, *The Strange Career of Jim Crow,* 3rd ed. (New York: Oxford University Press, 1974).

17. Kenneth Going, *The NAACP Comes of Age: The Defeat of Judge John J. Parker* (Bloomington: Indiana University Press, 1990).

18. Walton, *The Native Son Presidential Candidate,* 130.

19. Michael B. Preston, "The Election of Harold Washington: An Examination of the SES Model in the 1983 Chicago Mayoral Election," in Preston, Henderson, and Puryear, *The New Black Politics,* 139–72. For the 1992 candidate, see Harold Horton, "Ron Daniels: Profile of a Presidential Candidate," *Trotter Review* (Fall 1992): 32.

20. Gurin, Hatchett, and Jackson, *Hope and Independence,* 150.

21. Ibid. See Walton, *Black Political Parties.* Hardy Frye, *Black Parties and Political Power: A Case Study* (Massachusetts: G. K. Hall, 1980). And Hanes Walton, Jr., "The National Democratic Party of Alabama and Party Failure in America," in Kay Lawson and Peter Markl (eds.), *When Parties Fail* (Princeton: Princeton University Press, 1988), 365–88.

22. James D. Williams, "Dr. Hooks Heats Up the 83rd NAACP Convention and Bids Farewell," *The Crisis Magazine* (August/September 1992): 6. See also Steven A. Holmes, "Perot Brings Mixed Record to His First Black Audience," *New York Times,* 1 July 1992.

23. Ibid.

24. Ibid.

25. Ibid. See also Peter Applebome, "Perot Speech Get Cool Reception at NAACP," *New York Times,* 12 July 1992.

26. Ibid.

27. Ibid. "Presidential Politics: Perot Bows Out, Says Election Would Be Decided in House," *Congressional Quarterly Weekly Report* (18 July 1992): 2131–2. See also "Excerpts from Perot's Nashville Talk."

28. Aplebome, "Perot Speech Get Cool Reception at NAACP."

29. Holmes, "Perot Brings Mixed Record to His First Black Audience."

30. Ibid.

31. Rhodes Cook, "Clinton Picks the GOP Lock on the Electoral College," *Congressional Quarterly Weekly Report* (7 November 1992): 3553. Steven Rosenstone, "Debate on the New Party: Electoral Myths, Political Realities," *Boston Review* (January/February 1993): 11–13. Jerry Watts, "Morality and Political Efficiency," *Boston Review* (January/February 1993): 13–14.

32. Interview with Reverend Calvin O. Butts, Savannah, Georgia, 10 March 1993.
33. Ibid.
34. Todd S. Purdum, "Perot Tags Black Minister," *New York Times,* 12 July 1992.
35. Calvin Sims, "Butts Comes Under Fire for Endorsement of Perot: Some Blacks Upset by Rebuff to Democrats," *New York Times,* 14 July 1992.
36. Calvin Sims, "Clergyman Lashes Out at Critics Who Attacks Perot Endorsement," *New York Times,* 16 July 1992.
37. Ibid.
38. Ibid.
39. Jan Fisher, "Butts Backs an Educator for President," *New York Times,* 20 July 1992.
40. Interview with Dr. Phyllis Mack, Savannah, Georgia, 9 March 1992.
41. Ibid.
42. Ibid.
43. Ibid.
44. Ibid.
45. Ibid.
46. Ibid.

18. AN AFRICAN AMERICAN PRESIDENTIAL CANDIDATE: THE FAILED PRESIDENTIAL CAMPAIGN OF GOVERNOR L. DOUGLAS WILDER

1. Thomas Byrne Edsall and Mary D. Edsall, *Chain Reaction: The Impact of Race, Rights, and Taxes on American Politics* (New York: Norton, 1991), 76.
2. Charles Hamilton, "Deracialization: Examination of a Political Strategy," *First World* 1 (March/April 1977): 3–5.
3. Joseph P. McCormick, II, and Charles E. Jones, "The Conceptualization of Deracialization: Thinking Through the Dilemma," in Georgia A. Persons (ed.), *Dilemmas of Black Politics,* 70.
4. Ibid.
5. Hamilton, "Deracialization," 3.
6. Ibid., 5.
7. Martin Kilson, "Problems of Black Politics: Some Progress, Many Difficulties," *Dissent* 36 (1989): 526–34.
8. Ibid., 526.
9. Ibid.
10. Ibid., 530.
11. McCormick and Jones, "The Conceptualization of Deracialization," 76.
12. Huey L. Perry, "Recent Advances in Black Electoral Politics," *PS: Political Science and Politics* 23 (1990a): 141. Huey L. Perry, "The Reelection of Sidney Barthelemy as Mayor of New Orleans," *PS: Political Science and Politics* 23 (1990b): 156–7. Huey L. Perry, "Deracialization as an Analytical Construct in American Urban Politics," *Urban Affairs Quarterly* 27 (1991a): 181–91. Huey L. Perry, "Toward Conceptual Clarity Regarding Deracialization: A Response to Professor Starks," *Urban Affairs Quarterly* 27 (1991b): 223–6. Mary E. Summers and Philip A. Klinker, "The Election of John Daniels as Mayor of New Orleans," *PS: Political Science and Politics* 23 (1990): 143–5. Mary E. Summers and Philip A. Klinker, "The Daniels Election in New Haven and the Failure of the Deracialization Hypothesis," *Urban Affairs Quarerly* 27 (1991): 202–15. J. Philip Thompson, "David Dinkins' Victory in New York City: The Decline of the Democratic Party and the Strengthening of Black Politics," *PS: Political Science and Politics* 23 (1990): 145–8. Sandra C. Ardrey and William E. Nelson, "The Maturation of Black Politics: The Case of Cleveland," *PS: Political Science and Politics* 23 (1990): 148–51. Carol Pierannunzi and John D. Hutchenson, Jr., "Electoral Change and

Regime Maintenance: Maynard Jackson's Seond Time Around," *PS: Political Science and Politics* 23 (1990): 151–3. Carol Pierannunzi and John D. Hutchenson, Jr., "Deracialization in the Deep South: Mayoral Politics in Atlanta," *Urban Affairs Quarterly* 27 (1991): 192–201. Alvin J. Schexnider, "The Politics of Pragmatism: An Analysis of the 1989 Gubernatorial Election in Virginia," *PS: Political Science and Politics* 23 (1990): 154–6. Robert C. Smith, "Recent Elections and Black Politics: The Maturation or Death of Black Politics," *PS: Political Science and Politics* 23 (1990): 160–62. Mylon Winn, "The Election of Norman Rice as Mayor of Seattle," *PS: Political Science and Politics* 23 (1990): 158–9. Robert T. Starks, "A Commentary and response to 'Exploring the Meaning and Implications of Deracialization in African American Urban Politics,' "*Urban Affairs Quarterly* 27 (1991): 216–22. Ruth Ann Strickland and Marcia Lynn Wicker, "Comparing the Wilder and Gantt Campaigns: A Model for Black Candidate Success in Statewide Elections," *PS: Political Science and Politics* 25 (1992): 204–11.

13. Summers and Klinker, "The Election of John Daniels as Mayor of New Orleans," 142–5.

14. Michael Barone and Grant Ujifusa, *The Almanac of American Politics: The Senators, the Representatives, and the Governors—Their Records and Election Results, Their States, and Districts* (Washington, DC: The National Journal, 1990), 1243–4.

15. Juan Williams, "One Man Show," *Washington Post* Magazine, 9 June 1991.

16. Ibid.

17. Charles E. Jones, "The Election of L. Douglas Wilder: The First Black Lieutenant Governor of Virginia," *The Western Journal of Black Studies* 15 (1991): 105–13.

18. B. Drummon Ayers, "Yankee Strategiest Plans Campaign to Put Wilder in White House," *New York Times,* 15 October 1991.

19. Williams, "One Man Show." Jones, "The Election of L. Douglas Wilder," 107–108.

20. Ibid.

21. Jones, "The Election of L. Douglas Wilder," 110–11.

22. Ayers, "Yankee Strategiest Plans Campaign to Put Wilder in White House."

23. Jones and Clemons, "A Model of Racial Crossover Voting."

24. Schexnider, "The Politics of Pragmatism," 155.

25. Schexnider, "The Politics of Pragmatism," 154.

26. David S. Broder and Donald P. Baker, "Wilder Tosses Hat Near Ring," *Washington Post,* 18 March 1991.

27. Richard L. Berke, "Wilder Explores a Run for President," *New York Times,* 28 March 1993.

28. Francis Beal, "U.S. Politics Will Never Be the Same," *The Black Scholar* 15 (1984): 10–18.

29. Adam Meyerson, "Low-Tax Liberal," *Policy Review* 55 (1991): 26–31.

30. Ibid., 20.

31. Ibid.

32. John F. Harris, "Wilder, Advisers Map Possible Strategies for Presidential Bid," *Washington Post,* 12 August 1991.

33. Donald P. Baker, "Sounding Like a Contender, Wilder Hits N.H.," *Washington Post,* 28 August 1991. Robin Toner, "Testing Waters, Wilder Says America's Needs Come First," *New York Times,* 28 August 1991.

34. Richard Cohen, "Wilder's Drug Stand: Bold, Thoughtful," *Washington Post,* 9 April 1991.

35. Donald P. Baker, "Contrite Wilder Says He Was Misunderstood," *Washington Post,* 8 July 1991.

36. Donald P. Baker, "New Hampshire's Word on Wilder," *Washington Post,* 2 September 1991.

37. Robin Toner, "Wilder is Pressed on Mideast Stand," *New York Times,* 29 August 1991.

38. Donald P. Baker and Dan Balz, "Robb Saga Knocks Wilder Out of '92, Pundits Say," *Washington Post,* 29 June 1991.

39. Baker, "Contrite Wilder Says He Was Misunderstood."

40. John F. Harris, "Jackson Takes on School Funding Inequities in Wilder's Backyard," *Washington Post,* 25 September 1991. John F. Harris, "Jackson Wows Rural Virginia," *Washington Post,* 26 September 1991.

41. John F. Harris, "Wilder Has Some 'Friendly' Advice for Jackson," *Washington Post,* 29 September 1991.

42. John F. Harris and Donald P. Baker, "Wilder Accuses Jesse Jackson of Working Against Campaign," *Washington Post,* 24 December 1991.

43. Baker, "Contrite Wilder Says He Was Misunderstood."

44. John F. Harris, "Wilder Exploratory Bid Slow to Raise Contributions," *Washington Post,* 15 July 1991. Donald P. Baker, "Wilder Halfway to Matching Funds," *Washington Post,* 15 October 1991.

45. Donald P. Baker, "Wilder, Launching Campaign in New Hampshire, Gets Granite Reception," *Washington Post,* 17 November 1991.

46. "Clinton Outpaces Wilder in Survey of Old Dominion,"*Washington Post,* 29 December 1991.

47. Dan Balz, "Clinton, Tsongas, Wilder Spar on New Hampshire TV,"*Washington Post,* 2 November 1991.

48. Gwen Ifill, "Pack is Off and Spining with First TV Debate," *New York Times,* 17 December 1991. "Digging Past Political Pearls," Editorial, *New York Times,* 17 December 1991. Leslie H. Gelb, "The TV Debate Fiasco," *New York Times,* 18 December 1991.

49. Donald P. Baker, "Wilder Taps a Former Jackson Aide," *Washington Post,* 12 November 1991.

50. Robin Toner, "Democrats Court Labor By Hammering at Bush," *New York Times,* 13 November 1991.

51. B. Drummon Ayers, "Wilder's '92 Campaign Looks for Black Votes," *New York Times,* 10 November 1991.

52. Donald P. Baker, "Wilder Slams GOP Administrations for 'Creating' a Climate for Racism," *Washington Post,* 25 November 1991.

53. Donald P. Baker, "Wilder Woos Supporters in Clinton's Backyard," *Washington Post,* 9 December 1991.

54. Baker, "Wilder, Launching Campaign in New Hampshire, Gets Granite Reception."

55. Ibid.

56. Donald P. Baker, "Wilder Ends Campaign," *Washington Post,* 9 January 1992.

57. B. Drummon Ayers, "In the End, Wilder Realized the Numbers Fell Short," *New York Times,* 11 January 1992.

58. "Why Governor Wilder Failed," *New York Times,* 10 January 1991.

PART 7. DECISIONS

1. Charles V. Dale, *The Civil Rights Act of 1991: A Legal Analysis of Various Proposals to Reform the Federal Equal Employment Opportunity Laws* (Washington, DC: Congressional Research Service: 91–757A, 21 October 1991).

2. Miller and Walton, "Congressional Support of Civil Rights Public Policy," 11–25.

3. Quoted in Walton, *When the Marching Stopped,* 122–75.

4. Ibid., 135.

5. Ibid.

6. Ibid., 135–137.

7. Ibid.

8. Walton, Johnson, Green, and Jordan, "An Analysis of the Civil Rights Regulatory Agenda of the Bush Administration," 17–28.

9. Ibid., 25.

10. Jeffery Elliot (ed.), *Black Voices in American Politics,* 173.

11. Maya Angelou, "Dare to Hope," *The Black Scholar* 22 (Winter 1991/92): 23.

12. Linda Greenhouse, "Court, 6–3, Applies Voting Rights Act to Judicial Races: Big Impact in the South; Ruling Could Put More Minority Judges on Nation's Benches," *New York Times,* 21 June 1991. Linda Greenhouse, "Court Backs Minority Voting Districts," *New York Times,* 3 March 1993.

13. *Martin v. Allain* 658 F. Supp. 183 (S.D. Miss., 1987).

14. Press release, 17 June 1993, from office of State Representative Tyrone Brooks, Atlanta, Georgia, and the American Civil Liberties Union, headed by Laughlin McDonald and Kathy Wilde, representing the African American plaintiffs. See also "Editorial: Stand by Plan for More Black Judges," *Atlanta Journal/Constitution,* 5 June 1993. Theresa White, "Brooks Case Settlement to Transform Georgia's Courts," *Savannah Herald,* 2 September 1992.

15. *U.S. v. Brooks County,* Civil Action No. 90–105, Thom Consent Decree, 1.

16. Ibid., 2.

17. Ibid., 2–3.

18. Interview with Larry Ward, the Justice Department attorney handling the case, Savannah, Georgia, May 19–20, 1992. Thanks to Mr. Ward for bringing this case to my attention.

19. Janet Hook, "Officials Seek Moderation in Party's Change," *Congressional Quarterly Weekly Report,* 9 March 1985: 457.

20. Ibid.

21. Rhodes Cook, "Many Democrats Cool to Redoing Party Rules," *Congressional Quarterly Weekly Report,* 24 August 1985: 1687–9. See May Louis, "Race and Presidential Politics: The Challenge to Go Another Way," *Trotter Review* (Fall 1992): 12–13.

22. Ibid.

23. Ibid.

24. Ibid.

25. Ibid.

26. Matthew Holden, Jr., *The President, Congress, and Race Relations* (Boulder: Ernest Patterson Memorial Lecture, University of Colorado, 1986), 59.

27. Walton, "Democrats and African Americans," 333–45. Peter A. Brown, " '85 Demo Report Urges De-Marketing of Party," *Houston Chronicle,* 17 April 1989.

28. Linn Washington, *Black Judges on Justice* (New York: The New Press, 1994), xxi, 18–21. See also Bruce M. Wright, *Black Robes, White Justice: Why Our Legal System Doesn't Work for Blacks* (Secaucus: Lyle Stuart, 1987).

29. Ibid., 171–185 for an interview with Judge Henry Bramwell. See Elliott, *Black Voices in American Politics,* 147–96, for interviews with other conservative black jurists.

30. Ibid., xxi.

31. Joel D. Aberback and Bert Rockman, "The Political Views of U.S. Senior Federal Executives, 1970–1992," unpublished paper, 4.

32. Quoted in Ibid., 1.

33. Ibid.

34. Ibid., 4.

35. Ibid., 3.

36. Ibid., 5.

37. Ibid., 11–12.

38. Ibid., 9.

39. Black American Political Association of California, "African Americans in the Presi-

dent's Cabinet . . . Other African American Appointments," (unpublished document sent to author 13 September 1993), 1–39. This pamphlet is an effort to provide a comprehensive list of all of President Clinton's African American appointees up until September 13, 1993.

19. AFRICAN AMERICANS AND THE CLINTON PRESIDENCY: POLITICAL APPOINTMENTS AS SOCIAL JUSTICE

1. Andrew Hacker, *Two Nations: Black and White: Separate, Hostile, Unequal* (New York: Scribner, 1992).

2. Kenneth J. Meier, Joseph Stewart, Jr., and Robert E. England, "Second-Generation Educational Discriminations and White Flight from Public Schools," *National Political Science Review* 1 (1989): 76, 90. Chandler Davidson (ed.), *Minority Vote Dilution* (Washington, DC: Howard University Press, 1984). Shelia Ards, "The Theory of Vouchers and Housing Availability in the Black Community," in James Jennings (ed.), *Race, Politics, and Economic Development* (New York: Verso, 1992), 131–40. Juan Williams, "The Black Elite," *Washington Press* Magazine, 4 January 1981.

3. Walton, *The Native Son Presidential Candidate.*

4. Rhodes Cook, "Clinton Picks the GOP Lock on the Electoral College," 3549.

5. Ibid.

6. Ibid.

7. Ibid. And "Profiles: The Names and Faces of the Convention: Ronald H. Brown," *Congressional Quarterly's Guide to the 1992 Democratic National Convention* (4 July 1992): 28–29.

8. Ibid.

9. Stephen Labaton, "Nominee's Lobbying to be Scrutinized," *New York Times,* 20 December 1992.

10. Jeffrey L. Katz, "Facing Forward," *Congressional Quarterly's Guide to the 1992 Democratic National Convention* 50 (4 July 1992): 20.

11. Ronald W. Walters, *Black Presidential Politics in America: A Strategic Approach* (Albany: State University of New Press, 1988), 85–107.

12. "Profiles: The Names and Faces of the Convention: Ronald H. Brown," 27–30.

13. Ibid.

14. Phil Duncan, "The Makeup, Mind-Set of the Party Today," *Congressional Quarterly's Guide to the 1992 Democratic National Convention* 50 (4 July 1992): 52.

15. Ibid.

16. Ibid., 43.

17. Ibid.

18. Ibid.

19. Ibid.

20. Ibid.

21. Ibid., 18.

22. Ibid., 18–19.

23. Ibid., 19.

24. Katz, "Facing Forward," 20.

25. Ibid.

26. See "The Platform: Party's Statement of Policies Mirrors Clinton's Goals," *Congressional Quarterly's Guide to the 1992 Democratic National Convention* 50 (4 July 1992): 49–53.

27. Peter Applebome, "Perot Speech Gets Cool Reception at NAACP," *New York Times,* 12 July 1992.

28. Pamela Kessler, "Clinton Plans for Smooth Start with Focus on the Economic,"

Congressional Quarterly Weekly Report 50 (7 November 1992): 3555–6. Pat Towell, "Clinton Outlines his Priorities, Economy Chief Among Them," *Congressional Quarterly Weekly Report* 50 (14 November 1992): 3631–2.

29. Walton, *The Native Son Presidential Candidate,* 120–30.

30. Towell, "Clinton Outlines his Priorities."

31. Chuck Alston, "Confirmation: Senate Zips Through Approval of Clinton Cabinet Picks," 51 *Congressional Quarterly Weekly Report* (23 January 1993): 168–9.

32. Neil Lewis, "Guerrilla Fighter for Civil Rights: Clinton Seeks to Bring Lani Guinier Back to the Justice Department," *New York Times,* 5 May 1993.

33. Ibid.

34. Ibid.

20. AFRICAN AMERICANS AND THE RESURGENT REPUBLICAN CONGRESS: THE DUALITY OF TRANSFORMATION

1. See Norman C. Amaker, *Civil Rights and the Reagan Administration* (Washington, D.C.: Urban Institute Press, 1988) and Drew Days, "Turning Back the Clock: The Reagan Administration and Civil Rights," *Harvard Civil Rights-Civil Liberties Law Review* 19 (Summer 1984): 309.

2. See Anthony Champagne and Edward J. Hayham, *The Attack on the Welfare State* (Prospect Heights, Ill: Waveland Press, 1984). The ideas in this moderately conservative book are taken to their logical conclusion in Robert Detlefsen, *Civil Rights Under Reagan* (San Francisco: Institute for Contemporary Studies, 1991). Detlefsen argues that the Reagan administration's greatest failure was its inability to turn back the clock on the civil rights movement.3. For the need for legislative research on African Americans beyond individual and demographic attributes, see Walton, *Black Politics,* 167–73 and his *Invisible Politics,* 167–212.

4. E. Terrence Jones, *Conducting Political Research* (Philadelphia: Harper and Row, 1984), 29–30.

5. Ibid.

6. Ibid., 31.

7. For a comprehensive analysis of the CBC by one of its members, see William Clay, *Just Permanent Interests: Black Americans in Congress, 1870–1991* (New York: Amistad Press, 1992), 107–58.

8. See Marguerite Ross Barnett, "The Congressional Black Caucus: Illusions and Realities of Power," in Preston, Henderson, and Puryear, *The New Black Politics,* 28–54; see also her, "The Congressional Black Caucus and the Institutionalization of Black Politics," *Journal of Afro-American Issues* 5 (Summer 1995): 202–27.

9. Ibid. The growing conservative literature includes Timonthy O'Rourke, *The Impact of Reapportionment* (New Brunswick: Transaction Books, 1980); Abigail Thernstrom, *Whose Votes Count: Affirmative Action and Minority Voting Rights* (Cambridge: Harvard University Press, 1987); Carol M. Swain, *Black Faces, Black Interests: The Representation of African Americans in Congress* (Cambridge: Harvard University Press, 1993).

10. Aaron Wildavsky, "President Reagan as a Political Strategist," in Kay Lehman Schlozman (ed.), *Elections in America* (Boston: Allen and Unwin, 1987), 231.

11. Sam Fulwood, III, "CBC Returns to Its Roots in 104th Congress," *Focus* 23 (January 1995): 6.

12. In 1992, after the reapportionments ordered in 1990, the number of African Americans in Congress jumped from 26 to 39 members.

13. "House Republicans Rehearse Taking Reins of Power," *Congressional Quarterly Weekly Report* 52 (17 December 1994): 3548.

14. Persons, "The Election of Gary Franks," 194–208.

15. For a look at the chairs and membership of the House of Representatives Committees and Subcommittees in the 104th Congress see "Committees," *Congressional Quarterly Weekly Report* 52 (17 December 1994): 3549–58 and (31 December 1994): 3681–92.

16. Walton, *Invisible Politics,* 206–7.

17. Robert C. Smith, "The Black Congressional Delegation," *Western Political Quarterly* 34 (June 1981): 214.

18. See Michael Malbin, *Unelected Representatives: Congressional Staff and the Future of Representative Government* (New York: Basic Books, 1980); Harrison Fox and Susan Hammond, *Congressional Staffs: The Invisible Force in American Lawmaking* (New York: Free Press, 1977); Christine DeGregorio, "Professional Committee Staff as Policymaking Partners in the U.S. Congress," *Congress and the Presidency* 21 (Spring 1994): 49–68; John Kingdom, *Congressmen's Voting Decisions* 2d ed. (New York: Harper and Row, 1981).

19. Barker and Jones, *African Americans and the American Political System,* 256.

20. Ibid.

21. Ibid.

22. Ibid.

23. Ibid., 257.

24. "Congressional Civil Rights Bills" Hearing before the Committee on Governmental Affairs, 101st Congress, 1st Session, 1989, p. 111. Congressman Louis Stokes, "Testimony of Ms. Jackie Parker: The Underrepresentation of African Americans in the U.S. Senate," *U.S. Congressional Record* 135 (149) 30 October 1989. Another reprint appeared in *Focus* magazine: Jackie Parker, "Closed Doors on Capitol Hill: Black Senate Staffers Seek More Minority Representation in Policy-Level Positions," *Focus* (October 1989): 7.

25. Ibid.

26. See Simeon Booker, "Ticker Tape," *Jet,* 4 September 1995, 10.

27. David S. Cloud, "GOP's House-Clearing Sweep Changes Rules, Cuts Groups," *Congressional Quarterly Weekly Report* 52 (10 December 1994): 3488.

28. Ibid.

29. Ibid.

30. Donna Cassata, "Black Caucus Chooses Payne," *Congressional Quarterly Weekly Report* 52 (17 December 1994): 3545.

31. Ibid.

32. Ceci Connolly, "GOP Accentuates the Positive; Hopefuls To Sign Compact," *Congressional Quarterly Weekly Report* 52 (24 September 1994): 2711–2.

33. Walton, *Invisible Politics,* 214.

34. Marguerite Ross Barnett, "The Congressional Black Caucus," in Harvey Mansfield, Sr., (ed.), *Congress Against the President* (New York: Praeger, 1975), 46.

35. Smith, "The Black Congressional Delegation," 220.

36. Juliana Gruenwald, "Health Tax Break Passes Senate," *Congressional Quarterly Weekly Report* 53 (25 March 1995): 861.

37. Donna Cassata, "Republicans Bask in Success of Rousing Performance," *Congressional Quarterly Weekly Report* 53 (8 April 1995): 986.

38. Clay, *Just Permanent Interests,* 341.

39. James Steels, "Wounded and Bleeding: The CBC in the 104th," *Black Political Agenda* 2 (Fourth Quarter 1994): 6.

40. Clarence Lusane, "Unity and Struggle! The Political Behavior of African American Members of Congress," *The Black Scholar* 24 (Fall 1994): 26. See also his "African Americans and the Mid-Term Elections," *Black Political Agenda* 2 (Fourth Quarter 1994): 10.

41. Ibid.

42. "Agenda Turns To Other Issues," *Congressional Quarterly Weekly Report* 53 (8 April 1995): 982–5.

43. See Congressman Donald Payne's introduction to this volume.

PART 8. POLICY

1. Rich, *Coleman Young and Detroit Politics,* 18.

2. Ibid., 261.

3. Michael Lipsky, *Street-Level Bureaucracy: Dilemma of the Individual in Public Service* (New York: Russell Sage, 1980), and his "Toward A Theory of Street-Level Bureaucracy," in Willis D. Hawley and Michael Lipsky (eds.), *Theoretical Perspectives in Urban Politics* (Englewood Cliff, NJ: Prentice-Hall, 1976).

4. Alex Poinsett, *Black Power, Gary Style: The Making of Mayor Richard G. Hatcher* (Chicago: Johnson Publications, 1970). Edward Greer, *Big Steel: Black Politics and Corporate Power in Gary, Indiana* (New York: Monthly Review Press, 1979).

5. Interview with Deanie Frazier, Savannah, Georgia, 31 March 1993.

6. Jennings, *The Politics of Black Enpowerment,* 15.

7. Ibid., 16.

8. Jennings, *Race, Politics, and Economic Development,* 3. See also John Hope Franklin and Eleanor Holmes *Martin, Black Initiative, and Governmental Responsibility* (Washington, DC: Joint Center for Political Studies, 1987).

9. Ibid.

10. Ibid.

11. Smith and Seltzer, *Race, Class, and Culture,* 81.

21. AFRICAN AMERICAN MAYORS AND NATIONAL URBAN POLICY: THE FISCAL POLITICS OF URBAN FEDERALISM

1. Kwame Ture and Charles V. Hamilton, *Black Power: The Politics of Liberation* (New York: Vintage, 1992), 146.

2. Ibid., 148.

3. Ibid., 149.

4. Walton, *Black Politics,* 201.

5. Ibid.

6. Bette Woody, *Managing Crisis Cities: The New Black Leadership and the Politics of Resource Allocation* (Connecticut: Greenwood Press, 1982), 189.

7. Ture and Hamilton, *Black Power,* 215–216.

8. Ibid.

9. Ibid.

10. Mack Jones, "Black Mayoral Leadership in Atlanta: A Comment" in Lucius J. Barker (ed.), *Black Electoral Politics* (New Brunswick, NJ: Transaction Books, 1990), 138–144. Persons, "Black Mayoralities and the New Black Politics," 38–65. Robert T. Stark and Michael Preston, "The Political Legacy of Harold Washington, 1983–1987," *National Political Science Review* 2 (1990): 161–8. J. Philip Thompson, "David Dinkins' Victory in New York City: The Decline of the Democratic Party Organization and the Strengthening of Black Politics," *PS: Political Science and Politics* 23 (June 1990): 145–8. Bruce Ransom, "Black Independent Electoral Politics in Philadelphia and the Election of Mayor W. Wilson Good," in Preston, Henderson, and Puryear, *The New Black Politics.* "Symposium: Big City Black Mayors: Have They Made a Difference," in *Black Electoral Politics,* 129–95. William Nelson, Jr., "Black Mayoral Leadership: A Twenty Year Perspective," in *Black Electoral Politics,* 188–95. Adolph Reed, Jr., "The Black Urban Regime: Structural Origins and Constraints," in *Power, Community, and the City* (New Brunswick, NJ: Transaction Publishers, 1988).

11. Ibid.

12. Ibid.

13. Ibid.

14. Ibid.

15. Ibid.

16. John Harrigan, *Political Change in the Metropolis,* 4th ed. (Boston: Scott, Foresman, 1989).

17. Ibid., 358.

18. Ibid.

19. U.S. Census Bureau, *City Government Finances: 1979–1989* (Washington, DC: Government Printing Office, 1979–89).

20. Paul Peterson, *City Limits* (Chicago: University of Chicago Press, 1981), 175–181.

21. Ibid., 58.

22. Woody, *Managing Crisis Cities,* 185.

23. On enterprise zones and empowerment zones see Dennis R. Judd and Todd Swanstrom, *City Politics: Private Power and Public Policy* (New York: Harper/Collins, 1993), 301–3; Nicholas Lemann, "The Myth of Community Development," *New York Times* Magazine, 9 January 1994.

24. Eric Siegel, "Baltimore Snags $100 Million Grant," *Baltimore Sun,* 21 December 1994.

25. Sandy Banisky, "All Around Town, Residents Hope Money Brings Change," *Baltimore Sun,* 21 December 1994.

26. See the Department of Housing and Urban Development news release, "Statement of Henry Cisneros on Announcement of Empowerment Zones and Enterprise Communities," 21 December 1994, Washington, D.C.

27. Quoted in Guy Gugliotta, "HUD Chooses Baltimore for $100 Million in Aid," *Washington Post,* 21 December 1994.

28. Lemann, "The Myth of Community Development," 54.

22. AFRICAN AMERICAN FOREIGN POLICY: FROM DECOLONIZATION TO DEMOCRACY

1. African diaspora refers to the black population of Europe, North and South America, and the Caribbean. This paper focuses on the predominantly black nations of the Caribbean islands.

2. See Geneva Smitherman, *Black Talk: Words and Phrases from the Hood to the Amen Corner* (New York: Houghton Mifflin, 1994), 92.

3. Walton, *Invisible Politics,* 280.

4. Ibid.

5. One of the exceptional books to address this is Ted Hopf, *Peripheral Visions: Deterrence Theory and American Foreign Policy in the Third World, 1965–1990* (Ann Arbor: University of Michigan Press, 1994). Hopf used content analysis of Russian official governmental documents, newspaper reports, and speeches to discern how the Soviets viewed the third world and U.S. activity in those regions.

6. Earl A. Henderson, *Afrocentrism and World Politics: Toward a New Paradigm* (Connecticut: Praeger, 1995). Henderson argues persuasively that Eurocentric racial considerations drive the foreign policies of all of the European powers.

7. "Protesting Nigeria Tyranny?" *The Tampa Tribune,* 3 April 1995.

8. Quoted in J. Clay Smith, Jr., "United States Foreign Policy and Goler Teal Butcher," *Howard Law Journal* 37 (Winter 1994): 156. This paper is a major contribution in that it explores both the domestic and foreign realms.

9. Ibid., 154.

10. Henry F. Jackson, *From the Congo to Soweto: U.S. Foreign Policy Toward Africa Since 1960* (New York: Morrow, 1982), 19–43.

11. Jake C. Miller, *The Black Presence in American Foreign Affairs* (Washington, DC:

University Press of America, 1978), 7. Rubin Weston, *Racism in U.S. Imperialism* (Columbia, SC: University of South Carolina Press, 1972).

12. Ibid.

13. Laurence Finkelstein, "Bunche and the Colonial World: From Trusteeship to Decolonization," in Benjamin Rivlin (ed.), *Ralph Bunche: The Man and His Times* (New York: Holmes and Meier, 1990), 110.

14. Ibid., 119.

15. Ibid. Brian Urquhart, *Ralph Bunche: An American Life* (New York: W. W. Norton, 1993), chap. 8.

16. Herschelle Challenor, "The Contribution of Ralph Bunche to Trusteeship and Decolonization," in *Ralph Bunche,* 143–4.

17. Finkelstein, "Bunche and the Colonial World," 124. See also Urquhart, 111–38.

18. Charles P. Henry, "Civil Rights and National Security: The Case of Ralph Bunche," in *Ralph Bunche,* 50–63; and Benjamin Rivlin, "The Legacy of Ralph Bunche," in *Ralph Bunche,* 23.

19. Ibid.

20. Henry J. Richardson, III, "African Americans and International Law: For Professor Goler Teal Butcher, with Appreciation," *Howard Law Journal* 37 (Winter 1994): 222, 223.

21. Ibid., 197.

22. Walton, *Invisible Politics,* 280–1.

23. Smith, "United States Foreign Policy and Goler Teal Butcher," 210.

24. Ibid.

25. The forerunner to this movement was the theoretical framework known as Pan-Africanism and its proponents. For a review and analysis of the literature on African American international politics and behavior see Lockley Edmonson, "Black Americans as a Mobilizing Diaspora: Some International Implications," in Gaberiel Sheffer (ed.), *Modern Diasporas in International Politics* (London: Croon Helm, 1986), 164–211. Frederic I. Solop, "African-Americans Confront Apartheid," in Paula D. McClain (ed.), *Minority Group Influence: Agenda Setting, Formulation, and Public Policy* (Connecticut: Greenwood Press, 1993), 55. Philip White, "The Black American Constituency for Southern Africa, 1940–1980" in Alfred O. Hero and John Barrett (eds.), *The American People and South Africa* (Massachusetts: Lexington Books, 1981). Steven Metz, "The Anti-Apartheid Movement and the Populist Instincts in American Politics," *Political Science Quarterly* 101 (1986): 379–95. Although anticommunism was not a policy warmly embraced by African Americans, it did have African American supporters. For a discussion of some of these African American anti-communists see Gerald Horne, *Black and Red: W. E. B. DuBois and the Afro-American Response to the Cold War, 1944–1963* (New York: State University of New York Press, 1987). John Clytus, *Black Man in Red Cuba* (Coral Gables: University of Miami Press, 1970).

26. Quoted in Smith, "United States Foreign Policy and Goler Teal Butcher," 174.

27. " 'Less Than Brillant' Administration Role . . . Contributed to Momentum for Sanctions," *Congressional Quarterly Alamanac,* (Washington, DC: Congressional Quarterly, 1986), 360–1.

28. Ibid.

29. Smith, "United States Foreign Policy and Goler Teal Butcher," 174.

30. Ibid., 101–24.

31. Ibid. Ronald Walters, "The United States and South Africa: Nuclear Collaboration Under the Reagan Administration," *Trans-Africa Forum* (Fall 1983): 17–30.

32. Ronald W. Walters, *South Africa and the Bomb: Responsibility and Deterrence* (Massachusetts: Lexington Books, 1987), 122–3.

33. Ibid., 11.

34. Ibid., 145.

35. Ibid., 142.

36. Hopf, *Peripheral Visions,* 234–40.

37. Ibid., 100.

38. Ibid.

39. Smith, "United States Foreign Policy and Goler Teal Butcher," 174. For the advisory panel reflections see "Shaping Post-Apartheid South Africa," *Focus* (March 1987): 3. Neil Lewis, "Chester Crocker: Inside Making Policy on Africa," *New York Times,* 9 June 1987. Christopher Coker, *The United States and South Africa, 1968–1985: Constructive Engagement and Its Critics* (Durham: Duke University Press, 1986).

40. Ibid., 186.

41. Herschelle Challenor, "The Influence of Black Africans in U.S. Foreign Policy Toward Africa," in A. A. Said (ed.), *Ethnicity and U.S. Foreign Policy* (New York: Praeger, 1977), 239–74. Richard B. Moore, "Africa Conscious Harlem," in John Henrik Clarke (ed.), *Harlem: A Community in Transition* (New York: Citadel, 1964). St. Clair Drake, "Negro Americans and the African Interest," in John P. Davis (ed.), *The American Negro Reference Book* (Englewood Cliff: Prentice-Hall, 1966). John A. Davis, "Black Americans and United States Foreign Policy Toward Africa," *Journal of International Affairs* 23 (1969): 231–49.

42. Bill Ong Hing, "Immigration Politics: Messages of Exclusion to African Americans," *Howard Law Journal* 37 (Winter 1994): 245. Milton Morris, *Immigration: The Beleaguered Bureaucracy* (Washington, DC: Brookings Institution, 1985).

43. Beverly Baker-Kelly, "United States Immigration: A Wake Up Call," *Howard Law Journal* 37 (Winter 1990): 295.

44. Ibid., 296.

45. Ibid.

46. Hing, "Immigration Politics," 237.

47. Baker-Kelly, "United States Immigration," 298.

48. Lucius Barker and Mack Jones, *African Americans and the American Political System,* 266.

49. Ibid.

50. Pearl T. Robinson, "Looking Toward the Future with an Eye on the Past," in Pearl T. Robinson and Elliott P. Skinner (eds.), *Transformation and Resiliency in Africa* (Washington, DC: Howard University Press, 1983), 268.

51. Elliott P. Skinner, "Afro-Americans in Search of Africa: The Scholars' Dilemma," in *Transformation and Resiliency in Africa,* 24.

52. Ibid.

53. Juan Williams, "Black Leaders Find a Hot New Issue: 'Free South Africa' Protests Revive a Moribund Movement, *Washington Post,* 12 December 1984. Michael Marriott, "TransAfrica in the Eye of the Storm: Young Activists on Hill Organize Anti-apartheid Protest," *Washington Post,* 12 December 1984.

54. Smith, "United States Foreign Policy and Goler Teal Butcher," 179.

55. Ibid., 178.

56. Ronald W. Walters, *Pan Africanism in the Africa Diaspora* (Detroit: Wayne State University Press, 1993), 265–71.

57. Smith, "United States Foreign Policy and Goler Teal Butcher," 176.

58. Ibid., 177.

59. Ibid. Ethel Payne, "Anti-Apartheid Campaign Revives Old Coalition," *Washington Afro-American,* 24 January 1986.

60. "Reagan Message on South African Sanctions Veto," *Congressional Quarterly Almanac* 42 (1987): 28-D.

61. Ibid.

62. Reagan had issued an Executive Order on September 9, 1985 but H.R. 4868 included

most of its provisions. See "Hill Overrides Veto of South Africa Sanctions," *Congressional Quarterly Almanac* 42 (1987): 360.

63. "President Reagan's Letter on South Africa Executive Order," *Congressional Quarterly Almanac* 42 (1987): 30-D.

64. Miller and Walton, "Congressional Support of Civil Rights Public Policy," 11–27.

65. "Editorial: Focusing on Nigerian Repression," *St. Petersburg Times,* 22 March 1995.

66. Kenoye K. Eke, *Nigeria's Foreign Policy Under Two Military Governments, 1966–1979* (Lewiston, Maine: Edwin Mellen, 1990), 72.

67. "Focusing on Nigeria Repression," *St. Petersburg Times,* 22 March 1995.

68. Bob Herbert, "The New Slavery," *Baltimore Sun,* 12 April 1995.

69. Jack Payton, "U.S. Group Campaigns to Defeat Nigeria Regime," *St. Petersburg Times,* 18 March 1995.

70. "Protesting Nigeria's Tyranny," *The Tampa Tribune,* 3 April 1995.

PART 9. PROSPECTS

1. Rosenstone and Hansen, *Mobilization,* 117. On the balance of power strategy, see Chuck Stone, *Black Political Power in America* (Indianapolis: Bobbs-Merrill, 1968). Henry Lee Moon, *Balance of Power: The Negro Vote* (New York: Doubleday, 1948).

2. "Dymally Creates Innovative Group to Monitor Urban Water Policies," *Los Angeles Sentinel,* 14 July 1994.

3. Ken Leiser, "Institute Tapping Into Local Water Board Elections," *Daily Breeze,* 25 September 1994. Duke Helfand, "Dymally Minority Slate Wins Seats on 3 Boards," *Los Angeles Times,* 10 November 1994.

4. Helfand, "Dymally Minority Slate Wins Seats on 3 Boards."

5. Duke Helfand, "Minority Candidates Win Seats on Water Boards," *Los Angeles Times,* 10 November 1994.

6. "Dymally Creates Innovative Group to Monitor Urban Water Policies."

7. Helfand, "Dymally Minority Slate Wins Seats on 3 Boards."

8. Ibid.

23. AFRICAN AMERICANS, POLITICAL CONTEXT, AND THE CLINTON PRESIDENCY: THE LEGACY OF THE PAST IN THE FUTURE

1. Institute of Contemporary Studies, *Fairmont Conference,* xii.

2. Gerald Pomper (ed.), "The Presidential Election," in Pomper, *The Election of 1992,* 134–139.

3. Ibid.

4. Greenshaw, *Elephants in the Cottonfields,* 1–5.

5. Walton, *The Native Son Presidential Candidate,* 129–30.

BIBLIOGRAPHY

Books and Chapters

Amaker, Norman C. *Civil Rights and the Reagan Administration.* Washington, D.C.: Urban Institute Press, 1988.

Anderson, Kristi. *The Creation of A Democratic Majority, 1928–1936.* Chicago: University of Chicago Press, 1979.

Apostel, Richard, et al. *The Anatomy of Racial Attitudes.* Berkleley: University of California Press, 1983.

Aptheker, Herbert. "A Disquieting Negro Petition to Congress, 1800." *A Documentary History of the Negro People in the United States.* New York: Citadel Press, 1951.

——. "The Earliest Extant Negro Petition to Congress," *A Documentary History of the Negro People in the United States.* New York: Citadel Press, 1951.

——. "A Plea Against Mere Money Making, 1859." *A Documentary History of the Negro People in the United States.* New York: Citadel Press, 1951.

Ards, Shelia. "The Theory of Vouchers and Housing Availability in the Black Community." In James Jennings (ed.), *Race, Politics, and Economic Develpment.* New York: Verso, 1992.

Arian, Asher, Arthur S. Goldberg, John Mollenkoff, and Edward Rogorosky. *Changing New York City Politcs.* New York: Rutledge, 1991.

Bailey, Jr., Harry A. "Negro Interest Group Strategies." In Lenneal J. Henderson, Jr. (ed.), *Black Political Life in the United States.* San Francisco: Chandler, 1972.

Ball, Thomas E. *Julian Bond vs. John Lewis: On the Campaign Trail with John Lewis and Julian Bond.* Atlanta: HBCCC Publishing, 1988.

Baldassare, Mark, (ed.). *The Los Angeles Riots: Lesson for the Urban Future.* Boulder: Westview, 1994.
Barker, Lucius J. *Our Time Has Come: A Delegate's Diary of Jesse Jackson's 1984 Presidential Campaign.* Urbana: University of Illinois Press, 1988.
——, (ed.) "Symposium: Big City Black Mayors: Have They Made a Difference?" *Black Electoral Politics.* New Brunswick: Transaction Publishers, 1990.
—— and Mack Jones. *African Americans and the American Political System,* 3rd ed. Englewood Cliffs, New Jersey: Prentice Hall, 1994.
—— and Ronald W. Walters (eds.), "Jesse Jackson's Candidacy in Political-Social Perspective: A Contextual Analysis." *Jesse Jackson's 1984 Presidential Campaign: Challenge and Change in American Politics.* Urbana: University of Illinois Press, 1989.
Barnett, Marguerite Ross. "The Congressional Black Caucus: Illusions and Realities of Power." In Michael Preston, Lenneal Henderson, and Paul Puryear (eds.), *The New Black Politics.* New York: Longman, 1982.
Barone, Michael and Grant Ujifusa. *The Almanac of American Politics: The Senators, the Representatives, and the Governors—Their Records and Election Results, Their States, and Districts.* Washington, DC: The National Journal, 1990.
Beatty, Bess. *A Revolution Gone Backward: The Black Response to National Politics 1876–1896.* Westport: Greenwood, 1987.
Bell, Harold H. *A Survey of the Negro Convention Movement, 1830–1861.* New York: Arno, 1969.
Bennett, Lerone. *Confrontation: Black and White.* Chicago: Johnson, 1965.
Bentley, Arthur F. *The Process of Government.* San Antonio: Principia, 1949.
Berlin, Ira. *Slaves Without Masters: The Free Negro in the Antebellum South.* New York: Vintage, 1976.
Black, Earl. *Southern Governors and Civil Rights: Racial Segregation as a Campaign Issue in the Second Reconstruction.* Massachussets: Harvard University Press, 1976.
Bobo, Lawrence D., James J. Johnson, Jr., Melvin L. Oliver, James Sidanium, Camille Zubrinsky. *Public Opinion Before and After a Spring of Discontent: A Preliminary Report on the 1992 Los Angeles County Social Survey* Vol. 3, Number 1. Los Angeles: UCLS Center for the Study of Urban Poverty Occasional Working Paper Series, 1992.
Bond, Julian. *Black Candidates: Southern Campaign Experiences.* Atlanta: Southern Regional Council, 1969.
Brooks, Roy L. *Rethinking the American Race Problem.* Berkeley: University of California Press, 1990.
Brown, Claude. *Manchild in the Promise Land.* New York: Macmillan, 1965.
Brown, Courtney. *Ballots of Tumult: A Portrait of Volatility in American Voting.* Ann Arbor: University of Michigan Press, 1991.
Brown, Courtney. *Serpents in the Sand: Essays on the Nonlinear Nature of Politics and Human Destiny.* Ann Arbor: University of Michigan Press, 1995.
Browning, Rufus P., Dale Rogers Marshall, and David H. Tabb (eds.). *Racial Politics in American Cities.* New York: Longman, 1990.
Bunche, Ralph and Dewey Grantham (eds.). *The Political Status of the Negro in the Age of FDR.* Chicago: University of Chicago Press, 1943.
Burk, Robert Fredrick. *The Eisenhower Administration and Black Civil Rights.* Knoxville: University of Tennessee Press, 1985.
Burnham, Walter Dean. "The Legacy of George Bush: Travails of an Understudy." In James Ceaser and Andrew Bush (eds.), *Upside Down, Inside Out: The 1992 Elections and American Politics.* Maryland: Rowman and Littlefield, 1993.
Button, James. *Black Violence: Political Impact of the 1960s Riots.* Princeton: Princeton University Press, 1978.

Canon, David T. *Actors, Athletes, and Astronauts: Political Amateurs in the United States Congress.* Chicago: University of Chicago Press, 1990.

Campbell, A., P. Converse, W. E. Miller, and D. Stokes. *The American Voter.* New York: Wiley, 1960.

Campbell, Bruce A. and Richard J. Trilling (eds.). *Realignment in American Politics: Toward A Theory.* Austin: University of Texas Press, 1980.

Campbell, Colin, S. J. Rockman, and Bert Rockman (eds.). *The Bush Presidency: First Appraisals.* Chatham, New Jersey: Chatham House, 1991.

Carmines, Edward and Robert Huckfeldt. "Politics in the Wake of the Voting Rights Act." In Bernard Grofman and Chandler Davidson (eds.), *Controversies in Minorities Voting: The Voting Rights Act in Perspective.* Washington, DC: Brookings Institute, 1992.

—— and James Stimson. *Issue Evolution: Race and the Transformation of American Politics.* Princeton: Princeton University Press, 1989.

Carroll, Susan J. *Women as Candidates in American Politics.* Bloomington: Indiana University Press, 1985.

Carson, Clayborne. *In Struggle: SNCC and the Black Awakening of the 1960s.* Cambridge: Harvard University Press, 1981.

Carter, Stephen L. "Foreword" in Lani Guinier, *The Tyranny of the Majority: Fundamental Fairness in Representative Democracy.* New York: Free Press, 1994.

Cavanaugh, Thomas E. and Lorin S. Foster. *Jesse Jackson's Campaign: The Primaries and Caucuses.* Washington, DC: Joint Center for Political Studies, 1984.

Ceasar, James and Andrew Bush. *Upside Down, Inside Out: The 1992 Elections and American Politics.* Maryland: Rowman and Littlefield, 1993.

Challenor, Herschelle. "The Contribution of Ralph Bunche to Trusteeship and Decolonization." In Brian Urquhart (ed.), *Ralph Bunche: An American Life.* New York: W. W. Norton, 1993.

——. "The Influence of Black Africans in U.S. Foreign Policy Toward Africa." In A. A. Said (ed.), *Ethnicity and U.S. Foreign Policy.* New York: Praeger, 1977.

Champayne, Anthony and Edward J. Hayham. *The Attack on the Welfare State.* Prospect Heights, IL: Waveland, 1984.

Chisholm, Shirley. *The Good Fight.* New York: Harper and Row, 1973.

Clay, William. *Just Permanent Interests: Black Americans in Congress, 1870–1991.* New York: Amistad Press, 1992.

Chrisman, Robert and Robert Allen. *Court of Appeal: The Black Community Speaks Out on the Racial and Sexual Politics of Thomas vs Hill.* New York: Ballantine, 1992.

Clytus, John. *Black Man in Red Cuba.* Coral Gables: University of Miami Press, 1970.

Coker, Christopher. *The United States and South Africa, 1968–1985: Constructive Engagement and Its Critics.* Durham: Duke University Press, 1986.

Coleman, Mary and Leslie McLemore. "Continuity and Change: The Power of Traditionalism in Biracial Politics in Mississippi's Second Congressional District." In Michael Preston and Lenneal Henderson, Jr. (eds.). *The New Black Politics: The Search for Political Power* 2d ed. New York: Longham, 1987.

Collins, Sheila D. *The Rainbow Challenge: The Jackson Campaign and the Rules of U.S. Politics.* New York: Monthly Review Press, 1986.

Combs, Michael and John Gruhl (eds.). *Affirmative Action: Theory and Analysis and Prospects.* North Carolina: McFarland, 1986.

Converse, Jean. *Survey Research in the United States: Roots and Emergence.* Berkeley: University of California Press, 1987.

Converse, Philip E. "V. O. Key, Jr. and the Study of Public Opinion." In Milton C. Cummings, Jr. (ed.), *V. O. Key, Jr. and the Study of American Politics.* Washington, DC: American Political Science Association, 1988.

Cook, Samuel Dubois. "Introduction." In Hanes Walton, Jr., *The Political Philosophy of Martin Luther King, Jr.* Westport, Connecticut: Greenwood, 1971.

Cook, Samuel Dubois. "The Politics of the Success of Failure." In Hanes Walton, Jr., *Black Political Parties: An Historical and Political Analysis.* New York: Free Press, 1972.

Cotton, Elizabeth. *The Jackson Phenomenon.* New York: Doubleday, 1989.

Cross, Jr., William E. *Shades of Black: Diversity in African-American Identity.* Philadelphia: Temple University Press, 1991.

Dahl, Robert A. *Who Governs?* New Haven: Yale University Press, 1961.

Dale, Charles V. *The Civil Rights Act of 1991: A Legal Analysis of Various Proposals to Reform the Federal Equal Employment Opportunity Laws.* Washington, DC: Congressional Research Service: 91–757A, October 21, 1991.

——. *Federal Civil Rights Decisions of the United States Supreme Court During the 1988–89 Term.* Washington, DC: Congressional Research Service: 89–439A, July 28, 1989.

Darcy, R., Susan Welch, and Janet Clark. *Women, Elections, and Representation.* New York: Longman, 1987.

Davidson, Chandler (ed.). *Minority Vote Dilution.* Washington, DC: Howard University Press, 1984.

——. "The Voting Rights Act: A Brief History." In Bernard Grofman and Chandler Davidson, (eds.), *Controversies in Minority Voting: The Voting Rights Act in Perspective.* Washington, DC: Brookings Institution, 1992.

Davis, Marilyn and Alex Willingham, "Andrew Young and the Georgia State Elections of 1990." In Georgia Persons (ed.), *Dilemmas of Black Politics.* New York: HarperCollins, 1993.

Dawson, Michael and Ernest Wilson, III. "Paradigms and Paradoxes: Political Science and African-American Politics." In William Crotty (ed.), *Political Science: Looking to the Future Vol. I.* Illinois: Northwestern University Press, 1991.

Dean, John. *The Making of a Black Mayor.* Washington, D.C.: Joint Center for Political Studies, 1973.

Detlefsen, Robert. *Civil Rights Under Reagan.* San Francisco: Institute for Contemporary Studies, 1991.

Drake, St. Clare. "Negro Americans and the African Interest." In John P. Davis, (ed.), *The American Negro Reference Book.* Englewood Cliff: Prentice-Hall, 1966.

DuBois, W. E. B. (ed.). *Atlanta University Publications.* Vol. I–III. New York: Octagon Books, 1968.

Eagles, Charles (ed.). *The Civil Rights Movement in America.* Jackson: University Press of Mississippi, 1986.

——. *Democracy Delayed: Congressional Reapportionment and Urban-Racial Conflict in the 1920s.* Athens: University of Georgia Press, 1990.

Edmonson, Lockley. "Black Americans as a Mobilizing Diaspora: Some International Implications." In Gabriel Sheffer (ed.), *Modern Diasporas in International Politics.* London: Croon Helm, 1986.

Edsall, Thomas Byrne and Mary D. Edsall. *Chain Reaction: The Impact of Race, Rights, and Taxes on American Politics.* New York: Norton, 1991.

Edward, III, George C. with Alex M. Gallup. *Presidential Approval: A Sourcebook.* Baltimore: John Hopkins University Press, 1990.

Eke, Kenoye K. *Nigeria's Foreign Policy Under Two Military Governments, 1966–1979.* Lewiston, Maine: Edwin Mellen Press, 1990.

Elliott, Jeffrey M. (ed.). *Black Voices in American Politics.* New York: Harcourt, Brace, Jovanovich, 1986.

Eulau, Heniz. *The Behavioral Persuasion in Politics.* New York: Random House, 1963.

Farr, Bob and Nancy Skelton. *Thunder in America: The Impeachable Presidential Campaign of Jesse Jackson.* Texas: Texas Monthly Press, 1986.

Feagin, Joe, et al. *A Case for the Case Study.* Chapel Hill: University of North Carolina Press, 1991.

Finkelstein, Laurence. "Bunche and the Colonial World: From Trusteeship to Decolonization." In Benjamin Rivlin (ed.), *Ralph Bunche: The Man and His Times.* New York: Holmes and Meier, 1990.

Fleming, G. James. *An All-Negro Ticket in Baltimore.* New York: Holt, Rinehart and Winston, 1969.

——. *Baltimore's Failure to Elect a Black Mayor in 1971.* Washington, D.C.: Joint Center for Political Studies, 1972.

Foster, Lorin (ed.). *The Voting Rights Act: Consequences and Implications.* New York: Praeger, 1985.

Fox, Harrison and Susan Hammond. *Congressional Staffs: The Invisible Force in American Lawmaking.* New York: Free Press, 1977.

Franklin, John Hope and Glenda Rae McNeil. *African Americans and the Living Constitution.* Washington, DC: Smithsonian Institution, 1995.

—— and A. A. Moss, Jr. *From Slavery to Freedom: A History of Negro Americans* 6th ed. New York: Alfred A. Knopf, 1988.

—— and Eleanor Holmes Norton. *Black Initiative and Governmental Responsibility.* Washington, D.C.: Joint Center for Political Studies, 1987.

Frazier, E. F. *The Negro Church in America.* New York: Schocken, 1974.

——. *The Negro in the United States.* New York: Macmillan, 1957.

Freer, Regina. "Black-Korean Conflict." In Mark Baldassare (ed.), *The Los Angeles Riots: Lesson for the Urban Future.* Boulder: Westview, 194.

Frye, Hardy. *Black Parties and Political Power: A Case Study.* Boston: G. K. Hall, 1980.

Gall, Peter. *Bring Us Together: The Nixon Team and the Civil Rights Retreat.* Philadelphia: J. B. Lippincott, 1971.

Gamm, Gerald H. *The Making of New Deal Democrats: Voting Behavior and Realignment in Boston, 1920–1940.* Chicago: University of Chicago Press, 1986.

Garcia, F. Chris. *Political Socialization of Chicano Children.* New York: Praeger, 1973.

Garrow, David. *Bearing the Cross: Martin Luther King, Jr. and the Southern Christian Leadership Conference, 1955–1968.* New York: Morrow, 1986.

——. *Protest at Selma: Martin Luther King, Jr. and the Voting Rights Act of 1965.* New Haven: Yale University Press, 1978.

Gillette, William. *Retreat from Reconstruction, 1869–1879.* Baton Rouge: Louisiana State University Press, 1979.

Glazer, Nathan. *Affirmative Discrimination: Ethnic Inequality and Public Policy.* New York: Basic Books, 1971.

Going, Kenneth. *The NAACP Comes of Age: The Defeat of Judge John J. Parker.* Bloomington: Indiana University Press, 1990.

Graham, Hugh David. *The Civil Rights Era: Origins and Development of National Policy, 1960–1972.* New York: Oxford University Press, 1990.

——. "Voting Rights and the American Regulatory State." In Bernard Grofman and Chandler Davidson (eds.), *Controversies in Minority Voting: The Voting Rights Act in Perspective.* Washington, DC: Brookings Institution, 1992.

Greenshaw, Wayne. *Elephants in the Cottonfields: Ronald Reagan and the New Republican South.* New York: Macmillan, 1982.

Greer, Edward. *Big Steel: Black Politics and Corporate Power in Gary, Indiana.* New York: Monthly Review Press, 1979.

Grossman, Lawrence. "Democrats and Blacks in the Gilded Age." In Peter Kowler (ed.), *Democrats and the American Idea.* Washington: Center for National Policy Press, 1992.

Gurin, Patricia, Shirley Hatchett, and James S. Jackson. *Hope and Independence: Blacks' Response to Electoral and Party Politics.* New York: Russell Sage, 1989.

Guteriz, Armando. "Jackson Campaign in the Hispanic Community: Problems and Prospects for a Black-Brown Colition." In L. J. Barker and R. W. Walter (eds.), *Jesse Jackson's 1984 Presidential Campaign.* Urbana and Chicago: University of Illinois Press, 1989.

Hacker, Andrew. *Two Nations Black and White: Separate, Hostile, Unequal.* New York: Scribner, 1992.

Hamilton, Charles V. *The Bench and the Ballot: Southern Federal Judges and Black Votes.* New York: Oxford University Press, 1973.

——. *Minority Politics in Black Belt Alabama.* New York: McGraw-Hill, 1962.

Harrigan, John. *Political Change in the Metropolis* 4th ed. Boston: Scott, Foresman, 1989.

Hartsfield, Annie Mary and Elston E. Roady. *Florida Votes* rev. ed. Tallahassee: Florida State University Institute for Social Research, 1972.

Haygood, David. *The Purge that Failed: Tammany v. Powell.* New York: McGraw-Hill, 1960.

Henderson, Earl A. *Afrocentrism and World Politics: Toward a New Paradigm.* Westport, Connecticut: Praeger, 1995.

Henderson, Jr., Lenneal J. (ed.). *Black Political Life in the United States.* San Francisco: Chandler, 1972.

Henry, Charles. *Culture and African American Politics.* Bloomington: Indiana University Press, 1990.

——. *Jesse Jackson: The Search for Common Ground.* California: The Black Scholar Press, 1991.

——. "Racial Factors in the 1982 California Gubernatorial Campaign: Why Bradley Lost." In Michael Preston, Lenneal Henderson, and Paul Puryear (eds.), *The New Black Politics: The Search for Political Power* 2d ed. New York: Longman, 1987.

Hill, R. B. *The Strengths of Black Families.* New York: National Urban League, 1972.

Hine, Darlene Clark. *Black Victory: The Rise and Fall of the White Primary in Texas.* New York: KTO Press, 1979.

Hirshon, Stanley. *Farwell to the Bloody Shirts: Northern Republicans and the Southern Negro, 1877–1883.* Bloomington: Indiana University Press, 1962.

Holden, Jr., Matthew. *The President, Congress, and Race Relations.* Boulder: University of Colorado, 1986.

——. "Race and Constitutional Change in the Twentieth Century." In Hohn Hope Franklin and Genna Rae McNeil (eds.), *African Americans and the Living Constitution.* Washington, D.C.: Smithsonian Institute Press, 1995.

Holloway, Harry. *The Politics of the Southern Negro: From Exclusion to Big City Organizations.* New York: Random House, 1969.

Hopf, Ted. *Peripheral Visions: Deterrence Theory and American Foreign Policy in the Third World, 1965–1990.* Ann Arbor: University of Michigan Press, 1994.

Horne, Gerald. *Black and Red: W. E. B. DuBois and the Afro-American Response to the Cold War, 1944–1963.* New York: State University of New York Press, 1987.

Howard-Pitney, David. *The Afro-American Jeremiad: Appeals for Justice in America.* Philadelphia: Temple University Press, 1990.

Hucksfeld, Robert and Carol Kohfeld. *Race and the Decline of Class in American Politics.* Urbana: University of Illinois Press, 1989.

Hull, Gloria T., Patricia Bell Scott, and Barbara Smith (eds.). *Black Women's Studies: All the Women are White, All the Men are Black, But Some of Us are Brave.* Old Westbury: Feminist Press, 1982.

Hyman, Herbert. *Political Socialization.* New York: Free Press, 1959.

——. *Secondary Analysis of Sample Surveys: Principles, Procedures, and Potentialities.* New York: John Wiley, 1972.

Institute for Contemporary Studies. *The Fairmont Papers: Black Alternatives Conference.* San Franciso: Institute for Contemporary Studies, 1981.

Jack, Hulan E. *Fifty Years a Democrat: The Autobiography of Hulan E. Jack.* New York: New Benjamin Franklin House, 1982.

Jackson, Brooks. *Honest Graft: Big Money and the American Political Process* 2d ed. Washington, D.C.: Farragut, 1990.

Jacobson, Gary C. *Money in Congressional Elections.* New Haven: Yale University Press, 1980.

——. "The Republican Advantage in Campaign Finance." In John E. Chubb and Paul Petterson (eds.), *The New Directions in American Politics.* Washington, D.C.: Brookings Institution, 1985.

Jackson, Henry F. *From the Congo to Soweto: U.S. Foreign Policy Toward Africa Since 1960.* New York: Morrow, 1982.

Jacobstein, Helen. *The Segregation Factor in the Florida Democratic Gubernatorial Primary of 1956.* Gainesville: University of Florida Press, 1972.

Jamieson, Kathleen Hall. *Dirty Politics.* New York: Oxford University Press, 1993.

Jennings, James. *The Politics of Black Empowerment: The Transformation of Black Activisms in Urban America.* Detroit: Wayne State University Press, 1992.

—— (ed.). *Race, Politics, and Economic Development: Community Perspectives.* New York: Verso, 1992.

Jennings, M. Kent. *Generations and Politics.* Princeton: Princeton University Press, 1981.

Joint Center for Political Studies. *Blacks and the 1988 Democratic Convention.* Washington, D.C.: Joint Center for Political Studies, 1988.

Jones, Charles and Michael L. Clemmons. "A Model of Racial Crossover Voting: An Assessment of the Wilder Victory." In Georgia A. Persons (ed.), *Dilemmas of Black Politics.* New York: HarperCollins, 1993.

Jones, E. Terrence. *Conducting Political Research.* Philadelphia: Harper and Row, 1984.

Jones, Mack. "Black Mayoral Leadership in Atlanta: A Comment." In Lucius J. Barker (ed.), *Black Electoral Politics.* New Brunswick: Transaction Publishing, 1990.

Kahneman, Daniel and Amos Tversky, "The Simulation Heuristic." In Daniel Kahneman, Paul Slovic, and Amos Tversky (eds.), *Judgement Under Uncertainty: Heuristics and Biases.* New York: Cambridge University Press, 1982.

Kaiser, Ernest (ed.). *The American Negro Academy Occasional Papers 1–22.* New York: Arno Press and the New York Times, 1969.

Keech, William. *The Impact of Negro Voting: The Role of the Vote in the Quest for Equality.* Chicago: Rand McNally, 1968.

Key, Jr., V. O. *Southern Politics.* New York: Vintage Books, 1949.

Kiecolt, K. Jill and Laura E. Nathan. *Secondary Analysis of Survey Data.* Beverly Hills: Sage, 1985.

Kilson, Martin. "Political Status of American Negroes in the Twentieth Century." In Martin Kilson and Robert I. Rothberg (eds.), *The African Dream: Interpretive Essays.* Cambridge: Harvard University Press, 1976.

King, Gary. *Unifying Political Methodology: The Likelihood Theory of Statistical Inference.* Cambridge: Cambridge University Press, 1989.

—— and Lynn Ragsdale. *The Elusive Executive: Discovering Statistical Patterns in the Presidency.* Washington, D.C.: Congressional Quarterly Press, 1988.

King, Jr., Martin Luther. *Where Do We Go From Here: Chaos or Community?* Boston: Beacon Hill, 1967.

Kingdom, John. *Congressman's Voting Decisions* 2d ed. New York: Harper and Row, 1981.

Kirschman, Joleen and Kathryn M. Neckerman. "We'd Love to Hire Them, But . . . : The Meaning of Race for Employers." In Christopher Jencks and Paul E. Peterson (eds.), *The Urban Underclass.* Washington, D.C.: The Brookings Institution, 1991.

Klein, Ethel. *Gender Politics.* Cambridge: Harvard University Press, 1985.

Kluggel, James R. and Eliot Smith. *Beliefs About Inequality.* New York: Aldine deGruyer, 1986.

Landess, T. H. and R. M. Quinn. *Jesse Jackson and the Politics of Race.* Ottawa: Jameson Books, 1985.

Lewinson, Paul. *Race, Class, and Party: A History of Negro Suffrage in the South.* New York: Russell and Russell, 1993.

Light, Paul. *The President's Agenda: Domestic Policy Choices from Kennedy to Carter.* Baltimore: Johns Hopkins University Press, 1985.

Lipsky, Michael. *Protest in City Politics.* Chicago: Rand McNally, 1969.

——. *Street-Level Bureaucracy: Dilemma of the Individual in Public Service.* New York: Russell Sage, 1980.

——. "Toward A Theory of Street-Level Bureaucracy." In Willis D. Hawley and Michael Lipsky (eds.), *Theoretical Perspectives in Urban Politics.* Englewood Cliffs: Prentice-Hall, 1976.

Lisio, Donald. *Hoover, Blacks and Lily-Whites: A Study of Southern Strategies.* Chapel Hill: University of North Carolina Press, 1985.

Litwack, Leon. *North of Slavery: The Negro in the Free States, 1790–1860.* Chicago: University of Chicago Press, 1961.

Logan, Rayford. *The Betrayal of the Negro: From Rutherford B. Hayes to Woodrow Wilson.* New York: Collier, 1965.

Lowi, Theodore. *The End of Liberalism.* New York: W. W. Norton, 1969.

Lukes, Steven (ed.). *Durkheim: The Rules of the Sociological Method and Selected Texts on Sociology and its Methods.* New York: Free Press, 1982.

Mahood, H. R. *Interest Group Politics in America: A New Intensity.* Englewood Cliffs: Prentice Hall, 1990.

Magleby, David and Candice J. Nelson. *The Money Chase: Congressional Campaign Reform.* Washington, D.C.: Brookings Institution, 1990.

Malbin, Michael. *Unelected Representatives: Congressional Staff and the Future of Representative Government.* New York: Basic Books, 1989.

Mansbridge, Jane. *Why We Lost the ERA.* Chicago: University of Chicago Press, 1986.

Matthews, Donald and James Prothro. *Negroes and the New Southern Politics.* New York: Harcourt, Brace, and World, 1966.

Mazmanian, Daniel. *Third Parties in Presidential Elections.* Washington, D.C.: Brookings Institution, 1974.

McCollough, Thomas E. *The Moral Imagination and Public Life: Raising the Ethical Question.* Chatham, New Jersey: Chatham House, 1991.

McCormick, II, Joseph P. and Charles E. Jones. "The Conceptualization of Deracialization: Thinking Through the Dilemma." In Georgia A. Persons (ed.), *Dilemmas of Black Politics: Issues of Leadership and Strategy.* New York: HarperCollins, 1993.

McMillan, Neil. *The Citizens' Council: Organized Resistance to the Second Reconstruction 1954–1964.* Urbana: University of Illinois Press, 1971.

Mendelberg, Tali. *The Politics of Racial Ambiguity: Origins and Consequences of Implicit Racial Appeals.* Ann Arbor: University of Michigan, unpublished doctoral dissertation, 1994.

Miller, Jake C. *The Black Presence in American Foreign Affairs.* Washington, D.C.: University Press of America, 1978.

Mollenknopf, John H. "New York: The Great Anomaly." In Rufus P. Browning, Dale Rogers

Marshall, and David H. Tabb (eds.), *Racial Politics in American Cities.* New York: Longman, 1990.

Moon, Henry Lee. *Balance of Power: The Negro Vote.* New York: Doubleday, 1948.

Moore, Richard. "Africa Conscious Harlem." In John Henrik Clarke, (ed.), *Harlem: A Community in Transition.* New York: Citadel, 1964.

Morgan, Richard. *Disabling America: The 'Rights' Industry in Our Time.* New York: Basic Books, 1984.

Morgan, Ruth. *The President and Civil Rights: Policy-Making by Executive Order.* New York: St. Martin, 1960.

Morris, Aldon. *The Origins of the Civil Rights Movement: Black Communities Organizing for Change.* New York: Free Press, 1984.

——, Shirley Hatchett, and Ronald Brown. "The Civil Rights Movement and Black Political Socialization." In R. S. Sigel (ed.), *Political Learning in Adulthood.* Chicago: University of Chicago, 1989.

Morris, Lorenzo (ed.). *The Social and Political Implications of the 1984 Jesse Jackson Presidential Campaign.* New York: Praeger, 1990.

Morris, Milton. *Immigration: The Beleaguered Bureaucracy.* Washington, D.C.: Brookings Institution, 1985.

Morrison, Toni (ed.). "Introduction" in *Race-ing Justice, Engender-ing Power: Essays on Anita Hill, Clarence Thomas, and the Construction of Social Reality.* New York: Pantheon, 1992.

Moss, Jr., Alfred A. *The American Negro Academy: Voice of the Talented Tenth.* Baton Rouge: Louisiana State University Press, 1981.

Murray, Charles. *Losing Ground: America's Social Policy, 1950–1980.* New York: Basic Books, 1984.

Mydral, Gunnar. *An American Dilemma.* New York: Harper and Row, 1944.

Nelson, Melany. *Even Mississippi.* Alabama: University of Alabama Press, 1989.

Nieman, Donald. *Promises To Keep: African-Americans and the Constitutional Order, 1776 to Present.* New York: Oxford University Press, 1991.

Niemi, Richard and Herbert Weisberg (eds.). *Controversies in American Voting Behavior.* San Franciso: W. H. Freeman, 1976.

Nelson, Jr., William. "Black Mayoral Leadership: A Twenty Year Perspective." In Lucius J. Barker, (ed.), *Black Electoral Politics.* New Brunswick: Transaction Publishers, 1990.

Odegard, Peter. *Pressure Politics: The Story of the Anti-Saloon League.* New York: Columbia Unversity Press, 1928.

O'Neill, Timothy. *Bakke and the Politics of Equality: Friends and Foes in the Classroom of Litigation.* Connecticut: Wesleyan University Press, 1985.

O'Neill, Tip and William Novak. *Man of the House: The Life and Political Memoirs of Speaker Tip O'Neill.* New York: Random House, 1987.

O'Rourke, Timothy. *The Impact of Reapportionment.* New Brunswick: Transaction Books, 1980.

Parker, Frank R. *Black Votes Count: Political Empowerment in Mississippi After 1965.* Chapel Hill: University of North Carolina Press, 1990.

Persons, Georgia A. "Black Mayoralties and the New Black Politics: From Insurgency to Racial Reconciliation." In Georgia A. Persons (ed.), *Dilemmas of Black Politics.* New York: HarperCollins, 1993.

——. "The Election of Gary Franks and the Ascendency of the New Black Conservatives." In *Dilemmas of Black Politics.*

Pettigrew, Thomas and Denise Alston. *Tom Bradley's Campaign for Governor: The Dilemma of Race and Political Strategies.* Washington, D.C.: Joint Center for Political Studies, 1988.

Pinderhughes, Dianne M. "Political Choices: A Realignment in Partisanship Among Black Voters." In J. D. Williams (ed.), *The State of Black Americans.* New York: Urban League, 1985.

——. "The Role of African American Political Organizations in the Mobilization of Voters." In Ralph Gomes and Linda Faye Williams (eds.), *From Exclusion to Inclusion: The Long Struggle for African American Political Power.* Westport: Greenwood Press, 1992.

Pinney, Edward L. and Robert S. Friedman. *Political Leadership and the School Desegregation Crisis in Louisiana.* New York: McGraw-Hill, 1963.

Pohlman, Marcus D. *Black Politics in Conservative America.* New York: Longman, 1990.

Pointsett, Alex. *Black Power, Gary Style: The Making of Mayor Richard G. Hatcher.* Chicago: Johnson, 1970.

Pomper, Gerald (ed.). *The Election of 1988.* Chatham, N.J.: Chatham House, 1989.

——. *Nominating the President: The Politics of Convention Choice.* New York: W. W. Norton, 1960.

—— (ed.). "The Presidential Election." In Gerald Pomper, (ed.), *The Election of 1992.* Chatham, N.J.: Chatham House, 1993.

Porter, Bruce and Marvin Dunn. *The Miami Riot of 1980: Crossing the Bounds.* Massachusetts: Lexington, 1984.

Price, Hugh D. *The Negro and Southern Politics: A Chapter of Florida History.* New York: New York University Press, 1957.

Price, Margaret. *The Negro and the Ballot.* Atlanta: Southern Regional Council, 1959.

——. *The Negro Voter in the South.* Atlanta: Southern Regional Council, 1957.

Preston, Michael B. "The Election of Harold Washington: An Examination of the SES Model in the 1983 Chicago Mayoral Election." in Michael Preston, Lenneal Henderson, Jr., Paul Puryear (eds.), *The New Black Politics* 2d ed. New York: Longman, 1987.

——. "Urban Politics and Public Policy: Mayoral Campaigns in Chicago, Cleveland, Detroit, New Orleans, and Philadelphia," in *The New Black Politics.*

Prewitt, Kenneth. *Institutional Racism in America.* Englewood Cliffs, NJ: Prentice Hall, 1970.

Quarles, Benjamin. *Black Abolitionists.* New York: W. W. Norton, 1960.

Quick, Paul. "Domestic Policy: Divided Government and Cooperative Presidential Leadership." In Colin Campbell, S. J. Rockman and Bert A. Rockman (eds.), *The Bush Presidency: First Appraisals.* Chatham, New Jersey: Chatham House, 1991.

Ransom, Bruce. "Black Independent Electoral Politics in Philadelphia and the Election of Mayor W. Wilson Good." In Michael Preston, Lenneal Henderson, Jr., and Paul Puryear (eds.), *The New Black Politics* 2d ed. New York: Longman, 1987.

Reagan, Ronald. "Reagan Message on South African Sanctions Veto." *Congressional Quarterly Alamanac* Vol. 42, 99th Congress, 2nd Session, 1986. Washington, D.C.: Congressional Quarterly, 1987.

Reed, Jr., Adolph. "The Black Urban Regime: Structural Origins and Constraints." In *Power, Community, and the City.* New Brunswick: Transaction Publishers, 1988.

——. *The Jesse Jackson Phenomenon.* New York: Yale University Press, 1985.

Rich, Wilbur C. *Coleman Young and Detroit Politics: From Social Activist to Power Broker.* Detroit: Wayne State University Press, 1989.

Riker, William H. *The Art of Political Manipulation.* New Haven: Yale University Press, 1986.

Riridon, William L. *Plunkitt of Tammany Hall.* New York: Bedford Books of St. Martin's Press, 1994.

Robinson, Pearl T. "Looking Toward the Future with an Eye on the Past." In Pearl T. Robinson and Elliott P. Skinner (eds.), *Transformation and Resiliency in Africa.* Washington, D.C.: Howard University Press, 1983.

Rose, Douglas, ed. *The Emergence of David Duke and the Politics of Race.* Chapel Hill: University of North Carolina Press, 1992.

Rose, Harold M. and Paula D. McClain. *Race, Place, and Risk: Black Homicide in Urban America.* Albany: State University of New York Press, 1990.

Rosenstone, Steven J., Roy L. Behr, and Edward H. Lazarus. *Third Parties in America: Citizen Response to Major Party Failure.* Princeton: Princeton University Press, 1984.

Rosenstone, Steven J. and John Mark Hansen. *Mobilization, Participation, and Democracy in America.* New York: Macmillan, 1993.

Rothenberg, Randall. *The Neoliberals: Creation of the New American Politics.* New York: Simon and Schuster, 1984.

Saloma, John. *Ominous Politics: The New Conservative Labyrinth.* New York: Hill and Wang, 1984.

Schuman, Howard, Charlotte C. Steeh, and Laurence Bobo. *Racial Attitudes in America: Trends and Interpretations.* Cambridge: Harvard University Press, 1988.

Scott, James C. *Domination and the Art of Resistance: Hidden Transcipts.* New Haven: Yale University Press, 1990.

Schwartz, Herman. *Packing the Courts: The Conservative Campaign to Rewrite the Constitution.* New York: Scribner, 1988.

Shafer, Byron E. (ed.). *The End of Realignment? Interpreting American Electoral Eras.* Madison: University of Wisconsin Press, 1991.

Sherrill, Robert. *Gothic Politics in the Deep South: Stars of the New Confederacy.* New York: Grossman, 1968.

Shull, Steven A. *The President and Civil Rights Policy: Leadership and Change.* Westport, Connecticut: Greenwood, 1989.

Sieglman, Lee and Susan Welch. *Black Americans' Views of Racial Inequality: The Dream Deferred.* New York: Cambridge University Press, 1991.

Sindler, Allan. *Negro Protest and Local Politics in Durham, N.C.* New York: McGraw-Hill, 1965.

Skinner, Elliott. "Afro-Americans in Search of Africa: The Scholars' Dilemma." In Pearl T. Robinson and Elliott P. Skinner (eds), *Transformation and Resiliency in Africa.* Washington, D.C.: Howard University Press, 1983.

Smallwood, Frank. *The Other Candidates: Third Parties in Presidential Elections.* Hanover: University Press of New England, 1983.

Smith, Robert C. and Richard Seltzer. *Race, Class, and Culture: A Study in Afro-American Mass Opinions.* Albany: State University of New York Press, 1992.

Smitherman, Geneva. *Black Talk: Words and Phrases from the Hood to the Amen Corner.* New York: Houghton Mifflin, 1994.

Somit, Albert and Joseph Tanenhaus. *The Development of American Political Science.* Boston: Allyn and Bacon, 1967.

Sorauf, Frank J. *Money in American Elections.* Boston: Scott Foresman, 1988.

—— and Paul Allen Breck. *Party Politics in America* 6th ed. Boston: Scott Foresman, Little Brown, 1988.

Sowell, Thomas. *Civil Rights: Rhetoric or Reality.* New York: Morrow, 1984.

Steinfels, Peter. *The Neoconservatives.* New York: Simon and Schuster, 1979.

Stone, Chuck. *Black Political Power in America.* Indianapolis: Bobbs-Merrill, 1968.

Strong, Donald. *Negroes, Ballots, and Judges: National Voting Rights Legislation in the Federal Courts.* Tuscaloosa: University of Alabama Press, 1958.

Swain, Carol M. *Black Faces, Black Interests: The Representation of African Americans in Congress.* Cambridge: Harvard University Press, 1993.

Tate, Katherine. *From Protest to Politics: The New Black Voters in American Elections.* Cambridge: Harvard University Press, 1993.

——, Ronald Brown, Shirley J. Hatchett, and James Jackson. *1984 National Black Election Study Sourcebook.* Ann Arbor: Institute for Social Research, University of Michigan, 1988.

Taylor, Shelley B. "The Availability Bias in Social Perception and Interaction." In Daniel Kahnerman, Paul Slovic, and Amos Tversky (eds.), *Judgement Under Uncertainty: Heuristics and Biases.* New York: Cambridge University Press, 1982.

Thernstrom, Abigail M. *Whose Votes Count: Affirmative Action and Minority Voting Rights.* Cambridge: Harvard University Press, 1987.

Tinder, Glenn. *Political Thinking: The Perennial Questions* 5th ed. New York: HarperCollins, 1991.

Tryman, M. Donald. *Afro-American Mass Political Integration.* Washington, D.C.: University Press of America, 1982.

Tulis, Jeffrey. *The Rhetorical President.* Princeton: Princeton University Press, 1987.

Ture, Kwame and Charles V. Hamilton. *Black Power: The Politics of Liberation.* New York: Vintage, 1992.

Urquhart, Brian. *Ralph Bunche: An American Life.* New York: W. W. Norton, 1993.

Walker, Jack L. *Sit-ins in Atlanta.* New York: McGraw-Hill, 1963. Walls, Dwayne. *The Chickenbone Special.* New York: Harcourt, Brace, Jovanovich, 1971.

Walters, Ronald. *Black Presidential Politics in America: A Strategic Approach.* Albany: State University of New York Press, 1988.

—— and Lucius Barker (eds). *Jesse Jackson's 1984 Presidential Campaign.* Urbana: University of Illinois Press, 1988.

Walters, Ronald. *Pan Africanism in the African Diaspora.* Detroit: Wayne State University Press, 1993.

——. *South Africa and the Bomb: Responsibility and Deterrence.* Lexington, Massachusetts: Lexington, 1987.

Walton, Jr., Hanes. "Black Female Presidential Candidates." In Hanes Walton, Jr. (ed.), *Black Politics and Black Political Behavior.* New York: Praeger, 1994.

——. *Black Political Parties: A Historical and Political Analysis.* New York: Free Press, 1972.

——. *Black Politics: A Theoretical and Structural Analysis.* Philadelphia: J. B. Lippincott, 1972.

——. "Black Presidential Participation and Critical Election Theory." In Lorenzo Morris (ed.), *The Social and Political Implications of the 1984 Jesse Jackson Presidential Campaign.* New York: Praeger, 1990.

——. *Black Republicans: The Politics of the Black and Tans.* New Jersey: Scarecrow Press, 1975.

——. "Blacks and Conservative Political Movements." In Lenneal Henderson (ed.), *Black Political Life in the United States.* San Francisco: Chandler, 1972.

——. "Democrats and African Americans: The American Idea." In Peter B. Kovler (ed.), *Democrats and the American Idea: A Bicentennial Appraisal.* Washington, D.C.: Center for National Policy Press, 1992.

——. *Invisible Politics: Black Political Behavior.* Albany: State University of New York Press, 1988.

——. "The National Democratic Party of Alabama and Party Failure in America." In Kay Lawson and Peter Markl (eds.), *When Parties Fail.* Princeton: Princeton University Press, 1988.

——. *The Native Son Presidential Candidate: The Carter Vote in Georgia.* New York: Praeger, 1992.

——. *The Negro in Third Party Politics.* Philadelphia: Dorrance, 1969.

——. *The Political Philosophy of Martin Luther King, Jr.* Connecticut: Greenwood Press, 1971.

——. "The Political Use of Absentee Ballots in a Rural Black Belt County: Dr. Merolyn Stewart's Campaign for Taliaferro County's School Superintendent Position." In Hanes Walton, Jr. (ed.), *Black Politics and Black Political Behavior: A Linkage Analysis.* New York: Praeger, 1994.

——. *When the Marching Stopped: The Politics of Civil Rights Regulatory Agencies.* Albany State University of New York Press, 1988.

——, Cheryl M. Miller, Joseph P. McCormick, II. "Race and Political Science: The Dual Traditions of Race Relations Politics and African-American Politics." In John Drezzek, James Farr, and Stephen Leonard, (eds.), *Political Science and Its History: Research Programs and Political Traditions.* New York: Cambridge University Press, 1994.

Ware, Gilbert. *William Hastie: Grace Under Pressure.* New York: Oxford University Press, 1984.

Wasby, Stephen. *Political Science: The Discipline and Its Dimensions.* New York: Charles Scribner and Sons, 1970.

Washington, Lyn. *Black Judges on Justice: Prospect from the Bench.* New York: The New Press, 1994.

Watson, Denton L. *Lion in the Lobby: Clarence Mitchell, Jr.'s Struggle for the Passage of Civil Rights Laws.* New York: William Morrow, 1990.

Weiss, Nancy T. "Creative Tensions in the Leadership of the Civil Rights Movement." In Charles W. Eagles (ed.), *The Civil Rights Movement in America.* Jackson: University Press of Mississippi, 1986.

——. *Farewell to the Party of Lincoln: Black Politics in the Age of FDR.* Princeton: Princeton University Pres, 1983.

Weissberg, Robert. "The Democratic Party and the Conflict over Racial Policy." In Benjamin Ginsbert and Alan Stone (eds.), *Do Elections Matter?* New York: M. E. Sharpe, 1986.

Weston, Rubin. *Racism in U.S. Imperialism.* Columbia: University of South Carolina Press, 1972.

Whalen, Charles and Barbara Whalen. *The Longest Debate: A Legislative History of the 1964 Civil Rights Act.* Cabin John, Maryland: Seven Locks Press, 1985.

White, Phillip. "The Black American Constituency for Southern Africa, 1940–1980." In Alfred O. Hero and John Barrett, (eds.), *The American People and South Africa.* Lexington, Massachusetts: Lexington Books, 1981.

Whittmore, L. H. *Together: A Reporter's Journey into the New Black Politics.* New York: William Morrow, 1971.

Wildavsky, Aaron. "Choosing Preferences by Constructing Institutions: A Cultural Theory of Preference Formation." in Arthur Asa Berger (ed.), *Political Culture and Public Opinion.* New Brunswick: Transaction Publishers, 1989.

——. "Industrial Politics in American Political Cultures." In Charles E. Barfield and William A. Schambra (eds.), *The Politics of Industrial Policy.* Washington, D.C.: American Enterprise Institute, 1986.

——. "President Reagan as a Political Strategist." In Kay Lehman Schlozman (ed.), *Elections in America.* Boston: Allen and Unwin, 1987.

Wilson, William J. *The Truly Disadvantaged: The Inner City, The Underclass, and Public Policy.* Chicago: University of Chicago Press, 1987.

Wilson, Zaphon. "Gantt Versus Helms: Deracialization Confronts Southern Traditionalism." In Georgia Persons (ed.), *Dilemmas of Black Politics.* New York: HarperCollins, 1993.

Woodard, C. Van. *The Origins of the New South, 1877–1913.* Baton Rouge: Louisiana State University Press, 1957.

——. *The Strange Career of Jim Crow,* 3rd ed. New York: Oxford University Press, 1974.

Woody, Bette. *Managing Crisis Cities: The New Black Leadership and the Politics of Resource Allocation.* Westport, Connecticut: Greenwood, 1982.

Wright, William E. *Memphis Politics: A Study in Racial Bloc Voting.* New York: McGraw-Hill, 1960.

Yin, Robert. *Case Study Research: Design and Methods* rev. ed. Beverly Hills: Sage, 1989.

Zilversmith, Arthur. *The First Emancipation: The Abolition of Slavery in the North.* Chicago: University of Chicago Press, 1967.

Articles

Abramowitz, Alan I. 1988. "Explaining Senate Outcomes." *American Political Science Review* 32: 385–403.
Abramson, Jill. "Thomas Down Play in a Congress Teeming with Sex and Harrassment." *Wall Street Journal,* 11 October 1991.
"Agenda Turns To Other Issues." *Congressional Quarterly Weekly Report* 53 (8 April 1995): 982–84.
Allen, Richard, Michael C. Dawson, and Ronald Brown. 1990. "Racial Belief Systems, Religious Guidance, and African American Political Participation." *National Political Science Review* 2: 22–44.
——. 1989. "A Schema-Based Approach to Modeling an African American Racial Belief System." *American Political Science Review* 32 (June): 420–42.
Alston, Chuck. "Confirmation: Senate Zips Through Approval of Clinton Cabinet Picks." *Congressional Quarterly Weekly Report* 51 (23 January 1993): 168–9.
Anderson, Jackson. "Did Bell Influence Savannah Annexation?" *Savannah Morning News,* 14 November 1975.
——. "Jack Anderson Defends His Column." *Savannah Morning News,* 14 November 1975.
——. "The Savannah Story: Corrections." *Savannah Morning News,* 27 November 1978.
Apple, Jr., R. W. "Senate Confirms Thomas, 52–48, Ending Week of Bitter Battle: 'Time for Healing,' Judge Says." *New York Times,* 15 October 1991.
Applebome, Peter. "Perot Speech Gets Cool Reception at NAACP." *New York Times,* 12 July 1992.
Ardrey, Sandra C. and William E. Nelson. 1990. "The Maturation of Black Politics: The Case of Cleveland." *PS: Political Science and Politics* 23: 148–51.
"Audit Explained to Council." *Claxton Enterprise,* 24 February 1983.
Ayers, B. Drummon. "In the End, Wilder Realized the Numbers Fell Short." *New York Times,* 11 January 1992.
——. "Wilder's 92 Campaign Looks for Black Votes." *New York Times,* 10 November 1991.
——. "Yankee Strategist Plans Campaign to Put Wilder in White House." *New York Times,* 15 October 1991.
Baker, Donald P. "Contrite Wilder Says He Was Misunderstood." *Washington Post,* 8 July 1991
——. "New Hampshire's Word on Wilder." *Washington Post,* 2 September 1991
——. "Sounding Like a Contender, Wilder Hits N.H." *Washington Post,* 28 August 1991.
——. "Wilder Ends Campaign." *Washington Post,* 9 January 1992.
——. "Wilder Halfway to Matching Funds." *Washington Post,* 15 October 1991.
——. "Wilder, Launching Campaign in New Hampshire, Gets Granite Reception." *Washington Post,* 17 November 1991.
——. "Wilder Taps a Former Jackson Aide." *Washington Post,* 12 November 1991.
——. "Wilder Slams GOP Administrations for 'Creating' a Climate for Racism." *Washington Post,* 25 November 1991.
——. "Wilder Woos Supporters in Clinton's Backyard." *Washington Post,* 9 December 1991.
—— and Dan Balz. "Robb Saga Knocks Wilder Out of '92 Pundits Say." *Washington Post,* 29 June 1991.
"Baker Resigns City Council Seat; Members Vote 5–1 to Accept Councilwoman Decision, Call Elections." *Claxton Enterprise,* 13 February 1992.

Baker-Kelly, Beverly. 1990. "United States Immigration: A Wake Up Call." *Howard Law Journal* 37 (Winter): 295.

Balz, Dan. "Clinton, Tsongas, Wilder Spar on New Hampshire TV." *Washington Post,* 2 November 1991.

"Banquet Features CSRA's First Elected Black Mayor." *Claxton Enterprise,* 18 March 1992.

Barnett, Marguerite Ross. 1985. "The Congressional Black Caucus and the Institutionalization of Black Politics." *Journal of Afro-American Issues* 5 (Summer): 202–27.

Beat, Francis. 1984. "U.S. Politics Will Never Be the Same." *The Black Scholar* 15: 10–18.

Beecher, Bobby. "America Needs God—Not Government." *Claxton Enterprise,* 14 May 1992.

——. "Black-on-Black Violence is Hard to Understand." *Claxton Enterprise,* 25 December 1991.

——. "Blacks Need New Leadership." *Claxton Enterprise,* 11 March 1993.

——. "A Clinton Supreme Court is Reason Enough to Vote for Bush." *Claxton Enterprise,* 2 July 1992.

——. "Coerced Integration Has Hurt More Than Helped Race Relations." *Claxton Enterprise,* 20 August 1992.

——. "Georgia Raped During Reapportionment." *Claxton Enterprise,* 9 April 1992.

——. "Justice Department's Action is Another Slap in the Face." *Claxton Enterprise,* 26 March 1992.

——. "President Bush Will Feel Patrick Buchanan's Heat." *Claxton Enterprise,* 19 December 1991.

——. "Presidential Candidate Clinton." *Claxton Enterprise,* 2 July 1992.

——. "Uncle Sam Too Black for Racial Discord." *Claxton Enterprise,* 27 February 1992.

"Behind on Payments: Claxton Still in Debt After Discussion." *Claxton Enterprise,* 18 September 1989.

Berke, Richard L. "Wilder Explores a Run for President." *New York Times,* 28 March 1993.

"Blacks Say Council Action 'Slanderous.' " *Claxton Enterprise,* 8 November 1980.

Blumenstyk, Goldie. "Justice Department Affirms Federal Backing for Black Colleges." *The Chronicle of Higher Education,* 15 October 1991: A41.

"Board of Education Members Named in Reapportionment Suit." *Claxton Enterprise,* 11 August 1983.

Booker, Simeon. "Ticker Tape." *Jet,* 4 September 1985.

Bowen, Bill. "Mitchell Ousts Jackson to End 20 Year Reign." *Savannah Times,* 17 November 1991.

Broder, David S. and Donald P. Baker. "Wilder Tosses Hat Near Ring." *Washington Post,* 18 March 1991.

Brown, Peter A. " '85 Demo Report Urges De-Marketing of Party." *Houston Chronicle,* 17 April 1989.

"Building Permit Utilities at Issue: Housing Authority Takes City to Court." *Claxton Enterprise,* 31 July 1980.

Bunche, Ralph. 1935. "A Critical Analysis of the Tactics and Programs of Minority Groups." *Journal of Negro Education* 4 (July): 308–320.

——. 1941. "The Negro in the Political Life of the United States." *Journal of Negro Education* 10 (July): 567–84.

——. 1939. "Programs of Organizations Devoted to Improvement of the Status of the American Negro." *Journal of Negro Education* 8 (October): 539–50.

Burke, Richard L. "Thomas's Accuser Assails Handling of Her Complaint." *New York Times,* 8 October 1991.

Caldwell, Carl. "Spector of Denial May Do Thomas In." *New York Daily News,* 11 October 1991.

Cagle, Monty. "Claxton City Council, Housing Authority Vow to Find New Low Rent Project Site." *Claxton Enterprise,* 17 April 1980.

——. "Council Moves to Block Housing with Rezoning Request." *Claxton Enterprise,* 26 June 1980.
——. "Court Rules in Favor of Housing Authority." *Claxton Enterprise,* 26 June 1980.
——. "Financial Discussion Bows to Housing Project Argument." *Claxton Enterprise,* 1 May 1980.
——. "Will Annexation End Claxton's Stagnation?" *Claxton Enterprise,* 19 March 1981.
"Campbell Savin in as Assistant Commerce Secretary." *Jet,* 25 January 1982.
Cannady, Dal. "Council Delays Committees, Appointees." *Claxton Enterprise,* 9 January 1992.
Cartoon of Jessie Jackson. *Claxton Enterprise,* 24 March 1988.
——. *Claxton Enterprise,* 31 March 1988.
——. *Claxton Enterprise,* 21 July 1988
—— of Andrew Young. *Claxton Enterprise,* 4 May 1989.
Cassata, Donna. "Black Caucus Chooses Payne." *Congressional Quarterly Weekly Reports* 52 (17 December 1994): 3545.
——. "Republicans Bask in Success of Rousing Performance." *Congressional Quarterly Weekly Report* 53 (8 April 1995): 986.
"City Expects Settlement on Redistricting Proposal." *Claxton Enterprise,* 19 July 1984.
"City Gives Big 'Yes' To Freeport: Woody, Harper Win Only Contested Race." *Claxton Enterprise,* 12 December 1984.
"City Preparing for Election at City Hall." *Claxton Enterprise,* 8 August 1989.
"City No Longer Eligible for UDAG Funds." *Claxton Enterprise,* 1 May 1980.
"City Ready for Elections." *Claxton Enterprise,* 6 December 1984.
"City Rejects Request for MLK Drive: Petitions Seek Change in Name of Church Street." *Claxton Enterprise,* 5 March 1992.
"City Voters to Elect Four Council Members December 4." *Claxton Enterprise,* 27 November 1986.
"City's Redistricting Plan May be in Trouble." *Claxton Enterprise,* 29 September 1983.
Clarke, Stuart Alan. 1989. "Liberalism and Black Political Thought." *National Political Science Review* 1: 5–14.
"Claxton Could Lose Federal Funds." *Claxton Enterprise,* 24 April 1980.
"Claxton To Lose UDAG Eligibility?" *Claxton Enterprise,* 24 April 1980.
"Clinton Outpaces Wilder in Survey of Old Dominion." *Washington Post,* 29 December 1991.
Cloud, David S. "GOP's House-Clearing Sweep Changes Rules, Cuts Groups." *Congressional Quarterly Weekly Report* 52 (10 December 1994): 3488.
Clubok, Alfred, John DeGrove, and Charles Farris. 1964. "The Manipulated Negro Vote: Preconditions and Consequences." *Journal of Politics* 26 (February): 112–29.
Cohen, Cathy J. and Michael C. Dawson. 1993. "Neighborhood Poverty and African-American Politics." *American Political Science Review* 87 (June): 286–302.
Cohen, Richard. "Wilder's Drug Stand: Bold, Thoughtless." *Washington Post,* 9 April 1991.
"Committees." *Congressional Quarterly Weekly Report* 52 (17 December 1994): 3549–58.
"Committee." *Congressional Quarterly Weekly Report* 52 (21 December 1994): 3681–92.
Connolly, Ceci. "GOP Accentuates the Positive: Hopefuls To Sign Compact." *Congressional Quarterly Weekly Report* 54 (24 September 1994): 2711–12.
"Consideration Sought for Original Plan: City Files Response to Redistricting." *Claxton Enterprise,* 23 November 1983.
Cook, Rhodes. "Clinton Picks the GOP Lock on the Electoral College." *Congressional Quarterly Weekly Report* 50 (7 November 1992): 3549.
——. "Many Democrats Cool to Redoing Party Rules." *Congressional Weekly Report* (24 August 1985): 1687–89.

Cook, Rhonda. "Redding Changes Tune, Pleads Guilty in Extortion Case." *Atlanta Journal/Constitution,* 20 August 1992.

——. "Redding Mulls Pleading Guilty to Taking Cash." *Atlanta Journal/Constitution,* 15 August 1992.

Cook, Samuel DuBois. 1964. "Political Movements and Organizations." *Journal of Politics* 26 (February): 130–53.

"Cornelius Alive and Well, Ready to Kill Food Stamps." *Jet,* 22 March 1982.

"Council Votes to Appeal Building Permit Verdict." *Claxton Enterprise,* 11 September 1989.

"Councilman Recognized." *Claxton Enterprise,* 18 December 1986.

"Court Rules Evans School System and Others Did Not Discriminate Against Black Kids." *Claxton Enterprise,* 5 July 1984.

"The Court Still Haggling Over Rights." *New York Times,* 16 June 1989.

"DA Asks for Full Inquiry into Claxton City Voting." *Claxton Enterprise,* 27 December 1979.

D'Ambrosio, Donna. "City Council Hears Proposal for 1993 Fiscal Budget." *Claxton Enterprise,* 5 June 1993.

——. "City Council Learns City Elections Fairly Conducted." *Claxton Enterprise,* 6 June 1992.

Daniels, Lee. "The New Black Consevatives." *New York Times* Sunday Magazine, 4 October 1981.

Daniels, William J. 1989. "The Constitution, The Supreme Court, and Racism: Compromises on the Way to Democracy." *National Political Science Review* 1: 126–30.

Darcy, R. and Charles D. Hadley. 1988. "Black Women in Politics: The Puzzle of Success." *Social Science Quarterly* 69: 629–45.

David, Maureen. "President Orders Aide to Review New Minority Scholarship Policy." *New York Times,* 18 December 1990.

Davis, John A. 1969. "Black American and United States Foreign Policy Toward Africa." *Journal of International Affairs* 23: 231–49.

Days, Drew. 1984. "Turning Back the Clock: The Reagan Administration and Civil Rights." *Harvard Civil Rights-Civil Liberties Law Review* 19 (Summer): 309.

DeGregorio, Christine. 1994. "Professional Committee Staff as Policymaking Partners in the U. S. Congress." *Congress and the Presidency* 21 (Spring): 49–68.

Denham, Scott. "Tempers Flare at Monday City Council Meetings." *Claxton Enterprise,* 23 March 1989.

Drake, W. Avon. 1990. "Electoral Politics, Affirmative Action, and the Supreme Court: The Case of Richmond v. Croson." *National Political Science Review* 2: 65–91.

Duke, Lynn. "Integration Agreements Could Be Reexamined: Fate of Historically Black College Muddled." *Washington Post,* 27 June 1992.

——. "Key Official on Black Colleges Fired." *Washington Post,* 14 February 1991.

Duncan, Phil. "The Makeup, Mind-Set of the Party Today." *Congressional Quarterly Guide to the 1992 Democratic National Convention* 50 (4 July 1992): 52.

Editorial. "Digging Past Political Pearls." *New York Times,* 17 December 1991.

Editorial. "Focusing on Nigerian Regression." *St. Petersburg Times,* 22 March 1995.

Editorial. "Poor Judgement?" *Claxton Enterprise,* 10 April 1986.

Editorial. "Stand By Plan for More Black Judges." *The Atlanta Journal Constitution,* 5 June 1993.

"Elders is Confirmed as Surgeon General." *Congressional Quarterly Almanac* 49 (1993): 356.

Engstrom, Richard and Michael McDonald. 1988. "Definitions, Measurements, and Statistics: Weeding Wildgen's Thicket." *Urban Lawyer* 20 (Winter): 174–91.

——. 1985. "Quantitative Evidence in Vote Dilution Litigation: Political Participation and Polarized Voting." *Urban Lawyer* 17 (Summer): 371–77.

——. 1987. "Quantitative Evidence in Vote Dilution Litigation: Part II: Minority Coalition and Multivariate Analysis." *Urban Lawyer* 19 (Winter): 65–75.

"EEOC Contender Shot During Ohio Bank Robbery." *Jet,* 22 February 1982.

Epstein, Aaron. "Mississippi's Segregated Colleges Unlawful, Supreme Court Says." *Philadelphia Inquirer,* 27 June 1992.

——. "Thomas Survives Controversey, Wins Senate Confirmation, 52–48, Bush Nominee Carries Closest Vote Since 1888." *Philadelphia Inquirer,* 15 October 1991.

—— and Karen Warren. ''2nd Woman Implicates Thomas." *Philadelphia Inquirer,* 11 October 1991.

"Evans Blacks Concerned about Possible Annexation." *Claxton Enterprise,* 30 April 1991.

"Evans School Sytem in Court in Savannah." *Claxton Enterprise,* 10 November 1983.

Fisher, Jan. "Butts Backs an Educator for President." *New York Times,* 20 July 1992.

Fleming, Eddie. "Anderson's Savannah Expose Called Lies." *Savannah Morning News,* 14 November 1975.

Fogelson, Robert. "From Resentment to Confrontation: The Police, the Negro, and the Outbreak of the Nineteen-Sixties Riots." *Political Science Quarterly* Vol. 82 (June, 1967): 217–47.

——. "White on Black: A Critique of the McCone Commission Report on the Los Angeles Riots, Political Riots." *Political Science Quarterly* 82 (September 1967): 337–67.

"Food Stamp Administration Named Aide to Head of Department of Agriculture." *Jet,* 7 February 1983.

Fraley, Colett. "Foster's Answers Keep His Bid for Surgeon General Alive." *Congressional Quarterly Weekly Report* 53 (5 May 1995): 1244–47.

"Freeport, Five City Council Post on December Ballot." *Claxton Enterprise,* 21 November 1984.

Fulwood, III, Sam. 1995. "CBC Returns to Its Roots in 104th Congress." *Focus* 23 (January): 6.

"GBI Probe Ends: Results Not Known." *Claxton Enterprise,* 17 January 1989.

Gelb, Leslie H. "The TV Debate Fiasco." *New York Times,* 18 December 1991.

Gilens, Martin. 1988. "Gender and Support for Reagan: A Comprehensive Model of Presidential Approval." *American Journal of Political Science* 32: 19–49.

"Group to File County Reapportionment Suit: Evans County, Claxton, Hagan Named in Action Charging Racial Discrimination." *Claxton Enterprise,* 4 August 1983.

Graham, Barbara Luck. 1989. "Executive Authority, Constitutional Interpretation, and Civil Rights." *National Political Science Review* 1: 114–20.

Graves, Kay Williams. "New Mayor, Old Problems." *Georgia Trend,* November, 1992: 50–53.

Gray, William. "UNCF CEO William Gray Praises President Bush for $375 Million Education Bill." *Jet,* 10 August 1992.

Greenhouse, Linda. "Bush Reverses U.S. Stance Against Black College Aid." *New York Times,* 22 October 1992.

Greenhouse, Linda. "Court, 6–3, Applies Voting Rights Act to Judicial Races: Big Impact in the South." *New York Times,* 21 June 1991.

——. "Court, 8–1, Faults Mississippi on Bias in College System." *New York Times,* 27 June 1992.

——. "Court Backs Minority Voting Districts." *New York Times,* 3 March 1993.

Gruenwald, Juliana. "Health Tax Break Passes Senate." *Congressional Quarterly Weekly Report* 53 (25 March 1995): 861.

Hamilton, Charles. 1977. "Deracialization: Examination of a Political Strategy." *First World* 1 (March/April): 3–5.

Hardy, Thomas. "Braun Rode Colorblind Coalition." *Chicago Tribune,* 8 November 1992.

Harris, John F. "Jackson Takes on School Funding Inequities in Wilder's Backyard." *Washington Post,* 25 September 1991.

——. "Jackson Wows Rural Virginia." *Washington Post,* 26 September 1991.

——. "Wilder, Advisers Map Possible Strategies for Presidential Bid." *Washington Post,* 12 August 1991.

——. "Wilder Exploratory Bid Slow to Raise Contributions." *Washington Post,* 15 July 1991.

——. "Wilder Has Some 'Friendly' Advice for Jackson." *Washington Post,* 15 October 1991.

—— and Donald P. Baker. "Wilder Accuses Jesse Jackson of Working Against Campaign." *Washington Post,* 24 December 1991.

Hawkins, B. Demise. "Enrollment of HBCUs Experience an Influx of White Students." *Black Issues in Higher Education* 63 (22 August 1992): 9.

Henderson, David. "Campaigning in Code." *Washington Post,* 1 July 1990.

Henry, Charles. "Money, Law, and Black Congressional Candidates." *Urban League Review* (Summer, 1984): 87–103.

——. "Tom Bradley's Defeat: The Impact of Racial Symbols on Political Campaigns." *The Black Scholar* (Fall, 1982): 32–45.

Herbert, Bob. "The New Slavery." *The Baltimore Sun,* 12 April 1995.

Holmes, Steven A. "Perot Brings Mixed Record to His First Black Audience." *New York Times,* 1 July 1992.

Hook, Janet. "Official Seek Moderation in Party's Change." *Congressional Quarterly Weekly Report* 43 (9 March 1985): 457.

Horton, Harold. "Ron Daniels: Profile of a Presidential Candidate." *Trotter Review* (Fall, 1992): 32.

"House Republicans Rehearse Taking Reins of Power." *Congressional Quarterly Weekly Report* Vol. 52 (17 December 1994): 3548.

"Housing Authority Wins Back Permit." *Claxton Enterprise,* 21 August 1980.

"Hundred Protest Closing of Agency to Aid Needy." *Jet,* 22 October 1981.

Ifll, Gwen. "Pack is Off and Spinning with First TV Debate." *New York Times,* 17 December 1991.

Innerst, Carol. "Bush Orders Switch on Black College Aid." *Washington Times,* 23 October 1991.

Jackson, Luther P. "Race and Suffrage in the South Since 1949." *New South* 1 (June/July, 1940).

Johnston, David. "In Justice Department of the 90's Focus Shifts from Rights." *New York Times,* 26 March 1991.

Jones, Charles E. 1991. "The Election of L. Douglas Wilder: The First Black Lieutenant Governor of Virginia." *The Western Journal of Black Studies* 15: 105–13.

Jones, Mack. 1992. "Political Science and the Black Political Experience: Issues in Epistemology and Relevance." *National Political Science Review* 3: 29–30.

"Judge Signs Claxton's Redistricting Plan." *Claxton Enterprise,* 8 August 1989.

Karlan, Pamela S. and Peyton McCrary. Book Review, "Without Fear and Without Research: Abigail Thernstrom on the Voting Rights Act." *Journal of Law and Politics* 4 (Spring 1988): 751–77.

Katz, Jeffrey L. "Facing Forward." *Congressional Quarterly Guide to the 1992 Democratic National Convention* 50 (4 July 1992): 20.

Kessler, Pamela. "Clinton Plans for Smooth Start with Focus on the Economic." *Congressional Quarterly Weekly Report* 50 (7 November 1992): 3555–6.

Kilson, Martin. "The Black Experience at Howard." *New York Times Magazine,* 2 September 1973.

——. 1989. "Problems of Black Politics: Some Progress, Many Difficulties." *Dissent* 36: 526–34.

King, Colbert I. "The Dilemma of Black Republicans." *Washington Post,* 22 September 1992.

"Klan Seeking Parade Permit: City Council Table." *Claxton Enterprise,* 21 June 1984.

"Klan's Claxton Visit Uneventful." *Claxton Enterprise,* 5 July 1984.

Kousser, J. Morgan. "The Voting Rights Act and the Two Reconstructions." *Journal of Law and Politics* (Spring 1988): 160–76.

Labaton, Stephen. "Nominee's Lobbying to be Scrutinized." *New York Times,* 20 December 1992.

LaFraniere, Sharon. "It is an Unpleasant Issue." *Washington Post,* 8 October 1991.

Lewis, Neil. "Chester Crocker: Inside Making Policy on Africa." *New York Times,* 9 June 1987.

——. "Guerrilla Fighter for Civil Rights: Clinton Seeks to Bring Lani Guinier Black to the Justice Department." *New York Times,* 5 May 1993.

Lichter, Linda S. 1985. "Who Speaks for Black America." *Public Opinion* 8: 47–70.

Lieske, Joel. "The Conditions of Racial Violence in American Cities: A Developmental Synthesis." *American Political Science Review* 72 (December 1978): 1324–40.

Lipsky, Michael. "Protest as a Political Resource." *American Political Science Review* 62 (1968): 114–5.

Louis, May. "Race and Presidential Politics: The Challenge to Go Another Way." *Trotter Review* (Fall 1992): 12–13.

Lublin, David Ian. "Quality, Not Quantity: Strategic Politicians in U. S. Senate Elections, 1952–1990." Paper under review.

Lusane, Clarence. 1994. "African Americans and the Mid-Term Elections." *Black Political Agenda* 2(4): 10.

——. 1994. "Unity and Struggle! The Political Behavior of African American Members of Congress." *The Black Scholar* 24 (Fall): 26.

MacPherson, Peter. "Surgeon General Nominee Chosen." *Congressional Quarterly Weekly Report* 53 (4 February 1995): 371.

Mansbridge, Jane and Katherine Tate. 1992. "Race Trumps Gender: The Thomas Nomination in the Black Community." *PS: Political Science and Politics* 25: 488–92.

Marcus, Ruth. "Justice Department Changes Position in Landmark Desegregation Case To Be Heard by Supreme Court." *Black Issues in Higher Education* (24 October 1991).

——. "The Shifting Sands of George Bush's Civil Rights Position." *Washington Post National Weekly,* 24–30 August 1992: 8–9.

——. "What Does Bush Really Believe?" *Washington Post,* 18 August 1992.

Marriott, Michael. "TransAfrica in the Eye of the Storm: Young Activists on High Organize Anti-Apartheid Protest." *Washington Post,* 12 December 1984.

Massey, Douglas S. and Nancy A. Denton. 1988. "Residential Segregation of Blacks, Hispanics, and Asians by Socioeconomic Status and Generation." *Social Science Quarterly* 69: 797–817.

McDonald, Langhlin. 1983. "The Quiet Revolution in Minority Voting Rights." *Vanderbilt Law Review* 51 (Fall): 1249–97.

McLemore, Leslie. "Mississippi Freedom Democratic Party." *Black Politicians* (October 1971): 19–23.

McPherson, Misty. "Controversy Surrounds Renaming of Long Street in Honor of Late Martin Luther King." *Claxton Enterprise,* 30 July 1992.

——. "Problems Apparent within City Council." *Claxton Enterprise,* 6 August 1992.

Meier, Kenneth J., Joseph Stewart, Jr., and Robert E. England. 1989. "Second Generation Educational Discriminations and White Flight from Public Schools." *National Political Science Review* 1: 76, 90.

Meiso, Patricia. "Panel Accused of Bias Against Black Colleges." *Baltimore Sun,* 13 October 1991.

——. "Plan to Improve MD's Black Institutions Clears First Huddle." *Washington Post,* 20 November 1991.

Mercer, Joyce. "Republican Lawyer is Administration's Choice to Head White House Effort on Black Colleges." *Chronicle of Higher Education* (6 June 1992).

Mercer, Joyce. "Some Black College Chiefs Angered Over Goodwin Firing." *Black Issues in Higher Education* (27 February 1992): 1.

Metz, Steven. 1986. "The Anti-Apartheid Movement and Populist Instincts in American Politics." *Political Science Quarterly* 101: 379–95.

Meyerson, Adam. 1991. "Low-Tax Liberal." *Policy Review* 55: 26–31.

Midlarsky, Manus. "Analyzing Diffusion and Contagion Effects: The Urban Disorder of the 1960's." *American Political Science Review* (December 1978): 1996–2008.

Milbrath, Lester. *Political Participation.* Chicago: Rand McNally, 1965.

—— and M. L. Gael. *Political Participation* 2d ed. Chicago: Rand McNally, 1977.

Miller, Ceryl M. and Hanes Walton, Jr. 1994. "Congressional Support of Civil Rights Public Policy: From Bipartisan to Partisan Convergence." *Congress and the Presidency* 21 (Spring): 11–27.

Milner, Laura. "Claxton Faces New Dispute on King Name." *Savannah Morning News and Evening Press,* 10 March 1992.

——. "Woman Quits Claxton City Council Post: Baker Levels Charges of Racism Against Mayor, Councilmen." *Savannah Morning News and Evening Press,* 6 February 1992.

"NAACP, School Systems Going to Court September 12." *Claxton Enterprise,* 23 June 1983.

"NAACP Wants More Black Teachers Hired: Dual Queens, Official Custom Abolished." *Claxton Enterprise,* 10 April 1986.

"NBA Argues for Black Colleges Before the U.S. Supreme Court." *National Bar Association Magazine* 6 (July 1992): 10.

Parker, Frank. "The 'Result' Test of Section 2 of the Voting Rights Act: Abandoning the Intent Standard." *Virginia Law Review* (May 1983): 715–84.

Parker, Jackie. "Closed Doors on Capitol Hill: Black Senate Staffers Seek More Minority Representation in Policy-Level Positions." *Focus,* 4 September 1995.

Payne, Ethel. "Anti-Apartheid Campaign Revives Old Coalition." *Washington Afro-American,* 24 January 1986.

Payton, Jack. "U. S. Group Campaigns to Defeat Nigeria Regime." *St. Petersburg Times,* 18 March 1995.

Peace, Mitchell. "City Borrows $126,000 to Pay Creditors." *Claxton Enterprise,* 2 August 1979.

——. "Claxton Council Members Overturn Mayor's Decision on Goode St. Work." *Claxton Enterprise,* 27 July 1989.

——. "Councilman Challenges Mayor." *Claxton Enterprise,* 8 November 1979.

——. "Grand Jury Action Not Expected on GBI's Probe of City Voting." *Claxton Enterprise,* 12 December 1979.

——. "Mayor's Vote Gives OK to Councilman's Contract." *Claxton Enterprise,* 20 July 1989.

——. "NAACP Charges School System Re-segregating Classes Here." *Clayton Enterprise,* 15 June 1989.

——. "Reapportionment Suit Update: County Commissioners, City Official Huddle with Attorneys To Map Courses of Action." *Claxton Enterprise,* 8 September 1983.

——. "Redistricting Plan Rejected: Clerk Calls Council Elections." *Claxton Enterprise,* 3 November 1983.

——. "Report Critical of City's Recent Grant Application." *Claxton Enterprise,* 4 June 1987.

——. "State Nixes Block Grant for Claxton." *Claxton Enterprise,* 23 April 1987.

Pierannunzi, Carol and John D. Hutchenson, Jr. 1991. "Deracialization in the Deep South: Mayoral Politics in Atlanta." *Urban Affairs Quarterly* 27: 192–201.

——. 1990. "Electoral Change and Regime Maintenance: Maynard Jackson's Second Time Around." *PS: Political Science and Politics* 23: 151–53.

Perry, Huey L. 1991. "Deracialization as an Analytical Construct in American Urban Politics." *Urban Affairs Quarterly* 27: 181–91.

——. 1990. "The Reelection of Sidney Barthelemy as Mayor of New Orleans." *PS: Political Science and Politics* 23: 156–7.

——. 1991. "Toward Conceptual Clarity Regarding Deracialization: A Response to Professor Starks." *Urban Affairs Quarterly* 27: 223–6.

Pinderhughes, Dianne. 1985. "Legal Strategies for Voting Rights: Political Science and the Law." *Howard Law Journal* 28: 515–40.

——. 1992. "Divisions in the Civil Rights Community." *PS: Political Science and Politics* 25: 485–7.

Political Advertisement. "If David Duke is Governor—You Need Alphonse Jackson." *Shreveport Sun,* 14 November 1991.

"Plans Okayed for Election on March 19." *Claxton Enterprise,* 13 February 1992.

"President Nominates Judge Clarence Thomas for Supreme Court Seat." *The Third Branch* (1 July 1992): 23.

"Presidential Politics: Perot Bows Out, Say Election Would Be Decided in House." *Congressional Quarterly Weekly Report* (18 July 1992): 2131–2.

"Protesting Nigeria Tyranny." *Tampa Tribune,* April 3, 1995: 6.

Purdum, Todd S. "Perot Taps Black Minister." *New York Times,* 12 July 1992.

Rappoport, Ronald B., Walter J. Stone, and Alan I. Abramowitz. 1991. "Do Endorsements Matter: Group Influence in the 1984 Democratic Caucuses." *American Political Science Review* 85: 193–203.

Rasberry, William. "A Double Disaster for EEOC." *Washington Post,* 18 November 1991.

——. "The Shame of the Supreme Court." *Washington Post,* 17 June 1989.

Reed, Jr., Adolph. "Race and the Disruption of the New Deal Coalition." *Urban Affairs Quarterly* 37 (December 1991): 326–33.

—— and Julian Bond. "Equality: Why We Can't Wait." *The Nation* (9 December 1991): 733–7.

"Renee Baker Defeats Mary Lee Harper in City Election: Others Return to Office Without Opposition." *Claxton Enterprise,* 12 December 1985.

"Renee Baker Graduates from UGA Bank Operations School." *Claxton Enterprise,* 5 November 1987.

"Rev. Jackson's Wife Visits Claxton." *Claxton Enterprise,* 15 March 1984.

Richardson, III, Henry J. 1994. "African Americans and International Law: For Professor Goler Teal Butcher, with Appreciation." *Howard Law Journal* 37 (Winter): 223–33.

Robinson, Pearl T. 1982. "Whither the Future of Blacks in the Republican Party?" *Political Science Quarterly* 97 (Summer): 207–31.

Rose, John C. "Negro Suffrage: The Constitutional Point of View." *American Political Science Review* 1 (November 1906): 17–43.

Rosenstone, Steven. "Debate on the New Party: Electoral Myths, Political Realities." *Boston Review* (January/February 1993): 11–13.

Ross, Sonya. "Black Colleges on a Limb: Court Decision Leaves Uncertainty Over Future." *Savannah Morning News,* 6 July 1992.

"Royal Protests Remarks on Attendance Record." *Claxton Enterprise,* 5 February 1992.

Satterthwaite, Jean. "Baker Resigns City Council Seat; Members Vote 5–1 to Accept Councilwoman's Decision, Call Election." *Claxton Enterprise,* 13 February 1992.

——. "Claxton Voters Get Ready for December City Elections." *Claxton Enterprise,* 29 November 1984.

——. "Unhappy with Committee Assignment: Woody Says He Will Resign Council." *Claxton Enterprise,* 7 February 1985.

Schexnider, Alvin J. 1990. "The Politics of Pragmatism: An Analysis of the 1989 Gubernatorial Election in Virginia." *PS: Political Science and Politics* 23: 154–6.

"School System Responds to NAACP Survey." *Claxton Enterprise,* 9 January 1986.

"Seems Like Old Times: Claxton Gaining City Debt." *Claxton Enterprise,* 9 April 1982.

Sellers, Richards. "Board Gets Settlement Proposal From 'Concerned Citizens' Group." *Claxton Enterprise,* 8 March 1984.

Sellers, Richards. "Candidates Absent at Voters' Seminar." *Claxton Enterprise,* 1 December 1983.

——. "Judge Now to Decide on Evidence: NAACP School Discrimination Suit Drawing to a Close." *Claxton Enterprise,* 19 January 1984.

"Shaping Post-Apartheid South Africa." *Focus,* March 1987.

Shapiro, Robert Y. and Harpreet Mahajan. 1986. "Gender Differences in Policy Preferences: A Summary of Trends from the 1960s." *Public Opinion Quarterly* 50: 42–61.

Simpson, Alan. "Atwater's Election as Howard University Trustee Sparks Dissension." *Washington Post,* 23 February 1989.

Sims, Calvin. "Butts Comes Under Fire for Endorsement of Perot: Some Blacks Upset by Rebuff to Democrats." *New York Times,* 16 July 1992.

——. "Clergyman Lashes Out at Critics Who Attack Perot Endorsement." *New York Times,* 16 July 1992.

"Six Candidates Now Qualified for City Council Elections." *Claxton Enterprise,* 5 November 1986.

Smith, J. Clay. 1983. "A Black Lawyer's Response to the Fairmont Papers." *Howard Law Journal* 26: 221–3.

——. 1994. "United States Foreign Policy and Goler Teal Butcher." *Howard Law Journal* 37 (Winter): 156.

Smith, Robert. "Historically Black Colleges and Universities are Justified." *Black Issues in Higher Education* 70 (27 August 1992): 14.

——. 1981. "The Black Congressional Delegation." *Western Political Quarterly* 34 (June): 220.

Smothers, Ronald. "Blacks Say GOP Ballot Challengers are Tactics to Harass Minority Voters." *New York Times,* 25 October 1992.

Squire, Peverill. 1989. "Challengers in U.S. Senate Elections." *Legislative Studies Quarterly* 14: 531–47.

Starks, Robert T. 1991. "Exploring the Meaning and Implications of Deracialization in African American Urban Politics." *Urban Affairs Quarterly* 27: 216–22.

Starks, Robert T. and Michael Preston. 1990. "The Political Legacy of Harold Washington, 1983–1987." *National Political Science Review* 2: 161–68.

Steele, James. 1994. "Wounded and Bleeding: The CBC in the 104th." *Black Political Agenda* 2(4): 6.

Stokes, Louis. "Testimony of Ms. Jackie Parker: The Underrepresentation of African Americans in U. S. Senate." *Congressional Record* House of Representatives 135, (30 October 1989):149–150.

Stone, Pauline. 1980. "Ambition Theory and the Black Politician." *Western Political Quarterly* 32 (March): 94–107.

Strickland, Ruth Ann and Marcia Lynn Wicker. 1992. "Comparing the Wilder and Gantt Campaigns: A Model for Black Candidate Success in Statewide Elections." *PS: Political Science and Politics* 25: 204–11.

"Suits Cost City over $5,000." *Claxton Enterprise,* 11 September 1980.

Sullivan, Louis W. "Alma Maters that Matter: The Unique Mission of Historically Black Colleges and Universities." *The Hilltop,* 13 September 1991.

Summers, Mary E. and Philip A. Klinker. 1990. "The Election of John Daniels as Mayor of New Haven." *PS: Political Science and Politics* 23: 143–5.

——. 1991. "The Daniels Election in New Haven and the Failure of the Deracialization Hypothesis." *Urban Affairs Quarterly* 27: 202–15.

Thernstrom, Abigail. "The Odd Evolution of the Voting Rights Act." *Public Interest* (Spring 1979): 49–76.

Thompson, J. Phillip. 1990. "David Dinkins' Victory in New York City: The Decline of the Democratic Party Organization and the Strengthening of Black Politics." *PS: Political Science and Politics* 23 (June): 145–8.

Toner, Robin. "Democrats Court Labor by Hammering at Bush." *New York Times,* 13 November 1991.

——. "Wilder is Pressed on Mideast Stand." *New York Times,* 29 August 1991.

"Two Council Members Air Complaint about Committee Post Assignments." *Claxton Enterprise,* 30 January 1992.

Towell, Pat. "Clinton Outlines his Priorities, Economy Chief Among Them." *Congressional Quarterly Weekly Report,* 14 November 1992: 3631–2.

Tryman, MFanya. "Black Majoralty Campaigns: Running the Race." *Phylon,* December 1974: 346–58.

Valelly, Richard and Jeffrey Tulis. "On the Study of Race and Politics." *CLIO,* 3 (Fall and Winter 1992/93): 1–10.

"Vote Drive Sponsored by Black Groups." *Claxton Enterprise,* 26 April 1982.

Walgemonth, Kathleen. 1959. "Wilson and Federal Segregation." *Journal of Negro History* 44 (April): 158–73.

——. 1988. "Woodrow Wilson's Appointment Policy and the Negro." *Journal of Southern History* 20 (November): 457–71.

Walters, Ronald. "The United States and South Africa: Nuclear Collaboration Under the Reagan Administration." *Trans-Africa Forum* 2 (Fall 1983): 17–30.

Walton, Jr., Hanes. 1968. "Race Relations Courses in Negro Colleges." *Negro Educational Review* 19 (October): 123–32.

——. 1985. "The Recent Literature on Black Politics." *PS: Political Science and Politics* 18 (Fall): 773–4.

——. 1970. "Black Political Thought: The Problem of Characterization." *Journal of Black Studies* (3): 214–18.

——. 1981. "Black Politics Payoff: Used and Unused Strategies." *Political Science Review* 20 (July-September): 288–97.

——. 1994. Review of "W. E. B. DuBois: Biography of a Race 1868–1919." *Journal of Negro Education* 63 (Fall): 675–6.

——. 1990. Review of "Race and the Decline of Class in American Politics." *Journal of American History* 77 (December): 1097–8.

——, et. al. 1991. "R. R. Wright, Congress, President Truman, and the First National Public African American Holiday: National Freedom Day." *PS: Political Science and Politics* 24 (December): 685–8.

Walton, Jr., Hanes and Mervyn M. Dymally. 1996. "Politics and Politicians." In *Encyclopedia of African American Culture and History.* New York, Macmillan.

——. "Presidents of the United States." 1996. In *Encyclopedia of African American Culture and History.* New York, Macmillan.

Walton, Jr., Hanes, Roosevelt Green, Jr., Willie E. Johnson, and Kenneth Jordan. 1990. "The Civil Rights Regulatory Agenda of the Bush Administration." *Urban League Review* 14 (Summer): 7–15.

Walton, Jr., Hanes and Clarence Martin. 1971. "The Black Electorate and the Maddox Administration." *Negro Educational Review* 1 (April): 112–14.

Walton, Jr., Hanes, Leslie McLemore, and C. Vernon Gray. 1973. "Black Politics: The View from the Readers." *American Politics Quarterly* 1 :43–50.

——. 1990. "The Pioneering Books on Black Politics and the Political Science Community, 1903–1965." *National Political Science Review* 2: 201.

Walton, Jr., Hanes and Joseph P. MacCornick, II. 1995. "The Study of African American Politics as Social Danger: Clues from the Disciplinary Journals." *National Political Science Review* 6 (1996).

Watson, Tom. "Blacks Say Racism is a Claxton Tradition." *USA Today,* 7 December 1994.

"We Must Re-elect Alphonse Jackson—We Must Defeat David Duke." Political advertisement, *Shreveport Sun,* 14 November 1991.

Wells, Janet. "Forty-three Blacks Win Elections in Three Southern States." *VEP News,* May 1969: 1–10.

Weiss, Nancy T. 1974/75. "The Negro and the New Freedom: Fighting Wilsonian Segregation." *Political Science Quarterly* 89 (Winter): 751–76.

Westlye, Mark C. 1983. "Competitiveness of Senate Seats and Voting Behavior in Senate Elections." *American Journal of Political Science* 27: 253–83.

White, Theresa. "Brooks Case Settlement to Transform Georgia's Courts." *Savannah Herald,* 2 September 1992.

"Why Governor Wilder Failed." *New York Times,* 10 January 1991.

Wildgen, John. 1988. "Adding Thornburg to the Thicket: The Ecological Fallacy and Parameter Control in Vote Dilution Cases." *Urban Lawyer* 20 (Winter): 155–73.

Wilkerson, Isabel. "Senate Race Tightens Amid Dispute Over Ethics." *New York Times,* 29 October 1992.

Williams, James D. "Dr. Hooks Heats Up the 83rd NAACP Convention and Bids Farewell." *Crisis Magazine,* August/September 1992: 6.

Williams, Juan. "The Black Elite." *Washington Post* Magazine, 4 January 1981.

——. "Black Leaders Find a Hot New Issue: Free South Africa Protests Revive a Moribund Movement." *Washington Post,* 12 December 1984.

——. "The Continuing Education of Franklyn Jenifer." *Washington Post Magazine,* 20 September 1992.

——. "One Man Show." *Washington Post* Magazine, 9 June 1991.

Williams, Linda. 1996. "White and Black Perceptions of the Electability of Black Politics Candidates." *National Political Science Review* 2 (1990): 45–64.

Willingham, Alex. "Voting Policy and Voter Participation: The Legacy of the 1980's." *Trotter Review* (Fall 1992): 25.

Winn, Mylon. 1990. "The Election of Norman Rice as Mayor of Seattle." *PS: Political Science and Politics* 23: 158–9.

"Woody Defeated, Incumbents Win." *Claxton Enterprise,* 11 December 1986.

"Woody 'Forces' Vote on Question: Council Rejects MLK Holiday Request." *Claxton Enterprise,* 10 April 1986.

Zoellner, Tom. "Claxton Town Clerk Given New Powers: Some on Council Protest Vote in Surprise Resolution." *Savannnah Morning News and Evening Press,* 7 February 1995.

Government Publications

Ayers, et. al. v. Fordice, No. 90–6588.

Concerned Citizens for Better Government for Evans County vs. DeLoach. No. Cu3–343 (S.D. Ga 1/13/84). Department of Justice Brief, pp. 32–33, 41. Department of Justice, Reply Brief, 9 October 1992.

Federal Election Commission. *FEC Reports on Financial Activity 1979–1980: Final Report: U.S. Senate and House Campaigns.* Washington, DC: Federal Election Commission, 1982.

Federal Election Commission. *FEC Reports on Financial Activity 1985–1986: Final Report: U.S. Senate and House Campaigns.* Washington, DC: Federal Election Commission, 1987.
Federal Election Commission. *FEC Reports on Financial Activity 1989–1990: Final Report: U.S. Senate and House Campaigns.* Washington, DC: Federal Election Commission, 1991.
Federal Election Commission. *FEC Reports on Financial Activity 1991–1992: Final Report: U.S. Senate and House Campaigns.* Washington, DC: Federal Election Commission, 1994.
Federal Election Commission. *FEC Reports on Financial Activity 1993–1994: Final Report: U.S. Senate and House Campaigns.* Washington, DC: Federal Election Commission, 1995.
Heart of Atlanta Motel v. United States (379 U.S. 341 1969).
Martin v. Allain 658 F. Supp. 183 (S.D. Miss., 198), pp. 1183 and 1205.
Presidential Documents, Executive Order 12577 of April 28, 1989. Historically Black Colleges and Universities." *Federal Register* 52 (2 May 1989): 18869–18871.
United States Census. *City Government Finances: 1979–1989.* Washington, DC: Government Printing Office, 1979–89.
United States Commission on Civil Rights. *Political Participation.* Washington, DC: Government Printing Office, 1968.
United States v. Brooks County, Civil Action No. 90–105, Thomas Consent Decree, p. 1.
United States v. Fordice, 112 Supreme Court 272 (1992).
South Carolina v. Katzenbach, 383 U.S. 301 (1966).
State of Mississippi United States v. Mabus.
Woody v. Evans County Board of Commissioners. CU692–073 (S.D. GA, December 7, 1992)

Interviews, Letters, and Memoranda

Interview, Enoch Mathis, Savannah, Georgia, June, 1986.
Interview, Alderman Otis Johnson, December, 1991.
Interview, Mayor John P. Rousaksis, City Hall, Savannah, Georgia, December, 1991.
Interview, Dr. Phyliss Mack, Dental Office, Savannah, Georgia, March 9, 1992, 5:45 to 6:15 p.m.
Interview, Larry Ward, Justice Department Attorney, Savannah State College, Payne Hall, Savannah, Georgia, May 19–20, 1992.
Interview, J. Clay Smith, Jr., Washington, DC, June 1, 1992 and several other dates.
Interview, Robert Goodwin, Points of Lights Foundation, June 1, 1992, Washington, DC, 6:00 p.m.
Interview, Telephone, Dr. Elias Blake, June 10, 1992.
Interview, Richard Smiley, Law Office of Attorney Barbara J. Mobley, Decatur, Georgia, November 13, 1992.
Interview, Attorney Barbara J. Mobley, Law Office, Decatur, Georgia, November 14, 1992.
Interview, Reverend Doctor Calvin O. Butts, Wiley-Willcox Gymnasium, Savannah State College, Savannah, Georgia, March 10, 1993, 12 p.m.
Interview, Attorney Clarence Martin, Savannah, Georgia, March 9, 1993.
Interview, Chatham County Commissioner Deanie Frazier, March 31, 1993, Savannah, Georgia, 3:00 p.m. to 4:00 p.m.
Interview, Mayor Perry DeLoach, Claxton, Georgia, February 3, 1995.
Interview, Renee Baker, Claxton, Georgia, February 5, 1995.
Interview, Councilman Jerome Woody, Claxton, Georgia, February 6, 1995.
Letter, J. Clay Smith, Jr. to Jay A. Parker, President Lincoln Institute for Research and Education, August 30, 1985.
Letter, Dr. James E. Cheek to President George W. Bush, June 26, 1991.
Letter, James E. Cheek to the Honorable C. Boyden Gray, September 13, 1991.

Letter, Samuel L. Myers to C. Boyden Gray, September 26, 1991.

Letter, James E. Cheek to the Honorable Louis W. Sullivan, October 2, 1991.

Letter, James E. Cheek to the Honorable C. Boyden Gray, October 5, 1991.

Letter, Hazel Mingo to Hanes Walton, Jr., July 15, 1992.

Paper, Aberbach, Joel and Bert Rockman. "The Political Views of U.S. Senior Federal Executives, 1970–92."

Mailgram to J. Clay Smith, Jr. from Jay A. Parker, President Lincoln Institute for Research and Education, July 10, 1985.

Meeting, Hazel Mingo, Acting Director of White House Initiatives on Black College and Universities, GSA Building, with Author and Professor Marion Orr, June 2, 1993, 2:30 p.m.

Memorandum, Dr. Elias Blake to Dr. William Harvey, Chair, HBCU Joint Board Committee, July 10, 1991.

Memorandum, Robert K. Goodwin, Executive Director, White House Initiatives on HBCUs to HBCU Presidents and Chancellors, October 11, 1991.

Press Release, State Representative Tyrone Brooks, Legislative Office, Room 511, Atlanta, Georgia and the American Civil Liberties Union Head, Laughlin McDonald and Kathy Wilde.

Statement, Dr. Arthur E. Thomas, President's Advisory Board on Historically Black Colleges and Universities, September 9, 1991.

CONTRIBUTORS

William H. Boome is chairman of the department of political science at Clark Atlanta University.

Ronald D. Clark holds a Ph.D. from the University of Illinois and teaches in Maryland.

Victor C. Cooper is a political science graduate of Savannah State University.

Michael C. Dawson is professor of political science at the University of Chicago.

Damon E. Elmore received his law degree from Emory University.

Pearl K. Ford is a graduate of Georgia Southern University and is in the Ph.D. program at Howard University.

William O. Generett, Jr. is a graduate of Morehouse College and the Emory University law school.

Amy Y. Graham is a graduate student at Georgia Southern University.

Roosevelt Green, Jr. is a professor of sociology and social work at Lock Haven University.

Simone Green is a graduate student in political science at Howard University.

Kimberlynn Hendricks is a graduate student at Georgia State University.

Oliver Jones, Jr. is the chairman of the department of political science at Florida A & M University.

Sesley Jones is a graduate of Clark Atlanta University.

Kenneth Jordan is an associate professor and director of the MPA program at Savannah State College.

Modibo M. Kadalie is an assistant professor of social and behavioral sciences at Savannah State College.

Renita D. Lipscomb is entering graduate school in political science.

Paula D. McClain is chair of the department of government and foreign affairs at the University of Virginia.

Marion E. Orr is assistant professor of political science at Duke University.

Donald L. Payne is a Congressman from the tenth district in New Jersey and chairman of the Congressional Black Caucus.

Katherine Tate is a professor of political science at Ohio State University.

Steven C. Tauber is a visiting instructor of American politics at the University of South Florida.

Hanes Walton, Jr. is professor of political science at the University of Michigan.

LaShawn Warren is a graduate of Howard University Law School and works in the attorney general's office in the state of Washington.

Renia Williams was a political science major at Savannah State College and is entering graduate school.

Stephanie Williams currently attends the University of Georgia law school.

INDEX